Windows® 2000
Registry

ISBN 0-13-030064-0

90000

9 780130 300645

PRENTICE HALL PTR MICROSOFT® TECHNOLOGIES SERIES

NETWORKING

- Microsoft Technology: Networking, Concepts, Tools
  Woodard, Gattuccio, Brain

- NT Network Programming Toolkit
  Murphy

- Building COM Applications with Internet Explorer
  Loveman

- Understanding DCOM
  Rubin, Brain

- Web Database Development for Windows Platforms
  Gutierrez

PROGRAMMING

- Introduction to Windows 98 Programming
  Murray, Pappas

- Developing Professional Applications for Windows 98 and NT Using MFC, Third Edition
  Brain, Lovette

- Win 32 System Services: The Heart of Windows 98 and Windows NT, Third Edition
  Brain

- Multithreaded Programming with Win32
  Pham, Garg

- Visual Basic 6: Design, Specification, and Objects
  Hollis

- ADO Programming in Visual Basic 6
  Holzner

- Visual Basic 6: Error Coding and Layering
  Gill

- Visual C++ Templates
  Murray, Pappas

- Introduction to MFC Programming with Visual C++
  Jones

- MFC Programming in C++ with the Standard Template Libraries
  Murray, Pappas

- COM-CORBA Interoperability
  Geraghty, Joyce, Moriarty, Noone

- Distributed COM Application Development Using Visual Basic 6.0
  Maloney

- Distributed COM Application Development Using Visual C++ 6.0
  Maloney

- Understanding and Programming COM+: A Practical Guide to Windows 2000 DNA
  Oberg

- ASP/MTS/ADSI Web Security
  Harrison

- Microsoft Site Server 3.0 Commerce Edition
  Libertone, Scoppa

- Building Microsoft SQL Server 7 Web Sites
  Byrne

- Windows 2000 Web Applications Developer's Guide
  Yager

- The Visual Basic Object and Component Handbook
  Vogel

- The COM and COM+ Programming Primer
  Gordon

- Developing Solutions with Office 2000 Components and VBA
  Aitken

- Windows Shell Programming
  Seely

- The Visual Basic Style Guide
  Patrick

ADMINISTRATION

- Windows 2000 Registry
  Sanna

- Configuring Windows 2000 Server
  Simmons

- Tuning and Sizing NT Server
  Aubley

- Windows NT Cluster Server Guidebook
  Libertone

- Windows NT 4.0 Server Security Guide
  Goncalves

- Windows NT Security
  McInerney

- Supporting Windows NT and 2000 Workstation and Server
  Mohr

- Zero Administration Kit for Windows
  McInerney

- Designing Enterprise Solutions with Microsoft Technologies
  Kemp, Kemp, Goncalves

PRENTICE HALL PTR MICROSOFT® TECHNOLOGIES SERIES

Paul Sanna

Windows 2000 Registry

Prentice Hall PTR, Upper Saddle River, NJ 07458
www.phptr.com

Library of Congress Cataloging-in-Publication Data

Sanna, Paul J.
  Windows 2000 registry / Paul Sanna.
    p. cm.
  ISBN 0-13-030064-0
  1. Microsoft Windows (Computer file) I. Title.

QA76.76.O63 S35525 1999
005.4'4769--dc21

99-055471

Acquisitions editor: Jill Pisoni
Editorial assistant: Justin Somma
Development editors: Jim Markham and Ralph Moore
Technical editor: Jim Kelly
Cover designer: Anthony Gemmellaro
Cover design director: Jerry Votta
Buyer: Maura Goldstaub
Marketing manager: Bryan Gambrel
Project coordinator: Anne Trowbridge
Compositor/Production services: Pine Tree Composition, Inc.

© 2000 by Prentice Hall PTR
Prentice-Hall, Inc.
Upper Saddle River, New Jersey 07458

Prentice Hall books are widely used by corporations and government agencies for training, marketing, and resale.

The publisher offers discounts on this book when ordered in bulk quantities. For more information contact:

Corporate Sales Department
Phone: 800–382–3419
Fax: 201–236–7141
E-mail: corpsales@prenhall.com

Or write:

Prentice Hall PTR
Corp. Sales Dept.
One Lake Street
Upper Saddle River, New Jersey 07458

Printed in the United States of America
10 9 8 7 6 5 4 3 2 1

ISBN: 0–13–030064–0

Prentice-Hall International (UK) Limited, *London*
Prentice-Hall of Australia Pty. Limited, *Sydney*
Prentice-Hall Canada Inc., *Toronto*
Prentice-Hall Hispanoamericana, S.A., *Mexico*
Prentice-Hall of India Private Limited, *New Delhi*
Prentice-Hall of Japan, Inc., *Tokyo*
Pearson Education Asia Pte. Ltd.
Editora Prentice-Hall do Brasil, Ltda., *Rio de Janeiro*

CONTENTS

The Registry. Such a simple sounding word, but in the world of Microsoft it is one of the core components for an operation system like Windows 2000 to function. No matter your skill level, there is always something new to learn about this most important component and the tools used to access it and, in some cases, modify it.

If you know about the Registry and its importance to Windows, feel free to skip ahead. But for many, the Registry is just another compu-speak word with little meaning. But it's not that complicated an idea. If you can imagine for a minute that Windows 2000 is a business, then the Registry would be its headquarters.

Just as a business can have multiple departments, with numerous duties and jobs and services, Windows 2000 does, too. We typically think of a business headquarters as the place where all the information needed to run that business is stored. Some of this information might be kept in satellite offices or even other cities, states, or countries. But in the end, there usually is one place that the important stuff resides (or at least a copy of it).

The Registry is the headquarters for Windows 2000. You will see that it contains more information than you'll probably ever have time to inspect. But all this information is 100% critical to Windows 2000's productivity and reliability.

By the time you finish the book, you'll see that the analogy between the Registry and a company headquarters isn't as far-fetched as it sounds. And you'll learn in the first chapter why Microsoft chose to create Windows 2000 in this manner.

Who This Book Is For

If you're a Windows 2000 Registry novice, you're going to learn a lot from this book. If you're a Windows 2000 Registry expert, you're also going to learn a lot from this book.

System and network administrators will find information that will save them time and energy that will translate to cost savings. If something can be manually configured on a server or desktop, a good bet is that there's a Registry setting that can accomplish the same task. Day-to-day users of Windows 2000 Professional will also find this book useful as long as they keep in mind that tinkering with the Registry without understanding the consequences will result in, well, consequences. But the good news is that knowing a little about the Registry can sometimes help typical users to do some things for themselves.

How This Book Is Organized

Following is a summary of the chapters and the information you will learn in each. Some of the information may not be needed by all readers, so feel free to skip ahead to the chapters that will benefit you most in your work and study.

Chapter 1: Introducing the Registry

Here, you learn what the Registry is, where it is stored, and why it even exists. Warnings will be provided here (and continually through the book) on the dangers that can befall your operating system should you make changes haphazardly. And finally, a detailed breakdown of how the Registry is structured is presented. This breakdown will give you the basic building blocks for how the Registry stores its information.

Chapter 2: Using the Editors to Inspect and Modify the Registry

The two major tools used to access the Registry are described in detail for you. Since there are two tools, you will also be shown when using one over the other will provide you with an advantage in performing your duties. Descriptions are also provided on how to customize the look and feel of each tool as well as to learn basic uses.

Chapter 3: Putting Security in and Around the Registry

There are issues with security that you will need to be aware of when accessing and modifying the Registry. Warnings are issued again and with good reason. Windows 2000 comes with many tools and you will no doubt be using these tools in conjunction with the Regedit and Regedt32 skills picked up in Chapter 2.

Chapter 4: Diagnosing, Repairing, and Preventing Windows 2000 Disasters

Okay, they happen. And you've got to know how to fix them. But knowing how to prevent them in the first place is a skill worth having. This chapter shows you how to use the Recovery Console, Emergency Repair Disks, and other options that can help "save the day." What do these things have to do with the Registry? Well, you'll see that much of the information that is used to repair a server or workstation is information pulled directly out of the Registry.

Chapter 5: Using the REG Utility

A new power tool is available in the Windows 2000 Resource Kit called the REG utility. Power users will love it and administrators will find themselves saving time by learning its intricacies.

Chapter 6: System and Startup Settings

Most people don't think about what goes on inside that machine when you flip the power switch. Windows 2000 performs myriad tasks before you ever get to the desktop. This chapter will walk you through the process and explain to you why the Registry is so important to the hardware as well as the software in your computer. You'll also be provided with details that will finally allow you to start customizing the Registry by making changes using the Registry editing tools described earlier.

Chapter 7: Configuring Quality of Life Settings

Don't like the way your desktop works or looks? Change it. You can use the power of the Registry to do some amazing things that will make your computing life easier (or at least easier to look at). This chapter provides you with the specific settings you can use to do all kinds of tricks. Some of these are simply shortcuts that you can do normally using the Control Panel. Others are "hidden" tricks that aren't that easy to do except from the Registry.

Chapter 8: Managing Desktop Configuration

The Registry stores a wide range of details about a workstation's desktop configuration. You can read in this chapter how to configure via the Registry a range of desktop elements, such as the command prompt, message display, Start menu, Control Panel, and more.

Chapter 9: Configuring Microsoft Office 2000

When you consider that one of Microsoft's most popular application suites is Office 2000, it makes sense that the Registry should allow you to do some customization of applications such as Word or Excel. From installation to that (sometimes) annoying help desk assistant, you'll learn how to make Office 2000 more enjoyable to install and use. As with earlier chapters, you're given specific Registry settings that can be set to customize your own Office desktop.

Chapter 10: Accessing the Registry from Code

Now that you have the basics down from earlier chapters, it's time to turn "Pro" with the Registry. The Regedit and Regedt32 tools are great, but sometimes you have to go to the source. Programmers and power users will find this information quite valuable and perhaps indispensable. For everyone else, just understanding how the Registry works with third party applications can give a better understanding of its importance.

Chapter 11: Network Tweaks in the Registry

Registry support for Windows 2000 network features and services is broad. This chapter will show you some of the more useful ways to manage network connections via the Registry.

Chapter 12: Working with Group Policy

Group policy is a tool available in Windows 2000 for system administrators to help manage and control users' desktop configurations. This chapter discusses how group policy works and how to use the group policy tools, as well as how to see all of the Registry keys and entries that support group policy.

Chapter 13: Hardware Management

Most users don't realize that the hardware in their computers isn't the entire story. There is software involved that allows the Windows 2000 operating system to "talk" to the hardware. And, no surprise, the Registry is where much of this information is stored. You will learn exactly where and how the Registry manages all the moving parts.

Appendix A: HKCU Entry Names and Keys

This appendix provides a listing that shows all the Registry keys sorted by entry name from HKEY_CURRENT_USER (HKCU). Specifically, the listing shows all entries by name and the key in which each resides.

Appendix B: Class ID Reference

This appendix includes a table that provides a reference of the CLSID to the object each one represents. The list is based on a fresh install of Windows 2000 with only Microsoft Office 2000 installed.

Appendix C: Object Reference

This appendix provides a table which shows the class ID for each of the objects installed into the Registry by Windows 2000. The table also reflects an installation of Windows 2000.

Conventions Used in This Book

Throughout the book, you will see various elements designed to help illustrate or highlight key information, such as the following:

- Figures and Tables—Use the figures to help you understand portions of the text, and make sure you study tables carefully.
- Tip Icon—The Tip icon contains useful, friendly information.
- Note Icon—The Note Icon contains an extra piece of information you may find helpful.
- Warning Icon—The Warning Icon points out some danger or issue you should remember for both the exam and real-world implementation.

Introducing the Registry

In This Part

Introducing
the Registry

As a user of the Registry, you probably fall into one of three knowledge levels: casual user, sophisticated user, or power user. If you're a casual user, you probably have no idea what the Registry is; it's possible you have never heard the word mentioned in the context of Windows and personal computers. If you're in the sophisticated user category, you probably know what the Registry is, and you might even take a look at it to see what those power users are talking about. You might even change a setting, such as a color or Windows desktop background preference, following the detailed instructions provided in a magazine or a book. Finally, if you are in the power user group, you most likely dive into the Registry often to tweak this entry and tune that value. You are familiar and comfortable with the Registry and know how to avoid trouble.

This chapter is designed to take the casual user to the level of sophisticated user and provide a review for the sophisticated user. However, if you think you're already a power user, be sure to review this chapter so you can anticipate questions you're bound to receive from the casual and sophisticated group! You'll also find a useful review of Registry data types later in the chapter.

Here's what you will find in this chapter:

- An overview of the Windows 2000 Registry
- A review of how the Registry is used by the operating system, hardware, and applications
- A discussion of how the Registry is organized
- A review of the major Registry subtrees
- An explanation of the different types of data stored in the Registry

The Registry Defined

This *entire* book actually is a definition for the Registry, but the following should establish a useful, working baseline for your understanding:

The Registry is a repository of configuration information for Windows 2000. This repository stores configuration information for the operating system, as well as for applications and hardware installed on your computer. The configuration information stored in the Registry spans the range of significance—from minor to major. For example, the Registry holds the name of the bitmap you use as wallpaper on the Windows desktop, and the Registry also stores data about the hardware installed on your computer and the interrupt each component uses, without which your machine would not boot.

Registry data is not stored in one large monolithic file on your computer. Rather, the Registry is stored in a number of files on your computer. You cannot view the contents of these files in their native format. You view the contents of the files using the Registry editor that ships with Windows 2000. There are a number of Registry editors available. These editors seem to make the Registry look *whole* by presenting all of the data from the external Registry files in one place. You can find instruction on the use of the Windows 2000 Registry in Chapter 2, "Using the Editors to Inspect and Modify the Registry," and you can find a review of other useful Registry tools in Chapter 5, "Using the REG Utility."

The structure of the Registry is identical regardless of what version of Windows 2000 you are running: Professional Server, Advanced Server, or Data Center Server. In fact, the structure of the Registry in Windows 2000 is almost identical to that in versions of Windows NT, Windows 95, and Windows 98.

Last, the Registry isn't just for managing the computer sitting across the desk from you. A system administrator or help desk engineer can access the Registry of another computer from across the network. This makes it possible to diagnose and fix problems from a remote location. In addition, because so much information about a system's configuration is stored in the Registry, it's easy to inspect a user's configuration without actually seeing the dialog boxes or windows where the user sets these options. For example, it's not difficult to determine how many games are installed on a worker's computer if you know where in the Registry to look.

The Use of the Registry

There are four primary consumers and providers of the Registry. These consumers both provide data to the Registry and take advantage of the data in it.

- Windows 2000 operating system
- Software installed on your computer
- Hardware installed on your computer
- You (you can add data to the Registry if you like)

Considering these four varied users of the Registry, the way the Registry is applied in everyday use is also quite varied. Another point to consider in how the Registry is used is that applications and hardware really aren't forced into using the Registry. It's a hit-or-miss proposition for applications as to whether their settings are stored in the Registry. The same holds true for the hardware attached to your computer. While most sophisticated applications use the Registry to store configuration data, these applications are not required to. It is entirely up to the developer of a software application whether and what data to store in the Registry. Of course, there are penalties associated with not following Microsoft guidelines for Registry use, from the relatively minor penalty of not being allowed to include the Windows logo on the application's packaging, to the more serious penalty of sacrificing certain functionality or services provided by the Windows 2000 operating system. The following sections summarize the major uses of the Registry. You will drill into these topics in later chapters of this book.

Hardware Management

Host machine data, such as CPU details, BIOS info, device driver information, and more is stored in the Registry. Here is a partial list of the hardware details found in the Registry:

- I/O ports used on the machine
- Device driver use of ports; memory addresses, interrupts, and DMA channels
- Plug-and-play device specifics
- Data about controller, bus, chipsets

Security

The Registry stores data about the different users, their account information, and the groups to which they belong. Policy data also is stored in the Registry. Policies in Windows 2000 determine control settings for users, such as whether they can modify system settings via the control panel, whether they can issue the Shut Down command, and even whether they can modify the

Registry. The security data in the Registry is not easy to identify or make sense of; this is presumably by design. There are methods, of course, for decoding the entries in the Registry, which you will learn in this book.

Software Configuration

Most software applications store configuration data in the Registry. What type of data might this be? There are as many answers to that question as there are software applications. Some applications store thousands of pieces of data in the Registry. For others, configuration of the Registry to support their needs may mean the creation of just one subkey with no associated entry data. Here are examples of configuration data stored by applications:

- Folder locations for different components of the application
- User preferences
- Version information
- Languages installed
- Driver support
- Licensing information for network and shared applications

Chapter 2, "Using the Editors to Inspect and Modify the Registry," provides a review of how a sampling of popular software applications use the Registry.

User Preferences

Almost any setting you can change in Windows 2000 is stored in the Registry. From the image that is displayed as the background in Windows 2000 to the mouse double-click speed, all user preference data is stored in the Registry on a user-by-user basis. This means that every user who has an account on a Windows 2000 machine will see his or her personal preferences reflected when logging on to the computer. A surprise for many new Registry users is that you cannot see the preferences of all users who have accounts on the machine at one time; data for a specific user is loaded into the Registry when the user logs on. Here is a list of preference data stored by Windows 2000 in the Registry:

- Accessibility options set in the Control Panel
- Name of temporary directories
- Colors used in command prompt window
- Printers available
- Remote access options, such as number of redial attempts

The Benefits of the Registry

So what's the big deal about the Registry? You can read about the evolution of the Registry in the next section, which tells part of the story of why this Registry is so valuable. For now, consider these two primary benefits to the Windows 2000 Registry:

- **As a central repository for (almost) all configuration information.** A central repository for all configuration information about Windows 2000 means that it's likely this type of information wouldn't be scattered around different places on a computer. You'll learn later in this chapter how, in early versions of Windows, configuration data could be spread across a hard drive in sometimes hundreds of small initialization files (called INI files). A central repository scheme makes it easy to access and back up all configuration information for the operating system, hardware components, and software applications.

- **The ability to share configuration information.** By storing all configuration in a common place, it is easy for the operating system, applications, and hardware to find the information they might need. Applications oftentimes need services from other applications, and information about these services is stored in the Registry. Applications also need information about hardware installed, and hardware needs to know about drivers installed to the operating system. The central location for this data, the Registry, makes it easy for each of the Windows 2000 components to share data about itself.

The Look of the Registry

You cannot look at the Registry in its native form. The Registry is really comprised of the data stored at least six files. All of the values in these files are represented in this thing we call the Registry. The list of the minimum files that comprise the Registry is found below in the "Hives" section. You can look at the information stored in the Registry using either of two utilities shipped with Windows 2000, REGEDIT.exe or Regdt32.exe. Use of these utilities is covered in Chapter 2, "Using the Editors to Inspect and Modify the Registry." In addition, the Windows 2000 Resource Kit contains some handy Registry editing tools.

Figure 1.1 presents what may be your first look at the Registry. You can find a discussion later about how the Registry is organized. For now, notice how the presentation of the Registry data is reminiscent of how Windows Explorer presents your hard disk, folders, and network resources. You can open a folder to see folders beneath it, and you can open the next folder, and so on. Eventually, when you have opened the folder at an entry level, you can see real data used by Windows 2000, Windows 2000 applications, and hard-

FIGURE 1.1   The Registry is typically presented in a hierarchical format.

ware. Keep in mind that the presentation of Registry data is dependent on the application that is doing the presenting. For example, you can write an application that might present Registry data in a format that a relational database application could use. The presentation used by the Registry editors, though, is the most common.

The Risk of the Registry

As you can probably tell, the Registry is probably the most significant component in Windows 2000. Like many good things, though, there is risk. There is no substitute or replacement for the Registry should you lose it. If you happen to delete an important file from Windows 2000, you can usually extract it from the Windows 2000 CD and recover your system. This is not the case with the Registry. While you can maintain and restore from backup copies of the Registry, you can't simply extract a new working copy from the CD. The importance of backing up the Registry, and your entire system in general, can't be stressed enough.

The Registry provides an attractive vehicle for inspecting configuration data about your system and, optionally, for changing preferences and settings. At the same time, this attraction could turn into a fatal attraction if you

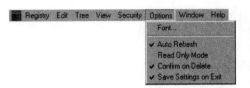

FIGURE 1.2   You can enable read-only mode in the Registry, thereby preventing accidental modification of any entry.

mistakenly change a critical setting that makes your system unusable or unbootable. While there is a read-only option in the Windows 2000 Registry editor to ensure changes made are not saved permanently (see Figure 1.2), you still must go through the effort of enabling this option. There are a number of options system administrators have for ensuring users do not damage their system by tweaking the Registry. For example, administrators can roll out Windows 2000 without the Registry editor tools that come with it. In addition, an administrator can set permissions on the Registry using Windows 2000 security features to ensure that only certain users have read-write access to the Registry. A policy can also be established that prevents users from accessing the Registry. You can find additional details on securing the Registry in Chapter 3, "Putting Security In and Around the Registry."

Forcing Read-Only Mode................

There is a Registry entry that enables read-only mode. By setting this entry's value to True, you can be sure that changes made to the Registry are not automatically saved unless you explicitly turn this option off from the menu. Read Chapter 2, "Using the Editors to Inspect and Modify the Registry," for details about settable Registry options.

The Roots of the Registry

Do you know that expression about history? "Those who don't respect history are doomed to repeat it." Well, Microsoft seems to have a healthy respect for history, especially with regards to the Registry. This is demonstrated by the significant enhancements made to the Registry over the course of the past few years and across all the operating system platforms the company develops.

The idea of a central configuration database isn't new with Windows 2000. This notion wasn't new with Windows 98, Windows 95, or Windows NT either. In fact, the idea of a central database has some origins in the 3.0 version of Windows, and a major step was made in Windows 3.1.

Windows 3.0 debuted configuration components known as *inee* files for the INI extensions of these files. The INI extension referred to the word *initialization*, which is exactly what these files did. Using a very specific format, these files include much of the information needed for Windows to boot and control the hardware and software installed on the computer. In Windows 3.0 and Windows 3.1, four main INI files were used: Win.ini, Progman.ini, Control.ini, and System.ini. The following is an excerpt from a fairly typical Win.ini. As you may be able to tell, this excerpt loads an application that reminds a user to register at line 1, sets the wallpaper used on the Desktop at line 5, and sets regional options starting at line 10:

```
1.       [windows]load=HPWHRC.EXE
C:\HP_XTRA\REGISTER\remind.exe
run=
     device=Canon BJC-4000,BJC4000,LPT1:

         [Desktop]
5.       Wallpaper=(None)
         TileWallpaper=0
         WallpaperStyle=2
         Pattern=(None)

10.      [intl]
         iCountry=1
         ICurrDigits=2
         iCurrency=0
         iDate=0
15.      sLongDate=dddd, MMMM dd, yyyy
         sShortDate=M/d/yy
         sThousand=,
         sTime=:

         [fonts]

         [FontSubstitutes]
         Helv=MS Sans Serif
         Tms Rmn=MS Serif
         Times=Times New Roman
         Helvetica=Arial
         MS Shell Dlg=MS Sans Serif
         MT Symbol=Symbol

         [Compatibility]
         _3DPC=0x00400000
         _BNOTES=0x224000
         _LNOTES=0x00100000
         ACAD=0x8000
```

In addition to Windows INI files, applications are shipped with their own INI files to store application-specific settings. So, for both Windows and third-party applications, there were at least three clear advantages to this INI file scheme:

■ Finally, in an improvement over DOS, there was a notion of a central point of system configuration.

- Users could view and edit settings easily via a simply organized file and a text editor.
- It was easy to identify all of the configuration data in Windows by seeking out all of the INI files on one's system.

These Windows 3.0 INI files yielded to the first Registry in Windows 3.1. Microsoft stored much of its configuration data in this small database, but applications still were free to access their own INI files. Why such a push to move away from INI file management of Windows and Windows applications? There were at least two solid reasons:

- **Proliferation of INI files.** Most third-party applications installed their own INI files to store configuration information. Seemingly, you could find on any computer running Windows 3.1 one INI file for each application ever installed, as well as one backup file for each. Because robust, reliable uninstall programs were fairly uncommon in the Windows 3.x days, INI files never seemed to disappear. Part of the reason for this was that many times the application would be installed to its own directory, while the INI file was loaded to the Windows directory.
- **Dangerous INI file editing.** INI files were, and still are, nothing but text files whose information is specially organized. Armed only with the Notepad application, users could tune and configure their Windows systems very easily. This ease of use also introduced the risk of dangerous edits and disastrous mistypes. The problem was that it was *too* easy to change these INI settings.

These INI files gave way to the Registry you see in use today in Windows 2000. Windows 95 introduced the widespread use of the Registry for both the operating system and applications. With Windows 98 and now Windows NT 4.0 and Windows 2000, it's difficult to find applications that still use either INI files.

The Registry Structure

The Registry is organized into a branch and leaf structure. This means that stemming from one of the main trunks of the Registry are branches, and stemming from those are other branches, or leaves. The branches represent sections of Registry data, such as information about hardware installed on your computer, as shown in Figure 1.3. The leaves represent pieces of data the Registry stores, such as the hardware interrupt assigned to a multimedia device, as shown in Figure 1.4. Like a tree that has branches and leaves, there are no rules that say branches at the bottom of the tree must be longer than those at the top of the tree. Nor are there rules that say leaves must appear only on branches that start at the trunk. Like a tree, the Registry's structure is determined by how it grows and the type of things that grow on it. The items

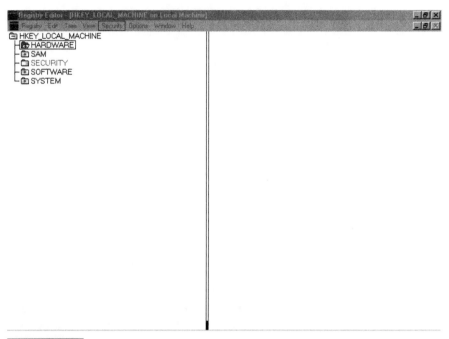

FIGURE 1.3   Figure 1.3 shows five subkeys of HKEY LOCAL MACHINE in the Windows 2000, as displayed in the Registry Editor

that determine the design are applications you install, hardware devices you configure, and options in Windows 2000 that you choose.

While it may seem that the structure of the database is free and very dynamic, there are some constants. These constants are the organizing units in the Registry. These units are the items that provide order and a system to the way data is presented and categorized. These organizing units are:

- Root keys
- Subkeys
- Hives
- Entries

The following sections provide details about these constants.

Root Keys

The *root key* is the major organizational unit in the Registry. All data in the Registry is grouped into one of the five root keys in the Registry. When you look at the Registry using one of the many Registry editing or viewing tools, you will see root keys at the top of the Registry structure. You may also refer to these root keys as *subtrees*.

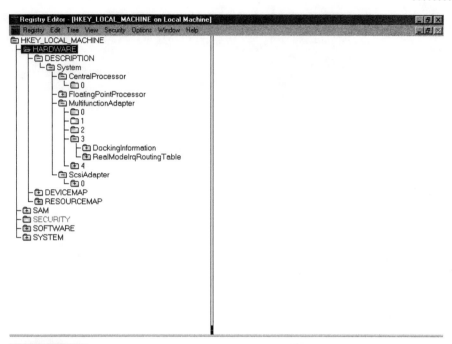

FIGURE 1.4   Figure 1.4 shows five subkeys of HKEY LOCAL MACHINE in the Windows 2000, as displayed in the Registry Editor, with Hardware hive expanded.

The root keys in the Registry can each be thought of as the root directory on a computer. Let's say that the single hard drive on your computer has been divided into six partitions. On each of those six partitions, you can create as many folders and subfolders as you need. The root keys can be thought of as those partitions. Root keys, like partitions, can store a wide and deep system of Registry subkeys and entries the same way partitions can store folders, and folders inside those folders, and eventually files and data.

These are the five root keys in the Windows 2000 Registry. They are displayed in Figure 1.5.

HKEY_CLASSES_ROOT

HKEY_CURRENT_USER

HKEY_LOCAL_MACHINE

HKEY_CURRENT_CONFIG

HKEY_USERS

The idea of the Registry being carved up into five root keys is a bit misleading. Actually, all of the Registry data can be found in only two of the root keys, HKEY_LOCAL_MACHINE and HKEY_CURRENT_USER. Registry data is

FIGURE 1.5   Figure 1.5 shows the five root hives in the Windows 2000, as displayed in the Registry Editor.

physically stored in only those two root keys. For usability and performance reasons, certain data is copied to other root keys. As an example, and as you'll learn in more detail later, all of the data under HKEY_CURRENT_USER can be found and is physically stored in the HKEY_CURRENT_USERS root key.

Registry Keys

A *key* is the organizing unit in the Registry. All data in the Registry is organized into a key. The top level key, as you learned in the prior section, is the root key. A key can store one or more keys. You can usually use the word key to refer to almost any point in the Registry. When you refer to a key that belongs to another key, you can refer to the subordinate key as a *subkey*. The only element of the Registry that is not considered a key is the actual entries that store Registry values.

Here are some rules of how a key should be named:

- A key name cannot include a backslash (\), an asterisk (*), a question mark (?), or a space.
- Only Windows 2000 can create a key name whose first character is a period (.).

FIGURE 1.6   A key can contain entries or it can stand alone.

- If you have the opportunity to inspect a version of Windows 2000 in a non-English language, look at the Registry. You will find that key names are English, though some of the values may be in the language of the operating system.

Entries

The *entry* is the most important part of the Registry. The entry is the last stop on the line for a root key, subkey, or key and is the element in the Registry that actually displays the data, as shown in Figure 1.6. Any key can have one or more entries. For certain keys, the only entry will be a default value. Other keys will store a default entry as well as a series of entries.

Every entry has three components:

- Name
- Data type of the value
- Value

You can tell if the key you click on when browsing the Registry is actually an entry by the display of the name, data type, and value in the right pane of the Registry editor. You can see an example of an entry in Figure 1.7.

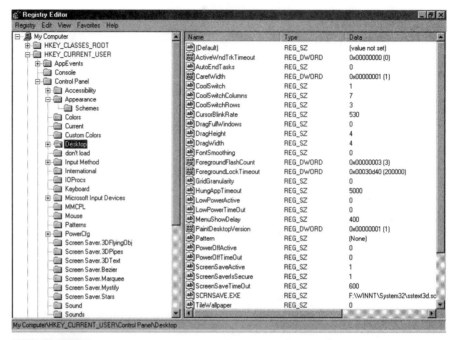

FIGURE 1.7 A subkey can have one or more entries.

Hives

A *hive* is a subsection of the Registry in which all of the subkeys and entries branch from the same subkey. For example, the SECURITY subkey under HKEY_LOCAL_MACHINE is known as a hive. Probably the most distinguishing feature of a hive is that all of its data is stored in a file separate from the rest of the Registry and the other hives. Actually, hive data is stored in two files. The primary file stores the actual Registry data, while a file with an extension of .LOG stores a record of changes made to the hive. There are a few exceptions to this rule, such as with the HKEY_CURRENT_CONFIG hive, for which the main System file is maintained as well as a copy named System.dat. By maintaining a copy rather than a log file of changes, it's presumably easy for Windows 2000 to recover from a near disaster. In addition, a System.sav file is maintained, which is a copy of the original HKEY_CUR-RENT_CONFIG hive. Hopefully this explains how Windows 2000 handles fault tolerance for the Registry. You can find advice on backing up the Registry yourself in Chapter 4, "Diagnosing, Repairing, and Preventing Windows 2000 Disasters."

Windows 2000 ships with a number of prebuilt hives, as shown in Table 1.1.

TABLE 1.1	Windows 2000 hives
Hive	**File**
HKEY_CURRENT_CONFIG	System, System.alt, System.
HKEY_CURRENT_USER	Ntuser.dat, Ntuser.dat.log
HKEY_LOCAL_MACHINE\SAM	Sam, Sam.log
HKEY_LOCAL_MACHINE\SECURITY	Security, Security.log
HKEY_LOCAL_MACHINE\SOFTWARE	Software, Software.log
HKEY_LOCAL_MACHINE\SYSTEM	System, System.log
HKEY_USERS\.DEFAULT	Default, Default.log

note

Some of the files shown in Table 1.1 are hidden. To see the files, open a command prompt window. Change to the directory where the file you want to view is stored. Next, type **dir /ah** and press the Enter key. The /ah is the parameter for the dir command that displays files that have an attribute of hidden.

Reviewing the Major Registry Sections

For organization and performance purposes, the Registry is divided into a number of sections called root keys. Root keys are the major organizing unit in the Registry. An oddity in the Registry is that you might see the same set of subkeys and data in more than one root key. While you might see the same data in more than one root key, generally, there is one place for every piece of Registry data. Each root key has a personality and a role, these determining what entries belong to which root key. In this section, you will be introduced to each root key and learn the use of each and what type of entries you can expect to see.

HKEY_CLASSES_ROOT

The HKEY_CLASSES_ROOT (HKCR) subkey is a mirror of the HKEY_LOCAL_MACHINE\Software\Classes subkey, which is covered in a later section. HKCR presents two types of data for just one purpose. The reason for HKCR is to provide support for applications and services compatible with the Windows 3.*x* Registry database. Here is a quick review of the two types of data you see in this root key.

FILE EXTENSION ASSOCIATION

Sorted to the top of this root key alphabetically because of the period as the first character, file extensions are the first items seen in this root key. For each file extension entry, a value is provided that associates an application installed in

Windows 2000 with the file extension. This is manifested when the user double-clicks on a file of a certain type and a particular application launches and loads the file. For example, on my computer, when I double-click on a file with a DOC extension, Microsoft Word starts. If I did not have Microsoft Word installed on my computer, the Wordpad application would start.

OLE CONFIGURATION

After the list of file extensions end in HKCR, entries for application components appear. The entries represent specific types of data managed by applications installed in Windows 2000. The data types, such as a Microsoft Word document or a DirectX image effect, are listed here so all applications understand how to associate a specific piece of data with the application that manages it. This is manifested to the user in a scenario when he or she embeds an object represented by some application in a document of another application, such as embedding a spreadsheet table in a word processing document. The settings in HKCR are responsible for the behavior seen when the menu system for the application associated with the embedded application appears in the host application when the user clicks on the embedded object (see Figure 1.8).

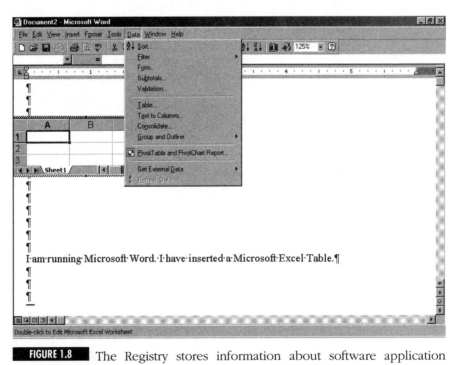

FIGURE 1.8   The Registry stores information about software application classes, which is reflected in situations when data is embedded in foreign applications, as well as in other situations.

HKEY_CURRENT_USER

The HKEY_CURRENT_USER (HKCU) root key stores user preference and desktop configuration details for the user currently logged on to the system. This preference and configuration information is reflected in a user's profile. Here are examples of the information stored in a user's profile and, hence, in HKCU:

- The shortcuts on the user's desktop
- The contents of the Start menu
- The contents of the Favorites menu
- The file extension/application associations (which override settings specified in HKCR and HKLM\software)

Data for HKCU is retrieved from the NTUSER files when a user logs on to the system. Figure 1.9 shows the main subkeys stored under the HKCU root key.

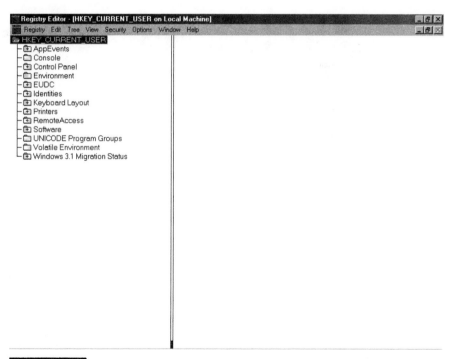

FIGURE 1.9   HKCU shows preference and configuration information for the user logged on to Windows 2000. You can see from the figure how Windows icon and window specifications are stored.

HKEY_USERS

The HKEY_USERS (HKU) subkey is almost identical to HKCU. Actually, one of the subkeys under HKU is populated from the same file as HKCU. In addition to profile information for the current user, HKU contains the same profile information for the default profile. This profile is used when a user logs on without a profile. Figure 1.10 shows how the HKU root key appears on my computer.

While Windows 2000 can manage thousands of user accounts, HKU presents data for just two user accounts, the default and currently logged on users. Considering this, HKEY_USERS will have the same appearance regardless of how many users accounts have profiles and whether the computer is logged onto the system. The name of the key features the SID of the currently logged on user. SID stands for Security Identifier. This value is the unique identifier in the domain for the user. You can find more details on SID in Chapter 8, "Managing Desktop Configuration." For now, take a look at HKU, where you can expect to see just three subkeys:

- **.DEFAULT.** The .DEFAULT key and its subkeys store the minimal profile information Windows 2000 needs to define the workspace when

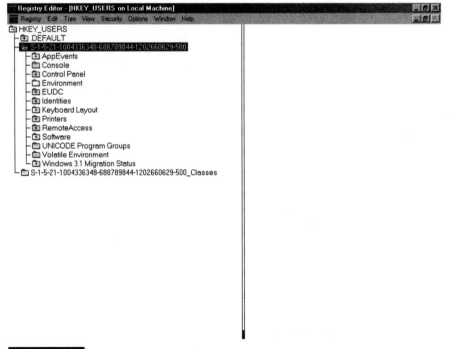

FIGURE 1.10   HKU contains all of the information Windows 2000 needs to reflect each user's Windows preferences.

Windows 2000 starts. This profile also is used as a template when a user logs on to a computer for the first time.

- **Current User SID.** The entry contains the configuration and preference information for the currently logged on user. The data stored in this key is the same as the data shown in HKCU.

- **Current User SID Classes.** The third and final key you will find under HKEY_USERS uses as a name the concatenation of the SID of the currently logged on user and the word *Classes*. So, if the current user's SID is S-1-5-21-1659004503-746137067-1343024091-500, then the third and final subkey under HKU would be S-1-5-21-1659004503-746137067-1343024091-500_Classes. This subkey contains any file extension association or component embedding information that overrides the defaults established for the installation in HKCR and HKLM\software

HKEY_LOCAL_MACHINE

The HKEY_LOCAL_MACHINE (HKLM) root key is the primary key responsible for representing the hardware configuration of the machine on which Windows 2000 is installed. You'll find hardware-specific settings in this root key, such as details about the processor(s), ports, bus data, plug-and-play settings, and so forth, as well as configuration information about installed applications. Think of this root key and its subordinates as specific to the machine on which Windows 2000 is running, irrespective of any user logged on or off. In addition, this root key stores security and network connections configuration data. Figure 1.11 shows an example of the HKLM section of a Windows 2000 Registry. The five major subkeys under HKLM are described in the next short sections.

HKEY_LOCAL_MACHINE\HARDWARE

This subkey reflects the hardware configuration of the computer. The subkey shows all the hardware attached to the computer and the interrupts the hardware devices use. Unlike many of the other subkeys in the Registry, the HKLM\Hardware subkey is not considered a hive. The HKLM\Hardware subkey is populated when Windows 2000 boots during kernel initialization. This means that the values for entries in the subkey, as well as entries themselves, are created when Windows 2000 boots and detects what hardware is installed and how it is configured. The following hardware types are detected during initialization. Upon detection, details for each of the devices found in the categories are written to the HKLM\Hardware section of the Registry.

- Bus/adapter type
- Communication and parallel ports
- Floating-point coprocessor
- Floppy disks

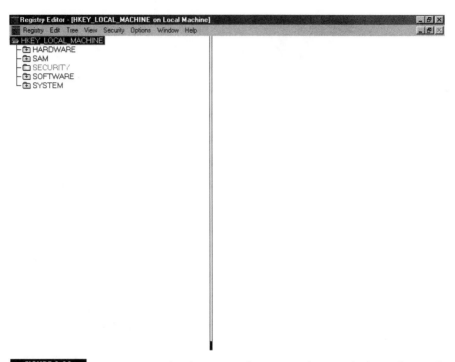

FIGURE 1.11   HKLM stores hardware configuration data, including plug-and-play support configuration information.

- Keyboard
- Pointing device (e.g., mouse)
- SCSI adapters
- Video adapters

Figure 1.12 shows the HKLM\Hardware subkey on a fairly standard desktop computer.

HKEY_LOCAL_MACHINE\SYSTEM

The System subkey under HKLM is used to store data Windows 2000 needs to boot your computer. Further subkeys under HKLM\System store what are known as *control sets*. Control sets each contain most of the data Windows 2000 uses at boot time. Why multiple control sets? Windows 2000 stores backups of control sets. The backup is created when Windows 2000 boots properly. When you use the Last Known Good Configuration to boot your system when you encounter trouble, you are using one of the backup control sets stored in this subkey (see Figure 1.13). In addition to control sets, this subkey also stores flags such as whether an install is in progress during the boot.

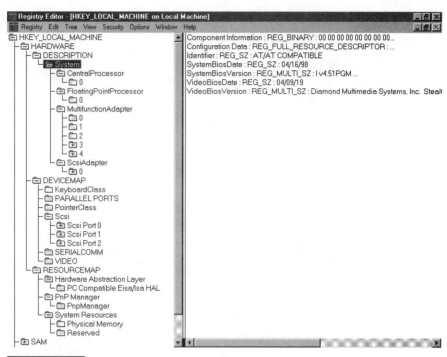

FIGURE 1.12 HKLM\Hardware subkey.

HKEY_LOCAL_MACHINE\SECURITY\SAM

The SECURITY\SAM subkey under HKLM stores all of the security-specific data for the local machine. Users, groups, the users assigned to groups, and policies are stored in this subkey. The great majority of the data in this subkey can be accessed and changed easily by using the tools that ship with Windows 2000 for modifying security settings. Considering this, you probably will not spend much time tweaking the values in this section of the Registry. Besides this convenience issue, another reason to avoid modifying entries in this subkey is that you can make your installation and network a more secure one by simply using the tools Windows ships for dealing with these incredibly critical system settings. The data you see in HKLM\SAM is mirrored from HKLM\SECURITY\SAM.

Browsing the Security Keys...............

You may have charged off to one of the Registry editors that ships with Windows 2000 in order to examine the SAM subkey firsthand. You may have been dismayed to find the SAM subkey grayed-out — hence, inaccessible. You might also have noticed the same for SECURITY. Here is how to overcome this roadblock. If you do not have any experience with the Registry editor, you may want to first review Chapter 2, "Using the Editors to Inspect and Modify the Registry." The first step is to be sure

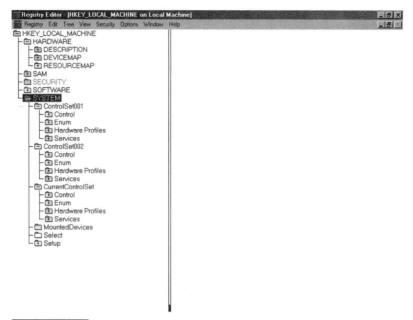

You can see the hardware profiles setup on your installation of Windows 2000 for each control set the Registry maintains.

you use the advanced Registry editor. This is the editor that allows you to set permissions for subkeys. Start the editor and open the HKLM root key window. Click on the SAM subkey and choose Permissions from the Security menu. If you do not see your user name in the list, choose Add and then select your user name and then OK. You should be back to the main Registry Key permissions dialog box. Be sure your user name is selected. Last, click on the Replace permissions option and choose OK. The SAM and SECURITY subkeys should now be enabled.

HKEY_LOCAL_MACHINE\SOFTWARE

The HKLM\Software subkey is concerned only with the software installed on Windows 2000. This subkey stores all of the data about the software installed on the local computer. This data is per-computer as opposed to per-user. This means that you can see a full inventory of the software loaded on the computer without regard to the user who installed it or what access to the software users might have.

HKLM\Software displays configuration information that determines how you work with the data of the application installed and how the applications installed work with each other.

How you work with files of a specific application is determined by how Windows 2000 associates a file with a specific application. In addition, software applications will use this subkey to store whatever configuration data is required. For America Online, this data is simply the version of the online client software installed. For Microsoft, this subkey represents hundreds of

TABLE 1.2	Registry Data Types
Data Type	**Description**
REG_BINARY	This data type stores, not surprisingly, binary data. In some cases, you'll be able to edit data of this type, such as of the value indicating a True or False condition. For example, some entries will have either a 0 value for False or a 1 value for True.
REG_DWORD	DWORD stands for double word. A double word value is 4 bytes on 8086-class, Pentium, and Pentium Pro machines. A double word data type is a significant amount of data. A double word value can be displayed in either hexadecimal or decimal value in the Registry editor.
REG_SZ	The REG_SZ data type is used to store string information. A string is a series of numbers and letters that you actually read and, perhaps, make some sense of. An example of a value with a REG_SZ data type might be a path, a default logon name, or an entry in the most recent used file list that normally appears at the end of the File menu in applications in which you work with documents.
REG_EXPAND_SZ	This data type is identical to the REGSZ data type except that a value of this type can contain expressions, macros, or environment variables that would expand the value beyond what is shown in the entry. For example, the %Systemroot% macro could be part of the value in an entry for this data type. When the value is **%systemroot%\Config32**, the Windows 2000 would interpret the entry as C:\WIN2000\Config32.
REG_MULTI_SZ	This data type is used to store multiple string values (REG_SZ) for a single entry. Each string value is separated by the Null character.
REG_DWORD_LITTLE_ENDIAN	This data type stores the same type of value as REG_DWORD. In this format, the lowest byte of the value and the highest byte in the value are stored. In little endian, the least significant byte of a value is stored first.
REG_DWORD_BIG_ENDIAN	This data type stores the same type of value as REG_DWORD. In this format, two bytes are stored: The highest byte of the value and the lowest byte in the value are stored. In big endian, the most significant byte of a value is stored first. Some IBM, Motorola, and HP systems store multibyte values in Big Endian format.
REG_QWORD	Data of this type is 64-bit.
REG_RESOURCE_LIST	This data type is reserved for the use by device drivers to store a list of the resources they use. It is uncommon for the end users to change entries of this data type.

subkeys and folders for all of the applications and small components installed.

HKEY_CURRENT_CONFIG

HKEY_CURRENT_CONFIG (HKCC) is another of those mirrored root keys in the Registry in which the data is really stored in a root key driven by an external hive. In the case of HKCC, the root key that is mirrored here is HKEY_LOCAL_MACHINE\System\CurrentControlSet\Hardware Profiles\Current. You probably won't be surprised to read that HKLM\System\CurrentControlSet\Hardware Profiles\Current stores the hardware configuration data for the control set that was used to successfully boot the system.

Understanding Registry Data Types

Entry values in the Registry are of a certain type. By assigning an entry a certain type, Windows 2000 and the applications that use the Registry can more quickly process the data in it. Also, specifying the data type of the value provides information to the Registry as to how the value should be stored. For example, let's say that a certain entry has a value of 2222. It helps Windows 2000 to know whether that value is the whole number larger than but not equal to 2221 and smaller than but not equal to 2223, or whether 2222 refers to a stream of letters or numbers that might be used, as an example, for a directory path. The data type of an entry in the Registry is significant. When an entry is created in the Registry by Windows 2000 or by an application or piece of hardware you install, the data type of the value must also be specified. If you manually create an entry in the Registry, you must also specify the data type. As you review data in the Registry, it's helpful to note the data type so you can make an accurate determination as to the use of the data. Last, if a program is written in Visual Basic, Java, C++, or any language, and you write a program that retrieves data from the Registry, you must be cognizant of the data type returned in order for your program to function properly.

Table 1.2 lists each Registry data type and provides a description.

note You can't count on the data type assigned to an entry to tell you exactly the type of data actually stored in an entry. It is entirely the choice of the application that writes data to the Registry to determine what data type the entry is categorized. You might say, "Wait a minute. How can a string, like a path, be a binary value?" That's a good question. An example of a scenario in which an entry's data type doesn't match the actual type of data in the entry might be the case when a series of numeric value must be stored. Rather than use multiple entries, an application might use the REG_MULTI_SZ data type to store each of the numeric values in one entry. The application would convert the numbers, stored as strings in the Registry, to actual values when the application needs to process them.

Using the Editors to Inspect and Modify the Registry

As much as you read dire warnings about the danger of changing Registry settings, of potentially rendering your system unstable, or, even worse, of making Windows 2000 inoperable, the fact remains that Windows 2000 ships with a handy utility called the *Registry editor*. In fact, the editor comes in two flavors. This editor makes it fairly easy to review keys and values in the Registry and to make changes both to the Registry on the computer you're working on or a network computer you're attached to. While you can find numerous Registry utilities that do many of things the Microsoft editors do, sometimes better, the editors that ship with Windows 2000 are free and supported. With this in mind, this chapter provides a review of the features and capabilities of the Registry editors. Here are the topics covered in this chapter:

- Determining which Registry editor to use
- Performing basic Registry review and editing tasks
- Connecting to a networked computer Registry
- Loading and unloading hives
- Working with Registry data in external files

Choosing Between REGEDIT and REGEDT32

Windows 2000 ships with two tools you can use to view and modify Registry data. Using these tools, you can inspect any root key, hive, key, entry, or value in the Registry. The tools are known collectively as the *Registry editors*. The two Registry editors that come with Windows 2000 are REGEDIT and REGEDT32.

Why are there two Registry editors? REGEDT32 is the editor Microsoft recommends you use. REGEDIT is a prior version that was first used with Windows 95. If Microsoft really didn't want you to use REGEDIT, it would not be installed with Windows 2000. The fact remains that REGEDIT does some things that REGEDT32 cannot. In fact, one of the most useful functions in REGEDIT, the ability to extract and then load Registry data from a text file, is missing from REGEDT32. At the same time, there are a number of must-have functions in REGEDT32 that are missing from REGEDIT. This written, it should become clear to you by the end of this chapter that it's difficult to administer the Registry without the use of both of these tools.

Table 2.1 will help you choose which editor is appropriate for the task you want to complete with the Registry.

Registry Editor Basics

As you gain experience in working with the Registry, you are sure to come across useful tools and larger applications that can help you administer and tweak the Registry. Until that time, you are left with the tools provided to you by Microsoft. These tools, REGEDIT and REGEDT32, are extremely useful, very reliable, and not hard to use. In this section of the chapter, you learn the

TABLE 2.1 REGEDIT versus REGEDT32	
If you want to . . .	**choose this editor**
review and make changes to the Registry	either
set permissions on keys	REGEDT32
set audit policy on keys	REGEDT32
set ownership on keys	REGEDT32
export data that can be edited and later loaded	REGEDIT
connect to another networked computer	either
copy a key name to the clipboard	REGEDIT
print all of the Registry	either
print a single key and all of its subordinates	either
search for a key, entry name, or value	either
load Registry data extracted from another computer	REGEDT32

basics involved in using the two Registry editors. Coverage of starting and stopping the editors and how to customize their appearance and behavior is provided, as well as of how to connect a remote computer's Registry.

Starting the Editor

Windows 2000 does not automatically create a menu choice or a desktop shortcut for either of the editors. You must issue the Run command to launch either REGEDIT or REGEDT32. To do so, open the start menu and then choose Run. When the Run dialog box appears, enter either **REGEDT32** or **REGEDIT,** and then click OK.

Both editors have the capability to remember how you had the screen organized the last time you used them. When you start REGEDT32 for the first time ever on Windows 2000, it appears as Figure 2.1. Figure 2.2 shows how REGEDIT will appear out of the box.

You may find it useful to place a shortcut to one or both of the Registry editors somewhere on the Desktop or on one of the menus. Here are two methods you can use to add easy access to either of the two Registry editors.

■ **To add a shortcut to the editor to the Start menu . . .**

Start Windows Explorer and open the Windows folder. Locate the appropriate file: REGEDIT.EXE or REGEDT32.EXE. REGEDT32 is stored in the System32 folder, while REGEDIT is stored in the Windows folder. When you have located the file, right-click on the file and drag it to the Start menu and then release the mouse button.

■ **To add a shortcut to a menu . . .**

Right-click on the taskbar and then choose Properties. Click the Advanced tab and then click the Advanced button. Navigate to the folder where you want to the shortcut to appear. Right-click, choose New and then Shortcut from the Context menu that appears. Finish creating the shortcut by supplying the path to the Registry editor you want to add it. REGEDIT.EXE is in the Windows folder, REGEDT32.EXE is in the Windows\System32 folder. Finish by supplying a name for the menu choice.

Closing the Editor

To shut down REGEDT32 or REGEDIT, choose Registry, Exit from the menu bar. Using REGEDT32, to close the Registry you have open but keep the editor running, choose Registry, Close from the menu. This technique is useful if you would like to end access to a remote computer's Registry. See "Accessing a Remote Computer's Registry" later in the chapter for details about administering the Registry of a remote computer on the network.

Opening the Local Registry

REGEDT32 gives you the ability to log on to another computer and view its Registry. After you complete work on the other computer, you will want to

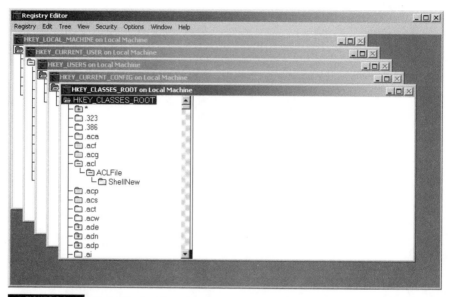

FIGURE 2.1 The REGEDT32 editor is one of two applications shipped with Windows 2000 that you can use to review and change Registry values.

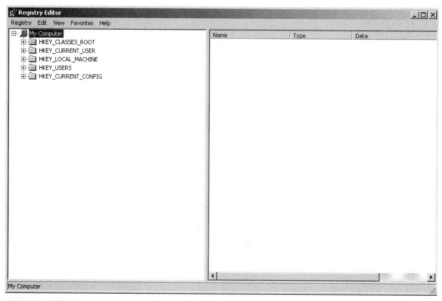

FIGURE 2.2 The REGEDIT editor shows all of the Registry keys in one window.

close that remote Registry. To open the Registry on the computer where REGEDT32 is running, choose Registry, Open Local from the menu.

Navigating REGEDIT

REGEDIT presents the Registry in Windows Explorer style. If you are comfortable using the Windows Explorer, then you should have little trouble navigating through the REGEDIT presentation of the Registry.

Root keys form the top level of the Registry hierarchy when viewed with REGEDIT. To see subordinate keys, click the plus (+) icon beside any folder. To see any values associated with a key, click once on the folder. To collapse a key, click on the minus (-) icon beside the folder icon. To see Registry keys listed beyond the bottom border of the screen, use the slider to move down the list. As you navigate through the Registry, you will click on keys. Entries associated with keys are displayed in the contents pane. Figure 2.3 shows you the components of REGEDIT you'll work with while navigating the editor.

Navigating REGEDT32

REGEDT32 presents the Registry in MDI fashion. MDI stands for multiple document interface. MDI is the term used to describe the category of Windows

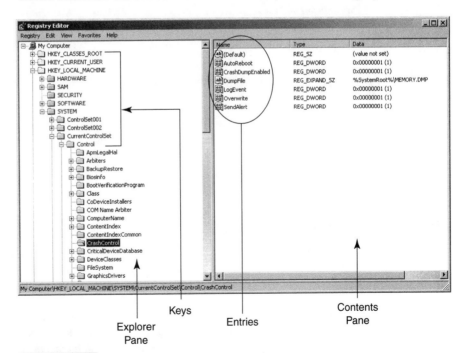

FIGURE 2.3   REGEDIT is a typical Windows application in that it uses standard controls, such as window panes and an Explorer-style presentation of data.

software applications, like REGEDT32, that use multiple windows within the application to display as many documents of information as is necessary. In the case of REGEDT32, each of the documents represents a root key. To see keys and entry for a specific root key, you must bring the appropriate windows to the foreground.

To see Registry data for a particular root key, click the Window menu and then choose the desired root key. Use any of the choices on the Window menu to organize the root key windows on the screen. Alternatively, you can minimize any of the root key windows until only the window you are interested is in view.

The root key is the topmost element in the hierarchy displayed in any of the root key windows. To see keys, double-click on any part of the root key. To navigate deeper into the root key, double-click on any key until the data that interests you is displayed. To hide keys, double-click on the open parent key.

REGEDT32 provides a menu interface to some of the navigation functions in the editor (see Figure 2.3). To open the selected key to see the next level subordinate keys, choose Tree, Expand One Level from the menu bar. To open the selected key to see all subordinate keys and values, choose Tree, Expand branch from the menu bar. To expand the entire hierarchy for the root key to see all keys, choose Tree, Expand All. Lastly, to close the selected open key, choose Tree, Collapse Branch. Figure 2.4 shows you the components of REGEDT32 you'll work with while navigating the editor.

Finding Information in the Registry

It's likely that at some point you'll need to see or modify data in the Registry but not be sure exactly where to find it. Both REGEDIT and REGEDT32 provide a search function to help you locate keys and entries. Of course, close study of this book should prepare you to locate any entry or key with just a small amount of information. Nevertheless, here is how to use the search functions in the editors.

SEARCH USING REGEDIT

To search the Registry using REGEDIT, choose Edit, Find from the menu bar. Enter the text you believe is contained in the key, entry name, or entry value of the data you are looking for. To limit the search results to just those keys, entries, or values whose text matches the text you entered exactly, check the Match whole string only option. To limit your search to only keys, entry name, or values, or some combination of the three, check the appropriate option. When you have specified all the relevant options, click OK. If the editor finds the text you specified, it will be selected on the screen. If you want to search for the next occurrence of the text you specified, press the F3 function key.

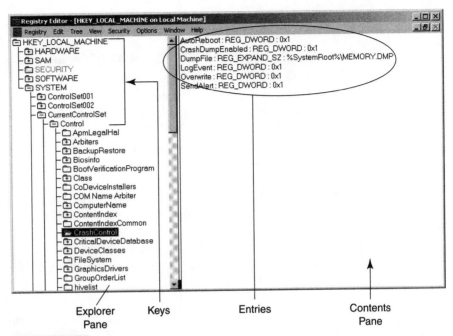

Explorer   Keys   Entries   Contents
Pane   Pane

FIGURE 2.4   The presentation of the Registry in REGEDT32 is very similar to that of files and folders in Windows Explorer.

SEARCH USING REGEDT32

To search the Registry using REGEDT32, choose View, Find Key from the menu. Enter the text you believe is contained in the key, entry name, or entry value of the data you are looking for. To limit the search results to just those keys, entries, or values whose text matches the text you entered exactly, check the Match Whole Word Only option. To limit your search to only keys, entry name, or values, or some combination of the three, check the appropriate option. When you have specified all the relevant option, click OK. If the editor finds the text you specified, it will be selected on the screen. If you want to search for the next occurrence of the text you specified, press the F3 function key.

Changing REGEDT32's Behavior and Display

A number of options are available in the REGEDT32 version of the editor to help you customize some aspects of how the editor works and looks. For example, you can specify that the editor operate in read-only mode. This way, any changes you make are not saved, hence eliminating any chance of doing damage to your Windows 2000 configuration. In addition, a number of options are available for you to customize the display of the data. Keep in mind that these options are not available in REGEDIT. Here is a review of the options:

- **To toggle between read-only mode and read-write mode . . .**
  Choose Options, Read Only Mode from the menu.

- **To save any of the settings you have made in REGEDT32 so they are applied the next time you start the editor . . .**
  Choose Options, Save Settings on Exit from the menu.

- **To force the editor to automatically display new Registry values as changes are made to the system configuration . . .**
  Choose Options, AutoRefresh from the menu.

- **To force the editor to immediately update Registry settings based on the current configuration just for the open root key window . . .**
  Choose View, Refresh Active from the menu.

- **To force the editor to immediately update all Registry settings based on the current configuration . . .**
  Choose View, Refresh All from the menu.

- **To be asked to confirm your choice before the editor deletes Registry data . . .**
  Choose Options, Confirm on Delete from the menu.

- **To display just the explorer pane . . .**
  Choose View, Tree Only from the menu.

- **If you have previously hidden either the explorer pane or the contents pane and now want to see both . . .**
  Choose View, Tree and Data from the menu.

- **To display just the contents pane . . .**
  Choose View, Data Only from the menu.

In addition to these choices, you can change the font used to display Registry keys and values, as well as use standard Windows techniques to organize the root key window. These options are available from the Options and Window menu, respectively.

Adding and Editing Keys, Entries, and Values

More than any other task you'll complete with the Registry editors, you will spend most of your time changing keys, entries, and values. As much as you can use REGEDT32 and REGEDIT to review Registry data, print keys, take ownership of keys, and more, you undoubtedly will spend most of your time *tweaking*. Tweaking is the word used informally to describe the process of adjusting Registry values in order for Windows 2000 to behave and appear exactly as you like. This section of the chapter explains how to use the features in the Registry editors to tweak keys and values.

TABLE 2.2	Registry Editor Capability Review
Task	**Editor**
Enter string value	both
Enter multi-string value	REGEDT32
Enter expand string	REGEDT32
Enter binary value	both
Enter binary value as hex	REGEDT32
Enter dword as binary	REGEDT32
Enter dword as decimal	both
Enter dword as hex	both

DATA TYPES USED IN THE REGISTRY EDITORS

The two Registry editors vary in their support and treatment of data types. For example, there are certain data types that are impossible to add when you use REGEDIT. Table 2.2 shows you which data types can be created in which editor, including which editor supports the creation of values in different numbering systems.

CREATING VALUES FOR DATA TYPES

Certain data types require a bit more instruction than the prompts provided in the dialog boxes in the Registry editors. The following is a guide to the specifics related to creating values of certain data types.

WORKING WITH MULTI-STRING VALUES • A multi-string data type value contains many strings. The application that uses the value parses the string by dividing the string into tokens delimited by the Null character. When you enter a multi-string value, which is possible only with the REGEDT32 editor, you press the Enter key after you enter each of the values (see Figure 2.5).

WORKING WITH EXPAND STRING VALUES • An expand string allows you to use system variables within the entry value. The variable is resolved to its true

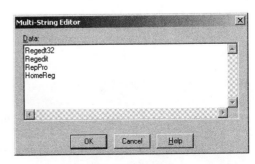

FIGURE 2.5   Each value in a multiple-string data type entry appears on a separate line.

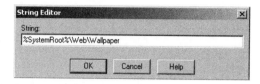

FIGURE 2.6 Environment variables can be used in the Registry with expand string variables.

value when the value is used. You can use the system variable as part of a string with literal characters, such as in the example provided in Figure 2.6. You should be sure to enclose the variable in percent symbols (%).

WORKING WITH BINARY VALUES • You use the Binary editor to create binary values (see Figure 2.7). The binary editor presents any binary data and can do so in binary or hex formats. The binary editor displays offset addresses for each line and column. The scale on the left of the edit field displays the offset for the entire line within the data block. The scale at the top of the edit field displays the offset within the line of data. You can switch the scale display from binary addresses to hex addresses by clicking the appropriate option button.

ADDING A NEW KEY

Adding a new key is a simple matter using either REGEDIT or REGEDT32. All you need to know in advance is the name of the key you will create and its location. It may be that you have no specific requirements for the name or location, or you may be asked to create a specific key in a specific spot. You need to know in advance these two pieces of information. The procedure is slightly different to add a key in REGEDIT compared to REGEDT32. Here are the details:

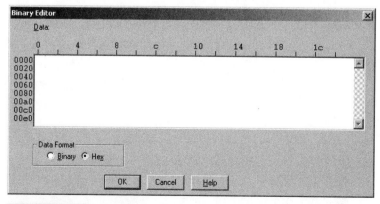

FIGURE 2.7 The binary editor in REGEDT32.

- **To add a key using REGEDIT.** Select the target key. Note that keys are added as subordinated to the key selected when the new key is added. Next, choose Edit, New key from the menu. A new empty key is created with the name field selected. Enter the new name and press Enter.

- **To add a key using REGEDT32.** Select the target key. Note that keys are added as subordinated to the key selected when the new key is added. Next, choose Edit, Add Key from the menu. The Add Key dialog box appears (see Figure 2.8). Enter the name of the key. Ignore the Class edit box. Click OK.

ADDING AN ENTRY

You will need to know four pieces of information before you add a new entry. With these pieces of information, you can add an entry to the Registry provided you have sufficient rights. For information on security as it applies to the Registry, refer to Chapter 3, "Putting Security In and Around the Registry."

- **Name.** You should know the name of the entry before you create it. It's easy with REGEDIT to rename a key name, so it's not a big deal if the name you specify when you create the key is not exact. Keep in mind, though, that if the reason you have to create the new key is in support of a requirement of some third-party application or piece of hardware, be sure to enter the exact name specified by the application or component.

- **Location.** You should know the target key of the new entry.

- **Data Type.** You must specify the data type of the entry when you create it. Unlike the name of the entry, you cannot change the data type of an entry. So, you must be sure to specify the data type correctly when you create the entry.

- **Value.** You may need to supply the value of the entry when you create it. Of course, if the entry will not be used immediately, or even if the value of the entry is not important or required, you can supply it later or simply ignore it.

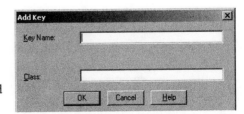

FIGURE 2.8 The dialog box used to enter new keys in REGEDT32.

Armed with these four pieces of data, follow these instructions to add the entry. The instructions vary based on the editor you use.

ADDING AN ENTRY USING REGEDIT • When you add an entry using REGEDIT, you are prompted only for the name of the new entry. While you must also select a data type, you are not forced to supply a value immediately.

To add an entry using REGEDIT, select the target key. Choose Edit, New from the menu, and then select from the choice of the data types that appear at the bottom of the menu for the entry you are creating: String value, Binary value, DWORD value. Immediately with your selection, an entry is created with the name field for the entry selected. Enter the name of the new entry and press the enter key.

To specify the value for the newly created entry, double-click on its name. Depending on the data type of the entry you created, the appropriate value editor will appear. Enter the value and then click OK.

ADDING AN ENTRY USING REGEDT32 • REGEDIT32 prompts you for all of the information required to create a new entry. Naturally, you can enter dummy information when the entry is created and return later to correct the data.

To add a new entry, select the target key and then choose Edit, Add Value from the menu. The dialog box shown in Figure 2.9 appears. Enter the name of the value and then select the data type for the value from the drop-down list. Click OK. Next, a dialog box appropriate to the data type you specified appears, giving you the opportunity to supply the value. For example, if the data type you specified was binary or DWORD, the binary editor appears. Enter the value and then click OK.

RENAMING A KEY OR ENTRY

You can rename a key or entry with only two mouse clicks. Unfortunately, this option is only available from REGEDIT. To rename a key or entry using REGEDT32, you must extract the hive supporting the data to an external file, make the name change in the file, and then reload the file into the Registry. You can find details about importing and exporting Registry data later in this chapter in the "Making Bulk Changes to the Registry" section. Regarding making name changes, again, the standard warnings are in effect: Be sure the new name you specify is correct. Your Windows 2000 system can simply stop working if you change the name of a critical key.

FIGURE 2.9   Adding an entry to a key in REGEDT32.

To change the name of a key or entry, select it, and then use one of these three techniques: (1) Choose Edit, Rename from the menu; (2) right-click on the key or entry, and choose Rename; or (2) press the F2 function key. Edit mode for the key's label will be enabled. Type the new name or edit the existing name and press the Enter key.

PRINTING THE REGISTRY

You might need to review a printed version of the Registry, including its structure and entry values. Printing probably seems like a fairly basic task, requiring little instruction. That's a correct assumption, and the only reason printing the Registry requires *any* instruction here is because of the Registry-specific options available at print time.

Even immediately following a new installation of Windows 2000 with minimal hardware and no new applications, the Registry still stores a significant amount of data. As an example, the contents of HKEY_CURRENT_USERS printed to a file with a Generic/Text print driver produces a file with more than 40,000 lines. Considering this, it makes sense that you have the option to specify how much of the Registry is printed when you choose Print from either of the two editors.

PRINTING FROM REGEDIT • To print from REGEDIT, select Registry, Print from the menu. If you do not want to export the entire Registry, it is helpful to first select the key to print before making the menu choice. The dialog box shown in Figure 2.10 appears.

FIGURE 2.10 The print option from REGEDIT lets you select how much of the Registry to print: all of it or just a particular key.

If you forgot to specify the key to print, click the Selected branch option at the bottom of the dialog box and then enter the full key name in the box provided. It may be easier simply to close the dialog box, click on the key to print, and then make the menu choice again.

To print the entire Registry, click the All option. Next, be sure the correct printer is selected, then click the Print button.

PRINTING FROM **REGEDT32** • To print Registry data using REGEDT32, select the key to print, and then choose Registry, Print Subtree from the menu. Unfortunately, to print the entire Registry at once, you must use the REGEDIT editor. The print job will start immediately. Considering this, you may want to first check the printer settings before starting printing. You can access the printer setup set of options from REGEDT32 by choosing Registry, Printer Setup from the menu.

Accessing a Remote Computer's Registry

Using REGEDT32, you can connect to the Registry on any computer you can see on the network, provided, of course, that you have sufficient rights. This allows you to inspect and modify another computer's Registry in a live environment. This contrasts to a scenario in which files are exchanged in order for one to inspect another's Registry.

To access a Registry on the network, choose Registry, Select Computer. The dialog box shown in Figure 2.11 appears with all the computers in your domain or workgroup displayed. Select the computer and then click OK. Two additional windows will appear in REGEDT32, one each for the HKLM and HKCU hives on the computer you selected. As Figure 2.12 shows, the title bar of the windows indicates which computer's Registry is displayed in the specific window.

Time for the standard warning again: Any changes you make to the remote computer's Registry will be reflected on the remote computer. Be extremely careful not to make a change you might later regret.

 Be sure to disconnect from the network computer before you shut down REGEDT32. If the option to Save Settings on Exit is enabled, the next time you start REGEDT32, the editor will attempt to reconnect to the remote computer you were last attached to. If the computer is not running or operable, you may experience a delay in the start of the editor.

When you want to disconnect from the remote computer's Registry, select one of the two windows displaying the remote computer's Registry. Then, choose Registry, Close from the menu.

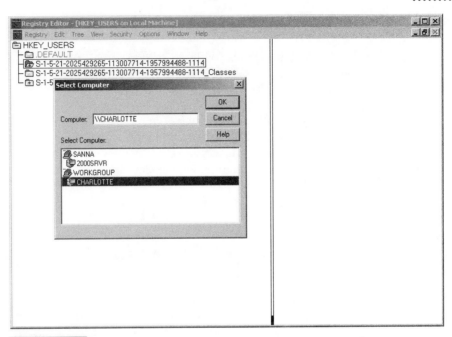

FIGURE 2.11   You can select the computer whose Registry you want to access from the Select Computer dialog box.

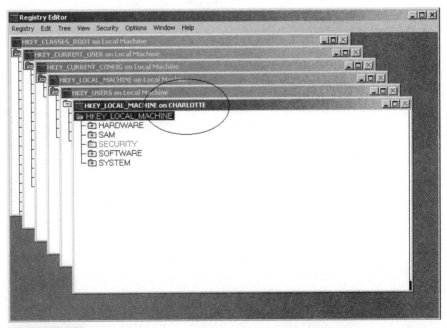

FIGURE 2.12   You can tell which Registry you're looking at by the title bar.

Making Bulk Changes to the Registry

Earlier in this chapter, you learned how to make changes to individual entries in the Registry. The techniques presented are useful for making a small number of changes, such as customizing some aspect of Windows 2000 behavior. It is likely, though, that you may need to make more substantial changes to the Registry, such as recreating an entire key, including all of the subordinate keys and value. This action might be required if a key was accidentally deleted. Consider yourself lucky if a careless mistake was made while working with the Registry and you can still start your Windows 2000. Another scenario in which you may work with bulk changes to the Registry is to exchange a series of keys and values with another computer. It's possible to extract an entire key from the Registry in one computer and then load the data in another. This makes it easy to mirror some Registry data in many computers. This section will show you the different functions available to make bulk changes to the Registry.

Loading and Unloading Hives with REGEDT32

REGEDT32 provides the ability to load and unload hives. As a review, a hive is a subtree of the Registry whose entire contents, including all subordinate keys and all values, is reflected in one file. As such, files created using the Save Key option (see next section) can be considered hives. As you learned in Chapter 1, only HKU and HKLM directly reflect data retrieved from an external file, so loading and unloading hives is only available for those two root keys.

The option to load and unload a hive is one of the best debugging and administrative tools in the Registry editors and in Windows 2000 in general. The option to load a hive allows you to inspect Registry values without impacting the Registry of the computer at which the inspection is taking place. Specifically, this option lets you load a hive into the Registry on the computer you are running and examine the keys and values of that hive. All the while, the settings and values of the Registry on the computer you are using stay intact, unaffected by the foreign hive loaded. Once the inspection is over, you can unload the hive so it no longer consumes memory.

LOADING THE HIVE

To load a hive, select either the top of the HKLM or HKCU root keys. Next, choose Registry, Load Hive from the menu. Browse through your computer or any computer you can see on the network. Locate the file you need to load. This file should have been created with the Save Key option in REGEDT32. Click Open. You are next prompted for a key to which the hive should be loaded, as shown in Figure 2.13. REGEDT32 will create this key for

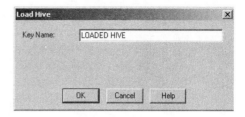

FIGURE 2.13   REGEDT32 prompts you for the name of the key it will create to house the hive you're loading.

you. Enter the name of the key, and click OK. The hive will appear in the key you specified (see Figure 2.14).

EDITING THE HIVE

As long as the hive is loaded into your REGEDT32, any changes you make to its keys or values are written to the file. It may be wise to immediately save the loaded hive to another file using the Save Key function (see the section entitled "Saving and Restoring Keys Using REGEDT32").

UNLOADING THE HIVE

When you no longer want to work with the hive you loaded, you may un-load it. To do so, select the key that was created when you loaded the hive. Next, select Registry, Unload Hive from the menu. The hive will disappear from the editor.

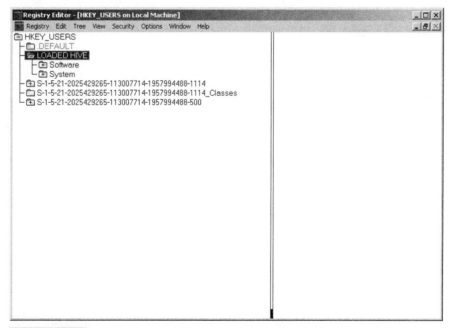

FIGURE 2.14   A loaded hive appears like hives stored on the host computer.

Saving and Restoring Keys Using REGEDT32

You can save a key to an external file and reload it quickly to any target key on either the computer that generated the file or another one using REGEDT32. This gives you the capability to move keys from one place to another in the Registry, as well as to very easily implement Registry keys and values on another computer regardless of the structure of the target Registry. This is also a valid option for diagnosing a problem on another computer that cannot access the network, hence eliminating the option to access the computer over the network.

This option differs from the import and export functions available in REGEDIT and the Save Subtree option in REGEDT32 in that the file is saved in binary format. It is impossible to inspect the contents of the file except when it is actually restored to a Registry. There are two important characteristics of the data saved when you use the Save Key option:

- No parent key information is saved. This means you must correctly specify the target when and if you later restore a key created with this option.

- Only the subordinate keys of the key you select are saved to the file, not the key itself. That means if you select, for example, the HKLM\Software\Microsoft key and then issue the Save Key command, just the keys beneath Microsoft are saved to the file, not the Microsoft key.

To save a key, first select the key to be saved. Next, choose Registry, Save Key from the menu. Select the location and supply a name, and then click OK.

You must have at least backup privileges on the computer to use Save Key.

To restore a key, select the target key. Next, choose Registry, Restore. Locate the file, select it, and then click OK. You will be prompted to confirm that you want to overwrite all keys subordinate to the target key with the contents of the file. If you are sure, click OK.

Working with Registry Data in Text Files

Both REGEDIT and REGEDT32 provide the facility to export Registry data to an external file. In both cases, this file can be edited with any application that can open text files, such as Notepad or Wordpad. Both editors also provide the option to update the Registry by loading an external file, such as an edited version of a file exported from the editor. There are a number of practical applications to this functionality:

- Update a number of Registry entries at one time.
- Change Registry structure quickly without use of an editor.
- Integrate Registry structure and values into many computers easily.

Exporting Data for Modification and Load Later

Of the two editors, REGEDIT is the only one that will allow you to export data, modify it in another application, and then reload the file to affect changes in the Registry.

When you export data from the Registry using REGEDIT, you have the option of exporting the entire Registry or just a selected key. If you select just a key to export, all subordinate keys and entries also are exported. Keep this point in mind, as the file created with the export can be very large.

To export the Registry from REGEDIT, select Registry, Export Registry File from the menu. If you do not want to export the entire Registry, it is helpful to first select the key to export before making this menu choice. The dialog box shown in Figure 2.15 appears.

If you forgot to specify the key to export, click the Selected branch option at the bottom of the dialog and then enter the full key name in the box

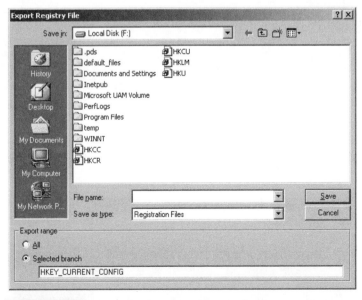

FIGURE 2.15   You can export the entire Registry or just one key from the Export Registry File dialog box.

provided. It may be easier simply to close the dialog box, click on the key to export, and then make the menu choice again.

To export the entire Registry, click the All option. When you have specified the Export range, specify the name of the file and its location, and then click OK. Depending upon how much data is exported and the speed of your computer, the export operation could take a few seconds.

Data exported from REGEDIT contains the full path to the entries exported, as well as the values and data type. This way, if the file were to be imported back into the Registry, the keys and entries would be loaded to their original position. Here is an example of the data exported from REGEDIT. You can tell both the data and format of the export file from the sample.

```
[HKEY_CURRENT_USER\Software\Microsoft\Windows NT\CurrentVersion\Network\User
Manager for Domains]
"SaveSettings"="1"

[HKEY_CURRENT_USER\Software\Microsoft\Windows NT\CurrentVersion\PrinterPorts]
"Fax"="winspool,Ne00:,15,45"
"Generic / Text Only"="winspool,FILE:,15,45"

[HKEY_CURRENT_USER\Software\Microsoft\Windows NT\CurrentVersion\Program Manager]

[HKEY_CURRENT_USER\Software\Microsoft\Windows NT\CurrentVersion\Program
Manager\Restrictions]
"EditLevel"=dword:00000000
"NoClose"=dword:00000000
"NoFileMenu"=dword:00000000
"NoRun"=dword:00000000
"NoSaveSettings"=dword:00000000
"Restrictions"=dword:00000000

[HKEY_CURRENT_USER\Software\Microsoft\Windows NT\CurrentVersion\Program
Manager\Settings]
"AutoArrange"=dword:00000001
"display.drv"="vga.drv"
"MinOnRun"=dword:00000000
"SaveSettings"=dword:00000001
"Window"="68 63 636 421 1"

[HKEY_CURRENT_USER\Software\Microsoft\Windows NT\CurrentVersion\Program
Manager\UNICODE Groups]

[HKEY_CURRENT_USER\Software\Microsoft\Windows NT\CurrentVersion\Setup]

[HKEY_CURRENT_USER\Software\Microsoft\Windows NT\CurrentVersion\Setup\Welcome]
"srvwiz"=dword:00000001

[HKEY_CURRENT_USER\Software\Microsoft\Windows NT\CurrentVersion\TaskManager]
"Preferences"=hex:70,01,00,00,e8,03,00,00,02,00,00,00,01,00,00,00,01,00,00,00,\
```

```
0a,00,00,00,0a,00,00,00,9e,01,00,00,c9,01,00,00,00,00,00,00,00,00,00,00,01,\

00,00,00,04,00,00,00,05,00,00,00,06,00,00,00,ff,ff,ff,ff,00,00,00,00,00,00,\
```

Exporting Data for Review Only

If you simply need to extract data from the Registry for review or archiving, you have a choice of either of the two editors. The presentation of exported data is easier to understand from REGEDT32, but a side benefit to using REGEDIT is that the file can be loaded back into the Registry. The previous section explained how to export data from REGEDIT. The process is slightly different in REGEDT32.

REGEDT32 relies on your selection of a key to determine what data to export. For example, if you click on HKLM\Software\Microsoft and then issue the export command, all of the keys and entries under Microsoft would be exported to the external file you specified. The only way to export the entire root key is to select the top of the hierarchy before you ask the editor to export.

To export data out of REGEDT32, select the key to export, and then choose Registry, Save Subtree As from the menu. Specify the name of the file and its location, and then click OK. Depending upon how much data is exported and the speed of your computer, the export operation could take a few seconds.

The following is an example of the data and format exported from the Registry using REGEDT32.

```
Key Name:          Software\Microsoft\Windows NT\CurrentVersion\Network\User
Manager for Domains
Class Name:        <NO CLASS>
Last Write Time:   8/4/99 - 4:01 PM
Value 0
  Name:            SaveSettings
  Type:            REG_SZ
  Data:            1

Key Name:          Software\Microsoft\Windows NT\CurrentVersion\PrinterPorts
Class Name:        <NO CLASS>
Last Write Time:   8/7/99 - 4:56 PM
Value 0
  Name:            Fax
  Type:            REG_SZ
  Data:            winspool,Ne00:,15,45

Value 1
  Name:            Generic / Text Only
  Type:            REG_SZ
  Data:            winspool,FILE:,15,45
```

```
Key Name:            Software\Microsoft\Windows NT\CurrentVersion\Program Manager
Class Name:          <NO CLASS>
Last Write Time:     8/4/99 - 4:01 PM

 Key Name:              Software\Microsoft\Windows NT\CurrentVersion\Program
Manager\Restrictions
Class Name:          <NO CLASS>
Last Write Time:     8/4/99 - 4:01 PM
Value 0
  Name:              EditLevel
  Type:              REG_DWORD
  Data:              0

Value 1
  Name:              NoClose
  Type:              REG_DWORD
  Data:              0

Value 2
  Name:              NoFileMenu
  Type:              REG_DWORD
  Data:              0

Value 3
  Name:              NoRun
  Type:              REG_DWORD
  Data:              0

Value 4
  Name:              NoSaveSettings
  Type:              REG_DWORD
  Data:              0

Value 5
  Name:              Restrictions
  Type:              REG_DWORD
  Data:              0

Key Name:            Software\Microsoft\Windows NT\CurrentVersion\Program
Manager\Settings
Class Name:          <NO CLASS>
Last Write Time:     8/4/99 - 4:01 PM
Value 0
  Name:              AutoArrange
  Type:              REG_DWORD
  Data:              0x1

Value 1
  Name:              display.drv
  Type:              REG_SZ
  Data:              vga.drv
```

```
Value 2
  Name:              MinOnRun
  Type:              REG_DWORD
  Data:              0

 Value 3
  Name:              SaveSettings
  Type:              REG_DWORD
  Data:              0x1

Value 4
  Name:              Window
  Type:              REG_SZ
  Data:              68 63 636 421 1

Key Name:          Software\Microsoft\Windows NT\CurrentVersion\Program
Manager\UNICODE Groups
Class Name:        <NO CLASS>
Last Write Time:   8/4/99 - 4:01 PM

Key Name:          Software\Microsoft\Windows NT\CurrentVersion\Setup
Class Name:        <NO CLASS>
Last Write Time:   8/4/99 - 4:01 PM

Key Name:          Software\Microsoft\Windows NT\CurrentVersion\Setup\Welcome
Class Name:        <NO CLASS>
Last Write Time:   8/4/99 - 4:01 PM
Value 0
  Name:              srvwiz
  Type:              REG_DWORD
  Data:              0x1

Key Name:          Software\Microsoft\Windows NT\CurrentVersion\TaskManager
Class Name:        REG_BINARY
Last Write Time:   8/5/99 - 7:23 AM
Value 0
  Name:              Preferences
  Type:              REG_BINARY
  Data:
00000000   70 01 00 00 e8 03 00 00 - 02 00 00 00 01 00 00 00   p...è..........
00000010   01 00 00 00 0a 00 00 00 - 0a 00 00 00 9e 01 00 00   ..............
00000020   c9 01 00 00 00 00 00 00 - 00 00 00 00 01 00 00 00   É..............
160        Ç...............
```

Importing Data with the Editor

If you used REGEDIT to create an external file, you can then use REGEDIT to load that same file into the Registry. The load process will update the Registry, reflecting the keys and values in the file. Of course, the requirement that a file to be loaded into the Registry be created with REGEDIT isn't really a strong requirement. As long as you can format a file to match REGEDIT's load format requirements, you can create the file from scratch.

You can use one of two methods to load a file into the Registry via REGEDIT:

- Choose Registry, Import Registry File from the menu. Select the file to load and then click Open.
- Use Windows Explorer to locate the file to load. Double-click on the file.

Regardless of the method you use, a message will appear on the screen confirming for you that the file was loaded.

Putting Security In and Around the Registry

The Registry is perhaps the most important component in Windows 2000. If even a small part of the Registry becomes corrupted or is improperly modified, there is little chance that your system will run properly, and there is a *great* chance you will need to fix your system, possibly to the extent of reinstalling Windows 2000. It makes sense, then, to secure the Registry, both from malicious modification and from accidental modification. This chapter will address security issues in and around the Registry from two perspectives: the tools you can use in Windows 2000 to secure the Registry and specific ways you can apply those tools.

Here's what you will find in this chapter:

- A review of the requirement for security in and around the Registry, including examples of the sensitive data contained in it.

- An overview of the security and system management tools delivered with Windows 2000.

- Some examples and specific techniques you can use today to secure the Registry both from a user's desktop and from across the Active Directory.

The Need for Registry Security

When you consider all of the elements of Windows 2000 that should be secured, such as critical files and folders, printers, policies, and certificates, the Registry should be at the top of the list. The Registry stores much data that would be considered private by the user, the network the machine belongs to, or the organization the user represents.

As an example, the security ID for each account-holding user on the workstation is stored in the Registry, and while cracking into the passwords associated with the SID is a difficult task, having the SID is a great start. In another example, the name of the user last logged on to the network is stored in the Registry (unless group policy has disabled this function), and details about the network to which the computer is attached can also be gleaned from the Registry. In short, protecting the Registry is critical to retain a secure environment for a standalone, as well as a networked machine.

The need for security in and around the Registry isn't to address just malicious threats or illegal or improper access. Ensuring that the casual user who might wander into the Registry via one of the editors or a third party tool also must be accounted for. By using one of the techniques in this chapter, you can secure the Registry so an inexperienced or careless user cannot harm the Registry, and, at the same time, still leave the Registry available for inspection by the user and diagnostics by you.

Using Windows 2000 Security Tools

Windows 2000 provides a number of security tools. How you use each either alone or in conjunction with another is a function of how comfortable you are with them, how familiar you are with them, and what level and type of security you want to apply to the Registry. In the next section, you will learn how to apply each of the following tools to real life scenarios:

- MMC
- Group Policy
- Security Template
- Permissions

Using the Microsoft Management Console

A popular tool used to secure the Registry is the Microsoft Management Console (MMC). The MMC is a new component provided with Windows 2000 that serves as a front-end to most administrative tools in the operating system. The MMC, though, isn't just a front-end or an attractive user-interface. The MMC is really a framework for packaging all administrative tools provided by both Microsoft in the operating system, as well as by independent software vendors (ISV). This framework provides a consistent interface to the user, as well as a consistent method for making changes across all administrative tasks.

Examples of use of the MMC include Computer Management, Event Viewer, Routing and Remote Access Administration Each is available from the Administrative Tools menu.

 If Administrative tools does not appear on the Programs menu, right-click on the Taskbar and choose Properties from the context menu that appears. Next, choose the Advanced tab, and then click on the Display Administrative Tools option from the list of Start Menu Settings. Click OK.

STARTING THE MMC

You can launch the MMC from any computer running Windows 2000. To do so, click Start and then choose Run. Type "MMC" and then press the Enter key. The MMC appears, as shown in Figure 3.1. The MMC derives its value from snap-ins, which are discussed in the next section.

MMC SNAP-INS

The MMC alone has almost no value. The MMC is a framework, and as such, it derives its usefulness from the applications and tools you use within it, called *snap-ins*. Each snap-in represents a set of features and functionality

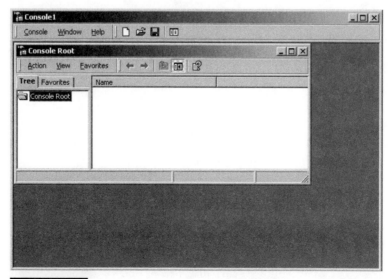

FIGURE 3.1   The MMC provides a consistent framework for developers and user interface for users to administer Windows 2000.

TABLE 3.1	Useful Snap-ins for Registry Security	
Snap-in	**Use**	**Platform**
Active Directory Users and Computers	Manages objects within the active directory; provides interface to group policy object for the domain, where Registry policy can be created and applied.	Domain controller only
Group Policy	Creates group policy objects, which can be applied to domain, OUs, sites, stand-alone computers, etc. GPOs can contain security policy for the Registry.	Any platform
Local Users and Groups	Creates user accounts and groups applied to the local computer.	Any platform other than domain controllers
Security Configuration and Analysis	Configures security from templates; performs security survey against baseline you provide and reports inconsistencies.	Any platform
Security Templates	Interface for editing security templates, which contains security configuration details applicable to any computer.	Any platform

used to administer some part of Windows 2000 or a Windows 2000 application. You can add snap-ins to the MMC whenever you need to use the functionality they contain. Table 3.1 shows you the most useful snap-ins for securing the Registry. The table includes a column that shows the platform where the snap-in is available.

You can usually tell what kind of functionality a snap-in provides by its name. However, a longer description accompanies many of the snap-ins at the bottom of the window, as shown in Figure 3.2. The list of snap-ins appears when you either create a new console or add a snap-in to a console that already exists. Creating a console is covered later in the "Creating a Console for Registry Security Use" section.

You can store on disk the state of the MMC with a particular snap-in loaded. This saved representation of the MMC is known as a *console*. You can also save a related set of snap-ins in a custom console.

A long list of snap-ins provides you with many of the administrative tools you'll need.

This way, when you open the console, all of the snap-ins are already loaded. You might create a console that contains all of the security related snap-ins. A number of prebuilt consoles are shipped with Windows 2000. Here are a few of the prebuilt consoles, as well as the snap-ins associated with each: Disk Defragmenter, Disk Management, Distributed file system, and DNS.

Because each snap-in provides a different kind of functionality, certain snap-ins do not behave in a standard manner. For example, when you load a typical snap-in, such as the group policy editor, its settings are reflected almost immediately in column and row format in the left pane. However, with the Group Policy snap-in, you are first prompted for the scope that the Group Policy will affect, such as the local computer that the MMC is running on, or perhaps the Active Director default group policy object (see Figure 3.3).

CREATING A CONSOLE FOR REGISTRY SECURITY USE

As an administrator, it makes sense to have a security console available. This console can act as your security toolset. Be sure to properly secure it. You can build this console on your own using the list of recommended security snap-ins in Table 3.1, or you can follow these steps to create one:

1. Click the Start menu, choose Run, and then enter MMC and press Enter. The Microsoft Management Console appears.

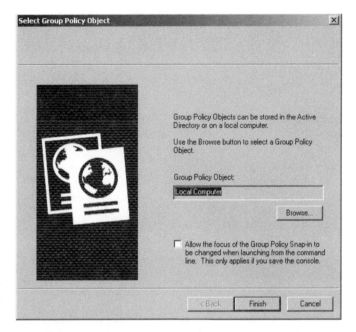

Select Group Policy Object

Group Policy Objects can be stored in the Active Directory or on a local computer.

Use the Browse button to select a Group Policy Object.

Group Policy Object:

Local Computer

Browse...

☐ Allow the focus of the Group Policy Snap-in to be changed when launching from the command line. This only applies if you save the console.

< Back   Finish   Cancel

FIGURE 3.3   The Group Policy snap-in prompts you for the scope.

2. Choose Console, Add-Remove Snap-in from the menu.

3. Click the Add button. The list of snap-ins appears.

4. Locate and then select the Security Templates snap-in. Click Add.

5. Locate and then select the Security Configuration and Analysis snap-in. Click Add.

6. Locate and then select the Group snap-in. Click Add. You are prompted for the Group Policy Object. If you are securing a standalone computer, click Finish. If you are securing elements of the Active Directory, click the Browse button. For now, choose the Default Domain Policy that appears under the Domains/OUs tab. You can select a different GPO when you need to. Click OK and then click Finish.

7. Locate, and then select the Active Directory Uses and Computers snap-in. This snap-in will be available if the computer you are working on is a domain controller. Click Add.

8. Click Close. You are returned to the Add/Remove Snap-in dialog.

9. Click OK.

10. Choose Console, Save as from the menu. Enter a name for the snap-in.

11. Select a location on the Start menu for the snap-in by navigating to the Documents and Settings folder in the Save in dropdown list. Next, open the folder for the appropriate user to have access to this snap-in.

Working with Group Policy

As a Windows 2000 system administrator, you can use group policy in your efforts to secure the Registry on each of your user's computers. Group policy is the set of rules that determines the configuration and access for managed Windows 2000 computers. The group policy function in Windows 2000 is extensive, and it's not the objective of this chapter (or book) to fully explain Active Directory management. However, the following discussion is a review of group policy, the components that make up policy, and how they can be applied to Registry security.

GROUP POLICY OVERVIEW

Group policy is the set of rules that determines the configuration and access for managed Windows 2000 computers. This management can occur over the network, in which case a network administrator defines the group policy that is applied either to computers when the network detects they are started up or to users when the network detects they have logged on. This management by group policy also can be applied to standalone, non-networked computers. Because the definition of group policy includes the words *access,* you might think that security is really the element that defines access. Correct, but you can integrate security settings into group policy so that all of the regulations and control of all resources in the enterprise are administered from as few places as possible.

An administrator defines group policy to determine what users can and cannot do and how their machines are configured. For example, group policy can be used to dictate what items appear on the users' Start menu, whether users have the rights to execute certain programs on their desktop, what Windows 2000 services users can start and stop, how often users must change their password, and much more. There are dozens of individual elements you can configure to define your own group policy. There are dozens of options available for the administrator to define group policy. Figure 3.4 shows an example of some of the options.

As an administrator, you can create sets of rules that apply to a group, such as all of the computers at headquarters. When you define a number of rules together in one group policy, this policy is known as a *group policy object (GPO).* An object in Windows 2000, such as a domain, OU, site, or local computer, can have multiple GPOs applied to it. For example, the domain might have three GPOs applied to it, one that manages the basic desktop configuration, another that defines public keys and IP security, and a third that manages Registry and file access. Naturally, you would want to ensure that elements of GPOs do not conflict with one another. To manage the problems that might arise from this flexibility, there are rules that determine the precedence when multiple GPOs are applied to one Windows 2000 component. These rules are covered in the next section.

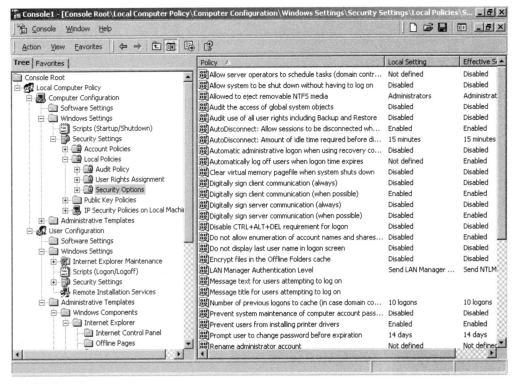

FIGURE 3.4   Group policy consists of a large number of individual settings and options.

ORDER OF POLICY

Group policy is enforced by all of the GPOs that apply to the objects receiving the policy. For example, a computer at a user's desk will receive policy from the local computer policy established at his or her computer, as well as from the domain if an Active Directory is set up, as well from an organizational unit if the computer belongs to one. In cases like this, there is an order in which policy is applied: The most recent policies applied supercede any policies applied earlier in the order.

The following is the order in which policy is applied:

1. **Local:** Policies applied to the local computer.

2. **Site:** Policy objects applied to the site.

3. **Domain:** Policy objects applied to the domain.

4. **Organization Unit:** Policy objects applied to the organizational unit.

Again, the policies that are applied later override those applied earlier. However, this does not mean that all rules defined in a policy are ignored when a policy is applied later—there may be some elements of a policy that are not enabled in a later-applied policy. In this case, the same element configured in an earlier-applied policy is enforced. For example, if a local policy stipulated that a shortcut to the REGEDT32 editor appears on the Start menu, and the Domain policy does not configure a Start menu policy, then the shortcut to REGEDT32 would appear.

PRECEDENCE AND INHERITANCE

By default, Windows 2000 applies the same GPO to all children of an object that receives the policy. Children objects are those objects that descend from another object. An example of a parent–child relationship would be a folder (parent) that contains a folder or file (children). Another example is related to the Registry. Subordinate keys are children to keys that closer to the top of the hierarchy where the root key is located.

As an example of host children object receiving the same policy as applied to the parent, all subordinate keys in the Registry receive the same policy as applied to the parent key. There are a few options that let you customize this behavior. The dialog box in Figure 3.5 shows an example of each.

The Block Policy Inheritance option restricts policy applied to the parent of the item you are working with to override the policy you are applying. For example, if you apply a GPO to a folder and that folder's parent has a

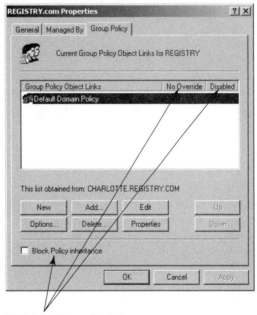

FIGURE 3.5 Two options help manage interoperability between GPOs.

GPO Inhertitance Controls

different GPO applied to it, the Block Policy Inheritance option will stop the parent's GPO from affecting the child folder.

Related to the Block Inheritance option is the No Override option. Actually, these options are related in that they produce opposite results. This option forces the GPO applied to the parent to be applied to all children of the item getting the policy, even if the children use the Block Policy Inheritance option.

Viewing and Modifying Group Policy

The policies and permissions established on the Active Directory or workstation where you are logged on might give you the rights to view, and possibly modify, group policy. Remember, group policy can be applied to a number of different objects, all of which can create policy for a single computer, users, group of computers, OU, and so on. So, just because you see a particular security setting specified in one GPO, do not assume that this setting will be applied to all users and computers. Follow these steps to inspect a global policy object.

1. Locate the object for which you want to view group policy. As an example, to view the group policy for the domain, you should open the Active Directory users and Computers snap-in.

2. Right-click on the object for which you want to view group policy and then choose Properties from the menu that appears.

3. Choose the Group Policy tab.

4. Click on any (if more than one shows) group policy object in the list and then click Edit.
   The Group Policy snap-in opens, as shown in Figure 3.6.

5. Navigate through the security and policy settings.

6. If your rights permit, you may modify security and policy settings from this snap-in. Naturally, be careful not to change a particularly sensitive setting. Also note that there is no concept of Save or Undo from this snap-in. When you make a change to a policy, it will be applied to all member assets.

7. When complete, choose Console, Exit from the menu. Next, click OK or Cancel in the Properties dialog box.

Security Templates

You can use a security template to apply the same set of security attributes to any group policy objects. Using a template means you can be sure a consistent set of security controls is applied. A security template contains all of the critical security settings. When a security template is applied to a group pol-

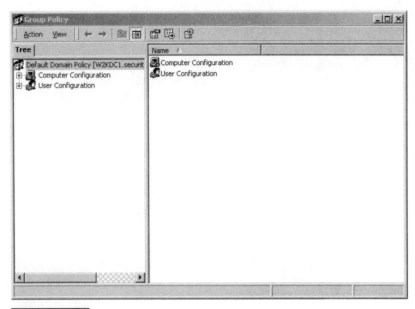

FIGURE 3.6   The Group Policy snap-in.

icy, any object to which the group policy is applied is affected by the contents of the template. Here is a list of the options that can be set with a security template:

- Password Policy
- Account Lockout Policy
- Kerberos Policy
- Audit Policy
- User Rights
- Security Option
- Event Log
- Restricted Groups
- System Services
- Registry
- File System

Windows 2000 ships with a number of prebuilt templates. For example, templates are available for basic workstation security, basic domain controller security, and more. You can use one of these predefined templates, modify one and then save it with a new name, or create a template from scratch. The templates show a variety of settings for different elements of security in the operating system. Depending on the setting you choose to inspect, the controls will vary. For example, the Maximum password age setting will display a control where you can enter days, while the Registry node forces you to select a Registry key and then assign permissions to it. Follow these steps to view, create, or modify a security template and then to assign it to a group policy object.

1. Start the MMC (refer to the "Using the Microsoft Management Console" section found earlier in this chapter).
2. Open a console that contains the Security Templates snap-in.
3. Open the Security Template node, and then open the node for the folder where the templates are stored. Your screen should appear like the one shown in Figure 3.7.
4. To inspect the settings for any of the predefined templates, click once on the name of the template and navigate through the various settings.

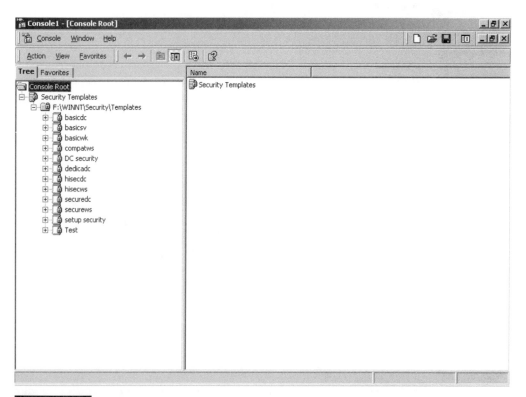

FIGURE 3.7 Windows 2000 ships with a number of predefined templates.

5. To create a new template, right-click on the folder node for the templates and then choose New Template from the menu that appears. Supply a name and description for the template and then click OK. Define the template by working with each of the appropriate security settings.

6. To create a new template from a predefined template, right-click on the template you want to use as a baseline and then choose Save as from the menu that appears. Supply a name and description for the template and then click OK. Define the template by working with each of the appropriate security settings.

7. When you complete defining or inspecting the template, choose Console, Exit from the menu. Note that there is no Save function; changes you make are stored to disk as you make them.

8. To apply a template to global policy, open the global policy object using the instructions provided earlier in the "Viewing and Modifying Group Policy" section.

warning   Be aware that the contents of the template will overwrite any security settings already created in this GPO. Choose a template and carefully make the decision to apply it.

9. Locate the Security Settings node under Computer Configuration. Right-click on the node and then choose Import Policy from the menu.

10. Select the template you want to apply and then click Open.

Registry Permissions

Windows 2000 uses permissions to secure many aspects of the network and the local computer. Permissions are the rights applied to almost any object in Windows 2000. These permissions determine what actions are legal for users to perform on the object. For example, a certain user might have permissions sufficient to read a file but not to delete it. You can assign permissions individually or via groups. For example, Joe from Accounting has Full Control permissions over the general ledger database files, but the Reporting group has just Read permissions over the database. Permissions only work with NTFS-formatted volumes. NTFS is the Windows 2000 file system. While you can run Windows 2000 on other file systems, NTFS is integrated into Windows 2000 and provides the features necessary to create a secure environment.

The owner of an object creates these permissions. The owner specifies what users have rights to the object and how powerful those rights are. The owner of an object is the person who creates it, and many times, especially for internal objects like parts of the Registry, the person who created an object is the default administrator account. The owner of an object also can grant Full Control permission of an object to another account, which would then give that target account the rights to assign permissions to the object.

PERMISSIONS AND OBJECTS

Almost any item in Windows 2000 can be considered an object. Objects in Windows 2000 are relevant to security because you may only use permissions to secure objects. Examples of objects that may be secured with permissions include files, folders, printers, policy objects, and more. Two objects to which you can apply permissions that can help you secure the Registry are (1) the executable file that launches one of the Registry editors by assigning permission to the file that launches the Registry editors. You can ensure only the approved users have the rights to use these tools: (a) for REGEDT32, this file is REGEDT32.EXE; (b) for REGEDIT, this file is REGEDIT.EXE. (2) The second object is a key in the Registry. By assigning permission to a key, you can be sure only approved users have the rights to work with a potentially critical key.

TYPES OF PERMISSIONS

Depending on the object, there maybe one or two types of permissions available for assignment:

- **Standard permissions.** Standard permissions are the typical permissions that can be applied to almost any type of object. Standard permissions include Read, Write, and Full Control. This list may vary based on the object, but you can usually depend on the options to assign Read, Write, and Full Control access to an object.

    In many cases, the standard permissions will be specific to the type of object. For example, the standard permission for a printer includes Print, Manage Printer, and Manage Documents. These permissions are not applicable to an object other than a printer, such a file.

    Figure 3.8 shows the standard permissions that may be applied to a file.

- **Advanced permissions.** Advanced permissions provide more control of the rights assigned to the objects. Advanced permissions are more customized to the type of object being secured than standard permissions. While standard permissions are relevant to the objects, advanced permissions provide even greater control.

    Figure 3.9 shows the advanced permissions that may be applied to a file.

REGISTRY KEY AND FILE PERMISSIONS

Depending on the level of security you want to apply to the Registry, you can create a strategy that mixes the use of permissions applied to the Registry editor executable file and Registry keys. The tables in this section explain the

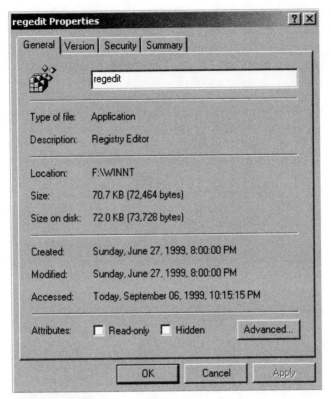

FIGURE 3.8   Permissions enable you to specify what users have and do not have the rights to read from or write to a file.

types of permissions available to secure files (like the Registry editor executable) and Registry keys.

Standard Registry key permissions may be acceptable for your use. Table 3.2 shows the standard permissions you can apply to a Registry key. Remember that only the owner of the key or an account granted Full Control by the owner may assign these permissions to other users.

Advanced Registry key permissions provide extraordinary control over access and use of a key. Table 3.3 shows the advanced permissions you can apply to a Registry key.

The file permissions are available for you to assign to the executable file that launches REGEDT32 or REGEDIT. The standard permissions, shown in Table 3.4, are more than sufficient for securing access to these files, so I won't show you the advanced permissions for files.

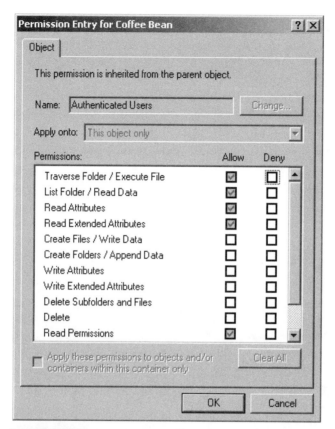

FIGURE 3.9 Advanced permissions give you the ability to assign rights for every task imaginable related to file.

TABLE 3.2 Standard Registry Key Permissions

Permission	Description
Read	This permission allows the key to be examined, including its subordinate keys and entries.
Full Control	This permission grants complete control to the key. This control includes the rights to delete and modify the key. This permission would also allow the bearer to assign permissions to the key.

TABLE 3.3	Advanced Registry Key Permissions
Permission	**Description**
Query Value	Determines whether the user has sufficient rights to read the value of an entry. This read might be achieved simply by using one of the Registry editors, or it might be achieved using an application.
Set Value	Determines whether the user has sufficient rights to modify or create for the first time the value of an entry. This edit operation might be achieved simply by using one of the Registry editors, or it might be achieved using an application.
Create Subkey	Determines whether the user has sufficient rights to create a subkey under the target key.
Enumerate Subkeys	Both Windows 2000 and Windows 2000 applications sometimes have a requirement to retrieve a list of the subordinate keys under another key. This process is known as enumeration. There is no concept of enumeration for a user with one of the Registry editors; enumeration is only relevant for a third-party application for Windows 2000.
Notify	The Registry has the capability to send messages when the value of a specific key changes. Which keys generate a message is determined by the application that is using the Registry. The Notify permission determines whether the user has sufficient rights for the notification event to occur should the value of the key change. While this permission might not seem relevant to the casual or even the power user, this permission could be critical to an internal process or application. Certain Registry values may need to be modified based on a modification to another key, and this notification mechanism enables this update to happen. If this permission is denied to the System or Administrator, unpredictable results might be returned.
Create Link	Determines whether the user has sufficient rights to create a link in the Registry. A Registry link is an element that points to another entry in the Registry.
Delete	Determines whether the user has sufficient rights to delete the target key.
Write DAC	Determines whether the user has the right to determine permissions on the target key for other users.
Write Owner	Determines whether the user has the rights to edit the key. If this permission is set to Deny, a user will be unable to see the key, including the structure of subordinate subkeys, as well as any entries for the key.
Read Control	Determines whether the user has the rights to view the key. If this permission is set to Deny, a user will be unable to see the key, including the structure of subordinate subkeys, as well as any entries for the key.

TABLE 3.4	Standard Registry Key Permissions
Permission	**Description**
Full Control	Grants complete control over the file, including deleting, editing, running, as well as granting other users permissions to the file.
Modify	Grants write privileges to the file. This means an account with Modify rights can edit the file. In the case of the Registry editor executables, this permission probably isn't relevant because it is impossible to edit one of these files with a hex or binary editor.
Read & Execute	Allows the user to run the file if it is an application and to open review the contents if the file is suitable for this operation. This would be the permission to assign to an account to allow the user to review the Registry but not to change its structure or values.
Read	Grants the right to open the file for inspection but not to save changes.
Write	Grants the right to open the file for inspection and to make permanent changes.

SUBORDINATE KEYS AND PERMISSION

You have the option to apply any permission assigned to a key to all of its subordinate keys as well. For example, you might grant Full Control permission of the HKLM\Software to a particular user. That user would also have Full Control rights to all of the subkeys under HKLM\Software. Other options include assigning the permission to just the key and not any of its subordinates (just HKLM\Software in our example), or to just the key's subordinates (all of HKLM\Software's subordinate keys, but not HKLM\Software).

PROPAGATION OF PERMISSIONS

You should be aware of any permission established for a parent key. If the option to propagate those permissions to children objects exists, then the effective rights for the key you are working on may also be affected by the parent key's permissions. Rights assigned by permission are cumulative. This means all permissions generated for the key, both by the parent and by explicitly setting permission on a key, are applied. In the case of a conflict—such as if User A has Full Control rights to a key and that permission has been set to apply to all child objects, but User A has no rights to one of the dependent keys—Windows 2000 will use the more restrictive setting. In this case, UserA will not have rights to the key.

The propagation of permission to child objects is not an automatic setting. You can turn this option off.

Remove or Deny.................

You may be tempted to remove a permission for a user if you do not want that user to have access to a particular Registry key. You should consider using a Deny-type permission instead of removing the user or the group from the list of permissions. The reason for this is that permissions applied from elsewhere in the system might give that user Allow-type access to the Registry key you are trying to secure. An example of this is where permissions from a Registry key are inherited from the permissions applied to the key's parent key.

The Registry

One of the most powerful tools for administering a secure Registry in Windows 2000 is the Registry. The Administrative Templates component of group policy stores its settings in the Registry.

Registry Security Solutions

The prior sections introduced you to tools and concepts for securing the Registry. In this section, you will learn how to use the tools and apply the concepts. Solutions are provided both for the standalone and the network computers. Table 3.5 shows which solution is appropriate for which platform.

Solution 1: Using Group Policy and Permissions to Secure the Editors

One of the best methods you can use to prevent users in the Active Directory from editing the Registry is to deny users the ability to use the editors. You can do this using the permissions function. If you properly define permissions, your system can be configured so that only administrators and other power users in your organization have the rights to use the editors. This

TABLE 3.5	Solution Checklist	
Solution	**Standalone**	**Network**
1		✓
2	✓	
3		✓
4	✓	
5	✓	✓
6	✓	✓

technique takes advantage of group policy and permissions. Refer to the first sections in this chapter for a review of both.

Follow these steps to apply permissions to the executable files that launch the Registry editors using group policy.

1. Open a console that displays the GPO you want to apply Registry to. You may also simply open the GPO by right-clicking on the item receiving the policy, such as a domain.

2. Navigate to Computer Configuration\Windows Settings\Security Settings\ File System.

3. Right-click in the right-side pane and then click Add File from the menu that appears.

   The dialog box shown in Figure 3.10 appears. Note that the drives displayed in the figure will most likely differ from those installed on your computer.

4. Navigate to the main Windows 2000 folder and then to the SYSTEM32 subfolder. Locate the file REGEDT32.EXE, click once on it, and then click OK.

   The Permissions dialog box appears.

5. The accounts with permissions assigned to the file appear in the list at the top of the dialog. You can click on each entry in the list to see the assigned permissions, which appear in the list at the bottom of the dialog box.

   If the check boxes appear gray, then permissions from the parent of this file (the folder where the file is located) are in force. To override parent permissions, clear the Allow inheritable permissions from parent check box.

6. If the list shows users who should not have the right to run the editor, click the name and then click Deny for each of the permissions shown.

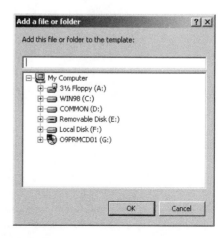

FIGURE 3.10   You select the files to secure on the computer where you define the policy; the policy figures out how to apply the files to the target computer.

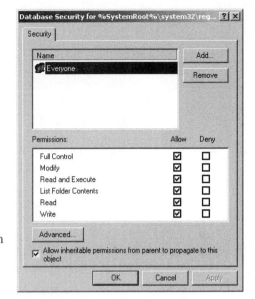

FIGURE 3.11 You define which users or groups will have Full Control permissions to the executable file for the editor.

7. Ensure that the administrator's group or some high-level group that you have created has Full Control permission to the key.

8. To define permission for an account or a group not shown in the list, click Add. The dialog box shown in Figure 3.11 appears.

Select the account or group from the list at the top of the dialog box and then click Add. You may select multiple accounts or groups and then set each permission individually. When the list at the bottom of the dialog shows all of the accounts or groups for which you want to specify permissions, click OK. Last, click on the account or group you just added to change and then select either Allow or Deny for the specific permission in the list at the bottom of the dialog box.

9. Click OK.

10. Repeat steps 3 through 8 for the REGEDIT.EXE file, which is stored in the main Windows folder.

11. Notice how the right-side pane shows variables for the name of the Windows folder. This way, the policy can be applied to the member computer regardless of where Windows is installed.

Solution 2: Using Permissions to Secure the Editors Locally

Permissions can be applied to assets on a standalone computer as easily as they can be used with group policy on the network. You can apply Deny permissions to the files that launch the two Registry editors to restrict users from running these tools. You would probably want to grant Full Control permissions of the files to Administrators.

Follow these steps to assign permissions to the Registry editor executable files on a standalone computer.

1. Log on to the computer whose Registry is to be secured with an account with administrator level rights.

2. Navigate to the folder where the executable file for the appropriate Registry editor is located. For REGEDIT, the location is the main Windows folder. For REGEDT32, the location is the SYSTEM32 subfolder in the main Windows folder.

3. Right-click on the file and choose Properties from the menu that appears.

4. Choose the Security tab. The dialog box shown in Figure 3.12 appears.

5. The account(s) or group(s) with permissions already established for the key appear in the list at the top of the dialog. You can click on each entry in the list to see the assigned permission, which appears in the list at the bottom of the dialog box.

   If the check boxes appear gray, then permissions from the parent of this file (the folder where the file is located) are in force. To override parent permissions, clear the Allow inheritable permissions from parent check box.

6. If the list shows users who should not have the right to run the editor, click the name and then choose Deny for each of the permissions shown.

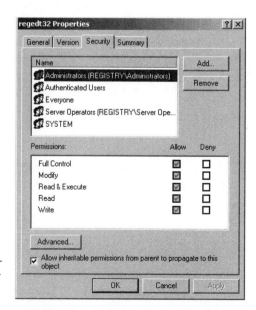

FIGURE 3.12   Permissions are defined by either the use name or by the group name.

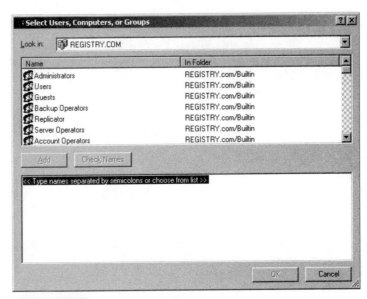

FIGURE 3.13   You define which users or groups will have Full Control permissions to the executable file for the editor.

7. Ensure that the administrator's group or some high-level group that you might have created has Full Control permission.

8. To define permission for an account or a group not shown in the list, click Add. The dialog box shown in Figure 3.13 appears.

   Select the account or group from the list at the top and then click Add. You may select multiple accounts or groups and then set their permissions individually. When the list at the bottom of the dialog shows all of the accounts or group for which you want to specify permissions, click OK. Last, click on the account or group you just added to change and then select either Allow or Deny for the specific permission in the list at the bottom of the dialog box.

9. Click OK.

Solution 3: Using a Security Template and Permissions to Secure Specific Keys

You can use a template to specify the keys in the Registry you want to secure. Using the template makes it easy to apply the Registry settings to any GPO you like. Using a template is not required for securing the Active Directory computer's Registry keys, but it makes it easy to apply security in a large forest of domains. Refer to the previous sections in this chapter for help on the Security Templates snap-in and working with templates.

You must be very careful when you assign permissions to individual Registry keys. You should not modify the default permissions for SYSTEM and administrators, and you should thoroughly test any changes you make to users' rights to keys.

Follow these steps to secure specific Registry keys on networked computers.

1. Open a console that gives you access to the Security templates snap-in.
2. Create a new template or edit an existing template.
3. Click once on the template.
4. Right-click on the Registry node and click Add Key from the menu that appears.

   The dialog box shown in Figure 3.14 appears.
5. Navigate to the key you want to secure and then click OK. The Permissions dialog box appears.
6. The accounts or groups of accounts with permissions assigned to the key appear in the list at the top of the dialog. You can click on each entry in the list to see the assigned permissions.

   If the check boxes appear gray, then permissions from the parent of this key are in force. To override parent permissions, clear the Allow inheritable permissions from parent check box.
7. If the list shows users who should not have the right to the key, click the name and then choose Deny for each of the permissions shown.

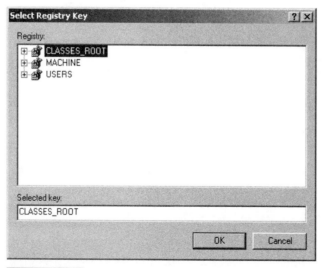

FIGURE 3.14   You select the key you would like to secure.

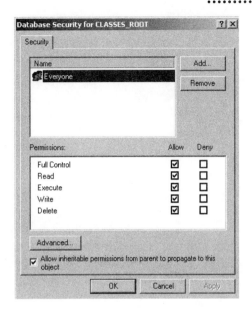

FIGURE 3.15 You define which users or groups will have Full Control permissions to the key.

8. To define permission for an account or a group not shown in the list, click Add. The dialog box shown in Figure 3.15 appears.

   Select the account or group from the list at the top and then click Add. You may select multiple accounts or groups and then set each permission individually. When the list at the bottom of the dialog shows all of the accounts or group for whom you want to specify permissions, click OK. Last, click on the account or group you just added to change and then select either Allow or Deny for the specific permission in the list at the bottom of the dialog box.

9. Click OK.

10. To assign advanced permissions, such as those listed in Table 3.3 above, or to specify the permission be applied to just subkeys of the key you selected, click the Advanced button.

11. Repeat steps 4 through 10 for each key to be secured.

12. Open a console that gives you access to the GPO where you want to apply this template. You may want to consider creating a GPO just to store the settings from the template.

12. Locate the Security Settings node under Computer Configuration. Right-click on the node and then choose Import Policy from the menu.

13. Select the template you just worked on and then choose Open.

    The Registry permissions you created in the template are applied to the GPO.

Solution 4: Using Permissions to Secure Keys at the Standalone Computer

Another application of the permissions feature in Windows 2000 is to secure the keys that a user might accidentally or maliciously change at each workstation. This solution requires the person doing the securing to open the Registry at each workstation to be secured. It also requires the person doing the securing to log on using an account with administrator level rights.

You must use extreme caution in setting permissions. You should test this technique thoroughly before using it on a wide basis. Windows 2000 will use administrative access to retrieve the data it needs from the Registry, so be sure to continue to allow administrator and SYSTEM continued Full Control access to all keys. If you fail to do so, Windows 2000 may not be able to retrieve the data it needs, so your system may not longer operate after your change. Also, while it is written many times in this book, be sure to back up the Registry before making any changes to permissions. This way, should any of the exhaustive tests you perform after changing the permissions return unacceptable results, you can be in a position to restore the Registry to its premodification state.

Assigning permissions for keys permits users to use a Registry editor, such as the two that ship with Windows 2000 but, depending on how the permissions are assigned, does not permit them to modify the data. Because only HKEY_LOCAL_MACHINE and HKEY_CURRENT_USER actually represent stored data in the Registry, these are the only two keys you need to secure. Follow these steps to assign permissions for these two keys:

1. Log on to the target computer with appropriate rights.

2. Launch the REGEDT32 Registry editor. If you are unfamiliar with this Registry editor, refer to Chapter 2, "Using the Editors to Inspect and Modify the Registry." You cannot use the REGEDIT editor for this task because it does not give you access to the NTFS permissions function.

3. Locate the window for HKEY_LOCAL_MACHINE and click once on the HKEY_LOCAL_MACHINE node.

4. Select Security, Permissions from the menu.

5. Click the Advanced button.
   The dialog box shown in Figure 3.16 appears.

6. Select the account name or group in the list you first want to modify.

7. To remove the permissions assigned, click the Remove button.

8. To modify or view the advanced permissions, click the View/Edit button.

9. Assign or deny advanced permissions by clicking the appropriate check box for each permission listed.
   To change the scope of these permissions, choose the appropriate option from the Applies onto dropdown list at the top of the dialog box.

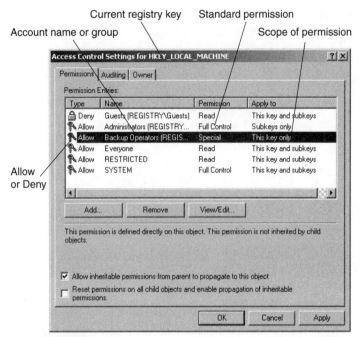

Current registry key   Standard permission

Account name or group   Scope of permission

Allow
or Deny

FIGURE 3.16   Advanced permissions show you users and groups and the permissions assigned to them for the current Registry key.

10. To define permissions for another account or group, click the Change button, select the account or group from the list that appears, click OK, and then repeat steps 7 and 8.

11. When you have completed defining permissions for HKLM, click until you are returned to the REGEDT32 window.

12. Locate the window for HKEY_CURRENT_USER and click once on the HKEY_CURRENT_USER node.

13. Repeat steps 4 through 9.

Solution 5: Removing the Editors from Users' Machines

A solution that prevents REGEDIT or REGEDT32 from being used to edit the Registry may be to remove the editors from a computer. To do so, locate the file REGEDIT.EXE in the Windows folder and delete it. Next, locate the REGEDT32.EXE file in the Windows\System32 folder and delete it. It's that easy.

You can easily restore the file by simply copying the same file from another machine to the correct location. The only drawback to this solution is that no one would have the use of the editors at the computer where they were deleted, not even a qualified administrator. Should you need to diagnose a problem on a machine where the editors where removed, you would need to copy the editor back to the machine or use another tool.

There are a few disadvantages to this scheme:

- All Registry work on a computer that has had the editors removed must be performed remotely. This means you must connect to the target computer from another computer on the network, and you must open the target computer's Registry using the Connect Registry feature in REGEDT32.

- This scheme is probably not sufficient alone because it does not prevent a user from using a third-party Registry editor tool to change the Registry, such as one downloaded from the Internet. In addition, this scheme does not prevent a user from writing a program that modifies the Registry.

Remove Registry Editors from Template.................

If your organization uses a standard workstation drive template, one that is copied to a new computer for a new employee, simply remove the two Registry editor executables from the template. This way, you can be sure the editors are not available on new computers when they are rolled out for new employees.

Solution 6: Forcing Read-only Mode

The REGEDT32 editor includes a feature to set the editor in Read-only mode. In Read-only mode, any changes made to the Registry are not saved. This rule applies regardless of the user and the permissions assigned. Read-only mode can be managed from the menu in REGEDT32, but this means that the user can turn this option off. Read-only mode can be set by modifying the Registry, though, which means the administrator has a few options to ensure that Read-only mode is always enabled.

The following key switches REGEDT32 to Read-only mode:

Key: HKEY_CURRENT_USER\Software\Microsoft\RegEdt32\Settings

Entry: ReadOnly:

Value: 1 for True, 0 for False

Here are some methods you can use to take advantage of Read-only mode.

- Create a GPO that modifies the ReadOnly entry in the Registry shown above. Next, scope the GPO so it applies to all appropriate users.

- Switch REGEDT32 to read-only manually on appropriate computers. Then, apply permissions to the ReadOnly key to ensure that a user does not change the value.

Diagnosing, Repairing, and Preventing Windows 2000 Disasters

The best planning and the most perfect computing conditions together are no guarantee that you or users you are responsible for won't experience serious trouble one day with Windows 2000. This trouble can range from an error message appearing on the screen to a Windows 2000 system that will not boot. Of course, if you or your users sometimes take risks, such as trying to install unsupported hardware drivers, then there is a better chance than otherwise that you will encounter a trouble situation. In either case, there are tools and procedures available to help diagnose and recover from these disasters, as well as to prepare for this type of situation. But what does the Registry have to do with Windows 2000 problems? Remember, there is a good chance that a service or device referenced in the Registry is a likely reason for problems at startup. Oftentimes, the Registry isn't the only culprit in a failed Windows 2000 system, but many times, the fix made will ultimately affect the Registry. Restoring the Registry using a handful of techniques is also a handy method for working past startup problems. In this chapter, you read about how to recover from failed Windows 2000 startups, as well as how to prepare for the occasion when Windows 2000 misbehaves.

What to Do When Windows 2000 Won't Start Normally

There are a number of reasons why Windows 2000 might not start normally. There may be problems with the disk on which Windows 2000 is installed, or perhaps problems just with the boot partition. While most users report that when Windows 2000 stopped working, they "had done nothing to the computer," most problems arise after some change was made to the system, such as adding or changing hardware. Adding a new operating system to the computer where Windows 2000 is running, installing new software, or simply modifying system files naturally are all good reasons for problems to occur with Windows 2000.

When Windows 2000 stops working, most users are less interested with why Windows 2000 won't start and more interested in how to get the operating system running normally again. Solving a Windows 2000 startup problem, though, many times requires the recognition of the symptoms associated with the Windows 2000 startup problem. So, be sure to take careful note of the messages you see and symptoms you experience when Windows 2000 won't start normally and encourage your users to do the same.

The following list shows some of the problems you and your users might experience and which of the solutions described later in this chapter might be most effective in solving the problem.

■ If at startup your system reports a problem with an unrecognized drive or partition, then damage or modification most likely occurred to the drive where Windows 2000 has been installed. In this case, you should consider using the Recovery Console to repair the drive.

■ If your system reports that it cannot find NTLDR, the most likely problem is that you attempted to boot your computer with a nonbootable floppy disk in the drive. If a floppy diskette is not in the drive, then you have a more serious problem. The message suggests a problem with the boot sector where the Windows 2000 boot files should be stored. This problem is a perfect candidate for treatment by the Emergency Repair Process with the ERD. You can also use the Recovery Console to repair problems with either the boot sector or to address other problems on the drive where Windows 2000 is installed.

■ If when you have made a change to Windows 2000 that now causes a problem with the operating system, you should consider removing the driver, application, or hardware you just added. Using the Advanced Startup options can help you get Windows 2000 to a point at which you can back out the change you made.

■ If you need to review the Registry to try and diagnose a problem, use one of the Advanced Startup options in order to access one of the two Registry editors available in the system. In addition, you can use the Recovery Console to access the REG tool. You can find details about the REG tool in Chapter 5.

•••••••••••••••••

Using Advanced Startup Options

When you start a computer running Windows 2000, you have the option to select the version of Windows 2000 installed and any other operating systems, as well as start Windows 2000 from a selection of advanced startup options. The most typical use of these startup options is to use one of the safe mode startup options. *Safe mode* is an option you can use when a change is made to Windows 2000 that makes it now unstartable. The word unstartable doesn't necessarily mean that the computer running Windows 2000 is completely unusable. You might use safe mode to address a problem as benign as the "Windows cannot start the service specified" message. In the opposite extreme, you might use safe mode to address a situation in which Windows 2000 crashes. Safe mode is an excellent first course of treatment in Windows 2000 problems. You will usually take advantage of one of the Advanced Startup options before attempting use of the Recovery Console or emergency repair disk (ERD). The Advanced Startup Options also are very helpful if you have a good idea of the change you made that is now causing problems with Windows 2000. The Advanced Startup options, specifically safe mode, make it easy to undo the change that caused the problem.

To access the list of Advanced Startup options, press F8 when the the list of startup options appears. The following list shows the options available:

- **Safe Mode** This mode starts the system with only basic service, such as for the mouse, video, storage access, and little more. This mode is designed to help you minimally start the system so you can manually address problems. This mode provides you access to the Registry, so you may be able to make manual changes to the configuration directly via the Registry, or you may be able to import a working version of the Registry or a specific hive for a backed-up text file.

- **Safe Mode With Networking** This mode is like Safe Mode, although basic support for attaching to the network also is provided. This mode is helpful because a driver needed to repair Windows 2000 is stored on a network resource. In addition, this mode can be used to start a troublesome Windows 2000 installation but also make available remote access to the Registry from another network resource. For help with understanding and using remote access to the Registry, consult Chapter 2, "Using the Editors to Inspect and Modify the Registry."

- **Safe Mode with Command Prompt** This mode is the same as the normal safe mode but provides system access only from the command line. This means that graphical user interface (known as the *shell*) you are used to working with is unavailable. If you are experiencing user interface problems, such as the system starting but the Explorer interface not starting (you can tell this by the absence of the Taskbar and Start menu), you may have a video problem or a change has been made to the key in the Registry that determines the shell. Whatever the problem, this mode provides access to the command line for direct access to the operating system.

In addition, there are a handful of other Advanced Startup options you can use in conjunction with the Safe Mode options described above:

- **Enable Boot Logging** This option creates a text file named NTBT-LOG.TXT in the main Windows 2000 folder when the system starts. The file contains detailed information about the boot process, such as the drivers loaded and the success or failure of these operations.

- **Last Known Good Configuration** The Last Known Good Configuration is a record of the Windows 2000 configuration used the last time the system booted properly. You can find details about how the Last Known Good Configuration is recorded and used in Chapter 6, "System and Startup Settings." By selecting Last Known Good Configuration, Windows 2000 will attempt to start using an older configuration. While this might seem like a foolproof option, the Last Known Good Configuration is not always completely reliable. Depending upon how far the startup process progressed before the problem occurred, the Last Known Good Configuration may have been updated with the configuration that you believe is faulty.

- **Directory Services Restore Mode** Available only on a Windows 2000 domain controller, this option repairs the Active Directory.

- **Debugging Mode** This startup option allows diagnostic information from the system experiencing trouble to be exchanged with another computer connected via a serial cable.

- **Boot Normally** This option starts the system as if the F8 key was not pressed to select an Advanced Startup option.

Using the Recovery Console

New to Windows in version 2000 is the Recovery Console. The Recovery Console is a command line interface to dozens of commands you can use to repair a Windows 2000 installation. When the Recovery Console is in use, you do not see the traditional Windows graphical-user interface (GUI). Instead, you see an interface that is identical to the window you see when you launch the command prompt. While the Recovery Console does not give you access to every command available from the Windows 2000 command prompt, it does provide access to just about any command line program you would need to fix a Windows 2000 startup problem.

Here are some of the ways you can use the Recovery Console:

- To stop a service that prevents the system from starting
- To recreate a master boot partition on a drive

- To display a list of all services installed
- To logon to any Windows 2000 installation found on the computer where the Recovery Console is running

When you start the Recovery Console, you are prompted to select which Windows 2000 installation to log onto, like the following:

```
1: F:\WINNT
2: H:\WINNT
```

You are prompted to enter the number of the installation and then press Enter. If only one Windows 2000 is detected, then the menu appears. In this case, or after you have selected an installation, you are next prompted to supply the password for the Administrator account. Naturally, administrator rights are required for almost any operation you would perform in attempting to recover a Windows 2000 installation, hence the requirement for the administrator password. After supplying the password and pressing Enter, the command line prompt appears, like the following:

```
F:\WINNT>
```

From the prompt, you can use any of the Recovery Console commands to fix the problem. A review of the commands is provided in the next section.

Recovery Console Commands

The Recovery Console provides access to more than twenty commands. You can use any of the commands to repair almost any aspect of a Windows 2000 installation on the computer where the Recovery Console is running. To see the list of commands displayed on the screen, type HELP and press Enter:

```
HELP
```

To see information on the screen about the command, including what parameters to supply and how the command should be used, type the command followed by /? And press enter, as follows:

```
DISKPART /?
```

Table 4.1 shows the commands available and their use.

Understanding Recovery Console Options

Two options are available for using the Recovery Console. Because you won't really use the Recovery Console on a regular basis (at least, you shouldn't), this point is really about how you make the Recovery Console available. The following are the two options:

TABLE 4.1	Recovery Console Commands
Command	**Use**
attrib	View or change the attributes of files and folders
batch	Execute commands in a text file
chdir	Change the current folder
cls	Clear the screen
copy	Copy files or folders
delete	Delete a file
dir	Display the contents of the current folder
disable	Change the startup for a system service to disabled
diskpart	Create or delete a partition on the current hard disk
enables	Enable a system service and allow you to specify the startup type (e.g., automatic, on demand, etc.)
exit	Close the recovery console
expand	Decompress a file, typically from the Windows 2000 installation media
fixboot	Create a new partition boot sector on the drive specified
fixmbr	Create a new master boot record on the specified storage device
format	Format the drive specified
help	Display help about the Recovery Console command specified
listsvc	List the names of all services, as well as startup state
logon	Display all local Windows 2000 installation and allow you to logon to selected one
map	Display map of physical storage devices to drive letters
mkdir	Create a folder
ren	Rename a file
rmdir	Remove a folder
set	Display and allow you to set Recovery Console environment variables
systemroot	Set the current system root for the current drive
type	Display the contents of the file specified

- **Install the Recovery Console for Easy Access** You can install the Recovery Console so that it is available from the startup menu. This way, you would need to use the Windows 2000 CD should you be required to use the console.

- **Launch the Recovery Console from the Windows 2000 Install Media** You may access the Recovery Console from either the Windows

2000 installation CD or from the four installation floppy diskettes. This way, if you did not make preparations for the occasion when your system is not startable, you can still use the Recovery Console.

The following two sections provide you the detail for installing the Recovery Console and for running it from Windows 2000 setup.

INSTALLING THE RECOVERY CONSOLE

Follow these steps to install the Recovery Console so it is always available from the Windows 2000 startup menu.

1. Load the Windows 2000 CD into the appropriate drive.
2. Change to the I386 directory.
3. Enter WINNT32 /CMDCONS and press the Enter key.
   The window shown in Figure 4.1 appears.

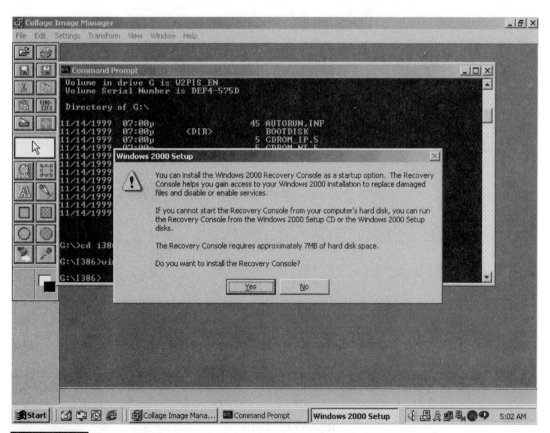

FIGURE 4.1   You install the Recovery Console from the Windows 2000 CD.

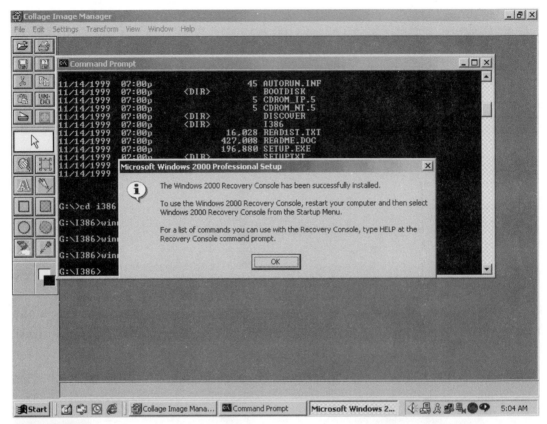

FIGURE 4.2   Click OK to finish installation of the Recovery Console.

4. Click OK.

Windows 2000 begins installing the Recovery Console.

When the installation is complete, the dialog box shown in Figure 4.2 appears.

5. Click OK.

LAUNCHING THE RECOVERY CONSOLE FROM SETUP

The Recovery Console is also available from the Windows 2000 installation media. You can use either the Windows 2000 CD or the setup diskettes, if you used them. Follow these steps to launch the Recovery Console from the Windows 2000 setup program.

1. If you can access a CD from the computer where the troublesome Windows 2000 installation is located either via another operating system installed on the same machine or perhaps via a boot CD with CD drivers,

then load the Windows 2000 CD into the drive. Right-click on the drive in My Computer and choose Autoplay from the menu. When the Windows 2000 Setup program starts, answer the prompts, including supplying the product key, until the system restarts and the text-based portion of setup begins. You can tell when the text-based portion of the Setup program begins when you are prompted to press Enter to continue Setup or press F3 to escape. Follow with step 3.

2. If you have the Windows Setup diskettes, load disk 1 and restart your computer. Follow the prompts to insert the remainder of the Setup program diskettes. Follow the prompts until you are prompted to press Enter to continue setup or press F3 to escape.

3. Press the Enter key.
   The Welcome to Setup screen appears.

4. Press the R key to start the Emergency Repair Process.
   The Windows 2000 Repair Options screen appears.

5. Press the C key to start the Recovery Console.
   The Recovery Console opens.

Using the Emergency Repair Process

The Emergency Repair Process is a set of procedures Windows 2000 uses to help recover a failed system. Unlike the Recovery Console, with which the user attempts to make the fix, and unlike the Advanced Startup options, which simply provide some alternatives to starting the system, the Emergency Repair Process is a direct, active attempt by the operating system (not the user) to identify and fix a problem. Here is a list of the operations the Emergency Repair Process can use to address a problem:

- **Fix problems with Windows 2000 startup files**
- **Review critical Windows 2000 system files** A system with problems affecting Windows 2000 system files can usually boot, but it is likely the system will not start after the user selects an operating system from the Startup menu.
- **Address problems with the Windows 2000 boot sector** The boot sector is the location on the drive where information about the Windows 2000 boot process can be found. If there are problems on the boot sector, then it is extremely likely you will not see any indication that Windows 2000 is installed on your computer when it starts. Most likely, startup fails just after the computer BIOS loads on a computer that has problems with the Windows 2000 sector.

The Emergency Repair Process is only available by launching setup either from the Windows 2000 CD or the Windows 2000 setup diskettes. The most important element of using the Emergency Repair Process is the ERD.

The information on the ERD contains the baseline data that Windows 2000 needs to establish what may have changed.

Creating an Emergency Repair Disk

Follow these steps to create an ERD. You can use the same procedure to update an ERD if you have made changes to the basic configuration of Windows 2000, such as adding a new and/or important user account or additional or changed hardware.

1. Have ready a spare 1.44 MB floppy diskette.

2. Click the Start menu and choose Programs, Accessories, System Tools, Backup from the menu.

   The Windows 2000 Backup and Recovery Tools window appears, as shown in Figure 4.3.

3. Click the Emergency Repair Disk button.

   The Emergency Repair window appears, as shown in Figure 4.4.

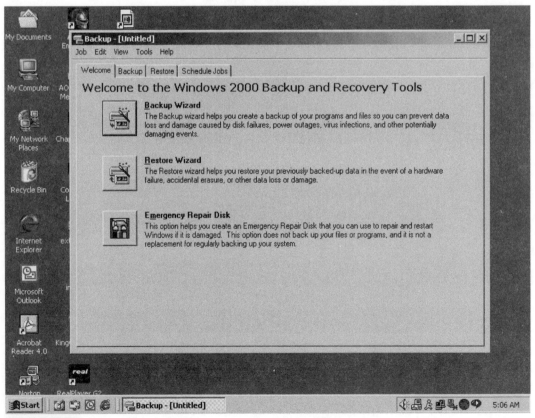

FIGURE 4.3   The Windows Backup window.

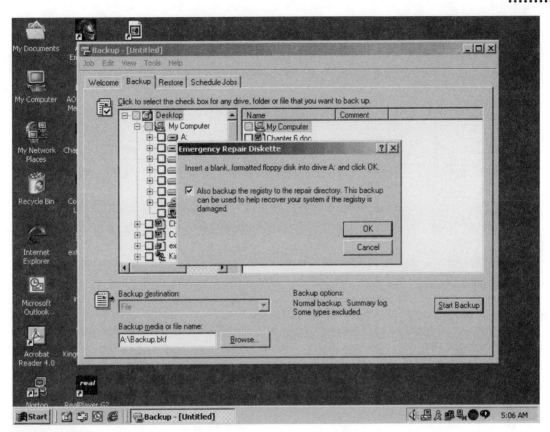

FIGURE 4.4   Choose whether to also backup the Registry to the Repair folder.

4. Click the option to also backup the Registry.

5. Insert the disk into the floppy drive.

6. Click OK.

   After you click OK, the system information, is copied to the diskette. When the process is complete, the message shown in Figure 4.5 appears.

7. Click OK.

8. Remove the diskette from the drive, label it appropriately, and choose Job Exit to close the backup window.

Last, if you are an experienced Windows NT user, you may be tempted to use the RDISK command to either create or update the ERD. This is not possible with Windows 2000. You must use the Windows 2000 Backup application, as described above, to work with the ERD.

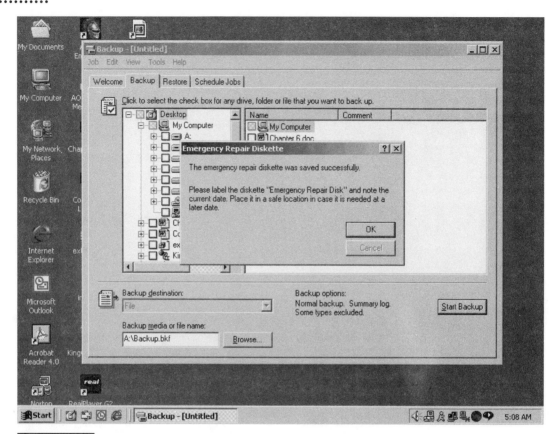

FIGURE 4.5   Click OK to finish installation.

Using the Emergency Repair Process

To start the Emergency Repair Process, you must start the Windows 2000 Setup program. You can use either the Windows 2000 CD to start the setup process if you still have access to the CD drive on the computer, or you can use the Setup program diskettes. Follow these steps:

1. When the Windows 2000 Setup program starts, answer the prompts, including supplying the product key, until the system restarts and the text-based portion of setup begins. You can tell when the text-based portion of the Setup program begins when you are prompted to press Enter to continue Setup or press F3 to escape.

2. Press the Enter key.
   The Welcome to Setup screen appears.

3. Press the R key to start the Emergency Repair Process.
   The Windows 2000 Repair Options screen appears.

4. Press the RC key to start the Emergency Repair Process.

5. There are two options available for using the Windows 2000 Repair process, Manual or Fast.

   If you use the manual process, you can select what type of inspection the repair process makes of your system, as well as how to treat each problem the repair process discovers. If you use the Fast process, Windows 2000 automatically identifies and fixes problems it finds. Both options involve copying configuration information from the ERD to the system. If you are what is considered a power user, and it's likely you are if you are reading this book, then you will probably prefer to use the manual process.

6. The first step in the Emergency Repair Process is to verify files on the troublesome Windows 2000 system with the same files referenced on the ERD. After the inspections occur, Windows 2000 reports differences between the current configuration and the configuration recorded on the ERD. You are given the option to repair any differences discovered, repair differences discovered on a case-by-case basis, or skip the particular problem reported.

   When you choose to fix a problem found, Windows 2000 copies the file it believes to be corrupt or missing from the Repair subfolder in the main Windows 2000 folder. Naturally, you should take care not to modify this folder in any way.

7. When Windows 2000 has checked every file, the system starts a reboot process.

8. If you still experience problems, it is worth the effort to rerun the Emergency Repair Process. If you still experience problems, it may be worth the effort now to attempt to start the system using one of the Advanced Startup Options described earlier in the chapter.

Preparing for Disasters

There are a few things you can do to ensure a smoother and shorter recovery process should your system fail to start properly. The following list shows the tasks you should complete to maintain a recoverable system. You can also legislate that users in your organization complete these tasks if you are a system administrator, or you can use the automation tools in Windows 2000, like group policy and the Windows scripting host, to complete these tasks for your user community.

- Create and maintain an ERD. When changes are made to the Windows 2000, be sure to update the ERD.
- Keep a copy of the HKLM and HKCU keys; minimally, maintain a backup copy of the HKLM\System. If you create an emergency repair

disk, you can specify an option to backup the Registry to the Repair folder under the main Windows 2000 folder when the ERD is created. This makes it easy to restore from the latest version of entries and values stored in the Registry. Use the instructions provided in Chapter 2, "Using the Editors to Inspect and Modify the Registry" for instruction on created text file version of the hives.

- Back up your system on a regular basis. Use the Windows Backup tool, which is free, or buy one of your choice. Be sure the backup process includes the Repair folder under the main Windows 2000 folder.

- Create the Startup floppy diskettes. While you can upgrade to Windows 2000 without creating the diskettes, if your system becomes unusable, you can use the diskettes to boot the system and access the Recovery Console and the emergency repair process tools.

Using the REG Utility

The Windows 2000 Resource Kit provides a useful tool, the REG utility, for command-line management of the Registry. The REG utility can accomplish a number of functions, each of which can also be accomplished by using one of the Registry editors shipped with Windows 2000. What the REG command alone provides, though, is an option for automating maintenance of the Registry. The user can use the REG command in batch scripts and other types of automation. In addition, the REG command provides a user interface for managing the Registry that, for some people, is easier and quicker to use than the standard Registry editors. In this chapter, you learn how to use the REG utility, including its eight different operation options. Note that the REG tool is not installed with Windows 2000. You must install the Windows 2000 Resource Kit to get the REG tool.

....

Using REG at the Command Line

During the installation process of the Windows 2000 Resource Kit, the path to the Resource Kit program files is added to the PATH environment variable. This means you can enter the REG command from any drive or folder on the workstation.

To issue the REG command, just enter the following:

```
REG operation parameters
```

where

operation indicates the specific Registry function you want to use. The following list shows the possible operations. You can find details on each of these operations later in the "REG Command Operations" section.

- Query
- Add
- Delete
- Copy
- Save
- Restore
- Load
- Unload
- Compare
- Export
- Import

parameters indicates the special information the REG command requires to complete the operation. The information entered for a parameter differs based on the operation required. For example, if you use the REG DELETE command, you must also supply as a parameter the key you want to delete.

REG Command Parameters Syntax

As noted above, the parameters component of the REG command syntax indicates the special options you specify for each use of the command. For example, you would use a parameter to indicate whether to delete all of the subkeys and associated entries for a key (which you also specify), or just the key itself. The description provided for each of the operations in the next major section explains what parameters are available, including which parameters are required and which are optional. In this section of this chapter, though, you can read about conventions used later to explain parameters to you:

- *Italicized* text indicates a placeholder. Replace the italicized text with data or text specific to your use of the command.
- Parameters shown in brackets ([ ]) indicate one of the set of options you can use to customize how the particular command works. Some commands provide a number of options. Each set of options would be shown in a separate set of brackets.
- The / symbol is used to precede a parameter. Providing the parameter alone is not sufficient. The / symbol also must be supplied.
- The | symbol separates choice of options within a bracketed set of options. Depending on the command, more than one of the options may be used.

Using the Key Parameter

The most important parameter you use with the REG command is the *key* parameter. The key parameter used in every variation of the REG command and tells the command what key(s) and/or entries the command should act upon. For example, the key parameter might indicate the Microsoft subkey in the HKEY_LOCAL_MACHINE\Software key on a machine named Lucky found somewhere on the network. Here is how the key parameter would appear in this example:

```
\\LUCKY\HKLM\Software\Microsoft
```

Naturally, a specific syntax must be used for the key parameter. The syntax is the same regardless of what variation of the REG command is used. The following is the syntax of the key parameter:

```
[\\Machine_name\]Rootkey\key_structure
```

where

> *Machine_name*\ is an optional parameter that specifies the computer name of a workstation somewhere on the network. This syntax is used if the REG command operation will be carried out on a remote computer, rather than the workstation where the command is issued. If the REG command is to be used against the Registry where the command is issued, then this syntax can be ignored.

> *Rootkey**key_structure* indicates the full path to the key the REG command should operate on. You can use special abbreviations for the root key portion:

HKLMHKEY_LOCAL_MACHINE

HKCUHKEY_CURRENT_USER

HKCRHKEY_CLASSES_ROOT

HKU HKEY_USERS

HKCCHKEY_CURRENT_CONFIG

REG Command Operations

Based on the eight operations you can execute with the REG command, there is little Registry maintenance you can't accomplish with the REG command. In this section, you can learn how to complete these operations. You can also learn about some of the variations and options available via parameters and switches.

Getting Information About a Key

The REG QUERY command displays the value of a single entry or the names of all the keys and their respective values under a key specified.

SYNTAX OF REG QUERY

Use this syntax for the REG QUERY command:

```
REG QUERY key [/v value | /ve] [/s]
```

where

key is the parameter that indicates the key to query with the command. If the REG QUERY command will be used to return the value of a single entry, the key parameter should indicate the key where the entry is stored. See the "Using the Key Parameter" section earlier for details on the use of this parameter.

`/v value | /ve` is an optional choice of switches that specify what value and/or entry to query. The `/ve` specifies the default entry specified by the key parameter. The `/v value` allows the user to specify by name the value belonging to the key parameter. Replace *value* with the name of the entry.

`/s` specifies that all of the keys and entries under the key specified by the key parameter should be queried. Do not use the `[/v value | /ve]` with this option.

EXAMPLE OF OUTPUT OF REG QUERY

The following syntax will produce information about all of the keys and entries under the HKEY_CURRENT_USER\Software\Microsoft\RegEdt32 key:

```
REG QUERY HKEY_CURRENT_USER\Software\Microsoft\RegEdt32 /s
```

The following shows the output from the command issued above:

```
HKEY_CURRENT_USER\Software\Microsoft\RegEdt32\Settings
        Left   REG_SZ  126
        Top    REG_SZ  80
        Width  REG_SZ  812
        Height REG_SZ  537
        Maximized     REG_SZ  1
        AutoRefresh   REG_SZ  1
        ReadOnly      REG_SZ  0
        ConfirmOnDelete      REG_SZ  1
        SaveSettings REG_SZ  1
        Registry      REG_SZ  __Local_Computer

HKEY_CURRENT_USER\Software\Microsoft\RegEdt32\__Local_
Computer
        Keys   REG_SZ  3,4,0,2,1
        HKEY_CURRENT_USER   REG_SZ  88,88,606,337,2,421
        HKEY_LOCAL_MACHINE REG_SZ  0,0,812,491,0,362
        HKEY_CLASSES_ROOT   REG_SZ  66,66,606,337,0,297
        HKEY_CURRENT_CONFIG       REG_SZ  44,44,606,337,0,297
        HKEY_USERS   REG_SZ  22,22,606,337,0,297
```

Adding Keys and Entries

You can use the REG ADD command to add keys and/or entries to an existing key. This command can also be used to specify the value for the new entry, as well as change the value for an existing entry.

SYNTAX OF REG ADD

Use this syntax for the REG ADD command:

```
REG ADD Key [/v Value | /ve] [/t data_type] [/s separator]
[/d data] [/f]
```

where

key is the parameter that indicates in what key the new entry will be created. See the "Using the Key Parameter" section earlier for details on the use of this parameter.

/v *Value* | /ve specifies what entry to add or modify. The /ve specifies the default entry specified by the key parameter. Naturally, this value does need to be created, though the REG ADD command can be used to specify the data for this entry. The /v *Value* allows the user to specify by name the value to create.

/t *data_type* specifies the data type of the entry to be created. If this parameter is not supplied, the REG_SZ data type is used. The following are the possible values.

- REG_SZ
- REG_MULTI_SZ
- REG_DWORD_BIG_ENDIAN
- REG_DWORD
- REG_BINARY
- REG_DWORD_LITTLE_ENDIAN
- REG_NONE
- REG_EXPAND_SZ

/s separator specifies the character used to delimit the list of values specified in the /d data parameter if the REG_MULTI_SZ. This parameter can be ignored if a data type other than REG_MULTI_SZ is specified with the /t data_type parameter.

/d *data* specifies the value of the entry added.

/f is an optional switch that indicates the value specified by the /d *data* parameter should overwrite an existing value for the entry if it exists without prompting by the command.

EXAMPLE OF OUTPUT OF REG ADD

The following use of the REG ADD command adds an entry named Complete with a value of −1 to the to the HKEY_CURRENT_USER\Software\RegistryBook \Chapter5 key.

```
REG ADD HKCU\Software\RegistryBook\Chapter5 /v Complete /d -1
```

Deleting Keys

The REG DELETE command is used to delete one value for a key, all values for a key, or all of the keys and values under another key. With an option to suppress any confirmation prompts, this command can easily be integrated into any automation processes, such as those built with Windows Scripting Host.

SYNTAX OF REG DELETE

Use this syntax when you use the REG DELETE command:

```
REG DELETE key [/v Value | /ve | /va] [/f]
```

where

key is the parameter that indicates what key is affected by the command. See the "Using the Key Parameter" section earlier for details on the use of this parameter.

/v *Value* | /ve | /va is an optional choice of switches that specify what value and/or entry to delete. The /va switch is the most powerful; it specifies that all values specified by the key parameter are deleted. The /ve indicates the default entry specified by the key parameter. The /v *Value* allows the user to specify by name the value belonging to the key parameter. To delete all of the keys, including subkeys, and all the values associated with each key, omit this parameter.

/f is an optional switch that suppresses any confirmation to carry out the delete. When this switch is used, the delete occurs immediately after the command is issued, without any further messages.

EXAMPLE OF OUTPUT OF REG DELETE

The following use of the REG DELETE command deletes all of the entries and associated keys under HKEY_CURRENT_USER\Software\Trash, doing so without any further prompt for confirmation from the user.

```
REG DELETE HKCU\Software\Trash /f
```

The following use of the REG DELETE command deletes the value of the default entry under the HKEY_LOCAL_MACHINE\Software\Example key. The command will prompt the user for confirmation to delete the value first:

```
REG DELETE HKLM\Software\Example /ve
```

Copying Keys and Entries

The REG COPY command is used to copy all of the entries for one key to another key, or it can be used to copy all of the subkeys and the associated entries of one key to another. An option you can use with REG COPY suppresses the display of messages from the command, so you can use REG COPY in a batch script or other similar application.

SYNTAX OF REG COPY

Use this syntax when you use the REG COPY command:

```
REG COPY SourceKey TargetKey [/s] [/f]
```

where

SourceKey indicates the key whose entries, and possibly whose subkeys, will be copied. See the "Using the Key Parameter" section earlier for details on the use of this parameter.

TargetKey is the key to which the entries and possibly subkeys specified by the *SourceKey* will be copied. See the "Using the Key Parameter" section earlier for details on the use of this parameter.

/s is an optional switch that indicates that all of the subkeys and associated values under the key specified by *SourceKey* should also be copied.

/f is an optional switch that specifies that the copy operation should start as soon as the REG COPY command is issued, thus suppressing display of any confirmation prompt.

EXAMPLE OF OUTPUT OF REG COPY

The following use of the REG COPY command copies all of the subkeys and associated entries in the HKEY_LOCAL_MACHINE\Software\RegistryBook key to the HKEY_LOCAL_MACHINE\Software\Backup\RegistryBook:

```
REG COPY HKLM\Software\RegistryBook
HKLM\Software\Backup\RegistryBook /s
```

Saving a Loaded Key

Use the REG SAVE command to save the selected key to an external file. This file is suitable for use with the LOAD command. The file is created in the System32 folder under the main Windows 2000 folder. Note that a file created with the Save command cannot be viewed with Notepad, Wordpad, or any other program capable of viewing a text file. This contrasts with files created with the Export command, which you can view with any application.

SYNTAX OF REG SAVE

Use this syntax with the REG SAVE command:

```
REG SAVE key file
```

where

key is the parameter that indicates what key is saved. See the "Using the Key Parameter" section earlier for details on the use of this parameter.

file is the name of the file created during the save operation.

EXAMPLE OF OUTPUT OF REG SAVE

The following use of the REG SAVE command saves the current selected key to a file named REGOUT.SAV.

```
REG SAVE REGOUT.SAV
```

Restoring a Key

The REG RESTORE key is used to restore a hive whose contents are overwritten by a loaded hive.

SYNTAX OF REG RESTORE

Use this syntax with the REG RESTORE command:

```
REG RESTORE key loaded_hive
```

where

> *key* is the parameter that indicates what key will be restored. See the "Using the Key Parameter" section earlier for details on the use of this parameter.

> *loaded_hive* is the name of the loaded hive file.

EXAMPLE OF OUTPUT OF REG RESTORE

The following use of the REG RESTORE restores the HKEY_LOCAL_MA-CHINE \Software\Registry key whose contents were populated by the file REGHIV.HVE.

```
REG RESTORE HKLM\Software\RegistryBook REGHIV.HVE
```

Loading a Key

The REG LOAD command is used to load a Registry hive created on another workstation into to the current workstation's Registry. Note that the file specified to be loaded must have been created with the Save command, which could have been issued from the command line with the REG SAVE command or from the Registry, Save Key menu choice. Refer to Chapter 2 for details on loading Registry hives.

SYNTAX OF REG LOAD

Use this syntax when you use the REG LOAD command:

```
REG LOAD target_key file
```

where

> *target_key* is the key to which the file should be loaded. This parameter should follow the format described above in the

> *file* is the name of the file to load.

EXAMPLE OF THE USE OF THE REG LOAD COMMAND

The following use of the REG LOAD command loads the file named EX-TRACT.HIV to the HKEY_LOCAL_MACHINE to the HKEY_LOCAL_MA-CHINE\TESTING \DIAGNOSTIC key.

```
REG LOAD HKLM\TESTING\DIAGNOSTIC extract.hiv
```

Unloading a Key

The REG UNLOAD command is used to unload a Registry hive previously loaded with the Load command, which could have been issued from the command line with the REG LOAD command or via the Registry, Load Hive menu choice (REGEDT32.EXE only). Refer to Chapter 2 for details on loading and unloading Registry hives.

SYNTAX OF REG UNLOAD

Use this syntax when you use the REG UNLOAD command:

```
REG UNLOAD key
```

where

key is the parameter that indicates what key to unload. The key should be in the format described above in the "Using the Key Parameter" section.

EXAMPLE OF THE USE OF THE REG UNLOAD COMMAND

The following use of the REG UNLOAD command unloads the hive named DIAGNOSTIC in the HKEY_LOCAL_MACHINE key previously loaded with the LOAD command:

```
REG UNLOAD HKEY_LOCAL_MACHINE HKLM\DIAGNOSTIC
```

Comparing Keys

The REG COMPARE command can be used to compare the value of one entry to the value of another entry. The command can be extended by using the special parameters to compare the values of all of the entries in one or more keys to the same named keys in another part of the Registry. The command also gives the user the option of specifying how the results of the compare are reported.

SYNTAX OF REG COMPARE

Use this syntax for the REG COMPARE command:

```
REG COMPARE first_key second_key [/v Value | /ve] [/oa |
/od | /os | /on] [/s]
```

where

first_key is the key parameter that indicates to what key the key specified by the first_key parameter should be compared.

second_key is the key parameter that indicates to what key the key specified by the `first_key` parameter should be compared. Supply a value of \\. for this parameter to indicate that the same key on the local machine should be compared to the key specified with the `first_key` parameter when `first_key` refers to a key on a remote computer.

`/v Value | /ve` is the choice of switches that specify what value and/or entry to compare. The `/ve` indicates the default entry specified by the key parameter. The `/v Value` allows the user to specify by name the value belonging to the key parameter by supplying the name of the entry in *Value*. If this parameter is omitted, then all of the entries in the key specified by the `first_key` parameter are compared to the same named entries in the key specified by the `second_key`.

`/oa | /od | /os | /on` is the choice of optional switches that indicates how to report the results of the compare back to the user. The `/oa` specifies that both differences and matches discovered during the compare are output from the program. The `/os` switch specifies that just the matches discovered during the compare are output from the program. The `/od` switch specifies that just the differences discovered during the compare are output from the program. The `/on` specifies that no information is returned from the program.

`/s` specifies that all of the dependent keys under the `first_key` parameter and all of those keys' entries should be compared to the same named keys under the `second_key` parameter. Using this parameter would not require the user to specify a value for the `/v Value | /ve` parameter.

EXAMPLE OF THE USE OF THE REG COMPARE COMMAND

The following use of the REG COMPARE command compares all of the entries in the ThisRegistryBook key under HKEY_LOCAL_MACHINE\Software to the entries in HKEY_CURRENT_USER\Software\AnotherRegistryBook.

```
REG COMPARE HKLM\Software\ThisRegistryBook\MyApp
HKCU\Software\AnotherRegistryBook
```

The following use of the REG COMPARE command compares all of the keys and values in the HKEY_LOCAL_MACHINE\SOFTWARE\Microsoft\Shared Tools on the remote computer named JUPITER to the same keys and values on the computer where the command is issued and reports only the differences discovered during the compare.

```
REG COMPARE \\JUPITER\HKLM\SOFTWARE\Microsoft\Shared Tools
\\. /s /od
```

Exporting Keys and Entries

The REG EXPORT command is used to create an external file storing Registry entries and keys. The file can be used for backup purposes or to examine the Registry entries and values. Refer to Chapter 2 for details on importing and exporting Registry data.

SYNTAX OF REG EXPORT

Use this syntax when you use the REG EXPORT command:

```
REG EXPORT key file.reg [/nt4]
```

where

> *key* is the parameter that indicates what key is affected by the command. See the "Using the Key Parameter" section earlier for details on the use of this parameter.
>
> *file.reg* is the name of the file to be created.
>
> /nt4 is an optional switch specifying the file should be created in an NT4 format.

EXAMPLE OF OUTPUT OF REG EXPORT

The following shows sample use of the REG EXPORT command:

```
REG EXPORT HKLM\Software\Adobe\Acrobat adobe.txt
```

The following shows the message displayed if the operation runs successfully:

```
The operation completed successfully
```

Importing Keys from an External File

Use the REG IMPORT command to import a Registry file that was created via the Registry Export command, which could have been issued from the command line using REG EXPORT or from the menu. Refer to Chapter 2 for details on importing and exporting Registry data.

SYNTAX OF REG IMPORT

Use this syntax when you use the REG IMPORT command:

```
REG IMPORT file.reg
```

where
    file.reg is the name of the file you want to import.

EXAMPLE OF OUTPUT OF REG IMPORT

Here is one sample usage of the REG IMPORT command:

```
REG IMPORT sample.reg
```

The following shows the message displayed if the operation runs successfully:

```
The operation completed successfully
```

If there is a problem, such as if the file specified does not exist, the following example appears:

```
Invalid File Format
```

Desktop Maintenance via the Registry

In This Part

System and Startup Settings

The Registry has much to do with the successful startup of Windows 2000. Once Windows 2000 starts, there are a number of settings you can modify in the Registry to control how the core operating system works, as well as to customize the startup process. In addition, the Registry stores data that, although you might not be able to successfully and safely change it, would tell you much about how the startup works. This chapter will help you understand the startup and shutdown processes in Windows 2000, as well as some of the system settings.

When Windows 2000 Boots

The Registry plays an important part in the Windows 2000 startup process. This chapter explains how to make changes in the Registry to customize the startup process. To help you understand that process, though, here is a review of what happens when you start your computer and run Windows 2000.

When you turn on your computer, the computer's BIOS (basic input/output system) performs a POST (power-on self-test). It also checks the memory loaded and the hardware installed on your machine.

If the computer starts without a serious error, the BIOS determines the location of the master boot record. The master boot record specifies the active partition on the computer. The BIOS then executes the boot sector on the active partition. For Windows 2000, the program on the boot sector that executes is Ntldr.exe.

Ntldr.exe switches the machines from a real mode into a flat 32-bit memory mode. Ntldr.exe next opens the Boot.ini file and presents to the user the list of operating systems that can be used to boot based on the options in the file. Assuming that the user selects Windows 2000, the hardware detection phase begins. This function is handled by two programs, Ntdetect.com and Ntoskrnl.exe. The following is the list of hardware components these programs look for:

- Bus/adapter type
- Communications port
- Storage device
- Parallel port
- Video adapter
- Keyboard
- Pointing device
- SCSI adapter
- Floating-point coprocessor

After Windows 2000 has collected information about hardware, the system is interested in which hardware configuration it should use. If the workstation has multiple hardware profiles set up, the user is presented with a list of those profiles. The user can select from one of the hardware profiles or select the Last Known Good Configuration by pressing F8 and picking it from a list (the Last Known Good Configuration is the configuration that was used the last time Windows 2000 booted successfully). The hardware profile and the Last Known Good Configuration are known as *ControlSets*. A ControlSet contains a complete set of keys and entries needed by Windows 2000 to launch. Windows 2000 stores a number of ControlSets, each identified by a number (e.g., ControlSet001, ControlSet002, etc.). More about ControlSets later.

note Windows 2000 stores copies of failed configurations, as well, so don't assume each ControlSet you see in the Registry is a *working* configuration.

Now, with a configuration selection in hand, the HKEY_LOCAL_ MACHINE \SYSTEM hive is populated. The hive is populated from the data in the SYSTEM. file, which is located in the System32\Config folder in the main Windows 2000 folder.

Next, the boot loader checks the Registry to see which ControlSet it should load. Entries in the HKEY_LOCAL_MACHINE\SYSTEM\Select key (see Figure 6.1) indicate what configuration is stored in each ControlSet. There are four entries in the HKEY_LOCAL_MACHINE\SYSTEM\Select key. The value of each entry indicates what ControlSet stores the appropriate configuration:

- Current
- Default
- Failed
- LastKnownGood

As an example, let's assume the user chooses Last Known Good Configuration. The Registry checks the Select key and finds the LastKnownGood entry. If the Last Known Good Configuration entry in the Select key has a

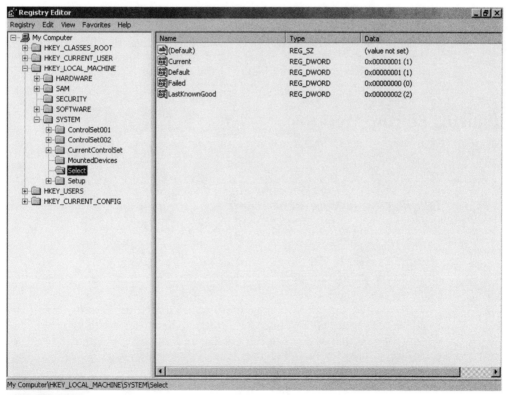

FIGURE 6.1   The Select key stores the numbers of the configurations stored in the Registry.

value of 3, then ControlSet003 stores the configuration that will be used to start Windows 2000 and the system loads it.

Next, the configuration selected by the user is copied to the Current-ControlSet key. Windows 2000 also updates the Current entry in HKEY_LOCAL_MACHINE\SYSTEM\Select key with the number of the Con-trolSet used. Windows 2000 next loads the services listed in the CurrentCon-trolSet. This marks the start of the kernel initialization phase. At this point in the startup process, the screen turns blue.

The first step in the kernel initialization is the population of the HKEY_LOCAL_MACHINE\HARDWARE key. This key is populated based on the data collected early in the startup process by Ntdetect.com and Ntoskrnl.exe. A snapshot of the configuration is taken at this point, as well. Here's how: Windows 2000 copies the configuration reflected in the Con-trolSet indicated by the Current entry in the HKEY_LOCAL_MACHINE\SYS-TEM\Select key (remember, the Current entry was updated after the user se-lects a configuration) to the Clone key. This way, Windows 2000 always has a copy of a configuration.

At this point, drivers are loaded, more services are started, and Win-dows 2000 starts the logon process. When a user successfully logs on, the configuration stored in the Clone set is copied to the Last Known Good Con-figuration key. This marks the end of the early startup process. The system continues the startup process by applying settings in the Registry based on a successful startup and on the identity of the user who has logged on.

Configuring Startup Options

The settings in this section enable you to configure aspects of Windows 2000's startup and logon process.

Displaying a Note at Startup

You can configure your workstation to display a message that appears as soon as the user presses Ctrl+Alt+Delete. This message can display any kind of warning regarding the legal ramifications of accessing the workstation or the network without proper authorization. Actually, the message can say any-thing, such as "Have a Nice Day."

To enable this feature, you must set at least one Registry entry, the LegalNoticeText entry, to define the text of the message. In addition, you can specify the text that appears in the title bar of the message with the LegalNo-ticeCaption entry.

Root Key: HKEY_LOCAL_MACHINE

Key: SOFTWARE\Microsoft\WindowsNT\CurrentVersion\Winlogon

Entry: LegalNoticeCaption

Entry: LegalNoticeText

Data Type: REG_SZ

Disable Warnings on Startup

You can suppress any error messages that might otherwise appear at Windows 2000 startup. Add this entry and set the value to 1. Note that the system and application logs will still record details about any startup problem, even if you configure this entry. If you enable this feature, make it a practice to review data in the system and error logs via the Event Viewer.

Root Key: HKEY_LOCAL_MACHINE

Key: SOFTWARE\Microsoft\WindowsNT\CurrentVersion\Winlogon

Entry: NoPopupsOnBoot

Data Type: REG_SZ

Show Logon Options

The logon dialog box, which appears at startup and when the user presses Ctrl+Alt+Del, has a button labeled Options. When the user clicks the Options button, the domain dropdown list becomes active, and the option to logon via a dial-up connection appears. The Domain dropdown list gives the user the opportunity to select the domain to which to log on, while the dial-up option lets the user select a dial-up connection to use. You can disable the Options button if you do not want these features to be available. Set the value of this entry to 0.

Root Key: HKEY_LOCAL_MACHINE

Key: SOFTWARE\Microsoft\WindowsNT\CurrentVersion\Winlogon

Entry: ShowLogonOptions

Data Type: REG_DWORD

AutoRestartShell

On occasion, the Windows 2000 shell program crashes. Unless you change your shell program, this program is Explorer.exe. By setting this entry value to 1, Windows 2000 will automatically restart the shell application. The alternative to Windows 2000 not automatically restarting your shell application in event of a problem is that all of the items typically found on your Desktop—icons, Taskbar, My Computer, everything—disappear.

Root Key: HKEY_LOCAL_MACHINE

Key: SOFTWARE\Microsoft\WindowsNT\CurrentVersion\Winlogon

Entry: AutoRestartShell

Data Type: REG_DWORD

System

When Windows 2000 starts, a number of programs launch in the protected system context. To see the applications that launch for the operating system, open the Registry and inspect this entry.

Root Key: HKEY_LOCAL_MACHINE

Key: SOFTWARE\Microsoft\WindowsNT\CurrentVersion\Winlogon

Entry: System

Data Type: REG_SZ

Display Configure Your Server Wizard

You can modify a user profile to determine whether the "Windows 2000 Configure Your Server" dialog box appears at startup. To continue to display the wizard, leave the value of this as 1. To disable the display of the wizard at startup, change the value to 0. The user may at any time display the wizard by choosing Programs\Administrative Tools\Configure Your Server from the Start menu.

Root Key: HKEY_CURRENT_USER

Key: \Software\Microsoft\WindowsNT\CurrentVersion\Setup\Welcome

Entry: srvwiz

Data Type: REG_DWORD

Configuring Script Options

A number of options are available to automate the logon, logoff, and shutdown script processes. You can use the Registry to control how these scripts run, such as if the commands in the script appear to the user as the script runs.

Running Logon Scripts Asynchronously

If you are familiar with logon scripts, then you may have experience in dealing with the problems caused when the shell portion of Windows 2000 starts before the logon script completes. This is usually a function more of the design of the logon script than a specific problem with Windows 2000. You can use the Registry to be sure that Windows 2000 does not start the user interface portion of the operating system until the logon script completes. To set this behavior, change the value of this entry to 1.

Root Key: HKEY_CURRENT_USER

Key:
Software\Microsoft\Windows\CurrentVersion\Policies\System

Entry: RunLogonScriptSync

Data Type: REG_DWORD

Forcing Asynchronous Running of Startup Scripts

You can configure startup scripts to run just before a user logs on. If you use more than one startup script, it is possible that one script will not wait for another script to finish before it starts. You can configure the Registry so that startup scripts run one at a time. Set the value of this entry to 1 to force startup scripts to run asynchronously.

Root Key: HKEY_CURRENT_USER

Key:
Software\Microsoft\Windows\CurrentVersion\Policies\System

Entry: RunStartupScriptSync

Data Type: REG_DWORD

Displaying Startup Script Commands

If you want the commands issued in a startup script to appear on the screen as the script runs, set this value to 0. If you do not want the commands to appear, either do not add this entry to the System key or set its value to 1.

Root Key: HKEY_CURRENT_USER

Key:
Software\Microsoft\Windows\CurrentVersion\Policies\System

Entry: HideStartupScripts

Data Type: REG_DWORD

Displaying Shutdown Script Commands

If you do not want the commands issued in a shutdown script to appear on the screen, set the value of this entry to 1.

Root Key: HKEY_CURRENT_USER

Key:
Software\Microsoft\Windows\CurrentVersion\Policies\System

Entry: HideShutdownScripts

Data Type: REG_DWORD

Managing Drive Sharing at Startup

You can configure whether the floppy and/or CD-ROM drives on a workstation can be shared over the network. A separate entry in the Registry is reserved for both drive types. For each entry, two options are available: a value of 0 indicates that only the user with administrative rights on the domain can access the drive remotely; a value of 1 indicates that only the user logged on locally at the workstation may access the drive.

> **Root Key:** HKEY_LOCAL_MACHINE
>
> **Key:** SOFTWARE\Microsoft\WindowsNT\CurrentVersion\Winlogon
>
> **Entry:** allocatedasd
>
> **Entry:** allocatecdroms
>
> **Entry:** allocatefloppydrives
>
> **Data Type:** REG_DWORD

Working with User Accounts

You can control certain aspects of how the user account is managed at system startup via the Registry. For example, you can specify that the user name for the last account logged onto the workstation not appear when the logon dialog box appears. As for another example, you can also control how early the prompt appears to remind users to change their passwords.

Don't Display the Last Logged On Username

When a user press Ctrl+Alt+Del to log on to Windows 2000, the logon dialog box appears. The logon dialog box automatically displays the username of the last account that was logged on to the machine. Some would view this as a security problem. This key can be used to disable the display of the name. Set the value of this entry to 1 to disable display of the last username logged on.

> **Root Key:** HKEY_LOCAL_MACHINE
>
> **Key:** HKEY_LOCAL_MACHINE\SOFTWARE\Microsoft\WindowsNT\ CurrentVersion \Winlogon
>
> **Entry:** DontDisplayLastUserName
>
> **Data Type:** REG_SZ

Managing Cached Logons

Windows 2000 networking is configured so that a user can log on to the network from any workstation on the Active Directory. A problem arises, though, when the network is down for some reason, such as through the inaccessibility of a domain controller. Each Windows 2000 machine, professional, server, or domain controller, stores the last ten user accounts that were successfully used to log on to the network at that workstation. This way, if the network does fail, a user can still log on to some workstation. For security reasons, you may feel that ten is too large a number of logons to cache. You can fine-tune that value using this entry.

Root Key: HKEY_LOCAL_MACHINE

Key: SOFTWARE\Microsoft\WindowsNT\CurrentVersion\Winlogon

Entry: cachedlogonscount

Data Type: REG_DWORD

Change Password Message

This entry allows you to specify how many days in advance a user receives a warning that he or she must change a password before actually being forced to.

Root Key: HKEY_LOCAL_MACHINE

Key: SOFTWARE\Microsoft\WindowsNT\CurrentVersion\Winlogon

Entry: passwordexpirywarning

Data Type: REG_DWORD

Restricting Lock Workstation

You can prevent the user of a workstation from locking it using the Windows 2000 Lock Workstation button on the Windows Security dialog box. For security reasons, you may not want to set this option, but it is available nonetheless. Set this entry to 1 to disable the Lock Workstation button. This entry does not appear by default in the Registry; you must add it.

Root Key: HKEY_LOCAL_MACHINE

Key: SOFTWARE\Microsoft\WindowsNT\CurrentVersion\Winlogon

Entry: DisableLockWorkstation

Data Type: REG_DWORD

Configuring System Options

When Windows 2000 boots, a number of system options can be configured, including the user interface used, which is known as the shell. In this section, you can read about the Registry settings you can manage to customize the system at startup.

Specifying an Alternate Shell

If you miss the familiar Program Manager interface from Windows 3.1, you can still use it in Windows 2000. To configure Windows 2000 to launch the Program Manager interface when Windows 2000 launches, you need to specify the shell program you want to run. Enter Program.exe for this key to launch Program Manager. What does Program Manager look like running on Windows 2000? Figure 6.2 provides you a look.

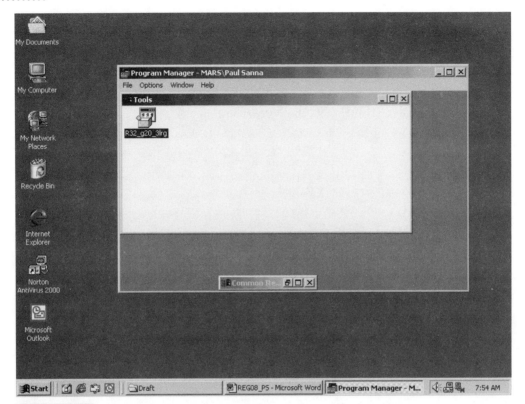

FIGURE 6.2   You can run Program Manager in Windows 2000 or as a replacement for Explorer in Windows 2000.

Note that if you start your computer with Program Manager and realize you have made a mistake, you need to change this Registry enter back to its original value. To restore the Explorer shell, the value of this entry should be Explorer.exe. To start the Registry editor from the Program Manger shell, choose File, Run from the Program Manager window. Enter Regedit.exe in the dialog box that appears, and then click OK.

> **Root Key:** HKEY_LOCAL_MACHINE
>
> **Key:** SOFTWARE\Microsoft\WindowsNT\CurrentVersion\Winlogon
>
> **Entry:** Shell
>
> **Data Type:** REG_SZ

Configuring Processor Priority

The Registry stores the setting that determines if applications running in the foreground receive preferential treatment from Windows 2000 in terms of processor time. All applications and services running on any computer require the use of the processor. In Windows 2000, as a multitasking operating system, all applications and services receive the same general amount of attention. The Application Response setting allows you to specify that certain applications receive a bit more processor time compared to other applications. What is the alternative? Depending on what software is loaded on your computer, a number of programs may be running without your knowing or noticing. Without setting the Foreground option, these applications and services receive the same number of slices of processor time as the application you are using on the Desktop, such as your browser, word processing program, whatever. Depending on the use of the computer running Windows 2000, you may want all applications to share equally in processor time.

> **Root Key:** HKEY_LOCAL_MACHINE
>
> **Key:** SYSTEM\ControlSet001\Control\PriorityControl
>
> **Entry:** Win32PrioritySeparation
>
> **Data Type:** REG_DWORD

Disabling Last Access Time on Files

The NTFS file system records the last time a file was accessed. You can disable this feature via a setting in the Registry. Set the value of this entry to 1 to do so. You will need to reboot your workstation to effect this change.

> **Root Key:** HKEY_LOCAL_MACHINE
>
> **Key:** System\CurrentControlSet\Control\FileSystem
>
> **Entry:** NtfsDisableLastAccessUpdate
>
> **Data Type:** REG_DWORD

Configuring Troubleshooting Options

You can add verbose logging to a number of events trapped by Windows 2000. Verbose logging means that Windows 2000 presents more than the normal amount of information. The details logged are stored in the event logs, which are accessible via the Event Viewer. You can specify verbose logging individually for the three different types of events, or you can make one Registry change that specifies verbose logging for all. Table 6.1 shows the types of events that can be logged with extra detail. The table also shows the entry whose value should be set to 1 to enable verbose logging.

> **Root Key:** HKEY_LOCAL_MACHINE
>
> **Key:** Software\Microsoft\WindowsNT\CurrentVersion\Diagnostics
>
> **Data Type:** REG_DWORD

TABLE 6.1	Event Logging Keys
Logging Option	**Key**
Verbose log all types of events	RunDiagnosticLoggingGlobal
Verbose log group policy events only	RunDiagnosticLoggingGroupPOlicy
Verbose log remote boot events	RunDiagnosticLoggingIntelliMirror
Verbose log group policy events for application installations	RunDiagnosticLoggingAppDeploy

Creating Multiple Pagefiles

Windows 2000 uses both the memory installed on your computer and disk space to create what is called *virtual memory*. The disk space Windows 2000 claims for memory is known as a *pagefile*. The pagefile on the Windows 2000 workstation is hidden, but you can see it by changing the option in Windows 2000 Explorer to see hidden files in any folder.

The limit on pagefile size is 4095 MB, and the user interface in Windows 2000 only allows you to create one pagefile on each volume. If you need more than one pagefile and you only have one drive available and just one volume on that drive, then you won't be able to create more than one pagefile for use on your workstation. Using the Registry, though, you can add support for multiple pagefiles on a single volume.

To do so, you must create a folder for each pagefile. Naturally, you won't be able to create the pagefile—this is Windows 2000's job—but you must create the folder where the pagefile will be stored. Next, you need to enter the locations, names, minimum size (in Kbytes), and maximum size (Kbytes) for each pagefile you want to create. Each of these values is entered into the Registry key specified below. The data type of the key is REG_MULTI_SZ, so you'll enter the information about each of the pagefiles in one entry. Here is the format:

c:*foldername*\pagefile.sys *minimum_size maximum_size*

c:*next folder name*\pagefile.sys *minimum_size maximum_size*

c:*last folder name*\pagefile.sys *minimum_size maximum_size*

Here is the detail on the Registry key you need to work with:

Root Key: HKEY_LOCAL_MACHINE

Key: System\CurrentControlSet\Control\SessionManager\ Memory Management

Entry: Pagingfiles

Checking the Registry Hive List

As you read in Chapter 1, the Registry is stored in a number of files. The Registry editors that ship with Windows 2000, as well as those tools you can purchase or download for free from the Internet, are simply tools to view this data. The Registry stores the location of each of the files, known as *hives*. You can use the entries storing these location simply to look at the location of the hives, or you can change the entries in order to change the location. The following is the location in the Registry where the hive locations are listed:

```
HKEY_LOCAL_MACHINE\SYSTEM\CurrentControlSet\Control\
HiveList
```

Figure 6.3 shows the appearance of the hive listing in the Registry.

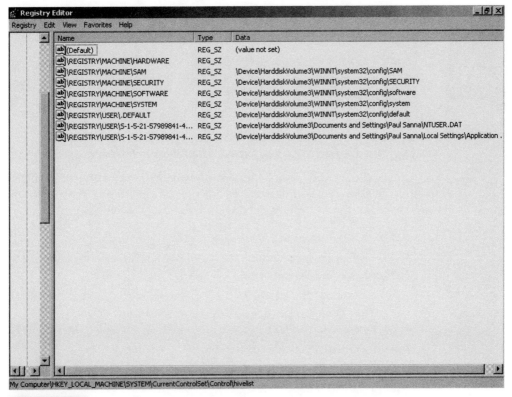

FIGURE 6.3   The location of Registry hives is stored in the Registry.

·················

Configuring Shutdown Options

The settings in this section will help you configure and customize Windows 2000 when you issue the command to shut down the system.

Shutting the Computer off After Shutdown

Some users, the author included, think it's a nuisance to have to shut off the computer after telling Windows 2000 to shut down the computer. A Registry entry is available to change this default behavior. Use a value of 1 in the PowerdownAfterShutdown entry to automatically power down the computer after entering the choosing Shutdown from the Logon dialog box.

Root Key: HKEY_LOCAL_MACHINE

Key: SOFTWARE\Microsoft\WindowsNT\CurrentVersion\Winlogon

Entry: PowerdownAfterShutdown

Data Type: REG_SZ

Disabling Shutdown Without Logon

This setting enables the user to shut down the server from the logon dialog box even if the user is not logged on. Set this value to 1 to enable this option.

Root Key: HKEY_LOCAL_MACHINE

Key: SOFTWARE\Microsoft\WindowsNT\CurrentVersion\Winlogon

Entry: ShutdownWithoutLogon

Data Type: REG_SZ

Setting the Default Logoff and Shutdown Choice

You can configure the default option implemented when the user selects logoff or shutdown. The following list shows the option and the value you would use. The list and values are the same for the two settings.

0 Logoff

1 Shutdown

2 Shutdown and Restart

3 Shutdown and Power Off

Root Key: HKEY_CURRENT_USER

Key: SOFTWARE\Microsoft\WindowsNT\CurrentVersion\Shutdown

Entry: LogoffSetting

Entry: ShutdownSetting

Data Type: REG_DWORD

Managing Problem Applications at Shutdown

It's probably impossible to find a user who has not experienced difficulty with an application he or she has installed into Windows 2000. Sometimes users do not know an application has halted until they issue the command to shut down Windows 2000. It's at that point that the operating system alerts the user that the operating system is having trouble with the application. The settings described in this section will help you manage halted applications when you shut down Windows 2000.

Checking for a Hung Application

When you issue the command to shutdown Windows 2000, the system contacts each running application with its own shutdown request. An application that is hung will not respond. Eventually, Windows 2000 will notify you that the application is not responding, and it will show you how much more time it will wait before attempting to forcibly shut it down. The default value for this entry is 20.

Root Key: HKEY_CURRENT_USER

Key: ControlPanel\Desktop

Entry: WaitToKillAppTimeout

Date Type: REG_SZ

Waiting for a Hung Application to Respond

You can configure the amount of time Windows 2000 waits for an unresponsive application to respond before Windows 2000 finally shuts it down. This setting is supplied in milliseconds. The default value is 5.

Root Key: HKEY_CURRENT_USER

Key: ControlPanel\Desktop

Entry: HungAppTimeout

Date Type: REG_SZ

Automatically Ending Hung Applications

If you are impatient, you might not want to wait for Windows 2000 to activate a halted application when you issue the shutdown command. Set this value of this entry to 1 to force Windows 2000 to shut down as soon as you enter command without attempting to shut down normally a hung application.

Root Key: HKEY_CURRENT_USER

Key: ControlPanel\Desktop

Entry: AutoEndTasks

Date Type: REG_SZ

Configuring Windows 2000 for a Crash

Almost all of the really usable configuration options for preparing for a crash in Windows 2000 can be set in the Registry. Don't think that working with these options is a frivolous activity. Either your installation of Windows 2000 or that of someone you know or administer will crash. You should expect it and take a few minutes to prepare for it. The traditional preparedness steps naturally involve backing up, storing the backups offsite, and other normal procedures. You won't learn how to back up here. Rather, I'll cover the options that control Windows 2000's behavior when it crashes.

Sending an Alert

You can configure Windows 2000 to send an alert to all members of the administrative group should the operating system crash. Set the value of the entry to 1 to send an administrative alert or set the value to 0 to disable.

Root Key: HKEY_LOCAL_MACHINE

Key: SYSTEM\ControlSet001\Control\CrashControl

Entry: SendAlert

Data Type: REG_DWORD

Configuring the Memory Dump File

It's difficult to miss the instant when Windows 2000 crashes. The screen background turns blue and streams of Windows 2000 internal technical data appear. This data is generally very useful, especially to a technical support engineer who may be able to determine why Windows 2000 crashed by examining that data. By examining this crash data, it is possible to determine what modules were loaded in memory when Windows 2000 crashed, what drivers were in use, the data at specific memory points, and more. The DumpFile setting allows you to redirect this data to an external file. This way, you can save the settings to examine at a later time, such as if the crash condition becomes malignant. With the data in file format, you can very easily share the data with an individual qualified to review it.

You can use two settings to save diagnostic data to an external file. The first one, CrashDumpEnabled, simply determines if the data will be saved to a file. Enter 1 to save the data externally; enter 0 not to. The second entry allows you to specify the name of the file that will store the crash data, as well as its location. The default location is %SystemRoot%\Memory.Dmp. The %SystemRoot% variable resolves to the main Windows 2000 directory. You might recall from Chapter 1 the point that the REG_EXPAND_SZ data type is used for Registry entries that contain variables that are resolved to the real value when the entry is used.

> **Root Key:** HKEY_LOCAL_MACHINE
>
> **Key:** SYSTEM\ControlSet001\Control\CrashControl
>
> **Entry:** CrashDumpEnabled
>
> **Data Type:** REG_DWORD
>
> **Entry:** DumpFile
>
> **Data Type:** REG_EXPAND_SZ

Automatically Reboot

When Windows 2000 crashes, the system freezes, and contents of memory, names of modules loaded, and so on is displayed on the screen against a blue background. This is commonly referred to as the *blue screen of death*. You can change this behavior so that Windows 2000 automatically reboots after a crash condition. The drawback to this option is that it might not be immediately obvious to you that the system crashed if you weren't working at it when the crash happened. Granted, you might wonder when you return to your workstation why the logon dialog appears to log back onto the system, but nothing is as familiar to an experienced Windows NT/2000 user, even from a good distance away, as the blue screen of death. If you use this option, be sure you enable the option to store the contents of the crash log to an external files. To enable this option, set the value of AutoReboot to 1.

> **Root Key:** HKEY_LOCAL_MACHINE
>
> **Key:** SYSTEM\ControlSet001\Control\CrashControl
>
> **Entry:** AutoReboot
>
> **Data Type:** REG_DWORD

Checking the Software That Runs at Startup

Windows 2000 runs a number of applications and services at startup. Applications are those programs that you may have installed. Some services launch automatically at system startup, such as your virus protection, others when they're needed, others when you manually start them, and some run just once. The Registry keeps track of those applications that need to be run just one time and notes when an application has been run so it doesn't run again. The same rules are in place for services. Services are programs that provide system support for Windows 2000. Examples of Windows 2000 services include the Network browser, which makes it possible for the workstation to see other computers on the network, and the Task Scheduler. A handful of

Registry entries control the applications and services that run at startup. It's useful to know where to find this list should you need to debug some problem at startup. The following list of keys show you where the run information is stored:

HKEY_LOCAL_MACHINE\SOFTWARE\Microsoft\Windows\
CurrentVersion\Run

HKEY_LOCAL_MACHINE\SOFTWARE\Microsoft\Windows\
CurrentVersion\RunOnce

HKEY_CURRENT_USER\Software\Microsoft\Windows\
CurrentVersion\Run

HKEY_CURRENT_USER\Software\Microsoft\Windows\
CurrentVersion\Runonce

Configuring Quality of Life Settings

Part of the experience of working with Windows 2000 is customizing the operating system so that it behaves and looks according to users' preferences. Not every feature and function a user customizes is work-related. Some elements of the operating system are customized just to make the system a bit easier and more pleasant to work with. These options enhance the users' quality of life when they work with Windows 2000. In this chapter, you can review the Registry settings available to enhance those quality of life aspects of Windows 2000. For example, you can find out how to customize Windows Explorer, the Desktop, colors, and the Start menu.

Customizing the Start Menu

The omnipresent Start menu presents some options to improve the user's quality of computing. You can configure how certain choices on the Start menu appear, as well as what special choices appear on the Start menu.

Scroll the Programs Menu

You can use a Registry setting to determine whether all of the choices on the Programs menu appear in one long list that you can scroll through or in multiple columns. To display the Programs menu in one scrollable list, set this entry to YES.

> **Root Key:** HKEY_CURRENT_USER
>
> **Key:** Software\Microsoft\Windows\CurrentVersion\Explorer\ Advanced
>
> **Name:** StartMenuScrollPrograms
>
> **Data Type:** REG_SZ

Displaying the Favorites Folder

Add this entry and then set its value to 1 to add the Favorites folder to the Start menu. This option provides quick access to any item in the Favorites folder without having to start the application associated with the item.

> **Root Key:** HKEY_CURRENT_USER
>
> **Key:** Software\Microsoft\Windows\CurrentVersion\Explorer\ Advanced
>
> **Name:** StartMenuFavorites
>
> **Data Type:** REG_SZ

Displaying Logoff

The Logoff command is usually available just from the Security dialog, which appears when the user presses Ctrl+Alt+Del. You can add the Logoff command to the Start menu by changing the value of this entry to 1.

> **Root Key:** HKEY_CURRENT_USER
>
> **Key:** Software\Microsoft\Windows\CurrentVersion\Explorer\ Advanced
>
> **Name:** StartMenuLogoff
>
> **Data Type:** REG_DWORD

Displaying the Administrative Tools Menu

The Administrative Tools menu appears on the Start menu when you set this option in the Taskbar and Start Menu Properties dialog box, which is displayed by right-clicking on the Taskbar. You can also set this option via the Registry by setting this key to YES.

Root Key: HKEY_CURRENT_USER

Key: Software\Microsoft\Windows\CurrentVersion\Explorer\
Advanced

Name: StartMenuAdminTools

Data Type: REG_SZ

Cascading Special Folders

The Start menu gives you access to special folders, such as Printers, Control Panel, My Documents, and Network Connections. When you open these folders from the Desktop, or, in the case of just the Printers folder, from the Start menu, the contents of the folder are displayed in the standard folder view. When you add these folders to the Start menu, their contents are displayed on a submenu, like the choices on the Programs or Accessories menus. You can use the Registry to control this option. Use a value of YES or NO to control whether contents of these special folders cascade from the Start menu.

Root Key: HKEY_CURRENT_USER

Key: Software\Microsoft\Windows\CurrentVersion\Explorer\
Advanced

Name: CascadeControlPanel

Name: CascadeMyDocuments

Name: CascadeNetworkConnections

Name: CascadePrinters

Data Type: REG_SZ

Working with Color

There's probably no greater example of customizing a user's computing experience than by changing the colors assigned to various elements of the system. Fortunately, Windows 2000 provides an opportunity to change the colors assigned to just about each element of the operating system.

Colors in Windows 2000 are created by combining levels of red, green, and blue. This method of specifying color is known as RGB. In Windows 2000, colors are assigned to Desktop elements, such as the border around Windows, the text that appears on a button, and others. These colors are assigned as RGB values. For example, the default background color for a button is 181 181 181.

Checking Default Color Schemes

You can use the Registry to define the colors used for many Desktop elements. Individual elements are stored as individual entries in the Control Panel\Colors key. This key can be found in two places: HKEY_CURRENT_

USER and HKEY_USERS\.Default. Changing a color in HKCU affects just the current user. To change a color for all new user accounts, modify the entry in the HKU\.Default root key. Table 7.1 shows the entry for each Windows 2000 Desktop element whose color can be changed, along with the default RGB value. Note that the individual R, G, and B values should be separated by a single space. Also note that the data type for these entries should be REG_SZ.

TABLE 7.1	Default Colors Selection		
Element	**R**	**G**	**B**
ActiveBorder	212	208	200
ActiveTitle	10	36	106
AppWorkSpace	128	128	128
Background	58	110	165
ButtonAlternateFace	181	181	181
ButtonDkShadow	64	64	64
ButtonFace	212	208	200
ButtonHilight	255	255	255
ButtonLight	212	208	200
ButtonShadow	128	128	128
ButtonText	0	0	0
GradientActiveTitle	166	202	240
GradientInactiveTitle	192	192	192
GrayText	128	128	128
Hilight	10	36	106
HilightText	255	255	255
HotTrackingColor	0	0	128
InactiveBorder	212	208	200
InactiveTitle	128	128	128
InactiveTitleText	212	208	200
InfoText	0	0	0
InfoWindow	255	255	225
Menu	212	208	200
MenuText	0	0	0
Scrollbar	212	208	200
TitleText	255	255	255
Window	255	255	255
WindowFrame	0	0	0
WindowText	0	0	0

Learning About Color Schemes

Windows 2000 ships with a number of color schemes. Using them lets a user add a prebuilt color personality to your Desktop very quickly. The color schemes also include information about typeface and size. Color scheme data is stored in the Registry in the Control Panel\Appearance key under the HKEY_CURRENT_USER and HKEY_USERS\.DEFAULT keys. The data is stored in a binary format, so it's tough to determine the specifics for any color scheme. Table 7.2 is provided to show you the RGB values for the colors used in each color scheme that ships with Windows 2000. Note that the current color scheme can be detected in the Registry with the HKEY_CURRENT_USER\Control Panel\Appearance key.

TABLE 7.2   Colors Used in Color Scheme

Element	R	G	B	Element	R	G	B
Lavender				**Tan256**			
ActiveBorder	174	168	217	ActiveBorder	202	184	149
ActiveTitle	128	128	128	ActiveTitle	0	0	0
AppWorkspace	90	78	177	AppWorkspace	156	129	78
Background	128	128	192	Background	128	64	64
ButtonDkShadow	0	0	0	ButtonDkShadow	0	0	0
ButtonFace	174	168	217	ButtonFace	202	184	149
ButtonHilight	216	213	236	ButtonHilight	228	220	203
ButtonLight	174	168	217	ButtonLight	202	184	149
ButtonShadow	90	78	177	ButtonShadow	156	129	78
ButtonText	0	0	0	ButtonText	0	0	0
GrayText	90	78	177	GrayText	156	129	78
Hilight	128	128	128	Hilight	0	0	0
HilightText	255	255	255	HilightText	255	255	255
InactiveBorder	174	168	217	InactiveBorder	202	184	149
InactiveTitle	90	78	177	InactiveTitle	156	129	78
InactiveTitleText	0	0	0	InactiveTitleText	0	0	0
Menu	174	168	217	Menu	202	184	149
MenuText	0	0	0	MenuText	0	0	0
InfoText	174	168	217	InfoText	202	184	149
InfoWindow	0	0	0	InfoWindow	0	0	0
Scrollbar	174	168	217	Scrollbar	202	184	149
TitleText	255	255	255	TitleText	255	255	255
Window	255	255	255	Window	255	255	255
WindowFrame	0	0	0	WindowFrame	0	0	0
WindowText	0	0	0	WindowText	0	0	0

(continued)

| **TABLE 7.2** | (continued) |

Element	R	G	B
Wheat256			
ActiveBorder	215	213	170
ActiveTitle	0	0	0
AppWorkspace	173	169	82
Background	0	64	64
ButtonDkShadow	0	0	0
ButtonFace	215	213	170
ButtonHilight	235	234	214
ButtonLight	215	213	170
ButtonShadow	173	169	82
ButtonText	0	0	0
GrayText	173	169	82
Hilight	0	0	0
HilightText	255	255	255
InactiveBorder	215	213	170
InactiveTitle	173	169	82
InactiveTitleText	0	0	0
Menu	215	213	170
MenuText	0	0	0
InfoText	215	213	170
InfoWindow	0	0	0
Scrollbar	215	213	170
TitleText	255	255	255
Window	255	255	255
WindowFrame	0	0	0
WindowText	0	0	0
Celery			
ActiveBorder	168	215	170
ActiveTitle	0	0	0
AppWorkspace	80	175	85
Background	32	18	46
ButtonDkShadow	0	0	0
ButtonFace	168	215	170
ButtonHilight	211	235	213
ButtonLight	168	215	170
ButtonShadow	85	175	85
ButtonText	0	0	0
GrayText	80	175	85

Element	R	G	B
Hilight	0	0	0
HilightText	255	255	255
InactiveBorder	168	215	170
InactiveTitle	80	175	75
InactiveTitleText	0	0	0
Menu	168	215	170
MenuText	0	0	0
InfoText	168	215	170
InfoWindow	0	0	0
Scrollbar	168	215	170
TitleText	255	255	255
Window	255	255	255
WindowFrame	0	0	0
WindowText	0	0	0
Rose			
ActiveBorder	207	175	183
ActiveTitle	128	128	128
AppWorkspace	159	96	112
Background	128	64	64
ButtonDkShadow	0	0	0
ButtonFace	207	175	183
ButtonHilight	231	216	220
ButtonLight	207	175	183
ButtonShadow	159	96	112
ButtonText	0	0	0
GrayText	159	96	112
Hilight	128	128	128
HilightText	255	255	255
InactiveBorder	207	175	183
InactiveTitle	159	96	112
InactiveTitleText	0	0	0
Menu	207	175	183
MenuText	0	0	0
InfoText	207	175	183
InfoWindow	0	0	0
Scrollbar	207	175	183
TitleText	255	255	255
Window	255	255	255

TABLE 7.2 (continued)

Element	R	G	B	Element	R	G	B
WindowFrame	0	0	0	ButtonText	0	0	0
WindowText	0	0	0	GrayText	69	139	186
Evergreen				Hilight	0	0	0
ActiveBorder	47	151	109	HilightText	255	255	255
ActiveTitle	0	0	0	InactiveBorder	164	198	221
AppWorkspace	31	101	73	InactiveTitle	69	139	186
Background	48	63	48	InactiveTitleText	0	0	0
ButtonDkShadow	0	0	0	Menu	164	198	221
ButtonFace	47	151	109	MenuText	0	0	0
ButtonHilight	137	218	186	InfoText	164	198	221
ButtonLight	47	151	109	InfoWindow	0	0	0
ButtonShadow	31	101	73	Scrollbar	164	198	221
ButtonText	0	0	0	TitleText	255	255	255
GrayText	31	101	73	Window	255	255	255
Hilight	0	0	0	WindowFrame	0	0	0
HilightText	255	255	255	WindowText	0	0	0
InactiveBorder	47	151	109	**Teal**			
InactiveTitle	31	101	73	ActiveBorder	192	192	192
InactiveTitleText	0	0	0	ActiveTitle	0	128	128
Menu	47	151	109	AppWorkspace	128	128	128
MenuText	0	0	0	Background	0	64	64
InfoText	47	151	109	ButtonDkShadow	0	0	0
InfoWindow	0	0	0	ButtonFace	192	192	192
Scrollbar	47	151	109	ButtonHilight	255	255	255
TitleText	255	255	255	ButtonLight	192	192	192
Window	255	255	255	ButtonShadow	128	128	128
WindowFrame	0	0	0	ButtonText	0	0	0
WindowText	0	0	0	GrayText	128	128	128
Blues				Hilight	0	128	128
ActiveBorder	161	198	221	HilightText	255	255	255
ActiveTitle	0	0	0	InactiveBorder	192	192	192
AppWorkspace	69	139	186	InactiveTitle	192	192	192
Background	0	0	64	InactiveTitleText	0	0	0
ButtonDkShadow	0	0	0	Menu	192	192	192
ButtonFace	164	198	221	MenuText	0	0	0
ButtonHilight	210	227	238	InfoText	192	192	192
ButtonLight	164	198	221	InfoWindow	0	0	0
ButtonShadow	69	139	186	Scrollbar	192	192	192

(continued)

TABLE 7.2   (continued)

Element	R	G	B	Element	R	G	B
TitleText	0	0	0	ButtonLight	192	192	192
Window	255	255	255	ButtonShadow	128	128	128
WindowFrame	0	0	0	ButtonText	0	0	0
WindowText	0	0	0	GrayText	128	128	128
TheReds				Hilight	0	0	128
ActiveBorder	192	192	192	HilightText	255	255	255
ActiveTitle	128	0	0	InactiveBorder	192	192	192
AppWorkspace	128	128	128	InactiveTitle	192	192	192
Background	64	0	0	InactiveTitleText	0	0	0
ButtonDkShadow	0	0	0	Menu	192	192	192
ButtonFace	192	192	192	MenuText	0	0	0
ButtonHilight	255	255	255	InfoText	192	192	192
ButtonLight	192	192	192	InfoWindow	0	0	0
ButtonShadow	128	128	128	Scrollbar	192	192	192
ButtonText	0	0	0	TitleText	255	255	255
GrayText	128	128	128	Window	255	255	255
Hilight	128	0	0	WindowFrame	0	0	0
HilightText	255	255	255	WindowText	0	0	0
InactiveBorder	192	192	192	**BlueAndBlack**			
InactiveTitle	192	192	192	ActiveBorder	192	192	192
InactiveTitleText	0	0	0	ActiveTitle	0	0	0
Menu	192	192	192	AppWorkspace	128	128	128
MenuText	0	0	0	Background	0	0	128
InfoText	192	192	192	ButtonDkShadow	0	0	0
InfoWindow	0	0	0	ButtonFace	192	192	192
Scrollbar	192	192	192	ButtonHilight	255	255	255
TitleText	255	255	255	ButtonLight	192	192	192
Window	255	255	255	ButtonShadow	128	128	128
WindowFrame	0	0	0	ButtonText	0	0	0
WindowText	0	0	0	GrayText	128	128	128
WindowsDefault				Hilight	255	255	0
ActiveBorder	192	192	192	HilightText	0	0	0
ActiveTitle	0	0	128	InactiveBorder	192	192	192
AppWorkspace	128	128	128	InactiveTitle	192	192	192
Background	0	128	128	InactiveTitleText	0	0	0
ButtonDkShadow	0	0	0	Menu	192	192	192
ButtonFace	192	192	192	MenuText	0	0	0
ButtonHilight	255	255	255	InfoText	192	192	192

TABLE 7.2	(continued)				

Element	R	G	B	Element	R	G	B
InfoWindow	0	0	0	ButtonText	0	0	0
Scrollbar	192	192	192	GrayText	128	128	128
TitleText	255	255	255	Hilight	128	128	0
Window	255	255	255	HilightText	0	0	0
WindowFrame	0	0	0	InactiveBorder	192	192	192
WindowText	0	0	0	InactiveTitle	192	192	192
Wheat				InactiveTitleText	0	0	0
ActiveBorder	192	192	192	Menu	192	192	192
ActiveTitle	128	128	0	MenuText	0	0	0
AppWorkspace	128	128	128	InfoText	192	192	192
Background	128	128	64	InfoWindow	0	0	0
ButtonDkShadow	0	0	0	Scrollbar	192	192	192
ButtonFace	192	192	192	TitleText	0	0	0
ButtonHilight	255	255	255	Window	255	255	255
ButtonLight	192	192	192	WindowFrame	0	0	0
ButtonShadow	128	128	128	WindowText	0	0	0

Changing Icons Associated with Document Types

The Registry provides you with the entries necessary to change the icons associated with documents, which are, in turn, associated with different types of applications. When a software program is installed in Windows 2000, the program usually registers itself with the operating system. The data collected in this registration process is stored, no surprise here, in the Registry. You can find out much more about the application-specific data stored in the Registry in Chapter 9, "Configuring Microsoft Office 2000." For now, here is information about how to change the icons that are assigned to documents associated with applications installed into Windows 2000.

The HKEY_CLASSES_ROOT (HKCR) is the most important root key for working with applications. The first set of keys in HKCR lists file extensions registered with Windows 2000. Each file extension known to Windows 2000 is represented by a key in HKCR. These keys are easily identified by the period used at the beginning of the key's name.

Like all other keys in the Registry, each of the file extension keys has a default entry. The default entry for the extension shows the name associated with the file extension. For example, if you look at the .BAT key, the default value is *batfile*. This name, also known as an *identifier,* is critical to changing an icon associated with an extension. Once you know the identifier for the extension, scroll through HKCR and find the identifier's key. If a default icon for the file extension has been established, you will see a DefaultIcon key in the identifier's key. The default value in the DefaultIcon key shows the name of the file storing the icon. If the file stores more than icon, then the index of the icon in the file follows the name of the file. These two pieces of data are separated by a comma. To change the default icon associated with the file type, change them on the file or change the index of the icon.

Changing How the Windows 2000 Shell Looks and Works

You might not know it, but there actually is a name for the user interface you use to work with Windows 2000. Actually, there is even another term used as an alternative to *user interface.* When you start Windows 2000, a *shell program* launches. This shell is the front-end to all of the programs, applications, and data associated with Windows 2000 and the applications and hardware you have installed on it. The shell in Windows 2000 is known as *Explorer.* Explorer is used to refer to the Windows 2000 Desktop and the interface used to open files, see folder contents, and more. In this section, a number of options are presented for controlling how Explorer looks and behaves.

Removing the My Documents Icon

The My Documents icon on the Desktop gives the user quick access to documents stored in that folder. If the My Documents shortcut is not typically used, it can be removed from the Desktop. Add this entry and the supporting key to the Registry and then set the value to 1 to disable display of the My Documents icon from the Desktop.

> **Root Key:** HKEY_CURRENT_USER
>
> **Key:** Software\Microsoft\Windows\CurrentVersion\Policies\ NonEnum
>
> **Name:** {450D8FBA-AD25-11D0-98A8-0800361B1103}
>
> **Data Type:** REG_DWORD

Removing the My Network Places Icon

If a workstation will not participate in the network or to prevent the user from browsing the network, the My Network Places icon can be removed from the Desktop. To do so, set the value of this entry to 1. It's likely the key and the entry will have to be added to the Registry first.

Root Key: HKEY_CURRENT_USER

Key: Software\Microsoft\Windows\CurrentVersion\Policies\
NonEnum

Name: NoNetHood

Data Type: REG_DWORD

Removing the Internet Explorer Icon

The Internet Explorer icon is a default choice on the Windows 2000 Desktop. You can remove it by deleting it, but then it is gone forever. Instead, you can use the Registry to hide it. A value of 1 for this entry hides the Internet Explorer icon.

Root Key: HKEY_CURRENT_USER

Key: Software\Microsoft\Windows\CurrentVersion\Policies\
Explorer

Name: NoInternetIcon

Data Type: REG_DWORD

Changing the Icon Text Layout

This entry determines if the text associated with an icon wraps to other lines or if the entire title appears on one line. Use a value of 1 to wrap the title and a value of 0 to stretch the title of the icon across one line.

Root Key: HKEY_CURRENT_USER

Key: Control Panel\Desktop\WindowMetrics

Name: IconTitleWrap

Data Type: REG_SZ

Changing the Horizontal Spacing Between Icons

This value in pixels determines the amount of horizontal space allocated to an icon. Increasing this value increases the space along rows between icons.

Root Key: HKEY_CURRENT_USER

Key: Control Panel\Desktop\WindowMetrics

Name: Iconspacing

Data Type: REG_SZ

Allowing Cool Task Switch

When the user presses Alt+Tab, a list of the running applications appears on the screen. This allows the user to switch to one of those applications. This feature is known as *cool switching*. This feature is enabled by default. To disable cool switching, change the value of this entry to 0.

> **Root Key:** HKEY_CURRENT_USER
>
> **Key:** Control Panel\Desktop
>
> **Name:** CoolSwitch
>
> **Data Type:** REG_SZ

Setting the Number of Task Switch Columns

This setting determines the number of columns that appear in the Cool Switch box. This box appears when the user presses Alt+Tab. The box shows icons representing each of the currently running applications.

> **Root Key:** HKEY_CURRENT_USER
>
> **Key:** Control Panel\Desktop
>
> **Name:** CoolSwitchColumns
>
> **Data Type:** REG_SZ

Setting the Number of Task Switch Rows

This setting determines the number of rows that appear in the Cool Switch box. This box appears when the user presses Alt+Tab. The box shows icons representing each of the currently running applications.

> **Root Key:** HKEY_CURRENT_USER
>
> **Key:** Control Panel\Desktop
>
> **Name:** CoolSwitchRows
>
> **Data Type:** REG_SZ

Changing the Cursor Blink Rate

By default, the cursor flashes every 530 milliseconds. Naturally, the cursor only blinks in certain applications, such as when text is being edited. You can tune that setting with this entry.

> **Root Key:** HKEY_CURRENT_USER
>
> **Key:** Control Panel\Desktop
>
> **Name:** CursorBlinkRate
>
> **Data Type:** REG_SZ

Changing the Desktop Wallpaper

You can supply the name of bitmap file you want to use as Desktop wallpaper. If the file is stored in the Web\Wallpaper subfolder under the main Windows 2000 folder, then you do not need to supply the path to the file, just the name of the file. If the file is stored in another location, then you must enter the full path to the file, as well as the filename.

Root Key: HKEY_CURRENT_USER

Key: Control Panel\Desktop

Name: Wallpaper

Data Type: REG_SZ

Setting Tiled Wallpaper

If you specify a bitmap image to use as a background image for the Desktop, you can also specify whether that image is centered in the middle of the Desktop or whether the image is copied across the Desktop to create a tile-like wallpaper effect. Set this entry to 1 to create the tile effect.

Root Key: HKEY_CURRENT_USER

Key: Control Panel\Desktop

Name: TileWallpaper

Data Type: REG_SZ

Determining Wallpaper Style

You can configure whether the wallpaper image you specify as a background for the desktop is stretched across the entire Desktop. Depending on the image, this option can distort the appearance of the image. To stretch the image, use a value of 2 for this entry. To use the default setting, or to use the tile option, set the value to 0.

Root Key: HKEY_CURRENT_USER

Key: Control Panel\Desktop

Name: WallpaperStyle

Data Type: REG_SZ

Controlling Window Dragging Options

When you drag windows in Windows 2000, you have your choice of two visual effects: the whole windows appears to move as you drag or only the outline of the window appears to move. Supply a value of 1 for this entry to drag the entire window, rather than just the outline.

Root Key: HKEY_CURRENT_USER

Key: Control Panel\Desktop

Name: DragFullWindows

Data Type: REG_SZ

Setting the Drag Height

Use this setting to determine the height of the window being dragged before the mouse determines that the window is being dragged. The default value is 4.

> **Root Key:** HKEY_CURRENT_USER
>
> **Key:** Control Panel\Desktop
>
> **Name:** DragHeight
>
> **Data Type:** REG_SZ

Setting the Drag Detection Width

This setting determines how far a window must be dragged horizontally before the mouse detects that the window is being dragged.

> **Root Key:** HKEY_CURRENT_USER
>
> **Key:** Control Panel\Desktop
>
> **Name:** DragWidth
>
> **Data Type:** REG_SZ

Setting Font Smoothing

You can the access Font Smoothing feature via the Registry, which smooths the edge of large fonts. Set this value to 1 to enable font smoothing.

> **Root Key:** HKEY_CURRENT_USER
>
> **Key:** Control Panel\Desktop
>
> **Name:** FontSmoothing
>
> **Data Type:** REG_SZ

Setting Menu Delay

You know that in Windows 2000, a menu can have a submenu, and choices on that submenu can have submenus as well, and so on. When the cursor stops over a choice on a menu that contains a submenu, there may be a slight delay before the submenu, known as a *cascading menu,* appears. You can configure the delay via the Registry. This value is entered in milliseconds. The default value is 400.

> **Root Key:** HKEY_CURRENT_USER
>
> **Key:** Control Panel\Desktop
>
> **Name:** MenuShowDelay
>
> **Data Type:** REG_SZ

Activating the Screen Saver

You can use this entry as a master switch for the screen saver function in Windows 2000. Naturally, you must configure other elements of the screen savers, such as the screen saver program to use and the amount of time that should lapse before the screen saver starts. This entry, though, controls whether the screen saver function is configured to run. Enter a value of 1 to start the screen saver.

Root Key: HKEY_CURRENT_USER

Key: Control Panel\Desktop

Name: ScreenSaveActive

Data Type: REG_SZ

Securing the Screen Saver

One of the nice features in the Windows 2000 screen saver program is that it can also be used to secure your system. You can configure the screen saver so that a password must be entered to stop the screen saver once it starts. Enter a value of 1 for this entry to use the password feature.

Root Key: HKEY_CURRENT_USER

Key: Control Panel\Desktop

Name: ScreenSaverIsSecure

Data Type: REG_SZ

Setting Screen Saver Start Time

This entry sets the amount of time the system must remain inactive before the screen saver starts. This value is entered in seconds.

Root Key: HKEY_CURRENT_USER

Key: Control Panel\Desktop

Name: ScreenSaveTimeOut

Data Type: REG_SZ

Configuring the Microsoft Mouse

Microsoft manufactures a mouse that provides a few extra features to help navigate through web sites and over web pages. A Registry entry helps control how the mouse works. You can configure how many lines are scrolled with one turn of the wheel on the mouse.

Root Key: HKEY_CURRENT_USER

Key: Control Panel\Desktop\WheelScrollLines

Name: WheelScrollLines

Data Type: REG_SZ

Removing the File Menu

To streamline the menu system in Windows Explorer, you can hide the File menu. The File menu is used to create folders and shortcuts and to delete and rename items. All of these functions are possible by right-clicking or using the keyboard. Change the value of this entry, which you most likely will have to create, to YES to hide the File menu.

Root Key: HKEY_CURRENT_USER

Key: Software\Microsoft\Windows\CurrentVersion\Policies\ Explorer

Name: NoFileMenu

Data Type: REG_SZ

Hiding File Extensions from View

The process of installing an application into Windows 2000 usually involves registering the files typically used by the application with the operating system. When new files are created, the file extension is used to associate files with an application. You can hide the extensions for these *known* files from view in My Computer and Windows Explorer. Set the value of this entry to 1 to hide file extensions. Note that extensions for files that Windows 2000 cannot associate with an application are displayed automatically.

Root Key: HKEY_CURRENT_USER

Key: Software\Microsoft\Windows\CurrentVersion\Explorer\ Advanced

Name: HideFileExt

Data Type: REG_DWORD

Stop Showing Startup Tips

Windows 2000 displays sometimes useful tips every time the system is accessed. Set the value of this entry to 0 to disable display of these tips.

Root Key: HKEY_CURRENT_USER

Key: Software\Microsoft\Windows\CurrentVersion\Explorer\ Advanced

Name: ShowInfoTip

Data Type: REG_DWORD

Hiding the Map Network Drive Button

If a workstation will not be connected to the network, the button that enables the user to map local drives to network resources can be hidden. Set the value of this entry to 0 to hide the Map Network Drives button.

Root Key: HKEY_CURRENT_USER

Key: Software\Microsoft\Windows\CurrentVersion\Explorer\Advanced

Name: MapNetDrvBtn

Data Type: REG_DWORD

Setting the Desktop as Web View

The Registry can be used to specify whether the Desktop is displayed as a web page. If the Desktop is displayed as a web page, the workstation can be configured so that live web content is delivered directly to the Desktop. Set the value of this entry to 1 to enable the Desktop as a web page.

Root Key: HKEY_CURRENT_USER

Key: Software\Microsoft\Windows\CurrentVersion\Explorer\Advanced

Name: WebView

Data Type: REG_DWORD

Displaying Operating System Files

By default, files used exclusively by Windows 2000 and its applications are hidden from Windows Explorer and My Computer. To display these files, change the value of this entry to 1.

Root Key: HKEY_CURRENT_USER

Key: Software\Microsoft\Windows\CurrentVersion\Explorer\Advanced

Name: ShowSuperHidden

Data Type: REG_DWORD

Setting the Windows Classic Desktop

An alternative to displaying the Windows 2000 Desktop as a Web page is to use the standard display, which includes no Web content. Set the value of this entry to 1 to enable the classic Desktop view.

Root Key: HKEY_CURRENT_USER

Key: Software\Microsoft\Windows\CurrentVersion\Explorer\Advanced

Name: ClassicViewState

Data Type: REG_DWORD

Setting Intelligent Menus

An enhancement in Windows, starting with Windows 2000, is intelligent menus. This feature configures menus so that only choices you usually make appear. If you want to see the full menu, you click on the double-arrow icon that appears on the bottom. To disable use of intelligent menus, set the value of this entry to NO. Otherwise, set the value to YES.

Root Key: HKEY_CURRENT_USER

Key: Software\Microsoft\Windows\CurrentVersion\Explorer\Advanced

Name: IntelliMenus

Data Type: REG_SZ

Managing Desktop Configuration

The Registry stores a wide range of details about a workstation's desktop configuration. *Desktop configuration* refers to the manner in which Windows 2000 is configured for a user to work every day. A user's impressions of working with Windows 2000 usually include personal preferences (colors and fonts) and how the system is configured (video settings, keyboard preferences, messages, etc.). This chapter focuses on the latter. You can read in this chapter how to configure a range of desktop elements, such as the command prompt, message display, Start menu, Control Panel, and more, via the Registry.

Working with Environment Variables

Environment variables are critical elements in Windows 2000, as they were in Windows NT and Windows 9x. Environment variables are dynamic placeholders for data. This data usually describes the current runtime environment of the operating system. For example, one of the most used environment variables is the one that stores the search path. Another widely used environment variable stores the location of the Temp folder. In addition, environment variables also represent configuration information, such as the type and number of processors installed on the computer.

Environment variables serve important functions. When problems arise in Windows 2000, checking the value of environment variables is as reasonable a diagnostic exercise as any other. Problems certainly can arise if the variable that represents the program that starts when the user chooses Command Prompt from the Accessories menu becomes corrupt, or if the wrong folder is represented by the TEMP or WINDIR variables.

Windows 2000 tracks two types of environment variables:

- those for the user currently logged on to the system
- those applicable regardless of which user is logged on

You can see the list of environment variables and their values in the Registry. Look in the following key to see the list of environment variables applied to all users:

```
HKEY_LOCAL_MACHINE\SYSTEM\CurrentControlSet\Control\
Session Manager\Environment
```

The following list shows the environment variables you can see in the key noted above, as well as sample values:

```
ComSpec = %SystemRoot%\system32\cmd.exe
NUMBER_OF_PROCESSORS = 1
OS = Windows_NT
Os2LibPath = %SystemRoot%\system32\os2\dll;
Path =
%SystemRoot%\system32;%SystemRoot%;%SystemRoot%\System32\
PATHEXT = .COM;.EXE;.BAT;.CMD;.VBS;.VBE;.JS;.JSE;.WSF;.WSH
PROCESSOR_ARCHITECTURE = x86
PROCESSOR_IDENTIFIER = x86 Family 6 Model 5 Stepping 1,
GenuineIntel
PROCESSOR_LEVEL = 6
PROCESSOR_REVISION = 0501
TEMP = %SystemRoot%\TEMP
TMP = %SystemRoot%\TEMP
Windir = %SystemRoot%
```

The most important environment variable Windows 2000 stores on a per user basis is the location of the Temp directory. This is the directory used by most applications to store files and data that can be discarded after use. It is unfortunate that most applications don't later delete the files created in the Temp folder once the applications no longer have use for them, but at least you know the contents of the Temp folder can be discarded with little concern.

Two entries govern the location of the Temp directory. The reason for two entries rather than one is the typical use of either one of two system variables indicating the location of the Temp folder. Some applications rely on the TEMP system variable; others rely on the use of the TMP system variable. An entry for each is stored in the following two keys:

```
HKCU\Environment
HKEY_LOCAL_MACHINE\system\CurrentControlSet
```

Both are assigned the data type REG_EXPAND_SZ so that other system variables may be used, such as %USERPROFILE%. This macro expands to the location of the location of the user's Documents and Settings folder, which is analogous to user's home directory on a network.

Setting Video and Display Options

The Display tool in the Control Panel folder gives the user access to the configuration options for the monitor, the video adapter that interfaces between the computer and the monitor, and the options the user can set to customize the display (see Figure 8.1). Many of the video and display options available

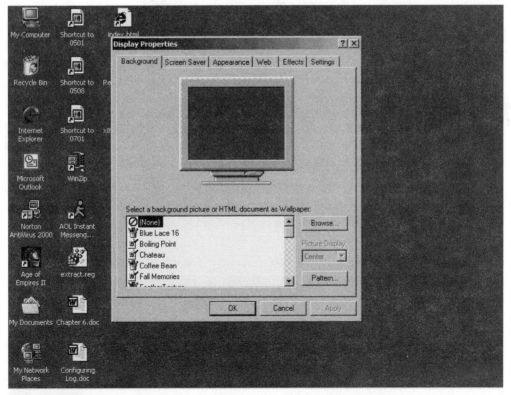

FIGURE 8.1   The Display tool helps the user manage everything from the screen saver to the monitor refresh frequency.

via the Registry are covered in Chapter 13, "Hardware Management," and Chapter 7, "Configuring Quality of Life Settings." This section presents a few more Registry entries you can use in a system administrator's role to control how and whether users can change the video and display configuration.

Disabling the Display Applet

The Display applet in the Control Panel controls the computer's display and video configuration. This covers everything from the colors used for Desktop items to the video adapter installed. To restrict users from changing and even viewing elements of the configuration, you can disable the Display applet. Add the following key and entry to the Registry and enter a value of 1. This will have the effect of removing the shortcut to the applet in the Control Panel folder.

> **Root Key:** HKEY_CURRENT_USER
>
> **Key:** Software\Microsoft\Windows\CurrentVersion\Policies\ System
>
> **Entry Name:** NoDispCPL
>
> **Entry Data Type:** REG_DWORD

Restrict Wallpaper Change

Many organizations have policies outlawing the use of any other than sanctioned wallpaper images, so that users do not use potentially offensive wallpapers and thus avoid possible personnel issues. Other organizations insist on the use of specific wallpaper, such as one with the corporate logo. You can use a Registry policy to restrict workstation users from changing the background wallpaper. Add the following key and entry to the Registry and enter a value of 1. This will have the effect of disabling all of the controls on the Appearance tab of the Display properties dialog box.

> **Root Key:** HKEY_CURRENT_USER
>
> **Key:** Software\Microsoft\Windows\CurrentVersion\Policies\ ActiveDesktop
>
> **Entry Name:** NoChangingWallPaper
>
> **Entry Data Type:** REG_DWORD

Hard-Coding the Wallpaper

You can specify the Desktop background wallpaper via the Registry. This option can help you maintain and roll out a standard configuration workstation without having to work with the Desktop applet in the Control Panel. You can specify the name of the bitmap that serves as the wallpaper, as well as the style of the image's appearance on the screen. In the key described below, enter the name and location of the bitmap file in the Wallpaper entry. For the WallpaperStyle entry, supply a value of 0 to center the image on the

Desktop, a value 2 to stretch the image to fill the Desktop, or supply a value of 1 to tile the image across the Desktop.

Root Key: HKEY_CURRENT_USER

Key: Software\Microsoft\Windows\CurrentVersion\Policies\ System

Entry Name: Wallpaper

Entry Name: WallpaperStyle

Entry Data Type: REG_SZ

Disabling the Appearance Tab

You can restrict users from displaying the Appearance tab on the Display Properties dialog box. This will prevent users from changing elements of their video and display configuration, such as the color of elements of the Windows 2000 interface, as well a color scheme. Add the following key and entry to the Registry and then enter a value of 1. This entry has the effect of removing the Appearance tab.

Root Key: HKEY_CURRENT_USER

Key: Software\Microsoft\Windows\CurrentVersion\Policies\ ActiveDesktop

Entry Name: NoDispAppearancePage

Entry Data Type: REG_DWORD

Removing the Background Tab

The Background tab in the Display dialog box shows the name of the file used as the Desktop background wallpaper. To prevent users from accessing this tab, add the following key and entry to the Registry and then supply a value of 1. This entry has the effect of removing the Background tab from the Display properties dialog box.

Root Key: HKEY_CURRENT_USER

Key: Software\Microsoft\Windows\CurrentVersion\Policies\ System

Entry Name: NoDispBackgroundPage

Entry Data Type: REG_DWORD

Disabling the Screen Saver Tab

Your organization might roll out workstations with a standard configuration in which the elements of the video and display setup are predefined by you (the administrator), such as the screen saver. You can disable the screen saver tab so that users cannot change this element of the configuration. Add the following key and entry to the Registry and enter a value of 1.

Root Key: HKEY_CURRENT_USER

Key: Software\Microsoft\Windows\CurrentVersion\Policies\ System

Entry Name: NoDispScrSavPage

Entry Data Type: REG_DWORD

Disabling the Settings Tab

The Settings tab of the Display properties dialog box presents the user with the option to change settings for the display adapter, as well as some of the other hardware-specific aspects of the video and display configuration. Naturally, mishandling some of these options can cause significant problems with the display aspects of the computer. Use the Registry to disable the Settings tab. Add the following key and entry to the Registry and enter a value of 1.

Root Key: HKEY_CURRENT_USER

Key: Software\Microsoft\Windows\CurrentVersion\Policies\ System

Entry Name: NoDispSettingsPage

Entry Data Type: REG_DWORD

Managing Keyboard Settings

You can use the Registry to control how the keyboard attached to a Windows 2000 computer operates. The relevant entries can be found in the following key:

HKEY_CURRENT_USER\ControlPanel

The options you can set via the Registry correspond to the options available in the Keyboard dialog box, which appears when you choose Keyboard from the Control Panel (see Figure 8.2).

Keyboard Delay

The keyboard delay value determines how long the delay before a character repeats on the screen when you press and hold that character's key on the keyboard. There are 4 possible values, 0, 1, 2, 3, with 0 indicating the shortest possible delay.

Root Key: HKEY_CURRENT_USER

Key: ControlPanel

Entry Name: CursorBlinkRate

Entry Data Type: REG_SZ

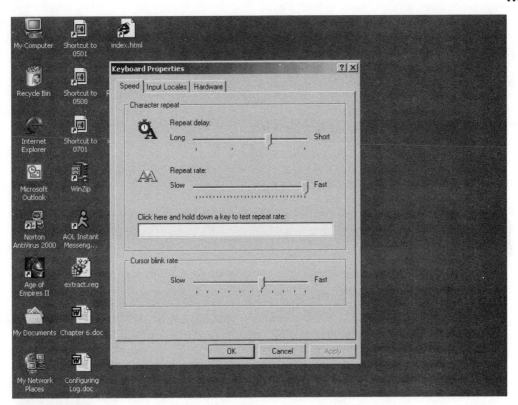

FIGURE 8.2   The Keyboard applet controls how the keyboard operates, including setting international keyboard layouts, repeat rates, and more.

Keyboard Repeat Speed

A cousin to the Keyboard Delay setting, the Keyboard Repeat speed also controls the keyboard's behavior when you press and hold a key on the keyboard. The Keyboard Repeat setting determines how quickly a character repeats when you press and hold its corresponding key on the keyboard. The values you can use range from 0 (slow repeat) to 31 (very fast repeat).

Root Key: HKEY_CURRENT_USER

Key: ControlPanel

Entry Name: KeyboardSpeed

Entry Data Type: REG_SZ

Cursor Blink Rate

The cursor blink rate determines how often the cursor blinks on the screen. You can set the value of the Cursor blink rate in increments of 100. The values you set in the Registry correspond to the stop points on the Cursor Blink Rate slider that appear in the Keyboard dialog.

Root Key: HKEY_CURRENT_USER

Key: ControlPanel

Entry Name: CursorBlinkRate

Entry Data Type: REG_SZ

Numlock Setting at Startup

You can control whether the Numlock state is set to on or off when the system is booted. A value 0 for InitialKeyboardIndicators entry indicates the setting should be off, while a value of 2 indicates Numlock should be enabled when the system boots.

Root Key: HKEY_CURRENT_USER

Key: ControlPanel

Entry Name: InitialKeyboardIndicators

Entry Data Type: REG_SZ

Display Input Locales on System Tray

The System Tray displays the keyboard locale in use if more than one is loaded. The small utility also allows the user to switch between keyboard locales extremely quickly. An application named INTERNAT.EXE. is used to control this small feature. It is located in the System32 subfolder in the main Windows 2000 folder. When you click on the option to display input locales on the taskbar, an entry is written to the Registry instructing the system to run this application.

Root Key: HKEY_CURRENT_USER

Key: Software\Microsoft\Windows\CurrentVersion\Run

Entry Name: Internat.exe

Entry Data Type: REG_SZ

Viewing International Settings

Windows 2000 can be configured to accommodate users from just about any country on the planet. These users, naturally, have specific requirements when it comes to the format of certain aspects of their everyday lives. Examples include the date and time format and the symbol used for currency. These settings are reflected in the dialog box that appears when you choose Regional Settings from the Control Panel. All of the settings can be modified in the Registry in the following key:

HKEY_CURRENT_USER\Control Panel\International

The following list shows the entries you can find in the key noted above, as well as sample values.

```
iCountry=1                       sLongDate=dddd, MMMM dd,
iCurrDigits=2                    yyyy
iCurrency=0                      sShortDate=M/d/yyyy
iDate=0                          sThousand=,
iDigits=2                        sTime=:
iLZero=1                         sTimeFormat=h:mm:ss tt
iMeasure=1                       iTimePrefix=0
iNegCurr=0                       sMonDecimalSep=.
iTime=0                          sMonThousandSep=,
iTLZero=0                        iNegNumber=1
Locale=00000409                  sNativeDigits=0123456789
s1159=AM                         NumShape=1
s2359=PM                         iCalendarType=1
sCountry=United States           iFirstDayOfWeek=6
sCurrency=$                      iFirstWeekOfYear=0
sDate=/                          sGrouping=3;0
sDecimal=.                       sMonGrouping=3;0
sLanguage=ENU                    sPositiveSign=
sList=,                          sNegativeSign=-
```

Configuring the Windows File Checker

The Registry provides a vehicle for disabling the Windows File Protection system. The Windows File Protection system protects critical system files, as well as any other files the administrator designates. Set the value of this entry to 1 to disable this feature. You will be prompted to reenable this WFP at startup. A value of 2 will disable the feature and suppress any warnings. A value of 3 will disable the SFC with no prompts only at the next boot up.

Root Key: HKEY_LOCAL_MACHINE

Key: Software\Microsoft\Windows NT\CurrentVersion\Winlogon

Entry Name: SFCDisable

Entry Data Type: REG_DWORD

The name of the folder where the SFC stores the cached version of control files for the SFC is DLLCACHE. By default, that folder is stored in the System32 subfolder in the main Windows 2000 folder. To change that default location, edit the following entry:

Entry Name: SFCDllCacheDir

Entry Data Type: REG_EXPAND_SZ

The following entry can be used to determine whether the progress meter is displayed as the SFS program runs. Use a value of 1 to display the progress meter. The default setting is 0, which means the progress meter is not displayed.

Entry Name: SFCShowProgress

Entry Data Type: REG_DWORD

Configuring the Command Prompt Window

The settings for the Windows 2000 command prompt are found in one place in the Registry. From this key, you can control all aspects of the window, from color to size of cursor to the number of commands stored in the history buffer. These settings correspond to the dialog box that appears when you open a command prompt window and then choose Properties from the menu (see Figure 8.3).

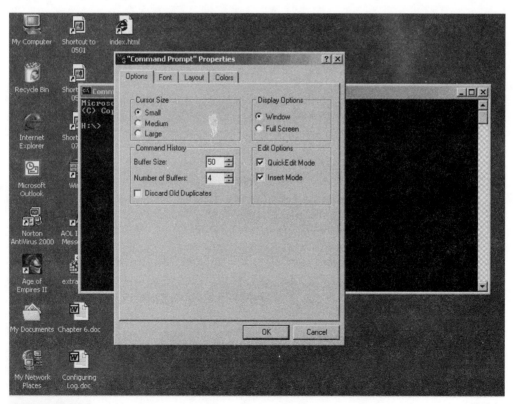

FIGURE 8.3 The Command Prompt Properties dialog box.

History Buffer Size

This HistoryBufferSize entry determines how many of the most recent commands a user enters at the command prompt window are stored. The user presses the Up arrow key to scroll through the stored commands. The default data type for this value is REG_DWORD, so you can enter a hexadecimal value as the real value for this setting. Be sure to select the Decimal option in the DWORD editor dialog box.

Root Key: HKEY_CURRENT_USER

Key: Console

Entry Name: HistoryBufferSize

Entry Data Type: REG_DWORD

Number of History Buffers

Windows 2000 can store the list of most recently issued commands for each open command prompt window (see History Buffer Size entry). The setting for NumberofHistoryBuffers must be equal to or greater than the number of command prompt windows for which the history must be maintained. The default data type for this value is REG_DWORD, so you can enter a hexadecimal value as the real value for this setting. Be sure to select the Decimal option in the DWORD editor dialog box.

Root Key: HKEY_CURRENT_USER

Key: Console

Entry Name: NumberOfHistoryBuffers

Entry Data Type: REG_DWORD

Setting Insert/Overtype Mode

Editing text on the command line is no different in most ways from editing text in a word processing program or Notepad. For example, you can set whether the command prompt works in insert or overtype mode. The default mode is insert mode. Change the value of the following entry to 0 to enable overtype mode:

Root Key: HKEY_CURRENT_USER

Key: Console

Entry Name: InsertMode

Entry Data Type: REG_DWORD

Setting Window Mode

By default, the command prompt window appears full screen. You can change this default behavior to window mode with the following entry. Use a value of 0:

Root Key: HKEY_CURRENT_USER

Key: Console

Entry Name: FullScreen

Entry Data Type: REG_DWORD

Configuring Windows 2000 Messages

The Registry provides some control over the number and content of status messages displayed by Windows 2000. You can also control the display of options via group policy, which is covered in Chapter 12, "Working with Group Policy."

Hide All System Messages from Windows 2000

You can suppress the display of all messages status from Windows 2000 via the Registry. If you enable this policy, users do not see messages, such as those reminding users to wait before powering down their computer while Windows 2000 closes programs and files. Set the value of this key to 1 to enable this feature.

Root Key: HKEY_CURRENT_USER

Key: Software\Microsoft\Windows\CurrentVersion\Policies\ System

Entry Name: DisableStatusMessages

Entry Data Type: REG_DWORD

Display Detailed Messages in Windows 2000

If the standard Windows 2000 does not provide you or users enough information, you can configure the system to display more detailed messages. Add the following key and entry and then set the value if the entry to 1 to see detailed status messages as Windows starts up and shuts down the system.

Root Key: HKEY_CURRENT_USER

Key: Software\Microsoft\Windows\CurrentVersion\Policies\ System

Entry Name: VerboseStatus

Entry Data Type: REG_DWORD

Hide Welcome Tips

You can prevent Windows 2000 from providing those helpful tips that appear when the user logs on. Add the following key and entry and then set the value of the entry to 1 to suppress the Welcome Tips dialog box from appearing:

Root Key: HKEY_CURRENT_USER

Key: Software\Microsoft\Windows\CurrentVersion\Policies\
Explorer

Entry Name: NoWelcomeScreen

Entry Data Type: REG_DWORD

Specifying the Location for User Profiles

The Registry stores the location of user profiles. User profiles determine each user's working environment in Windows 2000. Elements such as programs installed, content and arrangement of items on the Desktop, colors, and other options are components of the user profile. A user profile is really a combination of folders and subfolders and files stored in those folders.

Windows 2000 creates the user profile and the associated folder hierarchy when a user account is created. When a user makes changes to his or her Windows 2000 environment, such as by installing new software or changing the background wallpaper, the user profile is updated.

Windows 2000 also contains a default user profile. This is the profile that is applied to all new user accounts.

Last, Windows 2000 also maintains a user profile for *all users*. The All Users user profile is used to create the generic working environment. The elements in a specific user profile override the same elements as defined in the profile for All Users. Elements of the Windows 2000 environment that are common to all users are stored in the All Users profile.

You can use the Registry to see the names and locations of the three types of user profiles maintained by Windows 2000. The following key stores the relevant entries for user profiles:

```
HKEY_LOCAL_MACHINE\SOFTWARE\Microsoft\WindowsNT\Current-
Version\ProfileList
```

The most important entry in the key noted above is the ProfilesDirectory entry. This entry stores the location of all user profiles:

```
ProfilesDirectory = %Systemdrive%\Documents and Settings
```

Two entries stores the name of the subfolders under the main user profile folder, defined by the ProfilesDirectory entry, in which the all users and default user profiles are stored:

```
AllUsersProfile
DefaultUserProfile
```

So, if you append the value of the AllUsersProfile entry to the value of the ProfilesDirectory entry, you'll learn the folder location of these folders, which will allow you to view and change the components of the Windows 2000 environment. Naturally, if you change the value of the entries listed above, you can establish a new location for the storage of the profiles.

You can also see details about the user profile currently in use. Look for the one subkey of the HKEY_LOCAL_MACHINE\SOFTWARE\Microsoft\ Windows NT\CurrentVersion\ProfileList key. This subkey, a 36-character alphanumeric string, is the security identifier (SID) for the currently logged on user account. Open that key and look for the ProfileImagePath entry. The value indicates the location of the current user profile:

```
HKEY_LOCAL_MACHINE\SOFTWARE\Microsoft\WindowsNT\Current-
Version \ProfileList\S-1-5-21-57989841-492894223-
1957994488-1000

ProfileImagePath = %Systemdrive%\Documents and
Settings\Paul Sanna
```

Seeing Hotfixes

Microsoft delivers point fixes to Windows 2000 bugs in the form of *hotfixes*. A hotfix is simply an executable file that updates one or more Windows 2000 files to fix some verified problem. You can tell the hotfixes that have been applied to Windows 2000 by inspecting the following key:

```
HKEY_LOCAL_MACHINE\SOFTWARE\Microsoft\WindowsNT\Current-
Version\HotFix
```

Subkeys of the key noted above will have names the same as the number assigned to hotfixes. Lastly, the Installed entry under the hotfix key indicates whether the hotfix has been installed:

```
HKEY_LOCAL_MACHINE\SOFTWARE\Microsoft\WindowsNT\Current-
Version\HotFix\Q147222

Installed=00000001
```

Configuring the Start Menu

Windows 2000 provides the opportunity, via the Registry, to configure the Start menu. You can add and remove choices from the Start menu, as well as manage how certain choices, such as Documents, behave. Like the Control Panel, you can manage much of the configuration of the Start menu via group policy. Changes you make to the Start menu via the group policy snap-in, covered in Chapter 12, "Working with Group Policy," are reflected in the Registry as well. In this section, you can learn about the Start menu changes in the Registry you can make, both via group policy and through some more less obvious entries.

Removing Windows Update

Inquisitive users might be tempted to click on the Windows Update choice on the Start menu. This choice connects the computer to the Microsoft Web site, which launches an interrogation of the workstation to see which components are eligible for update. As an administrator of the organization to which the computer belongs, you might not want the configuration of the computer to change, especially with software fresh out of the Microsoft factory. Create this key and entry to remove the Windows Update choice from the menu. Note that this Registry change will not restrict a user from simply accessing the Windows Update site on Microsoft's site. Other policies and Registry fixes can restrict users from installing new software, however.

> **Root Key:** HKEY_CURRENT_USER
>
> **Key:** Software\Microsoft\Windows\CurrentVersion\Policies\ Explorer
>
> **Entry Name:** NoWindowsUpdate
>
> **Entry Data Type:** REG_DWORD

Restricting Common Groups

Certain choices appear on the Programs menu regardless of the current user logged on. This is usually a function of how the software registered itself with Windows 2000 when it was installed. You can use a Registry setting to restrict all but choices installed under the context of the user logged on when the software was installed to appear on the Programs menu. Add the following key and entry to the Registry and supply a value of 1 to disable the display of common options on the Programs menu.

> **Root Key:** HKEY_CURRENT_USER
>
> **Key:** Software\Microsoft\Windows\CurrentVersion\Policies\ Explorer
>
> **Entry Name:** NoCommonGroups
>
> **Entry Data Type:** REG_DWORD

Managing the Documents Menu

Some might consider the existence of a list of the documents most recently accessed by a user a security risk. This list, naturally, is displayed on the Documents menu on the Start menu. To remove the Documents menu, add this key and entry and set its value to 1.

Root Key: HKEY_CURRENT_USER

Key: Software\Microsoft\Windows\CurrentVersion\Policies\Explorer

Entry Name: NoRecentDocsMenu

Entry Data Type: REG_DWORD

An alternative to removing the Documents menu from the Start menu would be to clear that menu when a user shuts down Windows 2000 or logs off the workstation. Use the following Registry setting to enable this feature.

Root Key: HKEY_CURRENT_USER

Key: Software\Microsoft\Windows\CurrentVersion\Policies\Explorer

Entry Name: ClearRecentDocsOnExit

Entry Data Type: REG_DWORD

Yet another option for managing the Documents menu is to simply prevent Windows 2000 from recording recently opened documents. In this case, the Documents menu always appears on the Start menu, although no shortcuts are ever added to the menu. Use a value of 1 to enable this option.

Root Key: HKEY_CURRENT_USER

Key: Software\Microsoft\Windows\CurrentVersion\Policies\Explorer

Entry Name: NoRecentDocsHistory

Entry Data Type: REG_DWORD

Removing the Network and Dial-Up Connections Folder

You can deny users of a computer the right to open the Network and Dial-Up Connections folder. Doing so will prevent the users from manually establishing a connection to the LAN or a remote network, even the Internet, as well as from creating a new connection or seeing the details for a configured connection. Add this key and entry to the Registry and then set the value of the entry to 1.

Root Key: HKEY_CURRENT_USER

Key: Software\Microsoft\Windows\CurrentVersion\Policies\Explorer

Entry Name: NoNetworkConnections

Entry Data Type: REG_DWORD

Removing the Favorites Menu

Like the Documents menu, which displays the last fifteen documents opened by the user currently logged on the computer, some view the Favorites menu as a security risk, or at least an invasion of privacy. You can disable the capability to add the Favorites menu to the Start menu. A user adds the Favorites folder via the Taskbar and Start Menu dialog box. Restrict this option by adding entry and key and setting the value to 1.

> **Root Key:** HKEY_CURRENT_USER
>
> **Key:** Software\Microsoft\Windows\CurrentVersion\Policies\ Explorer
>
> **Entry Name:** NoFavoritesMenu
>
> **Entry Data Type:** REG_DWORD

Removing the Find Choice

You can use the Registry to remove the Find choice from the Start menu, as well as from Windows Explorer. Setting this option via the Registry also will prevent the Search dialog box from appearing when the user presses Alt+F. Add the following key and entry and set the value of the entry to 1.

> **Root Key:** HKEY_CURRENT_USER
>
> **Key:** Software\Microsoft\Windows\CurrentVersion\Policies\ Explorer
>
> **Entry Name:** NoFind
>
> **Entry Data Type:** REG_DWORD

Removing Run from the Start Menu

You can remove the Run choice from the Start menu using a Registry switch. If you need to restrict users from running programs from the command line, though, then you have more work to do than simply removing the Run choice. You should also use Windows 2000 security features to disable users from executing executable files. For now, set the value of this entry to 1 remove the Run choice from the Start menu.

> **Root Key:** HKEY_CURRENT_USER
>
> **Key:** Software\Microsoft\Windows\CurrentVersion\Policies\ Explorer
>
> **Entry Name:** NoRun
>
> **Entry Data Type:** REG_DWORD

Preventing Changes to the Start Menu

Users can modify the Start menu by dragging shortcuts to the Start button, as well as by right-clicking on the Start menu and making choices from the menu that appears. You can restrict users from changing the Start menu by enabling this policy from the Registry. Add the key and entry shown below and then set the value of the entry to 1.

Root Key: HKEY_CURRENT_USER

Key: Software\Microsoft\Windows\CurrentVersion\Policies\
Explorer

Entry Name: NoChangeStartMenu

Entry Data Type: REG_DWORD

Preventing Change of Taskbar and Start Menu Changes

To prevent the user from changing the display of the Context menu for the Taskbar, which appears when the user right-clicks on it, set the following Registry key, entry, and value. Doing so will prevent users from changing some elements of the Start menu, adding toolbars to the Taskbar, changing items that appear on the Taskbar tray, and a handful of other functions.

Root Key: HKEY_CURRENT_USER

Key: Software\Microsoft\Windows\CurrentVersion\Policies\
Explorer

Entry Name: NoTrayContextMenu

Entry Data Type: REG_DWORD

Managing Intelligent Menus

You or your users may have noticed how menus in Windows 2000, both for the operating system and the applications you install, display choices you often use and hide those you seldom use. This behavior occurs by default. If it annoys you not to see all the choices on a menu despite your recent activity on the menu, then you can disable this feature. There are two ways you can do this.

Windows 2000 records your activity. This recording mechanism is known as *instrumentation*. The data recorded by instrumentation is used to modify the menus. If you disable instrumentation, then there is no way for Windows 2000 to record your actions and, hence, to customize menus. Use a value of 1 for this entry to turn off instrumentation. Keep in mind, though, that certain applications or even Windows 2000 might rely on the data recorded by instrumentation for reasons other than menu customization, so you might cause problems using this entry.

Root Key: HKEY_CURRENT_USER

Key: Software\Microsoft\Windows\CurrentVersion\Policies\
Explorer

Entry Name: NoInstrumentation

Entry Data Type: REG_DWORD

A safer option to turn off the intelligent menus options might be to do just that: turn off intelligent menus. With this Registry change, you can simply prevent Windows 2000 from customizing menus without disabling instrumentation.

Root Key: HKEY_CURRENT_USER

Key: Software\Microsoft\Windows\CurrentVersion\Policies\
Explorer

Entry Name: NoIntellimenus

Entry Data Type: REG_DWORD

Adding Support for Safely Running 16-bit Applications

If users on a workstation still use older 16-bit applications, such as older Window programs or even DOS programs, you may want to enable the option to run these programs in a dedicated process. By default, all 16-bit applications run in a shared process. The problem with this model is that if one of the applications running in the process crashes, it could crash the other running programs. A user can force an application launched from the Run dialog box to run in its own dedicated process. To enable the feature, the user must check a box that does not appear by default. To add this option to the Run dialog box (see Figure 8.4), add the following key and entry and set the value to 1.

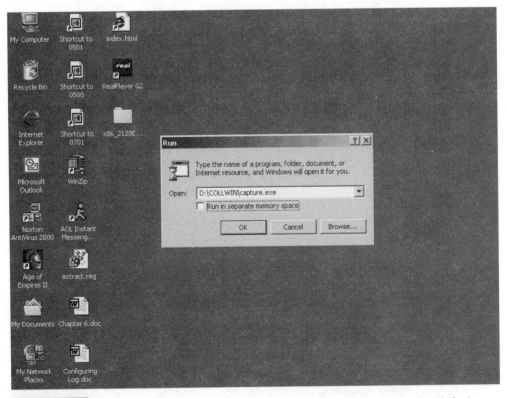

FIGURE 8.4 The option to protect 16-bit applications does not appear by default.

Root Key: HKEY_CURRENT_USER

Key: Software\Microsoft\Windows\CurrentVersion\Policies\Explorer

Entry Name: MemCheckBoxInRunDlg

Entry Data Type: REG_DWORD

Configuring the Control Panel

The Registry stores configuration details about the Control Panel. By using group policy, you can manage which, if any, Control applets are available for the user. The policy settings are stored in the Registry. In this section, you can see a handful of useful Registry keys and entries for managing the Control Panel. In addition to simply using the entries, you can get a flavor for the kinds of options group policy provides for managing the Control Panel. For more information on group policy, refer to Chapter 12, "Working with Group Policy."

Disabling the Control Panel Folder

You can truly lock down the configuration of a workstation by preventing users from accessing the Control Panel folder. Add the following key and entry and then set the value of the entry to 1 to disable the Control Panel:

Root Key: HKEY_CURRENT_USER

Key: Software\Microsoft\Windows\CurrentVersion\Policies\Explorer

Entry Name: NoControlPanel

Entry Data Type: REG_DWORD

Removing Specific Control Panel Tools

You can configure a workstation so that specific Control Panel tools are unavailable. This might be a better option than completely disabling the entire Control Panel if you want to ensure that users of the workstation do not cause problems in the system by incorrectly configuring one of the Control Panel tools.

You need to add a few keys and entries to the Registry in order to disable one or more Control Panel tools. The following is the first key, entry, and value to add.

Root Key: HKEY_CURRENT_USER

Key: Software\Microsoft\Windows\CurrentVersion\Policies\Explorer

Entry Name: DisallowCPL

Entry Data Type: REG_DWORD

Entry Value: 1

Next, add the following key to the key shown above. Note that the name of this key is the same as the entry you added above:

Key: DisallowCPL

The last step is to list the Control Panel tools that you want to prevent access to. The first step is to identify the file that manages the Control Panel tool, also known as an applet, whose use you want to restrict. To do so, open the System32 folder in the main the Windows 2000 folder. Search for all files with an extension of CPL. These files are the individual applets that appear in the Control Panel folder. You can usually figure out which applet the file controls by its name. For example, JOY.CPL manages the Game Controllers applet.

For each Control Panel applet you want to remove, add an entry to the DisallowRestrictCPL key you added above according to the following:

- The name of the entry should be the number of the applet you want to restrict. Start with 1 and then increment by 1 for each applet you want to remove.
- The data type of the entry should be REG_SZ.
- The value of the entry should be the name of the file that runs the applet.

Figure 8.5 shows an example of the Registry entries necessary to prevent display of the Display and Game Controller applets.

Displaying Only Specific Control Panel Tools

Earlier in this section you learned how to remove specific Control Panel applets from the folder. Another option available is to display just the applets you like. The process to do so is almost identical to the process described in the Removing Specific Control Panel Tools section above. Besides changing the approach used to solve the problem of controlling the Control panel (picking just those applets you want to show rather than those you want to hide), the only change is to substitute RestrictCPL as the name of the entry and key noted above in the two locations where you were instructed to add DisallowCPL. Here are the details:

Root Key: HKEY_CURRENT_USER
Key: Software\Microsoft\Windows\CurrentVersion\Policies\
Explorer
Entry Name: RestrictCPL
Entry Data Type: REG_DWORD
Entry Value: 1

Next, add the following key to the key shown above. Note that the name of this key is the same as the entry you added above:

Key: RestrictCPL

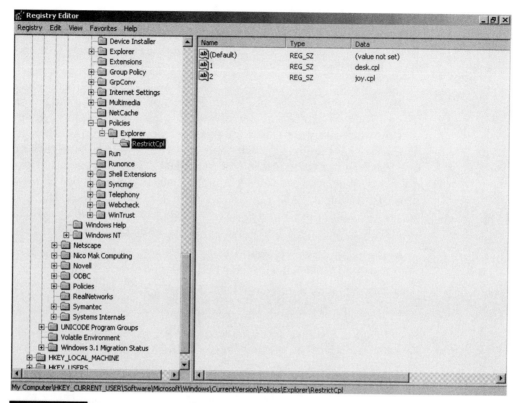

FIGURE 8.5 A handful of keys and entries are required to disable display of Control Panel applets.

A Few More Configuration Items

This section includes a few more Registry entries you can use to tune the Windows 2000 desktop configuration.

Enable or Disable Autorun

CDs and DVDs that include *autorun* software automatically launch when you load these disks into the appropriate drive. You may have experienced autorun in action when you loaded a new CD into the drive and the installation program for the software on the CD started automatically. You can't add autorun software to a CD after you get it; adding autorun is a choice of the developer of the CD. Even diskettes can include autorun software.

You can configure Windows 2000 so that the programs on these disks do not start automatically. Add the key shown below and then the appropriate entry/value combination. To disable autorun for all drives, including floppy, CD, and DVD drives, enter a value of 255. To disable autorun just for CD and DVD drives, use a value 181.

> **Root Key:** HKEY_LOCAL_MACHINE
>
> **Key:** Software\Microsoft\Windows\CurrentVersion\Policies\
> Explorer
>
> **Entry Name:** NoDriveTypeAutoRun
>
> **Entry Data Type:** REG_DWORD

Correcting Install from Hard Disk Problems

If you copied the installation files for Windows 2000 to your hard disk and then launched the installation from that location, you might experience problems later if Windows 2000 needs to load new files from the installation set. The problem comes from Windows 2000's practice to store as the installation drive the drive letter of the first drive it believes to be a CD-ROM, not the drive from which you installed the operating system. Update the SourcePath entry for the following key to the correct drive letter to avoid this problem. Be sure to include the colon symbol after the drive letter.

> **Root Key:** HKEY_LOCAL_MACHINE
>
> **Key:** Software\Microsoft\Windows\CurrentVersion\Setup
>
> **Entry Name:** SourcePath
>
> **Entry Data Type:** REG_SZ

Preventing Windows 2000 Shutdown

You can deny users on a workstation the capability to shut down Windows 2000. While users can simply power down a computer to achieve the same result, perhaps by running some program that shuts down the operating system, you can make the shutdown task more difficult by removing the Shut Down command from the Start menu. Add this key and entry to the Registry and then set the value of the entry to 1 to enable this policy. Note that this Registry change also disables the Shut Down button in the Windows Security dialog box.

> **Root Key:** HKEY_CURRENT_USER
>
> **Key:** Software\Microsoft\Windows\CurrentVersion\Policies\
> Explorer
>
> **Entry Name:** NoClose
>
> **Entry Data Type:** REG_DWORD

Configuring Microsoft Office 2000

One would expect Microsoft to do a reasonable job of taking advantage of the Registry in its own operating system to store details about its own productivity suite, namely Office. There's no disappointment along these lines. The Registry stores a wide range of details about the applications that make up Office, as well as the common components of the applications. In this chapter, you can read about the keys and entries that store Office 2000 information. The first part of the chapter reviews keys and entries common to the entire suite, followed by the specific product entries.

Common Office 2000 Registry Issues

While Microsoft Office consists of five major applications, some elements of the Office configuration apply to all of the products. In this section, you can find out about the Registry entries that apply to all of the Office 2000 products. Examples of these types of Registry entries include those related to installation, the Assistant help character, recent file list, and Help.

Recognizing the Office 2000 Version Number

The first thing you should know about Microsoft Office 2000 is that the suite's internal version number is 9. You probably will not find any Registry entries that refer to Office 2000, or at least any entries loaded into the Registry by the Office installation process. The following key shows you an example of how Office 2000 entries are organized into the Registry, as shown in Figure 9.1:

```
HKEY_CURRENT_USER\Software\Microsoft\Office\9.0
```

Reviewing the Recent File List

Office products, like most other Windows 2000 applications, maintain a list of the documents you recently opened. This makes it easy to access these documents later by simply selecting them from the bottom of the File menu. This list is commonly referred to as the MRU list for *most recently used*. Office stores the list of most recently accessed Office files in the Registry. These lists are stored on a per product basis, and the key name varies based on product.

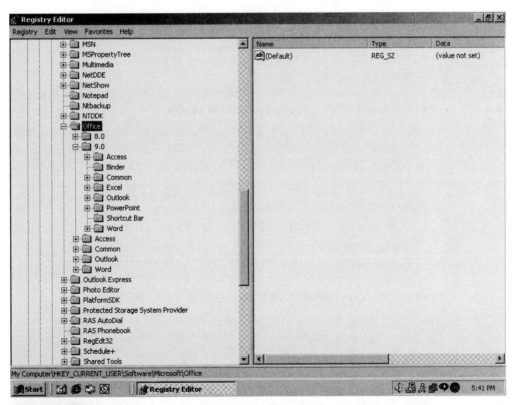

FIGURE 9.1   Office 2000 entries are stored under Office\9.0 Registry keys.

The list for each of the Office products can be found in the following keys. Note that each of the keys below is a subkey of HKEY_CURRENT_USER\ Software\Microsoft\Office\9.0:

```
Access\Settings
Excel\Recent File
Powerpoint\Recent File List
```

Managing the Assistant

The Assistant is the animated character that hops in and out of view when you use an Office 2000 application, providing advice and tips, solicited or otherwise. You can use the Registry to control how the Assistant works, such as what kind of advice the Assistant provides. Note that the Registry stores information about the Assistant in two locations, so note carefully the values of the Root key and Key fields supplied below.

CONTROL THE ASSISTANT'S APPEARANCE

To always show the Assistant, set the value of the following key to 21. To hide the Assistant, use a value of 22.

> **Root Key:** HKEY_CURRENT_USER
>
> **Key:** Software\Microsoft\Office\Common\Assistant
>
> **Entry Name:** AsstState

CONTROLLING THE ASSISTANT'S LOCATION

You can use the Registry to help determine at what location on the screen the Assistant appears. The top and left entries indicate the distance in pixels from the top of the screen and the left of the screen at which the Assistant appears.

> **Root Key:** HKEY_CURRENT_USER
>
> **Key:** Software\Microsoft\Office\Common\Assistant
>
> **Entry Name:** AsstLeft
>
> **Entry Name:** AsstTop

MANAGING THE ASSISTANT'S BEHAVIOR

You might think that you cannot control the assistant's behavior. This is not the case. Via the Registry, you can control how often and in what situations the Assistant appears. The following key is the home for a number of entries that control the Assistant's behavior:

```
HKEY_CURRENT_USER\Software\Microsoft\Office\9.0\Common\
Assistant
```

The following list shows you the name of the entry and how to use the entry to control the Assistant. In each case, use a value of 1 to turn the option on and a value of 0 to turn the option off.

`AsstAssistWithWizards:`   Determines whether the Assistant offers advice when you start to use a wizard.

`AsstShowTipOfDay:`   Controls whether the assistant displays a tip each time you start an Office 2000 application.

`AsstAssistWithHelp:`   Determines whether the Assistant appears when you press the F1 for Help or choose Help from the menu.

`AsstKeyboardShortcutTips:`   Use a value of 1 to determine if the Assistant should display the key combination for some action the Assistant detected.

Reviewing the Office Install Location

The Registry records the main target folder for the Office installation. Each of the Office products is installed to subfolders under the main Office folder. It is possible to install Office more than once on a single workstation to different target folders. If suddenly one of the Office products reports problems in locating some common component, such as the spell checker, images, or forms, you should consider looking in the Registry to check the location of the Office installation. Look for the following key in the appropriate product key under the main Office key:

```
InstallRoot
```

For example, to see the location by registered by Word as the main Office folder, look in the following key:

```
HKEY_LOCAL_MACHINE\SOFTWARE\Microsoft\Office\9.0\Word\
InstallRoot
```

The path entry will store the installed Office location.

Working with Help

Office 2000 uses a standard application for displaying Help in any of its applications. This application is known as the Help Viewer. When the Help Viewer is launched, it takes over a portion of the screen, consumes lots of memory, and takes an agonizingly long time to start. Via the Registry, you have a few options to control how the help Viewer works. Each of these entries can be found in the following key:

```
HKEY_CURRENT_USER\Software\Microsoft\Office\9.0\Common\
HelpViewer
```

> `IsFloating:` Determines whether the Help Viewer appears anchored to the right edge of the screen or in a floating window. A value of 1 indicates floating; a value of 0 indicates anchored.
>
> `FloatingSmall:` Determines the vertical size of the Help Viewer window when the window appears floating rather than anchored.
>
> `PaneSmall:` Determines the width of the Help Viewer window when anchored.

Reviewing Saved Searches

You probably have noticed that when you choose File, Open from the menu in an Office product, the same dialog box appears. You might also have noticed the option to search for files directly from this Open dialog box.

For Excel, an example of the key where saved searches can be found might be the following:

```
HKEY_CURRENT_USER\Software\Microsoft\Office\9.0\Common\
Open Find\Microsoft Excel\Saved Searches
```

A key is created for each search initiated by the user. The key has the same name as that given to the search. For example, if the user created a search by the name of "Budget Worksheets," the configuration of the search would be found in the following key:

```
HKEY_CURRENT_USER\Software\Microsoft\Office\9.0\Common\
Open Find\Microsoft Excel\Saved Searches\Budget Worksheets
```

The following list shows the entries that store the relevant parameters of the search. The names of the keys indicate which parameter of the search the entry stores.

```
Folder List
File Specification
File Type List cb
File Type List
Search Subdirs
Stem Words
Match Case
Match Byte
Wildcard Filenames
```

Seeing General Information about Office 2000

If you are experiencing problems with Office 2000 not specific to one of the products, you may have a problem related to the installation of the suite. One of the best ways to see information about how a product was installed is to examine the data Windows 2000 needs to uninstall the product. Naturally, the Registry stores detailed information about Office 2000 to manage the uninstall process. Office 2000 uninstall information is stored in the following key:

```
HKEY_LOCAL_MACHINE\SOFTWARE\Microsoft\Windows\
CurrentVersion\Uninstall\{00000409-78E1-11D2-B60F-
006097C998E7}
```

The following shows the list of some of the more useful entries you'll find in the key noted above:

`RegOwner`: Shows the name the user supplied to the installer when prompted.

`RegCompany`: Shows the name of the organization supplied the user when Office was installed.

`DisplayVersion`: Indicates the build number of the version of Office installed.

`InstallDate`: Indicates the date that Office was installed (in YYYY-MMDD format).

`InstallSource`: Shows the drive where the installation media was accessed. If Office was installed from a CD, then this entry will show the drive letter of the CD. If Office was installed from a network share, this entry will show the drive letter assigned to the network share.

`EstimatedSize`: In double word format, shows the size estimated by the Windows Installer program of the Office applications and tools selected by the user.

`VersionMajor`: Shows the version number of Office.

`WindowsInstaller`: Shows the version number of the Windows Installer program used to install Office.

Fixing Office Problems with Options and Preferences

An easy way to fix serious problems with Office applications is to rebuild the user preferences and options set of entries stored in the Registry. The next step in this process would be to restart the faulty application. If you are near wit's end in attempting to solve a problem and your next step is to reinstall Office, try this first:

Delete the following key and/or entry for the appropriate product. You may be asked to supply the installation CD for Office when you restart the application:

```
HKEY_CURRENT_USER\Software\Microsoft\Office\9.0\product\
Options
```
The UserData entry in the
```
HKEY_CURRENT_USER\Software\Microsoft \Office\9.0\product key
```

Managing Find Fast Performance

You may notice performance problems on your Windows 2000 workstation if you install the Find Fast feature in Office. This feature indexes your system, so that subsequent searches for documents run faster. As the indices are built and updated, your system will take a performance hit. Microsoft recommends in the Knowledge Base Article Q200306 the following Registry fix. Supply a value between 1000 and 10,000 to indicate the time in milliseconds that Fast Find should wait before starting the next index operation.

```
Root Key: HKEY_LOCAL_MACHINE
Key: Software\Microsoft\Office\9.0\Find Fast
Entry Name: SlowDown
Entry Data Type: REG_DWORD
```

Reviewing Word Entries

Much of the configuration information for Word stored in the Registry is in binary format, making it impossible to figure out what the values represent. While the names of the keys provide some insight as to the data type of data stored, its not easy. To browse through the Word entries, open the following key:

```
HKEY_CURRENT_USER\Software\Microsoft\Office\9.0\Word
```

Checking Word Conversion Options

Actually, one set of data that you can decipher relates to the conversion tools in Word. Office stores in the Registry details about the file import formats you selected when you installed Office. The data is found in the following key:

```
HKEY_LOCAL_MACHINE\SOFTWARE\Microsoft\Office\9.0\Word\Text
Converters\Import
```

In that key, you find one subkey for each converter you selected. Each key contains the following entries:

Extension: Indicates the extensions that Word should associate with converter (e.g., xls xlw xl5).

Name: Indicates the name of the file type (e.g., Microsoft Excel Worksheet).

Path: Indicates the location and the name of the converter program (e.g., H:\Program Files\Common Files\Microsoft Shared\TextConv\ EXCEL32 .CNV).

The following list shows a sample list of the keys, representing converters that you might find in the key noted above:

Lotus 1-2-3	Word 2.x for Windows
Microsoft Excel Worksheet	Word 4.x - 5.x for the
MS-DOS Text with Layout	Macintosh
Outlook Contacts	Word 6.0/95 for
Personal Address Book	Windows&Macintosh
Recover Text from Any File	Word 97
Schedule+ Contact List	WordPerfect 5.x
Text with Layout	WordPerfect 6.x - 7.0
Word (Asian Versions) 6.0/95	Works for Windows 4.0

Checking Path Variables

The Registry is the place where Word stores the folder locations it needs. For example, you can find the default location for templates, files recovered when Word crashes, and more in the Registry. The key in the Registry that stores this data is the following:

```
HKEY_CURRENT_USER\Software\Microsoft\Office\9.0\Word\
Options
```

The following is the list of key names where the appropriate folder is stored:

```
PROGRAMDIR
PICTURE-PATH
TOOLS-PATH
STARTUP-PATH
AUTOSAVE-PATH
```

Reviewing Excel Entries

For all of the power in Excel, the Registry provides little opportunity to tune and configure it. Many of the options are stored in binary format in one of the two following entries:

```
HKEY_CURRENT_USER\Software\Microsoft\Office\9.0\Excel
User Data

HKEY_CURRENT_USER\Software\Microsoft\Office\9.0\Excel\
Options
```

This scheme doesn't provide a lot of opportunity to tune and customize via the Registry. The following sections provide to you a few options for tuning Excel and fixing at least one problem.

Displaying Four-Place Year Values

Excel 2000 shipped with a bug in which only two places of a year display, even if you configure the Date/Time format in Windows 2000 to show the full four-place year. To remedy this problem, add the follow key and entry combination and then set the value to 1:

Root Key: HKEY_CURRENT_USER

Key: Software\Microsoft\Office\9.0\Excel\Options

Entry Name: EnableFourDigitYearDisplay

Entry Data Type: REG_DWORD

Defining the Default Font

You can define the default typeface and size for text you enter into Excel via the Registry. This option is also available in the Options dialog box in Excel. Enter the following key/entry combination, and then enter the name of the typeface, followed by a comma, and then the size. For example, to specify 10-pt. Arial as the default font, the value of the following entry would be Arial,10.

Root Key: HKEY_CURRENT_USER

Key: Software\Microsoft\Office\9.0\Excel\Options

Entry Name: Font

Entry Data Type: REG_SZ

Defining the Alternate Startup Folder

You can use the registry to specify an alternate startup location. Excel will also look in the folder you specify when it needs to open worksheets and other support Excel file. Note the data type of this entry is EXPAND_SZ, which means you can use environment variables as part of the value.

Root Key: HKEY_CURRENT_USER

Key: Software\Microsoft\Office\9.0\Excel\Options

Entry Name: AltStartup

Entry Data Type: REG_EXPAND_SZ

Providing for the Euro Currency Character in Small Sizes

Microsoft reports in Knowledge Base Article Q127124 that there is a problem with the Euro currency character when it is formatted with a size less than 8 pts and/or the worksheet is zoomed to 80 percent or smaller. The symptom of the problem is that that the character appears like the pipe symbol (|) under the conditions described. The problem occurs because Excel uses a special font set to display smaller fonts, such as with a small point size or when the worksheet is zoomed. To address this problem, you can configure Excel so that the small font set is not used. This configuration occurs in the registry. Use a value of 0 for the key described below to prevent use of the small font set:

Root Key: HKey_CURRENT_USER

Key: Software\Microsoft\Office\9.0\Excel\Options

Entry Name: FontSub

Entry Data Type: REG_DWORD

Reviewing Outlook Entries

Like the entries for Word, many of the Registry entries for Outlook are in binary form, making them difficult to decipher. Outlook, however, is such a robust application that it has many more entries in the Registry than the other applications in Office. That means that there is a fair amount of configuration flexibility available for Outlook via the registry. The following sections provide you the details necessary to configure aspects of Outlook's calendar, as well as printing and faxing capabilities, and more.

Seeing Details About Import and Export Functions

Just about any user who moves to Outlook from another PIM (personal information manager) converts data, such as contacts and appointments, to the Outlook format (see Figure 9.2). You can see some details about the programs used to import data into Outlook in the following key:

```
HKEY_LOCAL_MACHINE\SOFTWARE\Microsoft\Office\9.0\Outlook\
Operations
```

The key stores a separate subkey for each general category of data you can import and export into and out of Outlook. The following is a sample list of these keys. Note that the Registry prefixes each of the following with a number, which indicates in what order the options appear in Outlook.

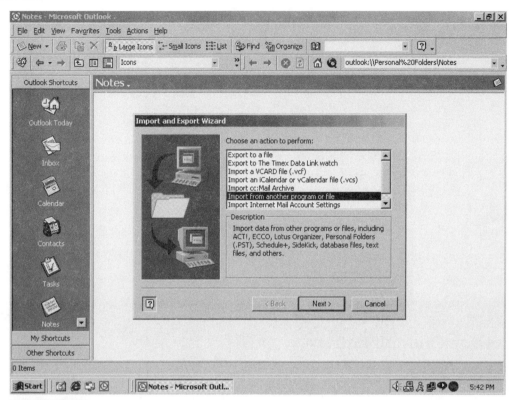

FIGURE 9.2 Outlook provides the capability to load data from many other popular PIMs and data sources, as well as to export in many formats.

```
ImportFile
ExportFile
ExportDataLink
ImportVCard
ImportAccounts
ImportVcalendar
ImportEudora
```

In each key, you can see entries reporting the description the user sees of each import/export option, as well as data Office uses to run the conversion.

Seeing Fax Details

You can use the Registry to view configuration details for Outlook's fax service. Open the following key to see the details:

```
HKEY_LOCAL_MACHINE\SOFTWARE\Microsoft\Office\9.0\Outlook\
OLFax\7.0\General
```

The following list shows the relevant entries. For each entry except for Retry Time (in seconds) and Retries (in number of attempts), use a value of 1 to enable the option or a value of 0 to disable it:

```
RxEnable
UseTapiTranslation
Retries
RetriesNoAnswer
Rings
Retry Time
MultiModDetectMode
```

In addition, you can also see details about the cover page Outlook uses for fax. Inspect the OutlookDefaultCover entry in the following key to see (or change) the default cover sheet. Note that this key lives in HKEY_LOCAL_ MACHINE, not HKEY_CURRENT_USER like the other entries noted in this section.

```
HKEY_LOCAL_MACHINE\Software\Microsoft\Office\9.0\Outlook\
OLFax\7.0\General
```

Configuring the Calendar

The Registry provides you access to the details about the configuration of the Outlook calendar in the following key:

```
HKEY_CURRENT_USER\Software\Microsoft\Office\9.0\Outlook\
Options\Calendar
```

You can modify or simply inspect the following entries with the following entry names:

FirstDOW: Indicates the first day of the week. 0 indicates Sunday through 6 for Saturday.

FirstWOY: Indicates the first week of the year. 0 indicates the week that starts on January 1, 1 indicates first 4-day week, and 2 indicates the first full week.

CalDefStart: Indicates the default start time for the day. This value is entered as the number of minutes since midnight. For example, 8 AM would be expressed as 480.

CalDefEnd: Indicates the default end time for the day. This value is entered as the number of minutes since midnight. For example, 5 PM would be expressed as 1020.

RemindDefault: Indicates the reminder time (in minutes).

Seeing Page Size Defaults

The following key stores details about the default page settings used during printing from Outlook:

```
HKEY_CURRENT_USER\Software\Microsoft\Office\9.0\Outlook\
Printing
```

The key stores the following entries. Note the values for each of the entries are expressed in thousandths of inches. For example, 8.5 inches would be entered as 85000.

```
Default Paper Width
Default Paper Height
```

Printing Tracking Information

Outlook provides you with the opportunity to view information about messages as they are delivered and read, as well as information about the recipient. You can use the Registry to determine whether that same information is printed when you print the message itself. Supply a value of 1 to the following entry to enable printing of tracking details. Use a value of 0 to turn this option off.

> **Root Key:** HKEY_CURRENT_USER
>
> **Key:** Software\Microsoft\Office\9.0\Outlook\Preferences
>
> **Entry Name:** PrintTrackingPref
>
> **Entry Data Type:** REG_DWORD

Restoring the Outlook Icon to the Desktop

The Recycle bin makes it easy to recover items you might have inadvertently deleted in Windows 2000. If you tried to delete the Outlook icon from the Desktop, however, you saw the message saying that there is no way to undelete the icon once you did delete. If you went on with the delete anyway and now you want to restore the Outlook icon to the Desktop, add the following key:

```
HKEY_LOCAL_MACHINE\SOFTWARE\Microsoft\Windows\
CurrentVersion\Explorer\Desktop \NameSpace\
{00020D75-0000-0000-C000-000000000046}
```

More Outlook Options

A number of other Outlook options can be configured from the Registry. Each of the entries in this section can be found in the following key:

```
HKEY_CURRENT_USER\Software\Microsoft\Office\9.0\Outlook\
Options
```

Note the subkey where the entries described below may be stored.

SENDING MAIL IMMEDIATELY

Set the value of this entry to 1 to force mail to be sent as you soon as the user clicks the Send button, as opposed to later when the Send/Receive command is given.

> **Subkey:** Mail
>
> **Entry Name:** Send Mail Immediately
>
> **Entry Data Type:** REG_DWORD

CHECK FOR MAIL TIME

Set the following entry (using a decimal value) for how often, in minutes, Outlook should check for new mail.

> **Subkey:** Mail
>
> **Entry Name:** Poll for Mail Interval
>
> **Entry Data Type:** REG_DWORD

SETTING THE MESSAGE FORMAT

Use a value of 1 in this key to specify MIME as the default mail message format. Use a value of 0 to specify Uuencode.

> **Subkey:** Mail
>
> **Entry Name:** Message Plain Format MIME
>
> **Entry Data Type:** REG_DWORD

FORCE OUTLOOK TO CHECK SPELLING

Set the value of this entry to 1 to force Outlook to always check spelling before a message is sent.

> **Subkey:** Spell
>
> **Entry Name:** Check
>
> **Entry Data Type:** REG_DWORD

Reviewing PowerPoint Entries

The PowerPoint in the hive stores a fair amount of entries related to its configuration. You can find the most relevant keys and entries related to PowerPoint in the following key:

```
HKEY_CURRENT_USER\Software\Microsoft\Office\9.0\PowerPoint
```

In the next few sections, you can read about the relevant data stored in the key noted above.

Getting Prompted with Wizard Help

Certain tasks in PowerPoint are made easier via the help of a wizard. You can make a change in the Registry to determine if you are prompted to use the appropriate wizard to help in completing the task. Change the entries in the following key to 1 to be prompted for help with the appropriate wizard:

```
HKEY_CURRENT_USER\Software\Microsoft\Office\9.0\
PowerPoint\Wizards
```

See Tips Triggered and Displayed

The Registry shows the number of tips that have been displayed in Power-Point, as well as those tips that were displayed as a result of a user action. A value of 1 indicates the tip has appeared, while a value of 0 indicates the tip has not appeared.

```
HKEY_CURRENT_USER\Software\Microsoft\Office\9.0\
PowerPoint\Tips
```

Setting the Link Size Threshold

By default, PowerPoint links rather than merges sound files greater than 100 KB. You can change this value in the Registry with this entry. Note that you need to enter the value in decimal format as the entry has a data type of REG_DWORD.

Root Key: HKEY_CURRENT_USER

Key: Software\Microsoft\Office\9.0\PowerPoint\Options

Entry Name: Link sound size

Entry Data Type: REG_DWORD

Beyond the Basics

In This Part

Accessing the Registry from Code

Microsoft generally recommends that Windows 2000 users *not* access the Registry directly, such as from the REGEDIT and REGEDT32 editors. Microsoft recommends using the user interface components provided in Windows 2000, such as the array of tools in Control Panel and the folder of administrative options, to change settings in the operating system. Regardless, and in contrast to Microsoft's recommendations, this book is written to show how to use and modify the Registry. Also, Microsoft *provides* the two editors mentioned earlier, practically begging you to tour and tune the Registry. So, if modifying the Registry by hand is frowned upon by Microsoft (even with a wink), imagine the attitude toward writing a software program that opens and tweaks the Registry! Though most software developers need to work with the Registry in order for Windows 2000 to support their applications, it is rare to find a system administrator or help desk engineer who must work with the Registry via code. Still, there may be the occasion when the automation provided by a coded solution is the best way to solve a problem, such as an automated way to be notified when certain keys change. For those occasions, this chapter provides a brief overview of the heart of Registry automation: the Registry API. The Registry API portion of the Windows Platform SDK provides all of the functions you need to check

Registry values, delete keys, write new entry value, load and unload hives, and more, This chapter will *not* teach you to program if you haven't before, nor will you find tips and tricks for Perl, Visual Basic, or C++. Instead, you'll find an overview of the Registry support in the Windows Platform SDK.

Registry API Functions Overview

The best way to understanding the support an API provides for a particular set of tasks or requirements, next to actually coding with the API, is to review a list of the functions and the service each provides. Table 10.1 provides a summary of the use of each Registry function.

TABLE 10.1   Registry Functions

Function	Description
RegCloseKey	Closes the Registry specified by the handle passed in. Returns ERROR_SUCCESS on completion.
RegConnectRegistry	Opens the Registry on a remote computer; returns a handle that can then be used with other functions to manipulate the remote Registry. You specify the remote computer by preceding its name with \\.
RegCreateKeyEx	Creates a key in the location and with the name you specify. You can specify a number of options for the new key with this version of the function, such as its data type and whether the key should be deleted when the system is restarted. If the key already exists, this function opens it.
RegCreateKey	Creates a key. This version of the RegCreateKey function is intended for use only with applications running on 16-bit versions of Windows.
RegDeleteKey	Deletes a subkey. You specify the subkey by passing in the name of the key and the handle of the key opened where the key is located. This function will not delete subkeys or values when run on a Windows 2000 platform. To delete all subkeys, you one of the enumeration functions to walk through each subordinate key.
RegDeleteValue	Deletes the entry whose name is passed to the function. This function also requires the handle of the key where the entry is located. If a NULL value is passed in place of he Value name, the entry specified by the RegSetValue function is deleted.
RegEnumKeyEx	Enumerates every subordinate key of the key specified, retrieving key name, class, and the date and time the key was last written.
RegEnumKey	Very similar to RegEnumKeyEx, though missing many of the options. It should be used for applications intended to run on 16-bit versions of Windows.

TABLE 10.1 (continued)	
Function	**Description**
RegEnumValue	Enumerates each entry of the open key specified by the handle passed in. The function returns the name of the entry, the data type, and its value.
RegFlushKey	Forces all pending Registry changes to be written to disk. While the Registry automatically flushes the buffer and writes to disk any pending changes, this function can be used to write changes immediately.
RegLoadKey	Duplicates the Load key feature available in the REGEDT32 editor. Loads a hive from an external file to a target key.
RegNotifyChangeKeyValue	Notifies the application using it when either a key or one of its attributes changes. An example of an attribute is the permissions assigned to the key.
RegOpenCurrentUser	New with the Windows 2000 version of the Platform SDK. This function returns a handle to the current user's key in the Registry from the HKEY_CURRENT_USERS rootkey. To use this function, you must pass it the type of access you need to the key.
RegOpenKey	Opens the specified key whose name is passed in. Similar to RegOpenKeyEx, but is designed for use with 16-bit version of Windows. The root key where the target key is located also must be passed in. A handle to the key opened is returned from this function. All Registry functions rely on such a handle to identify the key to be operated on, so this function is critical. This function is very similar to RegOpenKeyEx. This one should be used only with applications running on 16-bit versions of Windows.
RegOpenKeyEx	Opens the specified key whose name is passed in. The root key where the target key is located also must be passed in. A handle to the key opened is returned from this function. All Registry functions rely on such a handle to identify the key to be operated on, so this function is critical. This function is designed for use with the new version of Windows. This function's companion function, RegOpenKey, is designed for use with 16-bit version of Windows.
RegOpenUserClassesRoot	New with the Windows 2000 version of the Platform SDK. This function returns a handle to the current user's key in the Registry from the HKEY_CLASSES_ROOT rootkey. To use this function, you must pass it the type of access you need to the key.
RegQueryInfoKey	Retrieves information about a key, including the last time it was written to, the number of entries, the number of subordinate keys, the length of the key with the longest name, and more.
RegQueryMultipleValues	Retrieves the value and data type for the list of entries you pass in for an open key, whose handle you also pass in.

(continued)

TABLE 10.1 (continued)	
Function	**Description**
RegQueryValueEx	Retrieves the value for the entry you specify. You pass to this function a handle to the key where the entry is housed, the name of the entry, the buffer where the value is loaded, and its size.
RegReplaceKey	Replaces the key specified by the handle passed in with the contents of an external, whose name and location also are passed in.
RegRestoreKey	Behaves like the Restore key feature in the REGEDT32 editor. You pass a handle to an open key and the name and location of file created with the Save key feature (API or editor). The function restores the key.
RegSaveKey	Completes the same task as the Save Key feature in REGEDT32. The function writes to an external file all of the data in the subkey whose handle is passed to this function. The function also requires the name of the file to be created, as well as a security attribute structure.
RegSetValue	Sets the value of a Registry entry. This function is designed for use with 16-bit Windows applications.
RegSetValueEx	Sets the value for the entry you specify. The entry is created if it does not exist. This version of the function should be used with Windows 2000 applications.
RegUnloadKey	Has the same use as the Unload key feature available from the REGEDT32 Registry editor. With a handle to an open key and the name of the key to unload, this function drops from the Registry a key that had been previously loaded. As a refresher, the load and unload functions are used to review subkeys extracted from another computer's Registry without impacting the Registry of the computer where the key is being reviewed.

Registry API Data Types, Structures, and Constants

Handling Errors

Each of the functions listed in Table 10.1 returns a result code. These codes are known as *error codes,* although the first on the list below actually is a success code. Nonetheless, you should always check the return result from any function you call. If the function does not return a success, you may want to terminate the program based on the error code you receive. Not doing so could result in a crash of your program. Checking for a return code is a habit you should practice during the development of your program as well as in the final version of your application. Table 10.2 shows the error codes you will most likely encounter in working with the Registry API.

TABLE 10.2	Typical Registry API Error Codes	
Value	**Description**	**Code**
0	The function completed successfully.	ERROR_SUCCESS
1	Bad function call.	ERROR_INVALID_FUNCTION
2	The system cannot find the file specified.	ERROR_FILE_NOT_FOUND
5	The permissions of the individual logged on and running the program are not sufficient for the task attempted by the function.	ERROR_ACCESS_DENIED
6	Handle to the key passed to the function is not valid.	ERROR_INVALID_HANDLE
12	The access parameter passed to the function is not valid.	ERROR_INVALID_ACCESS
14	There is not enough memory to properly handle the return data the function requested.	ERROR_OUTOFMEMORY
64	Network name is no longer available.	ERROR_NETNAME_DELETED
65	Network access is denied.	ERROR_NETWORK_ACCESS_DENIED
69	Network BIOS session limit was exceeded.	ERROR_TOO_MANY_SESS
87	One of the parameters supplied is invalid.	ERROR_INVALID_PARAMETER
161	The specified path is invalid.	ERROR_BAD_PATHNAME
167	A region of the file cannot be locked.	ERROR_LOCK_FAILED
234	More data is available.	ERROR_MORE_DATA
259	No more data is available.	ERROR_NO_MORE_ITEMS
1009	Corrupt configuration Registry database.	ERROR_BADDB
1010	Invalid Registry key.	ERROR_BADKEY
1011	Problem opening configuration Registry key.	ERROR_CANTOPEN
1012	Problem reading configuration Registry key.	ERROR_CANTREAD
1013	Problem writing configuration Registry key.	ERROR_CANTWRITE
1014	Registry was recovered successfully.	ERROR_REGISTRY_RECOVERED
1015	The Registry is corrupted.	ERROR_REGISTRY_CORRUPT
1016	An I/O operation initiated by the Registry failed unrecoverably. The Registry could not read in, or write out, or flush, one of the files that contain the system's image of the Registry.	ERROR_REGISTRY_IO_FAILED
1017	The file intended in to be loaded or restored is not in the Registry file format.	ERROR_NOT_REGISTRY_FILE
1018	Target key has been marked for deletion.	ERROR_KEY_DELETED
1019	Could not allocate enough space in Registry.	ERROR_NO_LOG_SPACE
1020	There is a problem with one of the subkeys.	ERROR_KEY_HAS_CHILDREN
1369	The target Registry subtree is involved in a transaction incompatible with the requested operation.	ERROR_RXACT_INVALID_STATE

(continued)

TABLE 10.2	(continued)	
Value	**Description**	**Code**
7005	A problem was detected when the system tried to create a Registry key for event logging.	ERROR_CTX_CANNOT_MAKE_EVENTLOG_ENTRY

Registry Data Types

Some of the Registry API functions require you to pass in a data type, while others will return a data type value that you then need to interpret. The Registry data type definitions can help you in both cases. For projects built with the Windows 2000 Platform SDK, the definitions are located in WINNT.H. Table 10.3 shows the valid Registry data type definitions and their decimal value.

Registry Key Access Constants

You are required to specify the type of access you need to a key when you first open the Registry. This data is passed in the form of a key access value. Declarations for this parameter are found in WINNT.H. The following list shows the possible values for this type of constant:

> KEY_QUERY_VALUE
>
> KEY_SET_VALUE
>
> KEY_CREATE_SUB_KEY

TABLE 10.3	Registry API Data Type Constants
Declaration	**Value**
REG_NONE	0
REG_SZ	1
REG_EXPAND_SZ	2
REG_BINARY	3
REG_DWORD	4
REG_DWORD_LITTLE_ENDIAN	4
REG_DWORD_BIG_ENDIAN	5
REG_LINK	6
REG_MULTI_SZ	7
REG_RESOURCE_LIST	8
REG_FULL_RESOURCE_DESCRIPTOR	9
REG_RESOURCE_REQUIREMENTS_LIST	10
REG_QWORD	11
REG_QWORD_LITTLE_ENDIAN	11

TABLE 10.4	Root Key Constant Values
Declaration	**Value**
HKEY_CLASSES_ROOT	0x80000000
HKEY_CURRENT_USER	0x80000001
HKEY_LOCAL_MACHINE	0x80000002
HKEY_USERS	0x80000003
HKEY_PERFORMANCE_DATA	0x80000004
HEY_CURRENT_CONFIG	0x80000005
HKEY_DYN_DATA	0x80000006

KEY_ENUMERATE_SUB_KEYS

KEY_NOTIFY

KEY_CREATE_LINK

KEY_READ

KEY_WRITE

KEY_EXECUTE

KEY_ALL_ACCESS

KEY_QUERY_VALUE

KEY_SET_VALUE

KEY_CREATE_SUB_KEY

KEY_ENUMERATE_SUB_KEYS

KEY_NOTIFY

KEY_CREATE_LINK

Registry Root Key Constants

The root key is a parameter used in many functions. The definition for the root key values is found in WINREG.H. Table 10.4 shows the value for these constants.

Network Tweaks in the Registry

Registry support for Windows 2000 network features and services is broad. The Registry includes parameters for the network interface card, the services running against the card, as well as the number of protocols and services that Windows 2000 supports. The value that all of these entries provide is somewhat inconsistent, though, because many of the entries are for viewing only. You can see lots of information about the network, but your opportunities to change configuration aren't as plentiful as with other areas of the operating system. This doesn't mean that the network landscape is barren in the Registry. This chapter will show you some of the more useful ways to manage network connections via the Registry.

Active Directory Management

The Active Directory is the directory service component in Windows 2000 that provides the details about all of the users, computers, and printers on the network. All of the other components of a Windows 2000 network rely on the Active Directory to provide these services. Although the Active Directory is new in Windows 2000, there are already a few things you can do in the Registry to manage performance and functionality.

Allowing Changes—Active Directory Schema Change

The Active Directory is considered a database. You might not think of it as a typical relational database, with interrelated tables of column and row data, but the Active Directory is a database nonetheless.

As a database, the Active Directory has a schema. *Schema* is a term used with all types of databases, not just the Active Directory. A schema defines the organization of data in a database—the fields in a database, the fields' attributes, and more. Depending on the database, the schema may be changed, sometimes when the database is already populated with data. This is applicable to the Active Directory.

The Active Directory schema can be modified. Your organization might choose to add additional information about its members. Perhaps you might store each person's social security number or even the location of his or her cube or office. Another idea might be to store the number of the LAN port users plug their computers into. These are examples of data that is not stored by default in the Active Directory. You would have to modify the Active Directory schema in order to add these fields.

There are several things you need to know about changing the Active Directory schema before attempting to do so:

- The Active Directory schema may only be changed at a domain controller.
- You must be sure that the scope for the Active Directory Schema Manager is for Flexible Single Master Operations (FSMO). This ensures that only domain controller at one may time modify the schema.

Finally, to enable the workstation to make schema updates, change the value of the Schema Updates Allow entry to 1. To restrict the workstation from making schema updates, use a value of 0.

> **Root Key:** HKEY_LOCAL_MACHINE
>
> **Key:** System\Current Control Set\Services\NTDS\Parameters
>
> **Entry Name:** Schema Updates Allow
>
> **Data Type:** REG_DWORD

Controlling the Number of Objects Returned from an Active Directory Query

The Active Directory can store information about x objects. The objects typically are displayed in the Active Directory Users and Computers snap-in. The number of objects presented in the Active Directory Users and Computers snap-in isn't relevant for small networks. For large networks with thousands of users, though, requests made on the Active Directory to return the list of users to workstations that ask for it can be expensive, consuming a significant amount of memory. You can limit the number of objects returned to the client with a registry setting, thereby protecting the domain controller answering the request. By default, the Active Directory returns 10000 objects. You raise or lower this value with this Registry entry.

> **Root Key:** HKEY_CURRENT_USER
>
> **Key:** Software\Policies\Microsoft\Windows\Directory UI
>
> **Entry Name:** QueryLimit
>
> **Data Type:** REG_DWORD

Configuring Remote Access

You can create remote access servers with the Windows 2000 Server. Most of the functionality for the remote access server is provided by the user interface. In addition, the support for RADIUS server in Windows 2000 makes it easy to manage a number of remote access servers at one time. There are a handful of Registry entries you can use to customize how the remote access server operates.

Specifying the Allowable Number of Authentication Retries

Set this value to determine the number of time the remote access server will ask again for the correct password after the user initially enters an invalid password. The minimum value is 1, the maximum value is 10, and the default is 2.

> **Root Key:** HKEY_CURRENT_USER
>
> **Key:** System\CurrentControlSet\Services\RemoteAccess\ Parameters
>
> **Entry Name:** AuthenticateRetries

Time Limit for Authentication

Set this value, in seconds, to determine how long the remote access server will wait for the remote client to supply a user id and password. The minimum value is 20, the maximum is 600, and the default is 120.

> **Root Key:** HKEY_CURRENT_USER
>
> **Key:** System\CurrentControlSet\Services\RemoteAccess\ Parameters
>
> **Entry Name:** AuthenticateTime
>
> **Data Type:** REG_DWORD

CallBackTime

A handy feature built into Windows 2000 is the option to respond to a remote client's to establish a dial-in connection by calling the remote client back at a predetermined phone number. The minimum value, in minutes, is 2, the maximum is 12, and the default is 1.

Root Key: HKEY_CURRENT_USER

Key: System\CurrentControlSet\Services\RemoteAccess\ Parameters

Entry Name: CallbackTime

Time to Automatically Disconnect an Inactive Remote Client

A Windows 2000 remote access server will disconnect an inactive remote client after a certain amount of time of inactivity. You can tune the amount of time the server waits with this setting. The minimum value for this setting is 0 minutes. The maximum is value is 20 minutes.

Root Key: HKEY_CURRENT_USER

Key: System\CurrentControlSet\Services\RemoteAccess\ Parameters

Entry Name: AutoDisconnect

Data Type: REG_DWORD

Setting the Refresh Interval for Group Policy

Group policy is used in Windows 2000 to manage users and computers in a Windows 2000 network. Group policy is comprised of sets of rules, such as whether users can install software on their own computer or whether a computer can be joined to a domain.

Group policy affects users and computers differently. Group policy for users affect all users when they log on. Computers policies affect computers when they start, regardless of the user who might log on.

Administrators define group policy, and then the rules defined in the policy are copied to client computers. Group policy is passed down to client computers from domain controllers. When a change to group policy is made at one domain controller, the change is replicated.

You can use the registry to manage how often group policy is updated on client computers for computers and users, as well as from domain controller to domain controller. This setting is known as the *refresh interval*. This setting is made in minutes. In addition, to keep every computer on the network from getting updated at the same time, an offset interval also can be set. This offset interval ensures that not every workstation is updated at the same time.

Changing the Refresh Interval for Computers

You can fine-tune the rate that global policy is refreshed on computers in the domain. The default is 90 minutes. The acceptable range for this value is 0 to 64800. This setting is made on Active Directory domain controllers.

Root Key: HKEY_LOCAL_MACHINE

Key: Software\Policies\Microsoft\Windows\System

Entry Name: GroupPolicyRefreshTime

Data Type: REG_DWORD

Changing the Offset Interval for Computers

The Active Directory uses an offset value to determine when member computers in the domain are refreshed with group policy. While the GroupPolicyRefreshTime determines the standard interval at which computers are refreshed, the offset is used to ensure that the domain controller would not be forced to refresh all computers in the domain at the same time. The acceptable range for this value is 0 to 1440 with the default being 30.

Root Key: HKEY_LOCAL_MACHINE

Key: Software\Policies\Microsoft\Windows\ System

Entry Name: GroupPolicyRefreshTimeOffset

Data Type: REG_DWORD

Changing the Refresh Interval for Domain Controllers

The Active Directory refreshes group policy to all domain controllers when group policy at one domain controller changes. This way, all member computers in the domain are controlled by the same policy. The refresh rate for domain controllers is different than that of member computers. The acceptable range for this value is 0 to 64800. The default value is 5 minutes, but if you enter a 0, the refresh interval becomes 7 seconds.

Root Key: HKEY_LOCAL_MACHINE

Key: Software\Policies\Microsoft\Windows\ System

Entry Name: GroupPolicyRefreshTimeDC

Data Type: REG_DWORD

Changing the Offset Interval for Domain Controllers

To ensure that a domain controller does not refresh group policy to all domain controllers at one time, an offset interval is used. While the rate at which domain controllers are refreshed is governed by the GroupPolicyRefreshTimeDC setting, this entry controls the interval rate. The acceptable range for this value is 0 to 1440 with the default being 0.

Root Key: HKEY_LOCAL_MACHINE

Key: Software\Policies\Microsoft\Windows\ System

Entry Name: GroupPolicyRefreshTimeOffsetDC

Data Type: REG_DWORD

Managing Network Printers

You can manage how users work with printers you have made available over the network, as well as local printers, via the Registry. You can also configure workstations to work. For example, you can configure workstations so that printers cannot be deleted.

Restricting Printer Delete

Creating printers on workstations can be problematic because the printer drivers are not always readily available. To avoid the problem of having to recreate a printer on a user's workstation after it has been deleted, you can restrict users from deleting any printers created on their workstations via a Registry change. Set this value to 1 to restrict users from deleting local and network printers. You will most likely need to create the key and the value for this entry.

Root Key: HKEY_CURRENT_USER

Key: Software\Microsoft\Windows\CurrentVersion\Policies\ Explorer

Entry Name: NoDeletePrinter

Data Type: REG_DWORD

Restricting Printer Additions

You can restrict users from adding printers to their Windows 2000 configurations via this setting. Set the value of this entry to 1 to remove the icon for the Add Printer Wizard both from the Settings menu, as well as from the Control Panel folder. You most likely will need to add the key and entry for this setting.

Root Key: HKEY_CURRENT_USER

Key: Software\Microsoft\Windows\CurrentVersion\Policies\ Explorer

Entry Name: NoAddPrinter

Data Type: REG_DWORD

Configuring Browsing for Network Printers

This setting restricts the user from seeing the entire list of shared printers in the Active Directory when a printer is added using the Add Printer Wizard. If you do not add this key, users can browse through the list of printers to select one. If you set create this entry and the set this value to 0, users must enter the name of the printer they want to add. Note that this name is not the model name of the printer, such as Epson LQ-500. Rather, it is the name assigned to the printer by the person who installed it.

> **Root Key:** HKEY_CURRENT_USER
>
> **Key:** Software\Policies\Microsoft\WindowsNT\Printers\Wizard
>
> **Entry Name:** Downlevel Browse
>
> **Data Type:** REG_SZ

Providing a Default Network Printer Location

You can specify the default location users see when they browse the Active Directory in order to add a new printer via the Add Printer wizard. You should use the Universal Naming Convention (UNC) for specifying this location.

> **Root Key:** HKEY_CURRENT_USER
>
> **Key:** Software\Policies\Microsoft\WindowsNT\Printers\Wizard
>
> **Entry Name:** Default Search Scope
>
> **Data Type:** REG_DWORD

Providing a URL Location for Network Printers

You can configure the Add Printers wizard so that users can see the list of available printers on the network on a page displayed in their browser. When you add this setting, a button appears in the Add Printer Wizard allowing the user to browse to the page you specify.

> **Root Key:** HKEY_CURRENT_USER
>
> **Key:** Software\Policies\Microsoft\WindowsNT\Printers\Wizard
>
> **Entry Name:** Printers Page URL
>
> **Data Type:** REG_DWORD

Managing TCP/IP Settings

TCP/IP is the most important networking protocol in Windows 2000. While it is possible to launch a Windows 2000 network without TCP/IP, the network would be very small (nonrouted) and would not be unable to communicate with the Internet. The Registry provides you with opportunity to view and/or modify some of the TCP/IP settings for workstations and servers running TCP/IP.

Checking the DHCP Server Name

This setting reports the name of the DHCP server configured at the workstation. DHCP stands for Dynamic Host Control Protocol. While DHCP is technically a protocol, most persons think of DHCP as the service it provides to users. DHCP provides IP addresses to users when they log onto a specific network with a DHCP server. You can see the name of the DHCP server with this entry. If the name of the server is not available, then this entry will display the server's IP address.

Root Key: HKEY_LOCAL_MACHINE

Key: SYSTEM\CurrentControlSet\Services\Tcpip\Parameters

Entry Name: DhcpNameServer

Data Type: REG_SZ

Checking the Domain Name

The Domain entry shows the name of the domain of which the workstation is a member.

Root Key: HKEY_LOCAL_MACHINE

Key: SYSTEM\CurrentControlSet\Services\Tcpip\Parameters

Entry Name: Domain

Data Type: REG_SZ

Seeing the Host Name

The Hostname indicates the name of the workstation where TCP/IP is used. This is the name TCP/IP and TCP/IP service protocols will use when they attempt to create a DNS identity referring to the workstation. It's probably not best to change this value here. Instead, change the name of the workstation via the My Computer properties on the Desktop.

Root Key: HKEY_LOCAL_MACHINE

Key: SYSTEM\CurrentControlSet\Services\Tcpip\Parameters

Entry Name: Hostname

Data Type: REG_SZ

Checking the DNS Server's IP Address

The NameServer entry stores the IP address of the DNS server.

Root Key: HKEY_LOCAL_MACHINE

Key: SYSTEM\CurrentControlSet\Services\Tcpip\Parameters

Entry Name: NameServer

Data Type: REG_SZ

Enabling Use of Backup Gateway

This setting issued to determine if the backup gateway should be used if the default gateway is not available. If the value of this entry is 1, which is the default, then TCP/IP will move to the next gateway listed in the Advanced TCP/IP Settings dialog box.

Root Key: HKEY_LOCAL_MACHINE

Key: SYSTEM\CurrentControlSet\Services\Tcpip\Parameters

Entry Name: DeadGWDetectDefault

Data Type: REG_DWORD

Checking the DHCP Domain

This key indicates the name of the domain that provides the workstation with its IP address.

Root Key: HKEY_LOCAL_MACHINE

Key: SYSTEM\CurrentControlSet\Services\Tcpip\Parameters

Entry Name: DhcpDomain

Data Type: REG_SZ

Disallowing Access to Advanced TCP/IP Settings

This setting prevents users from accessing the Advanced TCP/IP properties for their network adapters. For security reasons, it may be advisable that users not see some of the advanced settings for TCP/IP on the network. Enter a value of 0 to restrict users from accessing this dialog box.

Root Key: HKEY_CURRENT_USER

Key: Software\Policies\Microsoft\Windows\Network Connections

Entry Name: NC_AllowAdvancedTCPIPConfig

Data Type: REG_SZ

Checking the IP Address Lease Start and Stop Times

Two Registry settings can tell you the time that the lease on the IP address in use on a workstation began and ends. Both times are provided in seconds using January 1, 1979, 12:00 AM as a baseline. Changing the values will have no effect on the lease of the IP address. In addition, the Lease entry tells you the duration of the lease, again, in seconds.

Root Key: HKEY_LOCAL_MACHINE

Key: \CurrentControlSet\Services\Tcpip\Parameters\
Interfaces*adapter_id*

Entry Names: LeaseObtainedTime

LeaseTerminatesTime

Lease

Data Type: REG_DWORD

Working with Group Policy

Group policy is a tool available in Windows 2000 for system administrators to help manage and control users' desktop configurations. Based on that description, it might not seem that group policy is immediately relevant to the Registry. Actually, group policy is extremely relevant to the Registry. Almost all of the individual policies that comprise group policy, such as whether users can download files from the Internet using Internet Explorer, are stored in the Registry. In fact, group policy is one of few components of Windows 2000 that uses the Registry in such an extremely clear, easy-to-decipher scheme. Because of this ease in understanding, you can simply manipulate the Registry to achieve the same results as if you used the group policy tools that ship with Windows 2000. In this chapter, you can read about both how group policy works and how to use the group policy tools, as well as learn how to see all of the Registry keys and entries that support group policy.

Understanding Group Policy

Group policy is the term given to the tools available to a system administrator to legislate the configuration of the Windows 2000 computers that the administrator is responsible for. Group policy can help determine exactly how Windows 2000 is configured on affected computers both from a user interface perspective (e.g., user cannot change the wallpaper), an operational perspective (e.g., user cannot install software), as well as a desktop customization perspective (e.g., My Network Places icon is removed from the Desktop; My Documents folder is located on user's home directory on a network server). Group policy in Windows 2000 provides a centralized point of administration for all the configuration and use rules legislated by the administrators of the workstations in the organization.

Group policy is made up of the following:

- **Administrative Templates**   The majority of group policy is collected under administrative templates. These policies define aspects of the user's desktop configuration. These policies are referred to as templates because the Registry on the local workstation to which the policy is applied is updated with details of the policy.

- **Security Settings**   Security settings are a collection of configuration options that define the overall security configuration at each workstation. Examples of security settings include the definition of how often users must change their passwords, the minimum length of a password, and details on the Kerberos authentication system used in Windows 2000.

- **Logon/Logoff Scripts**   Group policy is used to define scripts run when users log on and log off the network, as well as when the computer starts up and shuts down.

- **Software Rollout**   Group policy includes the option to install software on client workstations.

For the sake of this chapter, group policy refers to the configuration settings stored in the Registry and reflected in the administrative templates node. While Microsoft considers each of the general groups of configuration options above to be a part of group policy, this chapter will concentrate on the administrative templates group.

Examples of Group Policy and GPOs

As much as the group policy snap-in helps administrators define group policy, group policy is ultimately the collection of individual policies. There are dozens of individual policies that can be configured to make up group policy. Figure 12.1 shows just a small portion of the total collection of policies available. Note that the list presented includes policies related only to the general configuration of Internet Explorer. The policies shown in the figure are accessed via the management console in Windows 2000. You can find more information about the management console in the "Managing Group Policy" section.

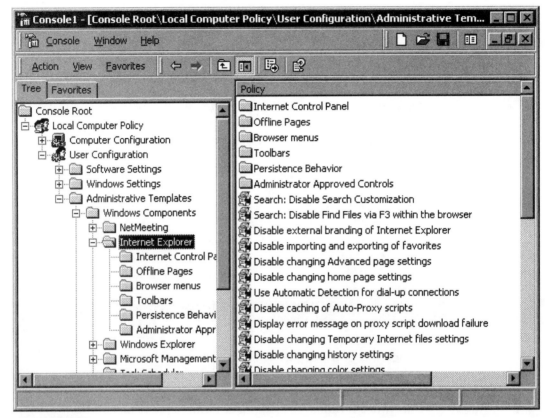

FIGURE 12.1   About thirty individual policies are available for tuning Internet Explorer.

A single collection of policies is known as a *GPO*. A GPO might also be composed of just one policy. The following list shows a few more examples of the individual policies that might be defined in a GPO:

- The Add/Remove Program applet is not available.
- A corporate standard screen saver is used, and users may not change or disable it.
- The list of printers available for users to configure at their desktops is available on a web page on the company intranet.
- The File Open dialog box does not show the location of files most recently opened.
- Logoff does not appear on the Start menu.
- Windows 2000 checks for changes made to important system files when the computer starts.
- CD-ROM and DVD drive autorun is disabled.

Categories of Group Policy

It may be helpful to think of group policy in terms of the two possible categories an individual policy in a GPO might fall into:

- **Computer Configuration**   Policies in the Computer Configuration group are in force as soon as computer starts up, regardless of the user who might later log on to the workstation and the network.
- **User Configuration**   Policies in the User Configuration group are applied to all users when they log on, regardless of the computer and the network from which they log on.

You can see how group policy is organized under these two major categories in Figure 12.2. Although some group policy folders appear under computer configuration *and* user configuration, individual policies exist in only

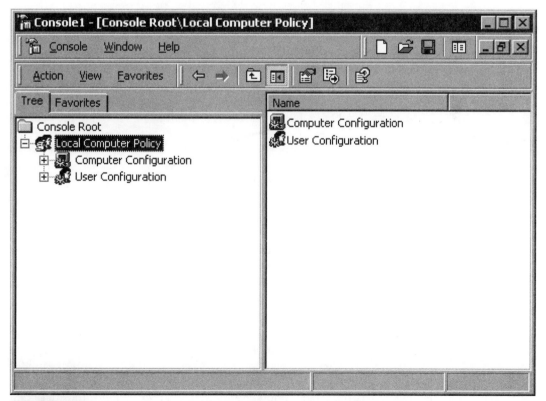

FIGURE 12.2   Group policy is composed of user configuration policies and computer configuration policies.

one place: user or computer. You will not find the same policy listed under user configuration and computer configuration.

Group Policy Hosts

Group policy is applied to various objects in the Active Directory, as well as to local workstations. The following list shows the object items that you can create and then apply a GPO. Note that you can create and apply multiple GPOs to a single object (except for a local workstation). For example, you might create four different GPOs to apply to the Engineering organizational unit (OU). Why do this? Rather than define all of the policies you need in one GPO, you might create multiple GPOs to store just a few related policies in each. This way, you can apply the same GPO to many objects.

- **A Site in the Active Directory** An Active Directory site can have its own group policy. A site is a group of Active Directory resources located on the same subnet. While group policy might be more applicable to a domain, local computer, or OU, you might still create group policy to customize some of the connection and bandwidth-sensitive configuration options that group policy gives you access to.

- **An OU in the Active Directory** Group policy may be created and applied to an OU, including any OU created in another OU, and so on. OUs are created to reflect an organization's business, organizational, departmental, or divisional structure. The responsibility of an OU can be delegated, which relieves the IT department from managing the user accounts and access to resources for a specific functional area, instead passing that responsibility to some member of the area. Applying group policy to an OU can be very useful, as it gives an organization the opportunity to fine-tune workstation's configuration to the specific requirements of the functional area.

- **An Entire Domain** At least one GPO typically is defined for the entire domain. Group policy applied to the domain affects every computer and every user in the Active Directory. This doesn't mean that you wouldn't define group policy for an organization unit, site, or local computer as well. It means that you would probably create one general set of rules for the domain that reflects the rules of the greater organization.

- **A Local Computer** Group policy can be defined at the local computer level. This is done by running the management console and adding the Group Policy snap-in. You can find instruction on this process below in the "Managing Group Policy" section. Group policy defined at the local computer affects all users who log on to that computer. Group policy is typically defined by an administrator, or at least by the person who maintains control over the workstation.

················

Group Policy Order

Depending on the size of an organization, such as the number of users, sites, and computers, as well as the amount of control the organization wishes to place on user's computing activities via group policy, there could be a large number of GPOs in force. These GPOs can be applied to local computers, as well as across the Active Directory. Considering this, there may be more than one GPO affecting a single object in the Active Directory. For example, a computer might belong to the Sales organization unit. This computer might be located in a remote location, so it might be part of an Active Directory site. In addition, some element of the group policy may have been configured directly at the computer. With this in mind, consider that any GPOs configured for the domain, the Sales OU, the site to which the computer belongs, as well as the policies applied at the computer's desktop, all would be configured at the computer. Naturally, there needs to be some sort of system that resolves conflicts between GPOs. Group policy order is the mechanism used to resolve conflicts between GPOs.

The following list shows the order in which group policy applied. Note that in the case of the list below, it doesn't always pay to be number one. Individual polices configured in GPOs applied later in the process override the same policy applied earlier in the sequence.

1. **Local Computer**   Policies configured through the Local Computer Policy scope on a workstation are applied first.

2. **Site Policies**   Policies configured in a GPO(s) applied to a site are applied to computers belonging to the site after policies configured for the Local Computer Policy are applied. This means that the same policies configured in a GPO applied to the domain or an OU to which the computer also belongs override the policy applied to the site.

3. **Domain**   Only a policy defined at an OU level can override a policy defined for the entire domain. Domain GPOs are typically used to define policy for the greater organization, such as an entire corporation.

4. **Organization Unit**   The most powerful GPO is the one applied last. The last types of objects to have GPOs applied in Windows 2000 are organization units. It may seem odd that the most powerful GPO platform is the OU, but there is a good reason behind this. The OU is used by group users, computers, and resources—logical groups that do not reflect geography or network infrastructure layout. The OU creates logical grouping of resources. Considering this, the typical OU has specific rules, policies, and ways it does business, perhaps differently than the rest of the organization.

Therefore, in the example provided above, policies applied at the local workstation would be applied first. Next, any GPOs applied to the site to which the computer is a member are applied. If the site GPO configured a policy that was also set at the local computer policy, the site policy would become the active one. Next, the GPOs applied to the domain would be applied to the computer. Any matching policies configured at the site or local computer would be overridden by the domain's version. Finally, any GPOs configured at the Sales OU would be applied to the member computer. Any policies already configured would be overridden in the same policies were configured at the Sales OU's GPO.

Understanding How Group Policy Works

You have read so far in this section what policies are, including some of the specific functions and features associated with GPOs. Here are the details of how group policy works on a practical, everyday basis. Note that these details are applicable to a Windows 2000 Active Directory network.

1. The configuration of users' computers in the organization and the rules about how users in the organization use organization resources are defined by the administrators of the system. These definitions are made as they relate to the list of policies that can be configured in Windows 2000, as well as how the policies relate to the Corporate Security Policy and other policies defined by the organization.

2. The administrator or administrator group plans how these policies will be implemented. This person or group defines how many GPOs will be needed, what policies will be configured in each, how the GPO will be applied, and how to educate users about the changes.

3. The administrator logs on to a domain controller in the network.

4. The administrator or the administrator group uses the tools provided in Windows 2000 (covered later in the "Managing Group Policy" section) to configure the individual policies in as many GPOs as needed.

5. The administrator sets any special options required for the GPO, such as rules about inheritance and/or whether it can be overridden.

6. On a regular basis, group policy is refreshed on all client computers in the Active Directory. This means that the changes made in the group policy settings at the domain controller are copied to appropriate client machines. When this occurs, the configurations and rules reflected in the policy are applied to the client machines. While there is a fixed interval for this refresh operation, the administrator can change this value.

Reviewing Group Policy and the Registry

As the introduction to this chapter described, group policy and the Registry are well integrated. All of the settings reflected in the administrative template node in the user and computer configuration nodes in group policy are stored in the Registry. The keys related to group policy are not created until the policy is configured on each computer. Fortunately, all of the group policy–related Registry keys are created in the same general location. This makes it easy to find and review the entries. Group policy–related keys are stored in either one of the following two locations. Naturally, policies in the computer configuration node are stored in HKEY_LOCAL_MACHINE, while policies stored in the user configuration node can be found in HKEY_CUR-RENT_USER:

```
HKEY_CURRENT_USER\SOFTWARE\Policies
HKEY_LOCAL_MACHINE\SOFTWARE\Policies
```

As you can read later in the "Group Policy Under the Hood" section, the set of group policy–related Registry entries is well documented. This makes it extremely easy to manage group policy via the Registry. Further, because the organization of group policy data in the Registry is so clean and well-documented, you can easily bypass the management console interface for managing group policy and simply implement the controls and configuration you want simply by modifying the Registry.

Managing Group Policy

Group policy can be managed from either a workstation, if the GPO created will be applied to the local computer, or from a domain controller to create and apply group policy to some Active Directory object, like an OU, site, or domain. Once created, it is up to the administrator to manage the individual policies that make up the GPO. This involves disabling a policy, so it does not apply to objects to which the GPO is applied, or this may involve enabling a policy, in which some option specific to the policy may need to be configured, such as specifying the maximum size of a file that may be sent using Microsoft NetMeeting. You can learn more about these specific tasks, also shown in the following list, in the following subsections of this chapter.

- Create a new GPO for an Active Directory object
- Change the policies applied to a workstation
- Examine the policies in an existing GPO
- Examine the policies configured at a workstation
- Change the individual policies in an Active Directory GPO or applied to a workstation

Creating a GPO for an Active Directory Object

The first step to managing group policy for computers and users in a Windows 2000 Active Directory network is to create a GPO. You'll probably create and manage a large number of GPOs, perhaps creating more than one for certain objects, like the domain or a particular OU. In this section, you can read the steps necessary to create a GPO for an Active Directory object.

Here are the steps:

1. Access the domain, site, or OU that the GPO will be created for. This will require logging on to a domain controller and starting the Active Directory Users and Computers snap-in.

2. Right-click on the domain, site, or OU for which the GPO will be created and then choose Properties from the menu that appears.

   The Properties dialog box appears, as shown in Figure 12.3.

3. Click once on the Group Policy tab and then click the New button.

   A new group policy object is added to the list of GPOs. The default name given to the new GPO is highlighted, as shown in Figure 12.4.

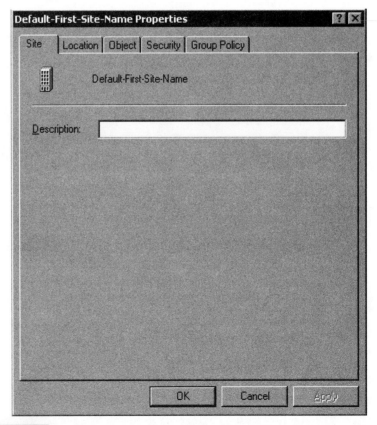

FIGURE 12.3   You can access group policy for an Active Directory object from its Properties dialog box.

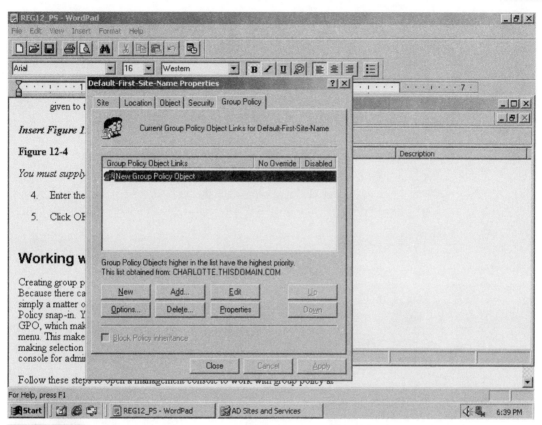

FIGURE 12.4   You must supply a name for a new GPO after it is created.

4. Enter the name for the GPO and then press the Enter key.

5. Click OK to finish creating the GPO.

Working with a GPO for a Local Computer

Creating group policy for application to a local computer is extremely easy. Because there can be only one GPO on a local computer, to create that GPO is simply a matter of opening a management console and then adding the Group Policy snap-in. You can save the management console to which you added the GPO, which makes the GPO easily available from the Administrative Tools menu. This makes it easy to administer the GPO at a later time simply by making a selection from the menu.

Follow these steps to open a management console to work with group policy at a local computer. These steps will also show you how to save the management console.

1. Click the Start menu and choose Run.

2. Enter MMC and press Enter or click OK.

   A new management console window appears.

3. Choose Console, Add/Remove Snap-in from the menu.

   The Add/Remove Snap-in dialog box appears, as shown in Figure 12.5.

4. Click the Add button.

   The Add Standalone Snap-in dialog box appears, as shown in Figure 12.6.

5. Scroll down the list and select Group Policy. Click Add.

   The Select Group Policy Object dialog box appears, as shown in Figure 12.7.

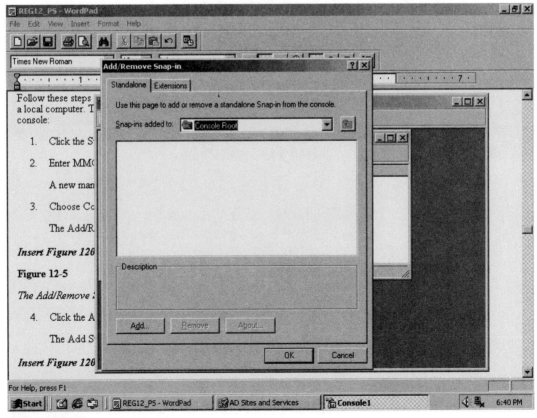

FIGURE 12.5 The Add/Remove Snap-in dialog box.

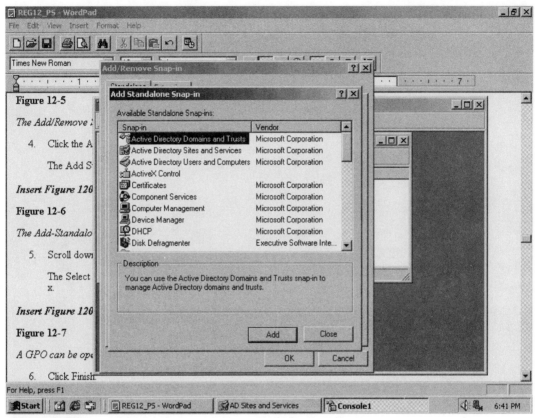

FIGURE 12.6   The Add Standalone Snap-in dialog box.

6. Click Finish.

   You are returned to the Add Standalone Snap-in dialog box.

7. Click Close.

   You are returned to the Add/Remove Snap-in dialog box.

8. Click OK.

   At this point, you can manage group policy for the local computer. To save the management console with the local group policy snap-in loaded, continue with step 9.

9. Choose Console, Save As from the menu.

   The Save As dialog box appears.

10. Enter a name for the management console in the File Name edit box. Local Group Policy seems like a good idea. Next, click Save.

    The management console is saved. You should be able to see it on the Program, Administrative Tools menu.

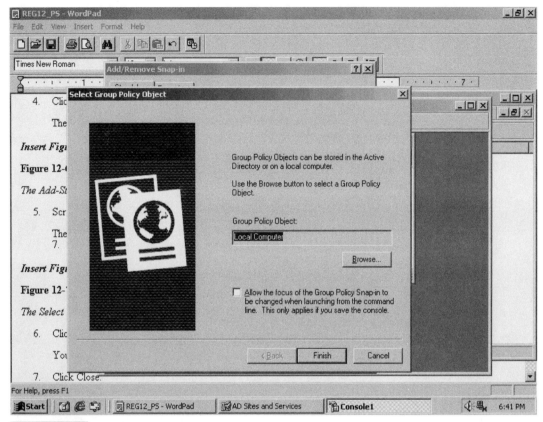

FIGURE 12.7 The Select Group Policy Object dialog box.

Opening an Existing Active Directory GPO

If you want to review group policy or change the individual policies in a GPO assigned to an Active Directory object, such as an OU, then you must open the GPO. There are two different methods you can use to open a GPO:

■ Find an object to which the GPO you want to work with is applied and then open the GPO via the object's properties dialog box.

■ Select the GPO you want to work with from a console opened with the Group Policy snap-in.

The following two sections provide the associated steps for each of the two methods listed.

OPENING A GPO FROM A MANAGEMENT CONSOLE

The management console is the tool used to manage group policy, as well as many other functions in Windows 2000. To edit a particular GPO, you can open a management console window and then access the GPO to change. When you have completed work on the GPO, you can save the management console, making it easy to open the GPO the next time and subsequent occasions when you want to work with it.

Follow these steps to open a GPO from a management console.

1. Click the Start menu and choose Run.

2. Enter MMC and press Enter or click OK.
   A new management console window appears.

3. Choose Console, Add/Remove Snap-in from the menu.
   The Add/Remove Snap-in dialog box appears.

4. Click the Add button.
   The Add Standalone Snap-in dialog box appears.

5. Scroll down the list and select Group Policy. Click Add.
   The Select Group Policy Object dialog box appears.

6. Click the Browse button.
   The Browse for a Group Policy Object dialog box appears, as shown in Figure 12.8.

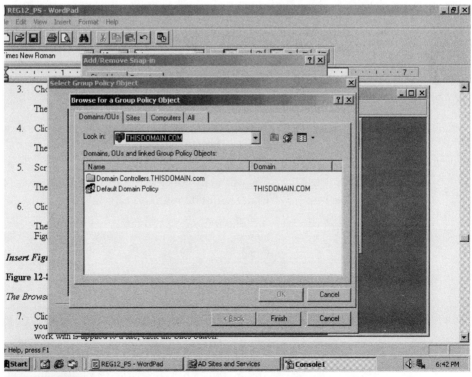

FIGURE 12.8 The Browse for a Group Policy Object dialog box.

7. Click on the tab for the type of Active Directory object to which the GPO you want to work with is applied. For example, if the GPO you want to work with is applied to a site, click the Sites button.

8. Click on the GPO you want to work with in the list of GPOs that appears in the Browse for a Group Policy Object dialog box.

9. Click OK.

You are returned to the Select Group Policy Object dialog box.

10. Click Finish.

You are returned to the Add Standalone Snap-in dialog box.

11. Click Close.

You are returned to the Add/Remove Snap-in dialog box.

12. Click OK.

You are returned to the management console window and are in a position to work with the GPO. Follow the steps below in the "Configuring Policies" section to learn how to edit the individual policies in a GPO.

OPENING A GPO DIRECTLY FROM THE OBJECT

An easy method you can use to open a GPO applied to an Active Directory object involves accessing the object directly and then opening the GPO via the object's Properties menu. This method represents the fastest way to open a GPO. Follow these steps to open a GPO directly from the object to which it is applied:

1. Access the domain, site, or OU that the GPO will be created for. This will require logging on to a domain controller and starting the Active Directory Users and Computers snap-in.

2. Right-click on the domain, site, or OU for which the GPO will be created and then choose Properties from the menu that appears.

The Properties dialog box appears.

3. Click once on the Group Policy tab.

4. Find the GPO in the list of GPOs and then click once on it.

5. Click the Edit button.

A management console window open to the GPO selected, as shown in Figure 12.9.

Managing Individual GPO Policies

In managing group policy, it is not enough simply to create GPOs for Active Directory objects or to manage group policy on a local workstation. The individual policies that comprise a GPO must also be managed. Each policy in a GPO can be enabled, disabled, or simply left in a not configured state. It is the responsibility of the administrator to enable or disable specific policies in each GPO created. The GPO is of no value to a system administrator or an

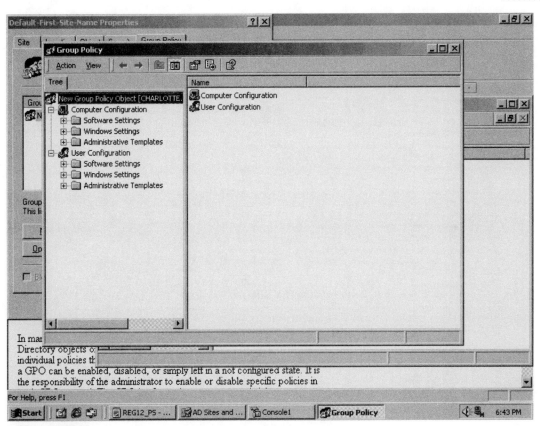

FIGURE 12.9 A managment console window opened to a GPO.

organization until the appropriate policies the GPO are managed. When you create a new GPO, all of its individual policies are in a *not configured* state, as shown in Figure 12.10.

UNDERSTANDING ENABLING POLICIES

Before learning how to manage individual policies, it's important to note the difference between policies that are *not configured* and those that are *disabled*. Just because a policy in a GPO is not configured is not an assurance that the behavior described by the policy, such as disabling Add/Remove programs, would not be explicitly denied or allowed. If a previously applied GPO, such as one defined at the local computer or site level, enabled a specific policy, that policy would be in force on all computers to which the GPO is applied unless a GPO applied later, perhaps at the domain or OU level, explicitly disabled the same policy. Think of the following:

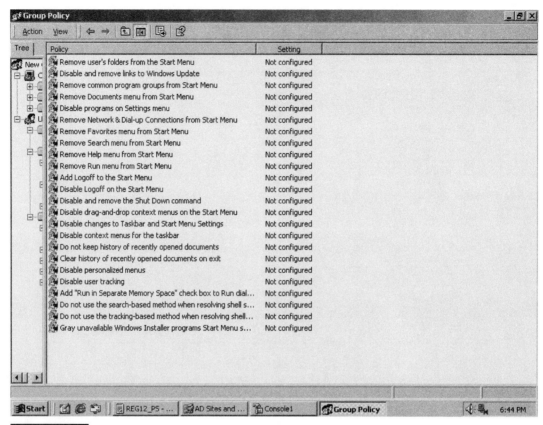

FIGURE 12.10 You must supply a name for a new GPO after it is created.

- Enabling a policy means *Yes,* prescribe the behavior in the policy.
- Disabling a policy means *No,* deny the behavior described in the policy.
- Not configuring a policy means *the GPO does not care.*

CONFIGURING POLICIES

Configuring an individual policy is a simple task that usually requires just one or two mouse clicks. Certain policies might require some text or numeric input from the user. For example, the Limit the bandwidth of Audio and Video policy for NetMeeting asks the administrator to supply the maximum amount of data, in kilobytes, that can be exchanged using NetMeeting (see Figure 12.11). In another example, the Browse a common web site to find printers policy asks the user to supply the URL where the users of the system can find the list of printers that can be installed (see Figure 12.12). Other policies, such as No screen saver, simply ask the administrator to specify whether this rule in force (see Figure 12.13).

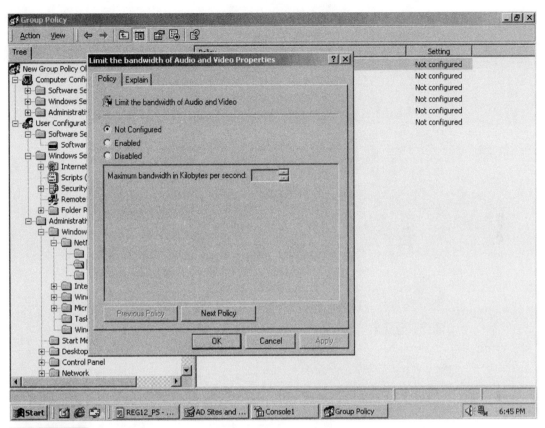

FIGURE 12.11 The Limit the bandwidth of Audio and Video policy.

To change a policy element in a GPO, follow these steps:

1. Open the GPO you want to edit. Follow the instructions above in the "Opening a GPO Directly from the Object" section for details on opening a GPO.

2. Navigate to the individual policy. Do this by opening any subfolders or nodes by clicking once on the + button that appears.

3. When the policy to be configured appears in the list of policies on the right side of the screen, double-click on the policy.
   The Properties dialog box for the policy appears.

4. Supply the information required by the policy. This could involve a combination of clicking on a selection or entering information. At the minimum, this step usually requires clicking on either the Enabled or Disabled option button. Click on the Explain tab to see more information about the policy.

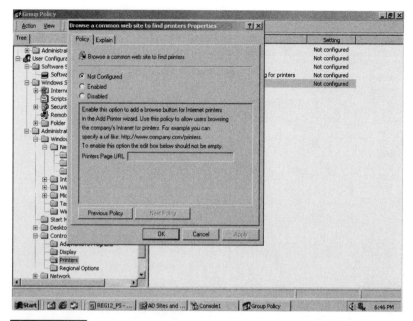

FIGURE 12.12 The Printer URL policy.

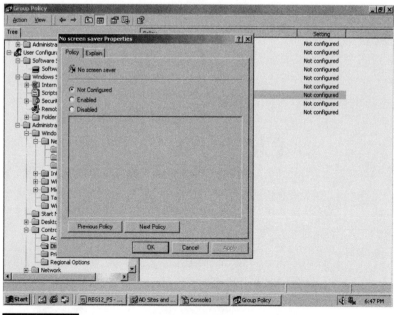

FIGURE 12.13 The No screen saver policy.

5. When you have supplied the information supplied by the policy, click OK.

6. Repeat steps 2 through 5 for every policy to be configured.

7. Choose Console, Exit to close the GPO.

Managing Group Policy Inheritance

The administrator does not need to visit every computer in the organization to implement group policy, even when the organization changes. Inheritance is used to ensure group policy is applied to all appropriate objects in the Active Directory. GPOs are applied to all computers that are members of the container where the GPO is applied. Examples of containers include sites and OUs.

For example, if a GPO named *PrintControl* is applied to the MARKET-ING OU, all computers that belong to the MARKETING OU have the policies of the *PrintControl* GPO applied. If an OU named DIRECT is added as a sub-OU to the MARKETING OU, then all computers in the MARKETING\DIRECT OU have applied the policies in PrintControl, as well as any GPOs applied to the DIRECT OU.

However, inheritance can be blocked. This means that a GPO can be configured so that any policies applied by a GPO to the parent would not override its policies.

1. Access the domain, site, or OU where the GPO is located. This will require logging on to a domain controller and starting the Active Directory Users and Computers snap-in.

2. Right-click on the object and then choose Properties from the menu.

3. When the Properties dialog box appears, click the Group Policy tab.

4. Click on the GPO and then click the Block Policy Inheritance option.

5. Click the Apply button and then click Close.

Group Policy Under the Hood

Windows 2000 provides, perhaps unwittingly, great tools to review the relationship between group policy and the entries in the Registry that support group policy. The two administrative template nodes in group policy (one in user configuration, the other in machine configuration) each are really just a representation of data stored in an external file. You can tell the name of the file by right-clicking on the Administrative Templates node and then choosing Add/Remove Templates from the menu that appears. A list appears showing the files represented in the policy (see Figure 12.14).

The files are also known as administrative template files. Each file is divided into numerous subsections with each subsection devoted to one policy.

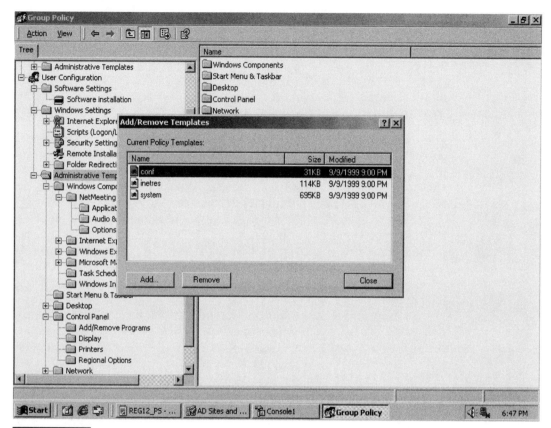

FIGURE 12.14 You can see the list of administrative templates loaded into a group policy.

The subsection begins with the keyword POLICY and ends with the keyword END POLICY. Here is an example:

```
POLICY !!Autorun
   KEYNAME
   "Software\Microsoft\Windows\CurrentVersion\Policies
   \Explorer"
   EXPLAIN !!Autorun_Help
    PART !!Autorun_Box            DROPDOWNLIST REQUIRED
        VALUENAME "NoDriveTypeAutoRun"
        ITEMLIST
            NAME !!Autorun_NoCD       VALUE NUMERIC 181
DEFAULT
  NAME !!Autorun_None   VALUE NUMERIC 255
       END ITEMLIST
  END PART
   END POLICY
```

Within the POLICY and END POLICY keywords, the administrative template files also provide the support for the management console to display information about the policy. The file includes the description you see about the policy, as well as information about any dropdown list, option lists, check boxes, or other user interface options that will be used to display the policy. These individual user interface elements are noted in the file with the word PART. If a list of items is required for the policy, such as the selections in a dropdown list, the individual items are noted with the ITEMLIST keyword. Finally, the EXPLAIN keyword indicates the label of the text that is displayed in the dialog box where you edit the policy. The value of the keyword is found at the end of the administrative template file. Here is an example:

```
[strings]
ABCDOnly="Restrict A, B, C and D drives only"
ABConly="Restrict A, B and C drives only"
ABOnly="Restrict A and B drives only"
ActiveDesktop="Active Desktop"
ActiveDirectory="Active Directory"
```

The most important information in the POLICY sections, though, is the names of the Registry entry where the policy data is stored. This data is preceded by the VALUENAME keyword. In addition, the VALUE keyword indicates the value for the entry required to enable or disable the policy. The key in which the entry is stored is indicated by the KEYNAME keyword.

The following excerpt shows the administrative template file that creates many of the policies available for customizing the Desktop:

```
CATEGORY !!Desktop

    KEYNAME
"Software\Microsoft\Windows\CurrentVersion\Policies\Explorer"

    POLICY !!NoDesktop
           EXPLAIN !!NoDesktop_Help
           VALUENAME "NoDesktop"
    END POLICY

    POLICY !!NoMyDocumentsIcon
        KEYNAME
"Software\Microsoft\Windows\CurrentVersion\Policies\NonEnum"
           EXPLAIN !!NoMyDocumentsIcon_Help
       VALUENAME "{450D8FBA-AD25-11D0-98A8-0800361B1103}"
    END POLICY

    POLICY !!NoNetHood
       EXPLAIN !!NoNetHood_Help
           VALUENAME "NoNetHood"
    END POLICY
```

```
POLICY !!NoInternetIcon
        EXPLAIN !!NoInternetIcon_Help
  VALUENAME "NoInternetIcon"
END POLICY

POLICY !!NoRecentDocsNetHood
  EXPLAIN !!NoRecentDocsNetHood_Help
        VALUENAME "NoRecentDocsNetHood"
END POLICY

POLICY !!DisablePersonalDirChange
        EXPLAIN !!DisablePersonalDirChange_Help
        VALUENAME "DisablePersonalDirChange"
END POLICY

POLICY !!sz_DB_DragDropClose
        EXPLAIN !!NoCloseDragDropBands_Help
        VALUENAME "NoCloseDragDropBands"
END POLICY

POLICY !!sz_DB_Moving
        EXPLAIN !!NoMovingBands_Help
        VALUENAME "NoMovingBands"
END POLICY

POLICY !!NoSaveSettings
        EXPLAIN !!NoSaveSettings_Help
        VALUENAME "NoSaveSettings"
END POLICY
```

Hardware Management

The Registry stores all the data it needs to manage the hardware attached to a computer running Windows 2000. While software applications can sometimes get away with storing configuration data in external files or databases, hardware devices usually cannot get away with this type of transgression. Thus, by inspecting the Registry, you can learn much about how your computer works with respect to its hardware and Windows 2000, as well as how to change some settings for tuning, configuration, and troubleshooting purposes. Keep in mind, though, that much of the Windows 2000 hardware-specific configuration is determined when the system boots as Windows 2000 detects the hardware. You still have the opportunity, though, to make some changes to the hardware configuration, as well as to collect information to help diagnose problems, by working with the registry. In this chapter, you will read about how the Registry organizes data about hardware, as well as how to tune some settings and fix some typical problems.

Reviewing Registry Hardware Support

Regardless of whether the hardware attached to your Windows 2000 system is giving you trouble or not, it is useful to know how the Registry organizes data about specific types of hardware. In this section, you will read about how the Registry stores data about video devices, network interface cards (NICs), keyboards, mice, and more, as well as what entries you can modify to change the performance or basic operation of a device.

Video Device Support

The first location to inspect in the Registry to understand the support provided to the video card and driver installed on a workstation is the following key:

```
HKEY_LOCAL_MACHINE\HARDWARE\DEVICEMAP\VIDEO
```

You can find more information on the HKEY_LOCAL_MACHINE\HARDWARE key later in this chapter in the "Understanding the HKLM\Hardware Hive" section, which discusses how hardware data is supported and configured. The discussion here, though, will focus just on video adapter support. The HKEY_LOCAL _MACHINE\HARDWARE\DEVICEMAP\VIDEO key lists any devices identified as a video adapter by Windows 2000 during startup. Open that key and identify any entry whose name starts with the following, where *nn* is the number of the device.

```
\Devicenn
```

The following shows a sample of the entries you might find on a computer with a Diamond Stealth II G460 adapter.

```
\\Device\\Video0=\\REGISTRY\\Machine\\System\\
ControlSet001\\Services\\i740\\Device0
\\Device\\Video1=\\REGISTRY\\Machine\\System\\
ControlSet001\\Services\\VgaSave\\Device0
\\Device\\Video2=\\REGISTRY\\Machine\\System\\
ControlSet001\\Services\\mnmdd\\Device0
VgaCompatible=\\Device\\Video1
```

 A Diamond Stealth II G460 is an AGP-type adapter (AGP for Accelerated Graphic Port). An AGP device improves video performance over PCI bus-based adapters. Note that the AGP card requires motherboard/chipset support.

The entries above are divided into two parts. The equals symbol is the delimiter between the two parts. The portion of the entry that *follows* the equals sign indicates the key in the Registry where configuration information about the adapter is stored. For example, entries related to the first video device found above, the i740 graphics chip, can be found in the following key:

```
\HKEY_LOCAL_MACHINE\SYSTEM\CONTROLSET001\SERVICES\I740\
DEVICE0
```

One of the most important entries in any of the keys referenced in HKEY_LOCAL_MACHINE\HARDWARE\DEVICEMAP\VIDEO, such as the key previously noted, is the ImagePath entry. The entry defines the file name of the driver. In addition, a number of standard entries are stored for every adapter, as well as some adapter-specific entries.

The following list (HKEY_LOCAL_MACHINE\SYSTEM\CONTROLSET001\ SERVICES\I740\DEVICE0) shows some of the typical configuration entries you will find for video adapter entries. Note that only the Device Description key, ImagePath, and device number in the Enum subkey present information in a form other than binary.

```
Type

Start

ErrorControl

Tag

ImagePath=System32\DRIVERS\i740nt5.sys

Devicen\InstalledDisplayDrivers

Devicen\VgaCompatible

Devicen\CapabilityOverride

Devicen\Device Description=Stealth II G460

Devicen\HardwareInformation.ChipType

Devicen\HardwareInformation.DacType

Devicen\HardwareInformation.MemorySize

Devicen\HardwareInformation.AdapterString

Devicen\HardwareInformation.BiosString

Devicen\HardwareInformation.Crc32

Security\Security

Enum\0=PCI\\VEN_8086&DEV_7800&SUBSYS_01001092&
REV_21\\3&2c3be70&0&0008

Enum\Count

Enum\NextInstance
```

SEEING CONFIGURATION DATA FOR THE VIDEO ADAPTER

In addition to hardware-specific configuration data, you can also see entries related to the current configuration of the video adapter as displayed in the Display applet found in the Control Panel folder. In some cases you can change the options that are normally available from the applet via the Registry. As an example, the XResolution and YResolution entries are the familiar resolution settings most users tinker with, such as changing between 640x480 and 864x1152. In other cases, you might not be able to change the values, even in the Control Panel.

These video adapter preference settings are found in the following key:

```
HKEY_LOCAL_MACHINE\SYSTEM\ControlSet00n\Hardware
Profiles\Current\System\CurrentControlSet\SERVICES key.
```

When you open the key, locate the name of the adapter and then click on the key related to the Device number assigned to the adapter. This device number is the same name of the entry for the adapter in the HKEY_LOCAL_MACHINE\ HARDWARE\DEVICEMAP\VIDEO key. Using as an example the same configuration described above, you can find this configuration data in the following key:

```
HKEY_LOCAL_MACHINE\SYSTEM\ControlSet001\Hardware
Profiles\Current\System\CurrentControlSet\
SERVICES\I740\DEVICE0
```

The following is the list of entries you can expect to find:

```
Attach.ToDesktop

DefaultSettings.BitsPerPel

DefaultSettings.XResolution

DefaultSettings.YResolution

DefaultSettings.VRefresh

DefaultSettings.Flags

DefaultSettings.XPanning

DefaultSettings.YPanning

Attach.RelativeX

Attach.RelativeY
```

Reviewing NIC Data in the Registry

You can review data stored about the network interface card(s) (NIC) installed on your computer, as well as configure some elements of its operation, in the Registry. The place in the Registry to start reviewing information about NICs installed on a computer is the following key:

HKEY_LOCAL_MACHINE\SOFTWARE\Microsoft\WindowsNT\Current-
Version\NetworkCards.

This key lists as entries all of the NICs installed on the computer. If you are surprised to think that a computer might have more than one NIC, consider the network server, which might have one card attached to the gateway to the Internet, while the other card is used to connect to the LAN.

 If you plan to configure a workstation or server with more than one network card, consider using different model cards. This way, it's easy to distinguish one card from the other when you review your system configuration or diagnose problems. A better idea is to use cards from different manufacturers.

Network cards are enumerated in separate keys, such as shown in Figure 13.1. For example, the first NIC found is found in HKEY_LOCAL_MACHINE\ SOFTWARE\Microsoft\WindowsNT\CurrentVersion\NetworkCards\1, while

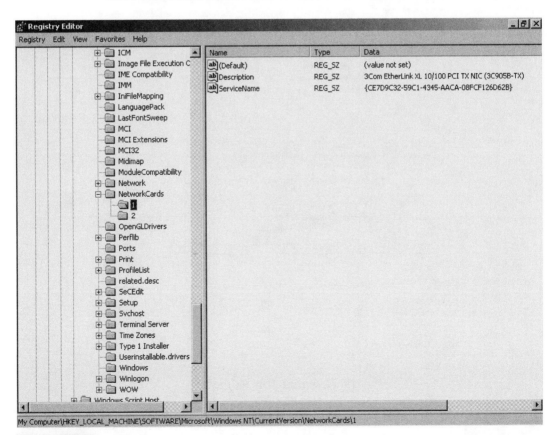

FIGURE 13.1 Network interface cards are enumerated in the Windows NT\Current Version\Network Cards key.

the next NIC would be found in HKEY_LOCAL_MACHINE\SOFTWARE\ Microsoft \WindowsNT\CurrentVersion\NetworkCards\2, and so on.

Each key has two important entries, as described below and shown in Figure 13.2:

- **Description**   This is the name of the card given by the manufacturer. If you have more than one NIC installed on your computer, use this entry to identify the one you're interested in.

- **ServiceName**   This entry stores the internal Windows 2000 class name for the NIC. This is the identifier to use when seeking information about the card. An example of a ServiceName is {CE7D9C32-59C1-4345-AACA-08FCF126D62B}.

Now, armed with the ServiceName and the NIC it represents, you can review the Registry for relevant data about a specific NIC. Knowing *where* to

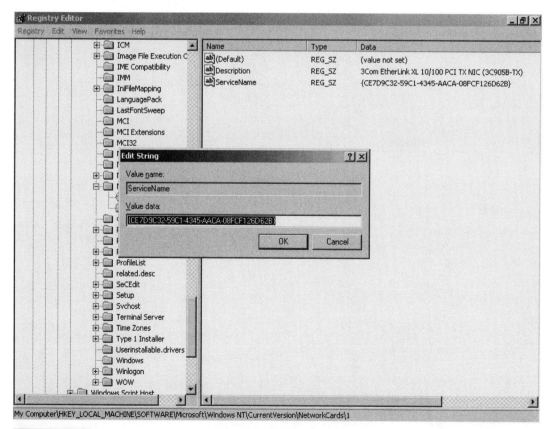

FIGURE 13.2   You can determine the internal ID assigned to a NIC by inspecting the Service-Name entry.

look for NIC data is addressed by knowing *what* to look for. Windows 2000 uses the following string to identify keys related to NICs:

{4D36E972-E325-11CE-BFC1-08002BE10318}

Details about NICs are mixed in the Registry with other connection devices that Windows 2000 knows about. NICs are known as *physical connections*. Remote access connections are known as *logical connections*. All of these connections are listed in dependent keys of the following key:

HKEY_LOCAL_MACHINE\SYSTEM\ControlSet00n\Control\
Class\{4D36E972-E325-11CE-BFC1-08002BE10318}

You can see an example of how the registry collects information about NICs in Figure 13.3.

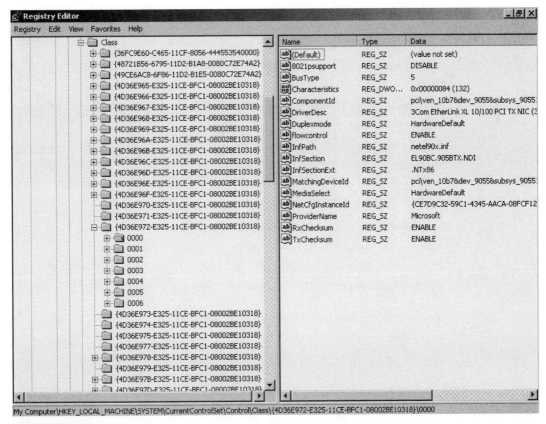

FIGURE 13.3   The Registry groups entries for both physical and logical network connections.

The following list shows an example of the different types of connection data stored under HKEY_LOCAL_MACHINE\SYSTEM\ControlSet00n\ Control\Class \{4D36E972-E325-11CE-BFC1-08002BE10318}:

```
DriverDesc=3Com EtherLink XL 10/100 PCI TX NIC (3C905B-TX)

DriverDesc=Direct Parallel

DriverDesc=RAS Async Adapter

DriverDesc=WAN Miniport (IP)

DriverDesc=WAN Miniport (L2TP)

DriverDesc=WAN Miniport (PPTP)
```

Naturally, the focus in this section of the chapter is on hardware, so the list below shows examples of the entries you might find for most NICs keys in the appropriate subkey of HKEY_LOCAL_MACHINE\SYSTEM\Control- Set00n \Control\Class\{4D36E972-E325-11CE-BFC1-08002BE10318}:

```
Characteristics

BusType=5

ComponentId=pci\\ven_10b7&dev_9055&subsys_905510b7

8021psupport=DISABLE

Duplexmode=HardwareDefault

flowcontrol=ENABLE

MediaSelect=HardwareDefault

RxChecksum=ENABLE

TxChecksum=ENABLE

InfPath=netel90x.inf

InfSection=EL90BC.905BTX.NDI

InfSectionExt=.NTx86

ProviderName=Microsoft

MatchingDeviceId=pci\\ven_10b7&dev_9055&subsys_905510b7

DriverDesc=3Com EtherLink XL 10/100 PCI TX NIC (3C905B-TX)

NetCfgInstanceId={CE7D9C32-59C1-4345-AACA-08FCF126D62B}
```

Reviewing Modem Data in the Registry

The Registry organizes data about common components with a class id. The class id for modems is {4D36E96D-E325-11CE-BFC1-08002BE10318}. You can find a list of the modems on a workstation by browsing through the subkeys belonging to:

```
HKEY_LOCAL_MACHINE\SYSTEM\ControlSet00n\Control\
Class\{4D36E96D-E325-11CE-BFC1-08002BE10318}
```

Modems are enumerated in subkeys of the key noted above. For example, the first modem configured would be found in the 0000 subkey of the key noted above. You can find a significant amount of information about the configuration of a modem, including the driver, the associated COM port, the INF file that provides configuration values, as well the command strings to the modem. The following list shows some of the entries you might consider reviewing or tuning:

```
AttachedTo=COM3

FriendlyName=Unknown Modem

UINumber=dword:00000001

LoggingPath=H:\\WINNT\\ModemLog_Unknown Modem.txt

Manufacturer=(Standard Modem Types)

Model=Unknown Modem

EnumPropPages32=modemui.dll,ModemPropPagesProvider

ID=hex:62,0e,07,00

PermanentGuid=hex:4e,9f,8e,b8,e2,78,45,42,aa,9
d,47,0b,0a,6d,b8,84

ConfigDialog=modemui.dll

PortSubClass=hex:02

Reset=ATZ<cr>

DeviceType=hex:01

InfPath=mdmgen.inf

InfSection=Gen

ProviderName=Microsoft

MatchingDeviceId=mdmunk

DriverDesc=Unknown Modem

ResponsesKeyName=Unknown Modem::(Standard
Modem Types)::Microsoft

Answer\1=ATA<cr>

[HKEY_LOCAL_MACHINE\SYSTEM\CurrentControlSet\Control\
Class\{4D36E96D-E325-11CE-BFC1-
08002BE10318}\0000\Clients\Ras]

Clients\RAS\EnableForRas=dword:00000000

Clients\RAS\EnableForRouting=dword:00000000

Hangup\1=ATH<cr>

Init\1=AT<cr>

Init\2=ATE0V1<cr>

Monitor\1=ATS0=0<cr>
```

```
Monitor\2=None
Settings\Prefix=AT
Settings\Terminator=<cr>
Settings\DialPrefix=D
Settings\Pulse=P
Settings\Tone=T
Settings\FlowControl_Off=
Settings\FlowControl_Hard=
Settings\FlowControl_Soft=
```

Reviewing Mouse Settings

Control of the mouse configuration can be handled via the Registry. The Registry keys that control the mouse behavior mirror the options in the Mouse configuration utility in the Control panel folder. You can find mouse configuration data in the following key:

```
HKEY_CURRENT_USER\Control Panel\Mouse
```

Table 13.1 shows the entries related to mouse behavior and their uses.

TABLE 13.1	Mouse Entries
DoubleClickHeight	Determines the allowable vertical movement between clicks to still interpret the two-click action as a mouse double-click.
DoubleClickSpeed	Determines how quickly the user must click a second time for Windows 2000 to interpret the two clicks as a double-click action. Minimum is 100; maximum is 900.
DoubleClickWidth	Determines the allowable horizontal movement between clicks to still interpret the two-click action as a mouse double-click.
MouseSpeed	Determines how fast the mouse pointer moves across the screen relative to the speed at which the user moves the mouse.
SnapToDefaultButton	Automatically moves the mouse pointer to the default control in a dialog box, such as the OK button. Set this value to 1 enable this feature.
SwapMouseButtons	Switches interpretation of clicks on the right-button on the mouse as a left-mouse click in Windows 2000, and vice-versa. Use a value of 1 to swap mouse buttons.

It's also worth looking at how the Registry stores information about the driver that controls the mouse. Like other generic types of hardware, the first clue about the support provided for a mouse is found in the following key:

```
HKEY_LOCAL_MACHINE\HARDWARE\DEVICEMAP\PointerClass
```

The value for the only entry in the key indicates to you what key elsewhere in the Registry stores configuration and driver details about the pointer device:

```
HKEY_LOCAL_MACHINE\SYSTEM\ControlSet00n\Services\mouclass
```

If you inspect the key shown above, you'll find a number of root entries, as well as entries in the Enum and Parameters subkeys. Of interest is the ImagePath entry in the key noted above, which indicates the name and location of the driver used for the mouse:

```
ImagePath = System32\DRIVERS\mouclass.sys
```

Last, in the case of a mouse discovered and configured at boot up, you can find mouse-related plug-and-play entries in the Registry as well. Details about a mouse discovered at start-up, at least in the case of a standard PS/2 mouse, can be found in the following key:

```
HKEY_LOCAL_MACHINE\SYSTEM\ControlSet00n\Enum\
Root\*PNP0F12\1_0_21_0_31_0
```

You might wonder how to know to look in the key noted above. Good question. An entry in HKEY_LOCAL_MACHINE\SYSTEM\ControlSet00n\ Services\mouclass\Enum, as described earlier in this section, indicates the location of plug and play data:

```
Root\*PNP0F12\1_0_21_0_31_0
```

Plug and Play in Windows 2000

Support for plug-and-play devices is expanded in Windows 2000 compared to Windows NT. *Plug and play* refers to the support provided in Windows for the operating system to detect and configure hardware attached to a computer with little to no intervention by the user. The name given to these technologies, plug and play, is accurate. You plug the hardware in and then it plays. However, plug and play is not only a function of the operating system.

Hardware drivers must be provided that are plug-and-play compatible. The device itself, naturally, also must be configured for plug-and-play operability.

The Registry, naturally, can tell you much about the plug and play. You can see the devices discovered and configured via plug and play in the following key:

```
HKEY_LOCAL_MACHINE\SYSTEM\CurrentControlSet\Enum
```

The subkeys under the Enum key are the enumerators the Registry uses to classify the various types of devices that are discovered. Devices may be enumerated by their specific type, and some devices are enumerated by the parent bus of the type, such as PCI. Table 13.2 explains the types of enumerators collected under Enum.

Under each enumerator key are subkeys for each particular device belonging to the enumerator category. You can open each device key to see information about the discovered device. Keep in mind that the entries in these keys should not be modified.

Understanding the HKLM\Hardware Hive

One of the most interesting areas of the Registry, which illustrates about how hardware is supported and configured, is the following key:

```
HKEY_LOCAL_MACHINE\HARDWARE
```

TABLE 13.2	Plug-and-Play Enumerator Types
Type	**Function**
DISPLAY	Monitor
DOT4	Printers
DOT4PRT	Printers
FDC	Floppy drives
IDE	Devices connected to the IDE controller, such as a CD/DVD drive
ISAPNP	ISA plug-and-play devices
LPTENUM	Devices connected to a parallel port
PCI	Devices connected to the PCI bus
PCIIDE	Primary IDE channel
SCSI	SCSI devices
SERENUM	Serial port devices
STORAGE	Storage volumes and removable media
SW	Software devices

This key has three subkeys. These subkeys indicate what generic hardware the system identified at startup, as well as the resources used by the hardware installed. The three subkeys are:

```
Description
```

```
DeviceMap
```

```
ResourceMap
```

In the following three sections, you can read about the purpose of these keys.

The Description Key

The Description key stores data about the computer's CPU(s) and multifunction adapters, such as the PCI bus and SCSI adapters. As an example, data about the system and video BIOS are stored in the Registry in the HKEY_LOCAL_MACHINE\HARDWARE\DESCRIPTION\System key. The following list shows the name of the entries storing the relevant data:

```
SystemBiosDate
```

```
SystemBiosVersion
```

```
VideoBiosDate
```

```
VideoBiosVersion
```

In addition, the HKEY_LOCAL_MACHINE\HARDWARE\DESCRIPTION\ System key stores data about the CPU. You can find data about your processor(s) in the following key:

```
HKEY_LOCAL_MACHINE\HARDWARE\DESCRIPTION\System\
CentralProcessor
```

For each processor installed on you motherboard, you will find a subkey. The subkey of the first CPU is 0. Subsequent CPUs are numbered 1 to n. Table 13.3 lists and explains the use of the entries you'll find for each CPU.

TABLE 13.3 CPU Entries	
Entry	**Use**
Component Information	Binary data
Identifier	The class of the processor, such as x86 Family 6 Model 5 Stepping 1
Configuration Data	Binary data related to resource used by CPU
VendorIdentifier	The manufacturer of the CPU
FeatureSet	Binary data
~MHz	The speed of the processor
Update Signature	Binary data
Update Status	Binary data
Previous Update Signature	Binary data

Last, you can find some detail about any SCSI adapter(s) in use on your system. Browse down to the following key to see, minimally, the name of the SCSI controller Windows 2000 discovered:

```
HKEY_LOCAL_MACHINE\HARDWARE\DESCRIPTION\System\
ScsiAdapter\0\DiskController\0
```

If you are having trouble getting a new SCSI controller to work, it may be worth looking here to see if the controller was properly identified. It's likely, though, that if you experience trouble with a SCSI adapter, you may not be able to boot your system at all, which makes the chance of inspecting the Registry not good.

The DeviceMap Key

The DeviceMap subkey under the HKEY_LOCAL_MACHINE\HARDWARE\ DEVICEMAP provides information about the standard devices installed on the computer, such as the keyboard, serial port, parallel port, and a few others, as well as the location of the drivers for certain devices. The following list shows subkeys:

```
KeyboardClass
PARALLEL PORTS
PointerClass
Scsi
SERIAL COMM
VIDEO
```

Most of the entries in this key will indicate the matching registry key where settings for the device are stored. For example, in the case of the Keyboard, the first keyboard found has an entry value of \REGISTRY\ MACHINE\SYSTEM\ControlSet001\Services\kbdclass. This indicates the location of entries specific to the keyboard and the driver. The following list shows an example of the entries:

```
ErrorControl=dword:00000001
Group=Keyboard Class
Start=dword:00000001
Tag=dword:00000001
Type=dword:00000001
DisplayName=Keyboard Class Driver
Parameters\ConnectMultiplePorts=dword:00000000
Parameters\KeyboardDataQueueSize=dword:00000064
Parameters\KeyboardDeviceBaseName=KeyboardClass
```

```
Parameters\MaximumPortsServiced=dword:00000003
Parameters\SendOutputToAllPorts=dword:00000001
Enum\0=Root\\*PNP030b\\1_0_22_0_32_0
Enum\Count=dword:00000001
Enum\NextInstance=dword:00000001
```

The ResourceMap Key

The ResourceMap key stores entries related to the HAL manager, the plug-and-play manager, and system resources. Specifically, you can see the physical resources assigned to the devices managed by HAL and plug-and-play manager. To see the resources, double-click on any entry in the following key:

HKEY_LOCAL_MACHINE\HARDWARE\RESOURCEMAP

The Resource Lists dialog box appears, as shown in Figure 13.4.

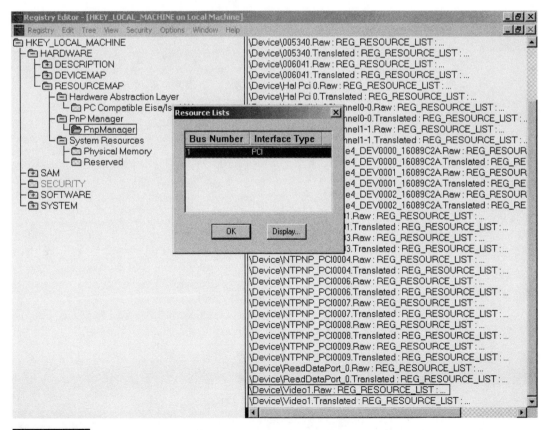

FIGURE 13.4 You can use the Registry to see the interfaces that require resources via the Registry.

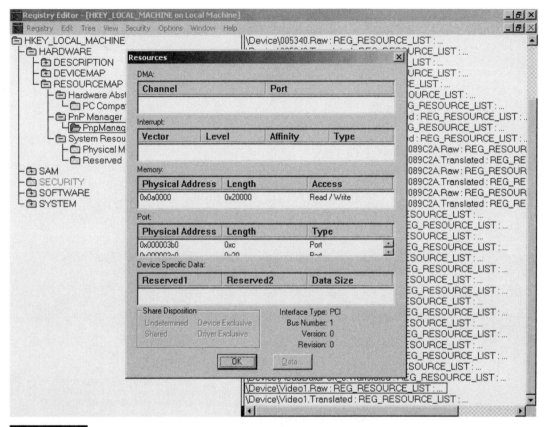

FIGURE 13.5 The Registry gives you the opportunity to view the specific resources used by hardware/interface combinations.

The Resource Lists dialog box shows the bus and the interface for each resource represented by the device you selected. It's possible that just one line of data appears in the box, so do not be concerned if you do not see more than one. To see detailed information about the device's use of resources specific to the interface, double-click on the appropriate line in the Resource Lists dialog box. The Resources dialog box appears, as shown in Figure 13.5. The dialog box shows you all of the resources associated with the device/interface combination you chose, including interrupt, memory address, and more.

Fixing Specific Hardware Problems

You can address a number of hardware problems by tweaking and tuning registry entries. In this section, you can read about solutions for solving certain hardware problems.

Debugging Zip Drive Problems

Your Windows 2000 installation might not properly detect a Zip drive interfaced through your parallel port. If you experience this problem, supply 00000001 as the value for this entry. Reboot your machine for the change to take effect.

Root Key: HKEY_LOCAL_MACHINE

Key: \SYSTEM\CurrentControlSet\Services\Parallel\ Parameters

Entry Name: ParEnableLegacyZip

Data Type: REG_DWORD

Knowing Where to Find the Driver Cabinet File

When Windows 2000 detects new hardware attached to a computer, the system will first try to use a driver stored in the Driver.cab file. As a method to prevent automatic installation of new hardware, Microsoft, in Knowledge Base Article Q230644, recommends the Driver.cab file be removed or renamed. You can use the Registry to identify the location of the Driver.cab file. Open the following key:

HKEY_LOCAL_MACHINE\SOFTWARE\Microsoft\Windows\ CurrentVersion\Setup

The DriverCachePath entry will indicate the location of the file.

Fixing Microsoft Wheel Mouse Problems

Microsoft reports a problem when you connect a Microsoft Wheel mouse to the PS/2 port on a computer. Specifically, the problem is that the computer hangs. Add the following key and value to address this problem. Enter a value of 0 to not use the wheel feature or enter a value of 1 to use the wheel feature without chance of the system hanging. If you use a value of 1 and the wheel does not work, try a value of 2.

Root Key: HKEY_LOCAL_MACHINE

Key: \System\CurrentControlSet\Services\I8042PRT\ Parameters

Entry Name: EnableWheelDetection

HKCU Entry Names and Keys

Many resources on the registry available today provide registry listings. These lists are sometimes nothing more than printed presentations of the file created when you open the Registry using one of the editors. Hopefully, you feel this listing is more valuable than that.

This listing shows all the Registry keys sorted by entry name from HKEY_CURRENT_USER (HKCU). Specifically, the listing shows all entries by name and the key in which each resides. The listing is useful because it allows you to inspect the HKCU subkey by the data it stores. This contrasts to the presentation the editors give of the Registry, in which data is organized, in effect, by use: by root key, category, vendor, names assigned to each piece of data. Most of the user-friendly and eminently modifiable keys exist in HKCU.

The listing represents an extract from the Registry running in the Windows 2000 server. The listing was captured immediately after installation with all options installation selected. Default entries have been omitted. Also of note is the omission of HKLM. Given the abundance of machine-specific settings in the root key, it would not be relevant to present keys based on hardware configuration when, presumably, you, the reader, would be running on a different type of hardware.

. . . .

Entry Name	**Key**
%SHARED_DESKTOP%	[HKCU\Software\Microsoft\Windows\ CurrentVersion\GrpConv\MapGroups]
(None)	[HKCU\Control Panel\Patterns]
\"C:\\PROGRA~1\\WINDOW~2\\ mplayer2.exe\"	[HKCU\Software\Netscape\Netscape Navigator\User Trusted External Applications]
\"C:\\Program Files\\Windows Media Player\\mplayer2.exe\"	[HKCU\Software\Netscape\Netscape Navigator\User Trusted External Applications]
_HasNotif	[HKCU\Software\Microsoft\Windows\ CurrentVersion\Explorer\MountPoints\D]
_UB	[HKCU\Software\Microsoft\Windows\ CurrentVersion\Explorer\MountPoints\A]
_UB	[HKCU\Software\Microsoft\Windows\ CurrentVersion\Explorer\MountPoints\C]
_UB	[HKCU\Software\Microsoft\Windows\ CurrentVersion\Explorer\MountPoints\D]
{01E04581-4EEE-11D0-BFE9- 00AA005B4383}	[HKCU\Software\Microsoft\Internet Explorer\Toolbar\ShellBrowser]
{0E5CBF21-D15F-11D0-8301- 00AA005B4383}	[HKCU\Software\Microsoft\Internet Explorer\Toolbar\ShellBrowser]
{c95fe080-8f5d-11d2-a20b- 00aa003c157a}	[HKCU\Software\Microsoft\Internet Explorer\Extensions\CmdMapping]
{CFBFAE00-17A6-11D0-99CB- 00C04FD64497}	[HKCU\Software\Microsoft\Internet Explorer\URLSearchHooks]
{FBF23B40-E3F0-101B-8488- 00AA003E56F8}	[HKCU\Software\Microsoft\Windows\ CurrentVersion\Explorer\ NewShortcutHandlers]
~SubsInfo	[HKCU\Software\Microsoft\Windows\ CurrentVersion\Webcheck\Store.1\{02C09 C60-E687-01BE-0000-00004BFBD552}]
0	[HKCU\Software\Microsoft\Windows\ CurrentVersion\Explorer\StreamMRU]
1	[HKCU\Keyboard Layout\Preload]
1	[HKCU\Software\Microsoft\Windows\ CurrentVersion\Explorer\StreamMRU]
1001	[HKCU\Software\Microsoft\Windows\ CurrentVersion\Internet Settings\Zones\0]
1001	[HKCU\Software\Microsoft\Windows\ CurrentVersion\Internet Settings\Zones\1]
1001	[HKCU\Software\Microsoft\Windows\ CurrentVersion\Internet Settings\Zones\2]
1001	[HKCU\Software\Microsoft\Windows\ CurrentVersion\Internet Settings\Zones\3]

Entry Name	Key
1001	[HKCU\Software\Microsoft\Windows\CurrentVersion\Internet Settings\Zones\4]
1004	[HKCU\Software\Microsoft\Windows\CurrentVersion\Internet Settings\Zones\0]
1004	[HKCU\Software\Microsoft\Windows\CurrentVersion\Internet Settings\Zones\1]
1004	[HKCU\Software\Microsoft\Windows\CurrentVersion\Internet Settings\Zones\2]
1004	[HKCU\Software\Microsoft\Windows\CurrentVersion\Internet Settings\Zones\3]
1004	[HKCU\Software\Microsoft\Windows\CurrentVersion\Internet Settings\Zones\4]
1200	[HKCU\Software\Microsoft\Windows\CurrentVersion\Internet Settings\Zones\0]
1200	[HKCU\Software\Microsoft\Windows\CurrentVersion\Internet Settings\Zones\1]
1200	[HKCU\Software\Microsoft\Windows\CurrentVersion\Internet Settings\Zones\2]
1200	[HKCU\Software\Microsoft\Windows\CurrentVersion\Internet Settings\Zones\3]
1200	[HKCU\Software\Microsoft\Windows\CurrentVersion\Internet Settings\Zones\4]
1201	[HKCU\Software\Microsoft\Windows\CurrentVersion\Internet Settings\Zones\0]
1201	[HKCU\Software\Microsoft\Windows\CurrentVersion\Internet Settings\Zones\1]
1201	[HKCU\Software\Microsoft\Windows\CurrentVersion\Internet Settings\Zones\2]
1201	[HKCU\Software\Microsoft\Windows\CurrentVersion\Internet Settings\Zones\3]
1201	[HKCU\Software\Microsoft\Windows\CurrentVersion\Internet Settings\Zones\4]

....

Entry Name	Key
1400	[HKCU\Software\Microsoft\Windows\CurrentVersion\Internet Settings\Zones\0]
1400	[HKCU\Software\Microsoft\Windows\CurrentVersion\Internet Settings\Zones\1]
1400	[HKCU\Software\Microsoft\Windows\CurrentVersion\Internet Settings\Zones\2]
1400	[HKCU\Software\Microsoft\Windows\CurrentVersion\Internet Settings\Zones\3]
1400	[HKCU\Software\Microsoft\Windows\CurrentVersion\Internet Settings\Zones\4]
1402	[HKCU\Software\Microsoft\Windows\CurrentVersion\Internet Settings\Zones\0]
1402	[HKCU\Software\Microsoft\Windows\CurrentVersion\Internet Settings\Zones\1]
1402	[HKCU\Software\Microsoft\Windows\CurrentVersion\Internet Settings\Zones\2]
1402	[HKCU\Software\Microsoft\Windows\CurrentVersion\Internet Settings\Zones\3]
1402	[HKCU\Software\Microsoft\Windows\CurrentVersion\Internet Settings\Zones\4]
1405	[HKCU\Software\Microsoft\Windows\CurrentVersion\Internet Settings\Zones\0]
1405	[HKCU\Software\Microsoft\Windows\CurrentVersion\Internet Settings\Zones\1]
1405	[HKCU\Software\Microsoft\Windows\CurrentVersion\Internet Settings\Zones\2]
1405	[HKCU\Software\Microsoft\Windows\CurrentVersion\Internet Settings\Zones\3]
1405	[HKCU\Software\Microsoft\Windows\CurrentVersion\Internet Settings\Zones\4]
1406	[HKCU\Software\Microsoft\Windows\CurrentVersion\Internet Settings\Zones\0]

Entry Name	Key
1406	[HKCU\Software\Microsoft\Windows\CurrentVersion\Internet Settings\Zones\1]
1406	[HKCU\Software\Microsoft\Windows\CurrentVersion\Internet Settings\Zones\2]
1406	[HKCU\Software\Microsoft\Windows\CurrentVersion\Internet Settings\Zones\3]
1406	[HKCU\Software\Microsoft\Windows\CurrentVersion\Internet Settings\Zones\4]
1407	[HKCU\Software\Microsoft\Windows\CurrentVersion\Internet Settings\Zones\0]
1407	[HKCU\Software\Microsoft\Windows\CurrentVersion\Internet Settings\Zones\1]
1407	[HKCU\Software\Microsoft\Windows\CurrentVersion\Internet Settings\Zones\2]
1407	[HKCU\Software\Microsoft\Windows\CurrentVersion\Internet Settings\Zones\3]
1407	[HKCU\Software\Microsoft\Windows\CurrentVersion\Internet Settings\Zones\4]
1601	[HKCU\Software\Microsoft\Windows\CurrentVersion\Internet Settings\Zones\0]
1601	[HKCU\Software\Microsoft\Windows\CurrentVersion\Internet Settings\Zones\1]
1601	[HKCU\Software\Microsoft\Windows\CurrentVersion\Internet Settings\Zones\2]
1601	[HKCU\Software\Microsoft\Windows\CurrentVersion\Internet Settings\Zones\3]
1601	[HKCU\Software\Microsoft\Windows\CurrentVersion\Internet Settings\Zones\4]
1604	[HKCU\Software\Microsoft\Windows\CurrentVersion\Internet Settings\Zones\0]
1604	[HKCU\Software\Microsoft\Windows\CurrentVersion\Internet Settings\Zones\1]

Entry Name	Key
1604	[HKCU\Software\Microsoft\Windows\CurrentVersion\Internet Settings\Zones\2]
1604	[HKCU\Software\Microsoft\Windows\CurrentVersion\Internet Settings\Zones\3]
1604	[HKCU\Software\Microsoft\Windows\CurrentVersion\Internet Settings\Zones\4]
1605	[HKCU\Software\Microsoft\Windows\CurrentVersion\Internet Settings\Zones\0]
1605	[HKCU\Software\Microsoft\Windows\CurrentVersion\Internet Settings\Zones\1]
1605	[HKCU\Software\Microsoft\Windows\CurrentVersion\Internet Settings\Zones\2]
1605	[HKCU\Software\Microsoft\Windows\CurrentVersion\Internet Settings\Zones\3]
1605	[HKCU\Software\Microsoft\Windows\CurrentVersion\Internet Settings\Zones\4]
1606	[HKCU\Software\Microsoft\Windows\CurrentVersion\Internet Settings\Zones\0]
1606	[HKCU\Software\Microsoft\Windows\CurrentVersion\Internet Settings\Zones\1]
1606	[HKCU\Software\Microsoft\Windows\CurrentVersion\Internet Settings\Zones\2]
1606	[HKCU\Software\Microsoft\Windows\CurrentVersion\Internet Settings\Zones\3]
1606	[HKCU\Software\Microsoft\Windows\CurrentVersion\Internet Settings\Zones\4]
1607	[HKCU\Software\Microsoft\Windows\CurrentVersion\Internet Settings\Zones\0]
1607	[HKCU\Software\Microsoft\Windows\CurrentVersion\Internet Settings\Zones\1]
1607	[HKCU\Software\Microsoft\Windows\CurrentVersion\Internet Settings\Zones\2]

Entry Name	Key
1607	[HKCU\Software\Microsoft\Windows\CurrentVersion\Internet Settings\Zones\3]
1607	[HKCU\Software\Microsoft\Windows\CurrentVersion\Internet Settings\Zones\4]
1800	[HKCU\Software\Microsoft\Windows\CurrentVersion\Internet Settings\Zones\0]
1800	[HKCU\Software\Microsoft\Windows\CurrentVersion\Internet Settings\Zones\1]
1800	[HKCU\Software\Microsoft\Windows\CurrentVersion\Internet Settings\Zones\2]
1800	[HKCU\Software\Microsoft\Windows\CurrentVersion\Internet Settings\Zones\3]
1800	[HKCU\Software\Microsoft\Windows\CurrentVersion\Internet Settings\Zones\4]
1802	[HKCU\Software\Microsoft\Windows\CurrentVersion\Internet Settings\Zones\0]
1802	[HKCU\Software\Microsoft\Windows\CurrentVersion\Internet Settings\Zones\1]
1802	[HKCU\Software\Microsoft\Windows\CurrentVersion\Internet Settings\Zones\2]
1802	[HKCU\Software\Microsoft\Windows\CurrentVersion\Internet Settings\Zones\3]
1802	[HKCU\Software\Microsoft\Windows\CurrentVersion\Internet Settings\Zones\4]
1803	[HKCU\Software\Microsoft\Windows\CurrentVersion\Internet Settings\Zones\0]
1803	[HKCU\Software\Microsoft\Windows\CurrentVersion\Internet Settings\Zones\1]
1803	[HKCU\Software\Microsoft\Windows\CurrentVersion\Internet Settings\Zones\2]
1803	[HKCU\Software\Microsoft\Windows\CurrentVersion\Internet Settings\Zones\3]

Entry Name

Key

Entry Name	Key
1803	[HKCU\Software\Microsoft\Windows\CurrentVersion\Internet Settings\Zones\4]
1804	[HKCU\Software\Microsoft\Windows\CurrentVersion\Internet Settings\Zones\0]
1804	[HKCU\Software\Microsoft\Windows\CurrentVersion\Internet Settings\Zones\1]
1804	[HKCU\Software\Microsoft\Windows\CurrentVersion\Internet Settings\Zones\2]
1804	[HKCU\Software\Microsoft\Windows\CurrentVersion\Internet Settings\Zones\3]
1804	[HKCU\Software\Microsoft\Windows\CurrentVersion\Internet Settings\Zones\4]
1805	[HKCU\Software\Microsoft\Windows\CurrentVersion\Internet Settings\Zones\0]
1805	[HKCU\Software\Microsoft\Windows\CurrentVersion\Internet Settings\Zones\1]
1805	[HKCU\Software\Microsoft\Windows\CurrentVersion\Internet Settings\Zones\2]
1805	[HKCU\Software\Microsoft\Windows\CurrentVersion\Internet Settings\Zones\3]
1805	[HKCU\Software\Microsoft\Windows\CurrentVersion\Internet Settings\Zones\4]
1A00	[HKCU\Software\Microsoft\Windows\CurrentVersion\Internet Settings\Zones\0]
1A00	[HKCU\Software\Microsoft\Windows\CurrentVersion\Internet Settings\Zones\1]
1A00	[HKCU\Software\Microsoft\Windows\CurrentVersion\Internet Settings\Zones\2]
1A00	[HKCU\Software\Microsoft\Windows\CurrentVersion\Internet Settings\Zones\3]
1A00	[HKCU\Software\Microsoft\Windows\CurrentVersion\Internet Settings\Zones\4]

Entry Name	**Key**
1A02	[HKCU\Software\Microsoft\Windows\CurrentVersion\Internet Settings\Zones\0]
1A02	[HKCU\Software\Microsoft\Windows\CurrentVersion\Internet Settings\Zones\1]
1A02	[HKCU\Software\Microsoft\Windows\CurrentVersion\Internet Settings\Zones\2]
1A02	[HKCU\Software\Microsoft\Windows\CurrentVersion\Internet Settings\Zones\3]
1A02	[HKCU\Software\Microsoft\Windows\CurrentVersion\Internet Settings\Zones\4]
1A03	[HKCU\Software\Microsoft\Windows\CurrentVersion\Internet Settings\Zones\0]
1A03	[HKCU\Software\Microsoft\Windows\CurrentVersion\Internet Settings\Zones\1]
1A03	[HKCU\Software\Microsoft\Windows\CurrentVersion\Internet Settings\Zones\2]
1A03	[HKCU\Software\Microsoft\Windows\CurrentVersion\Internet Settings\Zones\3]
1A03	[HKCU\Software\Microsoft\Windows\CurrentVersion\Internet Settings\Zones\4]
1C00	[HKCU\Software\Microsoft\Windows\CurrentVersion\Internet Settings\Zones\0]
1C00	[HKCU\Software\Microsoft\Windows\CurrentVersion\Internet Settings\Zones\1]
1C00	[HKCU\Software\Microsoft\Windows\CurrentVersion\Internet Settings\Zones\2]
1C00	[HKCU\Software\Microsoft\Windows\CurrentVersion\Internet Settings\Zones\3]
1C00	[HKCU\Software\Microsoft\Windows\CurrentVersion\Internet Settings\Zones\4]
1E05	[HKCU\Software\Microsoft\Windows\CurrentVersion\Internet Settings\Zones\0]

Entry Name	Key
1E05	[HKCU\Software\Microsoft\Windows\CurrentVersion\Internet Settings\Zones\1]
1E05	[HKCU\Software\Microsoft\Windows\CurrentVersion\Internet Settings\Zones\2]
1E05	[HKCU\Software\Microsoft\Windows\CurrentVersion\Internet Settings\Zones\3]
1E05	[HKCU\Software\Microsoft\Windows\CurrentVersion\Internet Settings\Zones\4]
2	[HKCU\Software\Microsoft\Windows\CurrentVersion\Explorer\StreamMRU]
50% Gray	[HKCU\Control Panel\Patterns]
a	[HKCU\Software\Microsoft\Windows\CurrentVersion\Explorer\ComDlg32\LastVisitedMRU]
a	[HKCU\Software\Microsoft\Windows\CurrentVersion\Explorer\ComDlg32\OpenSaveMRU*]
a	[HKCU\Software\Microsoft\Windows\CurrentVersion\Explorer\ComDlg32\OpenSaveMRU\reg]
a	[HKCU\Software\Microsoft\Windows\CurrentVersion\Explorer\ComDlg32\OpenSaveMRU\TXT]
a	[HKCU\Software\Microsoft\Windows\CurrentVersion\Explorer\FileExts\.msc\OpenWithList]
a	[HKCU\Software\Microsoft\Windows\CurrentVersion\Explorer\FileExts\.reg\OpenWithList]
a	[HKCU\Software\Microsoft\Windows\CurrentVersion\Explorer\FileExts\.TXT\OpenWithList]
a	[HKCU\Software\Microsoft\Windows\CurrentVersion\Explorer\RecentDocs]
a	[HKCU\Software\Microsoft\Windows\CurrentVersion\Explorer\RecentDocs\.TXT]
a	[HKCU\Software\Microsoft\Windows\CurrentVersion\Explorer\RecentDocs\Folder]
a	[HKCU\Software\Microsoft\Windows\CurrentVersion\Explorer\RunMRU]
Active1	[HKCU\Control Panel\Screen Saver.Mystify]

Entry Name	Key
Active2	[HKCU\Control Panel\Screen Saver.Mystify]
ActiveBorder	[HKCU\Control Panel\Colors]
ActiveTitle	[HKCU\Control Panel\Colors]
ActiveWindowTracking	[HKCU\Control Panel\Mouse]
ActiveWndTrkTimeout	[HKCU\Control Panel\Desktop]
ActualSizeKB	[HKCU\Software\Microsoft\Windows\ CurrentVersion\Webcheck\Store.1 \ {02C09C60-E687-01BE-0000- 00004BFBD552}]
AlwaysOnTop	[HKCU\Software\Microsoft\Fax\UserInfo]
Anchor Color Visited	[HKCU\Software\Microsoft\Internet Explorer\Settings]
Anchor Color	[HKCU\Software\Microsoft\Internet Explorer\Settings]
Anchor Underline	[HKCU\Software\Microsoft\Internet Explorer\Main]
AppData	[HKCU\Software\Microsoft\Windows\ CurrentVersion\Explorer\Shell Folders]
AppData	[HKCU\Software\Microsoft\Windows\ CurrentVersion\Explorer\User Shell Folders]
APPDATA	[HKCU\Volatile Environment]
application/x-iphone	[HKCU\Software\Netscape\Netscape Navigator\Viewers]
application/x-mplayer2	[HKCU\Software\Netscape\Netscape Navigator\Suffixes]
application/x-mplayer2	[HKCU\Software\Netscape\Netscape Navigator\Viewers]
AppWorkSpace	[HKCU\Control Panel\Colors]
audio/aiff	[HKCU\Software\Netscape\Netscape Navigator\Suffixes]
audio/aiff	[HKCU\Software\Netscape\Netscape Navigator\Viewers]
audio/basic	[HKCU\Software\Netscape\Netscape Navigator\Suffixes]
audio/basic	[HKCU\Software\Netscape\Netscape Navigator\Viewers]
audio/mid	[HKCU\Software\Netscape\Netscape Navigator\Suffixes]
audio/mid	[HKCU\Software\Netscape\Netscape Navigator\Viewers]
audio/midi	[HKCU\Software\Netscape\Netscape Navigator\Suffixes]
audio/midi	[HKCU\Software\Netscape\Netscape Navigator\Viewers]
audio/mpeg	[HKCU\Software\Netscape\Netscape Navigator\Suffixes]

Entry Name	**Key**
audio/mpeg	[HKCU\Software\Netscape\Netscape Navigator\Viewers]
audio/wav	[HKCU\Software\Netscape\Netscape Navigator\Suffixes]
audio/wav	[HKCU\Software\Netscape\Netscape Navigator\Viewers]
audio/x-aiff	[HKCU\Software\Netscape\Netscape Navigator\Suffixes]
audio/x-aiff	[HKCU\Software\Netscape\Netscape Navigator\Viewers]
audio/x-midi	[HKCU\Software\Netscape\Netscape Navigator\Suffixes]
audio/x-midi	[HKCU\Software\Netscape\Netscape Navigator\Viewers]
audio/x-mpegurl	[HKCU\Software\Netscape\Netscape Navigator\Suffixes]
audio/x-mpegurl	[HKCU\Software\Netscape\Netscape Navigator\Viewers]
audio/x-wav	[HKCU\Software\Netscape\Netscape Navigator\Suffixes]
audio/x-wav	[HKCU\Software\Netscape\Netscape Navigator\Viewers]
AutoArrange	[HKCU\Software\Microsoft\Windows NT\CurrentVersion\Program Manager\Settings]
AutoConfigProxy	[HKCU\Software\Microsoft\Windows\CurrentVersion\Internet Settings]
AutoEndTasks	[HKCU\Control Panel\Desktop]
AutoRefresh	[HKCU\Software\Microsoft\RegEdt32\Settings]
AutoRepeatDelay	[HKCU\Control Panel\Accessibility\Keyboard Response]
AutoRepeatRate	[HKCU\Control Panel\Accessibility\Keyboard Response]
b	[HKCU\Software\Microsoft\Windows\CurrentVersion\Explorer\ComDlg32\LastVisitedMRU]
b	[HKCU\Software\Microsoft\Windows\CurrentVersion\Explorer\ComDlg32\OpenSaveMRU*]
b	[HKCU\Software\Microsoft\Windows\CurrentVersion\Explorer\ComDlg32\OpenSaveMRU\reg]
b	[HKCU\Software\Microsoft\Windows\CurrentVersion\Explorer\ComDlg32\OpenSaveMRU\TXT]
b	[HKCU\Software\Microsoft\Windows\CurrentVersion\Explorer\FileExts\.reg\OpenWithList]

Entry Name	Key
b	[HKCU\Software\Microsoft\Windows\CurrentVersion\Explorer\FileExts\.TXT\OpenWithList]
b	[HKCU\Software\Microsoft\Windows\CurrentVersion\Explorer\RecentDocs]
b	[HKCU\Software\Microsoft\Windows\CurrentVersion\Explorer\RecentDocs\.TXT]
b	[HKCU\Software\Microsoft\Windows\CurrentVersion\Explorer\RunMRU]
b086b6fafe513bc3	[HKCU\Software\Microsoft\Advanced INF Setup\IE40.BrowseUI\RegBackup\0]
b086b6fafe513bc3	[HKCU\Software\Microsoft\Advanced INF Setup\IE40.BrowseUI\RegBackup\0.map]
Background Color	[HKCU\Software\Microsoft\Internet Explorer\Settings]
Background	[HKCU\Control Panel\Colors]
BackgroundColor	[HKCU\Control Panel\Screen Saver.Marquee]
BaseClass	[HKCU\Software\Microsoft\Windows\CurrentVersion\Explorer\MountPoints\A]
BaseClass	[HKCU\Software\Microsoft\Windows\CurrentVersion\Explorer\MountPoints\C]
BaseClass	[HKCU\Software\Microsoft\Windows\CurrentVersion\Explorer\MountPoints\D]
Beep	[HKCU\Control Panel\Sound]
BorderWidth	[HKCU\Control Panel\Desktop\WindowMetrics]
BounceTime	[HKCU\Control Panel\Accessibility\Keyboard Response]
Boxes	[HKCU\Control Panel\Patterns]
Brick	[HKCU\Control Panel\Appearance\Schemes]
BrowseNewProcess	[HKCU\Software\Microsoft\Windows\CurrentVersion\Explorer\BrowseNew-Process]
BuildNumber	[HKCU\Software\Microsoft\Windows NT\CurrentVersion\Winlogon]
ButtonAlternateFace	[HKCU\Control Panel\Colors]
ButtonDkShadow	[HKCU\Control Panel\Colors]
ButtonFace	[HKCU\Control Panel\Colors]
ButtonHilight	[HKCU\Control Panel\Colors]
ButtonLight	[HKCU\Control Panel\Colors]
ButtonShadow	[HKCU\Control Panel\Colors]
ButtonText	[HKCU\Control Panel\Colors]
c	[HKCU\Software\Microsoft\Windows\CurrentVersion\Explorer\ComDlg32\OpenSaveMRU*]

....

Entry Name	Key
c	[HKCU\Software\Microsoft\Windows\CurrentVersion\Explorer\ComDlg32\OpenSaveMRU\reg]
c	[HKCU\Software\Microsoft\Windows\CurrentVersion\Explorer\ComDlg32\OpenSaveMRU\TXT]
c	[HKCU\Software\Microsoft\Windows\CurrentVersion\Explorer\RecentDocs]
c	[HKCU\Software\Microsoft\Windows\CurrentVersion\Explorer\RecentDocs\.TXT]
C:\\PROGRA~1\\WINDOW~2\\mplayer2.exe	[HKCU\Software\Netscape\Netscape Navigator\User Trusted External Applications]
CabView	[HKCU\Software\Microsoft\Windows\CurrentVersion\Explorer\Streams\0]
CabView	[HKCU\Software\Microsoft\Windows\CurrentVersion\Explorer\Streams\1]
CabView	[HKCU\Software\Microsoft\Windows\CurrentVersion\Explorer\Streams\2]
Cache	[HKCU\Software\Microsoft\Internet Explorer\International\CpMRU]
Cache	[HKCU\Software\Microsoft\Windows\CurrentVersion\Explorer\MountPoints\A_Autorun]
Cache	[HKCU\Software\Microsoft\Windows\CurrentVersion\Explorer\MountPoints\A_DIL]
Cache	[HKCU\Software\Microsoft\Windows\CurrentVersion\Explorer\MountPoints\C_Autorun]
Cache	[HKCU\Software\Microsoft\Windows\CurrentVersion\Explorer\MountPoints\C_DIL]
Cache	[HKCU\Software\Microsoft\Windows\CurrentVersion\Explorer\MountPoints\C_DriveFlags]
Cache	[HKCU\Software\Microsoft\Windows\CurrentVersion\Explorer\MountPoints\C_GFA]
Cache	[HKCU\Software\Microsoft\Windows\CurrentVersion\Explorer\MountPoints\C_GVI]
Cache	[HKCU\Software\Microsoft\Windows\CurrentVersion\Explorer\MountPoints\D_Autorun]
Cache	[HKCU\Software\Microsoft\Windows\CurrentVersion\Explorer\MountPoints\D_DIL]

Entry Name	Key
Cache	[HKCU\Software\Microsoft\Windows\CurrentVersion\Explorer\MountPoints\D_LabelFromReg]
Cache	[HKCU\Software\Microsoft\Windows\CurrentVersion\Explorer\MountPoints\D_DriveFlags]
Cache	[HKCU\Software\Microsoft\Windows\CurrentVersion\Explorer\Shell Folders]
Cache	[HKCU\Software\Microsoft\Windows\CurrentVersion\Explorer\User Shell Folders]
Cache_Update_Frequency	[HKCU\Software\Microsoft\Internet Explorer\Main]
CacheLimit	[HKCU\Software\Microsoft\Windows\CurrentVersion\Internet Settings\5.0\Cache\Content]
CacheLimit	[HKCU\Software\Microsoft\Windows\CurrentVersion\Internet Settings\5.0\Cache\Cookies]
CacheLimit	[HKCU\Software\Microsoft\Windows\CurrentVersion\Internet Settings\5.0\Cache\Extensible Cache\MSHist011999081419990815]
CacheLimit	[HKCU\Software\Microsoft\Windows\CurrentVersion\Internet Settings\5.0\Cache\History]
CacheLimit	[HKCU\Software\Microsoft\Windows\CurrentVersion\Internet Settings\Cache\Content]
CacheLimit	[HKCU\Software\Microsoft\Windows\CurrentVersion\Internet Settings\Cache\Cookies]
CacheLimit	[HKCU\Software\Microsoft\Windows\CurrentVersion\Internet Settings\Cache\History]
CacheOptions	[HKCU\Software\Microsoft\Windows\CurrentVersion\Internet Settings\5.0\Cache\Extensible Cache\MSHist011999081419990815]
CachePath	[HKCU\Software\Microsoft\Windows\CurrentVersion\Internet Settings\5.0\Cache\Extensible Cache\MSHist011999081419990815]
CachePrefix	[HKCU\Software\Microsoft\Windows\CurrentVersion\Internet Settings\5.0\Cache\Content]
CachePrefix	[HKCU\Software\Microsoft\Windows\CurrentVersion\Internet Settings\5.0\Cache\Cookies]

Entry Name	Key
CachePrefix	[HKCU\Software\Microsoft\Windows\ CurrentVersion\Internet Settings\5.0\Cache\Extensible Cache\MSHist011999081419990815]
CachePrefix	[HKCU\Software\Microsoft\Windows\ CurrentVersion\Internet Settings\5.0\Cache\History]
CaptionFont	[HKCU\Control Panel\Desktop\ WindowMetrics]
CaptionHeight	[HKCU\Control Panel\Desktop\ WindowMetrics]
CaptionWidth	[HKCU\Control Panel\Desktop\ WindowMetrics]
CaretWidth	[HKCU\Control Panel\Desktop]
CD Quality	[HKCU\Software\Microsoft\Multimedia\ Audio\WaveFormats]
Certificates	[HKCU\Software\Microsoft\System- Certificates\Root\ProtectedRoots]
CharSet	[HKCU\Control Panel\Screen Saver.Marquee]
CleanShutdown	[HKCU\Software\Microsoft\Windows\ CurrentVersion\Explorer]
Clear Screen	[HKCU\Control Panel\Screen Saver.Mystify]
Client ID	[HKCU\Software\Microsoft\ MediaPlayer\Player\Settings]
CLIENTNAME	[HKCU\Volatile Environment]
ClrBackColor	[HKCU\Software\Microsoft\Media- Player\Control\PlayBar]
ClrDownload	[HKCU\Software\Microsoft\Media- Player\Control\PlayBar]
ClrForeColor	[HKCU\Software\Microsoft\Media- Player\Control\PlayBar]
ClrHighlight	[HKCU\Software\Microsoft\Media- Player\Control\PlayBar]
ClrShadow	[HKCU\Software\Microsoft\Media- Player\Control\PlayBar]
ClrStatic	[HKCU\Software\Microsoft\Media- Player\Control\PlayBar]
ClrViewed	[HKCU\Software\Microsoft\Media- Player\Control\PlayBar]
Color Schemes	[HKCU\Control Panel\Current]
ColorA	[HKCU\Control Panel\Custom Colors]
ColorB	[HKCU\Control Panel\Custom Colors]
ColorC	[HKCU\Control Panel\Custom Colors]
ColorD	[HKCU\Control Panel\Custom Colors]
ColorE	[HKCU\Control Panel\Custom Colors]
ColorF	[HKCU\Control Panel\Custom Colors]

Entry Name	Key
ColorG	[HKCU\Control Panel\Custom Colors]
ColorH	[HKCU\Control Panel\Custom Colors]
ColorI	[HKCU\Control Panel\Custom Colors]
ColorJ	[HKCU\Control Panel\Custom Colors]
ColorK	[HKCU\Control Panel\Custom Colors]
ColorL	[HKCU\Control Panel\Custom Colors]
ColorM	[HKCU\Control Panel\Custom Colors]
ColorN	[HKCU\Control Panel\Custom Colors]
ColorO	[HKCU\Control Panel\Custom Colors]
ColorP	[HKCU\Control Panel\Custom Colors]
ColorTable00	[HKCU\Console]
ColorTable01	[HKCU\Console]
ColorTable02	[HKCU\Console]
ColorTable03	[HKCU\Console]
ColorTable04	[HKCU\Console]
ColorTable05	[HKCU\Console]
ColorTable06	[HKCU\Console]
ColorTable07	[HKCU\Console]
ColorTable08	[HKCU\Console]
ColorTable09	[HKCU\Console]
ColorTable10	[HKCU\Console]
ColorTable11	[HKCU\Console]
ColorTable12	[HKCU\Console]
ColorTable13	[HKCU\Console]
ColorTable14	[HKCU\Console]
ColorTable15	[HKCU\Console]
Communications	[HKCU\Software\Microsoft\Windows\CurrentVersion\GrpConv\MapGroups]
CompletionChar	[HKCU\Software\Microsoft\Command Processor]
ComponentsPositioned	[HKCU\Software\Microsoft\Internet Explorer\Desktop\General]
ConfirmOnDelete	[HKCU\Software\Microsoft\RegEdt32\Settings]
Cookies	[HKCU\Software\Microsoft\Windows\CurrentVersion\Explorer\Shell Folders]
Cookies	[HKCU\Software\Microsoft\Windows\CurrentVersion\Explorer\User Shell Folders]
CoolSwitch	[HKCU\Control Panel\Desktop]
CoolSwitchColumns	[HKCU\Control Panel\Desktop]
CoolSwitchRows	[HKCU\Control Panel\Desktop]
Count	[HKCU\Software\Microsoft\Windows\CurrentVersion\Group Policy\GroupMembership]
CoverPageDir	[HKCU\Software\Microsoft\Fax\Setup]
CoverPageEditor	[HKCU\Software\Microsoft\Fax\Setup]
Critters	[HKCU\Control Panel\Patterns]
Current	[HKCU\Control Panel\Appearance]

Entry Name	**Key**
CurrentLevel	[HKCU\Software\Microsoft\Windows\CurrentVersion\Internet Settings\Zones\0]
CurrentLevel	[HKCU\Software\Microsoft\Windows\CurrentVersion\Internet Settings\Zones\1]
CurrentLevel	[HKCU\Software\Microsoft\Windows\CurrentVersion\Internet Settings\Zones\2]
CurrentLevel	[HKCU\Software\Microsoft\Windows\CurrentVersion\Internet Settings\Zones\3]
CurrentLevel	[HKCU\Software\Microsoft\Windows\CurrentVersion\Internet Settings\Zones\4]
CurrentPowerPolicy	[HKCU\Control Panel\PowerCfg]
CurrentState	[HKCU\Software\Microsoft\Internet Explorer\Desktop\Components\0]
CursorBlinkRate	[HKCU\Control Panel\Desktop]
CursorSize	[HKCU\Console]
d	[HKCU\Software\Microsoft\Windows\CurrentVersion\Explorer\ComDlg32\OpenSaveMRU*]
d	[HKCU\Software\Microsoft\Windows\CurrentVersion\Explorer\ComDlg32\OpenSaveMRU\reg]
d	[HKCU\Software\Microsoft\Windows\CurrentVersion\Explorer\ComDlg32\OpenSaveMRU\TXT]
d	[HKCU\Software\Microsoft\Windows\CurrentVersion\Explorer\RecentDocs]
d	[HKCU\Software\Microsoft\Windows\CurrentVersion\Explorer\RecentDocs\.TXT]
DebugOptions	[HKCU\Software\Microsoft\Windows NT\CurrentVersion\Windows]
DefaultColor	[HKCU\Software\Microsoft\Command Processor]
DefaultFormat	[HKCU\Software\Microsoft\Multimedia\Audio]
DelayBeforeAcceptance	[HKCU\Control Panel\Accessibility\Keyboard Response]
Density	[HKCU\Control Panel\Screen Saver.Stars]
Description	[HKCU\Control Panel\Microsoft Input Devices\Mouse\Exceptions\584]
Description	[HKCU\Control Panel\PowerCfg\PowerPolicies\0]

Entry Name	Key
Description	[HKCU\Control Panel\PowerCfg\PowerPolicies\1]
Description	[HKCU\Control Panel\PowerCfg\PowerPolicies\2]
Description	[HKCU\Control Panel\PowerCfg\PowerPolicies\3]
Description	[HKCU\Control Panel\PowerCfg\PowerPolicies\4]
Description	[HKCU\Control Panel\PowerCfg\PowerPolicies\5]
Description	[HKCU\Software\Microsoft\Windows\CurrentVersion\Internet Settings\Zones\0]
Description	[HKCU\Software\Microsoft\Windows\CurrentVersion\Internet Settings\Zones\1]
Description	[HKCU\Software\Microsoft\Windows\CurrentVersion\Internet Settings\Zones\2]
Description	[HKCU\Software\Microsoft\Windows\CurrentVersion\Internet Settings\Zones\3]
Description	[HKCU\Software\Microsoft\Windows\CurrentVersion\Internet Settings\Zones\4]
Desert	[HKCU\Control Panel\Appearance\Schemes]
DeskHtmlMinorVersion	[HKCU\Software\Microsoft\Internet Explorer\Desktop\Components]
DeskHtmlVersion	[HKCU\Software\Microsoft\Internet Explorer\Desktop\Components]
Desktop	[HKCU\Software\Microsoft\Windows\CurrentVersion\Explorer\Shell Folders]
Desktop	[HKCU\Software\Microsoft\Windows\CurrentVersion\Explorer\User Shell Folders]
DesktopChanged	[HKCU\Software\Microsoft\Internet Connection Wizard]
DesktopComponent	[HKCU\Software\Microsoft\Windows\CurrentVersion\Webcheck\Store.1\{02C09C60-E687-01BE-0000-00004BFBD552}]
Diamonds	[HKCU\Control Panel\Patterns]
Directory Name	[HKCU\Identities\{0ACE9E60-3362-4310-B2E4-66E22371AB5E}]
Disable Script Debugger	[HKCU\Software\Microsoft\Internet Explorer\Main]
Display Inline Images	[HKCU\Software\Microsoft\Internet Explorer\Main]

Entry Name	Key
Display	[HKCU\Software\Microsoft\Internet Explorer\Desktop\Scheme]
display.drv	[HKCU\Software\Microsoft\Windows NT\CurrentVersion\Program Manager\Settings]
DisplayName	[HKCU\Software\Microsoft\Windows\CurrentVersion\Internet Settings\Zones\0]
DisplayName	[HKCU\Software\Microsoft\Windows\CurrentVersion\Internet Settings\Zones\1]
DisplayName	[HKCU\Software\Microsoft\Windows\CurrentVersion\Internet Settings\Zones\2]
DisplayName	[HKCU\Software\Microsoft\Windows\CurrentVersion\Internet Settings\Zones\3]
DisplayName	[HKCU\Software\Microsoft\Windows\CurrentVersion\Internet Settings\Zones\4]
Do404Search	[HKCU\Software\Microsoft\Internet Explorer\Main]
Documents	[HKCU\Software\Microsoft\Windows NT\CurrentVersion\Windows]
DontPrettyPath	[HKCU\Software\Microsoft\Windows\CurrentVersion\Explorer\Advanced]
DosPrint	[HKCU\Software\Microsoft\Windows NT\CurrentVersion\Windows]
DoubleClickHeight	[HKCU\Control Panel\Mouse]
DoubleClickSpeed	[HKCU\Control Panel\Mouse]
DoubleClickWidth	[HKCU\Control Panel\Mouse]
DragFullWindows	[HKCU\Control Panel\Desktop]
DragHeight	[HKCU\Control Panel\Desktop]
DragWidth	[HKCU\Control Panel\Desktop]
e	[HKCU\Software\Microsoft\Windows\CurrentVersion\Explorer\ComDlg32\OpenSaveMRU*]
e	[HKCU\Software\Microsoft\Windows\CurrentVersion\Explorer\ComDlg32\OpenSaveMRU\reg]
e	[HKCU\Software\Microsoft\Windows\CurrentVersion\Explorer\RecentDocs]
Edit	[HKCU\Software\Microsoft\Internet Explorer\Desktop\Scheme]
EditLevel	[HKCU\Software\Microsoft\Windows NT\CurrentVersion\Program Manager\Restrictions]
Eggplant	[HKCU\Control Panel\Appearance\Schemes]

Entry Name	Key
Empty	[HKCU\Software\Microsoft\Windows\ CurrentVersion\Explorer\CLSID\{645FF04 0-5081-101B-9F08- 00AA002F954E}\DefaultIcon]
Enable	[HKCU\Software\Microsoft\Internet Explorer\International\CpMRU]
Enabled	[HKCU\Software\Microsoft\Internet Explorer\Security\P3Global]
EnableExtensions	[HKCU\Software\Microsoft\Command Processor]
EnableHttp1_1	[HKCU\Software\Microsoft\Windows\ CurrentVersion\Internet Settings]
EnableJIT	[HKCU\Software\Microsoft\Java VM]
EnableLogging	[HKCU\Software\Microsoft\Java VM]
EnableManualAnswer	[HKCU\Software\Microsoft\Fax\UserInfo]
EnableResend	[HKCU\Software\Microsoft\NetShow\ Player\Remote]
EndColor1	[HKCU\Control Panel\Screen Saver.Mystify]
EndColor2	[HKCU\Control Panel\Screen Saver.Mystify]
ExcludeProfileDirs	[HKCU\Software\Microsoft\Windows NT\CurrentVersion\Winlogon]
ExtendedSounds	[HKCU\Control Panel\Sound]
f	[HKCU\Software\Microsoft\Windows\ CurrentVersion\Explorer\ComDlg32\ OpenSaveMRU*]
f	[HKCU\Software\Microsoft\Windows\ CurrentVersion\Explorer\ComDlg32\ OpenSaveMRU\reg]
FaceName	[HKCU\Console]
Factor	[HKCU\Software\Microsoft\Internet Explorer\International\CpMRU]
FaultCount	[HKCU\Software\Microsoft\Windows\ CurrentVersion\Explorer]
FaultTime	[HKCU\Software\Microsoft\Windows\ CurrentVersion\Explorer]
Favorites	[HKCU\Software\Microsoft\Windows\ CurrentVersion\Explorer\Shell Folders]
Favorites	[HKCU\Software\Microsoft\Windows\ CurrentVersion\Explorer\User Shell Folders]
FaxNumber	[HKCU\Software\Microsoft\Fax\UserInfo]
file	[HKCU\Software\Microsoft\Windows\ CurrentVersion\Internet Settings\ZoneMap\ProtocolDefaults]
File0	[HKCU\Identities\{0ACE9E60-3362-4310- B2E4-66E22371AB5E}\Software\ Microsoft\Outlook Express\5.0\Recent Stationery List]

Entry Name	Key
File1	[HKCU\Identities\{0ACE9E60-3362-4310-B2E4-66E22371AB5E}\Software\Microsoft\Outlook Express\5.0\Recent Stationery List]
File1	[HKCU\Software\Microsoft\Microsoft Management Console\Recent File List]
File2	[HKCU\Identities\{0ACE9E60-3362-4310-B2E4-66E22371AB5E}\Software\Microsoft\Outlook Express\5.0\Recent Stationery List]
File3	[HKCU\Identities\{0ACE9E60-3362-4310-B2E4-66E22371AB5E}\Software\Microsoft\Outlook Express\5.0\Recent Stationery List]
File4	[HKCU\Identities\{0ACE9E60-3362-4310-B2E4-66E22371AB5E}\Software\Microsoft\Outlook Express\5.0\Recent Stationery List]
File5	[HKCU\Identities\{0ACE9E60-3362-4310-B2E4-66E22371AB5E}\Software\Microsoft\Outlook Express\5.0\Recent Stationery List]
File6	[HKCU\Identities\{0ACE9E60-3362-4310-B2E4-66E22371AB5E}\Software\Microsoft\Outlook Express\5.0\Recent Stationery List]
FileName	[HKCU\Control Panel\Microsoft Input Devices\Mouse\Exceptions\584]
Filter	[HKCU\Software\Microsoft\Windows\CurrentVersion\Explorer\Advanced]
FindFlags	[HKCU\Software\Microsoft\Windows\CurrentVersion\Applets\Regedit]
First Home Page	[HKCU\Software\Microsoft\Internet Explorer\Main]
Flags	[HKCU\Control Panel\Accessibility\HighContrast]
Flags	[HKCU\Control Panel\Accessibility\Keyboard Response]
Flags	[HKCU\Control Panel\Accessibility\MouseKeys]
Flags	[HKCU\Control Panel\Accessibility\SoundSentry]
Flags	[HKCU\Control Panel\Accessibility\StickyKeys]
Flags	[HKCU\Control Panel\Accessibility\TimeOut]
Flags	[HKCU\Control Panel\Accessibility\ToggleKeys]

Entry Name	Key
Flags	[HKCU\Software\Microsoft\Internet Explorer\Desktop\Components\0]
Flags	[HKCU\Software\Microsoft\System-Certificates\ACRS\PhysicalStores\.LocalMachine]
Flags	[HKCU\Software\Microsoft\Windows\CurrentVersion\Internet Settings\Zones\0]
Flags	[HKCU\Software\Microsoft\Windows\CurrentVersion\Internet Settings\Zones\1]
Flags	[HKCU\Software\Microsoft\Windows\CurrentVersion\Internet Settings\Zones\2]
Flags	[HKCU\Software\Microsoft\Windows\CurrentVersion\Internet Settings\Zones\3]
Flags	[HKCU\Software\Microsoft\Windows\CurrentVersion\Internet Settings\Zones\4]
Font	[HKCU\Control Panel\Screen Saver.Marquee]
FontFamily	[HKCU\Console]
Fonts	[HKCU\Software\Microsoft\Windows\CurrentVersion\Explorer\Shell Folders]
FontSize	[HKCU\Console]
FontSmoothing	[HKCU\Control Panel\Desktop]
FontWeight	[HKCU\Console]
ForegroundFlashCount	[HKCU\Control Panel\Desktop]
ForegroundLockTimeout	[HKCU\Control Panel\Desktop]
FriendlyName	[HKCU\Software\Microsoft\Internet Explorer\Desktop\Components\0]
fSavePageSettings	[HKCU\Software\Microsoft\Notepad]
fSaveWindowPositions	[HKCU\Software\Microsoft\Notepad]
FSTextEffect	[HKCU\Control Panel\Accessibility\SoundSentry]
ftp	[HKCU\Software\Microsoft\Windows\CurrentVersion\Internet Settings\ZoneMap\ProtocolDefaults]
Full	[HKCU\Software\Microsoft\Windows\CurrentVersion\Explorer\CLSID\{645FF040-5081-101B-9F08-00AA002F954E}\DefaultIcon]
FullName	[HKCU\Software\Microsoft\Fax\UserInfo]
FullPath	[HKCU\Software\Microsoft\Windows\CurrentVersion\Explorer\CabinetState]
FullScreen	[HKCU\Console]
fWrap	[HKCU\Software\Microsoft\Notepad]

Entry Name	Key
g	[HKCU\Software\Microsoft\Windows\CurrentVersion\Explorer\ComDlg32\OpenSaveMRU*]
g	[HKCU\Software\Microsoft\Windows\CurrentVersion\Explorer\ComDlg32\OpenSaveMRU\reg]
Games	[HKCU\Software\Microsoft\Windows\CurrentVersion\GrpConv\MapGroups]
GeneralFlags	[HKCU\Software\Microsoft\Internet Explorer\Desktop\Components]
GradientActiveTitle	[HKCU\Control Panel\Colors]
GradientInactiveTitle	[HKCU\Control Panel\Colors]
GrayText	[HKCU\Control Panel\Colors]
GridGranularity	[HKCU\Control Panel\Desktop]
Group0	[HKCU\Software\Microsoft\Windows\CurrentVersion\Group Policy\GroupMembership]
Group1	[HKCU\Software\Microsoft\Windows\CurrentVersion\Group Policy\GroupMembership]
Group2	[HKCU\Software\Microsoft\Windows\CurrentVersion\Group Policy\GroupMembership]
Group3	[HKCU\Software\Microsoft\Windows\CurrentVersion\Group Policy\GroupMembership]
Group4	[HKCU\Software\Microsoft\Windows\CurrentVersion\Group Policy\GroupMembership]
Group5	[HKCU\Software\Microsoft\Windows\CurrentVersion\Group Policy\GroupMembership]
Group6	[HKCU\Software\Microsoft\Windows\CurrentVersion\Group Policy\GroupMembership]
Group7	[HKCU\Software\Microsoft\Windows\CurrentVersion\Group Policy\GroupMembership]
h	[HKCU\Software\Microsoft\Windows\CurrentVersion\Explorer\ComDlg32\OpenSaveMRU*]
height	[HKCU\Software\Microsoft\Internet Explorer\Document Windows]
Height	[HKCU\Software\Microsoft\RegEdt32\Settings]
Hidden	[HKCU\Software\Microsoft\Windows\CurrentVersion\Explorer\Advanced]
HideFileExt	[HKCU\Software\Microsoft\Windows\CurrentVersion\Explorer\Advanced]

Entry Name	Key
HideIcons	[HKCU\Software\Microsoft\Windows\CurrentVersion\Explorer\Advanced]
High Contrast #1 (extra large)	[HKCU\Control Panel\Appearance\Schemes]
High Contrast #1 (large)	[HKCU\Control Panel\Appearance\Schemes]
High Contrast #1	[HKCU\Control Panel\Appearance\Schemes]
High Contrast #2 (extra large)	[HKCU\Control Panel\Appearance\Schemes]
High Contrast #2 (large)	[HKCU\Control Panel\Appearance\Schemes]
High Contrast #2	[HKCU\Control Panel\Appearance\Schemes]
High Contrast Black extra large)	[HKCU\Control Panel\Appearance\Schemes]
High Contrast Black (large)	[HKCU\Control Panel\Appearance\Schemes]
High Contrast Black	[HKCU\Control Panel\Appearance\Schemes]
High Contrast Scheme	[HKCU\Control Panel\Accessibility\HighContrast]
High Contrast White (extra large)	[HKCU\Control Panel\Appearance\Schemes]
High Contrast White (large)	[HKCU\Control Panel\Appearance\Schemes]
High Contrast White	[HKCU\Control Panel\Appearance\Schemes]
Hilight	[HKCU\Control Panel\Colors]
HilightText	[HKCU\Control Panel\Colors]
History	[HKCU\Software\Microsoft\Windows\CurrentVersion\Explorer\Shell Folders]
History	[HKCU\Software\Microsoft\Windows\CurrentVersion\Explorer\User Shell Folders]
HistoryBufferSize	[HKCU\Console]
HotTrackingColor	[HKCU\Control Panel\Colors]
HRZR_EHACNGU	[HKCU\Software\Microsoft\Windows\CurrentVersion\Explorer\UserAssist\{75048700-EF1F-11D0-9888-006097DEACF9}\Count]
HRZR_EHACNGU:P:\\Cebtenz Svyrf\\Vagrearg Rkcybere\\Pbaarpgvba Jvmneq\\vpjpbaa1.rkr	[HKCU\Software\Microsoft\Windows\CurrentVersion\Explorer\UserAssist\{75048700-EF1F-11D0-9888-006097DEACF9}\Count]
HRZR_EHACNGU:P:\\JVAAG\\ertrqvg.rkr	[HKCU\Software\Microsoft\Windows\CurrentVersion\Explorer\UserAssist\{75048700-EF1F-11D0-9888-006097DEACF9}\Count]

....

Entry Name	**Key**
HRZR_EHACNGU:P:\\JVAAG\\flfgrz32\\ABGRCNQ.RKR	[HKCU\Software\Microsoft\Windows\CurrentVersion\Explorer\UserAssist\{75048700-EF1F-11D0-9888-006097DEACF9}\Count]
HRZR_EHACNGU:P:\\JVAAG\\flfgrz32\\ehaqyy32.rkr	[HKCU\Software\Microsoft\Windows\CurrentVersion\Explorer\UserAssist\{75048700-EF1F-11D0-9888-006097DEACF9}\Count]
HRZR_EHACNGU:P:\\JVAAG\\Flfgrz32\\ertrqg32.rkr	[HKCU\Software\Microsoft\Windows\CurrentVersion\Explorer\UserAssist\{75048700-EF1F-11D0-9888-006097DEACF9}\Count]
HRZR_EHACNGU:P:\\JVAAG\\flfgrz32\\pzq.rkr	[HKCU\Software\Microsoft\Windows\CurrentVersion\Explorer\UserAssist\{75048700-EF1F-11D0-9888-006097DEACF9}\Count]
HRZR_EHACNGU:P:\\JVAAG\\Flfgrz32\\zfgvavg.rkr	[HKCU\Software\Microsoft\Windows\CurrentVersion\Explorer\UserAssist\{75048700-EF1F-11D0-9888-006097DEACF9}\Count]
HRZR_EHACNGU:P:\\JVAAG\\flfgrz32\\ZZP.rkr	[HKCU\Software\Microsoft\Windows\CurrentVersion\Explorer\UserAssist\{75048700-EF1F-11D0-9888-006097DEACF9}\Count]
HRZR_EHACVQY	[HKCU\Software\Microsoft\Windows\CurrentVersion\Explorer\UserAssist\{75048700-EF1F-11D0-9888-006097DEACF9}\Count]
HRZR_EHACVQY:%pfvqy2%\\Bhgybbx Rkcerff.yax	[HKCU\Software\Microsoft\Windows\CurrentVersion\Explorer\UserAssist\{75048700-EF1F-11D0-9888-006097DEACF9}\Count]
HRZR_EHACVQY:%pfvqy2%\\Fgneghc	[HKCU\Software\Microsoft\Windows\CurrentVersion\Explorer\UserAssist\{75048700-EF1F-11D0-9888-006097DEACF9}\Count]
HRZR_EHACVQY:%pfvqy2%\\Npprffbevrf	[HKCU\Software\Microsoft\Windows\CurrentVersion\Explorer\UserAssist\{75048700-EF1F-11D0-9888-006097DEACF9}\Count]
HRZR_EHACVQY:%pfvqy2%\\Npprffbevrf\\Abgrcnq.yax	[HKCU\Software\Microsoft\Windows\CurrentVersion\Explorer\UserAssist\{75048700-EF1F-11D0-9888-006097DEACF9}\Count]
HRZR_EHACVQY:%pfvqy2%\\Npprffbevrf\\Cnvag.yax	[HKCU\Software\Microsoft\Windows\CurrentVersion\Explorer\UserAssist\{75048700-EF1F-11D0-9888-006097DEACF9}\Count]

Entry Name	**Key**
HRZR_EHACVQY:%pfvqy2%\\ Npprffbevrf\\Flapuebavmr.yax	[HKCU\Software\Microsoft\Windows\ CurrentVersion\Explorer\UserAssist\ {75048700-EF1F-11D0-9888- 006097DEACF9}\Count]
HRZR_EHACVQY:%pfvqy2%\\ Npprffbevrf\\Flfgrz Gbbyf	[HKCU\Software\Microsoft\Windows\ CurrentVersion\Explorer\UserAssist\ {75048700-EF1F-11D0-9888- 006097DEACF9}\Count]
HRZR_EHACVQY:%pfvqy2%\\ Npprffbevrf\\JbeqCnq.yax	[HKCU\Software\Microsoft\Windows\ CurrentVersion\Explorer\UserAssist\ {75048700-EF1F-11D0-9888- 006097DEACF9}\Count]
HRZR_EHACVQY:%pfvqy2%\\ Npprffbevrf\\Jvaqbjf Rkcybere.yax	[HKCU\Software\Microsoft\Windows\ CurrentVersion\Explorer\UserAssist\ {75048700-EF1F-11D0-9888- 006097DEACF9}\Count]
HRZR_EHACVQY:%pfvqy2%\\ Npprffbevrf\\Npprffvovyvgl	[HKCU\Software\Microsoft\Windows\ CurrentVersion\Explorer\UserAssist\ {75048700-EF1F-11D0-9888- 006097DEACF9}\Count]
HRZR_EHACVQY:%pfvqy2%\\ Npprffbevrf\\Nqqerff Obbx.yax	[HKCU\Software\Microsoft\Windows\ CurrentVersion\Explorer\UserAssist\ {75048700-EF1F-11D0-9888- 006097DEACF9}\Count]
HRZR_EHACVQY:%pfvqy2%\\ Npprffbevrf\\Pbzzhavpngvba	[HKCU\Software\Microsoft\Windows\ CurrentVersion\Explorer\UserAssist\ {75048700-EF1F-11D0-9888- 006097DEACF9}\Count]
HRZR_EHACVQY:%pfvqy2%\\ Npprffbevrf\\Pbzznaq Cebzcg.yax	[HKCU\Software\Microsoft\Windows\ CurrentVersion\Explorer\UserAssist\ {75048700-EF1F-11D0-9888- 006097DEACF9}\Count]
HRZR_EHACVQY:%pfvqy2%\\ Npprffbevrf\\Pnyphyngbe.yax	[HKCU\Software\Microsoft\Windows\ CurrentVersion\Explorer\UserAssist\ {75048700-EF1F-11D0-9888- 006097DEACF9}\Count]
HRZR_EHACVQY:%pfvqy2%\\ Npprffbevrf\\Ragregnvazrag	[HKCU\Software\Microsoft\Windows\ CurrentVersion\Explorer\UserAssist\ {75048700-EF1F-11D0-9888- 006097DEACF9}\Count]
HRZR_EHACVQY:%pfvqy2%\\ Npprffbevrf\\Tnzrf	[HKCU\Software\Microsoft\Windows\ CurrentVersion\Explorer\UserAssist\ {75048700-EF1F-11D0-9888- 006097DEACF9}\Count]
HRZR_EHACVQY:%pfvqy2%\\ Npprffbevrf\\Vzntvat.yax	[HKCU\Software\Microsoft\Windows\ CurrentVersion\Explorer\UserAssist\ {75048700-EF1F-11D0-9888- 006097DEACF9}\Count]

Entry Name

Key

HRZR_EHACVQY:%pfvqy2%\\
Npprffbevrf\\Zvpebfbsg
Fpevcg Qrohttre

[HKCU\Software\Microsoft\Windows\
CurrentVersion\Explorer\UserAssist\
{75048700-EF1F-11D0-9888-
006097DEACF9}\Count]

HRZR_EHACVQY:%pfvqy2%\\
Nqzvavfgengvir Gbbyf

[HKCU\Software\Microsoft\Windows\
CurrentVersion\Explorer\UserAssist\
{75048700-EF1F-11D0-9888-
006097DEACF9}\Count]

HRZR_EHACVQY:%pfvqy2%\\
Nqzvavfgengvir Gbbyf\\
Argjbex Zbavgbe.yax

[HKCU\Software\Microsoft\Windows\
CurrentVersion\Explorer\UserAssist\
{75048700-EF1F-11D0-9888-
006097DEACF9}\Count]

HRZR_EHACVQY:%pfvqy2%\\
Nqzvavfgengvir Gbbyf\\
Cresbeznapr.yax

[HKCU\Software\Microsoft\Windows\
CurrentVersion\Explorer\UserAssist\
{75048700-EF1F-11D0-9888-
006097DEACF9}\Count]

HRZR_EHACVQY:%pfvqy2%\\
Nqzvavfgengvir Gbbyf\\
DbF Nqzvffvba Pbageby.yax

[HKCU\Software\Microsoft\Windows\
CurrentVersion\Explorer\UserAssist\
{75048700-EF1F-11D0-9888-
006097DEACF9}\Count]

HRZR_EHACVQY:%pfvqy2%\\
Nqzvavfgengvir Gbbyf\\
Ebhgvat naq Erzbgr Npprff.yax

[HKCU\Software\Microsoft\Windows\
CurrentVersion\Explorer\
UserAssist\{75048700-EF1F-11D0-9888-
006097DEACF9}\Count]

HRZR_EHACVQY:%pfvqy2%\\
Nqzvavfgengvir Gbbyf\\
Erzbgr Fgbentr.yax

[HKCU\Software\Microsoft\Windows\
CurrentVersion\Explorer\
UserAssist\{75048700-EF1F-11D0-9888-
006097DEACF9}\Count]

HRZR_EHACVQY:%pfvqy2%\\
Nqzvavfgengvir Gbbyf\\
Freire Rkgrafvbaf
Nqzvavfgengbe.yax

[HKCU\Software\Microsoft\Windows\
CurrentVersion\Explorer\

UserAssist\{75048700-EF1F-11D0-9888-
006097DEACF9}\Count]

HRZR_EHACVQY:%pfvqy2%\\
Nqzvavfgengvir Gbbyf\\
Freivprf.yax

[HKCU\Software\Microsoft\Windows\
CurrentVersion\Explorer\
UserAssist\{75048700-EF1F-11D0-9888-
006097DEACF9}\Count]

HRZR_EHACVQY:%pfvqy2%\\
Nqzvavfgengvir Gbbyf\\
Grezvany Freivprf
Pbasvthengvba.yax

[HKCU\Software\Microsoft\Windows\
CurrentVersion\Explorer\UserAssist\
{75048700-EF1F-11D0-9888-
006097DEACF9}\Count]

HRZR_EHACVQY:%pfvqy2%\\
Nqzvavfgengvir Gbbyf\\
Grezvany Freivprf Pyvrag
Perngbe.yax

[HKCU\Software\Microsoft\Windows\
CurrentVersion\Explorer\UserAssist\
{75048700-EF1F-11D0-9888-
006097DEACF9}\Count]

HRZR_EHACVQY:%pfvqy2%\\
Nqzvavfgengvir Gbbyf\\
Grezvany Freivprf
Yvprafvat.yax

[HKCU\Software\Microsoft\Windows\
CurrentVersion\Explorer\UserAssist\
{75048700-EF1F-11D0-9888-
006097DEACF9}\Count]

Entry Name	Key
HRZR_EHACVQY:%pfvqy2%\\ Nqzvavfgengvir Gbbyf\\ Grezvany Freivprf Znantre.yax	[HKCU\Software\Microsoft\Windows\ CurrentVersion\Explorer\UserAssist\ {75048700-EF1F-11D0-9888- 006097DEACF9}\Count]
HRZR_EHACVQY:%pfvqy2%\\ Nqzvavfgengvir Gbbyf\\JVAF.yax 006097DEACF9}\Count]	[HKCU\Software\Microsoft\Windows\ {75048700-EF1F-11D0-9888- CurrentVersion\Explorer\UserAssist\
HRZR_EHACVQY:%pfvqy2%\\ Nqzvavfgengvir Gbbyf\\ Pbaarpgvba Znantre Nqzvavfgengvba Xvg.yax	[HKCU\Software\Microsoft\Windows\ CurrentVersion\Explorer\UserAssist\ {75048700-EF1F-11D0-9888- 006097DEACF9}\Count]
HRZR_EHACVQY:%pfvqy2%\\ Nqzvavfgengvir Gbbyf\\ Pbasvther Lbhe Freire.yax	[HKCU\Software\Microsoft\Windows\ CurrentVersion\Explorer\UserAssist\ {75048700-EF1F-11D0-9888- 006097DEACF9}\Count]
HRZR_EHACVQY:%pfvqy2%\\ Nqzvavfgengvir Gbbyf\\ Pbzcbarag Freivprf.yax	[HKCU\Software\Microsoft\Windows\ CurrentVersion\Explorer\UserAssist\ {75048700-EF1F-11D0-9888- 006097DEACF9}\Count]
HRZR_EHACVQY:%pfvqy2%\\ Nqzvavfgengvir Gbbyf\\ Pbzchgre Znantrzrag.yax	[HKCU\Software\Microsoft\Windows\ CurrentVersion\Explorer\UserAssist\ {75048700-EF1F-11D0-9888- 006097DEACF9}\Count]
HRZR_EHACVQY:%pfvqy2%\\ Nqzvavfgengvir Gbbyf\\QAF.yax	[HKCU\Software\Microsoft\Windows\ CurrentVersion\Explorer\UserAssist\ {75048700-EF1F-11D0-9888- 006097DEACF9}\Count]
HRZR_EHACVQY:%pfvqy2%\\ Nqzvavfgengvir Gbbyf\\ Qngn Fbheprf (BQOP).yax	[HKCU\Software\Microsoft\Windows\ CurrentVersion\Explorer\UserAssist\ {75048700-EF1F-11D0-9888- 006097DEACF9}\Count]
HRZR_EHACVQY:%pfvqy2%\\ Nqzvavfgengvir Gbbyf\\QUPC.yax	[HKCU\Software\Microsoft\Windows\ CurrentVersion\Explorer\UserAssist\ {75048700-EF1F-11D0-9888- 006097DEACF9}\Count]
HRZR_EHACVQY:%pfvqy2%\\ Nqzvavfgengvir Gbbyf\\ Qverpgbel Freivpr Zvtengvba Gbby.yax	[HKCU\Software\Microsoft\Windows\ CurrentVersion\Explorer\UserAssist\ {75048700-EF1F-11D0-9888- 006097DEACF9}\Count]
HRZR_EHACVQY:%pfvqy2%\\ Nqzvavfgengvir Gbbyf\\ Qvfgevohgrq Svyr Flfgrz.yax	[HKCU\Software\Microsoft\Windows\ CurrentVersion\Explorer\UserAssist\ {75048700-EF1F-11D0-9888- 006097DEACF9}\Count]
HRZR_EHACVQY:%pfvqy2%\\ Nqzvavfgengvir Gbbyf\\ Rirag Ivrjre.yax	[HKCU\Software\Microsoft\Windows\ CurrentVersion\Explorer\UserAssist\ {75048700-EF1F-11D0-9888- 006097DEACF9}\Count]

Entry Name   **Key**

HRZR_EHACVQY:%pfvqy2%\\   [HKCU\Software\Microsoft\Windows\
Nqzvavfgengvir Gbbyf\\   CurrentVersion\Explorer\UserAssist\
Vagrearg Freivprf Znantre.yax   {75048700-EF1F-11D0-9888-
                                        006097DEACF9}\Count]

HRZR_EHACVQY:%pfvqy2%\\   [HKCU\Software\Microsoft\Windows\
Nqzvavfgengvir Gbbyf\\   CurrentVersion\Explorer\UserAssist\
Vagrearg Nhguragvpngvba   {75048700-EF1F-11D0-9888-
Freivpr.yax   006097DEACF9}\Count]
HRZR_EHACVQY:%pfvqy2%\\   [HKCU\Software\Microsoft\Windows\
Nqzvavfgengvir Gbbyf\\   CurrentVersion\Explorer\UserAssist\
Ybpny Frphevgl Cbyvpl.yax   {75048700-EF1F-11D0-9888-
                                        006097DEACF9}\Count]

HRZR_EHACVQY:%pfvqy2%\\   [HKCU\Software\Microsoft\Windows\
Nqzvavfgengvir Gbbyf\\   CurrentVersion\Explorer\UserAssist\
Yvprafvat.yax   {75048700-EF1F-11D0-9888-
                                        006097DEACF9}\Count]

HRZR_EHACVQY:%pfvqy2%\\   [HKCU\Software\Microsoft\Windows\
Vagrearg Rkcybere.yax   CurrentVersion\Explorer\UserAssist\
                                        {75048700-EF1F-11D0-9888-
                                        006097DEACF9}\Count]

HRZR_EHAJZPZQ   [HKCU\Software\Microsoft\Windows\
                                        CurrentVersion\Explorer\UserAssist\
                                        {5E6AB780-7743-11CF-A12B-
                                        00AA004AE837}\Count]

HRZR_EHAJZPZQ   [HKCU\Software\Microsoft\Windows\
                                        CurrentVersion\Explorer\UserAssist\
                                        {75048700-EF1F-11D0-9888-
                                        006097DEACF9}\Count]

HRZR_EHAJZPZQ:0k1   130
                                        [HKCU\Software\Microsoft\
                                        Windows\CurrentVersion\
                                        Explorer\UserAssist\
                                        {75048700-EF1F-11D0-9888-
                                        006097DEACF9}\Count]

HRZR_EHAJZPZQ:0k1   132
                                        [HKCU\Software\Microsoft\
                                        Windows\CurrentVersion\
                                        Explorer\UserAssist\
                                        {75048700-EF1F-11D0-9888-
                                        006097DEACF9}\Count]

HRZR_EHAJZPZQ:0k1   191
                                        [HKCU\Software\Microsoft\
                                        Windows\CurrentVersion\
                                        Explorer\UserAssist\
                                        {75048700-EF1F-11D0-9888-
                                        006097DEACF9}\Count]

HRZR_EHAJZPZQ:0k1   1sn

Entry Name	Key
	[HKCU\Software\Microsoft\ Windows\CurrentVersion\ Explorer\UserAssist\ {75048700-EF1F-11D0-9888- 006097DEACF9}\Count]
HRZR_EHAJZPZQ:0k2	n220 [HKCU\Software\Microsoft\ Windows\CurrentVersion\ Explorer\UserAssist\ {5E6AB780-7743-11CF-A12B- 00AA004AE837}\Count]
HRZR_HVFPHG	[HKCU\Software\Microsoft\Windows\ CurrentVersion\Explorer\UserAssist\ {75048700-EF1F-11D0-9888- 006097DEACF9}\Count]
HRZR_PGYFRFFVBA	[HKCU\Software\Microsoft\Windows\ CurrentVersion\Explorer\UserAssist\ {5E6AB780-7743-11CF-A12B- 00AA004AE837}\Count]
HRZR_PGYFRFFVBA	[HKCU\Software\Microsoft\Windows\ CurrentVersion\Explorer\UserAssist\ {75048700-EF1F-11D0-9888- 006097DEACF9}\Count]
HRZR_PGYPHNPbhag:pgbe	[HKCU\Software\Microsoft\Windows\ CurrentVersion\Explorer\UserAssist\ {5E6AB780-7743-11CF-A12B- 00AA004AE837}\Count]
HRZR_PGYPHNPbhag:pgbe	[HKCU\Software\Microsoft\Windows\ CurrentVersion\Explorer\UserAssist\ {75048700-EF1F-11D0-9888- 006097DEACF9}\Count]
HTMLExtractTimeout	[HKCU\Software\Microsoft\Windows\ CurrentVersion\Explorer\Thumbnail View]
http	[HKCU\Software\Microsoft\Windows\ CurrentVersion\Internet Settings\ZoneMap\ProtocolDefaults]
https	[HKCU\Software\Microsoft\Windows\ CurrentVersion\Internet Settings\ZoneMap\ProtocolDefaults]
HungAppTimeout	[HKCU\Control Panel\Desktop]
i	[HKCU\Software\Microsoft\Windows\ CurrentVersion\Explorer\ComDlg32\ OpenSaveMRU*]
iCodePage	[HKCU\Software\Microsoft\Notepad]
Icon	[HKCU\Software\Microsoft\Windows\ CurrentVersion\Internet Settings\Zones\0]

Entry Name	Key
Icon	[HKCU\Software\Microsoft\Windows\CurrentVersion\Internet Settings\Zones\1]
Icon	[HKCU\Software\Microsoft\Windows\CurrentVersion\Internet Settings\Zones\2]
Icon	[HKCU\Software\Microsoft\Windows\CurrentVersion\Internet Settings\Zones\3]
Icon	[HKCU\Software\Microsoft\Windows\CurrentVersion\Internet Settings\Zones\4]
IconFont	[HKCU\Control Panel\Desktop\WindowMetrics]
IconSpacing	[HKCU\Control Panel\Desktop\WindowMetrics]
IconTitleWrap	[HKCU\Control Panel\Desktop\WindowMetrics]
IconVerticalspacing	[HKCU\Control Panel\Desktop\WindowMetrics]
iCountry	[HKCU\Control Panel\International]
iCurrDigits	[HKCU\Control Panel\International]
iCurrency	[HKCU\Control Panel\International]
iDate	[HKCU\Control Panel\International]
iDigits	[HKCU\Control Panel\International]
IE5_UA_Backup_Flag	[HKCU\Software\Microsoft\Windows\CurrentVersion\Internet Settings]
iFormat	[HKCU\Software\Microsoft\Clock]
iLZero	[HKCU\Control Panel\International]
iMeasure	[HKCU\Control Panel\International]
Implementing	[HKCU\Software\Microsoft\Windows\CurrentVersion\Explorer\Discardable\PostSetup\Component Categories\{00021493-0000-0000-C000-000000000046}\Enum]
Implementing	[HKCU\Software\Microsoft\Windows\CurrentVersion\Explorer\Discardable\PostSetup\Component Categories\{00021494-0000-0000-C000-000000000046}\Enum]
InactiveBorder	[HKCU\Control Panel\Colors]
InactiveTitle	[HKCU\Control Panel\Colors]
InactiveTitleText	[HKCU\Control Panel\Colors]
iNegCurr	[HKCU\Control Panel\International]
InfoText	[HKCU\Control Panel\Colors]
InfoWindow	[HKCU\Control Panel\Colors]
ini	[HKCU\Software\Microsoft\Windows NT\CurrentVersion\Extensions]
InitAllowed	[HKCU\Software\Microsoft\NetDDE\DDE Trusted Shares\DDEDBi26ACB1B8\Chat$]

Entry Name	**Key**
InitAllowed	[HKCU\Software\Microsoft\NetDDE\DDE Trusted Shares\DDEDBi26ACB1B8\CLPBK$]
InitAllowed	[HKCU\Software\Microsoft\NetDDE\DDE Trusted Shares\DDEDBi26ACB1B8\Hearts$]
InitHits	[HKCU\Software\Microsoft\Internet Explorer\International\CpMRU]
InitialKeyboardIndicators	[HKCU\Control Panel\Keyboard]
InsertMode	[HKCU\Console]
Installed	[HKCU\Software\Microsoft\Fax\Setup]
InstallType	[HKCU\Software\Microsoft\Fax\Setup]
Internet Tools	[HKCU\Software\Microsoft\Windows\CurrentVersion\GrpConv\MapGroups]
IntranetName	[HKCU\Software\Microsoft\Windows\CurrentVersion\Internet Settings\ZoneMap]
iPointSize	[HKCU\Software\Microsoft\Notepad]
ITBarLayout	[HKCU\Software\Microsoft\Internet Explorer\Toolbar\ShellBrowser]
iTime	[HKCU\Control Panel\International]
iTLZero	[HKCU\Control Panel\International]
iWindowPosDX	[HKCU\Software\Microsoft\Notepad]
iWindowPosDY	[HKCU\Software\Microsoft\Notepad]
iWindowPosX	[HKCU\Software\Microsoft\Notepad]
iWindowPosY	[HKCU\Software\Microsoft\Notepad]
j	[HKCU\Software\Microsoft\Windows\CurrentVersion\Explorer\ComDlg32\OpenSaveMRU*]
Key Modifiers	[HKCU\Control Panel\Input Method\Hot Keys\00000010]
Key Modifiers	[HKCU\Control Panel\Input Method\Hot Keys\00000011]
Key Modifiers	[HKCU\Control Panel\Input Method\Hot Keys\00000012]
Key Modifiers	[HKCU\Control Panel\Input Method\Hot Keys\00000070]
Key Modifiers	[HKCU\Control Panel\Input Method\Hot Keys\00000071]
Key Modifiers	[HKCU\Control Panel\Input Method\Hot Keys\00000072]
Key Modifiers	[HKCU\Control Panel\Input Method\Hot Keys\00000200]
Key Modifiers	[HKCU\Control Panel\Input Method\Hot Keys\00000201]
Key Modifiers	[HKCU\Control Panel\Input Method\Hot Keys\00000202]
KeyboardDelay	[HKCU\Control Panel\Keyboard]
KeyboardSpeed	[HKCU\Control Panel\Keyboard]
Keys	[HKCU\Software\Microsoft\RegEdt32__Local_Computer]

Entry Name	Key
Last User ID	[HKCU\Identities]
Last Username	[HKCU\Identities]
LastCountryID	[HKCU\Software\Microsoft\Fax\UserInfo]
LastRecipientAreaCode	[HKCU\Software\Microsoft\Fax\UserInfo]
LastUpdate	[HKCU\Software\Microsoft\Windows\ CurrentVersion\Explorer\MountPoints\A\ _Autorun]
LastUpdate	[HKCU\Software\Microsoft\Windows\ CurrentVersion\Explorer\MountPoints\A\ _DIL]
LastUpdate	[HKCU\Software\Microsoft\Windows\ CurrentVersion\Explorer\MountPoints\C\ _Autorun]
LastUpdate	[HKCU\Software\Microsoft\Windows\ CurrentVersion\Explorer\MountPoints\C\ _DIL]
LastUpdate	[HKCU\Software\Microsoft\Windows\ CurrentVersion\Explorer\MountPoints\C\ _DriveFlags]
LastUpdate	[HKCU\Software\Microsoft\Windows\ CurrentVersion\Explorer\MountPoints\C\ _GFA]
LastUpdate	[HKCU\Software\Microsoft\Windows\ CurrentVersion\Explorer\MountPoints\C\ _GVI]
LastUpdate	[HKCU\Software\Microsoft\Windows\ CurrentVersion\Explorer\MountPoints\D\ _Autorun]
LastUpdate	[HKCU\Software\Microsoft\Windows\ CurrentVersion\Explorer\MountPoints\D\ _DIL]
LastUpdate	[HKCU\Software\Microsoft\Windows\ CurrentVersion\Explorer\MountPoints\D\ _LabelFromReg]
LastUpdate	[HKCU\Software\Microsoft\Windows\ CurrentVersion\Explorer\MountPoints\D\ _DriveFlags]
LastUseDialingRules	[HKCU\Software\Microsoft\Fax\UserInfo]
LastUserIniSyncTime	[HKCU\Software\Microsoft\Windows NT\CurrentVersion\Terminal Server]
Left	[HKCU\Software\Microsoft\RegEdt32\ Settings]
lfCharSet	[HKCU\Software\Microsoft\Notepad]
lfClipPrecision	[HKCU\Software\Microsoft\Notepad]
lfEscapement	[HKCU\Software\Microsoft\Notepad]
lfFaceName	[HKCU\Software\Microsoft\Notepad]
lfItalic	[HKCU\Software\Microsoft\Notepad]
lfOrientation	[HKCU\Software\Microsoft\Notepad]
lfOutPrecision	[HKCU\Software\Microsoft\Notepad]

Entry Name	Key
lfPitchAndFamily	[HKCU\Software\Microsoft\Notepad]
lfQuality	[HKCU\Software\Microsoft\Notepad]
lfStrikeOut	[HKCU\Software\Microsoft\Notepad]
lfUnderline	[HKCU\Software\Microsoft\Notepad]
lfWeight	[HKCU\Software\Microsoft\Notepad]
Lilac (large)	[HKCU\Control Panel\Appearance\ Schemes]
Lilac	[HKCU\Control Panel\Appearance\ Schemes]
Lines1	[HKCU\Control Panel\Screen Saver.Mystify]
Lines2	[HKCU\Control Panel\Screen Saver.Mystify]
LinksFolderName	[HKCU\Software\Microsoft\Internet Explorer\Toolbar]
load	[HKCU\Software\Microsoft\Windows NT\CurrentVersion\Windows]
LoadConIme	[HKCU\Console]
Local AppData	[HKCU\Software\Microsoft\Windows\ CurrentVersion\Explorer\Shell Folders]
Local AppData	[HKCU\Software\Microsoft\Windows\ CurrentVersion\Explorer\User Shell Folders]
Local Page	[HKCU\Software\Microsoft\Internet Explorer\Main]
Local Settings	[HKCU\Software\Microsoft\Windows\ CurrentVersion\Explorer\Shell Folders]
Local Settings	[HKCU\Software\Microsoft\Windows\ CurrentVersion\Explorer\User Shell Folders]
Locale	[HKCU\Control Panel\International]
Locale	[HKCU\Software\Microsoft\Active Setup\Installed Components\>{60B49E34-C7CC-11D0-8953-00A0C90347FF}MICROS]
Locale	[HKCU\Software\Microsoft\Active Setup\Installed Components\ {2179C5D3-EBFF-11CF-B6FD-00AA00B4E220}]
Locale	[HKCU\Software\Microsoft\Active Setup\Installed Components\{22d6f312-b0f6-11d0-94ab-0080c74c7e95}]
Locale	[HKCU\Software\Microsoft\Active Setup\Installed Components\{44BBA840-CC51-11CF-AAFA-00AA00B6015C}]
Locale	[HKCU\Software\Microsoft\Active Setup\Installed Components\{44BBA842-CC51-11CF-AAFA-00AA00B6015B}]
Locale	[HKCU\Software\Microsoft\Active Setup\Installed Components\{7790769C-0471-11d2-AF11-00C04FA35D02}]

....

Entry Name	Key
Locale	[HKCU\Software\Microsoft\Active Setup\Installed Components\{89820200-ECBD-11cf-8B85-00AA005B4340}]
Locale	[HKCU\Software\Microsoft\Active Setup\Installed Components\{89820200-ECBD-11cf-8B85-00AA005B4383}]
Log	[HKCU\Software\Microsoft\Windows\ CurrentVersion\GrpConv]
LOGONSERVER	[HKCU\Volatile Environment]
LowPowerActive	[HKCU\Control Panel\Desktop]
LowPowerTimeOut	[HKCU\Control Panel\Desktop]
Maple	[HKCU\Control Panel\Appearance\ Schemes]
MapNetDrvBtn	[HKCU\Software\Microsoft\Windows\ CurrentVersion\Explorer\Advanced]
Marine (high color)	[HKCU\Control Panel\Appearance\ Schemes]
Maximized	[HKCU\Software\Microsoft\Internet Explorer\Document Windows]
Maximized	[HKCU\Software\Microsoft\Windows Help]
MaximumSpeed	[HKCU\Control Panel\Accessibility\ MouseKeys]
Menu	[HKCU\Control Panel\Colors]
MenuFont	[HKCU\Control Panel\Desktop\ WindowMetrics]
MenuHeight	[HKCU\Control Panel\Desktop\ WindowMetrics]
MenuShowDelay	[HKCU\Control Panel\Desktop]
MenuText	[HKCU\Control Panel\Colors]
MenuWidth	[HKCU\Control Panel\Desktop\ WindowMetrics]
MessageFont	[HKCU\Control Panel\Desktop\ WindowMetrics]
Migrated Schemes	[HKCU\AppEvents]
Migrated5	[HKCU\Identities]
MigrateIni	[HKCU\Software\Microsoft\ Schedule+\Microsoft Schedule+]
MigrateIniPrint	[HKCU\Software\Microsoft\ Schedule+\Microsoft Schedule+]
MigrateProxy	[HKCU\Software\Microsoft\Windows\ CurrentVersion\Internet Settings]
MigToLWP	[HKCU\Software\Microsoft\Outlook Express\5.0\Shared Settings\Setup]
MigToLWPVer	[HKCU\Software\Microsoft\Outlook Express\5.0\Shared Settings\Setup]
MimeExclusionListForCache	[HKCU\Software\Microsoft\Windows\ CurrentVersion\Internet Settings]
MinLevel	[HKCU\Software\Microsoft\Windows\ CurrentVersion\Internet Settings\Zones\1]

Entry Name	Key
MinLevel	[HKCU\Software\Microsoft\Windows\CurrentVersion\Internet Settings\Zones\2]
MinLevel	[HKCU\Software\Microsoft\Windows\CurrentVersion\Internet Settings\Zones\3]
MinLevel	[HKCU\Software\Microsoft\Windows\CurrentVersion\Internet Settings\Zones\4]
MinOnRun	[HKCU\Software\Microsoft\Windows NT\CurrentVersion\Program Manager\Settings]
Mode	[HKCU\Control Panel\Screen Saver.Marquee]
MouseSpeed	[HKCU\Control Panel\Mouse]
MouseThreshold1	[HKCU\Control Panel\Mouse]
MouseThreshold2	[HKCU\Control Panel\Mouse]
MRUList	[HKCU\Software\Microsoft\Windows\CurrentVersion\Explorer\ComDlg32\LastVisitedMRU]
MRUList	[HKCU\Software\Microsoft\Windows\CurrentVersion\Explorer\ComDlg32\OpenSaveMRU*]
MRUList	[HKCU\Software\Microsoft\Windows\CurrentVersion\Explorer\ComDlg32\OpenSaveMRU\reg]
MRUList	[HKCU\Software\Microsoft\Windows\CurrentVersion\Explorer\ComDlg32\OpenSaveMRU\TXT]
MRUList	[HKCU\Software\Microsoft\Windows\CurrentVersion\Explorer\FileExts\.msc\OpenWithList]
MRUList	[HKCU\Software\Microsoft\Windows\CurrentVersion\Explorer\FileExts\.reg\OpenWithList]
MRUList	[HKCU\Software\Microsoft\Windows\CurrentVersion\Explorer\FileExts\.TXT\OpenWithList]
MRUList	[HKCU\Software\Microsoft\Windows\CurrentVersion\Explorer\RecentDocs]
MRUList	[HKCU\Software\Microsoft\Windows\CurrentVersion\Explorer\RecentDocs\.TXT]
MRUList	[HKCU\Software\Microsoft\Windows\CurrentVersion\Explorer\RecentDocs\Folder]
MRUList	[HKCU\Software\Microsoft\Windows\CurrentVersion\Explorer\RunMRU]
MRUListEx	[HKCU\Software\Microsoft\Windows\CurrentVersion\Explorer\StreamMRU]

••••••••••••••••

Entry Name	Key
MVB	[HKCU\Control Panel\IOProcs]
My Pictures	[HKCU\Software\Microsoft\Windows\CurrentVersion\Explorer\Shell Folders]
My Pictures	[HKCU\Software\Microsoft\Windows\CurrentVersion\Explorer\User Shell Folders]
Name	[HKCU\Control Panel\PowerCfg\PowerPolicies\0]
Name	[HKCU\Control Panel\PowerCfg\PowerPolicies\1]
Name	[HKCU\Control Panel\PowerCfg\PowerPolicies\2]
Name	[HKCU\Control Panel\PowerCfg\PowerPolicies\3]
Name	[HKCU\Control Panel\PowerCfg\PowerPolicies\4]
Name	[HKCU\Control Panel\PowerCfg\PowerPolicies\5]
Name	[HKCU\Software\Microsoft\Windows\CurrentVersion\Webcheck\Store.1\{02C09C60-E687-01BE-0000-00004BFBD552}]
ncpa.cpl	[HKCU\Control Panel\don't load]
NetHood	[HKCU\Software\Microsoft\Windows\CurrentVersion\Explorer\Shell Folders]
NetHood	[HKCU\Software\Microsoft\Windows\CurrentVersion\Explorer\User Shell Folders]
NetMessage	[HKCU\Software\Microsoft\Windows NT\CurrentVersion\Windows]
NextId	[HKCU\Software\Microsoft\Internet Explorer\Extensions\CmdMapping]
NoClose	[HKCU\Software\Microsoft\Windows NT\CurrentVersion\Program Manager\Restrictions]
NoDriveTypeAutoRun	[HKCU\Software\Microsoft\Windows\CurrentVersion\Policies\Explorer]
NoFileMenu	[HKCU\Software\Microsoft\Windows NT\CurrentVersion\Program Manager\Restrictions]
NoJITSetup	[HKCU\Software\Microsoft\Internet Explorer\Main]
NoNetAutodial	[HKCU\Software\Microsoft\Windows\CurrentVersion\Internet Settings]
NoOfOldWorkAreas	[HKCU\Software\Microsoft\Internet Explorer\Desktop\Old WorkAreas]
NoRun	[HKCU\Software\Microsoft\Windows NT\CurrentVersion\Program Manager\Restrictions]
NoSaveSettings	[HKCU\Software\Microsoft\Windows NT\CurrentVersion\Program Manager\Restrictions]

Entry Name	Key
NoUpdateCheck	[HKCU\Software\Microsoft\Internet Explorer\Main]
NullPort	[HKCU\Software\Microsoft\Windows NT\CurrentVersion\Windows]
NumberOfHistoryBuffers	[HKCU\Console]
odbccp32.cpl	[HKCU\Control Panel\don't load]
OldWorkAreaRects	[HKCU\Software\Microsoft\Internet Explorer\Desktop\Old WorkAreas]
On	[HKCU\Control Panel\Accessibility\ Blind Access]
On	[HKCU\Control Panel\Accessibility\ Keyboard Preference]
On	[HKCU\Control Panel\Accessibility\ ShowSounds]
OnTaskBar	[HKCU\Software\Microsoft\Fax\UserInfo]
OpenEncodingType	[HKCU\Software\Microsoft\ SystemCertificates\ACRS\PhysicalStores \.LocalMachine]
OpenFlags	[HKCU\Software\Microsoft\ SystemCertificates\ACRS\PhysicalStores \.LocalMachine]
OpenParameters	[HKCU\Software\Microsoft\ SystemCertificates\ACRS\PhysicalStores \.LocalMachine]
OpenStoreProvider	[HKCU\Software\Microsoft\ SystemCertificates\ACRS\PhysicalStores \.LocalMachine]
Order	[HKCU\Software\Microsoft\Windows\ CurrentVersion\Explorer\MenuOrder\Star t Menu]
Order	[HKCU\Software\Microsoft\Windows\ CurrentVersion\Explorer\MenuOrder\Star t Menu\Programs]
Order	[HKCU\Software\Microsoft\Windows\ CurrentVersion\Explorer\MenuOrder\Star t Menu\Programs\Accessories]
Order	[HKCU\Software\Microsoft\Windows\ CurrentVersion\Explorer\MenuOrder\Star t Menu\Programs\Administrative Tools]
OriginalStateInfo	[HKCU\Software\Microsoft\Internet Explorer\Desktop\Components\0]
PaintDesktopVersion	[HKCU\Control Panel\Desktop]
Paisley	[HKCU\Control Panel\Patterns]
ParseAutoexec	[HKCU\Software\Microsoft\Windows NT\CurrentVersion\Winlogon]
Pattern	[HKCU\Control Panel\Desktop]
Pattern	[HKCU\Control Panel\Patterns]
Personal	[HKCU\Software\Microsoft\Windows\ CurrentVersion\Explorer\Shell Folders]

....

Entry Name	Key
Personal	[HKCU\Software\Microsoft\Windows\CurrentVersion\Explorer\User Shell Folders]
PerUserItem	[HKCU\Software\Microsoft\Windows\CurrentVersion\Internet Settings\5.0\Cache\Content]
PerUserItem	[HKCU\Software\Microsoft\Windows\CurrentVersion\Internet Settings\5.0\Cache\Cookies]
PerUserItem	[HKCU\Software\Microsoft\Windows\CurrentVersion\Internet Settings\5.0\Cache\History]
Plum (high color)	[HKCU\Control Panel\Appearance\Schemes]
Policies	[HKCU\Control Panel\PowerCfg\GlobalPowerPolicy]
Policies	[HKCU\Control Panel\PowerCfg\PowerPolicies\0]
Policies	[HKCU\Control Panel\PowerCfg\PowerPolicies\1]
Policies	[HKCU\Control Panel\PowerCfg\PowerPolicies\2]
Policies	[HKCU\Control Panel\PowerCfg\PowerPolicies\3]
Policies	[HKCU\Control Panel\PowerCfg\PowerPolicies\4]
Policies	[HKCU\Control Panel\PowerCfg\PowerPolicies\5]
PopupColors	[HKCU\Console]
Position	[HKCU\Software\Microsoft\Internet Explorer\Desktop\Components\0]
PowerOffActive	[HKCU\Control Panel\Desktop]
PowerOffTimeOut	[HKCU\Control Panel\Desktop]
Presentation Cache	[HKCU\Software\Microsoft\Windows\CurrentVersion\Controls Folder]
Presentation LCID	[HKCU\Software\Microsoft\Windows\CurrentVersion\Controls Folder]
PrintHood	[HKCU\Software\Microsoft\Windows\CurrentVersion\Explorer\Shell Folders]
PrintHood	[HKCU\Software\Microsoft\Windows\CurrentVersion\Explorer\User Shell Folders]
Priority	[HKCU\Software\Microsoft\msdaipp\Providers\{9FECD570-B9D4-11d1-9C78-0000F875AC61}]
Priority	[HKCU\Software\Microsoft\msdaipp\Providers\{9FECD571-B9D4-11d1-9C78-0000F875AC61}]

Entry Name	Key
Priority	[HKCU\Software\Microsoft\ SystemCertificates\ACRS\PhysicalStores \.LocalMachine]
Programs	[HKCU\Software\Microsoft\Windows NT\CurrentVersion\Windows]
Programs	[HKCU\Software\Microsoft\Windows\ CurrentVersion\Explorer\Shell Folders]
Programs	[HKCU\Software\Microsoft\Windows\ CurrentVersion\Explorer\User Shell Folders]
Provider	[HKCU\Software\Microsoft\Internet Explorer\SearchUrl]
ProxyByPass	[HKCU\Software\Microsoft\Windows\ CurrentVersion\Internet Settings\ZoneMap]
Pumpkin (large)	[HKCU\Control Panel\Appearance\ Schemes]
Quick Launch	[HKCU\Software\Microsoft\Windows\ CurrentVersion\GrpConv\MapGroups]
QuickEdit	[HKCU\Console]
Quilt	[HKCU\Control Panel\Patterns]
Radio Quality	[HKCU\Software\Microsoft\ Multimedia\Audio\WaveFormats]
Rainy Day	[HKCU\Control Panel\Appearance\ Schemes]
ReadOnly	[HKCU\Software\Microsoft\RegEdt32\ Settings]
Reason Setting	[HKCU\Software\Microsoft\Windows\ CurrentVersion\Explorer]
Recent	[HKCU\Software\Microsoft\Windows\ CurrentVersion\Explorer\Shell Folders]
Recent	[HKCU\Software\Microsoft\Windows\ CurrentVersion\Explorer\User Shell Folders]
RecommendedLevel	[HKCU\Software\Microsoft\Windows\ CurrentVersion\Internet Settings\ Zones\1]
RecommendedLevel	[HKCU\Software\Microsoft\Windows\ CurrentVersion\Internet Settings\ Zones\2]
RecommendedLevel	[HKCU\Software\Microsoft\Windows\ CurrentVersion\Internet Settings\ Zones\3]
RecommendedLevel	[HKCU\Software\Microsoft\Windows\ CurrentVersion\Internet Settings\ Zones\4]
RecurseFlags	[HKCU\Software\Microsoft\Windows\ CurrentVersion\Webcheck\Store.1\{02C09 C60-E687-01BE-0000-00004BFBD552}]

....

Entry Name	Key
Red	White
and Blue (VGA)	[HKCU\Control Panel\Appearance\Schemes]
Registry	[HKCU\Software\Microsoft\RegEdt32\Settings]
RequestMakeCall	[HKCU\Software\Microsoft\Windows\CurrentVersion\Telephony\HandoffPriorities]
RestoredStateInfo	[HKCU\Software\Microsoft\Internet Explorer\Desktop\Components\0]
Restrictions	[HKCU\Software\Microsoft\Windows NT\CurrentVersion\Program Manager\Restrictions]
Revocation Checking	[HKCU\Identities\{0ACE9E60-3362-4310-B2E4-66E22371AB5E}\Software\Microsoft\Outlook Express\5.0]
Rose (large)	[HKCU\Control Panel\Appearance\Schemes]
Rose	[HKCU\Control Panel\Appearance\Schemes]
s1159	[HKCU\Control Panel\International]
s2359	[HKCU\Control Panel\International]
Safety Warning Level	[HKCU\Software\Microsoft\Internet Explorer\Security]
Save_Session_History_On_Exit	[HKCU\Software\Microsoft\Internet Explorer\Main]
SaveConnections	[HKCU\Software\Microsoft\Windows NT\CurrentVersion\Network\Persistent Connections]
SaveSettings	[HKCU\Software\Microsoft\RegEdt32\Settings]
SaveSettings	[HKCU\Software\Microsoft\Windows NT\CurrentVersion\Network\Event Viewer]
SaveSettings	[HKCU\Software\Microsoft\Windows NT\CurrentVersion\Network\Server Manager]
SaveSettings	[HKCU\Software\Microsoft\Windows NT\CurrentVersion\Network\User Manager]
SaveSettings	[HKCU\Software\Microsoft\Windows NT\CurrentVersion\Network\User Manager for Domains]
SaveSettings	[HKCU\Software\Microsoft\Windows NT\CurrentVersion\Program Manager\Settings]
Scottie	[HKCU\Control Panel\Patterns]
sCountry	[HKCU\Control Panel\International]

Entry Name	Key
ScreenBufferSize	[HKCU\Console]
ScreenColors	[HKCU\Console]
ScreenSaveActive	[HKCU\Control Panel\Desktop]
ScreenSaverIsSecure	[HKCU\Control Panel\Desktop]
ScreenSaveTimeOut	[HKCU\Control Panel\Desktop]
SCRNSAVE.EXE	[HKCU\Control Panel\Desktop]
Scrollbar	[HKCU\Control Panel\Colors]
ScrollHeight	[HKCU\Control Panel\Desktop\ WindowMetrics]
ScrollWidth	[HKCU\Control Panel\Desktop\ WindowMetrics]
sCurrency	[HKCU\Control Panel\International]
sDate	[HKCU\Control Panel\International]
sDecimal	[HKCU\Control Panel\International]
Search Page	[HKCU\Software\Microsoft\Internet Explorer\Main]
SearchOptions	[HKCU\Software\Microsoft\Windows\ CurrentVersion\Device Installer]
SelfHealCount	[HKCU\Software\Microsoft\Windows\ CurrentVersion\Internet Settings\ Zones]
Sending_Security	[HKCU\Software\Microsoft\Internet Explorer\Security]
SendTo	[HKCU\Software\Microsoft\Windows\ CurrentVersion\Explorer\Shell Folders]
SendTo	[HKCU\Software\Microsoft\Windows\ CurrentVersion\Explorer\User Shell Folders]
SeparateProcess	[HKCU\Software\Microsoft\Windows\ CurrentVersion\Explorer\Advanced]
SerialNumber	[HKCU\Software\Microsoft\NetDDE\DDE Trusted Shares\DDEDBi26ACB1B8\Chat$]
SerialNumber	[HKCU\Software\Microsoft\NetDDE\DDE Trusted Shares\DDEDBi26ACB1B8\CLPBK$]
SerialNumber	[HKCU\Software\Microsoft\NetDDE\DDE Trusted Shares\DDEDBi26ACB1B8\Hearts$]
Services	[HKCU\Software\Microsoft\Windows\ CurrentVersion\Applets\SysTray]
SESSIONNAME	[HKCU\Volatile Environment]
Settings	[HKCU\Software\Microsoft\Internet Explorer\Desktop\Components]
Settings	[HKCU\Software\Microsoft\Windows\ CurrentVersion\Explorer\CabinetState]
Settings	[HKCU\Software\Microsoft\Windows\ CurrentVersion\Explorer\DeskView]
Settings	[HKCU\Software\Microsoft\Windows\ CurrentVersion\Explorer\StuckRects2]
Shell Icon BPP	[HKCU\Control Panel\Desktop\ WindowMetrics]

Entry Name	Key
ShellState	[HKCU\Software\Microsoft\Windows\CurrentVersion\Explorer]
Shortcut0	[HKCU\Software\Microsoft\MediaPlayer\Setup\CreatedLinks]
Show Status	[HKCU\Control Panel\Input Method]
Show	[HKCU\Software\Microsoft\Windows\CurrentVersion\Explorer\tips]
Show_ChannelBand	[HKCU\Software\Microsoft\Internet Explorer\Main]
Show_FullURL	[HKCU\Software\Microsoft\Internet Explorer\Main]
Show_StatusBar	[HKCU\Software\Microsoft\Internet Explorer\Main]
Show_ToolBar	[HKCU\Software\Microsoft\Internet Explorer\Main]
Show_URLinStatusBar	[HKCU\Software\Microsoft\Internet Explorer\Main]
Show_URLToolBar	[HKCU\Software\Microsoft\Internet Explorer\Main]
ShowCompColor	[HKCU\Software\Microsoft\Windows\CurrentVersion\Explorer\Advanced]
ShowInfoTip	[HKCU\Software\Microsoft\Windows\CurrentVersion\Explorer\Advanced]
Shutdown Setting	[HKCU\Software\Microsoft\Windows\CurrentVersion\Explorer]
Signature	[HKCU\Software\Microsoft\Windows\CurrentVersion\Internet Settings\5.0\Cache]
Size	[HKCU\Control Panel\Screen Saver.Marquee]
Size	[HKCU\Software\Microsoft\Internet Explorer\International\CpMRU]
sLanguage	[HKCU\Control Panel\International]
Slate	[HKCU\Control Panel\Appearance\Schemes]
sList	[HKCU\Control Panel\International]
sLongDate	[HKCU\Control Panel\International]
SmCaptionFont	[HKCU\Control Panel\Desktop\WindowMetrics]
SmCaptionHeight	[HKCU\Control Panel\Desktop\WindowMetrics]
SmCaptionWidth	[HKCU\Control Panel\Desktop\WindowMetrics]
SnapToDefaultButton	[HKCU\Control Panel\Mouse]
SoundNotification	[HKCU\Software\Microsoft\Fax\UserInfo]
Source	[HKCU\Software\Microsoft\Internet Explorer\Desktop\Components\0]
Speed	[HKCU\Control Panel\Screen Saver.Marquee]

Entry Name	Key
Spinner	[HKCU\Control Panel\Patterns]
Spruce	[HKCU\Control Panel\Appearance\Schemes]
srvwiz	[HKCU\Software\Microsoft\Windows NT\CurrentVersion\Setup\Welcome]
sShortDate	[HKCU\Control Panel\International]
Start Menu	[HKCU\Software\Microsoft\Windows\CurrentVersion\Explorer\Shell Folders]
Start Menu	[HKCU\Software\Microsoft\Windows\CurrentVersion\Explorer\User Shell Folders]
Start Page	[HKCU\Software\Microsoft\Internet Explorer\Main]
StartApp	[HKCU\Software\Microsoft\NetDDE\DDE Trusted Shares\DDEDBi26ACB1B8\Chat$]
StartApp	[HKCU\Software\Microsoft\NetDDE\DDE Trusted Shares\DDEDBi26ACB1B8\CLPBK$]
StartApp	[HKCU\Software\Microsoft\NetDDE\DDE Trusted Shares\DDEDBi26ACB1B8\Hearts$]
StartColor1	[HKCU\Control Panel\Screen Saver.Mystify]
StartColor2	[HKCU\Control Panel\Screen Saver.Mystify]
StartMenuAdminTools	[HKCU\Software\Microsoft\Windows\CurrentVersion\Explorer\Advanced]
StartMenuInit	[HKCU\Software\Microsoft\Windows\CurrentVersion\Explorer\Advanced]
Startup	[HKCU\Software\Microsoft\Windows\CurrentVersion\Explorer\Shell Folders]
Startup	[HKCU\Software\Microsoft\Windows\CurrentVersion\Explorer\User Shell Folders]
State	[HKCU\Software\Microsoft\Windows\CurrentVersion\WinTrust\Trust Providers\Software Publishing]
StatusFont	[HKCU\Control Panel\Desktop\WindowMetrics]
sThousand	[HKCU\Control Panel\International]
sTime	[HKCU\Control Panel\International]
Storm (VGA)	[HKCU\Control Panel\Appearance\Schemes]
SubscribedURL	[HKCU\Software\Microsoft\Internet Explorer\Desktop\Components\0]
SuperHidden	[HKCU\Software\Microsoft\Windows\CurrentVersion\Explorer\Advanced]
SwapMouseButtons	[HKCU\Control Panel\Mouse]
SystemDefault	[HKCU\Control Panel\Sounds]
SystemDefaultEUDCFont	[HKCU\EUDC\1252]

••••••••••••••••

Entry Name	**Key**
SystemFormats	[HKCU\Software\Microsoft\Multimedia\Audio]
Target IME	[HKCU\Control Panel\Input Method\Hot Keys\00000010]
Target IME	[HKCU\Control Panel\Input Method\Hot Keys\00000011]
Target IME	[HKCU\Control Panel\Input Method\Hot Keys\00000012]
Target IME	[HKCU\Control Panel\Input Method\Hot Keys\00000070]
Target IME	[HKCU\Control Panel\Input Method\Hot Keys\00000071]
Target IME	[HKCU\Control Panel\Input Method\Hot Keys\00000072]
Target IME	[HKCU\Control Panel\Input Method\Hot Keys\00000200]
Target IME	[HKCU\Control Panel\Input Method\Hot Keys\00000201]
Target IME	[HKCU\Control Panel\Input Method\Hot Keys\00000202]
Taskbar	[HKCU\Software\Microsoft\Windows\CurrentVersion\Explorer\Streams\Desktop]
Teal (VGA)	[HKCU\Control Panel\Appearance\Schemes]
Telephone Quality	[HKCU\Software\Microsoft\Multimedia\Audio\WaveFormats]
TEMP	[HKCU\Environment]
Templates	[HKCU\Software\Microsoft\Windows\CurrentVersion\Explorer\Shell Folders]
Templates	[HKCU\Software\Microsoft\Windows\CurrentVersion\Explorer\User Shell Folders]
Text Color	[HKCU\Software\Microsoft\Internet Explorer\Settings]
Text	[HKCU\Control Panel\Screen Saver.Marquee]
text/h323	[HKCU\Software\Netscape\Netscape Navigator\Viewers]
text/iuls	[HKCU\Software\Netscape\Netscape Navigator\Viewers]
TextColor	[HKCU\Control Panel\Screen Saver.Marquee]
Thatches	[HKCU\Control Panel\Patterns]
ThreadSensitive	[HKCU\Software\Microsoft\msdaipp\Providers\{9FECD571-B9D4-11d1-9C78-0000F875AC61}]
TileWallpaper	[HKCU\Control Panel\Desktop]
TimeToMaximumSpeed	[HKCU\Control Panel\Accessibility\MouseKeys]

Entry Name	Key
TimeToWait	[HKCU\Control Panel\Accessibility\TimeOut]
TitleText	[HKCU\Control Panel\Colors]
TMP	[HKCU\Environment]
Toolbars	[HKCU\Software\Microsoft\Windows\CurrentVersion\Explorer\Streams\Desktop]
Top	[HKCU\Software\Microsoft\RegEdt32\Settings]
TTEnable	[HKCU\Software\Microsoft\Windows NT\CurrentVersion\TrueType]
TTonly	[HKCU\Software\Microsoft\Windows NT\CurrentVersion\TrueType]
Tulip	[HKCU\Control Panel\Patterns]
txt	[HKCU\Software\Microsoft\Windows NT\CurrentVersion\Extensions]
TYPE0	[HKCU\Software\Netscape\Netscape Navigator\Viewers]
TYPE1	[HKCU\Software\Netscape\Netscape Navigator\Viewers]
TYPE10	[HKCU\Software\Netscape\Netscape Navigator\Viewers]
TYPE11	[HKCU\Software\Netscape\Netscape Navigator\Viewers]
TYPE12	[HKCU\Software\Netscape\Netscape Navigator\Viewers]
TYPE13	[HKCU\Software\Netscape\Netscape Navigator\Viewers]
TYPE14	[HKCU\Software\Netscape\Netscape Navigator\Viewers]
TYPE15	[HKCU\Software\Netscape\Netscape Navigator\Viewers]
TYPE16	[HKCU\Software\Netscape\Netscape Navigator\Viewers]
TYPE17	[HKCU\Software\Netscape\Netscape Navigator\Viewers]
TYPE18	[HKCU\Software\Netscape\Netscape Navigator\Viewers]
TYPE19	[HKCU\Software\Netscape\Netscape Navigator\Viewers]
TYPE2	[HKCU\Software\Netscape\Netscape Navigator\Viewers]
TYPE20	[HKCU\Software\Netscape\Netscape Navigator\Viewers]
TYPE21	[HKCU\Software\Netscape\Netscape Navigator\Viewers]
TYPE3	[HKCU\Software\Netscape\Netscape Navigator\Viewers]
TYPE4	[HKCU\Software\Netscape\Netscape Navigator\Viewers]

....

Entry Name	Key
TYPE5	[HKCU\Software\Netscape\Netscape Navigator\Viewers]
TYPE6	[HKCU\Software\Netscape\Netscape Navigator\Viewers]
TYPE7	[HKCU\Software\Netscape\Netscape Navigator\Viewers]
TYPE8	[HKCU\Software\Netscape\Netscape Navigator\Viewers]
TYPE9	[HKCU\Software\Netscape\Netscape Navigator\Viewers]
UNCAsIntranet	[HKCU\Software\Microsoft\Windows\CurrentVersion\Internet Settings\ZoneMap]
URL	[HKCU\Software\Microsoft\Windows\CurrentVersion\Webcheck\Store.1\{02C09C60-E687-01BE-0000-00004BFBD552}]
url1	[HKCU\Software\Microsoft\Internet Explorer\TypedURLs]
url2	[HKCU\Software\Microsoft\Internet Explorer\TypedURLs]
Use Anchor Hover Color	[HKCU\Software\Microsoft\Internet Explorer\Settings]
Use_DlgBox_Colors	[HKCU\Software\Microsoft\Internet Explorer\Main]
User Agent	[HKCU\Software\Microsoft\Windows\CurrentVersion\Internet Settings]
User ID	[HKCU\Identities\{0ACE9E60-3362-4310-B2E4-66E22371AB5E}]
Username	[HKCU\Identities\{0ACE9E60-3362-4310-B2E4-66E22371AB5E}]
Username	[HKCU\Software\Microsoft\Active Setup\Installed Components\{44BBA840-CC51-11CF-AAFA-00AA00B6015C}]
UserPreferencesMask	[HKCU\Control Panel\Desktop]
UseSchannelDirectly	[HKCU\Software\Microsoft\Windows\CurrentVersion\Internet Settings]
Version	[HKCU\Control Panel\Microsoft Input Devices\Mouse\Exceptions\584]
Version	[HKCU\Software\Microsoft\Active Setup\Installed Components\>{60B49E34-C7CC-11D0-8953-00A0C90347FF}MICROS]
Version	[HKCU\Software\Microsoft\Active Setup\Installed Components\{2179C5D3-EBFF-11CF-B6FD-00AA00B4E220}]
Version	[HKCU\Software\Microsoft\Active Setup\Installed Components\{22d6f312-b0f6-11d0-94ab-0080c74c7e95}]
Version	[HKCU\Software\Microsoft\Active Setup\Installed Components\{44BBA840-CC51-11CF-AAFA-00AA00B6015C}]

Entry Name	Key
Version	[HKCU\Software\Microsoft\Active Setup\Installed Components\{44BBA842-CC51-11CF-AAFA-00AA00B6015B}]
Version	[HKCU\Software\Microsoft\Active Setup\Installed Components\{7790769C-0471-11d2-AF11-00C04FA35D02}]
Version	[HKCU\Software\Microsoft\Active Setup\Installed Components\{89820200-ECBD-11cf-8B85-00AA005B4340}]
Version	[HKCU\Software\Microsoft\Active Setup\Installed Components\{89820200-ECBD-11cf-8B85-00AA005B4383}]
Version	[HKCU\Software\Microsoft\Windows\CurrentVersion\Explorer\MountPoints\A]
Version	[HKCU\Software\Microsoft\Windows\CurrentVersion\Explorer\MountPoints\A_Autorun]
Version	[HKCU\Software\Microsoft\Windows\CurrentVersion\Explorer\MountPoints\A_DIL]
Version	[HKCU\Software\Microsoft\Windows\CurrentVersion\Explorer\MountPoints\C]
Version	[HKCU\Software\Microsoft\Windows\CurrentVersion\Explorer\MountPoints\C_Autorun]
Version	[HKCU\Software\Microsoft\Windows\CurrentVersion\Explorer\MountPoints\C_DIL]
Version	[HKCU\Software\Microsoft\Windows\CurrentVersion\Explorer\MountPoints\C_DriveFlags]
Version	[HKCU\Software\Microsoft\Windows\CurrentVersion\Explorer\MountPoints\C_GFA]
Version	[HKCU\Software\Microsoft\Windows\CurrentVersion\Explorer\MountPoints\C_GVI]
Version	[HKCU\Software\Microsoft\Windows\CurrentVersion\Explorer\MountPoints\D]
Version	[HKCU\Software\Microsoft\Windows\CurrentVersion\Explorer\MountPoints\D_Autorun]
Version	[HKCU\Software\Microsoft\Windows\CurrentVersion\Explorer\MountPoints\D_DIL]
Version	[HKCU\Software\Microsoft\Windows\CurrentVersion\Explorer\MountPoints\D_LabelFromReg]

Entry Name	Key
Version	[HKCU\Software\Microsoft\Windows\CurrentVersion\Explorer\MountPoints\D_DriveFlags]
Version	[HKCU\Software\Microsoft\Windows\CurrentVersion\Explorer\UserAssist\{5E6AB780-7743-11CF-A12B-00AA004AE837}]
Version	[HKCU\Software\Microsoft\Windows\CurrentVersion\Explorer\UserAssist\{75048700-EF1F-11D0-9888-006097DEACF9}]
VerStamp	[HKCU\Identities\{0ACE9E60-3362-4310-B2E4-66E22371AB5E}\Software\Microsoft\Outlook Express\5.0]
video/avi	[HKCU\Software\Netscape\Netscape Navigator\Suffixes]
video/avi	[HKCU\Software\Netscape\Netscape Navigator\Viewers]
video/mpeg	[HKCU\Software\Netscape\Netscape Navigator\Suffixes]
video/mpeg	[HKCU\Software\Netscape\Netscape Navigator\Viewers]
video/msvideo	[HKCU\Software\Netscape\Netscape Navigator\Suffixes]
video/msvideo	[HKCU\Software\Netscape\Netscape Navigator\Viewers]
video/quicktime	[HKCU\Software\Netscape\Netscape Navigator\Suffixes]
video/quicktime	[HKCU\Software\Netscape\Netscape Navigator\Viewers]
video/x-ivf	[HKCU\Software\Netscape\Netscape Navigator\Suffixes]
video/x-ivf	[HKCU\Software\Netscape\Netscape Navigator\Viewers]
video/x-la-asf	[HKCU\Software\Netscape\Netscape Navigator\Suffixes]
video/x-la-asf	[HKCU\Software\Netscape\Netscape Navigator\Viewers]
video/x-mpeg	[HKCU\Software\Netscape\Netscape Navigator\Suffixes]
video/x-mpeg	[HKCU\Software\Netscape\Netscape Navigator\Viewers]
video/x-mpeg2a	[HKCU\Software\Netscape\Netscape Navigator\Suffixes]
video/x-mpeg2a	[HKCU\Software\Netscape\Netscape Navigator\Viewers]
video/x-ms-asf	[HKCU\Software\Netscape\Netscape Navigator\Suffixes]
video/x-ms-asf	[HKCU\Software\Netscape\Netscape Navigator\Viewers]
video/x-ms-asf-plugin	[HKCU\Software\Netscape\Netscape Navigator\Suffixes]

Entry Name	Key
video/x-ms-asf-plugin	[HKCU\Software\Netscape\Netscape Navigator\Viewers]
video/x-msvideo	[HKCU\Software\Netscape\Netscape Navigator\Suffixes]
video/x-msvideo	[HKCU\Software\Netscape\Netscape Navigator\Viewers]
View	[HKCU\Software\Microsoft\MSInfo]
View	[HKCU\Software\Microsoft\Windows\CurrentVersion\Applets\Regedit]
Viewing_Security	[HKCU\Software\Microsoft\Internet Explorer\Security]
ViewView2	[HKCU\Software\Microsoft\Windows\CurrentVersion\Explorer\Streams\0]
ViewView2	[HKCU\Software\Microsoft\Windows\CurrentVersion\Explorer\Streams\1]
ViewView2	[HKCU\Software\Microsoft\Windows\CurrentVersion\Explorer\Streams\2]
ViewView2	[HKCU\Software\Microsoft\Windows\CurrentVersion\Explorer\Streams\Desktop]
Virtual Key	[HKCU\Control Panel\Input Method\Hot Keys\00000010]
Virtual Key	[HKCU\Control Panel\Input Method\Hot Keys\00000011]
Virtual Key	[HKCU\Control Panel\Input Method\Hot Keys\00000012]
Virtual Key	[HKCU\Control Panel\Input Method\Hot Keys\00000070]
Virtual Key	[HKCU\Control Panel\Input Method\Hot Keys\00000071]
Virtual Key	[HKCU\Control Panel\Input Method\Hot Keys\00000072]
Virtual Key	[HKCU\Control Panel\Input Method\Hot Keys\00000200]
Virtual Key	[HKCU\Control Panel\Input Method\Hot Keys\00000201]
Virtual Key	[HKCU\Control Panel\Input Method\Hot Keys\00000202]
VisitGallery	[HKCU\Software\Microsoft\Internet Explorer\Desktop\SafeMode\General]
VisualNotification	[HKCU\Software\Microsoft\Fax\UserInfo]
Waffle	[HKCU\Control Panel\Patterns]
WaitToKillAppTimeout	[HKCU\Control Panel\Desktop]
WalkRandom1	[HKCU\Control Panel\Screen Saver.Mystify]
WalkRandom2	[HKCU\Control Panel\Screen Saver.Mystify]
Wallpaper	[HKCU\Control Panel\Desktop]
Wallpaper	[HKCU\Software\Microsoft\Internet Explorer\Desktop\SafeMode\General]

Entry Name	Key
WallpaperFileTime	[HKCU\Software\Microsoft\Internet Explorer\Desktop\General]
WarnOnPost	[HKCU\Software\Microsoft\Windows\ CurrentVersion\Internet Settings]
WarpSpeed	[HKCU\Control Panel\Screen Saver.Stars]
Weave	[HKCU\Control Panel\Patterns]
WebView	[HKCU\Software\Microsoft\Windows\ CurrentVersion\Explorer\Advanced]
Wheat	[HKCU\Control Panel\Appearance\ Schemes]
WheelScrollLines	[HKCU\Control Panel\Desktop]
width	[HKCU\Software\Microsoft\Internet Explorer\Document Windows]
Width	[HKCU\Software\Microsoft\RegEdt32\ Settings]
Window	[HKCU\Control Panel\Colors]
Window	[HKCU\Software\Microsoft\Windows NT\CurrentVersion\Program Manager\Settings]
WindowFrame	[HKCU\Control Panel\Colors]
Windows Classic (extra large)	[HKCU\Control Panel\Appearance\ Schemes]
Windows Classic (large)	[HKCU\Control Panel\Appearance\ Schemes]
Windows Classic	[HKCU\Control Panel\Appearance\ Schemes]
Windows Standard (extra large)	[HKCU\Control Panel\Appearance\ Schemes]
Windows Standard (large)	[HKCU\Control Panel\Appearance\ Schemes]
Windows Standard	[HKCU\Control Panel\Appearance\ Schemes]
WindowsEffect	[HKCU\Control Panel\Accessibility\ SoundSentry]
WindowSize	[HKCU\Console]
WindowText	[HKCU\Control Panel\Colors]
wtx	[HKCU\Software\Microsoft\Windows NT\CurrentVersion\Extensions]
x	[HKCU\Software\Microsoft\Internet Explorer\Document Windows]
Xl	[HKCU\Software\Microsoft\Windows Help]
Xr	[HKCU\Software\Microsoft\Windows Help]
y	[HKCU\Software\Microsoft\Internet Explorer\Document Windows]
Yd	[HKCU\Software\Microsoft\Windows Help]
Yu	[HKCU\Software\Microsoft\Windows Help]

Class ID Reference

Every object registered in Windows 2000 is assigned a unique identifier. This identifier is known as the CLSID. The Registry collects information about objects based on the CLSID. Table B.1 provides you a reference of the CLSID to the object each represents. This list is based on a fresh install of Windows 2000 with only Microsoft Office 2000 installed.

| TABLE B.1 | CLSID Reference |

CLSID Object	**Reference**
{0000002F-0000-0000-C000-000000000046}	CLSID_RecordInfo
{00000100-0000-0010-8000-00AA006D2EA4}	DAO.DBEngine.36
{00000101-0000-0010-8000-00AA006D2EA4}	DAO.PrivateDBEngine.36
{00000103-0000-0010-8000-00AA006D2EA4}	DAO.TableDef.36
{00000104-0000-0010-8000-00AA006D2EA4}	DAO.Field.36
{00000105-0000-0010-8000-00AA006D2EA4}	DAO.Index.36
{00000106-0000-0010-8000-00AA006D2EA4}	DAO.Group.36
{00000107-0000-0010-8000-00AA006D2EA4}	DAO.User.36
{00000108-0000-0010-8000-00AA006D2EA4}	DAO.QueryDef.36
{00000109-0000-0010-8000-00AA006D2EA4}	DAO.Relation.36
{00000300-0000-0000-C000-000000000046}	StdOleLink
{00000303-0000-0000-C000-000000000046}	FileMoniker
{00000304-0000-0000-C000-000000000046}	ItemMoniker
{00000305-0000-0000-C000-000000000046}	AntiMoniker
{00000306-0000-0000-C000-000000000046}	PointerMoniker
{00000308-0000-0000-C000-000000000046}	PackagerMoniker
{00000309-0000-0000-C000-000000000046}	CompositeMoniker
{0000030B-0000-0000-C000-000000000046}	DfMarshal
{00000315-0000-0000-C000-000000000046}	Picture (Metafile)
{00000316-0000-0000-C000-000000000046}	Picture (Device Independent Bitmap)
{00000319-0000-0000-C000-000000000046}	Picture (Enhanced Metafile)
{0000031A-0000-0000-C000-000000000046}	ClassMoniker
{0000031D-0000-0000-C000-000000000046}	DCOMAccessControl
{00000320-0000-0000-C000-000000000046}	PSFactoryBuffer
{00000327-0000-0000-C000-000000000046}	objref
{0000032E-0000-0000-C000-000000000046}	PipePSFactory
{00000507-0000-0010-8000-00AA006D2EA4}	ADODB.Command
{0000050B-0000-0010-8000-00AA006D2EA4}	ADODB.Parameter
{00000514-0000-0010-8000-00AA006D2EA4}	ADODB.Connection
{0000051A-0000-0010-8000-00AA006D2EA4}	ADO 2.5
{0000051A-0000-0010-8000-00AA006D2EA4}	ADO Error Lookup
{00000535-0000-0010-8000-00AA006D2EA4}	ADODB.Recordset
{00000541-0000-0010-8000-00AA006D2EA4}	ADODB.Error
{00000542-0000-0010-8000-00AA006D2EA4}	ADODB Error Lookup Service
{00000560-0000-0010-8000-00AA006D2EA4}	ADODB.Record
{00000566-0000-0010-8000-00AA006D2EA4}	ADODB.Stream
{00000602-0000-0010-8000-00AA006D2EA4}	ADOX.Catalog.2.5
{00000609-0000-0010-8000-00AA006D2EA4}	ADOX.Table.2.5
{00000615-0000-0010-8000-00AA006D2EA4}	ADOX.Group.2.5

TABLE B.1	Continued

CLSID Object	Reference
{00000618-0000-0010-8000-00AA006D2EA4}	ADOX.User.2.5
{0000061B-0000-0010-8000-00AA006D2EA4}	ADOX.Column.2.5
{0000061E-0000-0010-8000-00AA006D2EA4}	ADOX.Index.2.5
{00000621-0000-0010-8000-00AA006D2EA4}	ADOX.Key.2.5
{00020000-0000-0000-C000-000000000046}	Microsoft AVI Files
{00020001-0000-0000-C000-000000000046}	AVI Compressed Stream
{00020003-0000-0000-C000-000000000046}	Microsoft Wave File
{0002000D-0000-0000-C000-000000000046}	IAVIStream & IAVIFile Proxy
{0002000F-0000-0000-C000-000000000046}	ACM Compressed Audio Stream
{00020344-0000-0000-C000-000000000046}	MAPILogonRemote
{0002034C-0000-0000-C000-000000000046}	OutlookAttachMoniker
{0002034E-0000-0000-C000-000000000046}	OutlookMessageMoniker
{00020420-0000-0000-C000-000000000046}	PSDispatch
{00020421-0000-0000-C000-000000000046}	PSEnumVariant
{00020422-0000-0000-C000-000000000046}	PSTypeInfo
{00020423-0000-0000-C000-000000000046}	PSTypeLib
{00020424-0000-0000-C000-000000000046}	PSOAInterface
{00020425-0000-0000-C000-000000000046}	PSTypeComp
{00020800-0000-0000-C000-000000000046}	Microsoft Graph 2000 Application
{00020803-0000-0000-C000-000000000046}	Microsoft Graph 2000 Chart
{00020810-0000-0000-C000-000000000046}	Microsoft Excel Worksheet
{00020811-0000-0000-C000-000000000046}	Microsoft Excel Chart
{00020812-0000-0000-C000-000000000046}	Microsoft Excel Application
{00020820-0000-0000-C000-000000000046}	Microsoft Excel Worksheet
{00020821-0000-0000-C000-000000000046}	Microsoft Excel Chart
{00020900-0000-0000-C000-000000000046}	Microsoft Word 6.0 - 7.0 Document
{00020901-0000-0000-C000-000000000046}	Microsoft Word 6.0 - 7.0 Picture
{00020906-0000-0000-C000-000000000046}	Microsoft Word Document
{00020907-0000-0000-C000-000000000046}	Microsoft Word Picture
{000209FE-0000-0000-C000-000000000046}	Microsoft Word Basic
{000209FF-0000-0000-C000-000000000046}	Microsoft Word Application
{00020C01-0000-0000-C000-000000000046}	Sound (OLE2)
{00020D05-0000-0000-C000-000000000046}	Inserted File
{00020D09-0000-0000-C000-000000000046}	Outlook Message Attachment
{00020D75-0000-0000-C000-000000000046}	Microsoft Outlook
{00021120-0000-0000-C000-000000000046}	FXO File Viewer
{00021290-0000-0000-C000-000000000046}	Microsoft Clip Gallery
{00021400-0000-0000-C000-000000000046}	Desktop
{00021400-0000-0000-C000-000000000046}	file://%userappdata%\Microsoft\ InternetExplorer\Desktop.htt

| TABLE B.1 | Continued |

CLSID Object	Reference
{00021401-0000-0000-C000-000000000046}	Shortcut
{00021401-0000-0000-C000-000000000046}	{00021401-0000-0000-C000-000000000046}
{00021700-0000-0000-C000-000000000046}	Microsoft Equation 2.0
{00022601-0000-0000-C000-000000000046}	Media Clip
{00022602-0000-0000-C000-000000000046}	Video Clip
{00022603-0000-0000-C000-000000000046}	MIDI Sequence
{00022613-0000-0000-C000-000000000046}	Multimedia File Property Sheet
{00024500-0000-0000-C000-000000000046}	Microsoft Excel Application
{00024502-0000-0000-C000-000000000046}	Microsoft Graph 2000 Application
{00024512-0000-0000-C000-000000000046}	RefEdit.Ctrl
{0002CC0F-0000-0000-C000-000000000046}	{0002CC1F-0000-0000-C000-000000000046}
{0002CC1F-0000-0000-C000-000000000046}	Microsoft Map
{0002CE02-0000-0000-C000-000000000046}	Microsoft Equation 3.0
{0002DF01-0000-0000-C000-000000000046}	Internet Explorer(Ver 1.0)
{0002E005-0000-0000-C000-000000000046}	Component Categories Manager
{0002E006-0000-0000-C000-000000000046}	Component Categories Manager With Class Store
{0002E500-0000-0000-C000-000000000046}	Microsoft Office Chart 9.0
{0002E510-0000-0000-C000-000000000046}	Microsoft Office Spreadsheet 9.0
{0002E520-0000-0000-C000-000000000046}	Microsoft Office PivotTable 9.0
{0002E530-0000-0000-C000-000000000046}	Microsoft Office Data Source Control 9.0
{0002E531-0000-0000-C000-000000000046}	Microsoft Office Record Navigation Control 9.0
{0002E532-0000-0000-C000-000000000046}	Microsoft Office Expand Control 9.0
{00030001-0000-0000-C000-000000000046}	Microsoft Excel Chart
{00030002-0000-0000-C000-000000000046}	Microsoft Excel 4.0 Macro
{00030003-0000-0000-C000-000000000046}	Microsoft Word 2.0 Document
{00030006-0000-0000-C000-000000000046}	{00020803-0000-0000-C000-000000000046}
{00030007-0000-0000-C000-000000000046}	Microsoft Drawing
{0003000a-0000-0000-C000-000000000046}	Paintbrush Picture
{0003000B-0000-0000-C000-000000000046}	Microsoft Equation
{0003000C-0000-0000-C000-000000000046}	Package
{0003000D-0000-0000-C000-000000000046}	Sound
{0003000E-0000-0000-C000-000000000046}	Media Clip
{00030026-0000-0000-C000-000000000046}	Microsoft ClipArt Gallery
{00041943-0000-0000-C000-000000000046}	Microsoft Organization Chart 1.0
{0004749F-0000-0000-C000-000000000046}	Microsoft Imager 1.0 Picture
{00061068-0000-0000-C000-000000000046}	Outlook Message Recall Item
{00062000-0000-0000-C000-000000000046}	Outlook TableView
{00062001-0000-0000-C000-000000000046}	Outlook TimelineView
{00062002-0000-0000-C000-000000000046}	Outlook CardView
{00062003-0000-0000-C000-000000000046}	Outlook CalendarView

| TABLE B.1 | Continued |

CLSID Object	Reference
{00062004-0000-0000-C000-000000000046}	Outlook IconView
{00067009-0000-0000-C000-000000000046}	Outlook PSOutlookMessageSite
{0006729A-0000-0000-C000-000000000046}	PSFactoryBuffer
{00067800-0000-0000-C000-000000000046}	Mail Management Module
{00067801-0000-0000-C000-000000000046}	Contact Management Module
{00067802-0000-0000-C000-000000000046}	Appointment Management Module
{00067803-0000-0000-C000-000000000046}	Task Management Module
{00067804-0000-0000-C000-000000000046}	Notes Management Module
{00067808-0000-0000-C000-000000000046}	Journal Module
{0006780A-0000-0000-C000-000000000046}	MAPI Search Module
{0006780B-0000-0000-C000-000000000046}	File Search Module
{00067820-0000-0000-C000-000000000046}	Outlook FAT Management Module
{00067821-0000-0000-C000-000000000046}	Outlook My Computer Management Module
{00067822-0000-0000-C000-000000000046}	Outlook Network Neighborhood Management Module
{00067823-0000-0000-C000-000000000046}	Outlook Network Share Management Module
{00067828-0000-0000-C000-000000000046}	IMAP Module
{0006F005-0000-0000-C000-000000000046}	Outlook Registered Central
{0006F006-0000-0000-C000-000000000046}	Outlook Central
{0006F011-0000-0000-C000-000000000046}	Outlook Recipient
{0006F017-0000-0000-C000-000000000046}	Outlook Namespace
{0006F018-0000-0000-C000-000000000046}	Outlook FAT Namespace
{0006F019-0000-0000-C000-000000000046}	Outlook Finder Stub
{0006F01A-0000-0000-C000-000000000046}	Microsoft Outlook Envelope Object
{0006F01E-0000-0000-C000-000000000046}	Outlook Office Explorer
{0006F01F-0000-0000-C000-000000000046}	Outlook Office Finder
{0006F020-0000-0000-C000-000000000046}	Outlook Form Factory
{0006F023-0000-0000-C000-000000000046}	Outlook Recipient Collection Edit OLE Control
{0006F024-0000-0000-C000-000000000046}	Outlook DocSite OLE Control
{0006F02A-0000-0000-C000-000000000046}	Outlook Header OLE Control
{0006F030-0000-0000-C000-000000000046}	Outlook Message Site Object
{0006F031-0000-0000-C000-000000000046}	Outlook File Attachment
{0006F032-0000-0000-C000-000000000046}	Outlook Message Attachment
{0006F033-0000-0000-C000-000000000046}	Microsoft Outlook 8.0 Object Library
{0006F03A-0000-0000-C000-000000000046}	Microsoft Outlook
{0006F045-0000-0000-C000-000000000046}	Outlook File Icon Extension
{0006F065-0000-0000-C000-000000000046}	Outlook View Control
{0006F068-0000-0000-C000-000000000046}	Outlook View Selector Control
{0006F069-0000-0000-C000-000000000046}	Outlook Object Model Access

· · · · · · · · · · · · · · · ·

TABLE B.1 Continued

CLSID Object	Reference
{0006F071-0000-0000-C000-000000000046}	Outlook Progress Ctl
{0006F07A-0000-0000-C000-000000000046}	Outlook Exception List Object
{0006F07B-0000-0000-C000-000000000046}	Outlook Junk EMail List Object
{0006F07C-0000-0000-C000-000000000046}	Outlook Adult Content List Object
{0006F081-0000-0000-C000-000000000046}	MimeDirItem Class
{0006F082-0000-0000-C000-000000000046}	MimeDirParser Class
{0006F083-0000-0000-C000-000000000046}	MimeDirWriter Class
{0006F084-0000-0000-C000-000000000046}	MimeDirProfile Class
{0006F085-0000-0000-C000-000000000046}	MapiCvt Class
{0006F08A-0000-0000-C000-000000000046}	WebPub.cWebPub
{0006F08D-0000-0000-C000-000000000046}	dlgCancl.cCancel
{000C0114-0000-0000-C000-000000000046}	Microsoft Office 9
{000C101C-0000-0000-C000-000000000046}	Msi install server
{000C101D-0000-0000-C000-000000000046}	Microsoft Windows Installer Message RPC
{000C1025-0000-0000-C000-000000000046}	Msi custom action server
{000C103E-0000-0000-C000-000000000046}	PSFactoryBuffer
{000C1090-0000-0000-C000-000000000046}	Microsoft Windows Installer
{000C1205-0000-0000-C000-000000000046}	Microsoft Script Editor Proxy
{004CE610-CCD1-11D0-A9BA-00A0C908DB5E}	Configuration Object for Java
{006A2A75-547F-11D1-B930-00A0C9A06D2D}	F:\WINNT\System32\dsadmin.dll
{009541A0-3B81-101C-92F3-040224009C02}	Kodak Image Admin Control
{009541A4-3B81-101C-92F3-040224009C02}	Kodak Image Admin Property Page
{00BB2763-6A77-11D0-A535-00C04FD7D062}	Microsoft AutoComplete
{00BB2764-6A77-11D0-A535-00C04FD7D062}	Microsoft History AutoComplete List
{00BB2765-6A77-11D0-A535-00C04FD7D062}	Microsoft Multiple AutoComplete List Container
{00C429C0-0BA9-11d2-A484-00C04F8EFB69}	CrBlinds
{00D20920-7E20-11D0-B291-00C04FC31D18}	RTP Source Filter
{00D20921-7E20-11D0-B291-00C04FC31D18}	RTP Render Filter
{00D20923-7E20-11D0-B291-00C04FC31D18}	RTP Render Filter
{010E6CBE-FE2B-11D0-B079-006008058A0E}	TriEditParse Class
{011BE22D-E453-11D1-945A-00C04FB984F9}	WSecEdit Security Manager Class
{01458CF0-A1A2-11D1-8F85-00600895E7D5}	Interface Proxy Stub
{01C3D4A0-A701-11D1-8324-00A024CAA292}	Microsoft Picture It! Picture
{01C3D4A1-A701-11D1-8324-00A024CAA292}	Microsoft Picture It! Picture
{01C3D4A2-A701-11D1-8324-00A024CAA292}	Microsoft Picture It! Picture
{01C3D4A3-A701-11D1-8324-00A024CAA292}	Microsoft Picture It! Picture
{01C3D4A4-A701-11D1-8324-00A024CAA292}	Microsoft Picture It! Picture
{01C3D4A5-A701-11D1-8324-00A024CAA292}	Microsoft Picture It! Picture
{01C3D4A6-A701-11D1-8324-00A024CAA292}	Microsoft Picture It! Picture

TABLE B.1	Continued

CLSID Object	Reference
{01C3D4A7-A701-11D1-8324-00A024CAA292}	Microsoft Picture It! Picture
{01C3D4A8-A701-11D1-8324-00A024CAA292}	Microsoft Picture It! Picture
{01c6b350-12c7-11ce-bd31-00aa004bbb1f}	Swedish_Default Word Breaker
{01E04581-4EEE-11d0-BFE9-00AA005B4383}	&Address
{027713F2-5FA8-11d2-875B-00A0C93C09B3}	RotateBvr Class
{0285b5c0-12c7-11ce-bd31-00aa004bbb1f}	Spanish_Modern Word Breaker
{02B01C80-E03D-101A-B294-00DD010F2BF9}	Image Document
{02C7E642-7E04-11D0-9D99-00A0C908DB96}	Glow Effect
{0368BFF0-9870-11D0-94AB-0080C74C7E95}	AMtoolbar Class
{039EA4C0-E696-11d0-878A-00A0C91EC756}	Jet Expression Service
{03C036F1-A186-11D0-824A-00AA005B4383}	Microsoft Shell Folder AutoComplete List
{03D9F3F2-B0E3-11D2-B081-006008039BF0}	JVIEW Profiler
{03F1F940-A0F2-11D0-BB77-00AA00A1EAB7}	Allows management of the SMTP messaging protocol
{0456C164-D0EF-11D0-A787-0000F80272EA}	DocPPG Class
{0468C085-CA5B-11D0-AF08-00609797F0E0}	DataCtl Class
{0482E074-C5B7-101A-82E0-08002B36A333}	Microsoft Schedule+ 7.0 Application
{04921709-B159-11d1-9207-0000F8758E66}	HeightField
{04CCE2FF-A7D3-11D0-B436-00A0244A1DD2}	ThreadManager Class
{04DF1015-7007-11D1-83BC-006097ABE675}	Microsoft FrontPage Application
{04e07f54-6e5c-11d0-9292-00c04fd919b7}	ICodecInfo_PSFactory
{050DA15F-9F13-11D0-9CE5-00C04FC9BCC4}	NWLink Configuration Notify Object
{0514B040-84EA-11D0-A8BF-00A0C9008A48}	DirectPlay2 3.0 Object
{05238C14-A6E1-11D0-9A84-00C04FD8DBF7}	PSFactoryBuffer
{05300401-BCBC-11d0-85E3-00C04FD85AB4}	MHTML Asychronous Pluggable Protocol Handler
{05589FA1-C356-11CE-BF01-00AA0055595A}	ActiveMovieControl Object
{05589FAF-C356-11CE-BF01-00AA0055595A}	Audio Renderer Property Page
{0578DF30-4383-11D2-B91E-0060089F5C5D}	Answer Wizard ProxyStub Factory
{058C1509-2201-11D2-BFC1-00805F858323}	Main Wizard class for the conflict resolver
{058C1536-2201-11D2-BFC1-00805F858323}	WzConflict.sortie
{05dc3bb0-4337-11d0-a5c8-00a0c922e752}	NSEPM COM Server
{05f6fe1a-ecef-11d0-aae7-00c04fc9b304}	IntDitherer Class
{060AF76C-68DD-11D0-8FC1-00C04FD9189D}	Seeking
{0618AA30-6BC4-11CF-BF36-00AA0055595A}	Full Screen Renderer Property Page
{06210E88-01F5-11D1-B512-0080C781C384}	PSFactoryBuffer
{06290BD0-48AA-11D2-8432-006008C3FBFC}	Object under which scriptlets may be created
{06290BD1-48AA-11D2-8432-006008C3FBFC}	Constructor that allows hosts better control creating scriptlets
{06290BD2-48AA-11D2-8432-006008C3FBFC}	Factory bindable using IPersistMoniker

··················

TABLE B.1	Continued

CLSID Object	Reference
{06290BD3-48AA-11D2-8432-006008C3FBFC}	Moniker to a Windows Script Component
{06290BD4-48AA-11D2-8432-006008C3FBFC}	Object for encoding scriptlets
{06290BD5-48AA-11D2-8432-006008C3FBFC}	Object for constructing type libraries for scriptlets
{06290BD8-48AA-11D2-8432-006008C3FBFC}	Constructor for Scriptlet Automation Handler
{06290BD9-48AA-11D2-8432-006008C3FBFC}	Constructor for Scriptlet Event Handler
{06290BDA-48AA-11D2-8432-006008C3FBFC}	Constructor for Scriptlet ASP Handler
{06290BDB-48AA-11D2-8432-006008C3FBFC}	Constructor for Scriptlet Behavior Handler
{063B79F5-7539-11D2-9773-00A0C9B4D50C}	Microsoft COM+ Services Meta Data
{063B79F6-7539-11D2-9773-00A0C9B4D50C}	Microsoft COM+ Services Meta Data
{064D91E4-E8CD-11D0-BD91-006097C99369}	DTC Runtime
{068B0700-718C-11d0-8B1A-00A0C91BC90E}	Microsoft NetMeeting Manager Object
{068B0800-718C-11d0-8B1A-00A0C91BC90E}	Microsoft NetMeeting Manager Object 3
{06A03425-C9EB-11d2-8CAA-0080C739E3E0}	Help Collection Wrapper Class
{06BE7323-EF34-11d1-ACD8-00C04FA31009}	Outlook Express Mail Object
{06CE0C3A-8917-11D1-AA78-00C04FC9B202}	RTP Class
{06DD38D3-D187-11CF-A80D-00C04FD74AD8}	ActiveXPlugin Object
{06EC6E16-8E4B-11D0-B225-080000185165}	AxPropertyBag Class
{07167665-5011-11CF-BF33-00AA0055595A}	Full Screen Renderer
{0725C3CB-FEFB-11D0-99F9-00C04FC2F8EC}	WMI Event Provider
{075BB8A1-B7D8-11D2-A1C6-00609778EA66}	Microsoft MPEG-4 Video Decompressor About Page
{07798131-AF23-11d1-9111-00A0C98BA67D}	Web Search
{07970B30-A4DA-11D2-B724-00104BC51339}	PSFactoryBuffer
{07A774A0-6047-11D1-BA20-006097D2898E}	Logagent Class
{07B65360-C445-11CE-AFDE-00AA006C14F4}	MIDI Renderer
{07D26616-6136-11D1-8C9C-00C04FC3261D}	F:\WINNT\System32\clbcatq.dll
{080d0d78-f421-11d0-a36e-00c04fb950dc}	ADs LDAP Pathname Descriptor Object
{08165EA0-E946-11CF-9C87-00AA005127ED}	WebCheckWebCrawler
{083863F1-70DE-11d0-BD40-00A0C911CE86}	ActiveMovie Filter Class Manager
{083863F1-70DE-11d0-BD40-00A0C911CE86}	{00D20920-7E20-11D0-B291-00C04FC31D18}
{083863F1-70DE-11d0-BD40-00A0C911CE86}	{00D20921-7E20-11D0-B291-00C04FC31D18}
{083863F1-70DE-11d0-BD40-00A0C911CE86}	{07167665-5011-11CF-BF33-00AA0055595A}
{083863F1-70DE-11d0-BD40-00A0C911CE86}	{129D7E40-C10D-11D0-AFB9-00AA00B67A42}
{083863F1-70DE-11d0-BD40-00A0C911CE86}	{1643E180-90F5-11CE-97D5-00AA0055595A}
{083863F1-70DE-11d0-BD40-00A0C911CE86}	{1AE60860-8297-11D0-9643-00AA00A89C1D}
{083863F1-70DE-11d0-BD40-00A0C911CE86}	{1B544C20-FD0B-11CE-8C63-00AA0044B51E}
{083863F1-70DE-11d0-BD40-00A0C911CE86}	{1DA08500-9EDC-11CF-BC10-00AA00AC74F6}
{083863F1-70DE-11d0-BD40-00A0C911CE86}	{1F73E9B1-8C3A-11D0-A3BE-00A0C9244436}
{083863F1-70DE-11d0-BD40-00A0C911CE86}	{22E24591-49D0-11D2-BB50-006008320064}

| TABLE B.1 | Continued |

CLSID Object	Reference
{083863F1-70DE-11d0-BD40-00A0C911CE86}	{26721E10-390C-11D0-8A22-00A0C90C9156}
{083863F1-70DE-11d0-BD40-00A0C911CE86}	{30355649-0000-0010-8000-00AA00389B71}
{083863F1-70DE-11d0-BD40-00A0C911CE86}	{31363248-0000-0010-8000-00AA00389B71}
{083863F1-70DE-11d0-BD40-00A0C911CE86}	{33363248-0000-0010-8000-00AA00389B71}
{083863F1-70DE-11d0-BD40-00A0C911CE86}	{336475D0-942A-11CE-A870-00AA002FEAB5}
{083863F1-70DE-11d0-BD40-00A0C911CE86}	{33FACFE0-A9BE-11D0-A520-00A0D10129C0}
{083863F1-70DE-11d0-BD40-00A0C911CE86}	{38BE3000-DBF4-11D0-860E-00A024CFEF6D}
{083863F1-70DE-11d0-BD40-00A0C911CE86}	{399D5C90-74AB-11D0-9CCF-00A0C9081C19}
{083863F1-70DE-11d0-BD40-00A0C911CE86}	{3DDDA000-88E4-11D0-9643-00AA00A89C1D}
{083863F1-70DE-11d0-BD40-00A0C911CE86}	{4009F700-AEBA-11D1-8344-00C04FB92EB7}
{083863F1-70DE-11d0-BD40-00A0C911CE86}	{48025243-2D39-11CE-875D-00608CB78066}
{083863F1-70DE-11d0-BD40-00A0C911CE86}	{4A2286E0-7BEF-11CE-9BD9-0000E202599C}
{083863F1-70DE-11d0-BD40-00A0C911CE86}	{4B428940-263C-11D1-A520-000000000000}
{083863F1-70DE-11d0-BD40-00A0C911CE86}	{4EB31670-9FC6-11CF-AF6E-00AA00B67A42}
{083863F1-70DE-11d0-BD40-00A0C911CE86}	{63F8AA94-E2B9-11D0-ADF6-00C04FB66DAD}
{083863F1-70DE-11d0-BD40-00A0C911CE86}	{640999A0-A946-11D0-A520-000000000000}
{083863F1-70DE-11d0-BD40-00A0C911CE86}	{640999A1-A946-11D0-A520-000000000000}
{083863F1-70DE-11d0-BD40-00A0C911CE86}	{640999A2-A946-11D0-A520-000000000000}
{083863F1-70DE-11d0-BD40-00A0C911CE86}	{6A08CF80-0E18-11CF-A24D-0020AFD79767}
{083863F1-70DE-11d0-BD40-00A0C911CE86}	{6B6D0800-9ADA-11D0-A520-00A0D10129C0}
{083863F1-70DE-11d0-BD40-00A0C911CE86}	{6E8D4A20-310C-11D0-B79A-00AA003767A7}
{083863F1-70DE-11d0-BD40-00A0C911CE86}	{70E102B0-5556-11CE-97C0-00AA0055595A}
{083863F1-70DE-11d0-BD40-00A0C911CE86}	{82CCD3E0-F71A-11D0-9FE5-00609778EA66}
{083863F1-70DE-11d0-BD40-00A0C911CE86}	{8596E5F0-0DA5-11D0-BD21-00A0C911CE86}
{083863F1-70DE-11d0-BD40-00A0C911CE86}	{9B8C4620-2C1A-11D0-8493-00A02438AD48}
{083863F1-70DE-11d0-BD40-00A0C911CE86}	{A0025E90-E45B-11D1-ABE9-00A0C905F375}
{083863F1-70DE-11d0-BD40-00A0C911CE86}	{A5EA8D20-253D-11D1-B3F1-00AA003761C5}
{083863F1-70DE-11d0-BD40-00A0C911CE86}	{A888DF60-1E90-11CF-AC98-00AA004C0FA9}
{083863F1-70DE-11d0-BD40-00A0C911CE86}	{A98C8400-4181-11D1-A520-00A0D10129C0}
{083863F1-70DE-11d0-BD40-00A0C911CE86}	{AF7D8180-A8F9-11CF-9A46-00AA00B7DAD1}
{083863F1-70DE-11d0-BD40-00A0C911CE86}	{B1B77C00-C3E4-11CF-AF79-00AA00B67A42}
{083863F1-70DE-11d0-BD40-00A0C911CE86}	{B4CA2970-DD2B-11D0-9DFA-00AA00AF3494}
{083863F1-70DE-11d0-BD40-00A0C911CE86}	{B6353564-96C4-11D2-8DDB-006097C9A2B2}
{083863F1-70DE-11d0-BD40-00A0C911CE86}	{B9D1F320-C401-11D0-A520-000000000000}
{083863F1-70DE-11d0-BD40-00A0C911CE86}	{B9D1F321-C401-11D0-A520-000000000000}
{083863F1-70DE-11d0-BD40-00A0C911CE86}	{B9D1F322-C401-11D0-A520-000000000000}
{083863F1-70DE-11d0-BD40-00A0C911CE86}	{B9D1F323-C401-11D0-A520-000000000000}
{083863F1-70DE-11d0-BD40-00A0C911CE86}	{B9D1F324-C401-11D0-A520-000000000000}
{083863F1-70DE-11d0-BD40-00A0C911CE86}	{B9D1F325-C401-11D0-A520-000000000000}

•••••••••••••••

| **TABLE B.1** | Continued |

CLSID Object	Reference
{083863F1-70DE-11d0-BD40-00A0C911CE86}	{B9D1F32E-C401-11D0-A520-000000000000}
{083863F1-70DE-11d0-BD40-00A0C911CE86}	{C69E8F40-D5C8-11D0-A520-145405C10000}
{083863F1-70DE-11d0-BD40-00A0C911CE86}	{C9076CE2-FB56-11CF-906C-00AA00A59F69}
{083863F1-70DE-11d0-BD40-00A0C911CE86}	{CC58E280-8AA1-11D1-B3F1-00AA003761C5}
{083863F1-70DE-11d0-BD40-00A0C911CE86}	{CD8743A1-3736-11D0-9E69-00C04FD7C15B}
{083863F1-70DE-11d0-BD40-00A0C911CE86}	{CDCDD6A0-C016-11D0-82A4-00AA00B5CA1B}
{083863F1-70DE-11d0-BD40-00A0C911CE86}	{CF49D4E0-1115-11CE-B03A-0020AF0BA770}
{083863F1-70DE-11d0-BD40-00A0C911CE86}	{D3588AB0-0781-11CE-B03A-0020AF0BA770}
{083863F1-70DE-11d0-BD40-00A0C911CE86}	{D42FEAC0-82A1-11D0-9643-00AA00A89C1D}
{083863F1-70DE-11d0-BD40-00A0C911CE86}	{D51BD5A0-7548-11CF-A520-0080C77EF58A}
{083863F1-70DE-11d0-BD40-00A0C911CE86}	{D51BD5A1-7548-11CF-A520-0080C77EF58A}
{083863F1-70DE-11d0-BD40-00A0C911CE86}	{D51BD5A2-7548-11CF-A520-0080C77EF58A}
{083863F1-70DE-11d0-BD40-00A0C911CE86}	{D51BD5A3-7548-11CF-A520-0080C77EF58A}
{083863F1-70DE-11d0-BD40-00A0C911CE86}	{D51BD5A4-7548-11CF-A520-0080C77EF58A}
{083863F1-70DE-11d0-BD40-00A0C911CE86}	{D51BD5A5-7548-11CF-A520-0080C77EF58A}
{083863F1-70DE-11d0-BD40-00A0C911CE86}	{D51BD5AE-7548-11CF-A520-0080C77EF58A}
{083863F1-70DE-11d0-BD40-00A0C911CE86}	{E2510970-F137-11CE-8B67-00AA00A3F1A6}
{083863F1-70DE-11d0-BD40-00A0C911CE86}	{E436EBB5-524F-11CE-9F53-0020AF0BA770}
{083863F1-70DE-11d0-BD40-00A0C911CE86}	{E436EBB6-524F-11CE-9F53-0020AF0BA770}
{083863F1-70DE-11d0-BD40-00A0C911CE86}	{EC941960-7DF6-11D0-9643-00AA00A89C1D}
{083863F1-70DE-11d0-BD40-00A0C911CE86}	{EC941961-7DF6-11D0-9643-00AA00A89C1D}
{083863F1-70DE-11d0-BD40-00A0C911CE86}	{ECB29E60-88ED-11D0-9643-00AA00A89C1D}
{083863F1-70DE-11d0-BD40-00A0C911CE86}	{EFD08EC1-EA11-11CF-9FEC-00AA00A59F69}
{083863F1-70DE-11d0-BD40-00A0C911CE86}	{F8388A40-D5BB-11D0-BE5A-0080C706568E}
{083863F1-70DE-11d0-BD40-00A0C911CE86}	{FDFE9681-74A3-11D0-AFA7-00AA00B67A42}
{083863F1-70DE-11d0-BD40-00A0C911CE86}	{FEB50740-7BEF-11CE-9BD9-0000E202599C}
{085C06A0-3CAA-11d0-A00E-00A024A85A2C}	Microsoft NetMeeting Quality of Service
{08B0E5C0-4FCB-11CF-AAA5-00401C608500}	Microsoft VM
{08B0E5C0-4FCB-11CF-AAA5-00401C608501}	Web Browser Applet Control
{08D32746-7AF6-11D0-B42A-00A0244A1DD2}	PSFactoryBuffer
{08EB4FA6-6FFD-11D1-B0E0-00C04FD8DCA6}	F:\WINNT\System32\dsadmin.dll
{0910dd01-df8c-11d1-ae27-00c04fa35813}	Terminal Server User Properties
{09474572-B2FB-11D1-A1A1-0000F875B132}	MMCListPadInfo Class
{09799AFB-AD67-11d1-ABCD-00C04FC30936}	Open With Context Menu Handler
{098f2470-bae0-11cd-b579-08002b30bfeb}	Null persistent handler
{098f2470-bae0-11cd-b579-08002b30bfeb}	{c3278e90-bea7-11cd-b579-08002b30bfeb}
{0996FF6F-B6A1-11D0-9292-00C04FB6678B}	Microsoft Certificate Authority Control
{0996FF70-B6A1-11D0-9292-00C04FB6678B}	Certificate Authority Property Page
{0998BB05-DFFD-11CF-927F-00AA00688A38}	Dsctl 1.0 Object

TABLE B.1 Continued

CLSID Object	Reference
{0A522730-A626-11D0-8D60-00C04FD6202B}	CLSID_CEudoraImport
{0A522732-A626-11D0-8D60-00C04FD6202B}	CLSID_CExchImport
{0A522733-A626-11D0-8D60-00C04FD6202B}	CLSID_CNetscapeImport
{0a75afcd-4680-11d1-a3b4-00c04fb950dc}	ADs PostalAddress Object
{0A89A860-D7B1-11CE-8350-444553540000}	Shell Automation Inproc Service
{0A9AE910-85C0-11D0-BD42-00A0C911CE86}	AVI mux Property Page1
{0ACE4881-8305-11CF-9427-444553540000}	MSWC.BrowserType
{0AFACED1-E828-11D1-9187-B532F1E9575D}	Folder Shortcut
{0AFACED1-E828-11D1-9187-B532F1E9575D}	{0AFACED1-E828-11D1-9187-B532F1E9575D}
{0AFACED1-E828-11D1-9187-B532F1E9575D}	{0AFACED1-E828-11D1-9187-B532F1E9575D}
{0AFACED1-E828-11D1-9187-B532F1E9575D}	{0AFACED1-E828-11D1-9187-B532F1E9575D}
{0B124F8C-91F0-11D1-B8B5-006008059382}	Installed Apps Enumerator
{0B89F2B1-3048-11D1-A727-006097C9947C}	URLPicker Class
{0B9A3960-8C3E-11d0-B797-00A02488FCDE}	HsmAdminData Class
{0BA686AA-F7D3-101A-993E-0000C0EF6F5E}	THREED CHECKBOX CONTROL
{0BA686AE-F7D3-101A-993E-0000C0EF6F5E}	THREED CHECKBOX PROPERTY PAGE
{0BA686AF-F7D3-101A-993E-0000C0EF6F5E}	THREED FRAME CONTROL
{0BA686B3-F7D3-101A-993E-0000C0EF6F5E}	THREED FRAME PROPERTY PAGE
{0BA686B4-F7D3-101A-993E-0000C0EF6F5E}	THREED COMMAND BUTTON CONTROL
{0BA686B8-F7D3-101A-993E-0000C0EF6F5E}	THREED COMMAND BUTTON PROPERTY PAGE
{0BA686B9-F7D3-101A-993E-0000C0EF6F5E}	THREED PANEL CONTROL
{0BA686BD-F7D3-101A-993E-0000C0EF6F5E}	THREED PANEL PROPERTY PAGE
{0BA686BE-F7D3-101A-993E-0000C0EF6F5E}	THREED OPTION BUTTON CONTROL
{0BA686C2-F7D3-101A-993E-0000C0EF6F5E}	THREED OPTION BUTTON PROPERTY PAGE
{0BA686C3-F7D3-101A-993E-0000C0EF6F5E}	THREED GROUP PUSH BUTTON CONTROL
{0BA686C7-F7D3-101A-993E-0000C0EF6F5E}	THREED GROUP PUSH BUTTON PROPERTY PAGE
{0BE35200-8F91-11CE-9DE3-00AA004BB851}	Font Property Page
{0BE35201-8F91-11CE-9DE3-00AA004BB851}	Color Property Page
{0BE35202-8F91-11CE-9DE3-00AA004BB851}	Picture Property Page
{0BE35203-8F91-11CE-9DE3-00AA004BB851}	CLSID_StdFont
{0BE35204-8F91-11CE-9DE3-00AA004BB851}	CLSID_StdPict
{0BFCC060-8C1D-11D0-ACCD-00AA0060275C}	DebugHelper Class
{0C0A3666-30C9-11D0-8F20-00805F2CD064}	Machine Debug Manager
{0C16C27E-A6E7-11D0-BFC3-0020F8008024}	Indexing Service Utility SSO V2
{0C7F3F20-8BAB-11d2-9432-00C04F8EF48F}	Downloadable Speech API
{0C7FF16C-38E3-11d0-97AB-00C04FC2AD98}	SQLOLEDB
{0C7FF16C-38E3-11d0-97AB-00C04FC2AD98}	SQLOLEDB Error Lookup
{0CD7A5C0-9F37-11CE-AE65-08002B2E1262}	Cabinet File

••••••••••••••••

| **TABLE B.1** | Continued |

CLSID Object	**Reference**
{0CF32AA1-7571-11D0-93C4-00AA00A3DDEA}	System Monitor Source Properties
{0CF774D0-F077-11D1-B1BC-00C04F86C324}	HTML Host Encode Object
{0CF774D1-F077-11D1-B1BC-00C04F86C324}	ASP Host Encode Object
{0D2E74C4-3C34-11d2-A27E-00C04FC30871}	%SystemRoot%\system32\shell32.dll
{0D3DEBB0-DEBE-11D1-8B87-00C04FD7A924}	AppExport Class
{0D43FE01-F093-11CF-8940-00A0C9054228}	FileSystem Object
{0D45D530-764B-11d0-A1CA-00AA00C16E65}	dsuiext.dll
{0df68130-4b62-11cf-ae2c-00aa006ebfb9}	NWCOMPAT Provider Object
{0E064AEC-9D99-11D0-ABE5-00AA0064D470}	Collaboration Data Objects Session Class
{0E59F1D5-1FBE-11D0-8FF2-00A0D10038BC}	ScriptControl Object
{0E5CBF21-D15F-11d0-8301-00AA005B4383}	&Links
{0E5EDCF0-9F3B-11D1-B3C3-0060977B463D}	FrontPage Editor Window
{0E6AE022-0C83-11D2-8CD4-00104BC75D9A}	MetaCreations Wormhole
{0E890F83-5F79-11D1-9043-00C04FD9189D}	DXSurface
{0EE708FE-94B4-11D0-9F66-00A0C9055CAC}	MDT OleUndoManager Class
{0F1BE7F7-45CA-11d2-831F-00A0244D2298}	IPConfMSP Class
{0F1BE7F8-45CA-11d2-831F-00A0244D2298}	H323MSP Class
{0F3621F1-23C6-11D1-AD97-00AA00B88E5A}	CMSnapin Class
{0F65B1BF-740F-11D1-BBE6-0060081692B3}	Remote Install Computer Property Pages
{0F6B957D-509E-11D1-A7CC-0000F87571E3}	Administrative Templates (Computers)
{0F6B957E-509E-11D1-A7CC-0000F87571E3}	Administrative Templates (Users)
{0FA9F4D5-A173-11D1-AA62-00C04FA34D72}	Microsoft Agent Voice Command Module Class
{0FB15084-AF41-11CE-BD2B-204C4F4F5020}	PSFactoryBuffer
{0fb32cc0-4b62-11cf-ae2c-00aa006ebfb9}	NWCOMPAT Namespace Object
{0FDE5092-AA2A-11D1-A7D4-0000F87571E3}	Group Policy About Information
{0FF15AA1-2F93-11d1-83B0-00C04FBD7C09}	CLSID_CCommNewsAcctImport
{10072CEC-8CC1-11D1-986E-00A0C955B42E}	PeerDraw Class
{101193C0-0BFE-11D0-AF91-00AA00B67A42}	Display
{101A8FB9-F1B9-11d1-9A56-00C04FA309D4}	CLSID_MessageStore
{105B80D2-95F1-11D0-B0A0-00AA00BDCB5C}	Microsoft DT DDS Form 2.0
{105B80D5-95F1-11D0-B0A0-00AA00BDCB5C}	Microsoft DT DDSform 2.1 FormPackage
{105B80DE-95F1-11D0-B0A0-00AA00BDCB5C}	Microsoft DT DDSform 2.1 FontNew
{105B80E0-95F1-11D0-B0A0-00AA00BDCB5C}	Microsoft DT DDSform 2.1 Font
{107045C5-06E0-11D2-8D6D-00C04F8EF8E0}	MetaCreations Water
{107045C8-06E0-11D2-8D6D-00C04F8EF8E0}	MetaCreations Light Wipe
{107045CA-06E0-11D2-8D6D-00C04F8EF8E0}	MetaCreations Lens
{107045CC-06E0-11D2-8D6D-00C04F8EF8E0}	MetaCreations Fade White
{107045CF-06E0-11D2-8D6D-00C04F8EF8E0}	MetaCreations Twister
{107045D1-06E0-11D2-8D6D-00C04F8EF8E0}	MetaCreations Burn Film

....

TABLE B.1 Continued	
CLSID Object	**Reference**
{1080B910-A636-11D0-A9EA-00AA00685C74}	PSFactoryBuffer
{10AE1B6E-6512-11D1-BB8E-0060083178D8}	ASFSession Class
{10AE1B71-6512-11D1-BB8E-0060083178D8}	FTSSession Class
{10CFC467-4392-11d2-8DB4-00C04FA31A66}	Offline Files Folder Options
{112981B2-1BA5-11D0-81B2-00A0C91180F2}	Remote Storage File
{112981B3-1BA5-11D0-81B2-00A0C91180F2}	FsaResourceNTFS Class
{11943940-36DE-11CF-953E-00C0A84029E9}	Microsoft Photo Editor 3.0 Photo
{11943941-36DE-11CF-953E-00C0A84029E9}	Microsoft Photo Editor 3.0 Scan
{1198A2C0-0940-11d1-838F-00C04FBD7C09}	CLSID_CCommunicatorImport
{11D59011-CF23-11D1-A02D-00C04FB6809F}	MSP Class
{11D5C91F-0A98-11D1-BB10-00C04FC9A3A3}	Computer Management 1.0 Object
{1241400f-4680-11d1-a3b4-00c04fb950dc}	ADs OctetList Object
{12518493-00B2-11d2-9FA5-9E3420524153}	Mounted Volume
{129D7E40-C10D-11D0-AFB9-00AA00B67A42}	DV Muxer
{131A6951-7F78-11D0-A979-00C04FD705A2}	ISFBand OC
{13709620-C279-11CE-A49E-444553540000}	Shell Automation Service
{13AA3650-BB6F-11D0-AFB9-00AA00B67A42}	DV Video Encoder
{13B3D462-43AD-11D0-BDC2-00A0C908DB96}	Wave Effect
{13D9E578-1CA8-11D0-A11B-00AA003E4672}	Microsoft SQLServer Database Reconciler
{141DBAF1-55FB-11D1-B83E-00A0C933BE86}	Explode
{14288070-1d42-11d0-9113-00aa00c147fa}	AVI Stream Source Filter
{1438E821-B6D2-11D0-8D86-00C04FD6202B}	CLSID_ApprenticeAcctMgr
{143A62C8-C33B-11D1-84FE-00C04FA34A14}	Microsoft Agent Character Property Sheet Handler
{1461AAC7-6810-11D0-918F-00AA00C18068}	SCard Class
{1461AACC-6810-11D0-918F-00AA00C18068}	SCardDatabase Class
{1461AAD1-6810-11D0-918F-00AA00C18068}	SCardLocate Class
{148BD520-A2AB-11CE-B11F-00AA00530503}	Scheduling Agent Task Object Class
{148BD52A-A2AB-11CE-B11F-00AA00530503}	Scheduling Agent Service Class
{14D0916D-9CDC-11D1-8C4A-00C04FC324A4}	ASP Tx Script Context
{14D0916E-9CDC-11D1-8C4A-00C04FC324A4}	ASP Tx Script Context
{14D0916F-9CDC-11D1-8C4A-00C04FC324A4}	ASP Tx Script Context
{14D09170-9CDC-11D1-8C4A-00C04FC324A4}	ASP Tx Script Context
{15b0bb4c-0f7d-11D1-b21f-00C04Fb9473f}	F:\WINNT\System32\clbcatq.dll
{15F0B130-CB2E-11D1-9596-00A0C90DCA5B}	OSE.Discussions
{15F0B132-CB2E-11D1-9596-00A0C90DCA5B}	OSE.Discussion
{15F0B134-CB2E-11D1-9596-00A0C90DCA5B}	OSE.Global
{15f88a55-4680-11d1-a3b4-00c04fb950dc}	ADs CaseIgnoreList Object
{1621F7C0-60AC-11CF-9427-444553540000}	MSWC.AdRotator
{163FDC20-2ABC-11d0-88F0-00A024AB2DBB}	dsquery.dll

TABLE B.1	Continued

CLSID Object	**Reference**
{1643E180-90F5-11CE-97D5-00AA0055595A}	Color Space Converter
{167701E3-FDCF-11D0-A48E-006097C549FF}	Microsoft Windows Report Control
{167701E4-FDCF-11D0-A48E-006097C549FF}	{167701E4-FDCF-11D0-A48E-006097C549FF}
{1698790a-e2b4-11d0-b0b1-00c04fd8dca6}	dsuiext.dll
{169A0691-8DF9-11d1-A1C4-00C04FD75D13}	In-pane search
{16B280C5-EE70-11D1-9066-00C04FD9189D}	Fade
{16B280C8-EE70-11D1-9066-00C04FD9189D}	BasicImage
{172BDDF8-CEEA-11D1-8B05-00600806D9B6}	Wbem Scripting Object Path
{176d6597-26d3-11d1-b350-080036a75b03}	ICM Scanner Management
{17869501-36C8-11d1-83B7-00C04FBD7C09}	CLSID_CNExpressAcctImport
{17CCA71B-ECD7-11D0-B908-00A0C9223196}	Generic WDM Filter Proxy
{17D6CCD8-3B7B-11D2-B9E0-00C04FD8DBF7}	DsObjectPicker
{1820FED0-473E-11D0-A96C-00C04FD705A2}	Shell DefView
{182C40F0-32E4-11D0-818B-00A0C9231C29}	COM+ Catalog Server
{183C259A-0480-11d1-87EA-00C04FC29D46}	LM Runtime Control
{18845040-0fa5-11d1-ba19-00c04fd912d0}	Microsoft HTML Load Options
{193B4137-0480-11D1-97DA-00C04FB9618A}	Microsoft DTC Transaction Unmarshaller (private, internal)
{19B7E2E2-FEBD-11d0-8827-00A0C955FC7E}	SCardAuth Class
{19B7E2E3-FEBD-11d0-8827-00A0C955FC7E}	SCardFileAccess Class
{19B7E2E4-FEBD-11d0-8827-00A0C955FC7E}	SCardManage Class
{19B7E2E5-FEBD-11d0-8827-00A0C955FC7E}	SCardVerify Class
{19B9A3F8-F975-11D1-97AD-00A0C9A06D2D}	F:\WINNT\System32\domadmin.dll
{1A04EA89-9414-11D0-906F-00AA00A1EAB7}	SmtpAdmin Class
{1A04EA8A-9414-11D0-906F-00AA00A1EAB7}	SmtpAdminService Class
{1A04EA8B-9414-11D0-906F-00AA00A1EAB7}	SmtpAdminVirtualServer Class
{1A04EA8C-9414-11D0-906F-00AA00A1EAB7}	SmtpAdminSessions Class
{1A04EA8D-9414-11D0-906F-00AA00A1EAB7}	SmtpAdminVirtualDirectory Class
{1A04EA8E-9414-11D0-906F-00AA00A1EAB7}	SmtpAdminAlias Class
{1A04EA8F-9414-11D0-906F-00AA00A1EAB7}	SmtpAdminUser Class
{1A04EA90-9414-11D0-906F-00AA00A1EAB7}	SmtpAdminDL Class
{1A04EA91-9414-11D0-906F-00AA00A1EAB7}	SmtpAdminDomain Class
{1A77E940-4E4E-11D0-B1E2-00C04FD70811}	DTCFramework Global Functions
{1A8766A0-62CE-11CF-A5D6-28DB04C10000}	WDM Streaming Standard Interface Handler
{1A9BA3A0-143A-11CF-8350-444553540000}	Shell Favorite Folder
{1AA06BA1-0E88-11d1-8391-00C04FBD7C09}	CLSID_CCommAcctImport
{1AA7F839-C7F5-11D0-A376-00C04FC9DA04}	Routing and Remote Access
{1AA7F83A-C7F5-11D0-A376-00C04FC9DA04}	Routing and Remote Access
{1AA7F83B-C7F5-11D0-A376-00C04FC9DA04}	Routing and Remote Access

TABLE B.1 Continued	
CLSID Object	**Reference**
{1AA7F83C-C7F5-11D0-A376-00C04FC9DA04}	AppleTalk Management
{1AA7F83D-C7F5-11D0-A376-00C04FC9DA04}	AppleTalk Management
{1AA7F83F-C7F5-11D0-A376-00C04FC9DA04}	RADIUS configuration object
{1AA7F840-C7F5-11D0-A376-00C04FC9DA04}	RADIUS configuration object
{1AA7F844-C7F5-11d0-A376-00C04FC9DA04}	remrras Class
{1AB4A8C0-6A0B-11d2-AD49-00C04FA31A86}	dsuiext.dll
{1ABAAF84-086F-11D2-95AF-0060B0576642}	IASStringAttributeEditor Class
{1ABCFC13-2340-11d2-B601-006097DF5BD4}	FTP Installer to handle FTP Associations
{1AE60860-8297-11D0-9643-00AA00A89C1D}	Intel RTP SPH for G.711/G.723.1
{1AEB1360-5AFC-11D0-B806-00C04FD706EC}	Office Graphics Filters Thumbnail Extractor
{1B0D38CF-941A-11D0-A675-00A0C903977C}	Standard COM Window
{1B1CAD8C-2DAB-11D2-B604-00104B703EFD}	Microsoft WBEM (non)Standard Marshaling for IEnumWbemClassObject
{1B53F360-9A1B-1069-930C-00AA0030EBC8}	HyperTerminal Connection Page Ext
{1B544C20-FD0B-11CE-8C63-00AA0044B51E}	AVI Splitter
{1B544C22-FD0B-11CE-8C63-00AA0044B51E}	VFW Capture Filter
{1B544C22-FD0B-11CE-8C63-00AA0044B51F}	VFW Capture Filter Property Page
{1BE1F766-5536-11D1-B726-00C04FB926AF}	EventSystemTier2
{1BE73E22-B843-11D0-8B40-00C0F00AE35A}	PermissionChecker Class
{1C3B4210-F441-11CE-B9EA-00AA006B1A69}	Microsoft Forms 2.1 DataObject
{1C82EAD9-508E-11D1-8DCF-00C04FB951F9}	Outlook Express Mime Editor
{1CB0A015-1676-11D0-825B-00A0C90395DF}	Component Services Add-In for VB 4.0
{1CE57F61-A88A-11D0-AB86-00C04FC3357A}	DHCP
{1cedc5da-3614-11d2-bf96-00c04fd8d5b0}	dsquery.dll
{1D0482E4-57E7-11d2-B10D-00805FC73204}	F:\WINNT\System32\catsrvut.dll
{1D1237A0-6CD6-11d2-96BA-00104B242E64}	ppDSFile Class
{1d2b4f40-1f10-11d1-9e88-00c04fdcab92}	ThumbCtl Class
{1D3ECD40-C835-11CE-9888-00608CC22020}	Kodak Image Shell Extension
{1DA08500-9EDC-11CF-BC10-00AA00AC74F6}	VGA 16 color ditherer
{1E54333B-2A00-11d1-8198-0000F87557DB}	DXLUTBuilder
{1E651CC0-B199-11D0-8212-00C04FC32C45}	Memory Allocator
{1E794A0A-86F4-11D1-ADD8-0000F87734F0}	RefDial Class
{1E9685E6-DB6D-11d0-BB63-00C04FC2F410}	Content Index Framework Control Object
{1EBDCF80-A200-11D0-A3A4-00C04FD706EC}	Thumbnails
{1EF94880-01A8-11D2-A90B-00AA00BF3363}	Microsoft NT DS Class Provider for WBEM
{1EFB6596-857C-11D1-B16A-00C0F0283628}	Microsoft TabStrip Control, version 6.0
{1F183F5A-5C4D-11D1-8B83-080036B11A03}	DefaultServer Class
{1F247DC0-902E-11D0-A80C-00A0C906241A}	Content Index ISearch Creator Object
{1F2E5C40-9550-11CE-99D2-00AA006E086C}	Security Shell Extension

∙∙∙∙∙∙∙∙∙∙∙∙∙∙∙∙∙

TABLE B.1 Continued

CLSID Object	Reference
{1F3C67C2-D153-11D0-BF8B-0000F81E8509}	MSDBGCallStack Class
{1f4de370-d627-11d1-ba4f-00a0c91eedba}	Search Results - Computers
{1f4de370-d627-11d1-ba4f-00a0c91eedba}	file://%webdir%\fsresult.htt
{1F73E9B1-8C3A-11D0-A3BE-00A0C9244436}	Indeo® video 5.10 Compression Filter
{1F7DD4F1-CAC3-11D0-A35B-00AA00BDCDFD}	Microsoft DT DDS Rectilinear GDD
{1F7DD4F2-CAC3-11D0-A35B-00AA00BDCDFD}	Microsoft DT DDS Rectilinear GDD Layout
{1F7DD4F3-CAC3-11D0-A35B-00AA00BDCDFD}	Microsoft DT DDS Rectilinear GDD Route
{1F823A6A-863F-11D1-A484-00C04FB93753}	Policy Settings Extension Snapin
{1FBA04EE-3024-11d2-8F1F-0000F87ABD16}	Toolbar Extension for Executable
{202D3AEF-2F0E-11D1-A1F6-0080C88593A5}	DfrgCtl Class
{203630C3-9110-11D0-AB6C-00A0C91E24A2}	EditorServices Class
{2048EEE6-7FA2-11D0-9E6A-00A0C9138C29}	Microsoft OLE DB Row Position Library
{2089ADC0-BE09-11CE-AAE4-CE6AC0F06E88}	VideoSoft FlexArray Property Page/Styles
{208D2C60-3AEA-1069-A2D7-08002B30309D}	My Network Places
{208D2C60-3AEA-1069-A2D7-08002B30309D}	file://%webdir%\nethood.htt
{20D04FE0-3AEA-1069-A2D8-08002B30309D}	My Computer
{20D04FE0-3AEA-1069-A2D8-08002B30309D}	file://%webdir%\folder.htt
{20EDB660-7CDD-11CF-8DAB-00AA006C1A01}	msrating.dll
{20FF6B80-C312-11D0-B4E4-00A0C9261445}	F:\PROGRA~1\MICROS~3\Office\ MDHELPER.DLL
{20ff6b80-c312-11d0-b4e4-0a0c9261445}	MD Helper
{210183C0-1E63-11d1-9693-00A0C90D04EF}	CLSID_COEAcctImport
{210DA8A2-7445-11d1-91F7-006097DF5BD4}	FTP Folder Web View Automation
{2179C5D3-EBFF-11CF-B6FD-00AA00B4E220}	Microsoft NetShow Player
{217FC9C0-3AEA-1069-A2DB-08002B30309D}	Shell Copy Hook
{21B22460-3AEA-1069-A2DC-08002B30309D}	File Property Page Extension
{21D6D48E-A88B-11D0-83DD-00AA003CCABD}	TAPI Class
{21EC2020-3AEA-1069-A2DD-08002B30309D}	Control Panel
{21EC2020-3AEA-1069-A2DD-08002B30309D}	file://%webdir%\controlp.htt
{2206CDB0-19C1-11D1-89E0-00C04FD7A829}	MSDAINITIALIZE Class
{2206CDB0-19C1-11D1-89E0-00C04FD7A829}	MSDASC Error Lookup
{2206CDB2-19C1-11D1-89E0-00C04FD7A829}	Microsoft OLE DB Service Component Data Links
{2206CDB3-19C1-11D1-89E0-00C04FD7A829}	MSDASC Error Lookup
{221E0DA0-36BA-11d0-BA93-00C04FD91A5E}	ISessionDescStore_PSFactory
{2227A280-3AEA-1069-A2DE-08002B30309D}	Printers
{2227A280-3AEA-1069-A2DE-08002B30309D}	%SystemRoot%\web\printfld.htm
{228136B0-8BD3-11D0-B4EF-00A0C9138CA4}	Catalog Class
{228136B8-8BD3-11D0-B4EF-00A0C9138CA4}	Cellset Class
{228D9A81-C302-11cf-9AA4-00AA004A5691}	LDAP Provider Object

| TABLE B.1 | Continued |

CLSID Object	Reference
{228D9A82-C302-11cf-9AA4-00AA004A5691}	LDAP Namespace Object
{2293C842-B001-11CF-90FA-00AA00A729EA}	H261 Color Values
{2293C845-B001-11CF-90FA-00AA00A729EA}	H263 Color Values
{22BF0C20-6DA7-11D0-B373-00A0C9034938}	Download Status
{22D6F312-B0F6-11D0-94AB-0080C74C7E95}	Windows Media Player
{22E24591-49D0-11D2-BB50-006008320064}	Windows Media Audio Decoder
{22EE26E5-2289-11d2-8F43-00C04FC2E0C7}	F:\WINNT\System32\catsrvut.dll
{233664b0-0367-11cf-abc4-02608c9e7553}	ADs Namespaces Object
{233A9692-667E-11d1-9DFB-006097D50408}	Outlook Express Message List
{233A9694-667E-11d1-9DFB-006097D50408}	Outlook Express Address Book
{2398E32F-5C6E-11D1-8C65-0060081841DE}	TextToSpeech Class
{239A3C5E-8D41-11D1-B675-00C04FA3C554}	AVGeneralNotification Class
{23DA323D-7006-11D1-8A98-006097B01206}	Windows Media On-Demand Wizard Control
{23DA323E-7006-11D1-8A98-006097B01206}	Pubwiz Property Page
{23E45B60-C598-11d0-B16F-00A0C916F120}	HsmWorkItem Class
{243E20B0-48ED-11D2-97DA-00A024D77700}	NtmsMgr Class
{24400D16-5754-11d2-8218-00C04FB687DA}	Index Cleaner Prop Bag
{24532D00-FCD8-11CF-A7D3-00A0C9056683}	G.723.1 Codec
{24532D01-FCD8-11CF-A7D3-00A0C9056683}	G.723.1 Codec Property Page
{247DF540-C558-11d0-B16F-00A0C916F120}	HsmWorkQueue Class
{24DCD5F2-6DBB-11D1-BEF5-00805FBE84A6}	Windows Media Unicast TraceView Control
{24F14F01-7B1C-11d1-838f-0000F80461CF}	%SystemRoot%\system32\shell32.dll
{24F14F02-7B1C-11d1-838f-0000F80461CF}	%SystemRoot%\system32\shell32.dll
{250770F3-6AF2-11CF-A915-008029E31FCD}	Marquee Control
{250e91a0-0367-11cf-abc4-02608c9e7553}	WinNT Namespace Object
{25336920-03f9-11cf-8fd0-00aa00686f13}	HTML Document
{25336921-03F9-11CF-8FD0-00AA00686F13}	Microsoft HTML Document 5.0
{2542F180-3532-1069-A2CD-00AA0034B50B}	Font Property Page
{254E8EA4-4924-11D0-A787-00A0C91BBEE1}	Invert Effect
{25959BEF-E700-11D2-A7AF-00C04F806200}	Msie Control
{25959BF0-E700-11D2-A7AF-00C04F806200}	Msie Property Page
{25BE9228-00AF-11D2-BF87-00C04FD8D5B0}	dsquery.dll
{25E609E0-B259-11CF-BFC7-444553540000}	Microsoft DirectInput Object
{25E609E1-B259-11CF-BFC7-444553540000}	Microsoft DirectInput Device Object
{2646205B-878C-11d1-B07C-0000C040BCDB}	NSIEMisc Class
{26721E10-390C-11D0-8A22-00A0C90C9156}	PCM Silence Suppressor
{26902120-114D-11D2-8FBF-0000F80272EA}	WebBrowserWrapper Class
{26B9ED02-A3D8-11D1-8B9C-080009DCC2FA}	MSWC.IISLog
{27016870-8E02-11D1-924E-00C04FBBBFB3}	MS Remote

....

| **TABLE B.1** | Continued |

CLSID Object	**Reference**
{273695A3-C77A-11d1-87F4-00C04FC2C17B}	DCOMExtAbout Class
{274fae1f-3626-11d1-a3a4-00c04fb950dc}	ADs LDAP NameTranslate Object
{275C23E2-3747-11D0-9FEA-00AA003F8646}	Multi Language Support
{275D9D50-5FF5-11CF-A5E1-00AA006BBF16}	Remote Debug Manager for Java
{275D9D51-5FF5-11CF-A5E1-00AA006BBF16}	Private Debug Manager for Java
{275DBBA0-805A-11CF-91F7-C2863C385E30}	MSFlexGrid Style Property Page Object
{280A3020-86CF-11D1-ABE6-00A0C905F375}	AC3 Parser Filter
{289228DE-A31E-11D1-A19C-0000F875B132}	ListPad Class
{28E6A820-A6C4-11D0-896F-00AA00A74BF2}	NntpVirtualRoot Class
{28FD8302-57CF-11D0-8A3E-00A0C90349CB}	PSFactoryBuffer
{2933BF90-7B36-11d2-B20E-00C04F983E60}	XML DOM Document
{2933BF91-7B36-11d2-B20E-00C04F983E60}	Free Threaded XML DOM Document
{295789F0-0949-11D1-B90C-00AA004AB12A}	ATM LAN Emulation Configuration Notify Object
{29729D01-CFE6-11D0-BE1D-0060977B4789}	Component Services Add-In for VB 5.0/6.0
{29822AB7-F302-11D0-9953-00C04FD919C1}	PSFactoryBuffer
{29822AB8-F302-11D0-9953-00C04FD919C1}	PSFactoryBuffer
{298942A3-C0FE-11D1-8D87-0060088F38C8}	GenerateMSI Class
{299D0193-6DAA-11d2-B679-006097DF5BD4}	FTP IDataObject impl
{29AB59D3-7E50-11D2-B520-00A0C98C01C9}	Redirect Effect
{29B5828C-CAB9-11D2-B35C-00105A1F8177}	Microsoft WBEM (non)Standard Marshaling for IWbemUnboundObjectSink
{29D44CA0-DD3A-11d0-95DF-00C04FD57E8C}	IMediaCatalogData Proxy/Stub
{2A005C11-A5DE-11CF-9E66-00AA00A3F464}	PropGroupManagerObject Class
{2A488070-6FD9-11D0-A808-00A0C906241A}	File System Client DocStore Locator Object
{2A54C904-07AA-11D2-8D6D-00C04F8EF8E0}	MetaCreations Jaws
{2A54C908-07AA-11D2-8D6D-00C04F8EF8E0}	MetaCreations Color Fade
{2A54C90B-07AA-11D2-8D6D-00C04F8EF8E0}	MetaCreations Flow Motion
{2A54C90D-07AA-11D2-8D6D-00C04F8EF8E0}	MetaCreations Vacuum
{2A54C911-07AA-11D2-8D6D-00C04F8EF8E0}	MetaCreations Grid
{2A54C913-07AA-11D2-8D6D-00C04F8EF8E0}	MetaCreations Glass Block
{2A54C915-07AA-11D2-8D6D-00C04F8EF8E0}	MetaCreations Threshold
{2a6eb050-7f1c-11ce-be57-00aa0051fe20}	French_French Stemmer
{2AABFCD0-1797-11D2-ABA2-00C04FB6C6FA}	WSecEdit Security Configuration Class
{2AFA62E2-5548-11D1-A6E1-006097C4E476}	ppDSApp Class
{2B11E9B0-9F09-11D0-9484-00A0C91110ED}	StdDataValue Object
{2B4F54B1-3D6D-11d0-8258-00C04FD5AE38}	Shell BindStatusCallback Proxy
{2BC0EF29-E6BA-11d1-81DD-0000F87557DB}	Convolution
{2C247F23-8591-11D1-B16A-00C0F0283628}	Microsoft ImageList Control, version 6.0
{2C37C621-9C6F-11D0-9BF1-00A0C9191768}	ProcedureEffects

TABLE B.1	Continued

CLSID Object	Reference
{2C875213-FCE5-11d1-A0B0-00C04FA31A86}	dsquery.dll
{2C96A89E-DA2E-11D1-BFCD-00C04FB9988E}	MachineData Class
{2CA8CA52-3C3F-11D2-B73D-00C04FB6BD3D}	Audio Input Mixer Properties
{2D1E3156-25DE-11D0-8073-00A0C905F098}	Remote Storage Engine
{2D360200-FFF5-11d1-8D03-00A0C959BC0A}	DHTML Edit Control for IE5
{2D360201-FFF5-11d1-8D03-00A0C959BC0A}	DHTML Edit Control Safe for Scripting for IE5
{2DE89781-DBF6-11D0-A30E-444553540000}	Indeo® video 5.10 Encode Parameters Property Page
{2dfb3a35-6071-11d1-8c13-00c04fd8d503}	Microsoft Locality Extension
{2E19B602-48EB-11d2-83CA-00104BCA42CF}	IAS Logging Snapin Class
{2E3A0EC0-89D7-11D0-A9E6-00AA00685C74}	SEODictionaryItem Class
{2E3ABB30-AF88-11D0-A9EB-00AA00685C74}	EventLock Class
{2EC5A8A5-E65B-11d0-8FAC-08002BE4E62A}	Telephony Audio Source
{2EC5A8A6-E65B-11d0-8FAC-08002BE4E62A}	Telephony Audio Destination
{2F155EE4-C332-11CD-B23C-0000C0058192}	THREED PANEL PROPERTY PAGE 2
{2F280288-BB6D-11D0-B948-00C04FD8D5B0}	DsPropertyPages.NTDS-Site-Settings
{2f2d0b90-1bc9-11d0-9113-00aa00c147fa}	IStreamBuffer_PSFactory
{2F42C693-C6A4-11D0-93E9-00AA0064D470}	Microsoft Exchange Events
{2F7FC18E-292B-11D2-A795-DFAA798E9148}	MSREdit Class
{2F94D7B0-BF63-11D1-A6A2-00C04FB9988E}	EndpointsTable Class
{2FAEBFA2-3F1A-11D0-8C65-00C04FD8FECB}	F:\WINNT\System32\dnsmgr.dll
{2FDD2BEA-73A5-11D0-9908-00A0C9058BF6}	CWsbLonglong Class
{2FE8F810-B2A5-11d0-A787-0000F803ABFC}	DirectPlayLobby Object
{2FEB9591-50CF-11D1-A6DF-006097C4E476}	ppDSMeta Class
{2ff47af0-1bcf-11d0-9113-00aa00c147fa}	IStreamSource_PSFactory
{30323449-0000-0010-8000-00AA00389B71}	I420/H261 Decode Filter
{30355649-0000-0010-8000-00AA00389B71}	Indeo® video 5.10 Decompression Filter
{3050F17F-98B5-11CF-BB82-00AA00BDCE0B}	Microsoft HTML Generic Page
{3050F1FC-98B5-11CF-BB82-00AA00BDCE0B}	Microsoft HTML Anchor Page
{3050F232-98B5-11CF-BB82-00AA00BDCE0B}	Microsoft HTML Background Page
{3050F296-98B5-11CF-BB82-00AA00BDCE0B}	Microsoft HTML Inline Style Page
{3050F391-98B5-11CF-BB82-00AA00BDCE0B}	Microsoft HTML Window Security Proxy
{3050F3B2-98B5-11CF-BB82-00AA00BDCE0B}	Microsoft HTML Javascript Pluggable Protocol
{3050f3B3-98b5-11cf-bb82-00aa00bdce0b}	%Microsoft Image Element Browse Property Page%
{3050f3B4-98b5-11cf-bb82-00aa00bdce0b}	%Microsoft Document Browse Property Page%
{3050f3BB-98b5-11cf-bb82-00aa00bdce0b}	%Microsoft Anchor Element Browse Property Page%
{3050F3BC-98B5-11CF-BB82-00AA00BDCE0B}	Microsoft HTML Resource Pluggable Protocol

TABLE B.1 Continued

CLSID Object	Reference
{3050F3C2-98B5-11CF-BB82-00AA00BDCE0B}	Microsoft HTML DwnBindInfo
{3050F3D6-98B5-11CF-BB82-00AA00BDCE0B}	IImgCtx
{3050F3D9-98B5-11CF-BB82-00AA00BDCE0B}	MHTML Document
{3050f3DA-98B5-11CF-BB82-00AA00BDCE0B}	Microsoft HTML Mailto Pluggable Protocol
{3050F406-98B5-11CF-BB82-00AA00BDCE0B}	Microsoft HTML About Pluggable Protocol
{3050f499-98b5-11cf-bb82-00aa00bdce0b}	Microsoft HTML Recalc
{3050F4CF-98B5-11CF-BB82-00AA00BDCE0B}	PeerFactory Class
{3050f4d8-98B5-11CF-BB82-00AA00BDCE0B}	HTML Application
{3050f4e1-98b5-11cf-bb82-00aa00bdce0b}	HtmlDlgHelper Class
{3050f4e7-98b5-11cf-bb82-00aa00bdce0b}	Microsoft HTML Server Document 5.0
{3050f4f0-98b5-11cf-bb82-00aa00bdce0b}	Microsoft Scriptlet svr om Uses
{3050f4f5-98B5-11CF-BB82-00AA00BDCE0B}	Trident HTMLEditor
{3050f4f8-98b5-11cf-bb82-00aa00bdce0b}	Microsoft Html Component
{3050f5be-98b5-11cf-bb82-00aa00bdce0b}	DownloadBehavior Class
{3060E8CE-7020-11D2-842D-00C04FA372D4}	Remote Installation Services
{30A095E2-9A0C-11D2-93BB-00105A994D2C}	F:\PROGRA~1\COMMON~1\MICROS~1\Euro\ MSOEURO.DLL
{30C3B080-30FB-11d0-B724-00AA006C1A01}	CoMapMIMEToCLSID Class
{30D02401-6A81-11d0-8274-00C04FD5AE38}	Microsoft SearchBand
{30E7F2A0-EC4C-11ce-8865-00805F742EF6}	SpeedDial
{31064da8-402e-11d1-9327-00c04fd919b7}	BASIC Authenticator Class
{31363248-0000-0010-8000-00AA00389B71}	H261 Decode Filter
{31430c59-bed1-11D1-8De8-00C04FC2E0C7}	F:\WINNT\System32\clbcatq.dll
{316B19B5-B5F8-11D0-8199-00A0C91BBEE3}	HtmLanguageService Class
{31C48C31-70B0-11d1-A708-006097C4E476}	ppDSClip Class
{31C48C32-70B0-11d1-A708-006097C4E476}	ppDSDetl Class
{31DCAB85-BB3E-11D0-9299-00C04FB6678B}	LogUI ncsa
{31DCAB86-BB3E-11D0-9299-00C04FB6678B}	LogUI odbc
{31DCAB87-BB3E-11D0-9299-00C04FB6678B}	LogUI msft
{31DCAB88-BB3E-11D0-9299-00C04FB6678B}	LogUI extnd
{31E0DFD7-2621-11D1-AFD7-006097C9A284}	HtmlHelp Class
{323991f0-7bad-11cf-b03d-00aa006e0975}	NDS Provider Object
{3241F066-6D68-11D0-8950-00AA00A74BF2}	NntpAdmin Class
{3241F06B-6D68-11D0-8950-00AA00A74BF2}	NntpAdminService Class
{3241F070-6D68-11D0-8950-00AA00A74BF2}	NntpAdminFeeds Class
{3241F075-6D68-11D0-8950-00AA00A74BF2}	NntpAdminGroups Class
{3241F07A-6D68-11D0-8950-00AA00A74BF2}	NntpAdminSessions Class
{32714800-2E5F-11d0-8B85-00AA0044F941}	%STR_WABFIND_FIND_PEOPLE%
{32B533BB-EDAE-11d0-BD5A-00AA00B92AF1}	AP Class Install Handler filter

TABLE B.1 Continued

CLSID Object	Reference
{32C35401-D04F-11d0-99B3-00AA004CD65C}	DirectSound Source Object
{32DA2B15-CFED-11D1-B747-00C04FC2B085}	Script Encoder Object
{33102459-4B30-11d2-A6DC-00C04F79E7C8}	CLSID_CNavNewsAcctImport
{33363248-0000-0010-8000-00AA00389B71}	H263 Decode Filter
{333C7BC4-460F-11D0-BC04-0080C7055A83}	Tabular Data Control
{334857cc-f934-11d2-ba96-00c04fb6d0d1}	ADs DN With String Object
{336475D0-942A-11CE-A870-00AA002FEAB5}	MPEG-I Stream Splitter
{33831ED4-42B8-11D2-93AD-00805F853771}	Microsoft NT DS Class Associations Provider for WBEM
{338E9310-7C07-11CE-8CA9-00AA0044BB60}	Microsoft Forms 2.1 ControlPalette
{33D9A760-90C8-11d0-BD43-00A0C911CE86}	ICM Class Manager
{33D9A761-90C8-11d0-BD43-00A0C911CE86}	ACM Class Manager
{33D9A762-90C8-11d0-BD43-00A0C911CE86}	WaveIn Class Manager
{33FACFE0-A9BE-11D0-A520-00A0D10129C0}	SAMI (CC) Reader
{3449A1C8-C56C-11D0-AD72-00C04FC29863}	MSDataShape
{349C6ABE-A30C-11D1-ABE5-00C04FC30999}	MSOLAPAuxiliaries Class
{349C6AC1-A30C-11D1-ABE5-00C04FC30999}	MSOLAPAuxiliarie Class
{34AB8E82-C27E-11D1-A6C0-00C04FB94F17}	Certificates 1.0 Object
{35053A22-8589-11D1-B16A-00C0F0283628}	Microsoft ProgressBar Control, version 6.0
{35172920-A700-11D0-A9EA-00AA00685C74}	EventManager Class
{352EC2B7-8B9A-11D1-B8AE-006008059382}	%DESC_AppMgr%
{35461E30-C488-11d1-960E-00C04FBD7C09}	CLSID_IMimeObjResolver
{35522CA0-67CE-11cf-9B8B-08005AFC3A41}	Voice Dictation Manager
{35CEC8A3-2BE6-11D2-8773-92E220524153}	SysTray
{369303C2-D7AC-11D0-89D5-00A0C90833E6}	Microsoft DirectAnimation Structured Graphics
{369647e0-17b0-11ce-9950-00aa004bbb1f}	Neutral Word Breaker
{369AF85F-BFF7-11D0-A5DA-00AA00BF93E3}	Microsoft NetShow 2.0 Real-Time Encoder Proxy
{3724B9A1-9503-11D1-B86A-00A0C90DC849}	WebGate Class
{372FCE38-4324-11D0-8810-00A0C903B83C}	CertConfig Class
{379E501F-B231-11d1-ADC1-00805FC752D8}	MsxmlIsland
{37EABAF0-7FB6-11D0-8817-00A0C903B83C}	CertAdmin Class
{3845A174-EB30-11D1-9A23-00A0C879FE5F}	ColorBvr Class
{388ED915-7FD2-11D0-A60B-00A0C90A43C9}	FrontPage Explorer
{388ED916-7FD2-11D0-A60B-00A0C90A43C9}	FrontPage Web Services
{388ED917-7FD2-11D0-A60B-00A0C90A43C9}	FrontPage Editor
{388ED918-7FD2-11D0-A60B-00A0C90A43C9}	FrontPage Editor Document
{388ED919-7FD2-11D0-A60B-00A0C90A43C9}	FrontPage ToDoList
{389E18D0-7EE3-11d0-9E35-00A0C916F120}	CWsbTrace Class
{38BE3000-DBF4-11D0-860E-00A024CFEF6D}	MPEG Layer-3 Decoder

TABLE B.1 Continued

CLSID Object	Reference
{38BE3001-DBF4-11D0-860E-00A024CFEF6D}	MPEG Layer-3 Decoder Property Page
{38BE3002-DBF4-11D0-860E-00A024CFEF6D}	MPEG Layer-3 Decoder About Page
{394C052E-B830-11D0-9A86-00C04FD8DBF7}	F:\WINNT\System32\els.dll
{3964D9A0-AC96-11D1-9851-00C04FD91972}	Application Data Control
{39981125-C287-11D0-8D8C-00C04FD6202B}	CLSID_CEudoraAcctImport
{39981127-C287-11D0-8D8C-00C04FD6202B}	CLSID_CNscpAcctImport
{39981129-C287-11D0-8D8C-00C04FD6202B}	CLSID_CMAPIAcctImport
{399A9AF4-DDE0-11D0-BD90-006097C99369}	DTC Framework Registrar
{399D5C90-74AB-11D0-9CCF-00A0C9081C19}	Intel RTP Demux Filter
{399D5C91-74AB-11D0-9CCF-00A0C9081C19}	Intel RTP Demux Filter Property Page
{39A2C2A6-4778-11D2-9BDB-204C4F4F5020}	DirectControl Class
{39A2C2A9-4778-11D2-9BDB-204C4F4F5020}	DirectContainer Class
{39b16f50-a8ba-11d1-aa91-00aa006bc80b}	MailMsg Class
{39F8D76B-0928-11D1-97DF-00C04FB9618A}	Microsoft DTC Transaction
{3A410F21-553F-11d1-8E5E-00A0C92C9D5D}	IDMRemoteServer_PSFactory
{3A94E09D-EC46-11d1-A7EC-0000F8758EAA}	Microsoft In-Memory Database Client Connection
{3AE86B20-7BE8-11D1-ABE6-00A0C905F375}	MPEG-2 Splitter
{3BBE95A4-C53F-11d1-B3A2-00A0C9083365}	TRUN Tx Begin Class
{3BBE95D0-C53F-11d1-B3A2-00A0C9083365}	Tip Gateway State-Machine
{3BBE95DA-C53F-11d1-B3A2-00A0C9083365}	Trun Gateway Tx Class
{3BBE95DF-C53F-11d1-B3A2-00A0C9083365}	Tip Gateway State-Machine
{3BBE95F5-C53F-11d1-B3A2-00A0C9083365}	Trun Gateway Tx Crash Recovery Class
{3BBE95FB-C53F-11d1-B3A2-00A0C9083365}	Trun Gateway Instance Class
{3BBE95FE-C53F-11d1-B3A2-00A0C9083365}	Trun Gateway Instance Scan Class
{3BC4F3A1-652A-11D1-B4D4-00C04FC2DB8D}	Microsoft Index Server Administration Object
{3BC4F3A3-652A-11D1-B4D4-00C04FC2DB8D}	Microsoft Index Server Catalog Administration Object
{3BC4F3A7-652A-11D1-B4D4-00C04FC2DB8D}	Microsoft Index Server Scope Administration Object
{3C374A40-BAE4-11CF-BF7D-00AA006946EE}	Microsoft Url History Service
{3C4BAEF5-3278-11D1-9A4B-0080ADAA5C4B}	DfsSnapinResultManager Class
{3C4F3BE3-47EB-101B-A3C9-08002B2F49FB}	Font
{3C4F3BE5-47EB-101B-A3C9-08002B2F49FB}	Print
{3C4F3BE7-47EB-101B-A3C9-08002B2F49FB}	Help
{3c94d400-4188-11d0-9123-00aa00c147fa}	RTP Stream Sink Filter
{3CB6973D-3E6F-11D0-95DB-00A024D77700}	NtmsMgr Class
{3CCF8A41-5C85-11d0-9796-00AA00B90ADF}	Shell DeskBarApp
{3D112E22-62B2-11D1-9FEF-00600832DB4A}	MMCTask Class
{3D2807C2-43DE-11D2-9900-0000F803FF7A}	Spin

| TABLE B.1 | Continued |

CLSID Object	Reference
{3DA165B6-CC41-11d2-BDC6-00C04F79EC6B}	shell32.dll
{3DA2AA3B-3D96-11D2-9BD2-204C4F4F5020}	AsyncPPProt Class
{3DA2AA3E-3D96-11D2-9BD2-204C4F4F5020}	AsyncMHandler Class
{3DC7A020-0ACD-11CF-A9BB-00AA004AE837}	The Internet
{3dd53d40-7b8b-11D0-b013-00aa0059ce02}	CDL: Asychronous Pluggable Protocol Handler
{3DD82D10-E6F1-11D2-B139-00105A1F77A1}	WBEM Power Event Provider
{3DDDA000-88E4-11D0-9643-00AA00A89C1D}	Intel RTP SPH for Generic Audio
{3E198485-919B-11D0-8C46-00C04FC2AB22}	DebugTextBuffer class
{3E4D4F1C-2AEE-11D1-9D3D-00C04FC30DF6}	oleprn Class
{3E669F1D-9C23-11d1-9053-00C04FD9189D}	DXSurface Modifier
{3E9BAF2D-7A79-11d2-9334-0000F875AE17}	NetMeeting Application
{3EA48300-8CF6-101B-84FB-666CCB9BCD32}	OLE Docfile Property Page
{3EE8A933-4D3F-11D0-97D0-00AA00BBB6E2}	Alpha Channel Blend
{3EFB1800-C2A1-11CF-960C-0080C7C2BA87}	Execute Object for Java
{3F037241-414E-11D1-A7CE-00A0C913F73C}	DirectMusicSection
{3F276EB4-70EE-11D1-8A0F-00C04FB93753}	Policy Settings Extension Snapin
{3F4DACA4-160D-11D2-A8E9-00104B365C9F}	VBScript Regular Expression
{3F4EEF80-BFE8-11d0-A3A5-00C04FD706EC}	Image List Cache
{3F69F351-0379-11D2-A484-00C04F8EFB69}	CrIris
{3F8A6C33-E0FD-11D0-8A8C-00A0C90C2BC5}	BlnMgr Class
{3FA7DEB3-6438-101B-ACC1-00AA00423326}	Active Messaging Session Object
{3FC0B520-68A9-11D0-8D77-00C04FD70822}	Display Control Panel HTML Extensions
{3FF292B6-B204-11CF-8D23-00AA005FFE58}	FoxOLEDB 1.0 Object
{4009F700-AEBA-11D1-8344-00C04FB92EB7}	ACELP.net Audio Decoder
{4037AE54-C812-11D1-9A88-00A0C9AF2B78}	Microsoft NsPptRex Control
{40710C26-4BC7-11D1-8B6F-080036B11A03}	MSPropertyTreeCtl Class
{40B6664F-4972-11D1-A7CA-0000F87571E3}	Scripts (Startup/Shutdown)
{40B66650-4972-11D1-A7CA-0000F87571E3}	Scripts (Logon/Logoff)
{40C1D161-52F2-11D0-A874-00AA00B5CA1B}	PCM Silence Suppressor Properties
{40dd6e20-7c17-11ce-a804-00aa003ca9f6}	Shell extensions for sharing
{410381DB-AF42-11D1-8F10-00C04FC2C17B}	COMNSView Class
{41116C00-8B90-101B-96CD-00AA003B14FC}	MAPIForm object
{4150F050-BB6F-11D0-AFB9-00AA00B67A42}	Format
{418AFB70-F8B8-11CE-AAC6-0020AF0B99A3}	Quality Management Property Page
{41E300E0-78B6-11ce-849B-444553540000}	PlusPack CPL Extension
{42071712-76d4-11d1-8b24-00a0c9068ff3}	Display Adapter CPL Extension
{42071713-76d4-11d1-8b24-00a0c9068ff3}	Display Monitor CPL Extension
{42071714-76d4-11d1-8b24-00a0c9068ff3}	Display Panning CPL Extension
{421516C1-3CF8-11D2-952A-00C04FA34F05}	Chroma

· · · · · · · · · · · · · · ·

TABLE B.1	Continued

CLSID Object	**Reference**
{424B71AF-0695-11D2-A484-00C04F8EFB69}	CrRadialWipe
{429AF92C-A51F-11d2-861E-00C04FA35C89}	%Trident API%
{43136EB5-D36C-11CF-ADBC-00AA00A80033}	NodeInit 1.0 Object
{4315D437-5B8C-11D0-BD3B-00A0C911CE86}	DeviceMoniker
{432DC4FC-6D93-11D0-B422-00A0244A1DD2}	Script LE
{435899C9-44AB-11D1-AF00-080036234103}	DSPrintQueue Class
{43668E21-2636-11D1-A1CE-0080C88593A5}	DfrgSnapin Class
{438755C2-A8BA-11D1-B96B-00A0C90312E1}	Browseui preloader
{438B8ECD-AD2A-11D1-ADEB-0000F87734F0}	TrialEnd Class
{438DA5E0-F171-11D0-984E-0000F80270F8}	TriEditDocument Class
{43A8F463-4222-11d2-B641-006097DF5BD4}	Shell Name Space ListView
{43AF3211-0887-11d1-8DCB-0080C7B89C95}	StreamWrapper Class
{43F8F289-7A20-11D0-8F06-00C04FC295E1}	CEnroll Class
{4419DD31-28A5-11d2-AE08-0080C7337EA1}	XML Viewer Behavior
{44EC053A-400F-11D0-9DCD-00A0C90391D3}	Registrar Class
{450D8FBA-AD25-11D0-98A8-0800361B1103}	My Documents
{4516EC41-8F20-11d0-9B6D-0000C0781BC3}	Direct3DRM Object
{4516EC43-8F20-11D0-9B6D-0000C0781BC3}	DirectXFile Object
{45588FF3-51FA-11D0-8236-00A0C908DB96}	XRAY Effect
{455ACF57-5345-11D2-99CF-00C04F797BC9}	PSFactoryBuffer
{4590F811-1D3A-11D0-891F-00AA004B2E24}	WBEM Locator
{4590F812-1D3A-11D0-891F-00AA004B2E24}	Microsoft WBEM WbemClassObject Marshalling proxy
{45AC8C62-23E2-11D1-A696-00C04FD58BC3}	System Information
{45AC8C63-23E2-11D1-A696-00C04FD58BC3}	System Information
{45AC8C64-23E2-11D1-A696-00C04FD58BC3}	System Information
{45AC8C65-23E2-11D1-A696-00C04FD58BC3}	System Information
{45E7E811-02C2-11D1-A6F0-006097C9947C}	SelectPPG Class
{45f9f4c0-6e5c-11d0-9292-00c04fd919b7}	NetShow Codec Manager
{45FFAAA0-6E1B-11D0-BCF2-444553540000}	QKsAudioIntfHandler
{4622AD11-FF23-11d0-8D34-00A0C90F2719}	Start Menu
{462F7758-8848-11D1-ADD8-0000F87734F0}	DialErr Class
{4656BAE3-F397-11CE-BFE1-00AA0057B34E}	Microsoft Data Tools Database Designer SQL Server Extra Column Properties Property Page
{4656BAE4-F397-11CE-BFE1-00AA0057B34E}	Microsoft Data Tools Database Designer SQL Server Table Browsing Property Page
{4656BAE5-F397-11CE-BFE1-00AA0057B34E}	Microsoft Data Tools Query Designer General property page
{4656bb14-f397-11ce-bfe1-00aa0057b34e}	DBConnectionManager Class

TABLE B.1	Continued

CLSID Object	**Reference**
{4656BB33-F397-11CE-BFE1-00AA0057B34E}	Microsoft Data Tools Query Designer ORC Personality
{4657278A-411B-11d2-839A-00C04FD918D0}	Shell Drag and Drop helper
{466D66FA-9616-11D2-9342-0000F875AE17}	MarshalableTI Class
{46763EE0-CAB2-11CE-8C20-00AA0051E5D4}	Obsolete Font
{4682C81B-B2FF-11D0-95A8-00A0C92B77A9}	Status ASP Component
{4682C82A-B2FF-11D0-95A8-00A0C92B77A9}	MyInfo ASP Component
{46CE9EDE-447C-11D0-98FC-00A0C9058BF6}	CWsbDbKey Class
{46DB591F-4101-11D2-912C-0000F8758E8D}	Microsoft In-Memory Database Transacted Property Group
{46E31370-3F7A-11CE-BED6-00AA00611080}	Microsoft Forms 2.0 MultiPage
{46E32B01-A465-11D1-B550-006097242D8D}	Voxware MetaVoice Audio Decoder
{4709E4E3-6B05-11D0-80E6-00AA006EC537}	Mask Effect
{473AA80B-4577-11D1-81A8-0000F87557DB}	DX2D Anti-Aliasing
{4753da60-5b71-11cf-b035-00aa006e0975}	ADs Provider Object
{47B0DFC7-B7A3-11D1-ADC5-006008A5848C}	DEInsertTableParam Class
{47C4815A-F70F-11d0-8C23-00C04FC31D21}	MSIMDB
{47D4D946-62E8-11cf-93BC-444553540000}	DirectSound Object
{47F410B9-5FA5-11D1-B647-00C04FA3C554}	PageAddress Class
{48025243-2D39-11CE-875D-00608CB78066}	Internal Text Renderer
{480D5CA0-F032-11CF-A7D3-00A0C9056683}	G.711 Codec Property Page
{480FF4B0-28B2-11D1-BEF7-00C04FBF8FEF}	DirectMusicCollection
{48123bc4-99d9-11d1-a6b3-00c04fd91555}	XML Document
{4834C721-DCC9-11D0-B211-00A0C9191768}	ProcedureAdditive
{4834C722-DCC9-11D0-B211-00A0C9191768}	ProcedureDistortion
{48EEA71A-3775-11D1-8C96-00A0C903A1A2}	PSFactoryBuffer
{49BD2028-1523-11D1-AD79-00C04FD8FDFF}	Microsoft WBEM Unsecured Apartment
{49c47ce0-9ba4-11d0-8212-00c04fc32c45}	SFilter Class
{49C47CE4-9BA4-11D0-8212-00C04FC32C45}	Stream Class
{49c47ce5-9ba4-11d0-8212-00c04fc32c45}	MMStream Class
{49FC0185-4B32-11d1-A40E-00600831F336}	DSDisplayPanel Class
{4A16043F-676D-11d2-994E-00C04FA309D4}	CLSID_DatabaseSession
{4A2286E0-7BEF-11CE-9BD9-0000E202599C}	MPEG Audio Codec
{4a7ded0a-ad25-11d0-98a8-0800361b1103}	MyDocs menu and properties
{4AF4A5FC-912A-11D1-B945-00A0C90312E1}	Microsoft Docking Bar Property Bag
{4AFBBA8C-FE10-11d0-B607-00C04FB6E866}	Gene
{4AFBBA8D-FE10-11d0-B607-00C04FB6E866}	Gene
{4AFBBA8E-FE10-11d0-B607-00C04FB6E866}	H.26
{4AFBBA8F-FE10-11d0-B607-00C04FB6E866}	H.26

....

TABLE B.1	Continued

CLSID Object	Reference
{4AFBBA90-FE10-11d0-B607-00C04FB6E866}	H.26
{4AFBBA91-FE10-11d0-B607-00C04FB6E866}	H.26
{4AFBBA92-FE10-11d0-B607-00C04FB6E866}	G.71
{4AFBBA93-FE10-11d0-B607-00C04FB6E866}	G.71
{4AFBBA94-FE10-11d0-B607-00C04FB6E866}	G.72
{4AFBBA95-FE10-11d0-B607-00C04FB6E866}	G.72
{4AFBBA96-FE10-11d0-B607-00C04FB6E866}	IV 4
{4AFBBA97-FE10-11d0-B607-00C04FB6E866}	IV 4
{4AFBBA98-FE10-11d0-B607-00C04FB6E866}	G.71
{4AFBBA99-FE10-11d0-B607-00C04FB6E866}	G.71
{4AFBBA9A-FE10-11d0-B607-00C04FB6E866}	LH P
{4AFBBA9B-FE10-11d0-B607-00C04FB6E866}	LH P
{4AFBBA9C-FE10-11d0-B607-00C04FB6E866}	IMC
{4AFBBA9D-FE10-11d0-B607-00C04FB6E866}	IMC
{4AFBBA9E-FE10-11d0-B607-00C04FB6E866}	Gene
{4AFBBA9F-FE10-11d0-B607-00C04FB6E866}	Gene
{4B106874-DD36-11D0-8B44-00A024DD9EFF}	Microsoft Local Troubleshooter
{4B106875-DD36-11D0-8B44-00A024DD9EFF}	Microsoft Local Troubleshooter Property Page
{4B2E958D-0393-11D1-B1AB-00AA00BA3258}	COM+ Active Process Iteration Server
{4B428940-263C-11D1-A520-000000000000}	Windows Media URL File Source
{4BA2C080-68BB-11d0-95BD-00C04FD57E8C}	IMediaCatalogAdviseSink Proxy/Stub
{4BA2C081-68BB-11d0-95BD-00C04FD57E8C}	IMediaCatalog Proxy/Stub
{4BAC124B-78C8-11D1-B9A8-00C04FD97575}	Agent Custom Proxy Class
{4BDAFC52-FE6A-11d2-93F8-00105A11164A}	IVolumeClient2_PSFactory
{4BF976C1-14CD-11D1-9A97-00AA00BB9C12}	Subscriber Replication Component
{4C3DDDD2-02CF-11D1-8C80-0000F80277C9}	AspParser Class
{4C4A5E40-732C-11D0-8816-00A0C903B83C}	CertServerPolicy Class
{4C599241-6926-101B-9992-00000B65C6F9}	Microsoft Forms 2.0 Image
{4C85388F-1500-11D1-A0DF-00C04FC9E20F}	Microsoft Office Field List 9.0
{4CB26C03-FF93-11d0-817E-0000F87557DB}	DXTaskManager
{4CCEA634-FBE0-11d1-906A-00C04FD9189D}	Pixelate
{4CECCEB1-8359-11D0-A34E-00AA00BDCDFD}	Microsoft DT DDS OrgChart GDD Layout
{4CECCEB2-8359-11D0-A34E-00AA00BDCDFD}	Microsoft DT DDS OrgChart GDD Route
{4CECCEB4-8359-11D0-A34E-00AA00BDCDFD}	Microsoft DT DDS OrgChart GDD
{4D2F086C-6EA3-101B-A18A-00AA00446E07}	MAPIPSFactory
{4D5C8C25-D075-11d0-B416-00C04FB90376}	&Tip of the Day
{4D5C8C2A-D075-11d0-B416-00C04FB90376}	Microsoft CommBand
{4D9E4505-6DE1-11CF-87A7-444553540000}	MSWC.NextLink
{4DDB6D36-3BC1-11d2-86F2-006008B0E5D2}	MSP Class

TABLE B.1 Continued	
CLSID Object	**Reference**
{4de7016c-5ef9-11d1-8c13-00c04fd8d503}	Microsoft User Extension
{4E14FBA2-2E22-11D1-9964-00C04FBBB345}	Event System
{4E3A7680-B77A-11D0-9DA5-00C04FD65685}	CLSID_IConverterSession
{4E3D9D1F-0C63-11D1-8BFB-0060081841DE}	DirectSR Class
{4E40F770-369C-11d0-8922-00A024AB2DBB}	Security Shell Extension
{4E7F49AD-E4B5-11D1-8D9D-006097DBEFEF}	mce.CCSproperty
{4E7F49AF-E4B5-11D1-8D9D-006097DBEFEF}	mce.CCSProperties
{4E7F49B6-E4B5-11D1-8D9D-006097DBEFEF}	mce.IMCEResource
{4E7F49B8-E4B5-11D1-8D9D-006097DBEFEF}	mce.MiniCubeEditor
{4E7F49CF-E4B5-11D1-8D9D-006097DBEFEF}	mce.RW
{4E7F49D5-E4B5-11D1-8D9D-006097DBEFEF}	mce.chartwizard
{4E934F30-341A-11D1-8FB1-00A024CB6019}	PSFactoryBuffer
{4EB31670-9FC6-11CF-AF6E-00AA00B67A42}	DV Splitter
{4EFE2452-168A-11d1-BC76-00C04FB9453B}	MidiOut Class Manager
{4F241DB1-EE9F-11D0-9824-006097C99E51}	Microsoft DirectAnimation Sequence
{4F664F91-FF01-11D0-8AED-00C04FD7B597}	OleSNMP Class
{4FB6BB00-3347-11d0-B40A-00AA005FF586}	Logical Disk Manager Administrative Service
{4FD2A832-86C8-11D0-8FCA-00C04FD9189D}	F:\WINNT\System32\ddrawex.dll
{4FE4FFE4-D006-11D0-BF8B-0000F81E8509}	MSSDBGCmdWin Class
{500202A0-731E-11D0-B829-00C04FD706EC}	LNK file thumbnail interface delegator
{503E9920-FE1F-11CF-99B0-00AA00B82E81}	Microsoft Windows Media File Transfer Service
{507708CC-A74A-11d2-9351-0000F875AE17}	NetMeeting NmSysInfo object
{50B6327F-AFD1-11d2-9CB9-0000F87A369E}	AD System Info Object
{50D3055F-9911-11D1-B9AF-00C04FD8D5B0}	DsPropertyPages.NTFRS-Subscriber
{50D30561-9911-11D1-B9AF-00C04FD8D5B0}	DsPropertyPages.Site-Link
{50D30562-9911-11D1-B9AF-00C04FD8D5B0}	DsPropertyPages.Site-Link-Bridge
{50D30572-9911-11D1-B9AF-00C04FD8D5B0}	DsPropertyPages.Rpc Container
{50E5E3D1-C07E-11D0-B9FD-00A0249F6B00}	RegWizCtrl
{50F16B26-467E-11D1-8271-00C04FC3183B}	Preview Class
{510a4910-7f1c-11ce-be57-00aa0051fe20}	German_German Stemmer
{51372af3-cae7-11cf-be81-00aa00a2fa25}	MTSPackage
{51d11c90-7b9d-11cf-b03d-00aa006e0975}	NDS Namespace Object
{51E2FE32-9693-11D0-9F68-00A0C9055CAC}	DataToolProxy Class
{51E2FE35-9693-11D0-9F68-00A0C9055CAC}	DataToolProxyMgr Class
{5220cb21-c88d-11cf-b347-00aa00a28331}	"Microsoft Licensed Class Manager 1.0"
{524CCE97-A886-11D0-AB86-00C04FC3357A}	DHCP
{525609F4-D232-11D0-B76F-00C04FC9BCC4}	AppleTalk Configuration Notify Object
{53230322-172B-11D0-AD40-00A0C90DC8D9}	ImexGridCtrl.1 Object
{53230327-172B-11D0-AD40-00A0C90DC8D9}	FieldListCtrl.1 Object

. . . .

TABLE B.1   Continued

CLSID Object	Reference
{532FD821-83AB-11D0-8032-00A0C90A8FE0}	FPNewSubCtl Class
{533AC2A4-1ACE-11D1-A787-0000F80272EA}	IHTMLColorPicker Class
{53937AA0-283B-11D0-8800-444553540000}	H263 Encode Options Property Page
{53961A01-459B-11d1-BE77-006008317CE8}	Yes/No Control
{53961A02-459B-11d1-BE77-006008317CE8}	Extension Control
{53961A03-459B-11d1-BE77-006008317CE8}	Phone Number Control
{53961A04-459B-11d1-BE77-006008317CE8}	Grammar Control
{53961A05-459B-11d1-BE77-006008317CE8}	Date Control
{53961A06-459B-11d1-BE77-006008317CE8}	Time Control
{53961A07-459B-11d1-BE77-006008317CE8}	Record Control
{53961A08-459B-11d1-BE77-006008317CE8}	Spelling Control
{53961A09-459B-11d1-BE77-006008317CE8}	Name Control
{53B6AA63-3F56-11D0-916B-00AA00C18068}	PSFactoryBuffer
{53B6AA67-3F56-11D0-916B-00AA00C18068}	SCardTypeConv Class
{53B6AA6C-3F56-11D0-916B-00AA00C18068}	SCardISO7816 Class
{53D01080-AF98-11D0-A9EB-00AA00685C74}	EventBindingManager Class
{53D6AB1D-2488-11D1-A28C-00C04FB94F17}	Certificates 1.0 Object
{5408B2F0-C816-11D1-8F99-00600895E7D5}	Interface Proxy Stub
{54274112-7A5E-11d2-875F-00A0C93C09B3}	EffectBvr Class
{545A2D1A-8ECB-11D1-94E8-00C04FA302A1}	PSFactoryBuffer
{545A2D1B-8ECB-11D1-94E8-00C04FA302A1}	MDM Callback
{545AE700-50BF-11D1-9FE9-00600832DB4A}	MMCCtrl Class
{54696EC0-36B2-11d0-BA93-00C04FD91A5E}	IEnumDisatch_PSFactory
{54702535-2606-11D1-999C-0000F8756A10}	Text Label Class
{549365d0-ec26-11cf-8310-00aa00b505db}	ADsDSOObject
{54AF9350-1923-11D3-9CA4-00C04F72C514}	MDACVer.Version
{54c37cd0-d944-11d0-a9f4-006097942311}	F:\WINNT\System32\urlmon.dll
{550dda30-0541-11d2-9ca9-0060b0ec3d39}	XML Data Source Object
{5512D110-5CC6-11CF-8D67-00AA00BDCE1D}	Microsoft Forms 2.0 HTML SUBMIT
{5512D112-5CC6-11CF-8D67-00AA00BDCE1D}	Microsoft Forms 2.0 HTML IMAGE
{5512D114-5CC6-11CF-8D67-00AA00BDCE1D}	Microsoft Forms 2.0 HTML RESET
{5512D116-5CC6-11CF-8D67-00AA00BDCE1D}	Microsoft Forms 2.0 HTML CHECKBOX
{5512D118-5CC6-11CF-8D67-00AA00BDCE1D}	Microsoft Forms 2.0 HTML OPTION
{5512D11A-5CC6-11CF-8D67-00AA00BDCE1D}	Microsoft Forms 2.0 HTML TEXT
{5512D11C-5CC6-11CF-8D67-00AA00BDCE1D}	Microsoft Forms 2.0 HTML Hidden
{5512D11E-5CC6-11CF-8D67-00AA00BDCE1D}	Microsoft Forms 2.0 HTML Password
{5512D122-5CC6-11CF-8D67-00AA00BDCE1D}	Microsoft Forms 2.0 HTML SELECT
{5512D124-5CC6-11CF-8D67-00AA00BDCE1D}	Microsoft Forms 2.0 HTML TextAREA
{55136805-B2DE-11D1-B9F2-00A0C98BC547}	ShellFavoritesNameSpace

TABLE B.1	Continued

CLSID Object	**Reference**
{55426A33-808E-11D0-A8AA-00A0C921A4D2}	TextManager class
{554667BB-7213-11cf-B210-00AA00A215ED}	Lexicon Enumerator
{555278E2-05DB-11D1-883A-3C8B00C10000}	Scale
{555AF860-68FF-11D0-B20E-080000185165}	Generic Control Hosting Component
{560E5A02-DEDE-11D1-A9F5-00A0248903EA}	PSFactoryBuffer
{56117100-C0CD-101B-81E2-00AA004AE837}	Shell Scrap DataHandler
{5645C8C0-E277-11CF-8FDA-00AA00A14F93}	NNTP filter
{5645C8C1-E277-11CF-8FDA-00AA00A14F93}	{5645C8C2-E277-11CF-8FDA-00AA00A14F93}
{5645C8C2-E277-11CF-8FDA-00AA00A14F93}	F:\WINNT\System32\mimefilt.dll
{5645C8C3-E277-11CF-8FDA-00AA00A14F93}	NNTP filter
{5645C8C4-E277-11CF-8FDA-00AA00A14F93}	{5645C8C2-E277-11CF-8FDA-00AA00A14F93}
{566F8E20-963C-11D0-9643-00AA00A89C1D}	Intel RTP RPH Property Page
{566F8E21-963C-11D0-9643-00AA00A89C1D}	Intel RTP RPH Property Page
{566F8E23-963C-11D0-9643-00AA00A89C1D}	Intel Common RPH Controls
{566F8E24-963C-11D0-9643-00AA00A89C1D}	Intel H26X RPH Controls
{568804CA-CBD7-11d0-9816-00C04FD91972}	Menu Shell Folder
{56EE2738-BDF7-11d1-8C28-00C04FB995C9}	MC Japanese Lexical Analyzer
{56FDF344-FD6D-11d0-958A-006097C9A090}	Task Bar Communication
{5728F10E-27CC-101B-A8EF-00000B65C5F8}	Microsoft Forms 2.1 SubForm95
{57651662-CE3E-11D0-8D77-00C04FC99D61}	CmdFileIcon
{5791BC26-CE9C-11D1-97BF-0000F81E849C}	WBEM Scripting Object Path
{57C06EAA-8784-11D0-83D4-00A0C911E5DF}	Microsoft Client Configuration Notify Object
{58221C65-EA27-11CF-ADCF-00AA00A80033}	FILEMGMT 1.0 Object
{58221C66-EA27-11CF-ADCF-00AA00A80033}	SvcVwr 1.0 Object
{58221C67-EA27-11CF-ADCF-00AA00A80033}	Computer Management 1.0 Object
{58221C69-EA27-11CF-ADCF-00AA00A80033}	FILEMGMT 1.0 Object
{58221C6A-EA27-11CF-ADCF-00AA00A80033}	SvcVwr 1.0 Object
{582C2191-4016-11D1-8C55-0060081841DE}	VDict Class
{58712b20-0a93-11d0-8dba-00aa00b90c3b}	IMediaPlayer_PSFactory
{58712b21-0a93-11d0-8dba-00aa00b90c3b}	IEnumMedia_PSFactory
{58712b22-0a93-11d0-8dba-00aa00b90c3b}	IMediaSession_PSFactory
{58712b23-0a93-11d0-8dba-00aa00b90c3b}	IEnumMediaSession_PSFactory
{58712b24-0a93-11d0-8dba-00aa00b90c3b}	IMediaSessionManager_PSFactory
{5880CD5C-8EC0-11d1-9570-0060B0576642}	NAPSnapin Class
{58A2E406-8304-11D2-9533-0060b0C3C4F4}	ActionBvr Class
{58AB2366-D597-11d1-B90E-00C04FC9B263}	EapTlsCfg Class
{58C2B4D0-46E7-11D1-89AC-00A0C9054129}	DirectMusicSynth
{58ECEE30-E715-11CF-B0E3-00AA003F000F}	FoxOLEDB 1.0 Object
{59099400-57FF-11CE-BD94-0020AF85B590}	Disk Copy Extension

• • • • • • • • • • • • • • • •

TABLE B.1	Continued

CLSID Object	Reference
{593817A0-7DB3-11CF-A2DE-00AA00B93356}	DirectDraw Clipper Object
{59850400-6664-101B-B21C-00AA004BA90B}	Microsoft Office Binder
{59850401-6664-101B-B21C-00AA004BA90B}	Microsoft Office Binder Unbind
{59850403-6664-101B-B21C-00AA004BA90B}	Microsoft Office Binder Briefcase Reconciler
{59850404-6664-101B-B21C-00AA004BA90B}	Microsoft Office Binder Briefcase Notifier
{598EBA02-B49A-11D2-A1C1-00609778EA66}	Microsoft MPEG-4 Video Decompressor Property page
{59be4990-f85c-11ce-aff7-00aa003ca9f6}	Shell extensions for Microsoft Windows Network objects
{59CCB4A0-727D-11CF-AC36-00AA00A47DD2}	Timer Object
{59CE6880-ACF8-11CF-B56E-0080C7C4B68A}	Performance Property Page
{59e09780-8099-101b-8df3-00000b65c3b5}	English_US Word Breaker
{59e097e4-8099-101b-8df3-00000b65c3b5}	English_UK Word Breaker
{59e09848-8099-101b-8df3-00000b65c3b5}	French_French Word Breaker
{5A435BAF-BA94-11D0-972A-0080C71CAE8C}	PSFactoryBuffer
{5A435BB0-BA94-11D0-972A-0080C71CAE8C}	SCardSSP Class
{5A580C11-E5EB-11d1-A86E-0000F8084F96}	CLSID_IHTTPMailTransport
{5a61f7a0-cde1-11cf-9113-00aa00425c62}	IIS Shell Extention
{5A7B63E0-F9BC-11D2-BBE5-00C04F86AE3B}	Internet Explorer Snapin About Information
{5A96F2D8-736E-11D1-BD0D-00C04FD8D5B6}	DsPropertyPages.Container
{5AAF51B2-B1F0-11d1-B6AB-00A0C90833E9}	Microsoft Scriptlet Element Behavior Handler
{5AAF51B3-B1F0-11d1-B6AB-00A0C90833E9}	Microsoft Scriptlet HiFiTimer Uses
{5ADF5BF6-E452-11D1-945A-00C04FB984F9}	WSecEdit Security Configuration Class
{5AE1DAE0-1461-11d2-A484-00C04F8EFB69}	CrWheel
{5B035261-40F9-11D1-AAEC-00805FC1270E}	Network Configuration Component Object
{5B175DF9-6A86-11D1-B651-00C04FA3C554}	PageTerminals Class
{5B18AB61-091D-11D1-97DF-00C04FB9618A}	Microsoft DTC Transaction Manager
{5b4dae26-b807-11d0-9815-00c04fd91972}	Menu Band
{5B5E7E70-E653-11CF-84A5-0000C08C00C4}	F:\WINNT\System32\msr2c.dll
{5b80820f-4755-11d1-9077-00a0c90ab504}	FaxSnapinAbout Class
{5BDDC640-AE09-11D0-8974-00AA00A74BF2}	NntpFeed Class
{5BDDC641-AE09-11D0-8974-00AA00A74BF2}	NntpOneWayFeed Class
{5BEDF7DE-98CF-11D0-B255-00C04FC9E292}	NWLink Client Configuration Notify Object
{5BF46533-282D-11D0-81BE-00A0C91180F2}	CWsbUlong Class
{5C0786ED-1847-11D2-ABA2-00C04FB6C6FA}	WSecEdit Security Configuration Class
{5C0786EE-1847-11D2-ABA2-00C04FB6C6FA}	WSecEdit Security Configuration Class
{5c24f661-415b-11d0-ba94-00c04fd91a5e}	NMSA Composite Video Media Description Object (Ver 1.0)
{5C659257-E236-11D2-8899-00104B2AFB46}	WMISnapin Class

CLSID Object	Reference
{5C659258-E236-11D2-8899-00104B2AFB46}	Allows configuration and control of the Windows Management Instrumentation (WMI) service.
{5C85DCB0-F967-11D0-81ED-00C04FC99D4C}	ppDShowNet Class
{5cb66670-d3d4-11cf-acab-00a024a55aef}	COM+ Extended Transaction Context Component
{5D02926A-212E-11D0-9DF9-00A0C922E6EC}	Microsoft InfoTech IStorage System
{5D08B586-343A-11D0-AD46-00C04FD8FDFF}	Microsoft WBEM Event Subsystem
{5D1A1AD2-C658-11d0-991E-00A0C9058BF6}	CWsbDbSys Class
{5D6179C8-17EC-11D1-9AA9-00C04FD8FE93}	Microsoft Local Users and Groups MMC Snap-in
{5D6179D2-17EC-11D1-9AA9-00C04FD8FE93}	Microsoft Local Users and Groups MMC Snap-in About Provider
{5D62A639-0FB0-11D2-8DB2-006097DBEFEF}	mce.IMCEResources
{5D8D8F1A-8B89-11D1-ADDB-0000F87734F0}	SmartStart Class
{5D9DD151-65F4-11CE-900D-00AA00445589}	Microsoft DTC Transaction Manager Proxy (private, internal)
{5DB2625A-54DF-11D0-B6C4-0800091AA605}	ICM Monitor Management
{5DC41690-C6A6-11d1-9D35-006008B0E5CA}	F:\WINNT\System32\catsrvut.dll
{5DC41691-C6A6-11d1-9D35-006008B0E5CA}	F:\WINNT\System32\catsrvut.dll
{5DC41692-C6A6-11d1-9D35-006008B0E5CA}	F:\WINNT\System32\catsrvut.dll
{5DC41693-C6A6-11d1-9D35-006008B0E5CA}	F:\WINNT\System32\catsrvut.dll
{5DC41694-C6A6-11d1-9D35-006008B0E5CA}	F:\WINNT\System32\catsrvut.dll
{5E6AB780-7743-11CF-A12B-00AA004AE837}	Microsoft Internet Toolbar
{5E71F04C-551F-11CF-8152-00AA00A40C25}	MicrosoftRDO.rdoEngine
{5e941d80-bf96-11cd-b579-08002b30bfeb}	Plain Text persistent handler
{5e941d80-bf96-11cd-b579-08002b30bfeb}	{c1243ca0-bf96-11cd-b579-08002b30bfeb}
{5EBB68F5-3BF1-11CF-814C-00AA00A40C25}	MicrosoftRDO.RdoQuery
{5ef4af3a-f726-11d0-b8a2-00c04fc309a4}	Recycle Bin Cleaner
{5EFB2260-89EE-11d0-B605-00A0C922E851}	FilePackage Class
{5F3E04C3-4612-11D0-A113-00A024B50363}	Symantec User Registration
{5F3E04C4-4612-11D0-A113-00A024B50363}	Dial-up Data Transport
{5F3E04C6-4612-11D0-A113-00A024B50363}	Symantec User Information Object
{5F5295E0-429F-1069-A2E2-08002B30309D}	Drive Property Page Extension
{5F7B221A-086B-11D2-95AF-0060B0576642}	IASEnumerableAttributeEditor Class
{600FD9A3-F1D3-11D1-828E-00C04F990690}	PSFactoryBuffer
{60254CA5-953B-11CF-8C96-00AA00B8708C}	Shell Extension For Windows Script Host
{603D3800-BD81-11d0-A3A5-00C04FD706EC}	Background Task Scheduler
{603D3801-BD81-11d0-A3A5-00C04FD706EC}	Shared Task Scheduler
{607d8680-7cd2-11d0-8dfa-00aa00b90c3b}	IMediaEventCallback_PSFactory
{607d8681-7cd2-11d0-8dfa-00aa00b90c3b}	ISimpleMediaEventRegistry_PSFactory
{607fd4e8-0a03-11d1-ab1d-00c04fc9b304}	CoICOFilter Class

. . . .

TABLE B.1 Continued	
CLSID Object	**Reference**
{609b7e3a-c918-11d1-aa5e-00c04fa35b82}	NTFS Store Driver Class
{60A0C080-E505-11D1-AA1C-00600895FB99}	MetaStream
{60AF234A-D7D3-11D0-ABB0-00C04FC3357A}	WINS
{60AF234B-D7D3-11D0-ABB0-00C04FC3357A}	WINS
{60AF234C-D7D3-11D0-ABB0-00C04FC3357A}	WINS
{60F41BE4-06DF-11D2-95AA-0060B0576642}	AttributeInfo Class
{60F6E464-4DEF-11d2-B2D9-00C04F8EEC8C}	Old Files In Root Prop Bag
{60F6E465-4DEF-11d2-B2D9-00C04F8EEC8C}	Temp Files Prop Bag
{60F6E466-4DEF-11d2-B2D9-00C04F8EEC8C}	Setup Files Prop Bag
{60F6E467-4DEF-11d2-B2D9-00C04F8EEC8C}	Uninstall Prop Bag
{6131A8EC-78CE-11d2-A3F2-3078302C2030}	F:\WINNT\System32\catsrvut.dll
{6165A063-5F6A-11D0-B8F1-000000000000}	Shadow Effect
{61738644-F196-11D0-9953-00C04FD919C1}	IIS WAMREG Admin
{6182E342-9C57-11D0-B4A9-00A0C90D63B5}	Intel RTP RPH Generic Audio Property Page
{61935832-FC85-11d0-8FAE-08002BE4E62A}	Audio Record Object
{61ccd0e6-908a-11d0-b4b7-00c04fc9dab7}	IMediaSessionMonitor_PSFactory
{61ccd0e7-908a-11d0-b4b7-00c04fc9dab7}	IMediaSessionMonitorRegistry_PSFactory
{61E218E0-65D3-101B-9F08-061CEAC3D50D}	ShellFind
{61F0B790-82D9-11d0-9E35-00A0C916F120}	HsmStoragePool Class
{61FB9D74-893E-11D1-B4B5-00600895A311}	BlnSetUser Proxy
{62112AA1-EBE4-11cf-A5FB-0020AFE7292D}	Shell Automation Folder View
{62392950-1AF8-11D0-B267-00A0C90F56FC}	DCOM-ZAW Class Access
{623E2882-FC0E-11d1-9A77-0000F8756A10}	Gradient
{62544620-AB83-11D0-B83F-00A0244A1DE2}	Java LE Debug Manager
{6262D3A0-531B-11CF-91F6-C2863C385E30}	Microsoft FlexGrid Control, version 6.0
{626BAFE1-E5D6-11D1-B1DD-006097D503D9}	CLSID_OERulesManager
{6295DF27-35EE-11d1-8707-00C04FD93327}	Mobsync Dll
{6295DF2D-35EE-11d1-8707-00C04FD93327}	Mobsync
{6295DF2E-35EE-11d1-8707-00C04FD93327}	Mobsync Proxy
{62AE1F9A-126A-11D0-A14B-0800361B1103}	dsuiext.dll
{62BE5D10-60EB-11d0-BD3B-00A0C911CE86}	System Device Enumerator
{62C81794-A9EC-11D0-8198-00A0C91BBEE3}	HtmDocData Class
{6316D324-2238-101B-9E66-00AA003BA905}	F:\PROGRA~1\COMMON~1\System\Mapi\1033\NT\CNFNOT32.EXE
{6319EEA0-531B-11CF-91F6-C2863C385E30}	MSFlexGrid General Property Page Object
{6342E1B6-94DB-11D1-ADE2-0000F87734F0}	INSHandler Class
{63500AE2-0858-11D2-8CE4-00C04F8ECB10}	CrShatter
{636B9F10-0C7D-11D1-95B2-0020AFDC7421}	DirectMusic
{6384E23E-736D-11D1-BD0D-00C04FD8D5B6}	DsPropertyPages.Default

TABLE B.1	Continued

CLSID Object	**Reference**
{63B51F81-C868-11D0-999C-00C04FD655E1}	Shell Icon Overlay Manager
{63da6ec0-2e98-11cf-8d82-444553540000}	Microsoft FTP Folder
{63da6ec0-2e98-11cf-8d82-444553540000}	file://F:\WINNT\web\ftp.htt
{63F8AA94-E2B9-11D0-ADF6-00C04FB66DAD}	Windows Media Multiplexer
{640999A0-A946-11D0-A520-000000000000}	ASX File Parser
{640999A1-A946-11D0-A520-000000000000}	ASX v.2 File Parser
{640999A2-A946-11D0-A520-000000000000}	NSC File Parser
{6413BA2C-B461-11d1-A18A-080036B11A03}	Augmented Merge Shell Folder
{64455860-5153-101C-816F-0E6013114B7F}	Image Property Page
{64577982-86D7-11d1-BDFC-00C04FA31009}	CLSID_IHashTable
{645FF040-5081-101B-9F08-00AA002F954E}	Recycle Bin
{645FF040-5081-101B-9F08-00AA002F954E}	file://%webdir%\recycle.htt
{64818D10-4F9B-11CF-86EA-00AA00B929E8}	Microsoft PowerPoint Presentation
{64818D11-4F9B-11CF-86EA-00AA00B929E8}	Microsoft PowerPoint Slide
{649D583D-3401-11D1-8C47-0080C7C43E7F}	WinFaxRasterize Class
{64AB4BB7-111E-11d1-8F79-00C04FC2FBE1}	Microsoft Shell UI Helper
{64B8F404-A4AE-11D1-B7B6-00C04FB926AF}	PSFactoryBuffer
{64D9163F-BA0F-11D0-979C-00A0C908612D}	Tools ASP Component
{64FD16F3-B7A5-11d1-8F93-00600895E7D5}	TipConnectionMgr
{65014010-9F62-11d1-A651-00600811D5CE}	Microsoft CrSource 4.0
{65040069-0D17-11D1-B4B2-00A0244A1DD2}	LE Callback
{65303443-AD66-11D1-9D65-00C04FC30DF6}	OleCvt Class
{654C2A40-71B6-11CE-A850-444553540000}	OPWNoLink
{66182EC4-AFD1-11d2-9CB9-0000F87A369E}	WinNT System Info Object
{66523042-35FE-11D1-8C4D-0060081841DE}	VCommand Class
{665A4443-D905-11D0-A30E-444553540000}	Indeo® video 5.10 Decode Sequence Property Page
{665A4444-D905-11D0-A30E-444553540000}	Indeo® video 5.10 Decode Frame Property Page
{665A4445-D905-11D0-A30E-444553540000}	Indeo® video 5.10 Encode Sequence Property Page
{665A4448-D905-11D0-A30E-444553540000}	Indeo® video 5.10 Decode OA
{665A444A-D905-11D0-A30E-444553540000}	Indeo® video 5.10 Encode OA
{66742402-F9B9-11D1-A202-0000F81FEDEE}	Version Column Provider
{66833FE6-8583-11D1-B16A-00C0F0283628}	Microsoft Toolbar Control, version 6.0
{66A2DB1A-D706-11D0-A37B-00C04FC9DA04}	PSFactoryBuffer
{66b37110-8bf2-11ce-be59-00aa0051fe20}	Dutch_Dutch Word Breaker
{66E10DE0-7E2D-11D0-B5FD-00A0C922E851}	FileService service
{674B6698-EE92-11D0-AD71-00C04FD8FDFF}	Microsoft WBEM Call Context
{674D3E3D-A1A8-11D0-A886-00C04FC99C9C}	ATMUNI Call Manager Configuration Notify Object

....

| **TABLE B.1** | Continued |

CLSID Object	Reference
{6756A641-DE71-11d0-831B-00AA005B4383}	MRU AutoComplete List
{675F097E-4C4D-11D0-B6C1-0800091AA605}	ICM Printer Management
{67741683-547D-11D0-8236-00A0C908DB96}	Flip Vertical Effect
{677A2D94-28D9-11D1-A95B-008048918FB1}	DfsSnapinScopeManager Class
{679d9e37-f8f9-11d2-8deb-00c04f6837d5}	Helper for IMoniker support in legacy code
{67DCC487-AA48-11d1-8F4F-00C04FB611C7}	CommunicationManager
{67EA19A0-CCEF-11d0-8024-00C04FD75D13}	CDF Extension Copy Hook
{68385DF9-CD7D-11D0-B443-00A0244A1DD2}	Session Debug Manager
{6853E76A-BD3E-11D1-9A4D-00C04FC297EB}	CertManageModule Class (policy legacy support)
{68883F00-85D8-11D0-8A50-00A0C90349CB}	PSFactoryBuffer
{692A8956-1089-11D2-8837-00104B2AFB46}	NSDrive Description
{692E33B0-AF9D-11D0-B976-00A0C9190447}	Remote Storage Properties
{6980ACA1-CFB6-11D0-BF8B-0000F81E8509}	Debugger Class
{6980ACA5-CFB6-11D0-BF8B-0000F81E8509}	MSSDBGDocument Class
{6980ACA9-CFB6-11D0-BF8B-0000F81E8509}	ProjView Class
{698C4280-BDCD-11D0-B218-00C04FD70811}	Choices Engine
{699DDBCC-DC7E-11D0-BCF7-00C04FC2FB86}	MSStdFmt Format Property Page Object
{69A25C12-1811-11D2-A52B-0000F803A951}	Certificates 1.0 Object
{69A25C14-1811-11D2-A52B-0000F803A951}	Certificates 1.0 Object
{69AD90EF-1C20-11d1-8801-00C04FC29D46}	Microsoft DirectAnimation Windowed Control
{69E2DD40-5321-101C-96BF-040224009C02}	Kodak Image Admin Help Page
{6A01FDA0-30DF-11d0-B724-00AA006C1A01}	CoSniffStream Class
{6A08CF80-0E18-11CF-A24D-0020AFD79767}	ACM Wrapper
{6A1B634D-99C8-11D1-ABE1-00C04FC30999}	MSOLAPDatabases Class
{6A1B6350-99C8-11D1-ABE1-00C04FC30999}	MSOLAPDatabase Class
{6A1B6353-99C8-11D1-ABE1-00C04FC30999}	MSOLAPSources Class
{6A1B6356-99C8-11D1-ABE1-00C04FC30999}	MSOLAPSource Class
{6A1B6359-99C8-11D1-ABE1-00C04FC30999}	MSOLAPModels Class
{6A1B635C-99C8-11D1-ABE1-00C04FC30999}	MSOLAPModel Class
{6A1B635F-99C8-11D1-ABE1-00C04FC30999}	MSOLAPDimensions Class
{6A1B6362-99C8-11D1-ABE1-00C04FC30999}	MSOLAPDimension Class
{6A1B6365-99C8-11D1-ABE1-00C04FC30999}	MSOLAPDetails Class
{6A1B6368-99C8-11D1-ABE1-00C04FC30999}	MSOLAPDetail Class
{6A8DEEA9-4101-11D2-912C-0000F8758E8D}	Microsoft In-Memory Database Transacted Property
{6AF50C90-B297-11D0-A2D4-00AA00A3EFFF}	TrackSelection Class
{6B6D0800-9ADA-11D0-A520-00A0D10129C0}	Windows Media splitter
{6B6D0803-9ADA-11D0-A520-00A0D10129C0}	Stub Source Filter
{6B6D0808-9ADA-11D0-A520-00A0D10129C0}	CD Audio filter

TABLE B.1	Continued

CLSID Object	Reference
{6B91AFEF-9472-11D1-8574-00C04FC31FD3}	Routers or Remote Access Servers
{6BA3F852-23C6-11D1-B91F-00A0C9A06D2D}	F:\WINNT\System32\dsuiwiz.dll
{6BC09698-0CE6-11D1-BAAE-00C04FC2E20D}	IAS Data Source Class
{6BC09699-0CE6-11D1-BAAE-00C04FC2E20D}	IAS Dictionary Class
{6BC0969D-0CE6-11D1-BAAE-00C04FC2E20D}	IAS Audit Channel Class
{6BC0969F-0CE6-11D1-BAAE-00C04FC2E20D}	IAS NT Event Log Class
{6BC096A0-0CE6-11D1-BAAE-00C04FC2E20D}	IAS Information Base Class
{6BC096B0-0CE6-11D1-BAAE-00C04FC2E20D}	IAS Request Attribute
{6BC096B1-0CE6-11D1-BAAE-00C04FC2E20D}	IAS Request
{6BC096B2-0CE6-11D1-BAAE-00C04FC2E20D}	IAS Pipeline Stage
{6BC096B3-0CE6-11D1-BAAE-00C04FC2E20D}	IAS Pipeline
{6BC096B8-0CE6-11D1-BAAE-00C04FC2E20D}	IAS Accounting provider
{6BC096BC-0CE6-11D1-BAAE-00C04FC2E20D}	IAS Helper COM Component
{6BC096BF-0CE6-11D1-BAAE-00C04FC2E20D}	IAS Pipeline Manager
{6BC096C4-0CE6-11D1-BAAE-00C04FC2E20D}	IAS OLE-DB Data Store
{6BC096C6-0CE6-11D1-BAAE-00C04FC2E20D}	IAS Active Directory Data Store
{6BC096C8-0CE6-11D1-BAAE-00C04FC2E20D}	IAS Networking Data Store
{6BC096D5-0CE6-11D1-BAAE-00C04FC2E20D}	IAS User Restrictions Handler
{6BC096DA-0CE6-11D1-BAAE-00C04FC2E20D}	IAS RADIUS Client Class
{6BC09894-0CE6-11D1-BAAE-00C04FC2E20D}	IAS RADIUS Protocol Class
{6BC09896-0CE6-11D1-BAAE-00C04FC2E20D}	IAS NT-SAM Authentication Provider
{6BC09897-0CE6-11D1-BAAE-00C04FC2E20D}	IAS MS-CHAP Error Provider
{6BC09898-0CE6-11D1-BAAE-00C04FC2E20D}	IAS BaseCamp Extension Host
{6BC09899-0CE6-11D1-BAAE-00C04FC2E20D}	IAS Authorization Extension Host
{6BC0989A-0CE6-11D1-BAAE-00C04FC2E20D}	IAS EAP Provider
{6BC0989C-0CE6-11D1-BAAE-00C04FC2E20D}	IAS NT-SAM Per-User Attributes Provider
{6BC0989D-0CE6-11D1-BAAE-00C04FC2E20D}	IAS NT-SAM Names Provider
{6BC098A4-0CE6-11D1-BAAE-00C04FC2E20D}	IAS Attribute Match Constraint
{6BC098A5-0CE6-11D1-BAAE-00C04FC2E20D}	IAS NT Group Membership Constraint
{6BC098A6-0CE6-11D1-BAAE-00C04FC2E20D}	IAS Time of Day Constraint
{6BC098A7-0CE6-11D1-BAAE-00C04FC2E20D}	IAS Network Policy Enforcer
{6BF191E1-9BF9-11d0-B047-0000C040BCDB}	Microsoft NetShow Path Dialog
{6C1303DC-BA00-11D1-B949-00A0C9A06D2D}	F:\WINNT\System32\dnsmgr.dll
{6C1303DD-BA00-11D1-B949-00A0C9A06D2D}	F:\WINNT\System32\dnsmgr.dll
{6C19BE35-7500-11D1-AD94-00C04FD8FDFF}	Microsoft WBEM Event filter marshaling proxy
{6C5C43A0-9CEA-11CF-90FA-00AA00A729EA}	H263 Video Effects Property Page
{6C5C43A1-9CEA-11CF-90FA-00AA00A729EA}	H261 Video Effects Property Page
{6CFFE322-6E97-11D1-8C1C-00C04FB995C9}	Media Catalog Path Moniker
{6d36ce10-7f1c-11ce-be57-00aa0051fe20}	Italian_Italian Stemmer

| **TABLE B.1** | Continued |

CLSID Object	Reference
{6D40D820-0BA7-11ce-A166-00AA004CD65C}	Voice Command Manager
{6D5313C0-8C62-11D1-B2CD-006097DF8C11}	Folder Options Property Page Extension
{6d7572ac-c939-11d1-aa5e-00c04fa35b82}	NTFS Property Stream Class
{6D835690-900B-11D0-9484-00A0C91110ED}	StdDataFormat Object
{6D940280-9F11-11CE-83FD-02608C3EC08A}	Kodak Image Edit Control
{6D940284-9F11-11CE-83FD-02608C3EC08A}	Kodak Image Edit Property Page
{6D940285-9F11-11CE-83FD-02608C3EC08A}	Kodak Image Annotation Control
{6D940289-9F11-11CE-83FD-02608C3EC08A}	Kodak Image Annotation Property Page
{6DAF9757-2E37-11D2-AEC9-00C04FB68820}	MOF Compiler
{6DC5746E-1A01-11D3-9ED6-00C04F79731E}	CertManageModule Class (exit legacy support)
{6DDE3061-736C-11D2-A5E8-00A0C967A25F}	ActorBvr Class
{6DFE6485-A212-11D0-BCD5-00C04FD8D5B6}	DsPropertyPages.User
{6DFE6486-A212-11D0-BCD5-00C04FD8D5B6}	DsPropertyPages.FPO
{6DFE6488-A212-11D0-BCD5-00C04FD8D5B6}	DsPropertyPages.Top
{6DFE6489-A212-11D0-BCD5-00C04FD8D5B6}	DsPropertyPages.Group
{6DFE648A-A212-11D0-BCD5-00C04FD8D5B6}	DsPropertyPages.Membership
{6DFE648B-A212-11D0-BCD5-00C04FD8D5B6}	DsPropertyPages.Managed-By
{6DFE648C-A212-11D0-BCD5-00C04FD8D5B6}	DsPropertyPages.Domain
{6DFE648E-A212-11D0-BCD5-00C04FD8D5B6}	DsPropertyPages.DomainPolicy
{6DFE648F-A212-11D0-BCD5-00C04FD8D5B6}	DsPropertyPages.LocalPolicy
{6DFE6490-A212-11D0-BCD5-00C04FD8D5B6}	DsPropertyPages.Volume
{6DFE6491-A212-11D0-BCD5-00C04FD8D5B6}	DsPropertyPages.Inter-Site-Transport
{6DFE6492-A212-11D0-BCD5-00C04FD8D5B6}	DsPropertyPages.Computer
{6DFE6493-A212-11D0-BCD5-00C04FD8D5B6}	DsPropertyPages.Printer-Queue
{6DFE6494-A212-11D0-BCD5-00C04FD8D5B6}	DsPropertyPages.Server
{6E182020-F460-11CE-9BCD-00AA00608E01}	Microsoft Forms 2.0 Frame
{6E449683-C509-11CF-AAFA-00AA00B6015C}	InstallEngineCtl Object
{6E449686-C509-11CF-AAFA-00AA00B6015C}	Microsoft Active Setup Engine
{6E65CBC0-926D-11D0-8E27-00C04FC99DCF}	Dial-Up Client Configuration Notify Object
{6E65CBC1-926D-11D0-8E27-00C04FC99DCF}	Dial-Up Server Configuration Notify Object
{6E65CBC3-926D-11D0-8E27-00C04FC99DCF}	NdisWan Configuration Notify Object
{6E65CBC4-926D-11D0-8E27-00C04FC99DCF}	PPTP Configuration Configuration Notify Object
{6E65CBC5-926D-11D0-8E27-00C04FC99DCF}	Steelhead Router Configuration Notify Object
{6E65CBC6-926D-11D0-8E27-00C04FC99DCF}	L2TP Configuration Configuration Notify Object
{6E8D4A20-310C-11D0-B79A-00AA003767A7}	Line 21 Decoder
{6E8E0081-19CD-11D1-AD91-00AA00B8E05A}	NSDrive Class
{6EB22881-8A19-11D0-81B6-00A0C9231C29}	Catalog Class
{6EBFA819-718B-11D1-8A98-006097B01206}	Windows Media Unicast Wizard Control
{6EBFA81A-718B-11D1-8A98-006097B01206}	Uniwiz Property Page

| **TABLE B.1** | Continued |

CLSID Object	**Reference**
{6EBFA82F-718B-11D1-8A98-006097B01206}	Windows Media Multicast Wizard Control
{6EBFA830-718B-11D1-8A98-006097B01206}	Multiwiz Property Page
{6F74FDC5-E366-11d1-9A4E-00C04FA309D4}	CLSID_MessageDatabase
{6F74FDC6-E366-11d1-9A4E-00C04FA309D4}	CLSID_FolderDatabase
{7007ACC1-3202-11D1-AAD2-00805FC1270E}	Dial-up Connection UI Class
{7007ACC2-3202-11D1-AAD2-00805FC1270E}	Direct Connection UI Class
{7007ACC3-3202-11D1-AAD2-00805FC1270E}	Inbound Connection UI Class
{7007ACC5-3202-11D1-AAD2-00805FC1270E}	LAN Connection UI Class
{7007ACC6-3202-11D1-AAD2-00805FC1270E}	VPN Connection UI Class
{7007ACC7-3202-11D1-AAD2-00805FC1270E}	Network and Dial-up Connections
{7007ACC7-3202-11D1-AAD2-00805FC1270E}	file://%webdir%\dialup.htt
{7007ACC8-3202-11D1-AAD2-00805FC1270E}	Network Connections Enum
{7007ACCF-3202-11D1-AAD2-00805FC1270E}	Network Connections Tray
{7007ACD1-3202-11D1-AAD2-00805FC1270E}	Network Common Connections Ui
{7007ACD3-3202-11D1-AAD2-00805FC1270E}	Net Connections UI Utilities Class
{7016F8FA-CCDA-11D2-B35C-00105A1F8177}	Microsoft WBEM (non)Standard Marshaling for IWbemMultiTarget
{7057e952-bd1b-11d1-8919-00c04fc2c836}	Microsoft DocHost User Interface Handler
{70618F72-D1ED-11d0-8FAC-08002BE4E62A}	Speech Tools Grammar Compiler
{706BCCF0-3686-11d1-95F3-00C04FD57E8C}	IMCLexicalAnalyzer Proxy/Stub
{7086AD76-44BD-11D0-81ED-00A0C90FC491}	DiskManagement.UITasks
{7087EBD9-B9CE-11d1-8F62-00C04FB611C7}	TimerEventManager
{70B51430-B6CA-11D0-B9B9-00A0C922E750}	PSFactoryBuffer
{70E102B0-5556-11CE-97C0-00AA0055595A}	Video Renderer
{711D9B80-02F2-11D1-B244-00AA00A74BFF}	Media Catalog Moniker
{71285C44-1DC0-11D2-B5FB-00104B703EFD}	Microsoft WBEM (non)Standard Marshaling for IWbemObjectSink
{71650000-E8A8-11d2-9652-00C04FC30871}	ThumbCtl Class
{7170F2E0-9BE3-11D0-A009-00AA00B605A4}	TAPI3 Terminal Manager Class
{717EF4FA-AC8D-11D0-B945-00C04FD8D5B0}	DsPropertyPages.Site
{717EF4FC-AC8D-11D0-B945-00C04FD8D5B0}	DsPropertyPages.NTDS-DSA
{717EF4FD-AC8D-11D0-B945-00C04FD8D5B0}	DsPropertyPages.NTDS-Connection
{717EF4FE-AC8D-11D0-B945-00C04FD8D5B0}	DsPropertyPages.User Special Info
{717EF500-AC8D-11D0-B945-00C04FD8D5B0}	DsPropertyPages.Licensing-Site-Settings
{7194CA22-B4D8-11D0-A8CF-00A0C921A4D2}	User Data class
{71E38F91-7E88-11CF-9EDE-0080C78B7F89}	MTxAS Object
{71EAF260-0CE0-11d0-A53E-00A0C90C2091}	ASP Read Cookie
{72267F6A-A6F9-11D0-BC94-00C04FB67863}	Active Desktop Mover
{72967901-68EC-11D0-B729-00AA0062CBB7}	WBEM Registry Property Provider

CLSID Object	Reference
{72967903-68EC-11D0-B729-00AA0062CBB7}	WBEM PerfMon Property Provider
{72d3edc2-a4c4-11d0-8533-00c04fd8d503}	ADs Property Entry Object
{730F6CDC-2C86-11D2-8773-92E220524153}	SysTrayInvoker
{7312498D-E87A-11d1-81E0-0000F87557DB}	CrBlur
{733AC4CB-F1A4-11d0-B951-00A0C90312E1}	WebView MIME Filter
{73647561-0000-0010-8000-00aa00389b71}	WDM Streaming Standard Data Type Handler
{7376D660-C583-11d0-A3A5-00C04FD706EC}	TridentImageExtractor
{73A4C9C1-D68D-11D0-98BF-00A0C90DC8D9}	Microsoft Access Application
{73AA8F59-DBC4-11D0-AF5C-00A02448799A}	Microsoft Development Environment
{73F2B3A3-5474-11D0-8236-00A0C908DB96}	Grayscale Effect
{73F7A062-8829-11D1-B550-006097242D8D}	Voxware MetaSound Audio Decoder
{73F7A062-8829-11D1-B550-006097242D8D}	0
{73FDDC80-AEA9-101A-98A7-00AA00374959}	WordPad Document
{74075FD1-AEE9-11D1-8645-0060089F6007}	Default Role Membership Policy
{74246bfc-4c96-11d0-abef-0020af6b0b7a}	Device Manager
{74304483-AC4B-11D1-A50A-00C04FD7A1BD}	MSIOff Control
{74304484-AC4B-11D1-A50A-00C04FD7A1BD}	MSIOff Property Page
{7444C717-39BF-11D1-8CD9-00C04FC29D45}	CryptPKO Class
{7444C719-39BF-11D1-8CD9-00C04FC29D45}	CryptSig Class
{74746E21-6141-11D1-85EA-0000F81E0CE1}	QA Hook
{7478EF61-8C46-11d1-8D99-00A0C913CAD4}	ComponentData Class
{7478EF65-8C46-11d1-8D99-00A0C913CAD4}	ComponentData Class
{7478EF69-8C46-11d1-8D99-00A0C913CAD4}	PerformanceAbout Class
{74864DA1-0630-11D0-A5B6-00AA00680C3F}	Microsoft WBEM Server
{7487cd30-f71a-11d0-9ea7-00805f714772}	Thumbnail Image
{75048700-EF1F-11D0-9888-006097DEACF9}	ActiveDesktop
{750fdf0e-2a26-11d1-a3ea-080036587f03}	Offline Files Menu
{750fdf0f-2a26-11d1-a3ea-080036587f03}	Temporary Offline Files Cleaner
{750fdf10-2a26-11d1-a3ea-080036587f03}	Offline Files Synchronization Handler
{75112880-1bc8-11d0-9113-00aa00c147fa}	IStreamSink_PSFactory
{753EDB4D-2E1B-11D1-9064-00A0C90AB504}	FaxSnapin Class
{7542E960-79C7-11D1-88F9-0080C7D771BF}	Event Subscription
{754FF233-5D4E-11d2-875B-00A0C93C09B3}	Cr Behavior Factory
{75718C9A-F029-11D1-A1AC-00C04FB6C223}	WBEM Scripting Sink
{75C9378A-7E89-11d2-B116-00805FC73204}	F:\WINNT\System32\catsrvut.dll
{75CA6903-A48C-11D0-8195-00A0C91BBEE3}	VsHtmEditorPackage Class
{760C4B83-E211-11D2-BF3E-00805FBE84A6}	Windows Media Services DRM Storage object
{7629CFA2-3FE5-101B-A3C9-08002B2F49FB}	Open / Save As
{7629CFA4-3FE5-101B-A3C9-08002B2F49FB}	Color

TABLE B.1	Continued

CLSID Object	**Reference**
{763A6C86-F30F-11D0-9953-00C04FD919C1}	WAM REG COM LAYER
{7658F2A2-0A83-11d2-A484-00C04F8EFB69}	CrStretch
{765901EA-C5A1-11D1-B10C-00104B243180}	F:\WINNT\System32\dsadmin.dll
{7669CAD6-BDEC-11D1-A6A0-00C04FB9988E}	ProtocolsTable Class
{76A64158-CB41-11D1-8B02-00600806D9B6}	WBEM Scripting Locator
{76E67A63-06E9-11D2-A840-006008059382}	Microsoft HTML Resource Pluggable Protocol
{772BBAD1-7A22-11D0-895D-00AA00A74BF2}	NntpAdminExpiration Class
{77597368-7b15-11d0-a0c2-080036af3f03}	Web Printer Shell Extension
{777D3984-11A3-11D0-A11A-00AA003E4672}	Microsft SQLServer Merge Replication Provider
{7823A620-9DD9-11CF-A662-00AA00C066D2}	PopupMenu Object
{787A1520-75B9-11CF-980D-444553540000}	ORG10SVR 1.0 Application
{78A51822-51F4-11D0-8F20-00805F2CD064}	ProcessDebugManager Class
{78af5016-3b7c-11d1-9326-00c04fd919b7}	NTLM Authenticator Class
{78b64540-f26d-11d0-a6a3-00a0c922e752}	PSFactoryBuffer
{78F30B82-48AA-11D2-9900-0000F803FF7A}	Roll
{78FF2710-F69B-11D2-B8F2-0050040AB917}	RemoteAcsSetup Class
{79176FB0-B7F2-11CE-97EF-00AA006D2776}	Microsoft Forms 2.0 SpinButton
{79376820-07D0-11CF-A24D-0020AFD79767}	DirectSound Audio Renderer
{7954DD9B-8C2A-11D1-ADDB-0000F87734F0}	ICWSystemConfig Class
{797F1E90-9EDD-11cf-8D8E-00AA0060F5BF}	Scheduling UI property sheet handler
{7988B571-EC89-11cf-9C00-00AA00A14F56}	Microsoft Disk Quota
{7988B573-EC89-11cf-9C00-00AA00A14F56}	Microsoft Disk Quota UI
{7999FC25-D3C6-11CF-ACAB-00A024A55AEF}	COM+ Transaction Context Component
{799ED9EA-FB5E-11D1-B7D6-00C04FC2AAE2}	Microsoft VBA for Outlook Addin
{79BA9E00-B6EE-11D1-86BE-00C04FBF8FEF}	DirectMusicBand
{79EAC9C3-BAF9-11CE-8C82-00AA004BA90B}	Hyperlinking ProxyStub Factory
{79eac9c9-baf9-11ce-8c82-00aa004ba90b}	IPersistMoniker
{79eac9d0-baf9-11ce-8c82-00aa004ba90b}	StdHlink
{79eac9d1-baf9-11ce-8c82-00aa004ba90b}	StdHlinkBrowseContext
{79eac9e0-baf9-11ce-8c82-00aa004ba90b}	URL Moniker
{79eac9e2-baf9-11ce-8c82-00aa004ba90b}	http: Asychronous Pluggable Protocol Handler
{79eac9e3-baf9-11ce-8c82-00aa004ba90b}	ftp: Asychronous Pluggable Protocol Handler
{79eac9e4-baf9-11ce-8c82-00aa004ba90b}	gopher: Asychronous Pluggable Protocol Handler
{79eac9e5-baf9-11ce-8c82-00aa004ba90b}	https: Asychronous Pluggable Protocol Handler
{79eac9e6-baf9-11ce-8c82-00aa004ba90b}	mk: Asychronous Pluggable Protocol Handler
{79eac9e7-baf9-11ce-8c82-00aa004ba90b}	file:, local: Asychronous Pluggable Protocol Handler
{79eac9f1-baf9-11ce-8c82-00aa004ba90b}	URLMoniker ProxyStub Factory
{79eac9f2-baf9-11ce-8c82-00aa004ba90b}	Async BindCtx

TABLE B.1	Continued

CLSID Object	**Reference**
{7A0227F6-7108-11D1-AD90-00C04FD8FDFF}	Microsoft WBEM Uninitialized WbemClassObject for transports
{7A707490-260A-11D1-83DF-00A0C90DC849}	WebViewCoord Class
{7A80E4A8-8005-11D2-BCF8-00C04F72C717}	ExtractIcon Class
{7AB96C22-2EDA-11D1-9CE0-0000F8040A53}	IWebDesignControlContext Class
{7AF60DD2-4979-11D1-8A6C-00C04FC33566}	Snmp Snapin Extension
{7AF60DD3-4979-11D1-8A6C-00C04FC33566}	Snmp Snapin Extension
{7AF60DD4-4979-11D1-8A6C-00C04FC33566}	Snmp Snapin Extension
{7B22FF22-1AD6-11D0-81B1-00A0C91180F2}	HsmActionRecall Class
{7B22FF23-1AD6-11D0-81B1-00A0C91180F2}	HsmActionRecycle Class
{7B22FF24-1AD6-11D0-81B1-00A0C91180F2}	HsmActionTruncate Class
{7B22FF26-1AD6-11D0-81B1-00A0C91180F2}	HsmActionValidate Class
{7B22FF28-1AD6-11D0-81B1-00A0C91180F2}	HsmActionMigrate Class
{7B22FF29-1AD6-11D0-81B1-00A0C91180F2}	HsmActionManage Class
{7B22FF2A-1AD6-11D0-81B1-00A0C91180F2}	HsmActionCopy Class
{7B22FF2B-1AD6-11D0-81B1-00A0C91180F2}	HsmActionMove Class
{7B22FF2C-1AD6-11D0-81B1-00A0C91180F2}	HsmCritMigrated Class
{7B22FF2D-1AD6-11D0-81B1-00A0C91180F2}	HsmCritPremigrated Class
{7B22FF2E-1AD6-11D0-81B1-00A0C91180F2}	HsmCritCompressed Class
{7B22FF2F-1AD6-11D0-81B1-00A0C91180F2}	HsmCritAccessTime Class
{7B22FF30-1AD6-11D0-81B1-00A0C91180F2}	HsmCritGroup Class
{7B22FF31-1AD6-11D0-81B1-00A0C91180F2}	HsmCritLogicalSize Class
{7B22FF32-1AD6-11D0-81B1-00A0C91180F2}	HsmCritModifyTime Class
{7B22FF33-1AD6-11D0-81B1-00A0C91180F2}	HsmCritOwner Class
{7B22FF34-1AD6-11D0-81B1-00A0C91180F2}	HsmCritPhysicalSize Class
{7B3125F4-F14D-11D1-BE0C-000000000000}	ComServersTable Class
{7b8a2d94-0ac9-11d1-896c-00c04Fb6bfc4}	Security Manager
{7b8a2d95-0ac9-11d1-896c-00c04Fb6bfc4}	URL Zone Manager
{7b9e38b0-a97c-11d0-8534-00c04fd8d503}	ADs Property Value Object
{7BA4C740-9E81-11CF-99D3-00AA004AE837}	Microsoft SendTo Service
{7BA4C742-9E81-11CF-99D3-00AA004AE837}	Microsoft BrowserBand
{7BC1C9C0-7FC2-11D0-A8AA-00A0C921A4D2}	TextView class
{7BD29E00-76C1-11CF-9DD0-00A0C9034933}	Temporary Internet Files
{7C07E0D0-4418-11D2-9212-00C04FBBBFB3}	MSPersist
{7C504FFC-44E0-11D1-ABD4-00C04FC30999}	PDOlapReport Class
{7C857801-7381-11CF-884D-00AA004B2E24}	PSFactoryBuffer
{7C8780B2-793F-11D0-94AB-0080C74C7E95}	SrcEditor Class
{7CBBABF0-36B9-11CE-BF0D-00AA0044BB60}	Microsoft Forms 2.1 ControlSelector
{7D045701-EDA1-11D0-A6E8-006097C9947C}	ImagePPG Class

TABLE B.1   Continued

CLSID Object	Reference
{7D0CD243-5910-11D0-823A-00A0C908DB96}	ChromaKey Transparency
{7D252A20-A4D5-11CE-8BF1-00608C54A1AA}	Imaging for Windows 1.0
{7D559C10-9FE9-11d0-93F7-00AA0059CE02}	Code Download Agent
{7DDE1826-4F86-11D0-9E22-00A0C916F120}	HsmTskMgr Class
{7DEBA670-68AB-11D0-98EB-00AA00BBB52C}	ASF Stream Description File
{7E3BF330-B28E-11D0-8BD8-00C04FD42E37}	SEOGenericMoniker Class
{7E3FCEA1-31B4-11d2-AE1F-0080C7337EA1}	XML Viewer Moniker
{7E8BC44E-AEFF-11D1-89C2-00C04FB6BFC4}	HomePage Class
{7e99c0a3-f935-11d2-ba96-00c04fb6d0d1}	ADs DN With Binary Object
{7E9EC061-F1A4-11D1-828E-00C04F990690}	PSFactoryBuffer
{7EBDAAE0-8120-11CF-899F-00AA00688B10}	MS Stock Font Property Page Object
{7EBDAAE1-8120-11CF-899F-00AA00688B10}	MS Stock Color Property Page Object
{7EBDAAE2-8120-11CF-899F-00AA00688B10}	MS Stock Picture Property Page Object
{7EC08DA1-69AE-11D0-BA9B-00C04FD91A5E}	Windows Media Program Manager Object
{7EC08DA2-69AE-11D0-BA9B-00C04FD91A5E}	Windows Media Program Manager Property Page
{7F1899DA-62A6-11D0-A2C6-00C04FD909DD}	ScopeTree 1.0 Object
{7F333A96-2BB5-11D1-BFFA-00C04FC307BD}	SmtpAdminService Class
{7F368827-9516-11D0-83D9-00A0C911E5DF}	Microsoft Server Configuration Notify Object
{7f73b8f6-c19c-11d0-aa66-00c04fc2eddc}	HHC file
{7F92DA04-AFB9-11D0-AE11-0080C7B89C95}	DSRefWrapper Class
{7f9609be-af9a-11d1-83e0-00c04fb6e984}	Fax Tiff Data Column Provider
{7FC0B86E-5FA7-11d1-BC7C-00C04FD929DB}	WebCheck SyncMgr Handler
{7febaf7c-18cf-11d2-993f-00a0c91f3880}	DefView Persistent history
{800DD100-DB43-11CE-914E-00A004000162}	Microsoft Schedule+ 7.0 Library
{80105023-50B1-11D1-B930-00A0C9A06D2D}	F:\WINNT\System32\dnsmgr.dll
{802BC939-CE74-11D0-B0B1-00C04FD61157}	DTC VB Runtime support
{803E14A0-B4FB-11D0-A0D0-00A0C90F574B}	WSecEdit Extension Class
{80EE4901-33A8-11d1-A213-0080C88593A5}	Defrag NTFS engine
{80EE4902-33A8-11d1-A213-0080C88593A5}	Defrag FAT engine
{80F49562-6A9A-11d2-875F-00A0C93C09B3}	PathBvr Class
{80F94176-FCCC-11d2-B991-00C04F8ECD78}	MessageView Class
{810E402F-056B-11D2-A484-00C04F8EFB69}	CrSlide
{812034D2-760F-11CF-9370-00AA00B8BF00}	Office Compatible 1.0
{819469D2-D0CF-11d1-8E0B-00C04FC2E0C7}	F:\WINNT\System32\clbcatq.dll
{81aa123e-b564-11d1-87f8-00a0c92b500f}	NetShow Playback Session Manager
{81aa123f-b564-11d1-87f8-00a0c92b500f}	McmServer Class
{81aa1240-b564-11d1-87f8-00a0c92b500f}	CougarAdmin Class
{82126854-FC89-11D0-9BA4-006097C9B2AE}	ADOConnectObject Class
{82126857-FC89-11D0-9BA4-006097C9B2AE}	AutomatableDBConnectObject Class

....

| TABLE B.1 | Continued |

CLSID Object	Reference
{8241F015-84D3-11d2-97E6-0000F803FF7A}	Shapes
{8278F931-2A3E-11d2-838F-00C04FD918D0}	Tracking Shell Menu
{82CCD3E0-F71A-11D0-9FE5-00609778EA66}	Microsoft MPEG-4 Video Decompressor
{834128A2-51F4-11D0-8F20-00805F2CD064}	ScriptDebugSvc Class
{8369AB20-56C9-11D0-94E8-00AA0059CE02}	Cleaner for Downloaded Program Files
{836D426B-AC66-11D0-ACBD-00A0C91E24A2}	AspView Class
{837BBD11-2F82-11d1-969E-00A0C90D04EF}	CLSID_CIMEPAcctImport
{83866CAD-740D-11D2-94E4-00C04FA379F1}	Advanced Queue Administration API
{83B8BCA6-687C-11D0-A405-00AA0060275C}	DebugDocumentHelper Class
{83BC5EC0-6F2A-11d0-A1C4-00AA00C16E65}	cmnquery.dll
{83D63730-94FD-11D0-A9E8-00AA00685C74}	SEORouter Class
{8422DAE3-9929-11CF-B8D3-004033373DA8}	HTML Inline Sound Control
{8422DAE7-9929-11CF-B8D3-004033373DA8}	HTML Inline Movie Control
{842D84C9-C347-11D1-8F64-00C04FB611C7}	Interface Proxy Stub
{842DFBE6-AD40-11D0-910F-0000F81E7FF2}	ScriptEngineSite Class
{8448DD80-7614-11d0-9E33-00A0C916F120}	HsmManagedResourceCollection Class
{844F4806-E8A8-11d2-9652-00C04FC30871}	WebViewFolderIcon Class
{84725EA1-2FBC-11D1-BC86-00A0C969FC67}	Indeo® video 5.10 About RTE Property Page
{847B4DF5-4B61-11D2-9BDB-204C4F4F5020}	RadioView Class
{84926CA0-2941-101C-816F-0E6013114B7F}	Kodak Image Scan Control
{84926CA4-2941-101C-816F-0E6013114B7F}	Kodak Image Scan Property Page
{8496e040-af4c-11d0-8212-00c04fc32c45}	AuStream Class
{84D586C4-A423-11D2-B943-00C04F79D22F}	CustRg Class
{85131630-480C-11D2-B1F9-00C04F86C324}	JS File Host Encode Object
{85131631-480C-11D2-B1F9-00C04F86C324}	VBS File Host Encode Object
{854D7AC5-BC3D-11D0-B421-00A0C90F9DC4}	VsHelpServices Class
{854D7ACA-BC3D-11D0-B421-00A0C90F9DC4}	VsHelpOptionPages Class
{8596E5F0-0DA5-11D0-BD21-00A0C911CE86}	File Writer
{85980D04-9851-11D1-A0F4-00C04FB67CF6}	Microsoft Picture It! Picture
{85980D05-9851-11D1-A0F4-00C04FB67CF6}	Microsoft Picture It! Picture
{85980D06-9851-11D1-A0F4-00C04FB67CF6}	Microsoft Picture It! Picture
{85980D07-9851-11D1-A0F4-00C04FB67CF6}	Microsoft Picture It! Picture
{85980D08-9851-11D1-A0F4-00C04FB67CF6}	Microsoft Picture It! Picture
{85980D13-9851-11D1-A0F4-00C04FB67CF6}	Microsoft Picture It! Picture
{85980D14-9851-11D1-A0F4-00C04FB67CF6}	Microsoft Picture It! Picture
{85980D15-9851-11D1-A0F4-00C04FB67CF6}	Microsoft Picture It! Picture
{85980D16-9851-11D1-A0F4-00C04FB67CF6}	Microsoft Picture It! Picture
{85980D17-9851-11D1-A0F4-00C04FB67CF6}	Microsoft Picture It! Picture
{85980D18-9851-11D1-A0F4-00C04FB67CF6}	Microsoft Picture It! Picture

TABLE B.1   Continued

CLSID Object	Reference
{85980D19-9851-11D1-A0F4-00C04FB67CF6}	Microsoft Picture It! Picture
{85980D1A-9851-11D1-A0F4-00C04FB67CF6}	Microsoft Picture It! Picture
{85980D1B-9851-11D1-A0F4-00C04FB67CF6}	Microsoft Picture It! Picture
{85980D1C-9851-11D1-A0F4-00C04FB67CF6}	Microsoft Picture It! Picture
{85980D1D-9851-11D1-A0F4-00C04FB67CF6}	Microsoft Picture It! Picture
{85980D1E-9851-11D1-A0F4-00C04FB67CF6}	Microsoft Picture It! Picture
{85980D1F-9851-11D1-A0F4-00C04FB67CF6}	Microsoft Picture It! Picture
{85980D20-9851-11D1-A0F4-00C04FB67CF6}	Microsoft Picture It! Picture
{85980D22-9851-11D1-A0F4-00C04FB67CF6}	Microsoft Picture It! Picture
{85980D23-9851-11D1-A0F4-00C04FB67CF6}	Microsoft Picture It! Picture
{85980D24-9851-11D1-A0F4-00C04FB67CF6}	Microsoft Picture It! Picture
{85980D25-9851-11D1-A0F4-00C04FB67CF6}	Microsoft Picture It! Picture
{85980D26-9851-11D1-A0F4-00C04FB67CF6}	Microsoft Picture It! Picture
{85980D27-9851-11D1-A0F4-00C04FB67CF6}	Microsoft Picture It! Picture
{85980D28-9851-11D1-A0F4-00C04FB67CF6}	Microsoft Picture It! Picture
{85980D29-9851-11D1-A0F4-00C04FB67CF6}	Microsoft Picture It! Picture
{85980D2A-9851-11D1-A0F4-00C04FB67CF6}	Microsoft Picture It! Picture
{85980D2B-9851-11D1-A0F4-00C04FB67CF6}	Microsoft Picture It! Picture
{85980D2C-9851-11D1-A0F4-00C04FB67CF6}	Microsoft Picture It! Picture
{85BBD920-42A0-1069-A2E4-08002B30309D}	Briefcase
{85BBD920-42A0-1069-A2E4-08002B30309D}	file://%webdir%\default.htt
{85BBD920-42A0-1069-A2E4-08002B30309D}	0x70000136
{860BB310-5D01-11d0-BD3B-00A0C911CE86}	VFW Capture Class Manager
{860d28d0-8bf4-11ce-be59-00aa0051fe20}	Dutch_Dutch Stemmer
{86422020-42A0-1069-A2E5-08002B30309D}	Network Context Menu Extension
{8652CE55-9E80-11D1-9053-00C04FD9189D}	DXRasterizer Class
{86747AC0-42A0-1069-A2E6-08002B30309D}	Briefcase Folder
{86C86720-42A0-1069-A2E8-08002B30309D}	.exe drop target
{86F19A00-42A0-1069-A2E9-08002B30309D}	.PIF file property pages
{86F19A00-42A0-1069-A2EB-08002B30309D}	.PIF file handler
{87099231-C7AF-11D0-B225-00C04FB6C2F5}	FaxTiff Class
{871C5380-42A0-1069-A2EA-08002B30309D}	Finds and displays information and Web sites on the Internet
{877E4351-6FEA-11d0-B863-00AA00A216A1}	Plug In Distributor: IKsClock
{87e9bbc0-863f-11d0-8e02-00aa00b90c3b}	IMediaManager_PSFactory
{883373C3-BF89-11D1-BE35-080036B11A03}	ShDocProp class
{884EA37B-37C0-11d2-BE3F-00A0C9A83DA1}	ShAVColumnProvider class
{8856F961-340A-11D0-A96B-00C04FD705A2}	Microsoft Web Browser
{88738460-8CA8-11CF-980D-444553540000}	ORG21SVR 1.0 Application

•••••••••••••••••

TABLE B.1	Continued

CLSID Object	Reference
{88895560-9AA2-1069-930E-00AA0030EBC8}	HyperTerminal Icon Ext
{888ADDCF-9993-11D0-A539-00A0C922E798}	PSFactoryBuffer
{888ADDDD-9993-11D0-A539-00A0C922E798}	PSFactoryBuffer
{888D5481-CABB-11D1-8505-00A0C91F9CA0}	VideoRenderCtl Class
{88C6C381-2E85-11D0-94DE-444553540000}	ActiveX Cache Folder
{88E729D6-BDC1-11D1-BD2A-00C04FB9603F}	Folder Redirection Editor
{8931FAC9-A4C7-11D1-A0FD-00C04FB67CF6}	Microsoft Picture It! Picture
{8931FACB-A4C7-11D1-A0FD-00C04FB67CF6}	Microsoft Picture It! Picture
{8936033C-4A50-11D1-98A4-00A0C90F27C6}	Microsoft Office UA Control
{89643D21-7B2A-11d1-8271-00A0C91F9CA0}	adbanner Class
{89B9D28B-AAEB-11D0-9796-00A0C908612D}	CounterCtl Class
{89E8C959-CCB2-11D0-B0B1-00C04FD61157}	DTC Designer
{89F70C30-8636-11ce-B763-00AA004CD65C}	Speech Recognition Enumerator/Share Object
{8A23E65E-31C2-11d0-891C-00A024AB2DBB}	{6B91AFEF-9472-11D1-8574-00C04FC31FD3}
{8A23E65E-31C2-11d0-891C-00A024AB2DBB}	For P&rinters...
{8A3F59E1-4994-11D1-A40D-00600831F336}	DSStatusBar Class
{8A4D3EDC-13A4-11D1-9A22-00C04FC2D6C1}	BMP Thumbnail Extractor
{8A58CDC0-CBDC-11D0-A9F8-00AA00685C74}	EventMetabaseDatabaseManager Class
{8A6443A5-ED5A-11CF-9662-00A0C905428A}	License Manager Library
{8AE029D3-08E3-11D1-BAA2-444553540000}	:-) VideoSoft FlexArray Control
{8AE029D6-08E3-11D1-BAA2-444553540000}	:-) VideoSoft FlexString Control
{8b20cd60-0f29-11cf-abc4-02608c9e7553}	WinNT Provider Object
{8B217746-717D-11CE-AB5B-D41203C10000}	F:\WINNT\System32\TLBINF32.DLL
{8B217752-717D-11CE-AB5B-D41203C10000}	F:\WINNT\System32\TLBINF32.DLL
{8B217755-717D-11CE-AB5B-D41203C10000}	F:\WINNT\System32\TLBINF32.DLL
{8B21775E-717D-11CE-AB5B-D41203C10000}	F:\WINNT\System32\TLBINF32.DLL
{8B342BD0-C889-11D0-898D-00AA00A74BF2}	Allows management of the NNTP news protocol
{8B88B770-F277-11D0-A6EC-006097C9947C}	LinkPPG Class
{8BAE8C50-4436-11D1-A540-00C04FC29CFB}	PSFactoryBuffer
{8BC3F05E-D86B-11D0-A075-00C04FB68820}	Windows Management Instrumentation
{8BD21D10-EC42-11CE-9E0D-00AA006002F3}	Microsoft Forms 2.0 TextBox
{8BD21D20-EC42-11CE-9E0D-00AA006002F3}	Microsoft Forms 2.0 ListBox
{8BD21D30-EC42-11CE-9E0D-00AA006002F3}	Microsoft Forms 2.0 ComboBox
{8BD21D40-EC42-11CE-9E0D-00AA006002F3}	Microsoft Forms 2.0 CheckBox
{8BD21D50-EC42-11CE-9E0D-00AA006002F3}	Microsoft Forms 2.0 OptionButton
{8BD21D60-EC42-11CE-9E0D-00AA006002F3}	Microsoft Forms 2.0 ToggleButton
{8BEBB290-52D0-11D0-B7F4-00C04FD706EC}	Thumbnails
{8C3ADF99-CCFE-11d2-AD10-00C04F72DD47}	Microsoft NetMeeting Applet Object
{8C4EB103-516F-11D1-A6DF-006097C4E476}	ppDSPropAdv Class

CLSID Object	Reference
{8C7461EF-2B13-11d2-BE35-3078302C2030}	Component Categories cache daemon
{8C758294-9351-11d1-9D1A-006008B0E5CA}	Com98rtc Class
{8C836AF9-FFAC-11D0-8ED4-00C04FC2C17B}	ReplicateCatalog Class
{8D4B04E1-1331-11d0-81B8-00C04FD85AB4}	CLSID_ImnAccountManager
{8D91090E-B955-11D1-ADC5-006008A5848C}	DEGetBlockFmtNamesParam Class
{8DB2180F-BD29-11D1-8B7E-00C04FD7A924}	COMComponentRegistrar Class
{8DD6C641-98CB-11D1-9846-00A024CFEF6D}	MPEG Layer-3 Decoder Statistics Page
{8E17FFF3-C5BA-11D1-8D8A-0060088F38C8}	MakeCab Class
{8E26BFC1-AFD6-11CF-BFFC-00AA003CFDFC}	Helper Object for Java
{8E27C92B-1264-101C-8A2F-040224009C02}	Calendar Control 9.0
{8E27C92F-1264-101C-8A2F-040224009C02}	Calendar General Property Page Object
{8E3867A3-8586-11D1-B16A-00C0F0283628}	Microsoft StatusBar Control, version 6.0
{8E6E6079-0CB7-11d2-8F10-0000F87ABD16}	Offline Pages Cleaner
{8E718888-423F-11D2-876E-00A0C9082467}	@msdxmLC.dll,-1@1033,&Radio
{8E71888A-423F-11D2-876E-00A0C9082467}	RadioServer Class
{8EAD3A12-B2C1-11d0-83AA-00A0C92C9D5D}	DiskManagement.SnapInExtension
{8ED14CC0-7A1F-11d0-92F6-00A0C922E6B2}	Microsoft NetMeeting Installable Codecs
{8EE20D86-6DEC-11d1-8C1C-00C04FB995C9}	IMediaCatalogPathMoniker Proxy/Stub
{8EE42293-C315-11D0-8D6F-00A0C9A06E1F}	CLSID_ApprenticeICW
{8F0C5675-AEEF-11d0-84F0-00C04FD43F8F}	AthWafer
{8F28A170-F329-11D0-A6EC-006097C9947C}	TablePPG Class
{8F2AC965-04A2-11D3-82BD-00C04F68928B}	F:\WINNT\System32\dsadmin.dll
{8f6b0360-b80d-11d0-a9b3-006097942311}	AP lzdhtml encoding/decoding Filter
{8F8F8DC0-5713-11D1-9551-0060B0576642}	IASSnapin Class
{8F8F8DC1-5713-11D1-9551-0060B0576642}	IASSnapin About Class
{8f92a857-478e-11d1-a3b4-00c04fb950dc}	ADs Email Object
{8FC0B734-A0E1-11D1-A7D3-0000F87571E3}	Group Policy
{8FE7E181-BB96-11D2-A1CB-00609778EA66}	Microsoft MS Audio Decompressor Control Property page
{90087284-d6d6-11d0-8353-00a0c90640bf}	Device Manager extension
{9036b028-a780-11d0-9b3d-0080c710ef95}	IIS Mimemap Object
{90810500-38F1-11D1-9345-00C04FC9DA04}	IPX Routing Management
{90810501-38F1-11D1-9345-00C04FC9DA04}	IPX Routing Management
{90810502-38F1-11D1-9345-00C04FC9DA04}	IPX RIP Routing Management
{90810503-38F1-11D1-9345-00C04FC9DA04}	IPX RIP Routing Management
{90810504-38F1-11D1-9345-00C04FC9DA04}	IPX SAP Routing Management
{90810505-38F1-11D1-9345-00C04FC9DA04}	IPX SAP Routing Management
{90901AF6-7A31-11D0-97E0-00C04FC3357A}	DHCP
{911685D1-350F-11d1-83B3-00C04FBD7C09}	CLSID_CAgentAcctImport

| **TABLE B.1** | Continued |

CLSID Object	Reference
{91493441-5A91-11CF-8700-00AA0060263B}	Microsoft Powerpoint Application
{91643D00-4AFA-11D1-A520-000000000000}	Windows Media Network Property Page
{91985A21-C80D-11D0-A5DE-00AA00BF93E3}	NetShow Real-Time Encoder Callback Class
{91EA3F8B-C99B-11d0-9815-00C04FD91972}	Augmented Shell Folder
{91ef9258-afec-11d1-9868-00a0c922e703}	IIS Computer Extension
{9209B1A6-964A-11D0-9372-00A0C9034910}	Machine Debug Manager
{92187326-72B4-11d0-A1AC-0000F8026977}	gcdef.dll
{92337A8C-E11D-11D0-BE48-00C04FC30DF6}	prturl Class
{92396AD0-68F5-11d0-A57E-00A0C9138C66}	RowsetHelper
{92396AD0-68F5-11d0-A57E-00A0C9138C66}	Rowset Helper Error Lookup Service
{92655FB1-ADF9-11d1-BEB9-006008317CE8}	Lexicon Dialog
{927971f5-0939-11d1-8be1-00c04fd8d503}	ADs Large Integer Object
{92A315C9-7B1E-11d2-84A2-00C04F990690}	Microsoft In-Memory Database Proxy Connection Manager
{92AABF20-39C8-11D1-95F6-00C04FD57E8C}	MC Euro Lexical Analyzer
{92ad68ab-17e0-11d1-b230-00c04fb9473f}	STClient Class
{93073C40-0BA5-11d2-A484-00C04F8EFB69}	CrInset
{9381D8F5-0288-11d0-9501-00AA00B911A5}	RDSServer.DataFactory
{93c4a549-6b3b-11d0-ba9c-00c04fd91a5e}	NMSA ASF Source Media Description Object (Ver 1.0)
{942A8E4F-A261-11D1-A760-00C04FB9603F}	Software installation
{94426DE2-3211-11d2-A0DB-00C04F8EDCEE}	F:\WINNT\System32\catsrvut.dll
{944AD531-B09D-11CE-B59C-00AA006CB37D}	PSFactoryBuffer
{944D4C00-DD52-11CE-BF0E-00AA0055595A}	DirectDraw Property Page
{945F5842-3A8D-11D1-9037-00C04FD9189D}	Ripple
{9461b922-3c5a-11d2-bf8b-00c04fb93661}	%DESK_SearchAssistant%
{9478f640-7f1c-11ce-be57-00aa0051fe20}	Swedish_Default Stemmer
{94a909a5-6f52-11d1-8c18-00c04fd8d503}	Microsoft Group Extension
{94abaf2a-892a-11d1-bbc4-00a0c90640bf}	About Device Manager
{958A1709-3B44-11D1-AD74-00C04FC2ADC0}	RM Enlistment Helper
{95A893C3-543A-11D0-AC45-00C04FD97575}	MSLwvTTS Engine Class
{95ad72f0-44ce-11d0-ae29-00aa004b9986}	Indexing Service Snapin
{95CE8412-7027-11D1-B879-006008059382}	Shell Tree Walker
{962FFCF3-965F-11D0-A881-00C04FC99C9C}	AppleTalk Configuration Notify Object
{964EB3C4-8B47-11D0-AB46-00805F84B59E}	Key Class
{97240642-F896-11D0-B255-006097C68E81}	MSDTHostCtrl Class
{972C4270-11FD-11CE-B841-00AA004CD6D8}	Microsoft Forms 2.1 Font
{975797FC-4E2A-11D0-B702-00C04FD8DBF7}	F:\WINNT\System32\els.dll
{978C9E23-D4B0-11CE-BF2D-00AA003F40D0}	Microsoft Forms 2.0 Label

TABLE B.1	Continued

CLSID Object	Reference
{97D6D376-23BB-11D1-A0E1-00C04FC9E20F}	DARef Class
{98315903-7BE5-11D2-ADC1-00A02463D6E7}	PSFactoryBuffer
{989D1DC0-B162-11d1-B6EC-D27DDCF9A923}	XML Script Engine
{98AFF3F0-5524-11D0-8812-00A0C903B83C}	CertRequest Class
{98de59a0-d175-11cd-a7bd-00006b827d94}	Microsoft Office Persistent Handler
{98de59a0-d175-11cd-a7bd-00006b827d94}	{f07f3920-7b8c-11cf-9be8-00aa004b9986}
{99169CB0-A707-11d0-989D-00C04FD919C1}	Web Application Manager Object
{99169CB1-A707-11d0-989D-00C04FD919C1}	Web Application Manager Object
{99180163-DA16-101A-935C-444553540000}	Reconciliation interface ProxyStub Factory
{992CFFA0-F557-101A-88EC-00DD010CCC48}	Network and Dial-up Connections
{99847C33-B1B4-11D1-8F10-00C04FC2C17B}	CCOMNSScopeImpl Class
{99B42120-6EC7-11CF-A6C7-00AA00A47DD2}	Label Object
{99FF4677-FFC3-11D0-BD02-00C04FC2FB86}	StdDataFormats Object
{9A407538-0A20-11D2-95B0-0060B0576642}	EnumerableAttributeInfo Class
{9A43A844-0831-11D1-817F-0000F87557DB}	Compositor
{9A653086-174F-11D2-B5F9-00104B703EFD}	WbemClassObject
{9A8831F0-A263-11D1-8DCF-00A0C90FFFC2}	MicrosoftRDO.rdoEngine
{9A8831F1-A263-11D1-8DCF-00A0C90FFFC2}	MicrosoftRDO.RdoConnection
{9A8831F2-A263-11D1-8DCF-00A0C90FFFC2}	MicrosoftRDO.RdoQuery
{9ADF33D0-8AAD-11d0-B606-00A0C922E851}	TextPackage Class
{9AED384E-CE8B-11D1-8B05-00600806D9B6}	WBEM Scripting Named Value Collection
{9b08e210-e51b-11cd-bc7f-00aa003db18e}	German_German Word Breaker
{9B0EFD60-F7B0-11D0-BAEF-00C04FC308C9}	Temporary Internet Files Cleaner
{9B2719DD-B696-11D0-A489-00C04FD91AC0}	SdpConferenceBlob Class
{9B27B462-FB5B-11CF-906C-00AA00A59F69}	H263 Encode OA
{9B3B23C0-E236-11d0-A5C9-0080C7195D7E}	IMediaCatalogGroup Proxy/Stub
{9B3B23C1-E236-11D0-A5C9-0080C7195D7E}	Media Catalog
{9B3B23C2-E236-11D0-A5C9-0080C7195D7E}	Media Catalog Group
{9B3B23C3-E236-11d0-A5C9-0080C7195D7E}	IMediaCatalogLexicon Proxy/Stub
{9B5D03A0-8DDB-11D1-A220-00A0C9055E81}	ExplorerWebs Class
{9B5D03A2-8DDB-11D1-A220-00A0C9055E81}	ExplorerWeb Class
{9B8C4620-2C1A-11D0-8493-00A02438AD48}	DVD Navigator
{9BA05971-F6A8-11CF-A442-00A0C90A8F39}	Microsoft Shell Folder View Router
{9BFF616C-3E02-11D2-A4CA-00C04FB93209}	Certificate Tempalte Shell Extensions
{9C2263B0-3E3C-11D2-9BD3-204C4F4F5020}	RadioPlayer Class
{9C61F46E-0530-11D2-8F98-00C04FB92EB7}	MetaCreations Roll Down
{9C7D6F13-1562-11D0-81AC-00A0C91180F2}	CWsbOrderedCollection Class
{9CDE7341-3C20-11D0-A330-00AA00B92C03}	
{9D148290-B9C8-11D0-A4CC-0000F80149F6}	Microsoft InfoTech Protocol for IE 3.0

| TABLE B.1 | Continued |

CLSID Object	Reference
{9D148291-B9C8-11D0-A4CC-0000F80149F6}	Microsoft InfoTech Protocols for IE 4.0
{9D3C85D1-F877-11D0-B083-00A0C95BED34}	About G.723.1 Codec
{9D47D76B-FA6F-11D1-ACC1-00A0C9AF2D2A}	Microsoft PptNsRex Control
{9DA6FD62-C63B-11D0-B94D-00C04FD8D5B0}	DsPropertyPages.Subnet
{9DA6FD63-C63B-11D0-B94D-00C04FD8D5B0}	DsPropertyPages.OU
{9DA6FD67-C63B-11D0-B94D-00C04FD8D5B0}	DsPropertyPages.TrustedDomain
{9DA6FD69-C63B-11D0-B94D-00C04FD8D5B0}	DsPropertyPages.NTFRS-Replica-Set
{9DA6FD6A-C63B-11D0-B94D-00C04FD8D5B0}	DsPropertyPages.NTFRS-Member
{9DBD2C50-62AD-11D0-B806-00C04FD706EC}	Summary Info Thumbnail handler (DOCFILES)
{9E12E76D-94D6-11D1-ADE2-0000F87734F0}	UserInfo Class
{9E51E0D0-6E0F-11d2-9601-00C04FA31A86}	dsfolder.dll
{9EC88934-C774-11d1-87F4-00C04FC2C17B}	DCOMCNFG Extension
{9f0bd3a0-ec01-11d0-a6a0-00a0c922e752}	IIS Admin Crypto Extension
{9f37f39c-6f49-11d1-8c18-00c04fd8d503}	Microsoft PrintQueue Extension
{9F4D2FA2-54A1-11d1-8267-00A0C91F9CA0}	gotobar Class
{9F82F020-F6FD-11D0-AA14-00AA006BC80B}	EventRouter Class
{A0025E90-E45B-11D1-ABE9-00A0C905F375}	Overlay Mixer2
{A0234992-6CC4-11D1-B3B2-0060977B463D}	FrontPage ActiveX Object Tag Property Page
{A0234993-6CC4-11D1-B3B2-0060977B463D}	FrontPage ActiveX Param Tags Property Page
{A04FABD8-98F7-11D1-A0F4-00C04FB67CF6}	Microsoft Picture It! Event Manager
{A04FABD9-98F7-11D1-A0F4-00C04FB67CF6}	Microsoft Picture It! Event Manager
{A04FABDA-98F7-11D1-A0F4-00C04FB67CF6}	Microsoft Picture It! Event Manager
{A04FABDB-98F7-11D1-A0F4-00C04FB67CF6}	Microsoft Picture It! Event Manager
{A04FABDC-98F7-11D1-A0F4-00C04FB67CF6}	Microsoft Picture It! Event Manager
{A04FABDD-98F7-11D1-A0F4-00C04FB67CF6}	Microsoft Picture It! Event Manager
{A04FABDE-98F7-11D1-A0F4-00C04FB67CF6}	Microsoft Picture It! Event Manager
{A04FABDF-98F7-11D1-A0F4-00C04FB67CF6}	Microsoft Picture It! Event Manager
{A04FABE1-98F7-11D1-A0F4-00C04FB67CF6}	Microsoft Picture It! Event Manager
{A04FABE2-98F7-11D1-A0F4-00C04FB67CF6}	Microsoft Picture It! Event Manager
{A04FABE3-98F7-11D1-A0F4-00C04FB67CF6}	Microsoft Picture It! Event Manager
{A04FABE4-98F7-11D1-A0F4-00C04FB67CF6}	Microsoft Picture It! Event Manager
{a07ccd00-8148-11d0-87bb-00c04fc33942}	MSOLAP
{a07ccd00-8148-11d0-87bb-00c04fc33942}	MSOLAP Error Lookup
{a07ccd02-8148-11d0-87bb-00c04fc33942}	MSOLAP ErrorLookup
{A07CCD15-8148-11D0-87BB-00C04FC33942}	ILaunchSlicer Class
{A08AF898-C2A3-11d1-BE23-00C04FA31009}	Outlook Express Envelope
{A08C11D2-A228-11d0-825B-00AA005B4383}	Address EditBox
{A0FF1F42-237A-11D0-81BA-00A0C91180F2}	CWsbGuid Class
{A1006DE3-2173-11d2-9A7C-00C04FA309D4}	CLSID_COE5Import

| **TABLE B.1** | Continued |

CLSID Object	Reference
{A1044801-8F7E-11D1-9E7C-00C04FC324A8}	WBEM Local Address Resolution Module
{A12D0F7A-1E84-11D1-9BD6-00C04FB683FA}	CertView Class
{A1A6B99D-497F-11D1-9217-00C04FBBBFB3}	Handler Class
{A1B9E020-3226-11D2-883E-00104B2AFB46}	CMSnapin Description
{A1B9E04A-3226-11D2-883E-00104B2AFB46}	SDSnapin Description
{A1E041D0-CD73-11D0-A9F8-00AA00685C74}	EventUtil Class
{A1F89741-F619-11CF-BC0F-00AA006111E0}	CLAPI.INETLOGINFORMATION
{A26D7620-6FA0-11ce-A166-00AA004CD65C}	Voice Command Object
{A28D553A-A703-11D0-9CEC-00C04FC9BCC4}	NetBEUI Configuration Notify Object
{A2B0DD40-CC59-11d0-A3A5-00C04FD706EC}	IE4 Suite Splash Screen
{A31357D0-7242-11d0-BAA0-00C04FD91A5E}	NetShow ODBC Wrapper Class
{A380D684-4A3B-11D0-A787-00A0C91BBEE1}	Motion Blur Effect
{A3863C2E-86EB-11D1-A9DB-00C04FB16F9E}	CWUpdInfo Class
{A3C63918-889D-11D1-83E9-00C04FC2C6D4}	Thumbnail Updater
{A3CCEDF7-2DE2-11D0-86F4-00A0C913F750}	CoPNGFilter Class
{A4463024-2B6F-11D0-BFBC-0020F8008024}	Indexing Service Query SSO V2.
{A470F8CF-A1E8-4f65-8335-227475AA5C46}	Add encryption item to context menus in explorer
{A4845882-333F-11D0-B724-00AA0062CBB7}	Microsoft WBEM Anonymous pipe transport
{A4AD47C0-20EA-11D0-8796-444553540000}	Internet Location Services Object
{A4BE1350-1051-11D1-AA1E-00AA006BC80B}	EventServiceObject Class
{A4C4671C-499F-101B-BB78-00AA00383CBB}	VBA Collection Object
{A4E91B6A-DCAE-11D2-A045-00C04F79DC55}	CA Shell Extensions
{a5062215-4681-11d1-a3b4-00c04fb950dc}	ADs FaxNumber Object
{a5276f50-12b0-11d0-8dbd-00aa00b90c3b}	File Transfer Media Player
{A5B69200-214B-11D0-81B7-00A0C91180F2}	PSFactoryBuffer
{A5CBEE43-6C2C-11cf-BCFD-00AA00C14806}	Windows Media Unicast Manager Admin Control
{A5E46E3A-8849-11D1-9D8C-00C04FC99D61}	Microsoft Browser Architecture
{A5E8B32E-442A-11D1-9EA0-006097D2D7CF}	CheckAccess Class
{A5EA8D20-253D-11D1-B3F1-00AA003761C5}	Cutlist File Source
{A5EA8D2F-253D-11D1-B3F1-00AA003761C5}	CutList Graph Builder
{A5EA8D30-253D-11D1-B3F1-00AA003761C5}	Simple Cut List
{A5EA8D31-253D-11D1-B3F1-00AA003761C5}	Video File Clip
{A5EA8D32-253D-11D1-B3F1-00AA003761C5}	Audio File Clip
{A5EA8D33-253D-11D1-B3F1-00AA003761C5}	Cutlist Cache Memory Manager
{A6CB8422-7EB8-11d0-8FC3-00A0C9190447}	HsmAdmin Class
{A741D3F6-31BE-11D1-9A4A-0080ADAA5C4B}	StandAloneDfs Class
{A741D3F9-31BE-11D1-9A4A-0080ADAA5C4B}	FaultTolerantDfs Class
{A741D3FB-31BE-11D1-9A4A-0080ADAA5C4B}	DfsRoot Class
{A741D3FE-31BE-11D1-9A4A-0080ADAA5C4B}	DfsReplica Class

....

| TABLE B.1 | Continued |

CLSID Object	Reference
{A741D400-31BE-11D1-9A4A-0080ADAA5C4B}	DfsJuntionPoint Class
{A7B93C92-7B81-11D0-AC5F-00C04FD97575}	Microsoft Agent Server 1.5
{A841B6C2-7577-11D0-BB1F-00A0C922E79C}	This snap-in administers the Microsoft Internet Information Services (IIS)
{A841B6D2-7577-11D0-BB1F-00A0C922E79C}	This snap-in administers the Microsoft Internet Information Services (IIS)
{A860CE50-3910-11d0-86FC-00A0C913F750}	CoDitherToRGB8 Class
{A888DF60-1E90-11CF-AC98-00AA004C0FA9}	AVI Draw Filter
{A88B0EC3-A024-11D1-BF67-000000000000}	DataStoreMdb Class
{A8A49CCE-964F-11D0-8D71-00A0C92B500F}	Microsoft NetShow Color Dialog
{A907657F-6FDF-11D0-8EFB-00C04FD912B2}	Microsoft TCP/IP Configuration Notify Object
{A92CC3E4-E7C4-11CE-A47B-00AA005119FB}	Microsoft Data Tools Query Designer SSV Personality
{A9397D66-3ED3-11D1-8D99-00C04FC2E0C7}	F:\WINNT\System32\clbcatq.dll
{A98C8400-4181-11D1-A520-00A0D10129C0}	.RAM Parser
{a9ae6c91-1d1b-11d2-b21a-00c04fa357fa}	LW Identities
{A9B48EAC-3ED8-11d2-8216-00C04FB687DA}	Content Indexer Cleaner
{A9E537F2-A0A6-11D0-B83C-00A0244A1DE2}	Java Debug Engine
{A9E69610-B80D-11D0-B9B9-00A0C922E750}	IIS Admin Service
{A9E69612-B80D-11D0-B9B9-00A0C922E750}	PSFactoryBuffer
{A9E6F356-317C-11d2-805D-0060B0576642}	IASGroupsAttributeEditor Class
{AA000926-FFBE-11CF-8800-00A0C903B83C}	CertServerPolicy Class
{AA0D4D03-06A3-11D2-8F98-00C04FB92EB7}	MetaCreations Ripple
{AA0D4D08-06A3-11D2-8F98-00C04FB92EB7}	MetaCreations Page Curl
{AA0D4D0A-06A3-11D2-8F98-00C04FB92EB7}	MetaCreations Liquid
{AA0D4D0C-06A3-11D2-8F98-00C04FB92EB7}	MetaCreations Center Curls
{AA0D4D0E-06A3-11D2-8F98-00C04FB92EB7}	MetaCreations Curls
{AA0D4D10-06A3-11D2-8F98-00C04FB92EB7}	MetaCreations Peel ABCD
{AA0D4D12-06A3-11D2-8F98-00C04FB92EB7}	MetaCreations Curtains
{AA205A4D-681F-11D0-A243-08002B36FCA4}	File System Client Filter Object
{AA527A40-4D9A-11D2-93AD-00805F853771}	Microsoft NT DS Instance Provider for WBEM
{AA70DDF4-E11C-11D1-ABB0-00C04FD9159E}	Microsoft WBEM View Provider
{AA9BB1E0-9FE2-11D0-B257-00C04FC9E292}	DHCP Server Configuration Notify Object
{AB481080-796C-11D0-A113-00A024B50363}	Symantec Standard About Box
{AB926900-77F8-11d1-B9A0-00A0C9190447}	HsmAdminData Extension Class
{AB939AD0-6D67-11d0-9E2E-00A0C916F120}	HsmManagedResource Class
{AB944620-79C6-11D1-88F9-0080C7D771BF}	Event Publisher
{ABBE31D0-6DAE-11D0-BECA-00C04FD940BE}	Subscription Mgr
{abc00000-0000-0000-0000-000000000000}	Outlook Express MsgTable Object

TABLE B.1 Continued	
CLSID Object	**Reference**
{AC0714F6-3D04-11D1-AE7D-00A0C90F26F4}	Addin Class
{AC0714F7-3D04-11D1-AE7D-00A0C90F26F4}	Microsoft Add-In Authouring Designer
{AC409538-741C-11D1-BBE6-0060081692B3}	Remote Install Service Property Pages
{AC48FFE0-F8C4-11d1-A030-00C04FB6809F}	RequestMakeCall Class
{AC680B41-CDA0-11D1-A936-0080C7C575C0}	Module Manager for Java
{AC985D53-983C-11D1-ABE1-00C04FC30999}	MSOLAPClient Class
{AC9F2F90-E877-11CE-9F68-00AA00574A4F}	Microsoft Forms 2.1 FormPackage
{ACA97E00-0C7D-11d2-A484-00C04F8EFB69}	CrSpiral
{ACE10358-974C-11D1-A48D-00C04FB93753}	Policy Settings Extension Snapin
{AD402346-00FC-11D0-819C-00A0C91180F2}	HsmJob Class
{AD40234B-00FC-11D0-819C-00A0C91180F2}	HsmJobDef Class
{AD402350-00FC-11D0-819C-00A0C91180F2}	HsmPolicy Class
{AD402355-00FC-11D0-819C-00A0C91180F2}	HsmActionDelete Class
{AD40235A-00FC-11D0-819C-00A0C91180F2}	HsmRule Class
{AD40235F-00FC-11D0-819C-00A0C91180F2}	HsmCritAlways Class
{AD402364-00FC-11D0-819C-00A0C91180F2}	HsmJobContext Class
{ADB880A6-D8FF-11CF-9377-00AA003B7A11}	HHCtrl Object
{ADC6CB86-424C-11D2-952A-00C04FA34F05}	DropShadow
{AE1A5812-5230-11D1-A6E0-006097C4E476}	ppDSView Class
{AE1A5813-5230-11D1-A6E0-006097C4E476}	ppDSOAdv Class
{AE1EF300-CD8F-11D0-A9F8-00AA00685C74}	EventComCat Class
{AE24FDAE-03C6-11D1-8B76-0080C744F389}	Microsoft Scriptlet Component
{AEB6717E-7E19-11d0-97EE-00C04FD91972}	URL Exec Hook
{AEB84C83-95DC-11D0-B7FC-B61140119C4A}	DiskManagement.Control
{AEB84C84-95DC-11D0-B7FC-B61140119C4A}	DiskManagement.Property Page
{AEC17CE3-A514-11D1-AFA6-00AA0024D8B6}	DirectMusicSynthSink
{AED6483E-3304-11d2-86F1-006008B0E5D2}	Video Render Dynamic Terminal
{AED6483F-3304-11d2-86F1-006008B0E5D2}	Media Streaming Dynamic Terminal
{AF0DF372-A631-11D0-8DD0-00AA0060DB00}	Alpha Transition
{AF0EB60E-0775-11D1-A77D-00C04FC2F5B3}	NewMail Class
{AF279B30-86EB-11D1-81BF-0000F87557DB}	Wipe
{AF320921-9381-11d1-9C3C-0000F875AC61}	MSDAIPP.DSO
{AF4F6510-F982-11d0-8595-00AA004CD6D8}	Registry Tree Options Utility
{AF604EFE-8897-11D1-B944-00A0C90312E1}	Microsoft Common Browser Architecture
{AF7D8180-A8F9-11CF-9A46-00AA00B7DAD1}	G.711 Codec
{AFC20920-DA4E-11CE-B943-00AA006887B4}	Microsoft Forms 2.1 FontNew
{AFC78D04-B917-11CE-AAE4-CE6AC0F06E88}	VideoSoft FlexArray Property Page/General
{AFC78D09-B917-11CE-AAE4-CE6AC0F06E88}	VideoSoft FlexString Property Page/General
{AFDB1F70-2A4C-11d2-9039-00C04F8EEB3E}	Offline Files Folder

• • • • • • • • • • • • • • • •

| **TABLE B.1** | Continued |

CLSID Object	Reference
{B00464B3-67D4-11D0-A464-00C04FC29CFB}	Windows Media Channel Manager Object
{B005E690-678D-11d1-B758-00A0C90564FE}	DocFind Command
{B0210780-89CD-11d0-AF08-00A0C925CD16}	DirectSoundCapture Object
{B0406340-B0C5-11d0-89A9-00A0C9054129}	Microsoft DT Diagram Surface 2
{B0406342-B0C5-11d0-89A9-00A0C9054129}	Microsoft DT DDS Circular Auto Layout Logic 2
{B0406343-B0C5-11d0-89A9-00A0C9054129}	Microsoft DT DDS Straight Line Routing Logic 2
{B0406344-B0C5-11d0-89A9-00A0C9054129}	Microsoft DT Simple Graphic Diagram Data 2
{b0516ff0-7f1c-11ce-be57-00aa0051fe20}	Spanish_Modern Stemmer
{B091E540-83E3-11CF-A713-0020AFD79762}	File Types Page
{B0A6BAE2-AAF0-11D0-A152-00A0C908DB96}	Microsoft DirectAnimation Sequencer
{b0b71247-4080-11d1-a3ac-00c04fb950dc}	ADs NetAddress Object
{B0D12372-6532-11D1-BB8F-0060083178D8}	NSLiteSession Class
{B0D12374-6532-11D1-BB8F-0060083178D8}	ASFSessionProp Class
{B0D12376-6532-11D1-BB8F-0060083178D8}	FTSSessionProp Class
{B0D17FC2-7BC4-11d1-BDFA-00C04FA31009}	CLSID_IFontCache
{B1549E58-3894-11D2-BB7F-00A0C999C4C1}	LM Behavior Factory
{B15B8DC0-C7E1-11d0-8680-00AA00BDCB71}	SoftDist
{B196B286-BAB4-101A-B69C-00AA00341D07}	PSFactoryBuffer
{B1AFF7D0-0C49-11D1-BB12-00C04FC9A3A3}	SendConsoleMessageApp Class
{B1B77C00-C3E4-11CF-AF79-00AA00B67A42}	DV Video Decoder
{B1BF0DE1-7D27-11D0-A8AA-00A0C921A4D2}	TextBuffer class
{B1F1A325-9601-11d0-8D70-00A0C92B500F}	Microsoft NetShow File Dialog
{B2104A32-2AE8-11D1-8EC0-00A0C90F26EA}	Microsoft Development Environment
{B23C35B7-9219-11D2-9E17-00C04FA322BA}	Microsoft SMTPSVC Categorizer
{b2538919-4080-11d1-a3ac-00c04fb950dc}	ADs Path Object
{B2AD2931-84FD-11d0-81E4-00A0C91180F2}	FsaFilterClientNTFS Class
{B2AD2932-84FD-11d0-81E4-00A0C91180F2}	FsaFilterRecallNTFS Class
{b3192190-1176-11d0-8ce8-00aa006c400c}	ASP Certificate Object
{B323F8E0-2E68-11D0-90EA-00AA0060F86C }	StillImage
{b33143cb-4080-11d1-a3ac-00c04fb950dc}	ADs TypedName Object
{B3449CE0-28F7-11D0-81BF-00A0C91180F2}	CWsbUshort Class
{B3449CE1-28F7-11D0-81BF-00A0C91180F2}	CWsbBool Class
{B3449CE7-28F7-11D0-81BF-00A0C91180F2}	CWsbLong Class
{B3449CE8-28F7-11D0-81BF-00A0C91180F2}	CWsbShort Class
{B3613D9F-E26E-11d0-8FAC-08002BE4E62A}	Speech Tools Log
{B3613DA0-E26E-11d0-8FAC-08002BE4E62A}	Logging Audio Source
{b3ad3e13-4080-11d1-a3ac-00c04fb950dc}	ADs Hold Object
{B3B443EF-0728-11D2-95AC-0060B0576642}	IASMultivaluedAttributeEditor Class
{b3cdae90-d170-11d0-802b-00c04fd75d13}	Channel Mgr

TABLE B.1	Continued

CLSID Object	**Reference**
{B45AFEC0-2AE6-11D1-859E-00C04FC9E292}	Microsoft SAP Agent Notify Object
{B45FF030-4447-11D2-85DE-00C04FA35C89}	SearchAssistantOC
{b477ca30-3821-11d0-8de6-00aa00b90c3b}	Streaming Media Player NG
{b47ccfd2-755d-11d0-bad6-0800365b0e03}	ASF Media Player
{B4B3AECB-DFD6-11d1-9DAA-00805F85CFE3}	F:\WINNT\System32\clbcatq.dll
{B4CA2970-DD2B-11D0-9DFA-00AA00AF3494}	Indeo® audio software
{B4CA2971-DD2B-11D0-9DFA-00AA00AF3494}	Indeo® audio software Property Page
{B4E90802-B83C-11D0-8B40-00C0F00AE35A}	ContentRotator Class
{b4f34438-afec-11d1-9868-00a0c922e703}	IIS App Extension
{B50F5260-0C21-11D2-AB56-00A0C9082678}	Compress Files Cleaner
{B54F3741-5B07-11cf-A4B0-00AA004A55E8}	VB Script Language
{B54F3742-5B07-11cf-A4B0-00AA004A55E8}	VB Script Language Authoring
{B54F3743-5B07-11cf-A4B0-00AA004A55E8}	VBScript Language Encoding
{B57467A6-50B5-11D1-BF97-0000F8773501}	AddPrint Class
{b5866878-bd99-11d0-b04b-00c04fd91550}	TypeFactory
{B58C2440-A1A3-11d1-B024-006097C9A284}	MsoHelp Key Search Dialog
{B58C2441-A1A3-11d1-B024-006097C9A284}	MsoHelp AW Search Dialog
{B5C45061-2729-11D1-A1D7-0080C88593A5}	This is the snapin created on 10/30
{B6353564-96C4-11D2-8DDB-006097C9A2B2}	Windows Media Update
{B67F993A-FC9D-11D0-8822-00A0C955FC7E}	KeyGeneration Class
{B695EC28-8333-11D0-B21D-080000185165}	ProfferService Class
{B6D1062C-4FBE-11D1-8D85-006097C9A2B2}	Windows Media Thinning Level Property Page
{B6FFC24C-7E13-11D0-9B47-00C04FC2F51D}	Microsoft DirectAnimation Control
{B722BCCD-4E68-101B-A2BC-00AA00404770}	Microsoft Office 9
{b75ac000-9bdd-11d0-852c-00c04fd8d503}	ADs Access Control Entry Object
{B7711240-A7D0-11CE-83FD-02608C3EC08A}	Annotation Property Page
{B7711241-A7D0-11CE-83FD-02608C3EC08A}	Annotation Button Property Page
{B7AAC060-2638-11d1-83A9-00C04FBD7C09}	CLSID_CAthena16Import
{B82F914A-9F4B-11D1-ABE4-00C04FC30999}	MSOLAPLevels Class
{B82F914D-9F4B-11D1-ABE4-00C04FC30999}	MSOLAPLevel Class
{B82F9150-9F4B-11D1-ABE4-00C04FC30999}	MSOLAPMeasures Class
{B82F9153-9F4B-11D1-ABE4-00C04FC30999}	MSOLAPMeasure Class
{B82F9156-9F4B-11D1-ABE4-00C04FC30999}	MSOLAPPartitions Class
{B82F9159-9F4B-11D1-ABE4-00C04FC30999}	MSOLAPPartition Class
{B82F915C-9F4B-11D1-ABE4-00C04FC30999}	MSOLAPAggregations Class
{B82F915F-9F4B-11D1-ABE4-00C04FC30999}	MSOLAPAggregation Class
{B82F9164-9F4B-11D1-ABE4-00C04FC30999}	MSOLAPExtLevels Class
{B82F9167-9F4B-11D1-ABE4-00C04FC30999}	MSOLAPExtLevel Class
{B82F916A-9F4B-11D1-ABE4-00C04FC30999}	MSOLAPExtMeasures Class

TABLE B.1   Continued

CLSID Object	Reference
{B82F916D-9F4B-11D1-ABE4-00C04FC30999}	MSOLAPExtMeasure Class
{b85ea052-9bdd-11d0-852c-00c04fd8d503}	ADs Access Control List Object
{B890AF56-AC8C-11D1-8CB7-00C04FC3261D}	CLBDTDispenser Class
{B8DA6310-E19B-11D0-933C-00A0C90DCAA9}	PSFactoryBuffer
{B8E1CD21-81D3-11d0-81E4-00A0C91180F2}	HsmWorkItem Class
{B91B6008-32D2-11D2-9888-00A0C925F917}	Compdata Class
{b958f73c-9bdd-11d0-852c-00c04fd8d503}	ADs Security Descriptor Object
{B977CB11-1FF5-11d2-9A7A-00C04FA309D4}	CLSID_CIMN1Import
{B98AC5E0-DE20-11d1-A7CE-0000F81E8509}	Java Class: com.ms.wfc.html.DhModule
{B9BD3860-44DB-101B-90A8-00AA003E4B50}	ISRShare_PSFactory
{B9D1F320-C401-11D0-A520-000000000000}	ASF DIB Handler
{B9D1F321-C401-11D0-A520-000000000000}	ASF ACM Handler
{B9D1F322-C401-11D0-A520-000000000000}	ASF ICM Handler
{B9D1F323-C401-11D0-A520-000000000000}	ASF URL Handler
{B9D1F324-C401-11D0-A520-000000000000}	ASF JPEG Handler
{B9D1F325-C401-11D0-A520-000000000000}	ASF DJPEG Handler
{B9D1F32E-C401-11D0-A520-000000000000}	ASF Animation Handler
{B9F11A90-90E3-11d0-8D77-00A0C9034A7E}	DirectSound Destination Object
{B9F11A95-90E3-11d0-8D77-00A0C9034A7E}	Microphone Setup Wizard
{B9F11A96-90E3-11d0-8D77-00A0C9034A7E}	Phoneme Converter
{BA126AD1-2166-11D1-B1D0-00805FC1270E}	Network Connection Manager Class
{BA126AD2-2166-11D1-B1D0-00805FC1270E}	Network Connection Manager Connection Enumerator Class
{BA126AD3-2166-11D1-B1D0-00805FC1270E}	LAN Connection Manager Class
{BA126AD4-2166-11D1-B1D0-00805FC1270E}	LAN Connection Manager Connection Enumerator Class
{BA126AD5-2166-11D1-B1D0-00805FC1270E}	WAN Connection Manager Class
{BA126AD6-2166-11D1-B1D0-00805FC1270E}	WAN Connection Manager Connection Enumerator Class
{BA126AD7-2166-11D1-B1D0-00805FC1270E}	Dial-up Connection Class
{BA126AD9-2166-11D1-B1D0-00805FC1270E}	Inbound Connection Class
{BA126ADB-2166-11D1-B1D0-00805FC1270E}	LAN Connection Class
{BA126ADD-2166-11D1-B1D0-00805FC1270E}	Inbound Connection Manager Class
{BA126ADE-2166-11D1-B1D0-00805FC1270E}	Inbound Connection Manager Connection Enumerator Class
{BA126ADF-2166-11D1-B1D0-00805FC1270E}	Network Install Queue
{BA2BC757-271E-11D2-8E77-00600893AF2D}	PDOlapAux Class
{BA4E57F0-FAB6-11cf-9D1A-00AA00A70D51}	MD COM Server
{BA60F742-6F72-11d2-875F-00A0C93C09B3}	SetBvr Class

| **TABLE B.1** | Continued |

CLSID Object	Reference
{BA634603-B771-11D0-9296-00C04FB6678B}	LogUI Control
{BA634604-B771-11D0-9296-00C04FB6678B}	LogUI Property Page
{BA634607-B771-11D0-9296-00C04FB6678B}	Rat Control
{BA634608-B771-11D0-9296-00C04FB6678B}	Rat Property Page
{BA63460B-B771-11D0-9296-00C04FB6678B}	Apps Control
{BA63460C-B771-11D0-9296-00C04FB6678B}	Apps Property Page
{bab33640-1280-11d2-aa30-00a0c91eedba}	DocFind Persistent history
{BACF5C8A-A3C7-11D1-A760-00C04FB9603F}	Software installation
{BB0D7187-3C44-11D2-BB98-3078302C2030}	CfgComp Class
{BB2B65B0-241E-101B-9E67-00AA003BA905}	F:\PROGRA~1\COMMON~1\System\ Mapi\1033\NT\CNFNOT32.EXE
{BB314F91-A010-11d1-A75A-006097C4E476}	ppDSMeta Class
{BB339A46-7C49-11d2-9BF3-00C04FA34789}	LM Auto Effect Behaivor
{BB64DF2F-88E4-11D0-9E87-00C04FD7081F}	Microsoft Agent DocFile Provider 1.5
{BB847B8A-054A-11d2-A894-0000F8084F96}	CLSID_IPropFindRequest
{BBBE3F40-964D-11D0-9643-00AA00A89C1D}	Intel RTP SPH Property Page
{BBBE3F41-964D-11D0-9643-00AA00A89C1D}	Intel RTP SPH Property Page
{BBBE3F43-964D-11D0-9643-00AA00A89C1D}	Intel RTP SPH Property Page
{BBD8F29B-6F61-11D0-A26E-08002B2C6F32}	Microsoft Certificate Mapping Control
{BBD8F29C-6F61-11D0-A26E-08002B2C6F32}	Certmap Property Page
{bbddbdec-c947-11d1-aa5e-00c04fa35b82}	NTFS Message Enumerator Class
{BC29A660-30E3-11d0-9E69-00C04FD7C15B}	WDM Streaming VPE Property Set Interface Handler
{bc36cde8-afeb-11d1-9868-00a0c922e703}	IIS Cert Map Extension
{BC5F0300-F7BC-11d0-B9ED-40A708C10000}	Dx3j Security Object
{BC5F1E50-5110-11D1-AFF5-006097C9A284}	BlnSet Proxy
{BC5F1E51-5110-11D1-AFF5-006097C9A284}	Bln Proxy
{BC5F1E53-5110-11D1-AFF5-006097C9A284}	BlnSink Proxy
{BC5F1E55-5110-11D1-AFF5-006097C9A284}	BlnUser Proxy
{BC94D813-4D7F-11d2-A8C9-00AA00A71DCA}	SdoService Class
{BCE9E2E7-1FDD-11d2-9A79-00C04FA309D4}	CLSID_COE4Import
{BCFD624E-705A-11d2-A2AF-00C04FC30871}	WebViewCoord Class
{BD010A01-000B-11D0-D0DD-00A0C9190459}	PSFactoryBuffer
{BD040C00-000B-11D0-D0DD-00A0C9190459}	CNtTapeIo Class
{BD050C00-000B-11D0-D0DD-00A0C9190459}	CNtFileIo Class
{BD090C00-000B-11D0-D0DD-00A0C9190459}	CFilterIo Class
{bd70c020-2d24-11d0-9110-00004c752752}	ASP auto file
{BD84B380-8CA2-1069-AB1D-08000948F534}	Fonts
{BD84B381-8CA2-1069-AB1D-08000948F534}	PANOSE Core Mapper

· · · · · · · · · · · · · · ·

TABLE B.1	Continued

CLSID Object	Reference
{BD95BA60-2E26-AAD1-AD99-00AA00B8E05A}	SDSnapin Class
{BD96C556-65A3-11D0-983A-00C04FC29E33}	RDS.DataControl
{BD96C556-65A3-11D0-983A-00C04FC29E36}	RDS.DataSpace
{BDD1F04B-858B-11D1-B16A-00C0F0283628}	Microsoft ListView Control, version 6.0
{BDEADE41-C265-11D0-BCED-00A0C90AB50F}	OWSComment Class
{BDEADE43-C265-11D0-BCED-00A0C90AB50F}	OWSBrowserUI Class
{BDEADE44-C265-11D0-BCED-00A0C90AB50F}	OWSMiscApis Class
{BDEADE47-C265-11D0-BCED-00A0C90AB50F}	OWSCommentThread Class
{BDEADE49-C265-11D0-BCED-00A0C90AB50F}	OWSEventSubscription Class
{BDEADE4A-C265-11D0-BCED-00A0C90AB50F}	OWSEventSubscriptions Class
{BDEADE4E-C265-11D0-BCED-00A0C90AB50F}	OWSDiscussionServers Class
{BDEADE7A-C265-11D0-BCED-00A0C90AB50F}	OWSNotificationSink Class
{BDEADE7B-C265-11D0-BCED-00A0C90AB50F}	OfficeWebServer SyncMgr Handler
{BDEADE7F-C265-11D0-BCED-00A0C90AB50F}	&Discuss
{BDEADEA1-C265-11D0-BCED-00A0C90AB50F}	OWSClientCollaboration Class
{BDEADEA5-C265-11D0-BCED-00A0C90AB50F}	OWSOfflineList Class
{BDEADEB0-C265-11D0-BCED-00A0C90AB50F}	Web Discussions
{BDEADEB1-C265-11D0-BCED-00A0C90AB50F}	Web Discussions
{BDEADEB2-C265-11D0-BCED-00A0C90AB50F}	Web Discussions
{BDEADF00-C265-11d0-BCED-00A0C90AB50F}	Web Folders
{BDEADF00-C265-11d0-BCED-00A0C90AB50F}	F:\Program Files\Common Files\Microsoft Shared\Web Folders\PUBPLACE.HTT
{BDF68FCE-0209-11D1-85C2-00C04FB960EA}	NNTP DirectoryDrop Class
{BE09F473-7FEB-11d2-9962-00C04FA309D4}	CLSID_MigrateMessageStore
{BE0A9830-2B8B-11D1-A949-0060181EBBAD}	WMI MSI ProviderMSIPROVApart
{BEA60F80-7EBA-11d0-81E4-00A0C91180F2}	HsmSession Class
{BEA60F81-7EBA-11d0-81E4-00A0C91180F2}	HsmScanner Class
{BEA60F8A-7EBA-11d0-81E4-00A0C91180F2}	HsmPhase Class
{bf0eaea8-c122-11d2-94f4-00c04f72d8c4}	WLBS Configuration Notify Object
{BF83CC10-7020-11D1-9730-00A024D77700}	NtmsMgr Class
{BF84C0C5-0C80-11D2-A497-00C04FB93209}	Policy Settings Extension Snapin
{BF87B6E0-8C27-11D0-B3F0-00AA003761C5}	Capture Graph Builder
{BF87B6E1-8C27-11D0-B3F0-00AA003761C5}	Capture Graph Builder 2
{BF981FDD-B743-11D1-A69A-00C04FB9988E}	MachineSettings Class
{BF984AD0-F0B6-11cf-84BD-00AA00BF93E3}	Windows Media Administration DLL
{BF984AD1-F0B6-11cf-84BD-00AA00BF93E3}	Windows Media Administration DLL
{BFC880F1-7484-11d0-8309-00AA00B6015C}	Download Site Manager
{BFFFD262-7705-11D0-B5DC-444553540000}	DirectPlayLobby 3.0 Object
{C04D65CF-B70D-11D0-B188-00AA0038C969}	Multi Language String

TABLE B.1	Continued

CLSID Object	**Reference**
{C04EFA90-E221-11D2-985E-00C04F575153}	PSFactoryBuffer
{C0932C62-38E5-11d0-97AB-00C04FC2AD98}	SQLOLEDB Error Lookup
{C0CD59AE-020D-11d1-81F2-00C04FC99D4C}	ppDShowPlay Class
{C0E13E61-0CC6-11d1-BBB6-0060978B2AE6}	Data Driven Cleaner
{C10B4771-4DA0-11D2-A2F5-00C04F86FB7D}	Winmgmt MOF Compiler
{C1172D01-751C-11D0-B6CF-00A024BF23EF}	Symantec Serialization Component
{c1243ca0-bf96-11cd-b579-08002b30bfeb}	Plain Text filter
{C1293E17-534E-11D2-8424-00C04FA372D4}	Remote Install DS Query Form
{C1C0FE00-F3C2-11D0-91D4-444553540000}	Indeo® video 5.10 About Encoder Property Page
{C2349702-EA0B-11CF-9FEC-00AA00A59F69}	H261 Encode OA
{C27CCE32-8596-11D1-B16A-00C0F0283628}	TreeView General Property Page Object
{C27CCE33-8596-11D1-B16A-00C0F0283628}	TabStrip General Property Page Object
{C27CCE34-8596-11D1-B16A-00C0F0283628}	Tab Property Page Object
{C27CCE35-8596-11D1-B16A-00C0F0283628}	ImageList General Property Page Object
{C27CCE36-8596-11D1-B16A-00C0F0283628}	Image Property Page Object
{C27CCE37-8596-11D1-B16A-00C0F0283628}	Toolbar General Property Page Object
{C27CCE38-8596-11D1-B16A-00C0F0283628}	Button Property Page Object
{C27CCE39-8596-11D1-B16A-00C0F0283628}	StatusBar General Property Page Object
{C27CCE3A-8596-11D1-B16A-00C0F0283628}	Panel Property Page Object
{C27CCE3B-8596-11D1-B16A-00C0F0283628}	Progress Bar General Property Page Object
{C27CCE3C-8596-11D1-B16A-00C0F0283628}	Slider General Property Page Object
{C27CCE3D-8596-11D1-B16A-00C0F0283628}	Slider Appearance Property Page Object
{C27CCE3E-8596-11D1-B16A-00C0F0283628}	ListView General Property Page Object
{C27CCE3F-8596-11D1-B16A-00C0F0283628}	ListView Sort Property Page Object
{C27CCE40-8596-11D1-B16A-00C0F0283628}	ListView Images Property Page Object
{C27CCE41-8596-11D1-B16A-00C0F0283628}	ListView Columns Property Page Object
{C27CCE42-8596-11D1-B16A-00C0F0283628}	ImageComboBox General Property Page Object
{C2BE6971-DF9E-11D1-8B87-00C04FD7A924}	AppImport Class
{C2E29801-B1BA-11d0-81E9-00A0C91180F2}	HsmRuleStack Class
{C2FBB630-2971-11d1-A18C-00C04FD75D13}	Microsoft CopyTo Service
{C2FBB631-2971-11d1-A18C-00C04FD75D13}	Microsoft MoveTo Service
{C2FE4500-D6C2-11D0-A37B-00C04FC9DA04}	IP Routing Management
{C2FE4501-D6C2-11D0-A37B-00C04FC9DA04}	IP Routing Management
{C2FE4502-D6C2-11D0-A37B-00C04FC9DA04}	IP Routing Management
{C2FE4503-D6C2-11D0-A37B-00C04FC9DA04}	IP Routing Management
{C2FE4504-D6C2-11D0-A37B-00C04FC9DA04}	IP Routing Management
{C2FE4505-D6C2-11D0-A37B-00C04FC9DA04}	IP Routing Management
{C2FE4506-D6C2-11D0-A37B-00C04FC9DA04}	IP Routing Management
{C2FE4507-D6C2-11D0-A37B-00C04FC9DA04}	IP Routing Management

TABLE B.1 Continued

CLSID Object	Reference
{C2FE4508-D6C2-11D0-A37B-00C04FC9DA04}	IGMP Snap-in
{C2FE4509-D6C2-11D0-A37B-00C04FC9DA04}	IGMP Snap-in
{C2FE450A-D6C2-11D0-A37B-00C04FC9DA04}	Router Configuration object for IP
{C2FE450B-D6C2-11D0-A37B-00C04FC9DA04}	IP Routing Management
{C2FE450C-D6C2-11D0-A37B-00C04FC9DA04}	IP Routing Management
{C2FEEEAC-CFCD-11D1-8B05-00600806D9B6}	Wbem Scripting Last Error
{c3278e90-bea7-11cd-b579-08002b30bfeb}	Null filter
{C3480406-A7F8-11D1-AA75-00C04FA34D72}	Microsoft Agent International DLL for Language 0x0406
{C3480407-A7F8-11D1-AA75-00C04FA34D72}	Microsoft Agent International DLL for Language 0x0407
{C3480409-A7F8-11D1-AA75-00C04FA34D72}	Microsoft Agent International DLL for Language 0x0409
{C348040B-A7F8-11D1-AA75-00C04FA34D72}	Microsoft Agent International DLL for Language 0x040b
{C348040C-A7F8-11D1-AA75-00C04FA34D72}	Microsoft Agent International DLL for Language 0x040c
{C3480410-A7F8-11D1-AA75-00C04FA34D72}	Microsoft Agent International DLL for Language 0x0410
{C3480413-A7F8-11D1-AA75-00C04FA34D72}	Microsoft Agent International DLL for Language 0x0413
{C3480414-A7F8-11D1-AA75-00C04FA34D72}	Microsoft Agent International DLL for Language 0x0414
{C3480416-A7F8-11D1-AA75-00C04FA34D72}	Microsoft Agent International DLL for Language 0x0416
{C348041D-A7F8-11D1-AA75-00C04FA34D72}	Microsoft Agent International DLL for Language 0x041d
{C3480816-A7F8-11D1-AA75-00C04FA34D72}	Microsoft Agent International DLL for Language 0x0816
{C3480C0A-A7F8-11D1-AA75-00C04FA34D72}	Microsoft Agent International DLL for Language 0x0c0a
{C3701884-B39B-11D1-9D68-00C04FC30DF6}	OleInstall Class
{C3701884-B39B-11D2-9D68-00C04FC30DF6}	PrtSum Class
{C3853C22-3F2E-11D2-9900-0000F803FF7A}	BlackHole
{C3A904FE-C4F2-11D1-B10B-00104B243180}	F:\WINNT\System32\dsadmin.dll
{c3b32488-afec-11d1-9868-00a0c922e703}	IIS Server Extension
{C3BDF740-0B58-11d2-A484-00C04F8EFB69}	CrBarn
{C3E5D3D2-1A03-11CF-942D-008029004347}	System Monitor General Properties
{C3E5D3D3-1A03-11CF-942D-008029004347}	System Monitor Graph Properties

TABLE B.1	Continued

CLSID Object	**Reference**
{C40FBD00-88B9-11d2-84AD-00C04FA31A86}	dsquery.dll
{c4376b00-f87b-11d0-a6a6-00a0c922e752}	IISAdmin Security Extension
{C47195EC-CD7A-11D1-8EA3-00C04F9900D7}	SysColorCtrl Class
{C49E32C6-BC8B-11D2-85D4-00105A1F8304}	Windows Management Instrumentation Backup and Recovery
{C4D2D8E0-D1DD-11CE-940F-008029004347}	System Monitor Control
{C4DF0040-2D33-11D0-A9CF-00AA00685C74}	SEORegDictionary Class
{C4DF0042-2D33-11D0-A9CF-00AA00685C74}	SEOMemDictionary Class
{C4DF0043-2D33-11D0-A9CF-00AA00685C74}	SEOMetaDictionary Class
{C4EAB3EB-F4AF-11d1-828E-00C04F990690}	IMDB Core Connection
{C4EE31F3-4768-11D2-BE5C-00A0C9A83DA1}	File and Folders Search ActiveX Control
{C54EC3BB-7442-11d2-A036-0060B0576642}	IASNASVendors Class
{C5598E60-B307-11D1-B27D-006008C3FBFB}	PSFactoryBuffer
{C59938DA-9B20-11D0-9CE3-00C04FC9BCC4}	NWLink Configuration Notify Object
{C5B86F32-69EE-11d2-875F-00A0C93C09B3}	MoveBvr Class
{C5F1645C-C8C9-11D0-BCDB-00C04FD8D5B6}	DsPropertyPages.Contact
{C62A69F0-16DC-11CE-9E98-00AA00574A4F}	Microsoft Forms 2.0 Form
{C6365470-F667-11d1-9067-00C04FD9189D}	Gradient DXSurface
{C63A2B30-5543-11b9-C000-5611722E1D15}	IVCmd_PSFactory
{C647B5C0-157C-11D0-BD23-00A0C911CE86}	AVI mux Property Page
{C6520AE1-2037-11D0-906C-00AA00A59F69}	H261 RTP Parameters Property Page
{C6520AE2-2037-11D0-906C-00AA00A59F69}	H263 RTP Parameters Property Page
{C69E8F40-D5C8-11D0-A520-145405C10000}	Indeo Video (r) 5.1 Progressive Download Source
{C69E8F41-D5C8-11D0-A520-145405C10000}	Indeo Video (r) 5.1 Progressive Download Source About
{C69E8F42-D5C8-11D0-A520-145405C10000}	Indeo Video (r) 5.1 Progressive Download Source Static Info
{C69E8F43-D5C8-11D0-A520-145405C10000}	Indeo Video (r) 5.1 Progressive Download Source Dynamic Info
{C6CC49B0-CE17-11D0-8833-00A0C903B83C}	CertGetConfig Class
{C71566F2-561E-11D1-AD87-00C04FD8FDFF}	Microsoft WBEM Universal Refresher
{c733e4af-576e-11d0-b28c-00c04fd7cd22}	Thread NotificationMgr
{C74190B6-8589-11D1-B16A-00C0F0283628}	Microsoft TreeView Control, version 6.0
{C76D83F8-A489-11D0-8195-00A0C91BBEE3}	HtmEditorFactory Class
{C76D83FD-A489-11D0-8195-00A0C91BBEE3}	VIDProtcol Class
{C7A3A54B-0250-11D3-9CD1-00105A1F4801}	Microsoft WBEM SMTP Event Consumer Provider
{C7B6C04A-CBB5-11d0-BB4C-00C04FC2F410}	IndexServer Simple Command Creator
{C7DAE17F-D8C1-11D2-B532-00104B9A3597}	Registry Class
{C7DAE181-D8C1-11D2-B532-00104B9A3597}	INIFile Class

● ● ● ● ● ● ● ● ● ● ● ● ● ●

TABLE B.1 Continued

CLSID Object	Reference
{c804d980-ebec-11d0-a6a0-00a0c922e752}	PSFactoryBuffer
{C83B5610-E0DF-11D0-9E00-00AA00AF3494}	About Indeo® audio software
{C854F6C6-A09F-11D0-A4AA-00C04FC29CFB}	CallbackProxy
{c8b522cb-5cf3-11ce-ade5-00aa0044773d}	MSDASQL
{c8b522cb-5cf3-11ce-ade5-00aa0044773d}	MSDASQL Error Lookup
{c8b522cc-5cf3-11ce-ade5-00aa0044773d}	MSDASQL ErrorLookup
{c8b522cd-5cf3-11ce-ade5-00aa0044773d}	MSDASQL Enumerator
{c8b522ce-5cf3-11ce-ade5-00aa0044773d}	MSDATT
{C8B522CF-5CF3-11CE-ADE5-00AA0044773D}	Microsoft OLE DB Error Collection Service
{c8b522d0-5cf3-11ce-ade5-00aa0044773d}	Microsoft OLE DB Root Enumerator
{c8b522d1-5cf3-11ce-ade5-00aa0044773d}	Microsoft OLE DB Data Conversion Library
{C9076CE1-FB56-11CF-906C-00AA00A59F69}	H263 Encode Parameters Property Page
{C9076CE2-FB56-11CF-906C-00AA00A59F69}	H263 Encode Transform Filter
{C962ABC9-1B2E-11D1-8DCE-00A0C92B500F}	ASFChopper Class
{C97912DE-997E-11D0-A5F6-00A0C922E752}	MdSync Class
{C9BC92DF-5B9A-11D1-8F00-00C04FC2C17B}	ComponentDataImpl Class
{CA38D8DA-C75D-11D1-8F99-00600895E7D5}	Interface Proxy Stub
{CA38D8DB-C75D-11D1-8F99-00600895E7D5}	Interface Proxy Stub
{CAE80521-F685-11d1-AF32-00C04FA31B90}	CLSID_OENote
{CB0E73C1-706A-11CF-A056-00A02416065A}	IPM.Note.FolderPub.Update
{CB0E73C2-706A-11CF-A056-00A02416065A}	IPM.Note.FolderPub.SyncState
{CB0E73C3-706A-11CF-A056-00A02416065A}	IPM.Note.FolderPub.Request
{CB0E73C7-706A-11CF-A056-00A02416065A}	IPM.Note.FolderPub.Update.Multiple
{CB2418D3-0709-11D2-95AB-0060B0576642}	IASIPAttributeEditor Class
{CB39A782-E5E4-11D1-8CC0-00C04FC3261D}	RegDBCompensator Class
{CB40F470-02F1-11D1-B244-00AA00A74BFF}	IMediaCatalogMoniker Proxy/Stub
{CB46E850-FC2F-11D2-B126-00805FC73204}	PSFactoryBuffer
{CB632C76-8DD4-11D1-ADDF-0000F87734F0}	TapiLocationInfo Class
{CB96B400-C743-11cd-80E5-00AA003E4B50}	Audio Destination Object
{CBE3FAA0-CC75-11D0-B465-00001A1818E6}	QKsAudIntfHandler
{CC2C83A6-9BE4-11D0-98E7-00C04FC2CAF5}	Microsoft JET 4.0 Briefcase Reconciler
{CC58E280-8AA1-11D1-B3F1-00AA003761C5}	Smart Tee Filter
{CC785860-B2CA-11CE-8D2B-0000E202599C}	MPEG Audio Decoder Property Page
{CCB4EC60-B9DC-11D1-AC80-00A0C9034873}	PDPO Class
{CCDD9080-8100-11D0-B6CF-00A024BF23EF}	Printer Data Transport
{CCE92A90-F11A-11d1-8FAF-00600895E7D5}	TMP Muxer
{CD000001-8B95-11D1-82DB-00C04FB1625D}	CDOMessage Class
{CD000002-8B95-11D1-82DB-00C04FB1625D}	CDOConfiguration Class
{CD000004-8B95-11D1-82DB-00C04FB1625D}	CDO DropDirectory class

| TABLE B.1 | Continued |

CLSID Object	Reference
{CD000005-8B95-11D1-82DB-00C04FB1625D}	SMTP OnArrival Script Host Sink Class
{CD000006-8B95-11D1-82DB-00C04FB1625D}	NNTP OnPost Script Host Sink Class
{CD000007-8B95-11D1-82DB-00C04FB1625D}	NNTP OnPostFinal Script Host Sink Class
{CD000008-8B95-11D1-82DB-00C04FB1625D}	SMTPConnector Class
{CD000009-8B95-11D1-82DB-00C04FB1625D}	NNTPPostConnector Class
{CD000010-8B95-11D1-82DB-00C04FB1625D}	NNTPFinalConnector Class
{CD000011-8B95-11D1-82DB-00C04FB1625D}	NNTPEarlyConnector Class
{CD000012-8B95-11D1-82DB-00C04FB1625D}	NNTP OnPostEarly Script Host Sink Class
{CD00007F-8B95-11D1-82DB-00C04FB1625D}	PSFactoryBuffer
{CD6C7868-5864-11D0-ABF0-0020AF6B0B7A}	CTreeView Control
{CD6C7869-5864-11D0-ABF0-0020AF6B0B7A}	CTreeView Property Page
{CD8743A1-3736-11D0-9E69-00C04FD7C15B}	Overlay Mixer
{CDA296F7-E065-11D1-BFD3-00C04FB9988E}	AppidData Class
{CDA42200-BD88-11d0-BD4E-00A0C911CE86}	Filter Mapper2
{CDBD8D00-C193-11D0-BD4E-00A0C911CE86}	CMediaPropertyBag
{CDBEC9C0-7A68-11D1-88F9-0080C7D771BF}	Event Class
{CDCDD6A0-C016-11D0-82A4-00AA00B5CA1B}	Microsoft PCM Audio Mixer
{CE292861-FC88-11D0-9E69-00C04FD7C15B}	VideoPort Object
{CEFC65D8-66D8-11D1-8D8C-0000F804B057}	Thumbnail Generator
{CF0F2F7C-F7BF-11d0-900D-00C04FD9189D}	MtStream Class
{cf3eb700-132b-11d0-8dbd-00aa00b90c3b}	Streaming Media Player
{CF49D4E0-1115-11CE-B03A-0020AF0BA770}	AVI Decompressor
{CF948561-EDE8-11CE-941E-008029004347}	System Monitor Data Properties
{CFADAC85-E12C-11D1-B34C-00C04F990D54}	ComClientExport Class
{CFB04621-1C9F-11D0-81B4-00A0C91180F2}	HsmCritLinked Class
{CFB04622-1C9F-11D0-81B4-00A0C91180F2}	HsmCritManageable Class
{CFBFAE00-17A6-11D0-99CB-00C04FD64497}	Microsoft Url Search Hook
{CFC2CAA4-DC5D-11D0-ADAD-00A0C90F5739}	DBNamespace Class
{CFC399AF-D876-11d0-9C10-00C04FC99C8E}	Msxml
{CFCCC7A0-A282-11D1-9082-006008059382}	Darwin App Publisher
{D0565000-9DF4-11D1-A281-00C04FCA0AA7}	EventSystem.EventObjectChange
{D14E3180-11FD-11CE-B841-00AA004CD6D8}	Microsoft Forms 2.1 Picture
{D1EB6D20-8923-11d0-9D97-00A0C90A43CB}	DirectPlay Object
{D1FE6762-FC48-11D0-883A-3C8B00C10000}	DXTransformFactory Class
{D2029F40-8AB3-11CF-85FB-00401C608501}	PSFactoryBuffer
{D2073C44-AB4F-11D0-A732-00A0C9082637}	Java Package Manager
{D20EA4E1-3957-11d2-A40B-0C5020524152}	Fonts
{D20EA4E1-3957-11d2-A40B-0C5020524153}	Administrative Tools
{d2423620-51a0-11d2-9caf-0060b0ec3d39}	XML Parser

TABLE B.1	Continued

CLSID Object	**Reference**
{d24d4450-1f01-11d1-8e63-006097d2df48}	Microsoft DT Icon Control
{d24d4451-1f01-11d1-8e63-006097d2df48}	Microsoft DT Label Control
{D24D4453-1F01-11d1-8E63-006097D2DF48}	Microsoft DT PolyLine Control 2
{D24FE500-C743-11cd-80E5-00AA003E4B50}	Audio Source Object
{D2AC2881-B39B-11D1-8704-00600893B1BD}	DirectMusicPerformance
{D2AC2882-B39B-11D1-8704-00600893B1BD}	DirectMusicSegment
{D2AC2883-B39B-11D1-8704-00600893B1BD}	DirectMusicSegmentState
{D2AC2884-B39B-11D1-8704-00600893B1BD}	DirectMusicGraph
{D2AC2885-B39B-11D1-8704-00600893B1BD}	DirectMusicTempoTrack
{D2AC2886-B39B-11D1-8704-00600893B1BD}	DirectMusicSeqTrack
{D2AC2887-B39B-11D1-8704-00600893B1BD}	DirectMusicSysExTrack
{D2AC2888-B39B-11D1-8704-00600893B1BD}	DirectMusicTimeSigTrack
{D2AC288A-B39B-11D1-8704-00600893B1BD}	DirectMusicStyle
{D2AC288B-B39B-11D1-8704-00600893B1BD}	DirectMusicChordTrack
{D2AC288C-B39B-11D1-8704-00600893B1BD}	DirectMusicCommandTrack
{D2AC288D-B39B-11D1-8704-00600893B1BD}	DirectMusicStyleTrack
{D2AC288E-B39B-11D1-8704-00600893B1BD}	DirectMusicMotifTrack
{D2AC288F-B39B-11D1-8704-00600893B1BD}	DirectMusicChordMap
{D2AC2890-B39B-11D1-8704-00600893B1BD}	DirectMusicComposer
{D2AC2892-B39B-11D1-8704-00600893B1BD}	DirectMusicLoader
{D2AC2894-B39B-11D1-8704-00600893B1BD}	DirectMusicBandTrack
{D2AC2896-B39B-11D1-8704-00600893B1BD}	DirectMusicChordMapTrack
{D2AC2897-B39B-11D1-8704-00600893B1BD}	DirectMusicAuditionTrack
{D2AC2898-B39B-11D1-8704-00600893B1BD}	DirectMusicMuteTrack
{D2BD7934-05FC-11D2-9059-00C04FD7A1BD}	PSFactoryBuffer
{D2BD7935-05FC-11D2-9059-00C04FD7A1BD}	OfficeObj Class
{D2C875C1-AD6E-11d1-9F2F-00A02488FCDE}	HsmActionOnResourcePreUnmanage Class
{D2D139E3-B6CA-11d1-9F31-00C04FC29D52}	Replica Class
{D2D588B5-D081-11D0-99E0-00C04FC2F8EC}	WMI Instance Provider
{D2D79DF5-3400-11d0-B40B-00AA005FF586}	IVolumeClient_PSFactory
{D2D79DF7-3400-11d0-B40B-00AA005FF586}	IDMNotify_PSFactory
{D30BCC65-60E8-11D1-A7CE-00A0C913F73C}	DirectMusicTemplate
{D3588AB0-0781-11CE-B03A-0020AF0BA770}	AVI/WAV File Source
{D3588AB1-0781-11CE-B03A-0020AF0BA770}	AVI DOC Writer
{D3938AB0-5B9D-11D1-8DD2-00AA004ABD5E}	SENS Subscriber for EventSystem EventObjectChange events
{D3AF5DB1-1DF8-11D0-81B6-00A0C91180F2}	HsmActionUnmanage Class
{D3AF5DB2-1DF8-11D0-81B6-00A0C91180F2}	HsmCritMbit Class
{D3E34B21-9D75-101A-8C3D-00AA001A1652}	Bitmap Image

TABLE B.1	Continued

CLSID Object	Reference
{D4023720-E4B9-11cf-8D56-00A0C9034A7E}	Instrumented Audio Source Object
{D4123720-E4B9-11cf-8D56-00A0C9034A7E}	Suspeding Audio Source Object
{D413C502-3FAA-11D0-B254-444553540000}	NPPAgent
{D42FEAC0-82A1-11D0-9643-00AA00A89C1D}	Intel RTP RPH for G.711/G.723.1
{D4480A50-BA28-11d1-8E75-00C04FA31A86}	Add Network Place
{D4523720-E4B9-11cf-8D56-00A0C9034A7E}	Audio Source from File Object
{D45FD2FC-5C6E-11D1-9EC1-00C04FD7081F}	Microsoft Agent Server 2.0
{D45FD2FF-5C6E-11D1-9EC1-00C04FD7081F}	Microsoft Agent DocFile Provider 2.0
{D45FD300-5C6E-11D1-9EC1-00C04FD7081F}	Microsoft Agent File Provider 2.0
{D45FD301-5C6E-11D1-9EC1-00C04FD7081F}	Microsoft Agent Flat File Provider 2.0
{D45FD31B-5C6E-11D1-9EC1-00C04FD7081F}	Microsoft Agent Control 2.0
{D45FD31C-5C6E-11D1-9EC1-00C04FD7081F}	MSLwvTTS 2.0 Engine Class
{D45FD31D-5C6E-11D1-9EC1-00C04FD7081F}	AgentNotifySink Custom Proxy Class
{D45FD31E-5C6E-11D1-9EC1-00C04FD7081F}	AgentCharacter Custom Proxy Class
{D4623720-E4B9-11cf-8D56-00A0C9034A7E}	Audio Destination to File Object
{D485DDC0-49C6-11d1-8E56-00A0C92C9D5D}	Logical Disk Manager Remote Client
{D4BE8632-0C85-11D2-91B1-00C04F8C8761}	IIS Certificate Wizard
{D4FE6221-1288-11D0-9097-00AA004254A0}	NMSA File System Media Description Object (Ver 1.0)
{d4fe6222-1288-11d0-9097-00aa004254a0}	NMSA File Transform Media Description Object (Ver 1.0)
{d4fe6223-1288-11d0-9097-00aa004254a0}	NMSA IP Media Description Object (Ver 1.0)
{d4fe6224-1288-11d0-9097-00aa004254a0}	NMSA Line-In Mic-In Media Description Object (Ver 1.0)
{d4fe6225-1288-11d0-9097-00aa004254a0}	NMSA Audio Transform Media Description Object (Ver 1.0)
{d4fe6226-1288-11d0-9097-00aa004254a0}	NMSA Media Description Object (Ver 1.0)
{d4fe6227-1288-11d0-9097-00aa004254a0}	NMSA Session Description Object (Ver 1.0)
{d4fe6228-1288-11d0-9097-00aa004254a0}	NMSA Session Description Object (Ver 1.0)
{D51BD5A0-7548-11CF-A520-0080C77EF58A}	QuickTime Movie Parser
{D51BD5A1-7548-11CF-A520-0080C77EF58A}	Wave Parser
{D51BD5A2-7548-11CF-A520-0080C77EF58A}	MIDI Parser
{D51BD5A3-7548-11CF-A520-0080C77EF58A}	Multi-file Parser
{D51BD5A4-7548-11CF-A520-0080C77EF58A}	Simple Text Reader
{D51BD5A5-7548-11CF-A520-0080C77EF58A}	File stream renderer
{D51BD5AE-7548-11CF-A520-0080C77EF58A}	XML-based ASX Parser
{D54EEE56-AAAB-11D0-9E1D-00A0C922E6EC}	Microsoft InfoTech IStorage for Win32 Files
{D56F34F2-7E89-11d2-9B4E-00A0C9697CD0}	Text3D
{D5778AE7-43DE-11D0-9171-00AA00C18068}	SCardCmd Class

TABLE B.1 Continued

CLSID Object	Reference
{D5978620-5B9F-11D1-8DD2-00AA004ABD5E}	SENS Network Events
{D5978630-5B9F-11D1-8DD2-00AA004ABD5E}	SENS Logon Events
{D5978640-5B9F-11D1-8DD2-00AA004ABD5E}	SENS OnNow Events
{D5C66BE1-C209-11d1-8DEC-00C04FC2E0C7}	F:\WINNT\System32\clbcatq.dll
{D5DE8D20-5BB8-11D1-A1E3-00A0C90F2731}	VBPropertyBag
{D601D57D-085B-11D2-95AF-0060B0576642}	IASVendorSpecificAttributeEditor Class
{D603F1F0-A9D9-11CF-8904-00AA00BDCB98}	FrontPage Editor
{D61A27C6-8F53-11D0-BFA0-00A024151983}	NtmsSvr Class
{D6277990-4C6A-11CF-8D87-00AA0060F5BF}	Scheduled Tasks
{D6277990-4C6A-11CF-8D87-00AA0060F5BF}	file://%webdir%\schedule.htt
{D62B3FF2-0463-11D1-A6F2-006097C9947C}	PageColorPPG Class
{D63A5850-8F16-11CF-9F47-00AA00BF345C}	WBEM Framework Instance Provider
{D66D6F99-CDAA-11D0-B822-00C04FC9B31F}	Multi Language ConvertCharset
{D67C0280-C743-11cd-80E5-00AA003E4B50}	Text to Speech Enumerator
{D68BD5B0-D6AA-11d0-9EDA-00A02488FCDE}	Remote Storage Recall Notification Client
{D68BD5B3-D6AA-11d0-9EDA-00A02488FCDE}	FsaRecallNotifyServer Class
{D68FC8F4-6B17-11D0-80E6-00AA006EC537}	DropShadow Effect
{d6bfa35e-89f2-11d0-8527-00c04fd8d503}	IIS Namespace Object
{D6D8C25A-4E83-11D2-8424-00C04FA372D4}	Remote Install New Computer Extension
{D7053240-CE69-11CD-A777-00DD01143C57}	Microsoft Forms 2.0 CommandButton
{D707877E-4D9C-11d2-8784-F6E920524153}	User Property Pages
{D70A2BEA-A63E-11D1-A7D4-0000F87571E3}	Group Policy
{D73733C8-CC80-11D0-B225-00C04FB6C2F5}	FaxServer Class
{D7546AAE-A77A-11D1-B901-00AA00585640}	OCFunc Class
{D7546ABD-A77A-11D1-B901-00AA00585640}	OCATP Class
{D76E2820-1563-11CF-AC98-00AA004C0FA9}	AVI Compressor
{D7A7D7C3-D47F-11D0-89D3-00A0C90833E6}	Microsoft DirectAnimation Path
{D7B70EE0-4340-11CF-B063-0020AFC2CD35}	DirectDraw Object
{D7FCB63B-5C55-11D1-8F00-00C04FC2C17B}	SnapinAboutImpl Class
{D82438F1-1C60-11d0-964E-00A0C905F099}	HsmCom Class
{D82438F4-1C60-11d0-964E-00A0C905F099}	ManVol Class
{D82BE2B0-5764-11D0-A96E-00C04FD705A2}	IShellFolderBand
{D857B813-5F40-11D2-B002-00C04FC30936}	Windows NT Server Solution
{d88966de-89f2-11d0-8527-00c04fd8d503}	IIS Provider Object
{D8BD2030-6FC9-11D0-864F-00AA006809D9}	PostAgent
{d9494fc0-31d7-11d0-911f-00aa00c147fa}	Thread Pool Class DLL
{D967F824-9968-11D0-B936-00C04FD8D5B0}	F:\WINNT\System32\dsadmin.dll
{D969A300-E7FF-11d0-A93B-00A0C90F2719}	Microsoft New Object Service
{D97A6DA0-A85D-11cf-83AE-00A0C90C2BD8}	ASP String List Object

TABLE B.1	Continued

CLSID Object	**Reference**
{D97A6DA0-A85F-11df-83AE-00A0C90C2BD8}	ASP Request Dictionary
{D97A6DA0-A861-11cf-93AE-00A0C90C2BD8}	ASP Request Object
{D97A6DA0-A862-11cf-84AE-00A0C90C2BD8}	ASP Write Cookie
{D97A6DA0-A864-11cf-83BE-00A0C90C2BD8}	ASP Response Object
{D97A6DA0-A865-11cf-83AF-00A0C90C2BD8}	ASP Session Object
{D97A6DA0-A866-11cf-83AE-10A0C90C2BD8}	ASP Application Object
{D97A6DA0-A867-11cf-83AE-01A0C90C2BD8}	ASP Server Object
{D97A6DA0-A868-11cf-83AE-00B0C90C2BD8}	ASP Scripting Context Object
{D97A6DA2-9C1C-11D0-9C3C-00A0C922E764}	PSFactoryBuffer
{D99E6E70-FC88-11D0-B498-00A0C90312F3}	PSFactoryBuffer
{d99f7670-7f1a-11ce-be57-00aa0051fe20}	English_UK Stemmer
{d9df823c-4425-11d1-932c-00c04fd919b7}	U2BASIC Authenticator Class
{D9E04211-14D7-11d1-9938-0060976A546D}	HsmActionOnResourcePostValidate Class
{D9E04212-14D7-11d1-9938-0060976A546D}	HsmActionOnResourcePreValidate Class
{D9E04213-14D7-11D1-9938-0060976A546D}	PSFactoryBuffer
{D9E04214-14D7-11d1-9938-0060976A546D}	HsmActionOnResourcePostUnmanage Class
{DA1E5A8E-1A89-11D2-95C9-00A0C90DCA5B}	OSE.DiscussionServer
{DA1E5A90-1A89-11D2-95C9-00A0C90DCA5B}	OSE.DiscussionServers
{da4e3da0-d07d-11d0-bd50-00a0c911ce86}	ActiveMovie Filter Categories
{da4e3da0-d07d-11d0-bd50-00a0c911ce86}	{083863F1-70DE-11d0-BD40-00A0C911CE86}
{da4e3da0-d07d-11d0-bd50-00a0c911ce86}	{0A4252A0-7E70-11D0-A5D6-28DB04C10000}
{da4e3da0-d07d-11d0-bd50-00a0c911ce86}	{2721AE20-7E70-11D0-A5D6-28DB04C10000}
{da4e3da0-d07d-11d0-bd50-00a0c911ce86}	{2EB07EA0-7E70-11D0-A5D6-28DB04C10000}
{da4e3da0-d07d-11d0-bd50-00a0c911ce86}	{33D9A760-90C8-11d0-BD43-00A0C911CE86}
{da4e3da0-d07d-11d0-bd50-00a0c911ce86}	{33D9A761-90C8-11d0-BD43-00A0C911CE86}
{da4e3da0-d07d-11d0-bd50-00a0c911ce86}	{33D9A762-90C8-11d0-BD43-00A0C911CE86}
{da4e3da0-d07d-11d0-bd50-00a0c911ce86}	{4EFE2452-168A-11d1-BC76-00C04FB9453B}
{da4e3da0-d07d-11d0-bd50-00a0c911ce86}	{65E8773D-8F56-11D0-A3B9-00A0C9223196}
{da4e3da0-d07d-11d0-bd50-00a0c911ce86}	{65e8773e-8f56-11d0-a3b9-00a0c9223196}
{da4e3da0-d07d-11d0-bd50-00a0c911ce86}	{860BB310-5D01-11d0-BD3B-00A0C911CE86}
{da4e3da0-d07d-11d0-bd50-00a0c911ce86}	{AD809C00-7B88-11D0-A5D6-28DB04C10000}
{da4e3da0-d07d-11d0-bd50-00a0c911ce86}	{CC7BFB41-F175-11d1-A392-00E0291F3959}
{da4e3da0-d07d-11d0-bd50-00a0c911ce86}	{CC7BFB46-F175-11d1-A392-00E0291F3959}
{da4e3da0-d07d-11d0-bd50-00a0c911ce86}	{CF1DDA2C-9743-11D0-A3EE-00A0C9223196}
{da4e3da0-d07d-11d0-bd50-00a0c911ce86}	{CF1DDA2D-9743-11D0-A3EE-00A0C9223196}
{da4e3da0-d07d-11d0-bd50-00a0c911ce86}	{E0F158E1-CB04-11d0-BD4E-00A0C911CE86}
{da4e3da0-d07d-11d0-bd50-00a0c911ce86}	{FBF6F530-07B9-11D2-A71E-0000F8004788}
{DA6A85E0-05C7-11D1-B243-006097CAD7E2}	System Information Extension
{DAB1A262-4FD7-11D1-842C-00C04FB6C218}	Route Class

••••••••••••••••

| TABLE B.1 | Continued |

CLSID Object	Reference
{DB35D732-21E9-11D0-81B8-00A0C91180F2}	CWsbIndexedEnum Class
{DB35D733-21E9-11D0-81B8-00A0C91180F2}	CWsbString Class
{DB57B100-853B-11D0-AF95-0080C71F7993}	java
{DB5D1FF4-09D7-11D1-BB10-00C04FC9A3A3}	FILEMGMT 1.0 Object
{DB5D1FF5-09D7-11D1-BB10-00C04FC9A3A3}	SvcVwr 1.0 Object
{DB6E8F48-FD3E-11D0-A0BC-00C04FC9E20F}	DPDVEvt Class
{DBCE2480-C732-101B-BE72-BA78E9AD5B27}	ICC Profile
{DBFCA500-8C31-11D0-AA2C-00A0C92749A3}	DiskManagement.SnapInComponent
{DC147890-91C2-11D0-8966-00AA00A74BF2}	Allows management of the NNTP news protocol.
{DC81C0CF-7800-11D1-BBAD-0060083178D8}	PSFactoryBuffer
{DC81C0D0-7800-11D1-BBAD-0060083178D8}	NSLiteServer Class
{dccc0bed-6066-11d1-8c13-00c04fd8d503}	Microsoft Organization Extension
{dd0efe08-8047-11d0-92a9-00c04fd919b7}	IMultimediaDeviceInfo_PSFactory
{DD2110F0-9EEF-11cf-8D8E-00AA0060F5BF}	Scheduling UI icon handler
{DD313E04-FEFF-11d1-8ECD-0000F87A470C}	User Assist
{DD9DA666-8594-11D1-B16A-00C0F0283628}	Microsoft ImageComboBox Control, version 6.0
{DDB008FE-048D-11d1-B9CD-00C04FC2C1D2}	Start Menu Task
{DDE5783A-88B9-11d2-84AD-00C04FA31A86}	dsquery.dll
{DDF5A600-B9C0-101A-AF1A-00AA0034B50B}	Color Property Page
{DE4874D1-FEEE-11d1-A0B0-00C04FA31A86}	dsquery.dll
{DE4874D2-FEEE-11d1-A0B0-00C04FA31A86}	dsquery.dll
{DE88C160-FF2C-11D1-BB6F-00C04FAE22DA}	JetEngine Class
{dea1bd90-f078-11cf-908b-00aa004254a0}	IEnumTrigger_PSFactory
{DEA8AFA0-CC85-11D0-9CE2-0080C7221EBD}	Create, Edit Internet Protocol Security Policies
{DEA8AFA1-CC85-11D0-9CE2-0080C7221EBD}	Create, Edit Internet Protocol Security Policies
{DEA8AFA2-CC85-11D0-9CE2-0080C7221EBD}	Create, Edit Internet Protocol Security Policies
{DEAAB3B2-8AAB-11d0-8FCD-00A0C9190447}	MedSet Class
{DEB58EBB-9CE2-11D1-9128-00C04FC30A64}	NNTP File System Driver Prepare Class
{DEBCE1BC-7D7E-11D2-BEA0-00805F0D8F97}	Microsoft In-Memory Database Transacted Property Group Manager
{dee35070-506b-11cf-b1aa-00aa00b8de95}	Microsoft.Jet.OLEDB.4.0
{dee35070-506b-11cf-b1aa-00aa00b8de95}	Microsoft Jet 4.0 OLE DB ProviderError Lookup
{dee35071-506b-11cf-b1aa-00aa00b8de95}	Microsoft Jet 4.0 OLE DB Provider Error Lookup
{DEE3B231-A3C2-11D0-896E-00AA00A74BF2}	NntpAdminRebuild Class
{DF0B3D60-548F-101B-8E65-08002B2BD119}	PSSupportErrorInfo
{DF0DAEF2-A289-11D1-8697-006008B0E5D2}	MDhcp Class
{DF3D9C23-AB4E-11D0-A732-00A0C9082637}	Code Store Database Manager
{DFA22B8E-E68D-11d0-97E4-00C04FC2AD98}	SQLOLEDB Enumerator
{dfc8bdc0-e378-11d0-9b30-0080c7e9fe95}	MSDAOSP

| TABLE B.1 | Continued |

CLSID Object	Reference
{DFD181E0-5E2F-11CE-A449-00AA004A803D}	Microsoft Forms 2.0 ScrollBar
{DFE49CFE-CD09-11D2-9643-00C04f79ADF0}	Cabview Data Object
{E01C01D0-F326-11D0-A6EC-006097C9947C}	TableCellPPG Class
{E02D16C0-C743-11cd-80E5-00AA003E4B50}	Speech Recognition Enumerator
{E05592E4-C0B5-11D0-A439-00A0C9223196}	Plug In Distributor: IKsQualityForwarder
{E0725551-286F-11d0-8E73-00A0C9083363}	Microsoft TTS Engine
{E07D3492-32B5-11D0-B724-00AA0062CBB7}	Microsoft WBEM Mailslot transport
{e0ca5340-4534-11cf-b952-00aa0051fe20}	HTML filter
{E0DD6CAB-2D10-11d2-8F1A-0000F87ABD16}	Toolbar Extension for Bands
{E0F158E1-CB04-11d0-BD4E-00A0C911CE86}	WaveOut and DSound Class Manager
{E0FA581D-2188-11D2-A739-00C04FA377A1}	Provider Binder for DS OLE DB Provider
{E1141BAB-08F6-11D1-B98A-00A0C9190447}	About Class
{E1211353-8E94-11D1-8808-00C04FC2C602}	DirectX6
{E126F8FF-A7AF-11D0-B88A-00C04FD424B9}	ByteBuffer Class
{E13B6686-3F39-11D0-96F6-00A0C9191601}	DiskManagement.SnapIn
{E13B6688-3F39-11D0-96F6-00A0C9191601}	DiskManagement.DataObject
{E13EF4E4-D2F2-11d0-9816-00C04FD91972}	Menu Site
{E14BB48F-3183-11D2-BE3C-3078302C2030}	AVPropServer Class
{E16C0593-128F-11D1-97E4-00C04FB9618A}	Simple File-based Log
{E16C0594-128F-11D1-97E4-00C04FB9618A}	ARIES Log Recovery Engine
{e17d4fc0-5564-11d1-83f2-00a0c90dc849}	Search Results
{e17d4fc0-5564-11d1-83f2-00a0c90dc849}	file://%webdir%/fsresult.htt
{E1A6B8A0-3603-101C-AC6E-040224009C02}	Kodak Image Thumbnail Control
{E1A6B8A4-3603-101C-AC6E-040224009C02}	Kodak Image Thumbnail Property Page
{E1D2BF40-A96B-11d1-9C6B-0000F875AC61}	MSDAIPP.BINDER
{E1D2BF42-A96B-11d1-9C6B-0000F875AC61}	Microsoft OLE DB Moniker Binder for Internet Publishing
{E237E260-155D-11D1-8C82-00A0C90FFFC0}	ColorHtml Service Class
{E23FDD70-B680-11D0-9C82-0000F8040A53}	BuilderWizardManager Class
{E2510970-F137-11CE-8B67-00AA00A3F1A6}	AVI mux
{E26D02A0-4C1F-11D1-9AA1-00C04FC3357A}	Telephony
{E26D02A1-4C1F-11D1-9AA1-00C04FC3357A}	Telephony
{E26D02A2-4C1F-11D1-9AA1-00C04FC3357A}	Telephony
{E301A009-F901-11D2-82B9-00C04F68928B}	F:\WINNT\System32\dsadmin.dll
{E30629D1-27E5-11CE-875D-00608CB78066}	Audio Renderer
{E30629D2-27E5-11CE-875D-00608CB78066}	Audio Capture Filter
{E31F0409-E9D8-11d0-8A96-00A0C90C2BC5}	Office Balloons ProxyStub Factory
{E355E538-1C2E-11D0-8C37-00C04FD8FE93}	F:\WINNT\System32\dsadmin.dll
{E3659FC1-EA13-11CF-9FEC-00AA00A59F69}	H261 Encode Parameters Property Page

| **TABLE B.1** | Continued |

CLSID Object	**Reference**
{E367E1A1-E917-11d0-AF5F-00A02448799A}	MDM Utilities
{E369A160-F3C2-11D0-91D4-444553540000}	Indeo® video 5.10 About Decoder Property Page
{E3A8BDE6-ABCE-11d0-BC4B-00C04FD929DB}	WebCheckChannelAgent
{E423AF7C-FC2D-11d2-B126-00805FC73204}	Remote Helper
{E436EBB1-524F-11CE-9F53-0020AF0BA770}	System Clock
{E436EBB2-524F-11CE-9F53-0020AF0BA770}	Filter Mapper
{E436EBB3-524F-11CE-9F53-0020AF0BA770}	Filter Graph
{E436EBB5-524F-11CE-9F53-0020AF0BA770}	File Source (Async.)
{E436EBB6-524F-11CE-9F53-0020AF0BA770}	File Source (URL)
{E436EBB7-524F-11CE-9F53-0020AF0BA770}	IPersistMoniker Plug In Distributor
{E436EBB8-524F-11CE-9F53-0020AF0BA770}	Filter Graph no thread
{E4C18D40-1CD5-101C-B325-00AA001F3168}	MS Organization Chart 2.0
{E5670E37-0D2F-11D2-9E65-00A0C904DD32}	Web Page Wizard
{E56829C9-2D59-11d2-BE38-3078302C2030}	Component Categories conditional cache daemon
{E5B42981-67DC-11D0-8547-00A0240B50F0}	Web Page Registration Data Transport
{E5B4EAA0-B2CA-11CE-8D2B-0000E202599C}	MPEG Video Decoder Property Page
{e5df9d10-3b52-11d1-83e8-00a0c90dc849}	WebViewFolderIcon Class
{E60A7940-4B3E-101C-96BF-040224009C02}	Kodak Image Admin Print Page
{E6CC6978-6B6E-11D0-BECA-00C04FD940BE}	ConnectionAgent
{E6E73D20-0C8A-11d2-A484-00C04F8EFB69}	CrZigzag
{E6FB5E20-DE35-11CF-9C87-00AA005127ED}	WebCheck
{E707D9B2-4F89-11D0-81CC-00A0C91180F2}	FsaServerNTFS Class
{E70C92A9-4BFD-11d1-8A95-00C04FB951F3}	CLSID_StoreNamespace
{E71AF890-4F3E-11CE-9872-0020AF68053F}	Microsoft Imager 2.0 Picture
{E791964C-208A-11CF-8146-00AA00A40C25}	MicrosoftRDO.RdoConnection
{E7D3DB4E-199C-11d1-9828-00C04FD91972}	Desktop Task
{E7E4BC40-E76A-11CE-A9BB-00AA004AE837}	Shell DocObject Viewer
{E80353D3-677D-11d2-875E-00A0C93C09B3}	ScaleBvr Class
{E846F0A0-D367-11D1-8286-00A0C9231C29}	F:\WINNT\System32\clbcatex.dll
{e8487246-70c9-11d0-baa0-00c04fd91a5e}	INetShowODBC_PSFactory
{E8BB6DC0-6B4E-11d0-92DB-00A0C90C2BD7}	TrayAgent
{e8cc4cbe-fdff-11d0-b865-00a0c9081c1d}	MSDAORA
{e8cc4cbe-fdff-11d0-b865-00a0c9081c1d}	MSDAORA ErrorLookup
{e8cc4cbf-fdff-11d0-b865-00a0c9081c1d}	MSDAORA ErrorLookup
{E8D83F00-CD78-11D0-B4D3-00A024BF23EF}	Online Registration Extension
{E8FB8620-588F-11D2-9D61-00C04F79C5FE}	PSFactoryBuffer
{E8FB8621-588F-11D2-9D61-00C04F79C5FE}	IisServiceControl Class
{E9218AE7-9E91-11D1-BF60-0080C7846BC0}	SdoMachine Class
{E9225296-C759-11d1-A02B-00C04FB6809F}	DispatchMapper Class

| TABLE B.1 | Continued |

CLSID Object	Reference
{E9ABBBB0-9757-11D1-83F7-00C04FA302A1}	PSFactoryBuffer
{E9ABBBB3-9757-11D1-83F7-00C04FA302A1}	Tree node callback
{E9B0E6C0-811C-11D0-AD51-00A0C90F5739}	Microsoft Data Tools Database Designer Oracle Table Property Page
{E9B0E6C1-811C-11D0-AD51-00A0C90F5739}	Microsoft Data Tools Database Designer Oracle Relationship Property Page
{E9B0E6C3-811C-11D0-AD51-00A0C90F5739}	Microsoft Data Tools Database Designer Oracle Index Property Page
{E9B0E6CB-811C-11D0-AD51-00A0C90F5739}	Microsoft Data Tools Query Designer
{E9B0E6CC-811C-11D0-AD51-00A0C90F5739}	Microsoft Data Tools Query Designer Definition Proxy
{E9B0E6D0-811C-11D0-AD51-00A0C90F5739}	Microsoft Data Tools Query Designer Query property page
{E9B0E6D1-811C-11D0-AD51-00A0C90F5739}	Microsoft Data Tools Query Designer Parameters property page
{E9B0E6D2-811C-11D0-AD51-00A0C90F5739}	Microsoft Data Tools Query Designer Join Line property page
{E9B0E6D3-811C-11D0-AD51-00A0C90F5739}	Microsoft Data Tools Query Designer ODBC Personality
{E9B0E6D4-811C-11D0-AD51-00A0C90F5739}	Microsoft Data Tools Database Designer
{E9B0E6D5-811C-11D0-AD51-00A0C90F5739}	Microsoft Data Tools Database Designer SQL Server Table Property Page
{E9B0E6D6-811C-11D0-AD51-00A0C90F5739}	Microsoft Data Tools Database Designer SQL Server Relationship Property Page
{E9B0E6D8-811C-11D0-AD51-00A0C90F5739}	Microsoft Data Tools Database Designer SQL Server Index Property Page
{E9B0E6D9-811C-11D0-AD51-00A0C90F5739}	MSDTDDGridCtrl2 Object
{E9B0E6DB-811C-11D0-AD51-00A0C90F5739}	Microsoft Data Tools DSRef Object
{E9C8B700-88B1-11d2-8C1F-00C04FA31009}	CLSID_OEHotMailWizard
{EA502722-A23D-11D1-A7D3-0000F87571E3}	Group Policy Object
{EA678830-235D-11d2-A8B6-0000F8084F96}	CLSID_IPropPatchRequest
{EAA46600-E736-11D0-B988-00A0C9190447}	PSFactoryBuffer
{EAB22AC3-30C1-11CF-A7EB-0000C05BAE0B}	Microsoft Web Browser Version 1
{EAB841A0-9550-11CF-8C16-00805F1408F3}	HTML Thumbnail Extractor
{EAE50EB0-4A62-11CE-BED6-00AA00611080}	Microsoft Forms 2.0 TabStrip
{EAF6F280-DD53-11d0-95DF-00C04FD57E8C}	IMediaCatalogQuery Proxy/Stub
{EB56EAE8-BA51-11d2-B121-00805FC73204}	F:\WINNT\System32\stclient.dll
{EB87E1BD-3233-11D2-AEC9-00C04FB68820}	WbemClassObject
{EB8F50E2-85D1-11D0-9D9D-00A0C908DB96}	Reveal Transition

CLSID Object	Reference
{EBC53A38-A23F-11D0-B09B-00C04FD8DCA6}	F:\WINNT\System32\domadmin.dll
{EBD0F6B6-4AED-11D1-9CDB-00805F0C62F5}	TIFFilter Class
{EC529B00-1A1F-11D1-BAD9-00609744111A}	WDM Streaming VPE VBI Property Set Interface Handler
{EC941960-7DF6-11D0-9643-00AA00A89C1D}	Intel RTP SPH for H.263/H.261
{EC941961-7DF6-11D0-9643-00AA00A89C1D}	Intel RTP RPH for H.263/H.261
{ecabaebb-7f19-11d2-978E-0000f8757e2a}	TrustManager Class
{ecabaebc-7f19-11d2-978E-0000f8757e2a}	PolicyManager Class
{ecabaebd-7f19-11d2-978E-0000f8757e2a}	Policy Package
{ecabaebf-7f19-11d2-978E-0000f8757e2a}	VolatilePolicyManager Class
{ecabaec0-7f19-11d2-978E-0000f8757e2a}	TrustGlobals Class
{ecabafaa-7f19-11d2-978e-0000f8757e2a}	Activity Property Unmarshal Class
{ecabafab-7f19-11d2-978e-0000f8757e2a}	SecurityEnvoy
{ecabafac-7f19-11d2-978e-0000f8757e2a}	Transaction Property Unmarshal Class
{ecabafad-7f19-11d2-978e-0000f8757e2a}	NonRootTransactionEnvoy
{ecabafae-7f19-11d2-978e-0000f8757e2a}	sca Class
{ecabafaf-7f19-11d2-978e-0000f8757e2a}	ClassFactory Activator Class
{ecabafb0-7f19-11d2-978e-0000f8757e2a}	obja Class
{ecabafb1-7f19-11d2-978e-0000f8757e2a}	stapa Class
{ecabafb2-7f19-11d2-978e-0000f8757e2a}	vca Class
{ecabafb3-7f19-11d2-978e-0000f8757e2a}	User Context Object
{ecabafb4-7f19-11d2-978e-0000f8757e2a}	User Context Properties Association Object
{ecabafb5-7f19-11d2-978e-0000f8757e2a}	PoolMgr Class
{ecabafb6-7f19-11d2-978e-0000f8757e2a}	Object Pool Activator Class
{ecabafb7-7f19-11d2-978e-0000f8757e2a}	Contruction Activator Class
{ecabafb9-7f19-11d2-978e-0000f8757e2a}	COM+ Instance Tracking Component
{ecabafbc-7f19-11d2-978e-0000f8757e2a}	COM+ Event Notification Server
{ecabafbe-7f19-11d2-978e-0000f8757e2a}	NtaHelper Class
{ecabafbf-7f19-11d2-978e-0000f8757e2a}	LceDisp Class
{ecabafc0-7f19-11d2-978e-0000f8757e2a}	cfw Class
{ECABAFC2-7F19-11D2-978E-0000F8757E2A}	Queued Components Recorder
{ecabafc3-7f19-11d2-978e-0000f8757e2a}	QC Listener Class
{ecabafc4-7f19-11d2-978e-0000f8757e2a}	Queued Components Player
{ecabafc6-7f19-11d2-978e-0000f8757e2a}	New Moniker
{ecabafc7-7f19-11d2-978e-0000f8757e2a}	Queue Moniker
{ecabafc9-7f19-11d2-978e-0000f8757e2a}	QC Queue Administration Class
{ecabafca-7f19-11d2-978e-0000f8757e2a}	COM+ QC Dead Letter Queue Listener Starter
{ecabafcb-7f19-11d2-978e-0000f8757e2a}	QC Marshal Interceptor Class
{ecabb0a8-7f19-11d2-978e-0000f8757e2a}	COM+ Services GetSecurityCallContext

TABLE B.1	Continued

CLSID Object	Reference
{ecabb0aa-7f19-11d2-978e-0000f8757e2a}	Byot Server Extended Object
{ecabb0ab-7f19-11d2-978e-0000f8757e2a}	MTSEvents Class
{ecabb0ac-7f19-11d2-978e-0000f8757e2a}	MTSLocator Class
{ecabb0bd-7f19-11d2-978e-0000f8757e2a}	CrmClerk Class
{ecabb0be-7f19-11d2-978e-0000f8757e2a}	CrmRecoveryClerk Class
{ecabb0bf-7f19-11d2-978e-0000f8757e2a}	MessageMover Class
{ecabb0c0-7f19-11d2-978e-0000f8757e2a}	DispenserManager
{ECABB0C3-7F19-11D2-978E-0000F8757E2A}	ComEvents.ComServiceEvents
{ECB29E60-88ED-11D0-9643-00AA00A89C1D}	Intel RTP RPH for Generic Audio
{ECCDF543-45CC-11CE-B9BF-0080C87CDBA6}	DfsShell Class
{ECD4FC4C-521C-11D0-B792-00A0C90312E1}	Shell DeskBar
{ECD4FC4D-521C-11D0-B792-00A0C90312E1}	Shell Rebar BandSite
{ECD4FC4E-521C-11D0-B792-00A0C90312E1}	Shell Band Site Menu
{ECD4FC4F-521C-11D0-B792-00A0C90312E1}	Menu Desk Bar
{ECDB03D2-6E99-11d2-875F-00A0C93C09B3}	NumberBvr Class
{ECF03A32-103D-11d2-854D-006008059367}	MyDocs Drop Target
{ECF03A33-103D-11d2-854D-006008059367}	mydocs.dll
{ED1343B0-A8A6-11D0-A9EA-00AA00685C74}	SEOStream Class
{ED8C108E-4349-11D2-91A4-00C04F7969E8}	XML HTTP Request
{edf016b0-1bcf-11d0-9113-00aa00c147fa}	IStreamFilter_PSFactory
{EE09B103-97E0-11CF-978F-00A02463E06F}	Scripting.Dictionary
{EE756760-C9C5-11D0-B967-00C04FC2F510}	Allows management of the SMTP messaging protocol.
{EEC6993A-B3FD-11D2-A916-00C04FB98638}	Microsoft USB PID Class Driver
{eec97550-47a9-11cf-b952-00aa0051fe20}	HTML File persistent handler
{eec97550-47a9-11cf-b952-00aa0051fe20}	{e0ca5340-4534-11cf-b952-00aa0051fe20}
{EEE78591-FE22-11D0-8BEF-0060081841DE}	DirectSS Class
{eeed4c20-7f1b-11ce-be57-00aa0051fe20}	English_US Stemmer
{ef206950-31d6-11d0-911f-00aa00c147fa}	IThreadPool_PSFactory
{EF3694A3-3C1C-11D1-ABD2-00C04FC30999}	PDOlapObject Class
{EF3694A6-3C1C-11D1-ABD2-00C04FC30999}	PDOlapDatasource Class
{EF3694A9-3C1C-11D1-ABD2-00C04FC30999}	PDOlapCollection Class
{EF3694AC-3C1C-11D1-ABD2-00C04FC30999}	PDOlapDimension Class
{EF3694AF-3C1C-11D1-ABD2-00C04FC30999}	PDOlapLevel Class
{EF3694B2-3C1C-11D1-ABD2-00C04FC30999}	PDOlapMeasure Class
{EF3694B5-3C1C-11D1-ABD2-00C04FC30999}	PDOlapCube Class
{EF3694B8-3C1C-11D1-ABD2-00C04FC30999}	PDCubeCreate Class
{ef636390-f343-11d0-9477-00c04fd36226}	OLE DB Rowset Proxy
{ef636391-f343-11d0-9477-00c04fd36226}	OLE DB Rowset Server

TABLE B.1	Continued

CLSID Object	**Reference**
{ef636392-f343-11d0-9477-00c04fd36226}	OLE DB Row Proxy
{ef636393-f343-11d0-9477-00c04fd36226}	OLE DB Row Server
{EF7C36A6-0E2C-11D1-A787-0000F80272EA}	InserterDialogs Class
{EF88CA72-B840-11D0-8B40-00C0F00AE35A}	PgCntObj Class
{EF8AD2D1-AE36-11D1-B2D2-006097DF8C11}	Global Folder Settings
{EFA24E61-B078-11d0-89E4-00C04FC9E26E}	Favorites Band
{EFA24E62-B078-11d0-89E4-00C04FC9E26E}	History Band
{EFA24E63-B078-11d0-89E4-00C04FC9E26E}	Channels Band
{EFA24E64-B078-11d0-89E4-00C04FC9E26E}	Explorer Band
{EFD08EC1-EA11-11CF-9FEC-00AA00A59F69}	H261 Encode Transform Filter
{EFD0E6BA-DB5F-11d0-8FAC-08002BE4E62A}	Speech Tools TTS Queue
{effc2928-37b1-11d2-a3c1-00c04fb1782a}	Offline Files Cleaner
{F00B4404-F8F1-11CE-A5B6-00AA00680C3F}	WBEM PerfMon Instance Provider
{F020E586-5264-11d1-A532-0000F8757D7E}	dsquery.dll
{f07f3920-7b8c-11cf-9be8-00aa004b9986}	Microsoft Office Filter
{F08DF954-8592-11D1-B16A-00C0F0283628}	Microsoft Slider Control, version 6.0
{F0975AFE-5C7F-11D2-8B74-00104B2AFB41}	WMI ADSI Extension
{F0E42D60-368C-11D0-AD81-00A0C90DC8D9}	Snapshot Viewer Control 9.0
{F0F08735-0C36-101B-B086-0020AF07D0F4}	SCC Quick Viewer
{F1029E5B-CB5B-11D0-8D59-00C04FD91AC0}	Rendezvous Class
{F117831B-C052-11d1-B1C0-00C04FC2F3EF}	TipGW Init
{F1631E43-47F8-11D0-80D4-00AA006EC537}	Lighting Effect
{F17E8672-C3B4-11D1-870B-00600893B1BD}	DirectMusicSignPostTrack
{F1D3FF84-4329-322A-E52D-0020AFC36E79}	Microsoft Office
{F1DC95A0-0BA7-11ce-A166-00AA004CD65C}	Voice Text Manager
{F1E752C3-FD72-11D0-AEF6-00C04FB6DD2C}	NodeInit 1.0 Object
{F2175210-368C-11D0-AD81-00A0C90DC8D9}	Snapshot Viewer General Property Page Object
{f2468580-af8a-11d0-8212-00c04fc32c45}	AuStream Class
{f27623a0-b2a1-11ce-ae4c-00aa00445589}	MSDTC Component Administrator
{f27623a1-b2a1-11ce-ae4c-00aa00445589}	MSDTC Contact Pool
{F27CE930-4CA3-11D1-AFF2-006097C9A284}	BlnMgr Proxy
{F2A39AA7-8D20-11D1-8E59-00600893AF2D}	MSOLAP.ConnectDialog
{F2C3FAAE-C8AC-11D0-BCDB-00C04FD8D5B6}	DsPropertyPages.OU
{f2e606e1-2631-11d1-89f1-00a0c90d061e}	DomainNames Object
{f2e606e3-2631-11d1-89f1-00a0c90d061e}	Cluster Object
{f2e606e5-2631-11d1-89f1-00a0c90d061e}	ClusApplication Object
{f2e606e7-2631-11d1-89f1-00a0c90d061e}	ClusResGroupPreferredOwnerNodes Object
{f2e606e9-2631-11d1-89f1-00a0c90d061e}	ClusResGroupResources Object
{f2e606eb-2631-11d1-89f1-00a0c90d061e}	ClusterNames Object

| TABLE B.1 | Continued |

CLSID Object	Reference
{f2e606ed-2631-11d1-89f1-00a0c90d061e}	ClusNetInterface Object
{f2e606ef-2631-11d1-89f1-00a0c90d061e}	ClusNetInterfaces Object
{f2e606f1-2631-11d1-89f1-00a0c90d061e}	ClusNetwork Object
{f2e606f3-2631-11d1-89f1-00a0c90d061e}	ClusNetworks Object
{f2e606f5-2631-11d1-89f1-00a0c90d061e}	ClusNetworkNetInterfaces Object
{f2e606f7-2631-11d1-89f1-00a0c90d061e}	ClusNode Object
{f2e606f9-2631-11d1-89f1-00a0c90d061e}	ClusNodes Object
{f2e606fb-2631-11d1-89f1-00a0c90d061e}	ClusNodeNetInterfaces Object
{f2e606fd-2631-11d1-89f1-00a0c90d061e}	ClusProperty Object
{f2e606ff-2631-11d1-89f1-00a0c90d061e}	ClusProperties Object
{f2e60701-2631-11d1-89f1-00a0c90d061e}	ClusRefObject Object
{f2e60703-2631-11d1-89f1-00a0c90d061e}	ClusResDependencies Object
{f2e60705-2631-11d1-89f1-00a0c90d061e}	ClusResGroup Object
{f2e60707-2631-11d1-89f1-00a0c90d061e}	ClusResGroups Object
{f2e60709-2631-11d1-89f1-00a0c90d061e}	ClusResource Object
{f2e6070b-2631-11d1-89f1-00a0c90d061e}	ClusResources Object
{f2e6070d-2631-11d1-89f1-00a0c90d061e}	ClusResPossibleOwnerNodes Object
{f2e6070f-2631-11d1-89f1-00a0c90d061e}	ClusResType Object
{f2e60711-2631-11d1-89f1-00a0c90d061e}	ClusResTypes Object
{f2e60713-2631-11d1-89f1-00a0c90d061e}	ClusResTypeResources Object
{f2e60715-2631-11d1-89f1-00a0c90d061e}	ClusVersion Object
{f2e60717-2631-11d1-89f1-00a0c90d061e}	ClusResTypePossibleOwnerNodes Object
{f2e60719-2631-11d1-89f1-00a0c90d061e}	ClusPropertyValue Object
{f2e6071b-2631-11d1-89f1-00a0c90d061e}	ClusPropertyValues Object
{f2e6071d-2631-11d1-89f1-00a0c90d061e}	ClusPropertyValueData Object
{f2e6071f-2631-11d1-89f1-00a0c90d061e}	ClusPartition Object
{f2e60721-2631-11d1-89f1-00a0c90d061e}	ClusPartitions Object
{f2e60723-2631-11d1-89f1-00a0c90d061e}	ClusDisk Object
{f2e60725-2631-11d1-89f1-00a0c90d061e}	ClusDisks Object
{f2e60727-2631-11d1-89f1-00a0c90d061e}	ClusScsiAddress Object
{f2e60729-2631-11d1-89f1-00a0c90d061e}	ClusRegistryKeys Object
{f2e6072b-2631-11d1-89f1-00a0c90d061e}	ClusCryptoKeys Object
{F30A9FD3-1BC4-11d0-964E-00A0C905F099}	ManVolLst Class
{F3364BA0-65B9-11CE-A9BA-00AA004AE837}	Shell File System Folder
{F3368374-CF19-11d0-B93D-00A0C90312e1}	OrderListExport
{F37C5810-4D3F-11d0-B4BF-00AA00BBB723}	Security Shell Extension
{f39a0dc0-9cc8-11d0-a599-00c04fd64433}	Channel
{f3aa0dc0-9cc8-11d0-a599-00c04fd64434}	Channel Shortcut
{f3ba0dc0-9cc8-11d0-a599-00c04fd64435}	Channel Handler Object

. . . .

TABLE B.1	Continued

CLSID Object	**Reference**
{F3BD7629-D1F0-11D0-B0B1-00C04FD61157}	DTC98 Registry Helper
{F3CA5665-C5DA-11CF-8F28-00AA0060FD48}	DirectSound 3.0 Object
{F3CA566B-C5DA-11CF-8F28-00AA0060FD48}	DirectDraw 3.0 Object
{F3CA5671-C5DA-11CF-8F28-00AA0060FD48}	DirectDrawClipper 3.0 Object
{F3CA5677-C5DA-11CF-8F28-00AA0060FD48}	Direct3dRMViewport 3.0 Object
{F3CA567D-C5DA-11CF-8F28-00AA0060FD48}	Direct3dRMDevice 3.0 Object
{F3CA5683-C5DA-11CF-8F28-00AA0060FD48}	Direct3dRMFrame 3.0 Object
{F3CA5689-C5DA-11CF-8F28-00AA0060FD48}	Direct3dRMMesh 31.0 Object
{F3CA568F-C5DA-11CF-8F28-00AA0060FD48}	Direct3dRMMeshBuilder 3.0 Object
{F3CA5695-C5DA-11CF-8F28-00AA0060FD48}	Direct3dRMFace 3.0 Object
{F3CA569B-C5DA-11CF-8F28-00AA0060FD48}	Direct3dRMLight 3.0 Object
{F3CA56A1-C5DA-11CF-8F28-00AA0060FD48}	Direct3dRMTexture 3.0 Object
{F3CA56A7-C5DA-11CF-8F28-00AA0060FD48}	Direct3dRMWrap 3.0 Object
{F3CA56AD-C5DA-11CF-8F28-00AA0060FD48}	Direct3dRMMaterial 3.0 Object
{F3CA56B3-C5DA-11CF-8F28-00AA0060FD48}	Direct3dRMAnimation 3.0 Object
{F3CA56B9-C5DA-11CF-8F28-00AA0060FD48}	Direct3dRMAnimationSet 3.0 Object
{F3CA56BF-C5DA-11CF-8F28-00AA0060FD48}	Direct3dRMUserVisual 3.0 Object
{F3CA56C5-C5DA-11CF-8F28-00AA0060FD48}	Direct3dRMShadow 3.0 Object
{F3CA56CB-C5DA-11CF-8F28-00AA0060FD48}	Direct3d 3.0 Object
{F3CA56D1-C5DA-11CF-8F28-00AA0060FD48}	Direct3dTexture 3.0 Object
{F3CA56D7-C5DA-11CF-8F28-00AA0060FD48}	Direct3dLight 3.0 Object
{F3CA56DD-C5DA-11CF-8F28-00AA0060FD48}	Direct3dMaterial 3.0 Object
{F3CA56E3-C5DA-11CF-8F28-00AA0060FD48}	Direct3dExecuteBuffer 3.0 Object
{F3CA56E9-C5DA-11CF-8F28-00AA0060FD48}	DirectDrawBitmap 3.0 Object
{F3CA56EF-C5DA-11CF-8F28-00AA0060FD48}	Direct3dViewport 3.0 Object
{F3CA56F5-C5DA-11CF-8F28-00AA0060FD48}	Direct3dRM 3.0 Object
{F3CA56FB-C5DA-11CF-8F28-00AA0060FD48}	Direct3dRMObject 3.0 Object
{F3CA5701-C5DA-11CF-8F28-00AA0060FD48}	Direct3dRMVisual 3.0 Object
{F3CA5707-C5DA-11CF-8F28-00AA0060FD48}	Direct3dRMWinDevice 3.0 Object
{F3CA570D-C5DA-11CF-8F28-00AA0060FD48}	DirectDrawSurface 3.0 Object
{F3CA5713-C5DA-11CF-8F28-00AA0060FD48}	DirectDrawPalette 3.0 Object
{F3CA571F-C5DA-11CF-8F28-00AA0060FD48}	DirectSoundBuffer 3.0 Object
{F3CA572B-C5DA-11CF-8F28-00AA0060FD48}	Direct3dRMDeviceArray 3.0 Object
{F3CA5731-C5DA-11CF-8F28-00AA0060FD48}	Direct3dRMViewportArray 3.0 Object
{F3CA5737-C5DA-11CF-8F28-00AA0060FD48}	Direct3dRMFrameArray 3.0 Object
{F3CA573D-C5DA-11CF-8F28-00AA0060FD48}	Direct3dRMVisualArray 3.0 Object
{F3CA5749-C5DA-11CF-8F28-00AA0060FD48}	Direct3dRMLightArray 3.0 Object
{F3CA574F-C5DA-11CF-8F28-00AA0060FD48}	Direct3dRMPickedArray 3.0 Object
{F3CA5755-C5DA-11CF-8F28-00AA0060FD48}	Direct3dRMFaceArray 3.0 Object

TABLE B.1	Continued

CLSID Object	**Reference**
{F3CA575B-C5DA-11CF-8F28-00AA0060FD48}	DirectInputDevice 3.0 Object
{F3CA5767-C5DA-11CF-8F28-00AA0060FD48}	DirectInput 3.0 Object
{F3CA57DF-C5DA-11CF-8F28-00AA0060FD48}	DirectInput 3.0 Object
{F3CA57E5-C5DA-11CF-8F28-00AA0060FD48}	Directsound3DLister 3.0 Object
{F3CA57EB-C5DA-11CF-8F28-00AA0060FD48}	DirectSound3DBufer 3.0 Object
{F3CFF120-9C41-11D1-863D-0060089F6007}	Role-based Security Policy
{f3da0dc0-9cc8-11d0-a599-00c04fd64437}	Channel Menu Handler Object
{f3ea0dc0-9cc8-11d0-a599-00c04fd64438}	Channel Shortcut Property Pages
{f414c260-6ac0-11cf-b6d1-00aa00bbbb58}	JScript Language
{f414c261-6ac0-11cf-b6d1-00aa00bbbb58}	JScript Language Authoring
{f414c262-6ac0-11cf-b6d1-00aa00bbbb58}	JScript Language Encoding
{F515306D-0156-11d2-81EA-0000F87557DB}	CrEmboss
{F515306E-0156-11d2-81EA-0000F87557DB}	CrEngrave
{F5175861-2688-11d0-9C5E-00AA00A45957}	Subscription Folder
{F55C5B4C-517D-11D1-AB57-00C04FD9159E}	Microsoft WBEM NT Eventlog Event Provider
{F5BE8BD2-7DE6-11D0-91FE-00C04FD701A5}	Microsoft Agent Control 1.5
{F5D121ED-C8AC-11D0-BCDB-00C04FD8D5B6}	DsPropertyPages.User
{F5D121EE-C8AC-11D0-BCDB-00C04FD8D5B6}	DsPropertyPages.Group
{F5D121EF-C8AC-11D0-BCDB-00C04FD8D5B6}	DsPropertyPages.Domain
{F5D121F0-C8AC-11D0-BCDB-00C04FD8D5B6}	DsPropertyPages.Contact
{F5D121F3-C8AC-11D0-BCDB-00C04FD8D5B6}	DsPropertyPages.Volume
{F5D121F4-C8AC-11D0-BCDB-00C04FD8D5B6}	DsPropertyPages.Computer
{f5d1badf-4080-11d1-a3ac-00c04fb950dc}	ADs ReplicaPointer Object
{F6167903-5479-11D0-8236-00A0C908DB96}	Flip Horizontal Effect
{F618C514-DFB8-11D1-A2CF-00805FC79235}	Catalog2 Class
{F61FFEC1-754F-11d0-80CA-00AA005B4383}	BandProxy
{F6FD0A00-43F0-11D1-BE58-00A0C90A4335}	FpStructureModification Class
{F6FD0A01-43F0-11D1-BE58-00A0C90A4335}	FpStructureElement Class
{F6FD0A0E-43F0-11D1-BE58-00A0C90A4335}	FpFile Class
{F6FD0A0F-43F0-11D1-BE58-00A0C90A4335}	FpMetaInfo Class
{F6FD0A11-43F0-11D1-BE58-00A0C90A4335}	FpFolder Class
{F6FD0A13-43F0-11D1-BE58-00A0C90A4335}	WebExtenderClient Class
{F748B5F0-15D0-11CE-BF0D-00AA0044BB60}	Microsoft Forms 2.1 Toolbox
{F778C6B4-C08B-11D2-976C-00C04F79DB19}	ISnapinAbout
{F7860350-AA27-11d0-B16D-00A0C916F120}	FsaPostIt Class
{F7974E22-6823-11d0-8FA3-00A0C9190447}	Cartridge Class
{F7A9C6E0-EFF2-101A-8185-00DD01108C6B}	OLE 2.0 Link
{F7CE2E13-8C90-11D1-9E7B-00C04FC324A8}	WBEM DCOM Transport V1
{F808DF6F-6049-11D1-BA20-006097D2898E}	PSFactoryBuffer

. . . .

TABLE B.1	Continued

CLSID Object	Reference
{f81e9010-6ea4-11ce-a7ff-00aa003ca9f6}	Shell extensions for sharing
{F8383852-FCD3-11d1-A6B9-006097DF5BD4}	Progress Dialog
{F8388A40-D5BB-11D0-BE5A-0080C706568E}	Infinite Pin Tee Filter
{F8860CCA-95A3-11D0-9F66-00A0C9055CAC}	Primer Class
{F8860CCC-95A3-11D0-9F66-00A0C9055CAC}	PrimerMgr Class
{F9043C85-F6F2-101A-A3C9-08002B2F49FB}	COMMON DIALOGS CONTROL
{f92e8c40-3d33-11d2-b1aa-080036a75b03}	Display TroubleShoot CPL Extension
{F935DC22-1CF0-11D0-ADB9-00C04FD58A0B}	Windows Script Host Shell Object
{F935DC26-1CF0-11D0-ADB9-00C04FD58A0B}	Windows Script Host Network Object
{F9A3F405-B068-11CF-858C-95A235C0163A}	DacCom 1.0 Object
{F9AE8980-7E52-11d0-8964-00C04FD611D7}	MSIDXS
{F9AE8980-7E52-11d0-8964-00C04FD611D7}	MSIDXS Error Lookup
{F9AE8981-7E52-11d0-8964-00C04FD611D7}	MSIDXS ErrorLookup
{F9D18BF8-E0ED-11d0-AB8B-08002BE4E3B7}	Telephony Controls Information Store
{FA77A74E-E109-11D0-AD6E-00C04FD8FDFF}	WBEM Registry Event Provider
{FA925E20-323B-11D0-8800-444553540000}	I420/H263 Decode Filter
{FAC1D9C0-0296-11D1-A840-00A0C92C9D5D}	DiskManagement.SnapInAbout
{FACB5ED2-7F99-11D0-ADE2-00A0C90DC8D9}	Snapshot File
{FAEDCF53-31FE-11D1-AAD2-00805FC1270E}	PSFactoryBuffer
{FB2FF4EB-337E-11D1-9B37-00C04FB9514E}	Tapi 3.0 Dialer Class
{FB6BA828-E616-11D1-8D27-00AA00B5BADA}	msodraa9.ShapeSelect
{FB8F0823-0164-101B-84ED-08002B2EC713}	Standard Font
{FB8F0824-0164-101B-84ED-08002B2EC713}	Standard Picture
{FBF23B40-E3F0-101B-8488-00AA003E56F8}	Internet Shortcut
{FBF23B41-E3F0-101B-8488-00AA003E56F8}	MIME File Types Hook
{FBF23B42-E3F0-101B-8488-00AA003E56F8}	Internet Explorer
{FC715823-C5FB-11D1-9EEF-00A0C90347FF}	Internet Explorer Maintenance
{FC7AF71D-FC74-101A-84ED-08002B2EC713}	Picture Property Page
{FC9E740F-6058-11D1-8C66-0060081841DE}	Telephony Class
{fcbf906f-4080-11d1-a3ac-00c04fb950dc}	ADs BackLink Object
{FCC152B7-F372-11D0-8E00-00C04FD7C08B}	DVD Graph Builder
{FCC764A0-2A38-11d1-B9C6-00A0C922E750}	IIS Servers Extension
{FCDC8671-7329-11d0-81DF-00A0C91180F2}	FsaFilterNTFS Class
{FCDECE00-A39D-11D0-ABE7-00AA0064D470}	ScriptoSys Class
{FD179533-D86E-11D0-89D6-00A0C90833E6}	Microsoft DirectAnimation Sprite
{FD2280A8-51A4-11D2-A601-3078302C2030}	IIS PropertyAttribute Object
{FD4F53E0-65DC-11D1-AB64-00C04FD9159E}	Microsoft WBEM NT Eventlog Instance Provider
{FD57D297-4FD9-11D1-854E-00C04FC31FD3}	QoS Admission Control
{FD57D29A-4FD9-11D1-854E-00C04FC31FD3}	QoS Admission Control

TABLE B.1	Continued

CLSID Object	**Reference**
{FD57D29C-4FD9-11D1-854E-00C04FC31FD3}	QoS Admission Control
{FD78D554-4C6E-11D0-970D-00A0C9191601}	DiskManagement.Connection
{FD853CD9-7F86-11d0-8252-00C04FD85AB4}	CLSID_IMimeInternational
{FD853CDB-7F86-11d0-8252-00C04FD85AB4}	CLSID_IMimeBody
{FD853CDC-7F86-11d0-8252-00C04FD85AB4}	CLSID_IMimeMessageParts
{FD853CDD-7F86-11d0-8252-00C04FD85AB4}	CLSID_IMimeAllocator
{FD853CDE-7F86-11d0-8252-00C04FD85AB4}	CLSID_IMimeSecurity
{FD853CDF-7F86-11d0-8252-00C04FD85AB4}	CLSID_IVirtualStream
{FD853CE0-7F86-11d0-8252-00C04FD85AB4}	CLSID_IMimeHeaderTable
{FD853CE1-7F86-11d0-8252-00C04FD85AB4}	CLSID_IMimePropertySet
{FD853CE2-7F86-11d0-8252-00C04FD85AB4}	CLSID_IMimeMessageTree
{FD853CE3-7F86-11d0-8252-00C04FD85AB4}	CLSID_IMimeMessage
{FD853CE6-7F86-11d0-8252-00C04FD85AB4}	CLSID_ISMTPTransport
{FD853CE7-7F86-11d0-8252-00C04FD85AB4}	CLSID_IPOP3Transport
{FD853CE8-7F86-11d0-8252-00C04FD85AB4}	CLSID_INNTPTransport
{FD853CE9-7F86-11d0-8252-00C04FD85AB4}	CLSID_IRASTransport
{FD853CEA-7F86-11d0-8252-00C04FD85AB4}	CLSID_IRangeList
{FD853CEB-7F86-11d0-8252-00C04FD85AB4}	CLSID_IIMAPTransport
{FD853CED-7F86-11d0-8252-00C04FD85AB4}	CLSID_IMimePropertySchema
{fd86b5d0-12c6-11ce-bd31-00aa004bbb1f}	Italian_Italian Word Breaker
{fd8d3a5f-6066-11d1-8c13-00c04fd8d503}	Microsoft OrganizationUnit Extension
{FD913802-5CA2-11d2-A1E6-00A0C913D1EF}	Downloadable Whistler 4.0
{FDFE9681-74A3-11D0-AFA7-00AA00B67A42}	QT Decompressor
{fe1290f0-cfbd-11cf-a330-00aa00c16e65}	Directory
{fe1290f0-cfbd-11cf-a330-00aa00c16e65}	{0D45D530-764B-11d0-A1CA-00AA00C16E65}
{fe1290f0-cfbd-11cf-a330-00aa00c16e65}	{163FDC20-2ABC-11d0-88F0-00A024AB2DBB}
{fe1290f0-cfbd-11cf-a330-00aa00c16e65}	{0D45D530-764B-11d0-A1CA-00AA00C16E65}
{fe1290f0-cfbd-11cf-a330-00aa00c16e65}	{0D45D530-764B-11d0-A1CA-00AA00C16E65}
{fe1290f0-cfbd-11cf-a330-00aa00c16e65}	{0D45D530-764B-11d0-A1CA-00AA00C16E65}
{fe1290f0-cfbd-11cf-a330-00aa00c16e65}	{163FDC20-2ABC-11d0-88F0-00A024AB2DBB}
{FE37FA01-3729-11D0-8CF4-00A0C9190459}	Remote Storage Media
{FE37FA02-3729-11D0-8CF4-00A0C9190459}	RmsLibrary Class
{FE37FA03-3729-11D0-8CF4-00A0C9190459}	RmsDriveClass Class
{FE37FA04-3729-11D0-8CF4-00A0C9190459}	RmsCartridge Class
{FE37FA05-3729-11D0-8CF4-00A0C9190459}	RmsDrive Class
{FE37FA06-3729-11D0-8CF4-00A0C9190459}	RmsStorageSlot Class
{FE37FA07-3729-11D0-8CF4-00A0C9190459}	RmsMediumChanger Class
{FE37FA08-3729-11D0-8CF4-00A0C9190459}	RmsIEPort Class
{FE37FA09-3729-11D0-8CF4-00A0C9190459}	RmsMediaSet Class

TABLE B.1	Continued

CLSID Object	**Reference**
{FE37FA10-3729-11D0-8CF4-00A0C9190459}	RmsRequest Class
{FE37FA11-3729-11D0-8CF4-00A0C9190459}	RmsPartition Class
{FE37FA12-3729-11D0-8CF4-00A0C9190459}	RmsClient Class
{FE37FA13-3729-11D0-8CF4-00A0C9190459}	RmsNTMS Class
{FE37FB02-3729-11D0-8CF4-00A0C9190459}	PSFactoryBuffer
{FE9AF5C0-D3B6-11CE-A5B6-00AA00680C3F}	WBEM Registry Instance Provider
{FE9E48A2-A014-11D1-855C-00A0C944138C}	PSFactoryBuffer
{FE9E48A4-A014-11D1-855C-00A0C944138C}	EnumTelnetClientsSvr Class
{FEB50740-7BEF-11CE-9BD9-0000E202599C}	MPEG Video Codec
{FF12FDC1-9A45-11D0-B4A9-00A0C90D63B5}	Intel RTP SPH Generic Audio Property Page
{FF151822-B0BF-11D1-A80D-000000000000}	Microsoft OLE DB Root Binder for Internet Publishing
{FF160657-DE82-11CF-BC0A-00AA006111E0}	MSASCIILog Control
{FF160658-DE82-11CF-BC0A-00AA006111E0}	MSASCIILog Property Page
{FF16065B-DE82-11CF-BC0A-00AA006111E0}	MSODBCLog Control
{FF16065C-DE82-11CF-BC0A-00AA006111E0}	MSODBCLog Property Page
{FF16065F-DE82-11CF-BC0A-00AA006111E0}	MSNCSALog Control
{FF160660-DE82-11CF-BC0A-00AA006111E0}	MSNCSALog Property Page
{FF160663-DE82-11CF-BC0A-00AA006111E0}	MSCustomLog Control
{FF160664-DE82-11CF-BC0A-00AA006111E0}	MSCustomLog Property Page
{FF2C7A52-78F9-11ce-B762-00AA004CD65C}	Voice Text Object
{FF37A93C-C28E-11D1-AEB6-00C04FB68820}	WBEM NT5 Base Perf Provider
{FF393560-C2A7-11CF-BFF4-444553540000}	History
{FF5903A8-78D6-11D1-92F6-006097B01056}	Fpsrvmmc Class
{FF67BB34-8430-11d0-81E4-00A0C91180F2}	HsmSessionTotals Class
{FF736B00-82CC-11D0-9E35-00A0C916F120}	PSFactoryBuffer
{FFD709F0-AF39-11D2-B854-0000F81E8872}	Java Class: com.ms.wfc.html.DhComponentWrapper$DhInnerSafeControl
{ffdc1a80-d527-11d0-a32c-34af06c10000}	Window List in Shell Process

Object
Reference

The Registry stores data configuration information about all objects installed into Windows 2000. You work with these objects every day, such as documents, databases, and even icons that appear on the desktop. The Registry organizes configuration information for these objects by their class ID. Table C.1 shows the class ID for each of the objects installed into the Registry by Windows 2000. The table also reflects an installation of Windows 2000. You probably will find the table below useful should you need to modify some aspect of one of the columns. With the table, you can find the class ID, and then access the class ID to make the change you require. An example of a change you might make would be to remove an icon from the desktop.

TABLE C.1	Windows 2000 Registry Objects

Object	**Class ID**
"Microsoft Licensed Class Manager 1.0"	{5220cb21-c88d-11cf-b347-00aa00a28331}
%DESC_AppMgr%	{352EC2B7-8B9A-11D1-B8AE-006008059382}
%DESK_SearchAssistant%	{9461b922-3c5a-11d2-bf8b-00c04fb93661}
%Microsoft Anchor Element Browse Property Page%	{3050f3BB-98b5-11cf-bb82-00aa00bdce0b}
%Microsoft Document Browse Property Page%	{3050f3B4-98b5-11cf-bb82-00aa00bdce0b}
%Microsoft Image Element Browse Property Page%	{3050f3B3-98b5-11cf-bb82-00aa00bdce0b}
%STR_WABFIND_FIND_PEOPLE%	{32714800-2E5F-11d0-8B85-00AA0044F941}
%SystemRoot%\system32\shell32.dll	{0D2E74C4-3C34-11d2-A27E-00C04FC30871}
%SystemRoot%\system32\shell32.dll	{24F14F01-7B1C-11d1-838f-0000F80461CF}
%SystemRoot%\system32\shell32.dll	{24F14F02-7B1C-11d1-838f-0000F80461CF}
%SystemRoot%\web\printfld.htm	{2227A280-3AEA-1069-A2DE-08002B30309D}
%Trident API%	{429AF92C-A51F-11d2-861E-00C04FA35C89}
&Address	{01E04581-4EEE-11d0-BFE9-00AA005B4383}
&Discuss	{BDEADE7F-C265-11D0-BCED-00A0C90AB50F}
&Links	{0E5CBF21-D15F-11d0-8301-00AA005B4383}
&Tip of the Day	{4D5C8C25-D075-11d0-B416-00C04FB90376}
.exe drop target	{86C86720-42A0-1069-A2E8-08002B30309D}
.PIF file handler	{86F19A00-42A0-1069-A2EB-08002B30309D}
.PIF file property pages	{86F19A00-42A0-1069-A2E9-08002B30309D}
.RAM Parser	{A98C8400-4181-11D1-A520-00A0D10129C0}
:-) VideoSoft FlexArray Control	{8AE029D3-08E3-11D1-BAA2-444553540000}
:-) VideoSoft FlexString Control	{8AE029D6-08E3-11D1-BAA2-444553540000}
@msdxmLC.dll,-1@1033,&Radio	{8E718888-423F-11D2-876E-00A0C9082467}
{00020803-0000-0000-C000-000000000046}	{00030006-0000-0000-C000-000000000046}
{00021401-0000-0000-C000-000000000046}	{00021401-0000-0000-C000-000000000046}
{0002CC1F-0000-0000-C000-000000000046}	{0002CC0F-0000-0000-C000-000000000046}
{00D20920-7E20-11D0-B291-00C04FC31D18}	{083863F1-70DE-11d0-BD40-00A0C911CE86}
{00D20921-7E20-11D0-B291-00C04FC31D18}	{083863F1-70DE-11d0-BD40-00A0C911CE86}
{07167665-5011-11CF-BF33-00AA0055595A}	{083863F1-70DE-11d0-BD40-00A0C911CE86}
{083863F1-70DE-11d0-BD40-00A0C911CE86}	{da4e3da0-d07d-11d0-bd50-00a0c911ce86}
{0A4252A0-7E70-11D0-A5D6-28DB04C10000}	{da4e3da0-d07d-11d0-bd50-00a0c911ce86}
{0AFACED1-E828-11D1-9187-B532F1E9575D}	{0AFACED1-E828-11D1-9187-B532F1E9575D}
{0AFACED1-E828-11D1-9187-B532F1E9575D}	{0AFACED1-E828-11D1-9187-B532F1E9575D}
{0AFACED1-E828-11D1-9187-B532F1E9575D}	{0AFACED1-E828-11D1-9187-B532F1E9575D}
{0D45D530-764B-11d0-A1CA-00AA00C16E65}	{fe1290f0-cfbd-11cf-a330-00aa00c16e65}
{0D45D530-764B-11d0-A1CA-00AA00C16E65}	{fe1290f0-cfbd-11cf-a330-00aa00c16e65}
{0D45D530-764B-11d0-A1CA-00AA00C16E65}	{fe1290f0-cfbd-11cf-a330-00aa00c16e65}
{0D45D530-764B-11d0-A1CA-00AA00C16E65}	{fe1290f0-cfbd-11cf-a330-00aa00c16e65}

TABLE C.1 Continued	
Object	**Class ID**
{129D7E40-C10D-11D0-AFB9-00AA00B67A42}	{083863F1-70DE-11d0-BD40-00A0C911CE86}
{163FDC20-2ABC-11d0-88F0-00A024AB2DBB}	{fe1290f0-cfbd-11cf-a330-00aa00c16e65}
{163FDC20-2ABC-11d0-88F0-00A024AB2DBB}	{fe1290f0-cfbd-11cf-a330-00aa00c16e65}
{1643E180-90F5-11CE-97D5-00AA0055595A}	{083863F1-70DE-11d0-BD40-00A0C911CE86}
{167701E4-FDCF-11D0-A48E-006097C549FF}	{167701E4-FDCF-11D0-A48E-006097C549FF}
{1AE60860-8297-11D0-9643-00AA00A89C1D}	{083863F1-70DE-11d0-BD40-00A0C911CE86}
{1B544C20-FD0B-11CE-8C63-00AA0044B51E}	{083863F1-70DE-11d0-BD40-00A0C911CE86}
{1DA08500-9EDC-11CF-BC10-00AA00AC74F6}	{083863F1-70DE-11d0-BD40-00A0C911CE86}
{1F73E9B1-8C3A-11D0-A3BE-00A0C9244436}	{083863F1-70DE-11d0-BD40-00A0C911CE86}
{22E24591-49D0-11D2-BB50-006008320064}	{083863F1-70DE-11d0-BD40-00A0C911CE86}
{26721E10-390C-11D0-8A22-00A0C90C9156}	{083863F1-70DE-11d0-BD40-00A0C911CE86}
{2721AE20-7E70-11D0-A5D6-28DB04C10000}	{da4e3da0-d07d-11d0-bd50-00a0c911ce86}
{2EB07EA0-7E70-11D0-A5D6-28DB04C10000}	{da4e3da0-d07d-11d0-bd50-00a0c911ce86}
{30355649-0000-0010-8000-00AA00389B71}	{083863F1-70DE-11d0-BD40-00A0C911CE86}
{31363248-0000-0010-8000-00AA00389B71}	{083863F1-70DE-11d0-BD40-00A0C911CE86}
{33363248-0000-0010-8000-00AA00389B71}	{083863F1-70DE-11d0-BD40-00A0C911CE86}
{336475D0-942A-11CE-A870-00AA002FEAB5}	{083863F1-70DE-11d0-BD40-00A0C911CE86}
{33D9A760-90C8-11d0-BD43-00A0C911CE86}	{da4e3da0-d07d-11d0-bd50-00a0c911ce86}
{33D9A761-90C8-11d0-BD43-00A0C911CE86}	{da4e3da0-d07d-11d0-bd50-00a0c911ce86}
{33D9A762-90C8-11d0-BD43-00A0C911CE86}	{da4e3da0-d07d-11d0-bd50-00a0c911ce86}
{33FACFE0-A9BE-11D0-A520-00A0D10129C0}	{083863F1-70DE-11d0-BD40-00A0C911CE86}
{38BE3000-DBF4-11D0-860E-00A024CFEF6D}	{083863F1-70DE-11d0-BD40-00A0C911CE86}
{399D5C90-74AB-11D0-9CCF-00A0C9081C19}	{083863F1-70DE-11d0-BD40-00A0C911CE86}
{3DDDA000-88E4-11D0-9643-00AA00A89C1D}	{083863F1-70DE-11d0-BD40-00A0C911CE86}
{4009F700-AEBA-11D1-8344-00C04FB92EB7}	{083863F1-70DE-11d0-BD40-00A0C911CE86}
{48025243-2D39-11CE-875D-00608CB78066}	{083863F1-70DE-11d0-BD40-00A0C911CE86}
{4A2286E0-7BEF-11CE-9BD9-0000E202599C}	{083863F1-70DE-11d0-BD40-00A0C911CE86}
{4B428940-263C-11D1-A520-000000000000}	{083863F1-70DE-11d0-BD40-00A0C911CE86}
{4EB31670-9FC6-11CF-AF6E-00AA00B67A42}	{083863F1-70DE-11d0-BD40-00A0C911CE86}
{4EFE2452-168A-11d1-BC76-00C04FB9453B}	{da4e3da0-d07d-11d0-bd50-00a0c911ce86}
{5645C8C2-E277-11CF-8FDA-00AA00A14F93}	{5645C8C1-E277-11CF-8FDA-00AA00A14F93}
{5645C8C2-E277-11CF-8FDA-00AA00A14F93}	{5645C8C4-E277-11CF-8FDA-00AA00A14F93}
{63F8AA94-E2B9-11D0-ADF6-00C04FB66DAD}	{083863F1-70DE-11d0-BD40-00A0C911CE86}
{640999A0-A946-11D0-A520-000000000000}	{083863F1-70DE-11d0-BD40-00A0C911CE86}
{640999A1-A946-11D0-A520-000000000000}	{083863F1-70DE-11d0-BD40-00A0C911CE86}
{640999A2-A946-11D0-A520-000000000000}	{083863F1-70DE-11d0-BD40-00A0C911CE86}
{65E8773D-8F56-11D0-A3B9-00A0C9223196}	{da4e3da0-d07d-11d0-bd50-00a0c911ce86}
{65e8773e-8f56-11d0-a3b9-00a0c9223196}	{da4e3da0-d07d-11d0-bd50-00a0c911ce86}
{6A08CF80-0E18-11CF-A24D-0020AFD79767}	{083863F1-70DE-11d0-BD40-00A0C911CE86}

....

| TABLE C.1 | Continued |

Object	Class ID
{6B6D0800-9ADA-11D0-A520-00A0D10129C0}	{083863F1-70DE-11d0-BD40-00A0C911CE86}
{6B91AFEF-9472-11D1-8574-00C04FC31FD3}	{8A23E65E-31C2-11d0-891C-00A024AB2DBB}
{6E8D4A20-310C-11D0-B79A-00AA003767A7}	{083863F1-70DE-11d0-BD40-00A0C911CE86}
{70E102B0-5556-11CE-97C0-00AA0055595A}	{083863F1-70DE-11d0-BD40-00A0C911CE86}
{82CCD3E0-F71A-11D0-9FE5-00609778EA66}	{083863F1-70DE-11d0-BD40-00A0C911CE86}
{8596E5F0-0DA5-11D0-BD21-00A0C911CE86}	{083863F1-70DE-11d0-BD40-00A0C911CE86}
{860BB310-5D01-11d0-BD3B-00A0C911CE86}	{da4e3da0-d07d-11d0-bd50-00a0c911ce86}
{9B8C4620-2C1A-11D0-8493-00A02438AD48}	{083863F1-70DE-11d0-BD40-00A0C911CE86}
{A0025E90-E45B-11D1-ABE9-00A0C905F375}	{083863F1-70DE-11d0-BD40-00A0C911CE86}
{A5EA8D20-253D-11D1-B3F1-00AA003761C5}	{083863F1-70DE-11d0-BD40-00A0C911CE86}
{A888DF60-1E90-11CF-AC98-00AA004C0FA9}	{083863F1-70DE-11d0-BD40-00A0C911CE86}
{A98C8400-4181-11D1-A520-00A0D10129C0}	{083863F1-70DE-11d0-BD40-00A0C911CE86}
{AD809C00-7B88-11D0-A5D6-28DB04C10000}	{da4e3da0-d07d-11d0-bd50-00a0c911ce86}
{AF7D8180-A8F9-11CF-9A46-00AA00B7DAD1}	{083863F1-70DE-11d0-BD40-00A0C911CE86}
{B1B77C00-C3E4-11CF-AF79-00AA00B67A42}	{083863F1-70DE-11d0-BD40-00A0C911CE86}
{B4CA2970-DD2B-11D0-9DFA-00AA00AF3494}	{083863F1-70DE-11d0-BD40-00A0C911CE86}
{B6353564-96C4-11D2-8DDB-006097C9A2B2}	{083863F1-70DE-11d0-BD40-00A0C911CE86}
{B9D1F320-C401-11D0-A520-000000000000}	{083863F1-70DE-11d0-BD40-00A0C911CE86}
{B9D1F321-C401-11D0-A520-000000000000}	{083863F1-70DE-11d0-BD40-00A0C911CE86}
{B9D1F322-C401-11D0-A520-000000000000}	{083863F1-70DE-11d0-BD40-00A0C911CE86}
{B9D1F323-C401-11D0-A520-000000000000}	{083863F1-70DE-11d0-BD40-00A0C911CE86}
{B9D1F324-C401-11D0-A520-000000000000}	{083863F1-70DE-11d0-BD40-00A0C911CE86}
{B9D1F325-C401-11D0-A520-000000000000}	{083863F1-70DE-11d0-BD40-00A0C911CE86}
{B9D1F32E-C401-11D0-A520-000000000000}	{083863F1-70DE-11d0-BD40-00A0C911CE86}
{c1243ca0-bf96-11cd-b579-08002b30bfeb}	{5e941d80-bf96-11cd-b579-08002b30bfeb}
{c3278e90-bea7-11cd-b579-08002b30bfeb}	{098f2470-bae0-11cd-b579-08002b30bfeb}
{C69E8F40-D5C8-11D0-A520-145405C10000}	{083863F1-70DE-11d0-BD40-00A0C911CE86}
{C9076CE2-FB56-11CF-906C-00AA00A59F69}	{083863F1-70DE-11d0-BD40-00A0C911CE86}
{CC58E280-8AA1-11D1-B3F1-00AA003761C5}	{083863F1-70DE-11d0-BD40-00A0C911CE86}
{CC7BFB41-F175-11d1-A392-00E0291F3959}	{da4e3da0-d07d-11d0-bd50-00a0c911ce86}
{CC7BFB46-F175-11d1-A392-00E0291F3959}	{da4e3da0-d07d-11d0-bd50-00a0c911ce86}
{CD8743A1-3736-11D0-9E69-00C04FD7C15B}	{083863F1-70DE-11d0-BD40-00A0C911CE86}
{CDCDD6A0-C016-11D0-82A4-00AA00B5CA1B}	{083863F1-70DE-11d0-BD40-00A0C911CE86}
{CF1DDA2C-9743-11D0-A3EE-00A0C9223196}	{da4e3da0-d07d-11d0-bd50-00a0c911ce86}
{CF1DDA2D-9743-11D0-A3EE-00A0C9223196}	{da4e3da0-d07d-11d0-bd50-00a0c911ce86}
{CF49D4E0-1115-11CE-B03A-0020AF0BA770}	{083863F1-70DE-11d0-BD40-00A0C911CE86}
{D3588AB0-0781-11CE-B03A-0020AF0BA770}	{083863F1-70DE-11d0-BD40-00A0C911CE86}
{D42FEAC0-82A1-11D0-9643-00AA00A89C1D}	{083863F1-70DE-11d0-BD40-00A0C911CE86}
{D51BD5A0-7548-11CF-A520-0080C77EF58A}	{083863F1-70DE-11d0-BD40-00A0C911CE86}

Object	Class ID
{D51BD5A1-7548-11CF-A520-0080C77EF58A}	{083863F1-70DE-11d0-BD40-00A0C911CE86}
{D51BD5A2-7548-11CF-A520-0080C77EF58A}	{083863F1-70DE-11d0-BD40-00A0C911CE86}
{D51BD5A3-7548-11CF-A520-0080C77EF58A}	{083863F1-70DE-11d0-BD40-00A0C911CE86}
{D51BD5A4-7548-11CF-A520-0080C77EF58A}	{083863F1-70DE-11d0-BD40-00A0C911CE86}
{D51BD5A5-7548-11CF-A520-0080C77EF58A}	{083863F1-70DE-11d0-BD40-00A0C911CE86}
{D51BD5AE-7548-11CF-A520-0080C77EF58A}	{083863F1-70DE-11d0-BD40-00A0C911CE86}
{e0ca5340-4534-11cf-b952-00aa0051fe20}	{eec97550-47a9-11cf-b952-00aa0051fe20}
{E0F158E1-CB04-11d0-BD4E-00A0C911CE86}	{da4e3da0-d07d-11d0-bd50-00a0c911ce86}
{E2510970-F137-11CE-8B67-00AA00A3F1A6}	{083863F1-70DE-11d0-BD40-00A0C911CE86}
{E436EBB5-524F-11CE-9F53-0020AF0BA770}	{083863F1-70DE-11d0-BD40-00A0C911CE86}
{E436EBB6-524F-11CE-9F53-0020AF0BA770}	{083863F1-70DE-11d0-BD40-00A0C911CE86}
{EC941960-7DF6-11D0-9643-00AA00A89C1D}	{083863F1-70DE-11d0-BD40-00A0C911CE86}
{EC941961-7DF6-11D0-9643-00AA00A89C1D}	{083863F1-70DE-11d0-BD40-00A0C911CE86}
{ECB29E60-88ED-11D0-9643-00AA00A89C1D}	{083863F1-70DE-11d0-BD40-00A0C911CE86}
{EFD08EC1-EA11-11CF-9FEC-00AA00A59F69}	{083863F1-70DE-11d0-BD40-00A0C911CE86}
{f07f3920-7b8c-11cf-9be8-00aa004b9986}	{98de59a0-d175-11cd-a7bd-00006b827d94}
{F8388A40-D5BB-11D0-BE5A-0080C706568E}	{083863F1-70DE-11d0-BD40-00A0C911CE86}
{FBF6F530-07B9-11D2-A71E-0000F8004788}	{da4e3da0-d07d-11d0-bd50-00a0c911ce86}
{FDFE9681-74A3-11D0-AFA7-00AA00B67A42}	{083863F1-70DE-11d0-BD40-00A0C911CE86}
{FEB50740-7BEF-11CE-9BD9-0000E202599C}	{083863F1-70DE-11d0-BD40-00A0C911CE86}
0	{73F7A062-8829-11D1-B550-006097242D8D}
0x70000136	{85BBD920-42A0-1069-A2E4-08002B30309D}
About Class	{E1141BAB-08F6-11D1-B98A-00A0C9190447}
About Device Manager	{94abaf2a-892a-11d1-bbc4-00a0c90640bf}
About G.723.1 Codec	{9D3C85D1-F877-11D0-B083-00A0C95BED34}
About Indeo® audio software	{C83B5610-E0DF-11D0-9E00-00AA00AF3494}
AC3 Parser Filter	{280A3020-86CF-11D1-ABE6-00A0C905F375}
ACELP.net Audio Decoder	{4009F700-AEBA-11D1-8344-00C04FB92EB7}
ACM Class Manager	{33D9A761-90C8-11d0-BD43-00A0C911CE86}
ACM Compressed Audio Stream	{0002000F-0000-0000-C000-000000000046}
ACM Wrapper	{6A08CF80-0E18-11CF-A24D-0020AFD79767}
ActionBvr Class	{58A2E406-8304-11D2-9533-0060b0C3C4F4}
Active Desktop Mover	{72267F6A-A6F9-11D0-BC94-00C04FB67863}
Active Messaging Session Object	{3FA7DEB3-6438-101B-ACC1-00AA00423326}
ActiveDesktop	{75048700-EF1F-11D0-9888-006097DEACF9}
ActiveMovie Filter Categories	{da4e3da0-d07d-11d0-bd50-00a0c911ce86}
ActiveMovie Filter Class Manager	{083863F1-70DE-11d0-BD40-00A0C911CE86}
ActiveMovieControl Object	{05589FA1-C356-11CE-BF01-00AA0055595A}
ActiveX Cache Folder	{88C6C381-2E85-11D0-94DE-444553540000}

TABLE C.1   Continued

Object	Class ID
ActiveXPlugin Object	{06DD38D3-D187-11CF-A80D-00C04FD74AD8}
Activity Property Unmarshal Class	{ecabafaa-7f19-11d2-978e-0000f8757e2a}
ActorBvr Class	{6DDE3061-736C-11D2-A5E8-00A0C967A25F}
AD System Info Object	{50B6327F-AFD1-11d2-9CB9-0000F87A369E}
adbanner Class	{89643D21-7B2A-11d1-8271-00A0C91F9CA0}
Add encryption item to context menus in explorer	{A470F8CF-A1E8-4f65-8335-227475AA5C46}
Add Network Place	{D4480A50-BA28-11d1-8E75-00C04FA31A86}
Addin Class	{AC0714F6-3D04-11D1-AE7D-00A0C90F26F4}
AddPrint Class	{B57467A6-50B5-11D1-BF97-0000F8773501}
Address EditBox	{A08C11D2-A228-11d0-825B-00AA005B4383}
Administrative Templates (Computers)	{0F6B957D-509E-11D1-A7CC-0000F87571E3}
Administrative Templates (Users)	{0F6B957E-509E-11D1-A7CC-0000F87571E3}
Administrative Tools	{D20EA4E1-3957-11d2-A40B-0C5020524153}
ADO 2.5	{0000051A-0000-0010-8000-00AA006D2EA4}
ADO Error Lookup	{0000051A-0000-0010-8000-00AA006D2EA4}
ADOConnectObject Class	{82126854-FC89-11D0-9BA4-006097C9B2AE}
ADODB Error Lookup Service	{00000542-0000-0010-8000-00AA006D2EA4}
ADODB.Command	{00000507-0000-0010-8000-00AA006D2EA4}
ADODB.Connection	{00000514-0000-0010-8000-00AA006D2EA4}
ADODB.Error	{00000541-0000-0010-8000-00AA006D2EA4}
ADODB.Parameter	{0000050B-0000-0010-8000-00AA006D2EA4}
ADODB.Record	{00000560-0000-0010-8000-00AA006D2EA4}
ADODB.Recordset	{00000535-0000-0010-8000-00AA006D2EA4}
ADODB.Stream	{00000566-0000-0010-8000-00AA006D2EA4}
ADOX.Catalog.2.5	{00000602-0000-0010-8000-00AA006D2EA4}
ADOX.Column.2.5	{0000061B-0000-0010-8000-00AA006D2EA4}
ADOX.Group.2.5	{00000615-0000-0010-8000-00AA006D2EA4}
ADOX.Index.2.5	{0000061E-0000-0010-8000-00AA006D2EA4}
ADOX.Key.2.5	{00000621-0000-0010-8000-00AA006D2EA4}
ADOX.Table.2.5	{00000609-0000-0010-8000-00AA006D2EA4}
ADOX.User.2.5	{00000618-0000-0010-8000-00AA006D2EA4}
ADs Access Control Entry Object	{b75ac000-9bdd-11d0-852c-00c04fd8d503}
ADs Access Control List Object	{b85ea052-9bdd-11d0-852c-00c04fd8d503}
ADs BackLink Object	{fcbf906f-4080-11d1-a3ac-00c04fb950dc}
ADs CaseIgnoreList Object	{15f88a55-4680-11d1-a3b4-00c04fb950dc}
ADs DN With Binary Object	{7e99c0a3-f935-11d2-ba96-00c04fb6d0d1}
ADs DN With String Object	{334857cc-f934-11d2-ba96-00c04fb6d0d1}
ADs Email Object	{8f92a857-478e-11d1-a3b4-00c04fb950dc}

| **TABLE C.1** | Continued |

Object	Class ID
ADs FaxNumber Object	{a5062215-4681-11d1-a3b4-00c04fb950dc}
ADs Hold Object	{b3ad3e13-4080-11d1-a3ac-00c04fb950dc}
ADs Large Integer Object	{927971f5-0939-11d1-8be1-00c04fd8d503}
ADs LDAP NameTranslate Object	{274fae1f-3626-11d1-a3a4-00c04fb950dc}
ADs LDAP Pathname Descriptor Object	{080d0d78-f421-11d0-a36e-00c04fb950dc}
ADs Namespaces Object	{233664b0-0367-11cf-abc4-02608c9e7553}
ADs NetAddress Object	{b0b71247-4080-11d1-a3ac-00c04fb950dc}
ADs OctetList Object	{1241400f-4680-11d1-a3b4-00c04fb950dc}
ADs Path Object	{b2538919-4080-11d1-a3ac-00c04fb950dc}
ADs PostalAddress Object	{0a75afcd-4680-11d1-a3b4-00c04fb950dc}
ADs Property Entry Object	{72d3edc2-a4c4-11d0-8533-00c04fd8d503}
ADs Property Value Object	{7b9e38b0-a97c-11d0-8534-00c04fd8d503}
ADs Provider Object	{4753da60-5b71-11cf-b035-00aa006e0975}
ADs ReplicaPointer Object	{f5d1badf-4080-11d1-a3ac-00c04fb950dc}
ADs Security Descriptor Object	{b958f73c-9bdd-11d0-852c-00c04fd8d503}
ADs TypedName Object	{b33143cb-4080-11d1-a3ac-00c04fb950dc}
ADsDSOObject	{549365d0-ec26-11cf-8310-00aa00b505db}
Advanced Queue Administration API	{83866CAD-740D-11D2-94E4-00C04FA379F1}
Agent Custom Proxy Class	{4BAC124B-78C8-11D1-B9A8-00C04FD97575}
AgentCharacter Custom Proxy Class	{D45FD31E-5C6E-11D1-9EC1-00C04FD7081F}
AgentNotifySink Custom Proxy Class	{D45FD31D-5C6E-11D1-9EC1-00C04FD7081F}
Allows configuration and control of the Windows Management Instrumentation (WMI) service.	{5C659258-E236-11D2-8899-00104B2AFB46}
Allows management of the NNTP news protocol.	{8B342BD0-C889-11D0-898D-00AA00A74BF2}
Allows management of the NNTP news protocol.	{DC147890-91C2-11D0-8966-00AA00A74BF2}
Allows management of the SMTP messaging protocol.	{03F1F940-A0F2-11D0-BB77-00AA00A1EAB7}
Allows management of the SMTP messaging protocol.	{EE756760-C9C5-11D0-B967-00C04FC2F510}
Alpha Channel Blend	{3EE8A933-4D3F-11D0-97D0-00AA00BBB6E2}
Alpha Transition	{AF0DF372-A631-11D0-8DD0-00AA0060DB00}
AMtoolbar Class	{0368BFF0-9870-11D0-94AB-0080C74C7E95}
Annotation Button Property Page	{B7711241-A7D0-11CE-83FD-02608C3EC08A}
Annotation Property Page	{B7711240-A7D0-11CE-83FD-02608C3EC08A}
Answer Wizard ProxyStub Factory	{0578DF30-4383-11D2-B91E-0060089F5C5D}
AntiMoniker	{00000305-0000-0000-C000-000000000046}
AP Class Install Handler filter	{32B533BB-EDAE-11d0-BD5A-00AA00B92AF1}
AP lzdhtml encoding/decoding Filter	{8f6b0360-b80d-11d0-a9b3-006097942311}

TABLE C.1 Continued

Object	Class ID
AppExport Class	{0D3DEBB0-DEBE-11D1-8B87-00C04FD7A924}
AppidData Class	{CDA296F7-E065-11D1-BFD3-00C04FB9988E}
AppImport Class	{C2BE6971-DF9E-11D1-8B87-00C04FD7A924}
AppleTalk Configuration Notify Object	{525609F4-D232-11D0-B76F-00C04FC9BCC4}
AppleTalk Configuration Notify Object	{962FFCF3-965F-11D0-A881-00C04FC99C9C}
AppleTalk Management	{1AA7F83C-C7F5-11D0-A376-00C04FC9DA04}
AppleTalk Management	{1AA7F83D-C7F5-11D0-A376-00C04FC9DA04}
Application Data Control	{3964D9A0-AC96-11D1-9851-00C04FD91972}
Appointment Management Module	{00067802-0000-0000-C000-000000000046}
Apps Control	{BA63460B-B771-11D0-9296-00C04FB6678B}
Apps Property Page	{BA63460C-B771-11D0-9296-00C04FB6678B}
ARIES Log Recovery Engine	{E16C0594-128F-11D1-97E4-00C04FB9618A}
ASF ACM Handler	{B9D1F321-C401-11D0-A520-000000000000}
ASF Animation Handler	{B9D1F32E-C401-11D0-A520-000000000000}
ASF DIB Handler	{B9D1F320-C401-11D0-A520-000000000000}
ASF DJPEG Handler	{B9D1F325-C401-11D0-A520-000000000000}
ASF ICM Handler	{B9D1F322-C401-11D0-A520-000000000000}
ASF JPEG Handler	{B9D1F324-C401-11D0-A520-000000000000}
ASF Media Player	{b47ccfd2-755d-11d0-bad6-0800365b0e03}
ASF Stream Description File	{7DEBA670-68AB-11D0-98EB-00AA00BBB52C}
ASF URL Handler	{B9D1F323-C401-11D0-A520-000000000000}
ASFChopper Class	{C962ABC9-1B2E-11D1-8DCE-00A0C92B500F}
ASFSession Class	{10AE1B6E-6512-11D1-BB8E-0060083178D8}
ASFSessionProp Class	{B0D12374-6532-11D1-BB8F-0060083178D8}
ASP Application Object	{D97A6DA0-A866-11cf-83AE-10A0C90C2BD8}
ASP auto file	{bd70c020-2d24-11d0-9110-00004c752752}
ASP Certificate Object	{b3192190-1176-11d0-8ce8-00aa006c400c}
ASP Host Encode Object	{0CF774D1-F077-11D1-B1BC-00C04F86C324}
ASP Read Cookie	{71EAF260-0CE0-11d0-A53E-00A0C90C2091}
ASP Request Dictionary	{D97A6DA0-A85F-11df-83AE-00A0C90C2BD8}
ASP Request Object	{D97A6DA0-A861-11cf-93AE-00A0C90C2BD8}
ASP Response Object	{D97A6DA0-A864-11cf-83BE-00A0C90C2BD8}
ASP Scripting Context Object	{D97A6DA0-A868-11cf-83AE-00B0C90C2BD8}
ASP Server Object	{D97A6DA0-A867-11cf-83AE-01A0C90C2BD8}
ASP Session Object	{D97A6DA0-A865-11cf-83AF-00A0C90C2BD8}

TABLE C.1 Continued	
Object	**Class ID**
ASP String List Object	{D97A6DA0-A85D-11cf-83AE-00A0C90C2BD8}
ASP Tx Script Context	{14D0916D-9CDC-11D1-8C4A-00C04FC324A4}
ASP Tx Script Context	{14D0916E-9CDC-11D1-8C4A-00C04FC324A4}
ASP Tx Script Context	{14D0916F-9CDC-11D1-8C4A-00C04FC324A4}
ASP Tx Script Context	{14D09170-9CDC-11D1-8C4A-00C04FC324A4}
ASP Write Cookie	{D97A6DA0-A862-11cf-84AE-00A0C90C2BD8}
AspParser Class	{4C3DDDD2-02CF-11D1-8C80-0000F80277C9}
AspView Class	{836D426B-AC66-11D0-ACBD-00A0C91E24A2}
ASX File Parser	{640999A0-A946-11D0-A520-000000000000}
ASX v.2 File Parser	{640999A1-A946-11D0-A520-000000000000}
Async BindCtx	{79eac9f2-baf9-11ce-8c82-00aa004ba90b}
AsyncMHandler Class	{3DA2AA3E-3D96-11D2-9BD2-204C4F4F5020}
AsyncPProt Class	{3DA2AA3B-3D96-11D2-9BD2-204C4F4F5020}
AthWafer	{8F0C5675-AEEF-11d0-84F0-00C04FD43F8F}
ATM LAN Emulation Configuration Notify Object	{295789F0-0949-11D1-B90C-00AA004AB12A}
ATMUNI Call Manager Configuration Notify Object	{674D3E3D-A1A8-11D0-A886-00C04FC99C9C}
AttributeInfo Class	{60F41BE4-06DF-11D2-95AA-0060B0576642}
Audio Capture Filter	{E30629D2-27E5-11CE-875D-00608CB78066}
Audio Destination Object	{CB96B400-C743-11cd-80E5-00AA003E4B50}
Audio Destination to File Object	{D4623720-E4B9-11cf-8D56-00A0C9034A7E}
Audio File Clip	{A5EA8D32-253D-11D1-B3F1-00AA003761C5}
Audio Input Mixer Properties	{2CA8CA52-3C3F-11D2-B73D-00C04FB6BD3D}
Audio Record Object	{61935832-FC85-11d0-8FAE-08002BE4E62A}
Audio Renderer	{E30629D1-27E5-11CE-875D-00608CB78066}
Audio Renderer Property Page	{05589FAF-C356-11CE-BF01-00AA0055595A}
Audio Source from File Object	{D4523720-E4B9-11cf-8D56-00A0C9034A7E}
Audio Source Object	{D24FE500-C743-11cd-80E5-00AA003E4B50}
Augmented Merge Shell Folder	{6413BA2C-B461-11d1-A18A-080036B11A03}
Augmented Shell Folder	{91EA3F8B-C99B-11d0-9815-00C04FD91972}
AuStream Class	{8496e040-af4c-11d0-8212-00c04fc32c45}
AuStream Class	{f2468580-af8a-11d0-8212-00c04fc32c45}
AutomatableDBConnectObject Class	{82126857-FC89-11D0-9BA4-006097C9B2AE}
AVGeneralNotification Class	{239A3C5E-8D41-11D1-B675-00C04FA3C554}
AVI Compressed Stream	{00020001-0000-0000-C000-000000000046}
AVI Compressor	{D76E2820-1563-11CF-AC98-00AA004C0FA9}

● ● ● ● ● ● ● ● ● ● ● ● ● ● ● ●

TABLE C.1   Continued

Object	Class ID
AVI Decompressor	{CF49D4E0-1115-11CE-B03A-0020AF0BA770}
AVI DOC Writer	{D3588AB1-0781-11CE-B03A-0020AF0BA770}
AVI Draw Filter	{A888DF60-1E90-11CF-AC98-00AA004C0FA9}
AVI mux	{E2510970-F137-11CE-8B67-00AA00A3F1A6}
AVI mux Property Page	{C647B5C0-157C-11D0-BD23-00A0C911CE86}
AVI mux Property Page1	{0A9AE910-85C0-11D0-BD42-00A0C911CE86}
AVI Splitter	{1B544C20-FD0B-11CE-8C63-00AA0044B51E}
AVI Stream Source Filter	{14288070-1d42-11d0-9113-00aa00c147fa}
AVI/WAV File Source	{D3588AB0-0781-11CE-B03A-0020AF0BA770}
AVPropServer Class	{E14BB48F-3183-11D2-BE3C-3078302C2030}
AxPropertyBag Class	{06EC6E16-8E4B-11D0-B225-080000185165}
Background Task Scheduler	{603D3800-BD81-11d0-A3A5-00C04FD706EC}
BandProxy	{F61FFEC1-754F-11d0-80CA-00AA005B4383}
BASIC Authenticator Class	{31064da8-402e-11d1-9327-00c04fd919b7}
BasicImage	{16B280C8-EE70-11D1-9066-00C04FD9189D}
Bitmap Image	{D3E34B21-9D75-101A-8C3D-00AA001A1652}
BlackHole	{C3853C22-3F2E-11D2-9900-0000F803FF7A}
Bln Proxy	{BC5F1E51-5110-11D1-AFF5-006097C9A284}
BlnMgr Class	{3F8A6C33-E0FD-11D0-8A8C-00A0C90C2BC5}
BlnMgr Proxy	{F27CE930-4CA3-11D1-AFF2-006097C9A284}
BlnSet Proxy	{BC5F1E50-5110-11D1-AFF5-006097C9A284}
BlnSetUser Proxy	{61FB9D74-893E-11D1-B4B5-00600895A311}
BlnSink Proxy	{BC5F1E53-5110-11D1-AFF5-006097C9A284}
BlnUser Proxy	{BC5F1E55-5110-11D1-AFF5-006097C9A284}
BMP Thumbnail Extractor	{8A4D3EDC-13A4-11D1-9A22-00C04FC2D6C1}
Briefcase	{85BBD920-42A0-1069-A2E4-08002B30309D}
Briefcase Folder	{86747AC0-42A0-1069-A2E6-08002B30309D}
Browseui preloader	{438755C2-A8BA-11D1-B96B-00A0C90312E1}
BuilderWizardManager Class	{E23FDD70-B680-11D0-9C82-0000F8040A53}
Button Property Page Object	{C27CCE38-8596-11D1-B16A-00C0F0283628}
Byot Server Extended Object	{ecabb0aa-7f19-11d2-978e-0000f8757e2a}
ByteBuffer Class	{E126F8FF-A7AF-11D0-B88A-00C04FD424B9}
CA Shell Extensions	{A4E91B6A-DCAE-11D2-A045-00C04F79DC55}
Cabinet File	{0CD7A5C0-9F37-11CE-AE65-08002B2E1262}
Cabview Data Object	{DFE49CFE-CD09-11D2-9643-00C04f79ADF0}
Calendar Control 9.0	{8E27C92B-1264-101C-8A2F-040224009C02}
Calendar General Property Page Object	{8E27C92F-1264-101C-8A2F-040224009C02}

TABLE C.1	Continued

Object	Class ID
CallbackProxy	{C854F6C6-A09F-11D0-A4AA-00C04FC29CFB}
Capture Graph Builder	{BF87B6E0-8C27-11D0-B3F0-00AA003761C5}
Capture Graph Builder 2	{BF87B6E1-8C27-11D0-B3F0-00AA003761C5}
Cartridge Class	{F7974E22-6823-11d0-8FA3-00A0C9190447}
Catalog Class	{228136B0-8BD3-11D0-B4EF-00A0C9138CA4}
Catalog Class	{6EB22881-8A19-11D0-81B6-00A0C9231C29}
Catalog2 Class	{F618C514-DFB8-11D1-A2CF-00805FC79235}
CCOMNSScopeImpl Class	{99847C33-B1B4-11D1-8F10-00C04FC2C17B}
CD Audio filter	{6B6D0808-9ADA-11D0-A520-00A0D10129C0}
CDF Extension Copy Hook	{67EA19A0-CCEF-11d0-8024-00C04FD75D13}
CDL: Asychronous Pluggable Protocol Handler	{3dd53d40-7b8b-11D0-b013-00aa0059ce02}
CDO DropDirectory class	{CD000004-8B95-11D1-82DB-00C04FB1625D}
CDOConfiguration Class	{CD000002-8B95-11D1-82DB-00C04FB1625D}
CDOMessage Class	{CD000001-8B95-11D1-82DB-00C04FB1625D}
Cellset Class	{228136B8-8BD3-11D0-B4EF-00A0C9138CA4}
CEnroll Class	{43F8F289-7A20-11D0-8F06-00C04FC295E1}
CertAdmin Class	{37EABAF0-7FB6-11D0-8817-00A0C903B83C}
CertConfig Class	{372FCE38-4324-11D0-8810-00A0C903B83C}
CertGetConfig Class	{C6CC49B0-CE17-11D0-8833-00A0C903B83C}
Certificate Authority Property Page	{0996FF70-B6A1-11D0-9292-00C04FB6678B}
Certificate Tempalte Shell Extensions	{9BFF616C-3E02-11D2-A4CA-00C04FB93209}
Certificates 1.0 Object	{34AB8E82-C27E-11D1-A6C0-00C04FB94F17}
Certificates 1.0 Object	{53D6AB1D-2488-11D1-A28C-00C04FB94F17}
Certificates 1.0 Object	{69A25C12-1811-11D2-A52B-0000F803A951}
Certificates 1.0 Object	{69A25C14-1811-11D2-A52B-0000F803A951}
CertManageModule Class (exit legacy support)	{6DC5746E-1A01-11D3-9ED6-00C04F79731E}
CertManageModule Class (policy legacy support)	{6853E76A-BD3E-11D1-9A4D-00C04FC297EB}
Certmap Property Page	{BBD8F29C-6F61-11D0-A26E-08002B2C6F32}
CertRequest Class	{98AFF3F0-5524-11D0-8812-00A0C903B83C}
CertServerPolicy Class	{4C4A5E40-732C-11D0-8816-00A0C903B83C}
CertServerPolicy Class	{AA000926-FFBE-11CF-8800-00A0C903B83C}
CertView Class	{A12D0F7A-1E84-11D1-9BD6-00C04FB683FA}
CfgComp Class	{BB0D7187-3C44-11D2-BB98-3078302C2030}
CFilterIo Class	{BD090C00-000B-11D0-D0DD-00A0C9190459}
cfw Class	{ecabafc0-7f19-11d2-978e-0000f8757e2a}
Channel	{f39a0dc0-9cc8-11d0-a599-00c04fd64433}
Channel Handler Object	{f3ba0dc0-9cc8-11d0-a599-00c04fd64435}

> ● ● ● ● ● ● ● ● ● ● ● ● ● ● ● ● ●

TABLE C.1	Continued

Object	Class ID
Channel Menu Handler Object	{f3da0dc0-9cc8-11d0-a599-00c04fd64437}
Channel Mgr	{b3cdae90-d170-11d0-802b-00c04fd75d13}
Channel Shortcut	{f3aa0dc0-9cc8-11d0-a599-00c04fd64434}
Channel Shortcut Property Pages	{f3ea0dc0-9cc8-11d0-a599-00c04fd64438}
Channels Band	{EFA24E63-B078-11d0-89E4-00C04FC9E26E}
CheckAccess Class	{A5E8B32E-442A-11D1-9EA0-006097D2D7CF}
Choices Engine	{698C4280-BDCD-11D0-B218-00C04FD70811}
Chroma	{421516C1-3CF8-11D2-952A-00C04FA34F05}
ChromaKey Transparency	{7D0CD243-5910-11D0-823A-00A0C908DB96}
CLAPI.INETLOGINFORMATION	{A1F89741-F619-11CF-BC0F-00AA006111E0}
ClassFactory Activator Class	{ecabafaf-7f19-11d2-978e-0000f8757e2a}
ClassMoniker	{0000031A-0000-0000-C000-000000000046}
CLBDTDispenser Class	{B890AF56-AC8C-11D1-8CB7-00C04FC3261D}
Cleaner for Downloaded Program Files	{8369AB20-56C9-11D0-94E8-00AA0059CE02}
CLSID_ApprenticeAcctMgr	{1438E821-B6D2-11D0-8D86-00C04FD6202B}
CLSID_ApprenticeICW	{8EE42293-C315-11D0-8D6F-00A0C9A06E1F}
CLSID_CAgentAcctImport	{911685D1-350F-11d1-83B3-00C04FBD7C09}
CLSID_CAthena16Import	{B7AAC060-2638-11d1-83A9-00C04FBD7C09}
CLSID_CCommAcctImport	{1AA06BA1-0E88-11d1-8391-00C04FBD7C09}
CLSID_CCommNewsAcctImport	{0FF15AA1-2F93-11d1-83B0-00C04FBD7C09}
CLSID_CCommunicatorImport	{1198A2C0-0940-11d1-838F-00C04FBD7C09}
CLSID_CEudoraAcctImport	{39981125-C287-11D0-8D8C-00C04FD6202B}
CLSID_CEudoraImport	{0A522730-A626-11D0-8D60-00C04FD6202B}
CLSID_CExchImport	{0A522732-A626-11D0-8D60-00C04FD6202B}
CLSID_CIMEPAcctImport	{837BBD11-2F82-11d1-969E-00A0C90D04EF}
CLSID_CIMN1Import	{B977CB11-1FF5-11d2-9A7A-00C04FA309D4}
CLSID_CMAPIAcctImport	{39981129-C287-11D0-8D8C-00C04FD6202B}
CLSID_CNavNewsAcctImport	{33102459-4B30-11d2-A6DC-00C04F79E7C8}
CLSID_CNetscapeImport	{0A522733-A626-11D0-8D60-00C04FD6202B}
CLSID_CNExpressAcctImport	{17869501-36C8-11d1-83B7-00C04FBD7C09}
CLSID_CNscpAcctImport	{39981127-C287-11D0-8D8C-00C04FD6202B}
CLSID_COE4Import	{BCE9E2E7-1FDD-11d2-9A79-00C04FA309D4}
CLSID_COE5Import	{A1006DE3-2173-11d2-9A7C-00C04FA309D4}
CLSID_COEAcctImport	{210183C0-1E63-11d1-9693-00A0C90D04EF}
CLSID_DatabaseSession	{4A16043F-676D-11d2-994E-00C04FA309D4}
CLSID_FolderDatabase	{6F74FDC6-E366-11d1-9A4E-00C04FA309D4}
CLSID_IConverterSession	{4E3A7680-B77A-11D0-9DA5-00C04FD65685}
CLSID_IFontCache	{B0D17FC2-7BC4-11d1-BDFA-00C04FA31009}
CLSID_IHashTable	{64577982-86D7-11d1-BDFC-00C04FA31009}

TABLE C.1	Continued

Object	Class ID
CLSID_IHTTPMailTransport	{5A580C11-E5EB-11d1-A86E-0000F8084F96}
CLSID_IIMAPTransport	{FD853CEB-7F86-11d0-8252-00C04FD85AB4}
CLSID_IMimeAllocator	{FD853CDD-7F86-11d0-8252-00C04FD85AB4}
CLSID_IMimeBody	{FD853CDB-7F86-11d0-8252-00C04FD85AB4}
CLSID_IMimeHeaderTable	{FD853CE0-7F86-11d0-8252-00C04FD85AB4}
CLSID_IMimeInternational	{FD853CD9-7F86-11d0-8252-00C04FD85AB4}
CLSID_IMimeMessage	{FD853CE3-7F86-11d0-8252-00C04FD85AB4}
CLSID_IMimeMessageParts	{FD853CDC-7F86-11d0-8252-00C04FD85AB4}
CLSID_IMimeMessageTree	{FD853CE2-7F86-11d0-8252-00C04FD85AB4}
CLSID_IMimeObjResolver	{35461E30-C488-11d1-960E-00C04FBD7C09}
CLSID_IMimePropertySchema	{FD853CED-7F86-11d0-8252-00C04FD85AB4}
CLSID_IMimePropertySet	{FD853CE1-7F86-11d0-8252-00C04FD85AB4}
CLSID_IMimeSecurity	{FD853CDE-7F86-11d0-8252-00C04FD85AB4}
CLSID_ImnAccountManager	{8D4B04E1-1331-11d0-81B8-00C04FD85AB4}
CLSID_INNTPTransport	{FD853CE8-7F86-11d0-8252-00C04FD85AB4}
CLSID_IPOP3Transport	{FD853CE7-7F86-11d0-8252-00C04FD85AB4}
CLSID_IPropFindRequest	{BB847B8A-054A-11d2-A894-0000F8084F96}
CLSID_IPropPatchRequest	{EA678830-235D-11d2-A8B6-0000F8084F96}
CLSID_IRangeList	{FD853CEA-7F86-11d0-8252-00C04FD85AB4}
CLSID_IRASTransport	{FD853CE9-7F86-11d0-8252-00C04FD85AB4}
CLSID_ISMTPTransport	{FD853CE6-7F86-11d0-8252-00C04FD85AB4}
CLSID_IVirtualStream	{FD853CDF-7F86-11d0-8252-00C04FD85AB4}
CLSID_MessageDatabase	{6F74FDC5-E366-11d1-9A4E-00C04FA309D4}
CLSID_MessageStore	{101A8FB9-F1B9-11d1-9A56-00C04FA309D4}
CLSID_MigrateMessageStore	{BE09F473-7FEB-11d2-9962-00C04FA309D4}
CLSID_OEHotMailWizard	{E9C8B700-88B1-11d2-8C1F-00C04FA31009}
CLSID_OENote	{CAE80521-F685-11d1-AF32-00C04FA31B90}
CLSID_OERulesManager	{626BAFE1-E5D6-11D1-B1DD-006097D503D9}
CLSID_RecordInfo	{0000002F-0000-0000-C000-000000000046}
CLSID_StdFont	{0BE35203-8F91-11CE-9DE3-00AA004BB851}
CLSID_StdPict	{0BE35204-8F91-11CE-9DE3-00AA004BB851}
CLSID_StoreNamespace	{E70C92A9-4BFD-11d1-8A95-00C04FB951F3}
ClusApplication Object	{f2e606e5-2631-11d1-89f1-00a0c90d061e}
ClusCryptoKeys Object	{f2e6072b-2631-11d1-89f1-00a0c90d061e}
ClusDisk Object	{f2e60723-2631-11d1-89f1-00a0c90d061e}
ClusDisks Object	{f2e60725-2631-11d1-89f1-00a0c90d061e}
ClusNetInterface Object	{f2e606ed-2631-11d1-89f1-00a0c90d061e}
ClusNetInterfaces Object	{f2e606ef-2631-11d1-89f1-00a0c90d061e}

....

TABLE C.1	Continued

Object	Class ID
ClusNetwork Object	{f2e606f1-2631-11d1-89f1-00a0c90d061e}
ClusNetworkNetInterfaces Object	{f2e606f5-2631-11d1-89f1-00a0c90d061e}
ClusNetworks Object	{f2e606f3-2631-11d1-89f1-00a0c90d061e}
ClusNode Object	{f2e606f7-2631-11d1-89f1-00a0c90d061e}
ClusNodeNetInterfaces Object	{f2e606fb-2631-11d1-89f1-00a0c90d061e}
ClusNodes Object	{f2e606f9-2631-11d1-89f1-00a0c90d061e}
ClusPartition Object	{f2e6071f-2631-11d1-89f1-00a0c90d061e}
ClusPartitions Object	{f2e60721-2631-11d1-89f1-00a0c90d061e}
ClusProperties Object	{f2e606ff-2631-11d1-89f1-00a0c90d061e}
ClusProperty Object	{f2e606fd-2631-11d1-89f1-00a0c90d061e}
ClusPropertyValue Object	{f2e60719-2631-11d1-89f1-00a0c90d061e}
ClusPropertyValueData Object	{f2e6071d-2631-11d1-89f1-00a0c90d061e}
ClusPropertyValues Object	{f2e6071b-2631-11d1-89f1-00a0c90d061e}
ClusRefObject Object	{f2e60701-2631-11d1-89f1-00a0c90d061e}
ClusRegistryKeys Object	{f2e60729-2631-11d1-89f1-00a0c90d061e}
ClusResDependencies Object	{f2e60703-2631-11d1-89f1-00a0c90d061e}
ClusResGroup Object	{f2e60705-2631-11d1-89f1-00a0c90d061e}
ClusResGroupPreferredOwnerNodes Object	{f2e606e7-2631-11d1-89f1-00a0c90d061e}
ClusResGroupResources Object	{f2e606e9-2631-11d1-89f1-00a0c90d061e}
ClusResGroups Object	{f2e60707-2631-11d1-89f1-00a0c90d061e}
ClusResource Object	{f2e60709-2631-11d1-89f1-00a0c90d061e}
ClusResources Object	{f2e6070b-2631-11d1-89f1-00a0c90d061e}
ClusResPossibleOwnerNodes Object	{f2e6070d-2631-11d1-89f1-00a0c90d061e}
ClusResType Object	{f2e6070f-2631-11d1-89f1-00a0c90d061e}
ClusResTypePossibleOwnerNodes Object	{f2e60717-2631-11d1-89f1-00a0c90d061e}
ClusResTypeResources Object	{f2e60713-2631-11d1-89f1-00a0c90d061e}
ClusResTypes Object	{f2e60711-2631-11d1-89f1-00a0c90d061e}
ClusScsiAddress Object	{f2e60727-2631-11d1-89f1-00a0c90d061e}
Cluster Object	{f2e606e3-2631-11d1-89f1-00a0c90d061e}
ClusterNames Object	{f2e606eb-2631-11d1-89f1-00a0c90d061e}
ClusVersion Object	{f2e60715-2631-11d1-89f1-00a0c90d061e}
CmdFileIcon	{57651662-CE3E-11D0-8D77-00C04FC99D61}
CMediaPropertyBag	{CDBD8D00-C193-11D0-BD4E-00A0C911CE86}
cmnquery.dll	{83BC5EC0-6F2A-11d0-A1C4-00AA00C16E65}
CMSnapin Class	{0F3621F1-23C6-11D1-AD97-00AA00B88E5A}
CMSnapin Description	{A1B9E020-3226-11D2-883E-00104B2AFB46}
CNtFileIo Class	{BD050C00-000B-11D0-D0DD-00A0C9190459}

TABLE C.1 Continued

Object	Class ID
CNtTapeIo Class	{BD040C00-000B-11D0-D0DD-00A0C9190459}
Code Download Agent	{7D559C10-9FE9-11d0-93F7-00AA0059CE02}
Code Store Database Manager	{DF3D9C23-AB4E-11D0-A732-00A0C9082637}
CoDitherToRGB8 Class	{A860CE50-3910-11d0-86FC-00A0C913F750}
CoICOFilter Class	{607fd4e8-0a03-11d1-ab1d-00c04fc9b304}
Collaboration Data Objects Session Class	{0E064AEC-9D99-11D0-ABE5-00AA0064D470}
Color	{7629CFA4-3FE5-101B-A3C9-08002B2F49FB}
Color Property Page	{0BE35201-8F91-11CE-9DE3-00AA004BB851}
Color Property Page	{DDF5A600-B9C0-101A-AF1A-00AA0034B50B}
Color Space Converter	{1643E180-90F5-11CE-97D5-00AA0055595A}
ColorBvr Class	{3845A174-EB30-11D1-9A23-00A0C879FE5F}
ColorHtml Service Class	{E237E260-155D-11D1-8C82-00A0C90FFFC0}
COM+ Active Process Iteration Server	{4B2E958D-0393-11D1-B1AB-00AA00BA3258}
COM+ Catalog Server	{182C40F0-32E4-11D0-818B-00A0C9231C29}
COM+ Event Notification Server	{ecabafbc-7f19-11d2-978e-0000f8757e2a}
COM+ Extended Transaction Context Component	{5cb66670-d3d4-11cf-acab-00a024a55aef}
COM+ Instance Tracking Component	{ecabafb9-7f19-11d2-978e-0000f8757e2a}
COM+ QC Dead Letter Queue Listener Starter	{ecabafca-7f19-11d2-978e-0000f8757e2a}
COM+ Services GetSecurityCallContext	{ecabb0a8-7f19-11d2-978e-0000f8757e2a}
COM+ Transaction Context Component	{7999FC25-D3C6-11CF-ACAB-00A024A55AEF}
Com98rtc Class	{8C758294-9351-11d1-9D1A-006008B0E5CA}
CoMapMIMEToCLSID Class	{30C3B080-30FB-11d0-B724-00AA006C1A01}
ComClientExport Class	{CFADAC85-E12C-11D1-B34C-00C04F990D54}
COMComponentRegistrar Class	{8DB2180F-BD29-11D1-8B7E-00C04FD7A924}
ComEvents.ComServiceEvents	{ECABB0C3-7F19-11D2-978E-0000F8757E2A}
COMMON DIALOGS CONTROL	{F9043C85-F6F2-101A-A3C9-08002B2F49FB}
CommunicationManager	{67DCC487-AA48-11d1-8F4F-00C04FB611C7}
COMNSView Class	{410381DB-AF42-11D1-8F10-00C04FC2C17B}
Compdata Class	{B91B6008-32D2-11D2-9888-00A0C925F917}
Component Categories cache daemon	{8C7461EF-2B13-11d2-BE35-3078302C2030}
Component Categories conditional cache daemon	{E56829C9-2D59-11d2-BE38-3078302C2030}
Component Categories Manager	{0002E005-0000-0000-C000-000000000046}
Component Categories Manager With Class Store	{0002E006-0000-0000-C000-000000000046}
Component Services Add-In for VB 4.0	{1CB0A015-1676-11D0-825B-00A0C90395DF}
Component Services Add-In for VB 5.0/6.0	{29729D01-CFE6-11D0-BE1D-0060977B4789}
ComponentData Class	{7478EF61-8C46-11d1-8D99-00A0C913CAD4}

TABLE C.1   Continued

Object	Class ID
ComponentData Class	{7478EF65-8C46-11d1-8D99-00A0C913CAD4}
ComponentDataImpl Class	{C9BC92DF-5B9A-11D1-8F00-00C04FC2C17B}
CompositeMoniker	{00000309-0000-0000-C000-000000000046}
Compositor	{9A43A844-0831-11D1-817F-0000F87557DB}
Compress Files Cleaner	{B50F5260-0C21-11D2-AB56-00A0C9082678}
Computer Management 1.0 Object	{11D5C91F-0A98-11D1-BB10-00C04FC9A3A3}
Computer Management 1.0 Object	{58221C67-EA27-11CF-ADCF-00AA00A80033}
ComServersTable Class	{7B3125F4-F14D-11D1-BE0C-000000000000}
Configuration Object for Java	{004CE610-CCD1-11D0-A9BA-00A0C908DB5E}
ConnectionAgent	{E6CC6978-6B6E-11D0-BECA-00C04FD940BE}
Constructor for Scriptlet ASP Handler	{06290BDA-48AA-11D2-8432-006008C3FBFC}
Constructor for Scriptlet Automation Handler	{06290BD8-48AA-11D2-8432-006008C3FBFC}
Constructor for Scriptlet Behavior Handler	{06290BDB-48AA-11D2-8432-006008C3FBFC}
Constructor for Scriptlet Event Handler	{06290BD9-48AA-11D2-8432-006008C3FBFC}
Constructor that allows hosts better control creating scriptlets	{06290BD1-48AA-11D2-8432-006008C3FBFC}
Contact Management Module	{00067801-0000-0000-C000-000000000046}
Content Index Framework Control Object	{1E9685E6-DB6D-11d0-BB63-00C04FC2F410}
Content Index ISearch Creator Object	{1F247DC0-902E-11D0-A80C-00A0C906241A}
Content Indexer Cleaner	{A9B48EAC-3ED8-11d2-8216-00C04FB687DA}
ContentRotator Class	{B4E90802-B83C-11D0-8B40-00C0F00AE35A}
Control Panel	{21EC2020-3AEA-1069-A2DD-08002B30309D}
Contruction Activator Class	{ecabafb7-7f19-11d2-978e-0000f8757e2a}
Convolution	{2BC0EF29-E6BA-11d1-81DD-0000F87557DB}
CoPNGFilter Class	{A3CCEDF7-2DE2-11D0-86F4-00A0C913F750}
CoSniffStream Class	{6A01FDA0-30DF-11d0-B724-00AA006C1A01}
CougarAdmin Class	{81aa1240-b564-11d1-87f8-00a0c92b500f}
CounterCtl Class	{89B9D28B-AAEB-11D0-9796-00A0C908612D}
Cr Behavior Factory	{754FF233-5D4E-11d2-875B-00A0C93C09B3}
CrBarn	{C3BDF740-0B58-11d2-A484-00C04F8EFB69}
CrBlinds	{00C429C0-0BA9-11d2-A484-00C04F8EFB69}
CrBlur	{7312498D-E87A-11d1-81E0-0000F87557DB}
Create, Edit Internet Protocol Security Policies	{DEA8AFA0-CC85-11D0-9CE2-0080C7221EBD}
Create, Edit Internet Protocol Security Policies	{DEA8AFA1-CC85-11D0-9CE2-0080C7221EBD}

TABLE C.1 Continued

Object	Class ID
Create, Edit Internet Protocol Security Policies	{DEA8AFA2-CC85-11D0-9CE2-0080C7221EBD}
CrEmboss	{F515306D-0156-11d2-81EA-0000F87557DB}
CrEngrave	{F515306E-0156-11d2-81EA-0000F87557DB}
CrInset	{93073C40-0BA5-11d2-A484-00C04F8EFB69}
CrIris	{3F69F351-0379-11D2-A484-00C04F8EFB69}
CrmClerk Class	{ecabb0bd-7f19-11d2-978e-0000f8757e2a}
CrmRecoveryClerk Class	{ecabb0be-7f19-11d2-978e-0000f8757e2a}
CrRadialWipe	{424B71AF-0695-11D2-A484-00C04F8EFB69}
CrShatter	{63500AE2-0858-11D2-8CE4-00C04F8ECB10}
CrSlide	{810E402F-056B-11D2-A484-00C04F8EFB69}
CrSpiral	{ACA97E00-0C7D-11d2-A484-00C04F8EFB69}
CrStretch	{7658F2A2-0A83-11d2-A484-00C04F8EFB69}
CrWheel	{5AE1DAE0-1461-11d2-A484-00C04F8EFB69}
CryptPKO Class	{7444C717-39BF-11D1-8CD9-00C04FC29D45}
CryptSig Class	{7444C719-39BF-11D1-8CD9-00C04FC29D45}
CrZigzag	{E6E73D20-0C8A-11d2-A484-00C04F8EFB69}
CTreeView Control	{CD6C7868-5864-11D0-ABF0-0020AF6B0B7A}
CTreeView Property Page	{CD6C7869-5864-11D0-ABF0-0020AF6B0B7A}
CustRg Class	{84D586C4-A423-11D2-B943-00C04F79D22F}
Cutlist Cache Memory Manager	{A5EA8D33-253D-11D1-B3F1-00AA003761C5}
Cutlist File Source	{A5EA8D20-253D-11D1-B3F1-00AA003761C5}
CutList Graph Builder	{A5EA8D2F-253D-11D1-B3F1-00AA003761C5}
CWsbBool Class	{B3449CE1-28F7-11D0-81BF-00A0C91180F2}
CWsbDbKey Class	{46CE9EDE-447C-11D0-98FC-00A0C9058BF6}
CWsbDbSys Class	{5D1A1AD2-C658-11d0-991E-00A0C9058BF6}
CWsbGuid Class	{A0FF1F42-237A-11D0-81BA-00A0C91180F2}
CWsbIndexedEnum Class	{DB35D732-21E9-11D0-81B8-00A0C91180F2}
CWsbLong Class	{B3449CE7-28F7-11D0-81BF-00A0C91180F2}
CWsbLonglong Class	{2FDD2BEA-73A5-11D0-9908-00A0C9058BF6}
CWsbOrderedCollection Class	{9C7D6F13-1562-11D0-81AC-00A0C91180F2}
CWsbShort Class	{B3449CE8-28F7-11D0-81BF-00A0C91180F2}
CWsbString Class	{DB35D733-21E9-11D0-81B8-00A0C91180F2}
CWsbTrace Class	{389E18D0-7EE3-11d0-9E35-00A0C916F120}
CWsbUlong Class	{5BF46533-282D-11D0-81BE-00A0C91180F2}
CWsbUshort Class	{B3449CE0-28F7-11D0-81BF-00A0C91180F2}
CWUpdInfo Class	{A3863C2E-86EB-11D1-A9DB-00C04FB16F9E}
DacCom 1.0 Object	{F9A3F405-B068-11CF-858C-95A235C0163A}
DAO.DBEngine.36	{00000100-0000-0010-8000-00AA006D2EA4}
DAO.Field.36	{00000104-0000-0010-8000-00AA006D2EA4}

TABLE C.1 Continued

Object	Class ID
DAO.Group.36	{00000106-0000-0010-8000-00AA006D2EA4}
DAO.Index.36	{00000105-0000-0010-8000-00AA006D2EA4}
DAO.PrivateDBEngine.36	{00000101-0000-0010-8000-00AA006D2EA4}
DAO.QueryDef.36	{00000108-0000-0010-8000-00AA006D2EA4}
DAO.Relation.36	{00000109-0000-0010-8000-00AA006D2EA4}
DAO.TableDef.36	{00000103-0000-0010-8000-00AA006D2EA4}
DAO.User.36	{00000107-0000-0010-8000-00AA006D2EA4}
DARef Class	{97D6D376-23BB-11D1-A0E1-00C04FC9E20F}
Darwin App Publisher	{CFCCC7A0-A282-11D1-9082-006008059382}
Data Driven Cleaner	{C0E13E61-0CC6-11d1-BBB6-0060978B2AE6}
DataCtl Class	{0468C085-CA5B-11D0-AF08-00609797F0E0}
DataStoreMdb Class	{A88B0EC3-A024-11D1-BF67-000000000000}
DataToolProxy Class	{51E2FE32-9693-11D0-9F68-00A0C9055CAC}
DataToolProxyMgr Class	{51E2FE35-9693-11D0-9F68-00A0C9055CAC}
Date Control	{53961A05-459B-11d1-BE77-006008317CE8}
DBConnectionManager Class	{4656bb14-f397-11ce-bfe1-00aa0057b34e}
DBNamespace Class	{CFC2CAA4-DC5D-11D0-ADAD-00A0C90F5739}
DCOMAccessControl	{0000031D-0000-0000-C000-000000000046}
DCOMCNFG Extension	{9EC88934-C774-11d1-87F4-00C04FC2C17B}
DCOMExtAbout Class	{273695A3-C77A-11d1-87F4-00C04FC2C17B}
DCOM-ZAW Class Access	{62392950-1AF8-11D0-B267-00A0C90F56FC}
DebugDocumentHelper Class	{83B8BCA6-687C-11D0-A405-00AA0060275C}
Debugger Class	{6980ACA1-CFB6-11D0-BF8B-0000F81E8509}
DebugHelper Class	{0BFCC060-8C1D-11D0-ACCD-00AA0060275C}
DebugTextBuffer class	{3E198485-919B-11D0-8C46-00C04FC2AB22}
Default Role Membership Policy	{74075FD1-AEE9-11D1-8645-0060089F6007}
DefaultServer Class	{1F183F5A-5C4D-11D1-8B83-080036B11A03}
Defrag FAT engine	{80EE4902-33A8-11d1-A213-0080C88593A5}
Defrag NTFS engine	{80EE4901-33A8-11d1-A213-0080C88593A5}
DefView Persistent history	{7febaf7c-18cf-11d2-993f-00a0c91f3880}
DEGetBlockFmtNamesParam Class	{8D91090E-B955-11D1-ADC5-006008A5848C}
DEInsertTableParam Class	{47B0DFC7-B7A3-11D1-ADC5-006008A5848C}
Desktop	{00021400-0000-0000-C000-000000000046}
Desktop Task	{E7D3DB4E-199C-11d1-9828-00C04FD91972}
Device Manager	{74246bfc-4c96-11d0-abef-0020af6b0b7a}
Device Manager extension	{90087284-d6d6-11d0-8353-00a0c90640bf}

....

TABLE C.1 Continued	
Object	**Class ID**
DeviceMoniker	{4315D437-5B8C-11D0-BD3B-00A0C911CE86}
DfMarshal	{0000030B-0000-0000-C000-000000000046}
DfrgCtl Class	{202D3AEF-2F0E-11D1-A1F6-0080C88593A5}
DfrgSnapin Class	{43668E21-2636-11D1-A1CE-0080C88593A5}
DfsJuntionPoint Class	{A741D400-31BE-11D1-9A4A-0080ADAA5C4B}
DfsReplica Class	{A741D3FE-31BE-11D1-9A4A-0080ADAA5C4B}
DfsRoot Class	{A741D3FB-31BE-11D1-9A4A-0080ADAA5C4B}
DfsShell Class	{ECCDF543-45CC-11CE-B9BF-0080C87CDBA6}
DfsSnapinResultManager Class	{3C4BAEF5-3278-11D1-9A4B-0080ADAA5C4B}
DfsSnapinScopeManager Class	{677A2D94-28D9-11D1-A95B-008048918FB1}
DHCP	{1CE57F61-A88A-11D0-AB86-00C04FC3357A}
DHCP	{524CCE97-A886-11D0-AB86-00C04FC3357A}
DHCP	{90901AF6-7A31-11D0-97E0-00C04FC3357A}
DHCP Server Configuration Notify Object	{AA9BB1E0-9FE2-11D0-B257-00C04FC9E292}
DHTML Edit Control for IE5	{2D360200-FFF5-11d1-8D03-00A0C959BC0A}
DHTML Edit Control Safe for Scripting for IE5	{2D360201-FFF5-11d1-8D03-00A0C959BC0A}
DialErr Class	{462F7758-8848-11D1-ADD8-0000F87734F0}
Dial-Up Client Configuration Notify Object	{6E65CBC0-926D-11D0-8E27-00C04FC99DCF}
Dial-up Connection Class	{BA126AD7-2166-11D1-B1D0-00805FC1270E}
Dial-up Connection UI Class	{7007ACC1-3202-11D1-AAD2-00805FC1270E}
Dial-up Data Transport	{5F3E04C4-4612-11D0-A113-00A024B50363}
Dial-Up Server Configuration Notify Object	{6E65CBC1-926D-11D0-8E27-00C04FC99DCF}
Direct Connection UI Class	{7007ACC2-3202-11D1-AAD2-00805FC1270E}
Direct3d 3.0 Object	{F3CA56CB-C5DA-11CF-8F28-00AA0060FD48}
Direct3dExecuteBuffer 3.0 Object	{F3CA56E3-C5DA-11CF-8F28-00AA0060FD48}
Direct3dLight 3.0 Object	{F3CA56D7-C5DA-11CF-8F28-00AA0060FD48}
Direct3dMaterial 3.0 Object	{F3CA56DD-C5DA-11CF-8F28-00AA0060FD48}
Direct3dRM 3.0 Object	{F3CA56F5-C5DA-11CF-8F28-00AA0060FD48}
Direct3DRM Object	{4516EC41-8F20-11d0-9B6D-0000C0781BC3}
Direct3dRMAnimation 3.0 Object	{F3CA56B3-C5DA-11CF-8F28-00AA0060FD48}
Direct3dRMAnimationSet 3.0 Object	{F3CA56B9-C5DA-11CF-8F28-00AA0060FD48}
Direct3dRMDevice 3.0 Object	{F3CA567D-C5DA-11CF-8F28-00AA0060FD48}
Direct3dRMDeviceArray 3.0 Object	{F3CA572B-C5DA-11CF-8F28-00AA0060FD48}

TABLE C.1	Continued

Object	Class ID
Direct3dRMFace 3.0 Object	{F3CA5695-C5DA-11CF-8F28-00AA0060FD48}
Direct3dRMFaceArray 3.0 Object	{F3CA5755-C5DA-11CF-8F28-00AA0060FD48}
Direct3dRMFrame 3.0 Object	{F3CA5683-C5DA-11CF-8F28-00AA0060FD48}
Direct3dRMFrameArray 3.0 Object	{F3CA5737-C5DA-11CF-8F28-00AA0060FD48}
Direct3dRMLight 3.0 Object	{F3CA569B-C5DA-11CF-8F28-00AA0060FD48}
Direct3dRMLightArray 3.0 Object	{F3CA5749-C5DA-11CF-8F28-00AA0060FD48}
Direct3dRMMaterial 3.0 Object	{F3CA56AD-C5DA-11CF-8F28-00AA0060FD48}
Direct3dRMMesh 31.0 Object	{F3CA5689-C5DA-11CF-8F28-00AA0060FD48}
Direct3dRMMeshBuilder 3.0 Object	{F3CA568F-C5DA-11CF-8F28-00AA0060FD48}
Direct3dRMObject 3.0 Object	{F3CA56FB-C5DA-11CF-8F28-00AA0060FD48}
Direct3dRMPickedArray 3.0 Object	{F3CA574F-C5DA-11CF-8F28-00AA0060FD48}
Direct3dRMShadow 3.0 Object	{F3CA56C5-C5DA-11CF-8F28-00AA0060FD48}
Direct3dRMTexture 3.0 Object	{F3CA56A1-C5DA-11CF-8F28-00AA0060FD48}
Direct3dRMUserVisual 3.0 Object	{F3CA56BF-C5DA-11CF-8F28-00AA0060FD48}
Direct3dRMViewport 3.0 Object	{F3CA5677-C5DA-11CF-8F28-00AA0060FD48}
Direct3dRMViewportArray 3.0 Object	{F3CA5731-C5DA-11CF-8F28-00AA0060FD48}
Direct3dRMVisual 3.0 Object	{F3CA5701-C5DA-11CF-8F28-00AA0060FD48}
Direct3dRMVisualArray 3.0 Object	{F3CA573D-C5DA-11CF-8F28-00AA0060FD48}
Direct3dRMWinDevice 3.0 Object	{F3CA5707-C5DA-11CF-8F28-00AA0060FD48}
Direct3dRMWrap 3.0 Object	{F3CA56A7-C5DA-11CF-8F28-00AA0060FD48}
Direct3dTexture 3.0 Object	{F3CA56D1-C5DA-11CF-8F28-00AA0060FD48}
Direct3dViewport 3.0 Object	{F3CA56EF-C5DA-11CF-8F28-00AA0060FD48}
DirectContainer Class	{39A2C2A9-4778-11D2-9BDB-204C4F4F5020}
DirectControl Class	{39A2C2A6-4778-11D2-9BDB-204C4F4F5020}
DirectDraw 3.0 Object	{F3CA566B-C5DA-11CF-8F28-00AA0060FD48}
DirectDraw Clipper Object	{593817A0-7DB3-11CF-A2DE-00AA00B93356}
DirectDraw Object	{D7B70EE0-4340-11CF-B063-0020AFC2CD35}
DirectDraw Property Page	{944D4C00-DD52-11CE-BF0E-00AA0055595A}
DirectDrawBitmap 3.0 Object	{F3CA56E9-C5DA-11CF-8F28-00AA0060FD48}
DirectDrawClipper 3.0 Object	{F3CA5671-C5DA-11CF-8F28-00AA0060FD48}
DirectDrawPalette 3.0 Object	{F3CA5713-C5DA-11CF-8F28-00AA0060FD48}
DirectDrawSurface 3.0 Object	{F3CA570D-C5DA-11CF-8F28-00AA0060FD48}
DirectInput 3.0 Object	{F3CA5767-C5DA-11CF-8F28-00AA0060FD48}
DirectInput 3.0 Object	{F3CA57DF-C5DA-11CF-8F28-00AA0060FD48}
DirectInputDevice 3.0 Object	{F3CA575B-C5DA-11CF-8F28-00AA0060FD48}
DirectMusic	{636B9F10-0C7D-11D1-95B2-0020AFDC7421}
DirectMusicAuditionTrack	{D2AC2897-B39B-11D1-8704-00600893B1BD}
DirectMusicBand	{79BA9E00-B6EE-11D1-86BE-00C04FBF8FEF}

TABLE C.1	Continued

Object	**Class ID**
DirectMusicBandTrack	{D2AC2894-B39B-11D1-8704-00600893B1BD}
DirectMusicChordMap	{D2AC288F-B39B-11D1-8704-00600893B1BD}
DirectMusicChordMapTrack	{D2AC2896-B39B-11D1-8704-00600893B1BD}
DirectMusicChordTrack	{D2AC288B-B39B-11D1-8704-00600893B1BD}
DirectMusicCollection	{480FF4B0-28B2-11D1-BEF7-00C04FBF8FEF}
DirectMusicCommandTrack	{D2AC288C-B39B-11D1-8704-00600893B1BD}
DirectMusicComposer	{D2AC2890-B39B-11D1-8704-00600893B1BD}
DirectMusicGraph	{D2AC2884-B39B-11D1-8704-00600893B1BD}
DirectMusicLoader	{D2AC2892-B39B-11D1-8704-00600893B1BD}
DirectMusicMotifTrack	{D2AC288E-B39B-11D1-8704-00600893B1BD}
DirectMusicMuteTrack	{D2AC2898-B39B-11D1-8704-00600893B1BD}
DirectMusicPerformance	{D2AC2881-B39B-11D1-8704-00600893B1BD}
DirectMusicSection	{3F037241-414E-11D1-A7CE-00A0C913F73C}
DirectMusicSegment	{D2AC2882-B39B-11D1-8704-00600893B1BD}
DirectMusicSegmentState	{D2AC2883-B39B-11D1-8704-00600893B1BD}
DirectMusicSeqTrack	{D2AC2886-B39B-11D1-8704-00600893B1BD}
DirectMusicSignPostTrack	{F17E8672-C3B4-11D1-870B-00600893B1BD}
DirectMusicStyle	{D2AC288A-B39B-11D1-8704-00600893B1BD}
DirectMusicStyleTrack	{D2AC288D-B39B-11D1-8704-00600893B1BD}
DirectMusicSynth	{58C2B4D0-46E7-11D1-89AC-00A0C9054129}
DirectMusicSynthSink	{AEC17CE3-A514-11D1-AFA6-00AA0024D8B6}
DirectMusicSysExTrack	{D2AC2887-B39B-11D1-8704-00600893B1BD}
DirectMusicTemplate	{D30BCC65-60E8-11D1-A7CE-00A0C913F73C}
DirectMusicTempoTrack	{D2AC2885-B39B-11D1-8704-00600893B1BD}
DirectMusicTimeSigTrack	{D2AC2888-B39B-11D1-8704-00600893B1BD}
Directory	{fe1290f0-cfbd-11cf-a330-00aa00c16e65}
DirectPlay Object	{D1EB6D20-8923-11d0-9D97-00A0C90A43CB}
DirectPlay2 3.0 Object	{0514B040-84EA-11D0-A8BF-00A0C9008A48}
DirectPlayLobby 3.0 Object	{BFFFD262-7705-11D0-B5DC-444553540000}
DirectPlayLobby Object	{2FE8F810-B2A5-11d0-A787-0000F803ABFC}
DirectSound 3.0 Object	{F3CA5665-C5DA-11CF-8F28-00AA0060FD48}
DirectSound Audio Renderer	{79376820-07D0-11CF-A24D-0020AFD79767}
DirectSound Destination Object	{B9F11A90-90E3-11d0-8D77-00A0C9034A7E}
DirectSound Object	{47D4D946-62E8-11cf-93BC-444553540000}
DirectSound Source Object	{32C35401-D04F-11d0-99B3-00AA004CD65C}
DirectSound3DBufer 3.0 Object	{F3CA57EB-C5DA-11CF-8F28-00AA0060FD48}
Directsound3DLister 3.0 Object	{F3CA57E5-C5DA-11CF-8F28-00AA0060FD48}

TABLE C.1 Continued	
Object	**Class ID**
DirectSoundBuffer 3.0 Object	{F3CA571F-C5DA-11CF-8F28-00AA0060FD48}
DirectSoundCapture Object	{B0210780-89CD-11d0-AF08-00A0C925CD16}
DirectSR Class	{4E3D9D1F-0C63-11D1-8BFB-0060081841DE}
DirectSS Class	{EEE78591-FE22-11D0-8BEF-0060081841DE}
DirectX6	{E1211353-8E94-11D1-8808-00C04FC2C602}
DirectXFile Object	{4516EC43-8F20-11D0-9B6D-0000C0781BC3}
Disk Copy Extension	{59099400-57FF-11CE-BD94-0020AF85B590}
DiskManagement.Connection	{FD78D554-4C6E-11D0-970D-00A0C9191601}
DiskManagement.Control	{AEB84C83-95DC-11D0-B7FC-B61140119C4A}
DiskManagement.DataObject	{E13B6688-3F39-11D0-96F6-00A0C9191601}
DiskManagement.Property Page	{AEB84C84-95DC-11D0-B7FC-B61140119C4A}
DiskManagement.SnapIn	{E13B6686-3F39-11D0-96F6-00A0C9191601}
DiskManagement.SnapInAbout	{FAC1D9C0-0296-11D1-A840-00A0C92C9D5D}
DiskManagement.SnapInComponent	{DBFCA500-8C31-11D0-AA2C-00A0C92749A3}
DiskManagement.SnapInExtension	{8EAD3A12-B2C1-11d0-83AA-00A0C92C9D5D}
DiskManagement.UITasks	{7086AD76-44BD-11D0-81ED-00A0C90FC491}
DispatchMapper Class	{E9225296-C759-11d1-A02B-00C04FB6809F}
DispenserManager	{ecabb0c0-7f19-11d2-978e-0000f8757e2a}
Display	{101193C0-0BFE-11D0-AF91-00AA00B67A42}
Display Adapter CPL Extension	{42071712-76d4-11d1-8b24-00a0c9068ff3}
Display Control Panel HTML Extensions	{3FC0B520-68A9-11D0-8D77-00C04FD70822}
Display Monitor CPL Extension	{42071713-76d4-11d1-8b24-00a0c9068ff3}
Display Panning CPL Extension	{42071714-76d4-11d1-8b24-00a0c9068ff3}
Display TroubleShoot CPL Extension	{f92e8c40-3d33-11d2-b1aa-080036a75b03}
dlgCancl.cCancel	{0006F08D-0000-0000-C000-000000000046}
DocFind Command	{B005E690-678D-11d1-B758-00A0C90564FE}
DocFind Persistent history	{bab33640-1280-11d2-aa30-00a0c91eedba}
DocPPG Class	{0456C164-D0EF-11D0-A787-0000F80272EA}
DomainNames Object	{f2e606e1-2631-11d1-89f1-00a0c90d061e}
Download Site Manager	{BFC880F1-7484-11d0-8309-00AA00B6015C}
Download Status	{22BF0C20-6DA7-11D0-B373-00A0C9034938}
Downloadable Speech API	{0C7F3F20-8BAB-11d2-9432-00C04F8EF48F}
Downloadable Whistler 4.0	{FD913802-5CA2-11d2-A1E6-00A0C913D1EF}
DownloadBehavior Class	{3050f5be-98b5-11cf-bb82-00aa00bdce0b}
DPDVEvt Class	{DB6E8F48-FD3E-11D0-A0BC-00C04FC9E20F}

TABLE C.1 Continued	
Object	**Class ID**
Drive Property Page Extension	{5F5295E0-429F-1069-A2E2-08002B30309D}
DropShadow	{ADC6CB86-424C-11D2-952A-00C04FA34F05}
DropShadow Effect	{D68FC8F4-6B17-11D0-80E6-00AA006EC537}
Dsctl 1.0 Object	{0998BB05-DFFD-11CF-927F-00AA00688A38}
DSDisplayPanel Class	{49FC0185-4B32-11d1-A40E-00600831F336}
dsfolder.dll	{9E51E0D0-6E0F-11d2-9601-00C04FA31A86}
DsObjectPicker	{17D6CCD8-3B7B-11D2-B9E0-00C04FD8DBF7}
DSPrintQueue Class	{435899C9-44AB-11D1-AF00-080036234103}
DsPropertyPages.Computer	{6DFE6492-A212-11D0-BCD5-00C04FD8D5B6}
DsPropertyPages.Computer	{F5D121F4-C8AC-11D0-BCDB-00C04FD8D5B6}
DsPropertyPages.Contact	{C5F1645C-C8C9-11D0-BCDB-00C04FD8D5B6}
DsPropertyPages.Contact	{F5D121F0-C8AC-11D0-BCDB-00C04FD8D5B6}
DsPropertyPages.Container	{5A96F2D8-736E-11D1-BD0D-00C04FD8D5B6}
DsPropertyPages.Default	{6384E23E-736D-11D1-BD0D-00C04FD8D5B6}
DsPropertyPages.Domain	{6DFE648C-A212-11D0-BCD5-00C04FD8D5B6}
DsPropertyPages.Domain	{F5D121EF-C8AC-11D0-BCDB-00C04FD8D5B6}
DsPropertyPages.DomainPolicy	{6DFE648E-A212-11D0-BCD5-00C04FD8D5B6}
DsPropertyPages.FPO	{6DFE6486-A212-11D0-BCD5-00C04FD8D5B6}
DsPropertyPages.Group	{6DFE6489-A212-11D0-BCD5-00C04FD8D5B6}
DsPropertyPages.Group	{F5D121EE-C8AC-11D0-BCDB-00C04FD8D5B6}
DsPropertyPages.Inter-Site-Transport	{6DFE6491-A212-11D0-BCD5-00C04FD8D5B6}
DsPropertyPages.Licensing-Site-Settings	{717EF500-AC8D-11D0-B945-00C04FD8D5B0}
DsPropertyPages.LocalPolicy	{6DFE648F-A212-11D0-BCD5-00C04FD8D5B6}

. . . .

TABLE C.1 Continued	
Object	**Class ID**
DsPropertyPages.Managed-By	{6DFE648B-A212-11D0-BCD5-00C04FD8D5B6}
DsPropertyPages.Membership	{6DFE648A-A212-11D0-BCD5-00C04FD8D5B6}
DsPropertyPages.NTDS-Connection	{717EF4FD-AC8D-11D0-B945-00C04FD8D5B0}
DsPropertyPages.NTDS-DSA	{717EF4FC-AC8D-11D0-B945-00C04FD8D5B0}
DsPropertyPages.NTDS-Site-Settings	{2F280288-BB6D-11D0-B948-00C04FD8D5B0}
DsPropertyPages.NTFRS-Member	{9DA6FD6A-C63B-11D0-B94D-00C04FD8D5B0}
DsPropertyPages.NTFRS-Replica-Set	{9DA6FD69-C63B-11D0-B94D-00C04FD8D5B0}
DsPropertyPages.NTFRS-Subscriber	{50D3055F-9911-11D1-B9AF-00C04FD8D5B0}
DsPropertyPages.OU	{9DA6FD63-C63B-11D0-B94D-00C04FD8D5B0}
DsPropertyPages.OU	{F2C3FAAE-C8AC-11D0-BCDB-00C04FD8D5B6}
DsPropertyPages.Printer-Queue	{6DFE6493-A212-11D0-BCD5-00C04FD8D5B6}
DsPropertyPages.Rpc Container	{50D30572-9911-11D1-B9AF-00C04FD8D5B0}
DsPropertyPages.Server	{6DFE6494-A212-11D0-BCD5-00C04FD8D5B6}
DsPropertyPages.Site	{717EF4FA-AC8D-11D0-B945-00C04FD8D5B0}
DsPropertyPages.Site-Link	{50D30561-9911-11D1-B9AF-00C04FD8D5B0}
DsPropertyPages.Site-Link-Bridge	{50D30562-9911-11D1-B9AF-00C04FD8D5B0}
DsPropertyPages.Subnet	{9DA6FD62-C63B-11D0-B94D-00C04FD8D5B0}
DsPropertyPages.Top	{6DFE6488-A212-11D0-BCD5-00C04FD8D5B6}
DsPropertyPages.TrustedDomain	{9DA6FD67-C63B-11D0-B94D-00C04FD8D5B0}
DsPropertyPages.User	{6DFE6485-A212-11D0-BCD5-00C04FD8D5B6}
DsPropertyPages.User	{F5D121ED-C8AC-11D0-BCDB-00C04FD8D5B6}
DsPropertyPages.User Special Info	{717EF4FE-AC8D-11D0-B945-00C04FD8D5B0}

TABLE C.1 Continued	
Object	**Class ID**
DsPropertyPages.Volume	{6DFE6490-A212-11D0-BCD5-00C04FD8D5B6}
DsPropertyPages.Volume	{F5D121F3-C8AC-11D0-BCDB-00C04FD8D5B6}
dsquery.dll	{163FDC20-2ABC-11d0-88F0-00A024AB2DBB}
dsquery.dll	{1cedc5da-3614-11d2-bf96-00c04fd8d5b0}
dsquery.dll	{25BE9228-00AF-11D2-BF87-00C04FD8D5B0}
dsquery.dll	{2C875213-FCE5-11d1-A0B0-00C04FA31A86}
dsquery.dll	{C40FBD00-88B9-11d2-84AD-00C04FA31A86}
dsquery.dll	{DDE5783A-88B9-11d2-84AD-00C04FA31A86}
dsquery.dll	{DE4874D1-FEEE-11d1-A0B0-00C04FA31A86}
dsquery.dll	{DE4874D2-FEEE-11d1-A0B0-00C04FA31A86}
dsquery.dll	{F020E586-5264-11d1-A532-0000F8757D7E}
DSRefWrapper Class	{7F92DA04-AFB9-11D0-AE11-0080C7B89C95}
DSStatusBar Class	{8A3F59E1-4994-11D1-A40D-00600831F336}
dsuiext.dll	{0D45D530-764B-11d0-A1CA-00AA00C16E65}
dsuiext.dll	{1698790a-e2b4-11d0-b0b1-00c04fd8dca6}
dsuiext.dll	{1AB4A8C0-6A0B-11d2-AD49-00C04FA31A86}
dsuiext.dll	{62AE1F9A-126A-11D0-A14B-0800361B1103}
DTC Designer	{89E8C959-CCB2-11D0-B0B1-00C04FD61157}
DTC Framework Registrar	{399A9AF4-DDE0-11D0-BD90-006097C99369}
DTC Runtime	{064D91E4-E8CD-11D0-BD91-006097C99369}
DTC VB Runtime support	{802BC939-CE74-11D0-B0B1-00C04FD61157}
DTC98 Registry Helper	{F3BD7629-D1F0-11D0-B0B1-00C04FD61157}
DTCFramework Global Functions	{1A77E940-4E4E-11D0-B1E2-00C04FD70811}
Dutch_Dutch Stemmer	{860d28d0-8bf4-11ce-be59-00aa0051fe20}
Dutch_Dutch Word Breaker	{66b37110-8bf2-11ce-be59-00aa0051fe20}
DV Muxer	{129D7E40-C10D-11D0-AFB9-00AA00B67A42}
DV Splitter	{4EB31670-9FC6-11CF-AF6E-00AA00B67A42}
DV Video Decoder	{B1B77C00-C3E4-11CF-AF79-00AA00B67A42}
DV Video Encoder	{13AA3650-BB6F-11D0-AFB9-00AA00B67A42}
DVD Graph Builder	{FCC152B7-F372-11D0-8E00-00C04FD7C08B}
DVD Navigator	{9B8C4620-2C1A-11D0-8493-00A02438AD48}
DX2D Anti-Aliasing	{473AA80B-4577-11D1-81A8-0000F87557DB}
Dx3j Security Object	{BC5F0300-F7BC-11d0-B9ED-40A708C10000}
DXLUTBuilder	{1E54333B-2A00-11d1-8198-0000F87557DB}
DXRasterizer Class	{8652CE55-9E80-11D1-9053-00C04FD9189D}

| TABLE C.1 | Continued |

Object	Class ID
DXSurface	{0E890F83-5F79-11D1-9043-00C04FD9189D}
DXSurface Modifier	{3E669F1D-9C23-11d1-9053-00C04FD9189D}
DXTaskManager	{4CB26C03-FF93-11d0-817E-0000F87557DB}
DXTransformFactory Class	{D1FE6762-FC48-11D0-883A-3C8B00C10000}
EapTlsCfg Class	{58AB2366-D597-11d1-B90E-00C04FC9B263}
EditorServices Class	{203630C3-9110-11D0-AB6C-00A0C91E24A2}
EffectBvr Class	{54274112-7A5E-11d2-875F-00A0C93C09B3}
EndpointsTable Class	{2F94D7B0-BF63-11D1-A6A2-00C04FB9988E}
English_UK Stemmer	{d99f7670-7f1a-11ce-be57-00aa0051fe20}
English_UK Word Breaker	{59e097e4-8099-101b-8df3-00000b65c3b5}
English_US Stemmer	{eeed4c20-7f1b-11ce-be57-00aa0051fe20}
English_US Word Breaker	{59e09780-8099-101b-8df3-00000b65c3b5}
EnumerableAttributeInfo Class	{9A407538-0A20-11D2-95B0-0060B0576642}
EnumTelnetClientsSvr Class	{FE9E48A4-A014-11D1-855C-00A0C944138C}
Event Class	{CDBEC9C0-7A68-11D1-88F9-0080C7D771BF}
Event Publisher	{AB944620-79C6-11D1-88F9-0080C7D771BF}
Event Subscription	{7542E960-79C7-11D1-88F9-0080C7D771BF}
Event System	{4E14FBA2-2E22-11D1-9964-00C04FBBB345}
EventBindingManager Class	{53D01080-AF98-11D0-A9EB-00AA00685C74}
EventComCat Class	{AE1EF300-CD8F-11D0-A9F8-00AA00685C74}
EventLock Class	{2E3ABB30-AF88-11D0-A9EB-00AA00685C74}
EventManager Class	{35172920-A700-11D0-A9EA-00AA00685C74}
EventMetabaseDatabaseManager Class	{8A58CDC0-CBDC-11D0-A9F8-00AA00685C74}
EventRouter Class	{9F82F020-F6FD-11D0-AA14-00AA006BC80B}
EventServiceObject Class	{A4BE1350-1051-11D1-AA1E-00AA006BC80B}
EventSystem.EventObjectChange	{D0565000-9DF4-11D1-A281-00C04FCA0AA7}
EventSystemTier2	{1BE1F766-5536-11D1-B726-00C04FB926AF}
EventUtil Class	{A1E041D0-CD73-11D0-A9F8-00AA00685C74}
Execute Object for Java	{3EFB1800-C2A1-11CF-960C-0080C7C2BA87}
Explode	{141DBAF1-55FB-11D1-B83E-00A0C933BE86}
Explorer Band	{EFA24E64-B078-11d0-89E4-00C04FC9E26E}
ExplorerWeb Class	{9B5D03A2-8DDB-11D1-A220-00A0C9055E81}
ExplorerWebs Class	{9B5D03A0-8DDB-11D1-A220-00A0C9055E81}
Extension Control	{53961A02-459B-11d1-BE77-006008317CE8}
ExtractIcon Class	{7A80E4A8-8005-11D2-BCF8-00C04F72C717}
F:\PROGRA~1\COMMON~1\MICROS~1\Euro\MSOEURO.DLL	{30A095E2-9A0C-11D2-93BB-00105A994D2C}

TABLE C.1 Continued	
Object	**Class ID**
F:\PROGRA~1\COMMON~1\System\Mapi\ 1033\NT\CNFNOT32.EXE	{6316D324-2238-101B-9E66-00AA003BA905}
F:\PROGRA~1\COMMON~1\System\Mapi\ 1033\NT\CNFNOT32.EXE	{BB2B65B0-241E-101B-9E67-00AA003BA905}
F:\PROGRA~1\MICROS~3\Office\MDHELPER.DLL	{20FF6B80-C312-11D0-B4E4-00A0C9261445}
F:\Program Files\Common Files\Microsoft Shared\ Web Folders\PUBPLACE.HTT	{BDEADF00-C265-11d0-BCED-00A0C90AB50F}
F:\WINNT\System32\catsrvut.dll	{1D0482E4-57E7-11d2-B10D-00805FC73204}
F:\WINNT\System32\catsrvut.dll	{22EE26E5-2289-11d2-8F43-00C04FC2E0C7}
F:\WINNT\System32\catsrvut.dll	{5DC41690-C6A6-11d1-9D35-006008B0E5CA}
F:\WINNT\System32\catsrvut.dll	{5DC41691-C6A6-11d1-9D35-006008B0E5CA}
F:\WINNT\System32\catsrvut.dll	{5DC41692-C6A6-11d1-9D35-006008B0E5CA}
F:\WINNT\System32\catsrvut.dll	{5DC41693-C6A6-11d1-9D35-006008B0E5CA}
F:\WINNT\System32\catsrvut.dll	{5DC41694-C6A6-11d1-9D35-006008B0E5CA}
F:\WINNT\System32\catsrvut.dll	{6131A8EC-78CE-11d2-A3F2-3078302C2030}
F:\WINNT\System32\catsrvut.dll	{75C9378A-7E89-11d2-B116-00805FC73204}
F:\WINNT\System32\catsrvut.dll	{94426DE2-3211-11d2-A0DB-00C04F8EDCEE}
F:\WINNT\System32\clbcatex.dll	{E846F0A0-D367-11D1-8286-00A0C9231C29}
F:\WINNT\System32\clbcatq.dll	{07D26616-6136-11D1-8C9C-00C04FC3261D}
F:\WINNT\System32\clbcatq.dll	{15b0bb4c-0f7d-11D1-b21f-00C04Fb9473f}
F:\WINNT\System32\clbcatq.dll	{31430c59-bed1-11D1-8De8-00C04FC2E0C7}
F:\WINNT\System32\clbcatq.dll	{819469D2-D0CF-11d1-8E0B-00C04FC2E0C7}
F:\WINNT\System32\clbcatq.dll	{A9397D66-3ED3-11D1-8D99-00C04FC2E0C7}
F:\WINNT\System32\clbcatq.dll	{B4B3AECB-DFD6-11d1-9DAA-00805F85CFE3}
F:\WINNT\System32\clbcatq.dll	{D5C66BE1-C209-11d1-8DEC-00C04FC2E0C7}
F:\WINNT\System32\ddrawex.dll	{4FD2A832-86C8-11D0-8FCA-00C04FD9189D}
F:\WINNT\System32\dnsmgr.dll	{2FAEBFA2-3F1A-11D0-8C65-00C04FD8FECB}
F:\WINNT\System32\dnsmgr.dll	{6C1303DC-BA00-11D1-B949-00A0C9A06D2D}
F:\WINNT\System32\dnsmgr.dll	{6C1303DD-BA00-11D1-B949-00A0C9A06D2D}
F:\WINNT\System32\dnsmgr.dll	{80105023-50B1-11D1-B930-00A0C9A06D2D}
F:\WINNT\System32\domadmin.dll	{19B9A3F8-F975-11D1-97AD-00A0C9A06D2D}
F:\WINNT\System32\domadmin.dll	{EBC53A38-A23F-11D0-B09B-00C04FD8DCA6}
F:\WINNT\System32\dsadmin.dll	{006A2A75-547F-11D1-B930-00A0C9A06D2D}

. . . .

| **TABLE C.1** | Continued |

Object	Class ID
F:\WINNT\System32\dsadmin.dll	{08EB4FA6-6FFD-11D1-B0E0-00C04FD8DCA6}
F:\WINNT\System32\dsadmin.dll	{765901EA-C5A1-11D1-B10C-00104B243180}
F:\WINNT\System32\dsadmin.dll	{8F2AC965-04A2-11D3-82BD-00C04F68928B}
F:\WINNT\System32\dsadmin.dll	{C3A904FE-C4F2-11D1-B10B-00104B243180}
F:\WINNT\System32\dsadmin.dll	{D967F824-9968-11D0-B936-00C04FD8D5B0}
F:\WINNT\System32\dsadmin.dll	{E301A009-F901-11D2-82B9-00C04F68928B}
F:\WINNT\System32\dsadmin.dll	{E355E538-1C2E-11D0-8C37-00C04FD8FE93}
F:\WINNT\System32\dsuiwiz.dll	{6BA3F852-23C6-11D1-B91F-00A0C9A06D2D}
F:\WINNT\System32\els.dll	{394C052E-B830-11D0-9A86-00C04FD8DBF7}
F:\WINNT\System32\els.dll	{975797FC-4E2A-11D0-B702-00C04FD8DBF7}
F:\WINNT\System32\mimefilt.dll	{5645C8C2-E277-11CF-8FDA-00AA00A14F93}
F:\WINNT\System32\msr2c.dll	{5B5E7E70-E653-11CF-84A5-0000C08C00C4}
F:\WINNT\System32\stclient.dll	{EB56EAE8-BA51-11d2-B121-00805FC73204}
F:\WINNT\System32\TLBINF32.DLL	{8B217746-717D-11CE-AB5B-D41203C10000}
F:\WINNT\System32\TLBINF32.DLL	{8B217752-717D-11CE-AB5B-D41203C10000}
F:\WINNT\System32\TLBINF32.DLL	{8B217755-717D-11CE-AB5B-D41203C10000}
F:\WINNT\System32\TLBINF32.DLL	{8B21775E-717D-11CE-AB5B-D41203C10000}
F:\WINNT\System32\urlmon.dll	{54c37cd0-d944-11d0-a9f4-006097942311}
Factory bindable using IPersistMoniker	{06290BD2-48AA-11D2-8432-006008C3FBFC}
Fade	{16B280C5-EE70-11D1-9066-00C04FD9189D}
FaultTolerantDfs Class	{A741D3F9-31BE-11D1-9A4A-0080ADAA5C4B}
Favorites Band	{EFA24E61-B078-11d0-89E4-00C04FC9E26E}
Fax Tiff Data Column Provider	{7f9609be-af9a-11d1-83e0-00c04fb6e984}
FaxServer Class	{D73733C8-CC80-11D0-B225-00C04FB6C2F5}
FaxSnapin Class	{753EDB4D-2E1B-11D1-9064-00A0C90AB504}
FaxSnapinAbout Class	{5b80820f-4755-11d1-9077-00a0c90ab504}
FaxTiff Class	{87099231-C7AF-11D0-B225-00C04FB6C2F5}
FieldListCtrl.1 Object	{53230327-172B-11D0-AD40-00A0C90DC8D9}
File and Folders Search ActiveX Control	{C4EE31F3-4768-11D2-BE5C-00A0C9A83DA1}
File Property Page Extension	{21B22460-3AEA-1069-A2DC-08002B30309D}
File Search Module	{0006780B-0000-0000-C000-000000000046}
File Source (Async.)	{E436EBB5-524F-11CE-9F53-0020AF0BA770}
File Source (URL)	{E436EBB6-524F-11CE-9F53-0020AF0BA770}
File stream renderer	{D51BD5A5-7548-11CF-A520-0080C77EF58A}
File System Client DocStore Locator Object	{2A488070-6FD9-11D0-A808-00A0C906241A}
File System Client Filter Object	{AA205A4D-681F-11D0-A243-08002B36FCA4}
File Transfer Media Player	{a5276f50-12b0-11d0-8dbd-00aa00b90c3b}

TABLE C.1 Continued	
Object	**Class ID**
File Types Page	{B091E540-83E3-11CF-A713-0020AFD79762}
File Writer	{8596E5F0-0DA5-11D0-BD21-00A0C911CE86}
file:, local: Asychronous Pluggable Protocol Handler	{79eac9e7-baf9-11ce-8c82-00aa004ba90b}
file://%userappdata%\Microsoft\Internet Explorer\ Desktop.htt	{00021400-0000-0000-C000-000000000046}
file://%webdir%\controlp.htt	{21EC2020-3AEA-1069-A2DD-08002B30309D}
file://%webdir%\default.htt	{85BBD920-42A0-1069-A2E4-08002B30309D}
file://%webdir%\dialup.htt	{7007ACC7-3202-11D1-AAD2-00805FC1270E}
file://%webdir%\folder.htt	{20D04FE0-3AEA-1069-A2D8-08002B30309D}
file://%webdir%\fsresult.htt	{1f4de370-d627-11d1-ba4f-00a0c91eedba}
file://%webdir%\fsresult.htt	{e17d4fc0-5564-11d1-83f2-00a0c90dc849}
file://%webdir%\nethood.htt	{208D2C60-3AEA-1069-A2D7-08002B30309D}
file://%webdir%\recycle.htt	{645FF040-5081-101B-9F08-00AA002F954E}
file://%webdir%\schedule.htt	{D6277990-4C6A-11CF-8D87-00AA0060F5BF}
file://F:\WINNT\web\ftp.htt	{63da6ec0-2e98-11cf-8d82-444553540000}
FILEMGMT 1.0 Object	{58221C65-EA27-11CF-ADCF-00AA00A80033}
FILEMGMT 1.0 Object	{58221C69-EA27-11CF-ADCF-00AA00A80033}
FILEMGMT 1.0 Object	{DB5D1FF4-09D7-11D1-BB10-00C04FC9A3A3}
FileMoniker	{00000303-0000-0000-C000-000000000046}
FilePackage Class	{5EFB2260-89EE-11d0-B605-00A0C922E851}
FileService service	{66E10DE0-7E2D-11D0-B5FD-00A0C922E851}
FileSystem Object	{0D43FE01-F093-11CF-8940-00A0C9054228}
Filter Graph	{E436EBB3-524F-11CE-9F53-0020AF0BA770}
Filter Graph no thread	{E436EBB8-524F-11CE-9F53-0020AF0BA770}
Filter Mapper	{E436EBB2-524F-11CE-9F53-0020AF0BA770}
Filter Mapper2	{CDA42200-BD88-11d0-BD4E-00A0C911CE86}
Finds and displays information and Web sites on the Internet	{871C5380-42A0-1069-A2EA-08002B30309D}
Flip Horizontal Effect	{F6167903-5479-11D0-8236-00A0C908DB96}
Flip Vertical Effect	{67741683-547D-11D0-8236-00A0C908DB96}
Folder Options Property Page Extension	{6D5313C0-8C62-11D1-B2CD-006097DF8C11}
Folder Redirection Editor	{88E729D6-BDC1-11D1-BD2A-00C04FB9603F}
Folder Shortcut	{0AFACED1-E828-11D1-9187-B532F1E9575D}
Font	{3C4F3BE3-47EB-101B-A3C9-08002B2F49FB}
Font Property Page	{0BE35200-8F91-11CE-9DE3-00AA004BB851}
Font Property Page	{2542F180-3532-1069-A2CD-00AA0034B50B}

. . . .

TABLE C.1 Continued	
Object	**Class ID**
Fonts	{BD84B380-8CA2-1069-AB1D-08000948F534}
Fonts	{D20EA4E1-3957-11d2-A40B-0C5020524152}
For P&rinters...	{8A23E65E-31C2-11d0-891C-00A024AB2DBB}
Format	{4150F050-BB6F-11D0-AFB9-00AA00B67A42}
FoxOLEDB 1.0 Object	{3FF292B6-B204-11CF-8D23-00AA005FFE58}
FoxOLEDB 1.0 Object	{58ECEE30-E715-11CF-B0E3-00AA003F000F}
FpFile Class	{F6FD0A0E-43F0-11D1-BE58-00A0C90A4335}
FpFolder Class	{F6FD0A11-43F0-11D1-BE58-00A0C90A4335}
FpMetaInfo Class	{F6FD0A0F-43F0-11D1-BE58-00A0C90A4335}
FPNewSubCtl Class	{532FD821-83AB-11D0-8032-00A0C90A8FE0}
Fpsrvmmc Class	{FF5903A8-78D6-11D1-92F6-006097B01056}
FpStructureElement Class	{F6FD0A01-43F0-11D1-BE58-00A0C90A4335}
FpStructureModification Class	{F6FD0A00-43F0-11D1-BE58-00A0C90A4335}
Free Threaded XML DOM Document	{2933BF91-7B36-11d2-B20E-00C04F983E60}
French_French Stemmer	{2a6eb050-7f1c-11ce-be57-00aa0051fe20}
French_French Word Breaker	{59e09848-8099-101b-8df3-00000b65c3b5}
FrontPage ActiveX Object Tag Property Page	{A0234992-6CC4-11D1-B3B2-0060977B463D}
FrontPage ActiveX Param Tags Property Page	{A0234993-6CC4-11D1-B3B2-0060977B463D}
FrontPage Editor	{388ED917-7FD2-11D0-A60B-00A0C90A43C9}
FrontPage Editor	{D603F1F0-A9D9-11CF-8904-00AA00BDCB98}
FrontPage Editor Document	{388ED918-7FD2-11D0-A60B-00A0C90A43C9}
FrontPage Editor Window	{0E5EDCF0-9F3B-11D1-B3C3-0060977B463D}
FrontPage Explorer	{388ED915-7FD2-11D0-A60B-00A0C90A43C9}
FrontPage ToDoList	{388ED919-7FD2-11D0-A60B-00A0C90A43C9}
FrontPage Web Services	{388ED916-7FD2-11D0-A60B-00A0C90A43C9}
FsaFilterClientNTFS Class	{B2AD2931-84FD-11d0-81E4-00A0C91180F2}
FsaFilterNTFS Class	{FCDC8671-7329-11d0-81DF-00A0C91180F2}
FsaFilterRecallNTFS Class	{B2AD2932-84FD-11d0-81E4-00A0C91180F2}
FsaPostIt Class	{F7860350-AA27-11d0-B16D-00A0C916F120}
FsaRecallNotifyServer Class	{D68BD5B3-D6AA-11d0-9EDA-00A02488FCDE}
FsaResourceNTFS Class	{112981B3-1BA5-11D0-81B2-00A0C91180F2}
FsaServerNTFS Class	{E707D9B2-4F89-11D0-81CC-00A0C91180F2}
FTP Folder Web View Automation	{210DA8A2-7445-11d1-91F7-006097DF5BD4}
FTP IDataObject impl	{299D0193-6DAA-11d2-B679-006097DF5BD4}
FTP Installer to handle FTP Associations	{1ABCFC13-2340-11d2-B601-006097DF5BD4}
ftp: Asychronous Pluggable Protocol Handler	{79eac9e3-baf9-11ce-8c82-00aa004ba90b}
FTSSession Class	{10AE1B71-6512-11D1-BB8E-0060083178D8}
FTSSessionProp Class	{B0D12376-6532-11D1-BB8F-0060083178D8}

TABLE C.1 Continued

Object	Class ID
Full Screen Renderer	{07167665-5011-11CF-BF33-00AA0055595A}
Full Screen Renderer Property Page	{0618AA30-6BC4-11CF-BF36-00AA0055595A}
FXO File Viewer	{00021120-0000-0000-C000-000000000046}
G.71	{4AFBBA92-FE10-11d0-B607-00C04FB6E866}
G.71	{4AFBBA93-FE10-11d0-B607-00C04FB6E866}
G.71	{4AFBBA98-FE10-11d0-B607-00C04FB6E866}
G.71	{4AFBBA99-FE10-11d0-B607-00C04FB6E866}
G.711 Codec	{AF7D8180-A8F9-11CF-9A46-00AA00B7DAD1}
G.711 Codec Property Page	{480D5CA0-F032-11CF-A7D3-00A0C9056683}
G.72	{4AFBBA94-FE10-11d0-B607-00C04FB6E866}
G.72	{4AFBBA95-FE10-11d0-B607-00C04FB6E866}
G.723.1 Codec	{24532D00-FCD8-11CF-A7D3-00A0C9056683}
G.723.1 Codec Property Page	{24532D01-FCD8-11CF-A7D3-00A0C9056683}
gcdef.dll	{92187326-72B4-11d0-A1AC-0000F8026977}
Gene	{4AFBBA8C-FE10-11d0-B607-00C04FB6E866}
Gene	{4AFBBA8D-FE10-11d0-B607-00C04FB6E866}
Gene	{4AFBBA9E-FE10-11d0-B607-00C04FB6E866}
Gene	{4AFBBA9F-FE10-11d0-B607-00C04FB6E866}
GenerateMSI Class	{298942A3-C0FE-11D1-8D87-0060088F38C8}
Generic Control Hosting Component	{555AF860-68FF-11D0-B20E-080000185165}
Generic WDM Filter Proxy	{17CCA71B-ECD7-11D0-B908-00A0C9223196}
German_German Stemmer	{510a4910-7f1c-11ce-be57-00aa0051fe20}
German_German Word Breaker	{9b08e210-e51b-11cd-bc7f-00aa003db18e}
Global Folder Settings	{EF8AD2D1-AE36-11D1-B2D2-006097DF8C11}
Glow Effect	{02C7E642-7E04-11D0-9D99-00A0C908DB96}
gopher: Asychronous Pluggable Protocol Handler	{79eac9e4-baf9-11ce-8c82-00aa004ba90b}
gotobar Class	{9F4D2FA2-54A1-11d1-8267-00A0C91F9CA0}
Gradient	{623E2882-FC0E-11d1-9A77-0000F8756A10}
Gradient DXSurface	{C6365470-F667-11d1-9067-00C04FD9189D}
Grammar Control	{53961A04-459B-11d1-BE77-006008317CE8}
Grayscale Effect	{73F2B3A3-5474-11D0-8236-00A0C908DB96}
Group Policy	{8FC0B734-A0E1-11D1-A7D3-0000F87571E3}
Group Policy	{D70A2BEA-A63E-11D1-A7D4-0000F87571E3}
Group Policy About Information	{0FDE5092-AA2A-11D1-A7D4-0000F87571E3}
Group Policy Object	{EA502722-A23D-11D1-A7D3-0000F87571E3}
H.26	{4AFBBA8E-FE10-11d0-B607-00C04FB6E866}
H.26	{4AFBBA8F-FE10-11d0-B607-00C04FB6E866}

....

| TABLE C.1 | Continued |

Object	Class ID
H.26	{4AFBBA90-FE10-11d0-B607-00C04FB6E866}
H.26	{4AFBBA91-FE10-11d0-B607-00C04FB6E866}
H261 Color Values	{2293C842-B001-11CF-90FA-00AA00A729EA}
H261 Decode Filter	{31363248-0000-0010-8000-00AA00389B71}
H261 Encode OA	{C2349702-EA0B-11CF-9FEC-00AA00A59F69}
H261 Encode Parameters Property Page	{E3659FC1-EA13-11CF-9FEC-00AA00A59F69}
H261 Encode Transform Filter	{EFD08EC1-EA11-11CF-9FEC-00AA00A59F69}
H261 RTP Parameters Property Page	{C6520AE1-2037-11D0-906C-00AA00A59F69}
H261 Video Effects Property Page	{6C5C43A1-9CEA-11CF-90FA-00AA00A729EA}
H263 Color Values	{2293C845-B001-11CF-90FA-00AA00A729EA}
H263 Decode Filter	{33363248-0000-0010-8000-00AA00389B71}
H263 Encode OA	{9B27B462-FB5B-11CF-906C-00AA00A59F69}
H263 Encode Options Property Page	{53937AA0-283B-11D0-8800-444553540000}
H263 Encode Parameters Property Page	{C9076CE1-FB56-11CF-906C-00AA00A59F69}
H263 Encode Transform Filter	{C9076CE2-FB56-11CF-906C-00AA00A59F69}
H263 RTP Parameters Property Page	{C6520AE2-2037-11D0-906C-00AA00A59F69}
H263 Video Effects Property Page	{6C5C43A0-9CEA-11CF-90FA-00AA00A729EA}
H323MSP Class	{0F1BE7F8-45CA-11d2-831F-00A0244D2298}
Handler Class	{A1A6B99D-497F-11D1-9217-00C04FBBBFB3}
HeightField	{04921709-B159-11d1-9207-0000F8758E66}
Help	{3C4F3BE7-47EB-101B-A3C9-08002B2F49FB}
Help Collection Wrapper Class	{06A03425-C9EB-11d2-8CAA-0080C739E3E0}
Helper for IMoniker support in legacy code	{679d9e37-f8f9-11d2-8deb-00c04f6837d5}
Helper Object for Java	{8E26BFC1-AFD6-11CF-BFFC-00AA003CFDFC}
HHC file	{7f73b8f6-c19c-11d0-aa66-00c04fc2eddc}
HHCtrl Object	{ADB880A6-D8FF-11CF-9377-00AA003B7A11}
History	{FF393560-C2A7-11CF-BFF4-444553540000}
History Band	{EFA24E62-B078-11d0-89E4-00C04FC9E26E}
HomePage Class	{7E8BC44E-AEFF-11D1-89C2-00C04FB6BFC4}
HsmActionCopy Class	{7B22FF2A-1AD6-11D0-81B1-00A0C91180F2}
HsmActionDelete Class	{AD402355-00FC-11D0-819C-00A0C91180F2}
HsmActionManage Class	{7B22FF29-1AD6-11D0-81B1-00A0C91180F2}
HsmActionMigrate Class	{7B22FF28-1AD6-11D0-81B1-00A0C91180F2}
HsmActionMove Class	{7B22FF2B-1AD6-11D0-81B1-00A0C91180F2}
HsmActionOnResourcePostUnmanage Class	{D9E04214-14D7-11d1-9938-0060976A546D}
HsmActionOnResourcePostValidate Class	{D9E04211-14D7-11d1-9938-0060976A546D}
HsmActionOnResourcePreUnmanage Class	{D2C875C1-AD6E-11d1-9F2F-00A02488FCDE}
HsmActionOnResourcePreValidate Class	{D9E04212-14D7-11d1-9938-0060976A546D}

| TABLE C.1 | Continued |

Object	Class ID
HsmActionRecall Class	{7B22FF22-1AD6-11D0-81B1-00A0C91180F2}
HsmActionRecycle Class	{7B22FF23-1AD6-11D0-81B1-00A0C91180F2}
HsmActionTruncate Class	{7B22FF24-1AD6-11D0-81B1-00A0C91180F2}
HsmActionUnmanage Class	{D3AF5DB1-1DF8-11D0-81B6-00A0C91180F2}
HsmActionValidate Class	{7B22FF26-1AD6-11D0-81B1-00A0C91180F2}
HsmAdmin Class	{A6CB8422-7EB8-11d0-8FC3-00A0C9190447}
HsmAdminData Class	{0B9A3960-8C3E-11d0-B797-00A02488FCDE}
HsmAdminData Extension Class	{AB926900-77F8-11d1-B9A0-00A0C9190447}
HsmCom Class	{D82438F1-1C60-11d0-964E-00A0C905F099}
HsmCritAccessTime Class	{7B22FF2F-1AD6-11D0-81B1-00A0C91180F2}
HsmCritAlways Class	{AD40235F-00FC-11D0-819C-00A0C91180F2}
HsmCritCompressed Class	{7B22FF2E-1AD6-11D0-81B1-00A0C91180F2}
HsmCritGroup Class	{7B22FF30-1AD6-11D0-81B1-00A0C91180F2}
HsmCritLinked Class	{CFB04621-1C9F-11D0-81B4-00A0C91180F2}
HsmCritLogicalSize Class	{7B22FF31-1AD6-11D0-81B1-00A0C91180F2}
HsmCritManageable Class	{CFB04622-1C9F-11D0-81B4-00A0C91180F2}
HsmCritMbit Class	{D3AF5DB2-1DF8-11D0-81B6-00A0C91180F2}
HsmCritMigrated Class	{7B22FF2C-1AD6-11D0-81B1-00A0C91180F2}
HsmCritModifyTime Class	{7B22FF32-1AD6-11D0-81B1-00A0C91180F2}
HsmCritOwner Class	{7B22FF33-1AD6-11D0-81B1-00A0C91180F2}
HsmCritPhysicalSize Class	{7B22FF34-1AD6-11D0-81B1-00A0C91180F2}
HsmCritPremigrated Class	{7B22FF2D-1AD6-11D0-81B1-00A0C91180F2}
HsmJob Class	{AD402346-00FC-11D0-819C-00A0C91180F2}
HsmJobContext Class	{AD402364-00FC-11D0-819C-00A0C91180F2}
HsmJobDef Class	{AD40234B-00FC-11D0-819C-00A0C91180F2}
HsmManagedResource Class	{AB939AD0-6D67-11d0-9E2E-00A0C916F120}
HsmManagedResourceCollection Class	{8448DD80-7614-11d0-9E33-00A0C916F120}
HsmPhase Class	{BEA60F8A-7EBA-11d0-81E4-00A0C91180F2}
HsmPolicy Class	{AD402350-00FC-11D0-819C-00A0C91180F2}
HsmRule Class	{AD40235A-00FC-11D0-819C-00A0C91180F2}
HsmRuleStack Class	{C2E29801-B1BA-11d0-81E9-00A0C91180F2}
HsmScanner Class	{BEA60F81-7EBA-11d0-81E4-00A0C91180F2}
HsmSession Class	{BEA60F80-7EBA-11d0-81E4-00A0C91180F2}
HsmSessionTotals Class	{FF67BB34-8430-11d0-81E4-00A0C91180F2}
HsmStoragePool Class	{61F0B790-82D9-11d0-9E35-00A0C916F120}
HsmTskMgr Class	{7DDE1826-4F86-11D0-9E22-00A0C916F120}
HsmWorkItem Class	{23E45B60-C598-11d0-B16F-00A0C916F120}
HsmWorkItem Class	{B8E1CD21-81D3-11d0-81E4-00A0C91180F2}
HsmWorkQueue Class	{247DF540-C558-11d0-B16F-00A0C916F120}

....

TABLE C.1 Continued	
Object	**Class ID**
HtmDocData Class	{62C81794-A9EC-11D0-8198-00A0C91BBEE3}
HtmEditorFactory Class	{C76D83F8-A489-11D0-8195-00A0C91BBEE3}
HTML Application	{3050f4d8-98B5-11CF-BB82-00AA00BDCE0B}
HTML Document	{25336920-03f9-11cf-8fd0-00aa00686f13}
HTML File persistent handler	{eec97550-47a9-11cf-b952-00aa0051fe20}
HTML filter	{e0ca5340-4534-11cf-b952-00aa0051fe20}
HTML Host Encode Object	{0CF774D0-F077-11D1-B1BC-00C04F86C324}
HTML Inline Movie Control	{8422DAE7-9929-11CF-B8D3-004033373DA8}
HTML Inline Sound Control	{8422DAE3-9929-11CF-B8D3-004033373DA8}
HTML Thumbnail Extractor	{EAB841A0-9550-11CF-8C16-00805F1408F3}
HtmLanguageService Class	{316B19B5-B5F8-11D0-8199-00A0C91BBEE3}
HtmlDlgHelper Class	{3050f4e1-98b5-11cf-bb82-00aa00bdce0b}
HtmlHelp Class	{31E0DFD7-2621-11D1-AFD7-006097C9A284}
http: Asychronous Pluggable Protocol Handler	{79eac9e2-baf9-11ce-8c82-00aa004ba90b}
https: Asychronous Pluggable Protocol Handler	{79eac9e5-baf9-11ce-8c82-00aa004ba90b}
Hyperlinking ProxyStub Factory	{79EAC9C3-BAF9-11CE-8C82-00AA004BA90B}
HyperTerminal Connection Page Ext	{1B53F360-9A1B-1069-930C-00AA0030EBC8}
HyperTerminal Icon Ext	{88895560-9AA2-1069-930E-00AA0030EBC8}
I420/H261 Decode Filter	{30323449-0000-0010-8000-00AA00389B71}
I420/H263 Decode Filter	{FA925E20-323B-11D0-8800-444553540000}
IAS Accounting provider	{6BC096B8-0CE6-11D1-BAAE-00C04FC2E20D}
IAS Active Directory Data Store	{6BC096C6-0CE6-11D1-BAAE-00C04FC2E20D}
IAS Attribute Match Constraint	{6BC098A4-0CE6-11D1-BAAE-00C04FC2E20D}
IAS Audit Channel Class	{6BC0969D-0CE6-11D1-BAAE-00C04FC2E20D}
IAS Authorization Extension Host	{6BC09899-0CE6-11D1-BAAE-00C04FC2E20D}
IAS BaseCamp Extension Host	{6BC09898-0CE6-11D1-BAAE-00C04FC2E20D}
IAS Data Source Class	{6BC09698-0CE6-11D1-BAAE-00C04FC2E20D}
IAS Dictionary Class	{6BC09699-0CE6-11D1-BAAE-00C04FC2E20D}
IAS EAP Provider	{6BC0989A-0CE6-11D1-BAAE-00C04FC2E20D}
IAS Helper COM Component	{6BC096BC-0CE6-11D1-BAAE-00C04FC2E20D}
IAS Information Base Class	{6BC096A0-0CE6-11D1-BAAE-00C04FC2E20D}
IAS Logging Snapin Class	{2E19B602-48EB-11d2-83CA-00104BCA42CF}

Object	Class ID
TABLE C.1 Continued	
Object	**Class ID**
IAS MS-CHAP Error Provider	{6BC09897-0CE6-11D1-BAAE-00C04FC2E20D}
IAS Network Policy Enforcer	{6BC098A7-0CE6-11D1-BAAE-00C04FC2E20D}
IAS Networking Data Store	{6BC096C8-0CE6-11D1-BAAE-00C04FC2E20D}
IAS NT Event Log Class	{6BC0969F-0CE6-11D1-BAAE-00C04FC2E20D}
IAS NT Group Membership Constraint	{6BC098A5-0CE6-11D1-BAAE-00C04FC2E20D}
IAS NT-SAM Authentication Provider	{6BC09896-0CE6-11D1-BAAE-00C04FC2E20D}
IAS NT-SAM Names Provider	{6BC0989D-0CE6-11D1-BAAE-00C04FC2E20D}
IAS NT-SAM Per-User Attributes Provider	{6BC0989C-0CE6-11D1-BAAE-00C04FC2E20D}
IAS OLE-DB Data Store	{6BC096C4-0CE6-11D1-BAAE-00C04FC2E20D}
IAS Pipeline	{6BC096B3-0CE6-11D1-BAAE-00C04FC2E20D}
IAS Pipeline Manager	{6BC096BF-0CE6-11D1-BAAE-00C04FC2E20D}
IAS Pipeline Stage	{6BC096B2-0CE6-11D1-BAAE-00C04FC2E20D}
IAS RADIUS Client Class	{6BC096DA-0CE6-11D1-BAAE-00C04FC2E20D}
IAS RADIUS Protocol Class	{6BC09894-0CE6-11D1-BAAE-00C04FC2E20D}
IAS Request	{6BC096B1-0CE6-11D1-BAAE-00C04FC2E20D}
IAS Request Attribute	{6BC096B0-0CE6-11D1-BAAE-00C04FC2E20D}
IAS Time of Day Constraint	{6BC098A6-0CE6-11D1-BAAE-00C04FC2E20D}
IAS User Restrictions Handler	{6BC096D5-0CE6-11D1-BAAE-00C04FC2E20D}
IASEnumerableAttributeEditor Class	{5F7B221A-086B-11D2-95AF-0060B0576642}
IASGroupsAttributeEditor Class	{A9E6F356-317C-11d2-805D-0060B0576642}
IASIPAttributeEditor Class	{CB2418D3-0709-11D2-95AB-0060B0576642}
IASMultivaluedAttributeEditor Class	{B3B443EF-0728-11D2-95AC-0060B0576642}
IASNASVendors Class	{C54EC3BB-7442-11d2-A036-0060B0576642}
IASSnapin About Class	{8F8F8DC1-5713-11D1-9551-0060B0576642}
IASSnapin Class	{8F8F8DC0-5713-11D1-9551-0060B0576642}
IASStringAttributeEditor Class	{1ABAAF84-086F-11D2-95AF-0060B0576642}

....

TABLE C.1 Continued	
Object	**Class ID**
IASVendorSpecificAttributeEditor Class	{D601D57D-085B-11D2-95AF-0060B0576642}
IAVIStream & IAVIFile Proxy	{0002000D-0000-0000-C000-000000000046}
ICC Profile	{DBCE2480-C732-101B-BE72-BA78E9AD5B27}
ICM Class Manager	{33D9A760-90C8-11d0-BD43-00A0C911CE86}
ICM Monitor Management	{5DB2625A-54DF-11D0-B6C4-0800091AA605}
ICM Printer Management	{675F097E-4C4D-11D0-B6C1-0800091AA605}
ICM Scanner Management	{176d6597-26d3-11d1-b350-080036a75b03}
ICodecInfo_PSFactory	{04e07f54-6e5c-11d0-9292-00c04fd919b7}
ICWSystemConfig Class	{7954DD9B-8C2A-11D1-ADDB-0000F87734F0}
IDMNotify_PSFactory	{D2D79DF7-3400-11d0-B40B-00AA005FF586}
IDMRemoteServer_PSFactory	{3A410F21-553F-11d1-8E5E-00A0C92C9D5D}
IE4 Suite Splash Screen	{A2B0DD40-CC59-11d0-A3A5-00C04FD706EC}
IEnumDisatch_PSFactory	{54696EC0-36B2-11d0-BA93-00C04FD91A5E}
IEnumMedia_PSFactory	{58712b21-0a93-11d0-8dba-00aa00b90c3b}
IEnumMediaSession_PSFactory	{58712b23-0a93-11d0-8dba-00aa00b90c3b}
IEnumTrigger_PSFactory	{dea1bd90-f078-11cf-908b-00aa004254a0}
IGMP Snap-in	{C2FE4508-D6C2-11D0-A37B-00C04FC9DA04}
IGMP Snap-in	{C2FE4509-D6C2-11D0-A37B-00C04FC9DA04}
IHTMLColorPicker Class	{533AC2A4-1ACE-11D1-A787-0000F80272EA}
IImgCtx	{3050F3D6-98B5-11CF-BB82-00AA00BDCE0B}
IIS Admin Crypto Extension	{9f0bd3a0-ec01-11d0-a6a0-00a0c922e752}
IIS Admin Service	{A9E69610-B80D-11D0-B9B9-00A0C922E750}
IIS App Extension	{b4f34438-afec-11d1-9868-00a0c922e703}
IIS Cert Map Extension	{bc36cde8-afeb-11d1-9868-00a0c922e703}
IIS Certificate Wizard	{D4BE8632-0C85-11D2-91B1-00C04F8C8761}
IIS Computer Extension	{91ef9258-afec-11d1-9868-00a0c922e703}
IIS Mimemap Object	{9036b028-a780-11d0-9b3d-0080c710ef95}
IIS Namespace Object	{d6bfa35e-89f2-11d0-8527-00c04fd8d503}
IIS PropertyAttribute Object	{FD2280A8-51A4-11D2-A601-3078302C2030}
IIS Provider Object	{d88966de-89f2-11d0-8527-00c04fd8d503}
IIS Server Extension	{c3b32488-afec-11d1-9868-00a0c922e703}
IIS Servers Extension	{FCC764A0-2A38-11d1-B9C6-00A0C922E750}
IIS Shell Extention	{5a61f7a0-cde1-11cf-9113-00aa00425c62}
IIS WAMREG Admin	{61738644-F196-11D0-9953-00C04FD919C1}
IISAdmin Security Extension	{c4376b00-f87b-11d0-a6a6-00a0c922e752}
IisServiceControl Class	{E8FB8621-588F-11D2-9D61-00C04F79C5FE}

Object	**Class ID**
ILaunchSlicer Class	{A07CCD15-8148-11D0-87BB-00C04FC33942}
Image Document	{02B01C80-E03D-101A-B294-00DD010F2BF9}
Image List Cache	{3F4EEF80-BFE8-11d0-A3A5-00C04FD706EC}
Image Property Page	{64455860-5153-101C-816F-0E6013114B7F}
Image Property Page Object	{C27CCE36-8596-11D1-B16A-00C0F0283628}
ImageComboBox General Property Page Object	{C27CCE42-8596-11D1-B16A-00C0F0283628}
ImageList General Property Page Object	{C27CCE35-8596-11D1-B16A-00C0F0283628}
ImagePPG Class	{7D045701-EDA1-11D0-A6E8-006097C9947C}
Imaging for Windows 1.0	{7D252A20-A4D5-11CE-8BF1-00608C54A1AA}
IMAP Module	{00067828-0000-0000-C000-000000000046}
IMC	{4AFBBA9C-FE10-11d0-B607-00C04FB6E866}
IMC	{4AFBBA9D-FE10-11d0-B607-00C04FB6E866}
IMCLexicalAnalyzer Proxy/Stub	{706BCCF0-3686-11d1-95F3-00C04FD57E8C}
IMDB Core Connection	{C4EAB3EB-F4AF-11d1-828E-00C04F990690}
IMediaCatalog Proxy/Stub	{4BA2C081-68BB-11d0-95BD-00C04FD57E8C}
IMediaCatalogAdviseSink Proxy/Stub	{4BA2C080-68BB-11d0-95BD-00C04FD57E8C}
IMediaCatalogData Proxy/Stub	{29D44CA0-DD3A-11d0-95DF-00C04FD57E8C}
IMediaCatalogGroup Proxy/Stub	{9B3B23C0-E236-11d0-A5C9-0080C7195D7E}
IMediaCatalogLexicon Proxy/Stub	{9B3B23C3-E236-11d0-A5C9-0080C7195D7E}
IMediaCatalogMoniker Proxy/Stub	{CB40F470-02F1-11D1-B244-00AA00A74BFF}
IMediaCatalogPathMoniker Proxy/Stub	{8EE20D86-6DEC-11d1-8C1C-00C04FB995C9}
IMediaCatalogQuery Proxy/Stub	{EAF6F280-DD53-11d0-95DF-00C04FD57E8C}
IMediaEventCallback_PSFactory	{607d8680-7cd2-11d0-8dfa-00aa00b90c3b}
IMediaManager_PSFactory	{87e9bbc0-863f-11d0-8e02-00aa00b90c3b}
IMediaPlayer_PSFactory	{58712b20-0a93-11d0-8dba-00aa00b90c3b}
IMediaSession_PSFactory	{58712b22-0a93-11d0-8dba-00aa00b90c3b}
IMediaSessionManager_PSFactory	{58712b24-0a93-11d0-8dba-00aa00b90c3b}
IMediaSessionMonitor_PSFactory	{61ccd0e6-908a-11d0-b4b7-00c04fc9dab7}
IMediaSessionMonitorRegistry_PSFactory	{61ccd0e7-908a-11d0-b4b7-00c04fc9dab7}
ImexGridCtrl.1 Object	{53230322-172B-11D0-AD40-00A0C90DC8D9}
IMultimediaDeviceInfo_PSFactory	{dd0efe08-8047-11d0-92a9-00c04fd919b7}
Inbound Connection Class	{BA126AD9-2166-11D1-B1D0-00805FC1270E}
Inbound Connection Manager Class	{BA126ADD-2166-11D1-B1D0-00805FC1270E}
Inbound Connection Manager Connection Enumerator Class	{BA126ADE-2166-11D1-B1D0-00805FC1270E}
Inbound Connection UI Class	{7007ACC3-3202-11D1-AAD2-00805FC1270E}
Indeo Video (r) 5.1 Progressive Download Source	{C69E8F40-D5C8-11D0-A520-145405C10000}
Indeo Video (r) 5.1 Progressive Download Source About	{C69E8F41-D5C8-11D0-A520-145405C10000}

●●●●●●●●●●●●●●●●●

TABLE C.1	Continued

Object	Class ID
Indeo Video (r) 5.1 Progressive Download Source Dynamic Info	{C69E8F43-D5C8-11D0-A520-145405C10000}
Indeo Video (r) 5.1 Progressive Download Source Static Info	{C69E8F42-D5C8-11D0-A520-145405C10000}
Indeo® audio software	{B4CA2970-DD2B-11D0-9DFA-00AA00AF3494}
Indeo® audio software Property Page	{B4CA2971-DD2B-11D0-9DFA-00AA00AF3494}
Indeo® video 5.10 About Decoder Property Page	{E369A160-F3C2-11D0-91D4-444553540000}
Indeo® video 5.10 About Encoder Property Page	{C1C0FE00-F3C2-11D0-91D4-444553540000}
Indeo® video 5.10 About RTE Property Page	{84725EA1-2FBC-11D1-BC86-00A0C969FC67}
Indeo® video 5.10 Compression Filter	{1F73E9B1-8C3A-11D0-A3BE-00A0C9244436}
Indeo® video 5.10 Decode Frame Property Page	{665A4444-D905-11D0-A30E-444553540000}
Indeo® video 5.10 Decode OA	{665A4448-D905-11D0-A30E-444553540000}
Indeo® video 5.10 Decode Sequence Property Page	{665A4443-D905-11D0-A30E-444553540000}
Indeo® video 5.10 Decompression Filter	{30355649-0000-0010-8000-00AA00389B71}
Indeo® video 5.10 Encode OA	{665A444A-D905-11D0-A30E-444553540000}
Indeo® video 5.10 Encode Parameters Property Page	{2DE89781-DBF6-11D0-A30E-444553540000}
Indeo® video 5.10 Encode Sequence Property Page	{665A4445-D905-11D0-A30E-444553540000}
Index Cleaner Prop Bag	{24400D16-5754-11d2-8218-00C04FB687DA}
Indexing Service Query SSO V2.	{A4463024-2B6F-11D0-BFBC-0020F8008024}
Indexing Service Snapin	{95ad72f0-44ce-11d0-ae29-00aa004b9986}
Indexing Service Utility SSO V2.	{0C16C27E-A6E7-11D0-BFC3-0020F8008024}
IndexServer Simple Command Creator	{C7B6C04A-CBB5-11d0-BB4C-00C04FC2F410}
INetShowODBC_PSFactory	{e8487246-70c9-11d0-baa0-00c04fd91a5e}
Infinite Pin Tee Filter	{F8388A40-D5BB-11D0-BE5A-0080C706568E}
INIFile Class	{C7DAE181-D8C1-11D2-B532-00104B9A3597}
In-pane search	{169A0691-8DF9-11d1-A1C4-00C04FD75D13}
Inserted File	{00020D05-0000-0000-C000-000000000046}
InserterDialogs Class	{EF7C36A6-0E2C-11D1-A787-0000F80272EA}
INSHandler Class	{6342E1B6-94DB-11D1-ADE2-0000F87734F0}
Installed Apps Enumerator	{0B124F8C-91F0-11D1-B8B5-006008059382}
InstallEngineCtl Object	{6E449683-C509-11CF-AAFA-00AA00B6015C}
Instrumented Audio Source Object	{D4023720-E4B9-11cf-8D56-00A0C9034A7E}
IntDitherer Class	{05f6fe1a-ecef-11d0-aae7-00c04fc9b304}
Intel Common RPH Controls	{566F8E23-963C-11D0-9643-00AA00A89C1D}
Intel H26X RPH Controls	{566F8E24-963C-11D0-9643-00AA00A89C1D}
Intel RTP Demux Filter	{399D5C90-74AB-11D0-9CCF-00A0C9081C19}
Intel RTP Demux Filter Property Page	{399D5C91-74AB-11D0-9CCF-00A0C9081C19}
Intel RTP RPH for G.711/G.723.1	{D42FEAC0-82A1-11D0-9643-00AA00A89C1D}

TABLE C.1 Continued	
Object	**Class ID**
Intel RTP RPH for Generic Audio	{ECB29E60-88ED-11D0-9643-00AA00A89C1D}
Intel RTP RPH for H.263/H.261	{EC941961-7DF6-11D0-9643-00AA00A89C1D}
Intel RTP RPH Generic Audio Property Page	{6182E342-9C57-11D0-B4A9-00A0C90D63B5}
Intel RTP RPH Property Page	{566F8E20-963C-11D0-9643-00AA00A89C1D}
Intel RTP RPH Property Page	{566F8E21-963C-11D0-9643-00AA00A89C1D}
Intel RTP SPH for G.711/G.723.1	{1AE60860-8297-11D0-9643-00AA00A89C1D}
Intel RTP SPH for Generic Audio	{3DDDA000-88E4-11D0-9643-00AA00A89C1D}
Intel RTP SPH for H.263/H.261	{EC941960-7DF6-11D0-9643-00AA00A89C1D}
Intel RTP SPH Generic Audio Property Page	{FF12FDC1-9A45-11D0-B4A9-00A0C90D63B5}
Intel RTP SPH Property Page	{BBBE3F40-964D-11D0-9643-00AA00A89C1D}
Intel RTP SPH Property Page	{BBBE3F41-964D-11D0-9643-00AA00A89C1D}
Intel RTP SPH Property Page	{BBBE3F43-964D-11D0-9643-00AA00A89C1D}
Interface Proxy Stub	{01458CF0-A1A2-11D1-8F85-00600895E7D5}
Interface Proxy Stub	{5408B2F0-C816-11D1-8F99-00600895E7D5}
Interface Proxy Stub	{842D84C9-C347-11D1-8F64-00C04FB611C7}
Interface Proxy Stub	{CA38D8DA-C75D-11D1-8F99-00600895E7D5}
Interface Proxy Stub	{CA38D8DB-C75D-11D1-8F99-00600895E7D5}
Internal Text Renderer	{48025243-2D39-11CE-875D-00608CB78066}
Internet Explorer	{FBF23B42-E3F0-101B-8488-00AA003E56F8}
Internet Explorer Maintenance	{FC715823-C5FB-11D1-9EEF-00A0C90347FF}
Internet Explorer Snapin About Information	{5A7B63E0-F9BC-11D2-BBE5-00C04F86AE3B}
Internet Explorer(Ver 1.0)	{0002DF01-0000-0000-C000-000000000046}
Internet Location Services Object	{A4AD47C0-20EA-11D0-8796-444553540000}
Internet Shortcut	{FBF23B40-E3F0-101B-8488-00AA003E56F8}
Invert Effect	{254E8EA4-4924-11D0-A787-00A0C91BBEE1}
IP Routing Management	{C2FE4500-D6C2-11D0-A37B-00C04FC9DA04}
IP Routing Management	{C2FE4501-D6C2-11D0-A37B-00C04FC9DA04}
IP Routing Management	{C2FE4502-D6C2-11D0-A37B-00C04FC9DA04}
IP Routing Management	{C2FE4503-D6C2-11D0-A37B-00C04FC9DA04}
IP Routing Management	{C2FE4504-D6C2-11D0-A37B-00C04FC9DA04}
IP Routing Management	{C2FE4505-D6C2-11D0-A37B-00C04FC9DA04}
IP Routing Management	{C2FE4506-D6C2-11D0-A37B-00C04FC9DA04}
IP Routing Management	{C2FE4507-D6C2-11D0-A37B-00C04FC9DA04}

....

TABLE C.1 Continued

Object	Class ID
IP Routing Management	{C2FE450B-D6C2-11D0-A37B-00C04FC9DA04}
IP Routing Management	{C2FE450C-D6C2-11D0-A37B-00C04FC9DA04}
IPConfMSP Class	{0F1BE7F7-45CA-11d2-831F-00A0244D2298}
IPersistMoniker	{79eac9c9-baf9-11ce-8c82-00aa004ba90b}
IPersistMoniker Plug In Distributor	{E436EBB7-524F-11CE-9F53-0020AF0BA770}
IPM.Note.FolderPub.Request	{CB0E73C3-706A-11CF-A056-00A02416065A}
IPM.Note.FolderPub.SyncState	{CB0E73C2-706A-11CF-A056-00A02416065A}
IPM.Note.FolderPub.Update	{CB0E73C1-706A-11CF-A056-00A02416065A}
IPM.Note.FolderPub.Update.Multiple	{CB0E73C7-706A-11CF-A056-00A02416065A}
IPX RIP Routing Management	{90810502-38F1-11D1-9345-00C04FC9DA04}
IPX RIP Routing Management	{90810503-38F1-11D1-9345-00C04FC9DA04}
IPX Routing Management	{90810500-38F1-11D1-9345-00C04FC9DA04}
IPX Routing Management	{90810501-38F1-11D1-9345-00C04FC9DA04}
IPX SAP Routing Management	{90810504-38F1-11D1-9345-00C04FC9DA04}
IPX SAP Routing Management	{90810505-38F1-11D1-9345-00C04FC9DA04}
ISessionDescStore_PSFactory	{221E0DA0-36BA-11d0-BA93-00C04FD91A5E}
ISFBand OC	{131A6951-7F78-11D0-A979-00C04FD705A2}
IShellFolderBand	{D82BE2B0-5764-11D0-A96E-00C04FD705A2}
ISimpleMediaEventRegistry_PSFactory	{607d8681-7cd2-11d0-8dfa-00aa00b90c3b}
ISnapinAbout	{F778C6B4-C08B-11D2-976C-00C04F79DB19}
ISRShare_PSFactory	{B9BD3860-44DB-101B-90A8-00AA003E4B50}
IStreamBuffer_PSFactory	{2f2d0b90-1bc9-11d0-9113-00aa00c147fa}
IStreamFilter_PSFactory	{edf016b0-1bcf-11d0-9113-00aa00c147fa}
IStreamSink_PSFactory	{75112880-1bc8-11d0-9113-00aa00c147fa}
IStreamSource_PSFactory	{2ff47af0-1bcf-11d0-9113-00aa00c147fa}
Italian_Italian Stemmer	{6d36ce10-7f1c-11ce-be57-00aa0051fe20}
Italian_Italian Word Breaker	{fd86b5d0-12c6-11ce-bd31-00aa004bbb1f}
ItemMoniker	{00000304-0000-0000-C000-000000000046}
IThreadPool_PSFactory	{ef206950-31d6-11d0-911f-00aa00c147fa}
IV 4	{4AFBBA96-FE10-11d0-B607-00C04FB6E866}
IV 4	{4AFBBA97-FE10-11d0-B607-00C04FB6E866}
IVCmd_PSFactory	{C63A2B30-5543-11b9-C000-5611722E1D15}
IVolumeClient_PSFactory	{D2D79DF5-3400-11d0-B40B-00AA005FF586}
IVolumeClient2_PSFactory	{4BDAFC52-FE6A-11d2-93F8-00105A11164A}
IWebDesignControlContext Class	{7AB96C22-2EDA-11D1-9CE0-0000F8040A53}
Java Class: com.ms.wfc.html.DhComponent-Wrapper$DhInnerSafeControl	{FFD709F0-AF39-11D2-B854-0000F81E8872}

TABLE C.1 Continued	
Object	**Class ID**
Java Class: com.ms.wfc.html.DhModule	{B98AC5E0-DE20-11d1-A7CE-0000F81E8509}
Java Debug Engine	{A9E537F2-A0A6-11D0-B83C-00A0244A1DE2}
Java LE Debug Manager	{62544620-AB83-11D0-B83F-00A0244A1DE2}
Java Package Manager	{D2073C44-AB4F-11D0-A732-00A0C9082637}
java:	{DB57B100-853B-11D0-AF95-0080C71F7993}
Jet Expression Service	{039EA4C0-E696-11d0-878A-00A0C91EC756}
JetEngine Class	{DE88C160-FF2C-11D1-BB6F-00C04FAE22DA}
Journal Module	{00067808-0000-0000-C000-000000000046}
JS File Host Encode Object	{85131630-480C-11D2-B1F9-00C04F86C324}
JScript Language	{f414c260-6ac0-11cf-b6d1-00aa00bbbb58}
JScript Language Authoring	{f414c261-6ac0-11cf-b6d1-00aa00bbbb58}
JScript Language Encoding	{f414c262-6ac0-11cf-b6d1-00aa00bbbb58}
JVIEW Profiler	{03D9F3F2-B0E3-11D2-B081-006008039BF0}
Key Class	{964EB3C4-8B47-11D0-AB46-00805F84B59E}
KeyGeneration Class	{B67F993A-FC9D-11D0-8822-00A0C955FC7E}
Kodak Image Admin Control	{009541A0-3B81-101C-92F3-040224009C02}
Kodak Image Admin Help Page	{69E2DD40-5321-101C-96BF-040224009C02}
Kodak Image Admin Print Page	{E60A7940-4B3E-101C-96BF-040224009C02}
Kodak Image Admin Property Page	{009541A4-3B81-101C-92F3-040224009C02}
Kodak Image Annotation Property Page	{6D940289-9F11-11CE-83FD-02608C3EC08A}
Kodak Image Annotation Control	{6D940285-9F11-11CE-83FD-02608C3EC08A}
Kodak Image Edit Property Page	{6D940284-9F11-11CE-83FD-02608C3EC08A}
Kodak Image Edit Control	{6D940280-9F11-11CE-83FD-02608C3EC08A}
Kodak Image Scan Property Page	{84926CA4-2941-101C-816F-0E6013114B7F}
Kodak Image Scan Control	{84926CA0-2941-101C-816F-0E6013114B7F}
Kodak Image Shell Extension	{1D3ECD40-C835-11CE-9888-00608CC22020}
Kodak Image Thumbnail Property Page	{E1A6B8A4-3603-101C-AC6E-040224009C02}
Kodak Image Thumbnail Control	{E1A6B8A0-3603-101C-AC6E-040224009C02}
L2TP Configuration Configuration Notify Object	{6E65CBC6-926D-11D0-8E27-00C04FC99DCF}
Label Object	{99B42120-6EC7-11CF-A6C7-00AA00A47DD2}
LAN Connection Class	{BA126ADB-2166-11D1-B1D0-00805FC1270E}
LAN Connection Manager Class	{BA126AD3-2166-11D1-B1D0-00805FC1270E}
LAN Connection Manager Connection Enumerator Class	{BA126AD4-2166-11D1-B1D0-00805FC1270E}
LAN Connection UI Class	{7007ACC5-3202-11D1-AAD2-00805FC1270E}
LceDisp Class	{ecabafbf-7f19-11d2-978e-0000f8757e2a}
LDAP Namespace Object	{228D9A82-C302-11cf-9AA4-00AA004A5691}
LDAP Provider Object	{228D9A81-C302-11cf-9AA4-00AA004A5691}

▶ ・・・・・・・・・・・・・・・・

TABLE C.1 Continued	
Object	**Class ID**
LE Callback	{65040069-0D17-11D1-B4B2-00A0244A1DD2}
Lexicon Dialog	{92655FB1-ADF9-11d1-BEB9-006008317CE8}
Lexicon Enumerator	{554667BB-7213-11cf-B210-00AA00A215ED}
LH P	{4AFBBA9A-FE10-11d0-B607-00C04FB6E866}
LH P	{4AFBBA9B-FE10-11d0-B607-00C04FB6E866}
License Manager Library	{8A6443A5-ED5A-11CF-9662-00A0C905428A}
Lighting Effect	{F1631E43-47F8-11D0-80D4-00AA006EC537}
Line 21 Decoder	{6E8D4A20-310C-11D0-B79A-00AA003767A7}
LinkPPG Class	{8B88B770-F277-11D0-A6EC-006097C9947C}
ListPad Class	{289228DE-A31E-11D1-A19C-0000F875B132}
ListView Columns Property Page Object	{C27CCE41-8596-11D1-B16A-00C0F0283628}
ListView General Property Page Object	{C27CCE3E-8596-11D1-B16A-00C0F0283628}
ListView Images Property Page Object	{C27CCE40-8596-11D1-B16A-00C0F0283628}
ListView Sort Property Page Object	{C27CCE3F-8596-11D1-B16A-00C0F0283628}
LM Auto Effect Behaivor	{BB339A46-7C49-11d2-9BF3-00C04FA34789}
LM Behavior Factory	{B1549E58-3894-11D2-BB7F-00A0C999C4C1}
LM Runtime Control	{183C259A-0480-11d1-87EA-00C04FC29D46}
LNK file thumbnail interface delegator	{500202A0-731E-11D0-B829-00C04FD706EC}
Logagent Class	{07A774A0-6047-11D1-BA20-006097D2898E}
Logging Audio Source	{B3613DA0-E26E-11d0-8FAC-08002BE4E62A}
Logical Disk Manager Administrative Service	{4FB6BB00-3347-11d0-B40A-00AA005FF586}
Logical Disk Manager Remote Client	{D485DDC0-49C6-11d1-8E56-00A0C92C9D5D}
LogUI Control	{BA634603-B771-11D0-9296-00C04FB6678B}
LogUI extnd	{31DCAB88-BB3E-11D0-9299-00C04FB6678B}
LogUI msft	{31DCAB87-BB3E-11D0-9299-00C04FB6678B}
LogUI ncsa	{31DCAB85-BB3E-11D0-9299-00C04FB6678B}
LogUI odbc	{31DCAB86-BB3E-11D0-9299-00C04FB6678B}
LogUI Property Page	{BA634604-B771-11D0-9296-00C04FB6678B}
LW Identities	{a9ae6c91-1d1b-11d2-b21a-00c04fa357fa}
Machine Debug Manager	{0C0A3666-30C9-11D0-8F20-00805F2CD064}
Machine Debug Manager	{9209B1A6-964A-11D0-9372-00A0C9034910}
MachineData Class	{2C96A89E-DA2E-11D1-BFCD-00C04FB9988E}
MachineSettings Class	{BF981FDD-B743-11D1-A69A-00C04FB9988E}
Mail Management Module	{00067800-0000-0000-C000-000000000046}
MailMsg Class	{39b16f50-a8ba-11d1-aa91-00aa006bc80b}
MakeCab Class	{8E17FFF3-C5BA-11D1-8D8A-0060088F38C8}
ManVol Class	{D82438F4-1C60-11d0-964E-00A0C905F099}

TABLE C.1 Continued	
Object	**Class ID**
ManVolLst Class	{F30A9FD3-1BC4-11d0-964E-00A0C905F099}
MAPI Search Module	{0006780A-0000-0000-C000-000000000046}
MapiCvt Class	{0006F085-0000-0000-C000-000000000046}
MAPIForm object	{41116C00-8B90-101B-96CD-00AA003B14FC}
MAPILogonRemote	{00020344-0000-0000-C000-000000000046}
MAPIPSFactory	{4D2F086C-6EA3-101B-A18A-00AA00446E07}
Marquee Control	{250770F3-6AF2-11CF-A915-008029E31FCD}
MarshalableTI Class	{466D66FA-9616-11D2-9342-0000F875AE17}
Mask Effect	{4709E4E3-6B05-11D0-80E6-00AA006EC537}
MC Euro Lexical Analyzer	{92AABF20-39C8-11D1-95F6-00C04FD57E8C}
MC Japanese Lexical Analyzer	{56EE2738-BDF7-11d1-8C28-00C04FB995C9}
mce.CCSProperties	{4E7F49AF-E4B5-11D1-8D9D-006097DBEFEF}
mce.CCSproperty	{4E7F49AD-E4B5-11D1-8D9D-006097DBEFEF}
mce.chartwizard	{4E7F49D5-E4B5-11D1-8D9D-006097DBEFEF}
mce.IMCEResource	{4E7F49B6-E4B5-11D1-8D9D-006097DBEFEF}
mce.IMCEResources	{5D62A639-0FB0-11D2-8DB2-006097DBEFEF}
mce.MiniCubeEditor	{4E7F49B8-E4B5-11D1-8D9D-006097DBEFEF}
mce.RW	{4E7F49CF-E4B5-11D1-8D9D-006097DBEFEF}
McmServer Class	{81aa123f-b564-11d1-87f8-00a0c92b500f}
MD COM Server	{BA4E57F0-FAB6-11cf-9D1A-00AA00A70D51}
MD Helper	{20ff6b80-c312-11d0-b4e4-0a0c9261445}
MDACVer.Version	{54AF9350-1923-11D3-9CA4-00C04F72C514}
MDhcp Class	{DF0DAEF2-A289-11D1-8697-006008B0E5D2}
MDM Callback	{545A2D1B-8ECB-11D1-94E8-00C04FA302A1}
MDM Utilities	{E367E1A1-E917-11d0-AF5F-00A02448799A}
MdSync Class	{C97912DE-997E-11D0-A5F6-00A0C922E752}
MDT OleUndoManager Class	{0EE708FE-94B4-11D0-9F66-00A0C9055CAC}
Media Catalog	{9B3B23C1-E236-11D0-A5C9-0080C7195D7E}
Media Catalog Group	{9B3B23C2-E236-11D0-A5C9-0080C7195D7E}
Media Catalog Moniker	{711D9B80-02F2-11D1-B244-00AA00A74BFF}
Media Catalog Path Moniker	{6CFFE322-6E97-11D1-8C1C-00C04FB995C9}
Media Clip	{00022601-0000-0000-C000-000000000046}
Media Clip	{0003000E-0000-0000-C000-000000000046}
Media Streaming Dynamic Terminal	{AED6483F-3304-11d2-86F1-006008B0E5D2}
MedSet Class	{DEAAB3B2-8AAB-11d0-8FCD-00A0C9190447}
Memory Allocator	{1E651CC0-B199-11D0-8212-00C04FC32C45}

• • • • • • • • • • • • • • • •

TABLE C.1 Continued

Object	Class ID
Menu Band	{5b4dae26-b807-11d0-9815-00c04fd91972}
Menu Desk Bar	{ECD4FC4F-521C-11D0-B792-00A0C90312E1}
Menu Shell Folder	{568804CA-CBD7-11d0-9816-00C04FD91972}
Menu Site	{E13EF4E4-D2F2-11d0-9816-00C04FD91972}
MessageMover Class	{ecabb0bf-7f19-11d2-978e-0000f8757e2a}
MessageView Class	{80F94176-FCCC-11d2-B991-00C04F8ECD78}
MetaCreations Burn Film	{107045D1-06E0-11D2-8D6D-00C04F8EF8E0}
MetaCreations Center Curls	{AA0D4D0C-06A3-11D2-8F98-00C04FB92EB7}
MetaCreations Color Fade	{2A54C908-07AA-11D2-8D6D-00C04F8EF8E0}
MetaCreations Curls	{AA0D4D0E-06A3-11D2-8F98-00C04FB92EB7}
MetaCreations Curtains	{AA0D4D12-06A3-11D2-8F98-00C04FB92EB7}
MetaCreations Fade White	{107045CC-06E0-11D2-8D6D-00C04F8EF8E0}
MetaCreations Flow Motion	{2A54C90B-07AA-11D2-8D6D-00C04F8EF8E0}
MetaCreations Glass Block	{2A54C913-07AA-11D2-8D6D-00C04F8EF8E0}
MetaCreations Grid	{2A54C911-07AA-11D2-8D6D-00C04F8EF8E0}
MetaCreations Jaws	{2A54C904-07AA-11D2-8D6D-00C04F8EF8E0}
MetaCreations Lens	{107045CA-06E0-11D2-8D6D-00C04F8EF8E0}
MetaCreations Light Wipe	{107045C8-06E0-11D2-8D6D-00C04F8EF8E0}
MetaCreations Liquid	{AA0D4D0A-06A3-11D2-8F98-00C04FB92EB7}
MetaCreations Page Curl	{AA0D4D08-06A3-11D2-8F98-00C04FB92EB7}
MetaCreations Peel ABCD	{AA0D4D10-06A3-11D2-8F98-00C04FB92EB7}
MetaCreations Ripple	{AA0D4D03-06A3-11D2-8F98-00C04FB92EB7}
MetaCreations Roll Down	{9C61F46E-0530-11D2-8F98-00C04FB92EB7}
MetaCreations Threshold	{2A54C915-07AA-11D2-8D6D-00C04F8EF8E0}
MetaCreations Twister	{107045CF-06E0-11D2-8D6D-00C04F8EF8E0}
MetaCreations Vacuum	{2A54C90D-07AA-11D2-8D6D-00C04F8EF8E0}
MetaCreations Water	{107045C5-06E0-11D2-8D6D-00C04F8EF8E0}
MetaCreations Wormhole	{0E6AE022-0C83-11D2-8CD4-00104BC75D9A}
MetaStream	{60A0C080-E505-11D1-AA1C-00600895FB99}
MHTML Asychronous Pluggable Protocol Handler	{05300401-BCBC-11d0-85E3-00C04FD85AB4}
MHTML Document	{3050F3D9-98B5-11CF-BB82-00AA00BDCE0B}
Microphone Setup Wizard	{B9F11A95-90E3-11d0-8D77-00A0C9034A7E}
Microsft SQLServer Merge Replication Provider	{777D3984-11A3-11D0-A11A-00AA003E4672}
Microsoft Access Application	{73A4C9C1-D68D-11D0-98BF-00A0C90DC8D9}

Object	**Class ID**
TABLE C.1 Continued	
Microsoft Active Setup Engine	{6E449686-C509-11CF-AAFA-00AA00B6015C}
Microsoft Add-In Authouring Designer	{AC0714F7-3D04-11D1-AE7D-00A0C90F26F4}
Microsoft Agent Character Property Sheet Handler	{143A62C8-C33B-11D1-84FE-00C04FA34A14}
Microsoft Agent Control 1.5	{F5BE8BD2-7DE6-11D0-91FE-00C04FD701A5}
Microsoft Agent Control 2.0	{D45FD31B-5C6E-11D1-9EC1-00C04FD7081F}
Microsoft Agent DocFile Provider 1.5	{BB64DF2F-88E4-11D0-9E87-00C04FD7081F}
Microsoft Agent DocFile Provider 2.0	{D45FD2FF-5C6E-11D1-9EC1-00C04FD7081F}
Microsoft Agent File Provider 2.0	{D45FD300-5C6E-11D1-9EC1-00C04FD7081F}
Microsoft Agent Flat File Provider 2.0	{D45FD301-5C6E-11D1-9EC1-00C04FD7081F}
Microsoft Agent International DLL for Language 0x0406	{C3480406-A7F8-11D1-AA75-00C04FA34D72}
Microsoft Agent International DLL for Language 0x0407	{C3480407-A7F8-11D1-AA75-00C04FA34D72}
Microsoft Agent International DLL for Language 0x0409	{C3480409-A7F8-11D1-AA75-00C04FA34D72}
Microsoft Agent International DLL for Language 0x040b	{C348040B-A7F8-11D1-AA75-00C04FA34D72}
Microsoft Agent International DLL for Language 0x040c	{C348040C-A7F8-11D1-AA75-00C04FA34D72}
Microsoft Agent International DLL for Language 0x0410	{C3480410-A7F8-11D1-AA75-00C04FA34D72}
Microsoft Agent International DLL for Language 0x0413	{C3480413-A7F8-11D1-AA75-00C04FA34D72}
Microsoft Agent International DLL for Language 0x0414	{C3480414-A7F8-11D1-AA75-00C04FA34D72}
Microsoft Agent International DLL for Language 0x0416	{C3480416-A7F8-11D1-AA75-00C04FA34D72}
Microsoft Agent International DLL for Language 0x041d	{C348041D-A7F8-11D1-AA75-00C04FA34D72}
Microsoft Agent International DLL for Language 0x0816	{C3480816-A7F8-11D1-AA75-00C04FA34D72}
Microsoft Agent International DLL for Language 0x0c0a	{C3480C0A-A7F8-11D1-AA75-00C04FA34D72}
Microsoft Agent Server 1.5	{A7B93C92-7B81-11D0-AC5F-00C04FD97575}
Microsoft Agent Server 2.0	{D45FD2FC-5C6E-11D1-9EC1-00C04FD7081F}
Microsoft Agent Voice Command Module Class	{0FA9F4D5-A173-11D1-AA62-00C04FA34D72}
Microsoft AutoComplete	{00BB2763-6A77-11D0-A535-00C04FD7D062}
Microsoft AVI Files	{00020000-0000-0000-C000-000000000046}
Microsoft Browser Architecture	{A5E46E3A-8849-11D1-9D8C-00C04FC99D61}
Microsoft BrowserBand	{7BA4C742-9E81-11CF-99D3-00AA004AE837}

●●●●●●●●●●●●●●●●●

TABLE C.1 Continued

Object	Class ID
Microsoft Certificate Authority Control	{0996FF6F-B6A1-11D0-9292-00C04FB6678B}
Microsoft Certificate Mapping Control	{BBD8F29B-6F61-11D0-A26E-08002B2C6F32}
Microsoft Client Configuration Notify Object	{57C06EAA-8784-11D0-83D4-00A0C911E5DF}
Microsoft Clip Gallery	{00021290-0000-0000-C000-000000000046}
Microsoft ClipArt Gallery	{00030026-0000-0000-C000-000000000046}
Microsoft COM+ Services Meta Data	{063B79F5-7539-11D2-9773-00A0C9B4D50C}
Microsoft COM+ Services Meta Data	{063B79F6-7539-11D2-9773-00A0C9B4D50C}
Microsoft CommBand	{4D5C8C2A-D075-11d0-B416-00C04FB90376}
Microsoft Common Browser Architecture	{AF604EFE-8897-11D1-B944-00A0C90312E1}
Microsoft CopyTo Service	{C2FBB630-2971-11d1-A18C-00C04FD75D13}
Microsoft CrSource 4.0	{65014010-9F62-11d1-A651-00600811D5CE}
Microsoft Data Tools Database Designer	{E9B0E6D4-811C-11D0-AD51-00A0C90F5739}
Microsoft Data Tools Database Designer Oracle Index Property Page	{E9B0E6C3-811C-11D0-AD51-00A0C90F5739}
Microsoft Data Tools Database Designer Oracle Relationship Property Page	{E9B0E6C1-811C-11D0-AD51-00A0C90F5739}
Microsoft Data Tools Database Designer Oracle Table Property Page	{E9B0E6C0-811C-11D0-AD51-00A0C90F5739}
Microsoft Data Tools Database Designer SQL Server Extra Column Properties Property Page	{4656BAE3-F397-11CE-BFE1-00AA0057B34E}
Microsoft Data Tools Database Designer SQL Server Index Property Page	{E9B0E6D8-811C-11D0-AD51-00A0C90F5739}
Microsoft Data Tools Database Designer SQL Server Relationship Property Page	{E9B0E6D6-811C-11D0-AD51-00A0C90F5739}
Microsoft Data Tools Database Designer SQL Server Table Browsing Property Page	{4656BAE4-F397-11CE-BFE1-00AA0057B34E}
Microsoft Data Tools Database Designer SQL Server Table Property Page	{E9B0E6D5-811C-11D0-AD51-00A0C90F5739}
Microsoft Data Tools DSRef Object	{E9B0E6DB-811C-11D0-AD51-00A0C90F5739}
Microsoft Data Tools Query Designer	{E9B0E6CB-811C-11D0-AD51-00A0C90F5739}
Microsoft Data Tools Query Designer Definition Proxy	{E9B0E6CC-811C-11D0-AD51-00A0C90F5739}
Microsoft Data Tools Query Designer General property page	{4656BAE5-F397-11CE-BFE1-00AA0057B34E}
Microsoft Data Tools Query Designer Join Line property page	{E9B0E6D2-811C-11D0-AD51-00A0C90F5739}
Microsoft Data Tools Query Designer ODBC Personality	{E9B0E6D3-811C-11D0-AD51-00A0C90F5739}
Microsoft Data Tools Query Designer ORC Personality	{4656BB33-F397-11CE-BFE1-00AA0057B34E}

TABLE C.1 Continued	
Object	**Class ID**
Microsoft Data Tools Query Designer Parameters property page	{E9B0E6D1-811C-11D0-AD51-00A0C90F5739}
Microsoft Data Tools Query Designer Query property page	{E9B0E6D0-811C-11D0-AD51-00A0C90F5739}
Microsoft Data Tools Query Designer SSV Personality	{A92CC3E4-E7C4-11CE-A47B-00AA005119FB}
Microsoft Development Environment	{73AA8F59-DBC4-11D0-AF5C-00A02448799A}
Microsoft Development Environment	{B2104A32-2AE8-11D1-8EC0-00A0C90F26EA}
Microsoft DirectAnimation Control	{B6FFC24C-7E13-11D0-9B47-00C04FC2F51D}
Microsoft DirectAnimation Path	{D7A7D7C3-D47F-11D0-89D3-00A0C90833E6}
Microsoft DirectAnimation Sequence	{4F241DB1-EE9F-11D0-9824-006097C99E51}
Microsoft DirectAnimation Sequencer	{B0A6BAE2-AAF0-11D0-A152-00A0C908DB96}
Microsoft DirectAnimation Sprite	{FD179533-D86E-11D0-89D6-00A0C90833E6}
Microsoft DirectAnimation Structured Graphics	{369303C2-D7AC-11D0-89D5-00A0C90833E6}
Microsoft DirectAnimation Windowed Control	{69AD90EF-1C20-11d1-8801-00C04FC29D46}
Microsoft DirectInput Device Object	{25E609E1-B259-11CF-BFC7-444553540000}
Microsoft DirectInput Object	{25E609E0-B259-11CF-BFC7-444553540000}
Microsoft Disk Quota	{7988B571-EC89-11cf-9C00-00AA00A14F56}
Microsoft Disk Quota UI	{7988B573-EC89-11cf-9C00-00AA00A14F56}
Microsoft DocHost User Interface Handler	{7057e952-bd1b-11d1-8919-00c04fc2c836}
Microsoft Docking Bar Property Bag	{4AF4A5FC-912A-11D1-B945-00A0C90312E1}
Microsoft Drawing	{00030007-0000-0000-C000-000000000046}
Microsoft DT DDS Circular Auto Layout Logic 2	{B0406342-B0C5-11d0-89A9-00A0C9054129}
Microsoft DT DDS Form 2.0	{105B80D2-95F1-11D0-B0A0-00AA00BDCB5C}
Microsoft DT DDS OrgChart GDD	{4CECCEB4-8359-11D0-A34E-00AA00BD-CDFD}
Microsoft DT DDS OrgChart GDD Layout	{4CECCEB1-8359-11D0-A34E-00AA00BD-CDFD}
Microsoft DT DDS OrgChart GDD Route	{4CECCEB2-8359-11D0-A34E-00AA00BD-CDFD}
Microsoft DT DDS Rectilinear GDD	{1F7DD4F1-CAC3-11D0-A35B-00AA00BD-CDFD}
Microsoft DT DDS Rectilinear GDD Layout	{1F7DD4F2-CAC3-11D0-A35B-00AA00BD-CDFD}
Microsoft DT DDS Rectilinear GDD Route	{1F7DD4F3-CAC3-11D0-A35B-00AA00BD-CDFD}
Microsoft DT DDS Straight Line Routing Logic 2	{B0406343-B0C5-11d0-89A9-00A0C9054129}

....

TABLE C.1   Continued

Object	Class ID
Microsoft DT DDSform 2.1 Font	{105B80E0-95F1-11D0-B0A0-00AA00BDCB5C}
Microsoft DT DDSform 2.1 FontNew	{105B80DE-95F1-11D0-B0A0-00AA00BDCB5C}
Microsoft DT DDSform 2.1 FormPackage	{105B80D5-95F1-11D0-B0A0-00AA00BDCB5C}
Microsoft DT Diagram Surface 2	{B0406340-B0C5-11d0-89A9-00A0C9054129}
Microsoft DT Icon Control	{d24d4450-1f01-11d1-8e63-006097d2df48}
Microsoft DT Label Control	{d24d4451-1f01-11d1-8e63-006097d2df48}
Microsoft DT PolyLine Control 2	{D24D4453-1F01-11d1-8E63-006097D2DF48}
Microsoft DT Simple Graphic Diagram Data 2	{B0406344-B0C5-11d0-89A9-00A0C9054129}
Microsoft DTC Transaction	{39F8D76B-0928-11D1-97DF-00C04FB9618A}
Microsoft DTC Transaction Manager	{5B18AB61-091D-11D1-97DF-00C04FB9618A}
Microsoft DTC Transaction Manager Proxy (private, internal)	{5D9DD151-65F4-11CE-900D-00AA00445589}
Microsoft DTC Transaction Unmarshaller (private, internal)	{193B4137-0480-11D1-97DA-00C04FB9618A}
Microsoft Equation	{0003000B-0000-0000-C000-000000000046}
Microsoft Equation 2.0	{00021700-0000-0000-C000-000000000046}
Microsoft Equation 3.0	{0002CE02-0000-0000-C000-000000000046}
Microsoft Excel 4.0 Macro	{00030002-0000-0000-C000-000000000046}
Microsoft Excel Application	{00020812-0000-0000-C000-000000000046}
Microsoft Excel Application	{00024500-0000-0000-C000-000000000046}
Microsoft Excel Chart	{00020811-0000-0000-C000-000000000046}
Microsoft Excel Chart	{00020821-0000-0000-C000-000000000046}
Microsoft Excel Chart	{00030001-0000-0000-C000-000000000046}
Microsoft Excel Worksheet	{00020810-0000-0000-C000-000000000046}
Microsoft Excel Worksheet	{00020820-0000-0000-C000-000000000046}
Microsoft Exchange Events	{2F42C693-C6A4-11D0-93E9-00AA0064D470}
Microsoft FlexGrid Control, version 6.0	{6262D3A0-531B-11CF-91F6-C2863C385E30}
Microsoft Forms 2.0 CheckBox	{8BD21D40-EC42-11CE-9E0D-00AA006002F3}
Microsoft Forms 2.0 ComboBox	{8BD21D30-EC42-11CE-9E0D-00AA006002F3}
Microsoft Forms 2.0 CommandButton	{D7053240-CE69-11CD-A777-00DD01143C57}
Microsoft Forms 2.0 Form	{C62A69F0-16DC-11CE-9E98-00AA00574A4F}
Microsoft Forms 2.0 Frame	{6E182020-F460-11CE-9BCD-00AA00608E01}
Microsoft Forms 2.0 HTML CHECKBOX	{5512D116-5CC6-11CF-8D67-00AA00BDCE1D}
Microsoft Forms 2.0 HTML Hidden	{5512D11C-5CC6-11CF-8D67-00AA00BDCE1D}

| **TABLE C.1** | Continued |

Object	Class ID
Microsoft Forms 2.0 HTML IMAGE	{5512D112-5CC6-11CF-8D67-00AA00BDCE1D}
Microsoft Forms 2.0 HTML OPTION	{5512D118-5CC6-11CF-8D67-00AA00BDCE1D}
Microsoft Forms 2.0 HTML Password	{5512D11E-5CC6-11CF-8D67-00AA00BDCE1D}
Microsoft Forms 2.0 HTML RESET	{5512D114-5CC6-11CF-8D67-00AA00BDCE1D}
Microsoft Forms 2.0 HTML SELECT	{5512D122-5CC6-11CF-8D67-00AA00BDCE1D}
Microsoft Forms 2.0 HTML SUBMIT	{5512D110-5CC6-11CF-8D67-00AA00BDCE1D}
Microsoft Forms 2.0 HTML TEXT	{5512D11A-5CC6-11CF-8D67-00AA00BDCE1D}
Microsoft Forms 2.0 HTML TextAREA	{5512D124-5CC6-11CF-8D67-00AA00BDCE1D}
Microsoft Forms 2.0 Image	{4C599241-6926-101B-9992-00000B65C6F9}
Microsoft Forms 2.0 Label	{978C9E23-D4B0-11CE-BF2D-00AA003F40D0}
Microsoft Forms 2.0 ListBox	{8BD21D20-EC42-11CE-9E0D-00AA006002F3}
Microsoft Forms 2.0 MultiPage	{46E31370-3F7A-11CE-BED6-00AA00611080}
Microsoft Forms 2.0 OptionButton	{8BD21D50-EC42-11CE-9E0D-00AA006002F3}
Microsoft Forms 2.0 ScrollBar	{DFD181E0-5E2F-11CE-A449-00AA004A803D}
Microsoft Forms 2.0 SpinButton	{79176FB0-B7F2-11CE-97EF-00AA006D2776}
Microsoft Forms 2.0 TabStrip	{EAE50EB0-4A62-11CE-BED6-00AA00611080}
Microsoft Forms 2.0 TextBox	{8BD21D10-EC42-11CE-9E0D-00AA006002F3}
Microsoft Forms 2.0 ToggleButton	{8BD21D60-EC42-11CE-9E0D-00AA006002F3}
Microsoft Forms 2.1 ControlPalette	{338E9310-7C07-11CE-8CA9-00AA0044BB60}
Microsoft Forms 2.1 ControlSelector	{7CBBABF0-36B9-11CE-BF0D-00AA0044BB60}
Microsoft Forms 2.1 DataObject	{1C3B4210-F441-11CE-B9EA-00AA006B1A69}
Microsoft Forms 2.1 Font	{972C4270-11FD-11CE-B841-00AA004CD6D8}
Microsoft Forms 2.1 FontNew	{AFC20920-DA4E-11CE-B943-00AA006887B4}
Microsoft Forms 2.1 FormPackage	{AC9F2F90-E877-11CE-9F68-00AA00574A4F}
Microsoft Forms 2.1 Picture	{D14E3180-11FD-11CE-B841-00AA004CD6D8}
Microsoft Forms 2.1 SubForm95	{5728F10E-27CC-101B-A8EF-00000B65C5F8}
Microsoft Forms 2.1 Toolbox	{F748B5F0-15D0-11CE-BF0D-00AA0044BB60}
Microsoft FrontPage Application	{04DF1015-7007-11D1-83BC-006097ABE675}
Microsoft FTP Folder	{63da6ec0-2e98-11cf-8d82-444553540000}

• • • • • • • • • • • • • • • • •

TABLE C.1   Continued

Object	Class ID
Microsoft Graph 2000 Application	{00020800-0000-0000-C000-000000000046}
Microsoft Graph 2000 Application	{00024502-0000-0000-C000-000000000046}
Microsoft Graph 2000 Chart	{00020803-0000-0000-C000-000000000046}
Microsoft Group Extension	{94a909a5-6f52-11d1-8c18-00c04fd8d503}
Microsoft History AutoComplete List	{00BB2764-6A77-11D0-A535-00C04FD7D062}
Microsoft HTML About Pluggable Protocol	{3050F406-98B5-11CF-BB82-00AA00BDCE0B}
Microsoft HTML Anchor Page	{3050F1FC-98B5-11CF-BB82-00AA00BDCE0B}
Microsoft HTML Background Page	{3050F232-98B5-11CF-BB82-00AA00BDCE0B}
Microsoft Html Component	{3050f4f8-98b5-11cf-bb82-00aa00bdce0b}
Microsoft HTML Document 5.0	{25336921-03F9-11CF-8FD0-00AA00686F13}
Microsoft HTML DwnBindInfo	{3050F3C2-98B5-11CF-BB82-00AA00BDCE0B}
Microsoft HTML Generic Page	{3050F17F-98B5-11CF-BB82-00AA00BDCE0B}
Microsoft HTML Inline Style Page	{3050F296-98B5-11CF-BB82-00AA00BDCE0B}
Microsoft HTML Javascript Pluggable Protocol	{3050F3B2-98B5-11CF-BB82-00AA00BDCE0B}
Microsoft HTML Load Options	{18845040-0fa5-11d1-ba19-00c04fd912d0}
Microsoft HTML Mailto Pluggable Protocol	{3050f3DA-98B5-11CF-BB82-00AA00BDCE0B}
Microsoft HTML Recalc	{3050f499-98b5-11cf-bb82-00aa00bdce0b}
Microsoft HTML Resource Pluggable Protocol	{3050F3BC-98B5-11CF-BB82-00AA00BDCE0B}
Microsoft HTML Resource Pluggable Protocol	{76E67A63-06E9-11D2-A840-006008059382}
Microsoft HTML Server Document 5.0	{3050f4e7-98b5-11cf-bb82-00aa00bdce0b}
Microsoft HTML Window Security Proxy	{3050F391-98B5-11CF-BB82-00AA00BDCE0B}
Microsoft ImageComboBox Control, version 6.0	{DD9DA666-8594-11D1-B16A-00C0F0283628}
Microsoft ImageList Control, version 6.0	{2C247F23-8591-11D1-B16A-00C0F0283628}
Microsoft Imager 1.0 Picture	{0004749F-0000-0000-C000-000000000046}
Microsoft Imager 2.0 Picture	{E71AF890-4F3E-11CE-9872-0020AF68053F}
Microsoft Index Server Administration Object	{3BC4F3A1-652A-11D1-B4D4-00C04FC2DB8D}
Microsoft Index Server Catalog Administration Object	{3BC4F3A3-652A-11D1-B4D4-00C04FC2DB8D}
Microsoft Index Server Scope Administration Object	{3BC4F3A7-652A-11D1-B4D4-00C04FC2DB8D}
Microsoft InfoTech IStorage for Win32 Files	{D54EEE56-AAAB-11D0-9E1D-00A0C922E6EC}
Microsoft InfoTech IStorage System	{5D02926A-212E-11D0-9DF9-00A0C922E6EC}
Microsoft InfoTech Protocol for IE 3.0	{9D148290-B9C8-11D0-A4CC-0000F80149F6}
Microsoft InfoTech Protocols for IE 4.0	{9D148291-B9C8-11D0-A4CC-0000F80149F6}
Microsoft In-Memory Database Client Connection	{3A94E09D-EC46-11d1-A7EC-0000F8758EAA}
Microsoft In-Memory Database Proxy Connection Manager	{92A315C9-7B1E-11d2-84A2-00C04F990690}

TABLE C.1   Continued

Object	Class ID
Microsoft In-Memory Database Transacted Property	{6A8DEEA9-4101-11D2-912C-0000F8758E8D}
Microsoft In-Memory Database Transacted Property Group	{46DB591F-4101-11D2-912C-0000F8758E8D}
Microsoft In-Memory Database Transacted Property Group Manager	{DEBCE1BC-7D7E-11D2-BEA0-00805F0D8F97}
Microsoft Internet Toolbar	{5E6AB780-7743-11CF-A12B-00AA004AE837}
Microsoft JET 4.0 Briefcase Reconciler	{CC2C83A6-9BE4-11D0-98E7-00C04FC2CAF5}
Microsoft Jet 4.0 OLE DB Provider Error Lookup	{dee35071-506b-11cf-b1aa-00aa00b8de95}
Microsoft Jet 4.0 OLE DB ProviderError Lookup	{dee35070-506b-11cf-b1aa-00aa00b8de95}
Microsoft ListView Control, version 6.0	{BDD1F04B-858B-11D1-B16A-00C0F0283628}
Microsoft Local Troubleshooter	{4B106874-DD36-11D0-8B44-00A024DD9EFF}
Microsoft Local Troubleshooter Property Page	{4B106875-DD36-11D0-8B44-00A024DD9EFF}
Microsoft Local Users and Groups MMC Snap-in	{5D6179C8-17EC-11D1-9AA9-00C04FD8FE93}
Microsoft Local Users and Groups MMC Snap-in About Provider	{5D6179D2-17EC-11D1-9AA9-00C04FD8FE93}
Microsoft Locality Extension	{2dfb3a35-6071-11d1-8c13-00c04fd8d503}
Microsoft Map	{0002CC1F-0000-0000-C000-000000000046}
Microsoft MoveTo Service	{C2FBB631-2971-11d1-A18C-00C04FD75D13}
Microsoft MPEG-4 Video Decompressor	{82CCD3E0-F71A-11D0-9FE5-00609778EA66}
Microsoft MPEG-4 Video Decompressor About Page	{075BB8A1-B7D8-11D2-A1C6-00609778EA66}
Microsoft MPEG-4 Video Decompressor Property page	{598EBA02-B49A-11D2-A1C1-00609778EA66}
Microsoft MS Audio Decompressor Control Property page	{8FE7E181-BB96-11D2-A1CB-00609778EA66}
Microsoft Multiple AutoComplete List Container	{00BB2765-6A77-11D0-A535-00C04FD7D062}
Microsoft NetMeeting Applet Object	{8C3ADF99-CCFE-11d2-AD10-00C04F72DD47}
Microsoft NetMeeting Installable Codecs	{8ED14CC0-7A1F-11d0-92F6-00A0C922E6B2}
Microsoft NetMeeting Manager Object	{068B0700-718C-11d0-8B1A-00A0C91BC90E}
Microsoft NetMeeting Manager Object 3	{068B0800-718C-11d0-8B1A-00A0C91BC90E}
Microsoft NetMeeting Quality of Service	{085C06A0-3CAA-11d0-A00E-00A024A85A2C}
Microsoft NetShow 2.0 Real-Time Encoder Proxy	{369AF85F-BFF7-11D0-A5DA-00AA00BF93E3}
Microsoft NetShow Color Dialog	{A8A49CCE-964F-11D0-8D71-00A0C92B500F}
Microsoft NetShow File Dialog	{B1F1A325-9601-11d0-8D70-00A0C92B500F}
Microsoft NetShow Path Dialog	{6BF191E1-9BF9-11d0-B047-0000C040BCDB}
Microsoft NetShow Player	{2179C5D3-EBFF-11CF-B6FD-00AA00B4E220}
Microsoft New Object Service	{D969A300-E7FF-11d0-A93B-00A0C90F2719}
Microsoft NsPptRex Control	{4037AE54-C812-11D1-9A88-00A0C9AF2B78}
Microsoft NT DS Class Associations Provider for WBEM	{33831ED4-42B8-11D2-93AD-00805F853771}

| **TABLE C.1** | Continued |

Object	Class ID
Microsoft NT DS Class Provider for WBEM	{1EF94880-01A8-11D2-A90B-00AA00BF3363}
Microsoft NT DS Instance Provider for WBEM	{AA527A40-4D9A-11D2-93AD-00805F853771}
Microsoft Office	{F1D3FF84-4329-322A-E52D-0020AFC36E79}
Microsoft Office 9	{000C0114-0000-0000-C000-000000000046}
Microsoft Office 9	{B722BCCD-4E68-101B-A2BC-00AA00404770}
Microsoft Office Binder	{59850400-6664-101B-B21C-00AA004BA90B}
Microsoft Office Binder Briefcase Notifier	{59850404-6664-101B-B21C-00AA004BA90B}
Microsoft Office Binder Briefcase Reconciler	{59850403-6664-101B-B21C-00AA004BA90B}
Microsoft Office Binder Unbind	{59850401-6664-101B-B21C-00AA004BA90B}
Microsoft Office Chart 9.0	{0002E500-0000-0000-C000-000000000046}
Microsoft Office Data Source Control 9.0	{0002E530-0000-0000-C000-000000000046}
Microsoft Office Expand Control 9.0	{0002E532-0000-0000-C000-000000000046}
Microsoft Office Field List 9.0	{4C85388F-1500-11D1-A0DF-00C04FC9E20F}
Microsoft Office Filter	{f07f3920-7b8c-11cf-9be8-00aa004b9986}
Microsoft Office Persistent Handler	{98de59a0-d175-11cd-a7bd-00006b827d94}
Microsoft Office PivotTable 9.0	{0002E520-0000-0000-C000-000000000046}
Microsoft Office Record Navigation Control 9.0	{0002E531-0000-0000-C000-000000000046}
Microsoft Office Spreadsheet 9.0	{0002E510-0000-0000-C000-000000000046}
Microsoft Office UA Control	{8936033C-4A50-11D1-98A4-00A0C90F27C6}
Microsoft OLE DB Data Conversion Library	{c8b522d1-5cf3-11ce-ade5-00aa0044773d}
Microsoft OLE DB Error Collection Service	{C8B522CF-5CF3-11CE-ADE5-00AA0044773D}
Microsoft OLE DB Moniker Binder for Internet Publishing	{E1D2BF42-A96B-11d1-9C6B-0000F875AC61}
Microsoft OLE DB Root Binder for Internet Publishing	{FF151822-B0BF-11D1-A80D-000000000000}
Microsoft OLE DB Root Enumerator	{c8b522d0-5cf3-11ce-ade5-00aa0044773d}
Microsoft OLE DB Row Position Library	{2048EEE6-7FA2-11D0-9E6A-00A0C9138C29}
Microsoft OLE DB Service Component Data Links	{2206CDB2-19C1-11D1-89E0-00C04FD7A829}
Microsoft Organization Chart 1.0	{00041943-0000-0000-C000-000000000046}
Microsoft Organization Extension	{dccc0bed-6066-11d1-8c13-00c04fd8d503}
Microsoft OrganizationUnit Extension	{fd8d3a5f-6066-11d1-8c13-00c04fd8d503}
Microsoft Outlook	{00020D75-0000-0000-C000-000000000046}
Microsoft Outlook	{0006F03A-0000-0000-C000-000000000046}
Microsoft Outlook 8.0 Object Library	{0006F033-0000-0000-C000-000000000046}
Microsoft Outlook Envelope Object	{0006F01A-0000-0000-C000-000000000046}
Microsoft PCM Audio Mixer	{CDCDD6A0-C016-11D0-82A4-00AA00B5CA1B}
Microsoft Photo Editor 3.0 Photo	{11943940-36DE-11CF-953E-00C0A84029E9}
Microsoft Photo Editor 3.0 Scan	{11943941-36DE-11CF-953E-00C0A84029E9}
Microsoft Picture It! Event Manager	{A04FABD8-98F7-11D1-A0F4-00C04FB67CF6}

TABLE C.1 Continued	
Object	**Class ID**
Microsoft Picture It! Event Manager	{A04FABD9-98F7-11D1-A0F4-00C04FB67CF6}
Microsoft Picture It! Event Manager	{A04FABDA-98F7-11D1-A0F4-00C04FB67CF6}
Microsoft Picture It! Event Manager	{A04FABDB-98F7-11D1-A0F4-00C04FB67CF6}
Microsoft Picture It! Event Manager	{A04FABDC-98F7-11D1-A0F4-00C04FB67CF6}
Microsoft Picture It! Event Manager	{A04FABDD-98F7-11D1-A0F4-00C04FB67CF6}
Microsoft Picture It! Event Manager	{A04FABDE-98F7-11D1-A0F4-00C04FB67CF6}
Microsoft Picture It! Event Manager	{A04FABDF-98F7-11D1-A0F4-00C04FB67CF6}
Microsoft Picture It! Event Manager	{A04FABE1-98F7-11D1-A0F4-00C04FB67CF6}
Microsoft Picture It! Event Manager	{A04FABE2-98F7-11D1-A0F4-00C04FB67CF6}
Microsoft Picture It! Event Manager	{A04FABE3-98F7-11D1-A0F4-00C04FB67CF6}
Microsoft Picture It! Event Manager	{A04FABE4-98F7-11D1-A0F4-00C04FB67CF6}
Microsoft Picture It! Picture	{01C3D4A0-A701-11D1-8324-00A024CAA292}
Microsoft Picture It! Picture	{01C3D4A1-A701-11D1-8324-00A024CAA292}
Microsoft Picture It! Picture	{01C3D4A2-A701-11D1-8324-00A024CAA292}
Microsoft Picture It! Picture	{01C3D4A3-A701-11D1-8324-00A024CAA292}
Microsoft Picture It! Picture	{01C3D4A4-A701-11D1-8324-00A024CAA292}
Microsoft Picture It! Picture	{01C3D4A5-A701-11D1-8324-00A024CAA292}
Microsoft Picture It! Picture	{01C3D4A6-A701-11D1-8324-00A024CAA292}
Microsoft Picture It! Picture	{01C3D4A7-A701-11D1-8324-00A024CAA292}
Microsoft Picture It! Picture	{01C3D4A8-A701-11D1-8324-00A024CAA292}
Microsoft Picture It! Picture	{85980D04-9851-11D1-A0F4-00C04FB67CF6}
Microsoft Picture It! Picture	{85980D05-9851-11D1-A0F4-00C04FB67CF6}
Microsoft Picture It! Picture	{85980D06-9851-11D1-A0F4-00C04FB67CF6}
Microsoft Picture It! Picture	{85980D07-9851-11D1-A0F4-00C04FB67CF6}
Microsoft Picture It! Picture	{85980D08-9851-11D1-A0F4-00C04FB67CF6}
Microsoft Picture It! Picture	{85980D13-9851-11D1-A0F4-00C04FB67CF6}
Microsoft Picture It! Picture	{85980D14-9851-11D1-A0F4-00C04FB67CF6}
Microsoft Picture It! Picture	{85980D15-9851-11D1-A0F4-00C04FB67CF6}
Microsoft Picture It! Picture	{85980D16-9851-11D1-A0F4-00C04FB67CF6}
Microsoft Picture It! Picture	{85980D17-9851-11D1-A0F4-00C04FB67CF6}
Microsoft Picture It! Picture	{85980D18-9851-11D1-A0F4-00C04FB67CF6}
Microsoft Picture It! Picture	{85980D19-9851-11D1-A0F4-00C04FB67CF6}
Microsoft Picture It! Picture	{85980D1A-9851-11D1-A0F4-00C04FB67CF6}
Microsoft Picture It! Picture	{85980D1B-9851-11D1-A0F4-00C04FB67CF6}
Microsoft Picture It! Picture	{85980D1C-9851-11D1-A0F4-00C04FB67CF6}
Microsoft Picture It! Picture	{85980D1D-9851-11D1-A0F4-00C04FB67CF6}
Microsoft Picture It! Picture	{85980D1E-9851-11D1-A0F4-00C04FB67CF6}
Microsoft Picture It! Picture	{85980D1F-9851-11D1-A0F4-00C04FB67CF6}

TABLE C.1 Continued

Object	Class ID
Microsoft Picture It! Picture	{85980D20-9851-11D1-A0F4-00C04FB67CF6}
Microsoft Picture It! Picture	{85980D22-9851-11D1-A0F4-00C04FB67CF6}
Microsoft Picture It! Picture	{85980D23-9851-11D1-A0F4-00C04FB67CF6}
Microsoft Picture It! Picture	{85980D24-9851-11D1-A0F4-00C04FB67CF6}
Microsoft Picture It! Picture	{85980D25-9851-11D1-A0F4-00C04FB67CF6}
Microsoft Picture It! Picture	{85980D26-9851-11D1-A0F4-00C04FB67CF6}
Microsoft Picture It! Picture	{85980D27-9851-11D1-A0F4-00C04FB67CF6}
Microsoft Picture It! Picture	{85980D28-9851-11D1-A0F4-00C04FB67CF6}
Microsoft Picture It! Picture	{85980D29-9851-11D1-A0F4-00C04FB67CF6}
Microsoft Picture It! Picture	{85980D2A-9851-11D1-A0F4-00C04FB67CF6}
Microsoft Picture It! Picture	{85980D2B-9851-11D1-A0F4-00C04FB67CF6}
Microsoft Picture It! Picture	{85980D2C-9851-11D1-A0F4-00C04FB67CF6}
Microsoft Picture It! Picture	{8931FAC9-A4C7-11D1-A0FD-00C04FB67CF6}
Microsoft Picture It! Picture	{8931FACB-A4C7-11D1-A0FD-00C04FB67CF6}
Microsoft Powerpoint Application	{91493441-5A91-11CF-8700-00AA0060263B}
Microsoft PowerPoint Presentation	{64818D10-4F9B-11CF-86EA-00AA00B929E8}
Microsoft PowerPoint Slide	{64818D11-4F9B-11CF-86EA-00AA00B929E8}
Microsoft PptNsRex Control	{9D47D76B-FA6F-11D1-ACC1-00A0C9AF2D2A}
Microsoft PrintQueue Extension	{9f37f39c-6f49-11d1-8c18-00c04fd8d503}
Microsoft ProgressBar Control, version 6.0	{35053A22-8589-11D1-B16A-00C0F0283628}
Microsoft SAP Agent Notify Object	{B45AFEC0-2AE6-11D1-859E-00C04FC9E292}
Microsoft Schedule+ 7.0 Application	{0482E074-C5B7-101A-82E0-08002B36A333}
Microsoft Schedule+ 7.0 Library	{800DD100-DB43-11CE-914E-00A004000162}
Microsoft Script Editor Proxy	{000C1205-0000-0000-C000-000000000046}
Microsoft Scriptlet Component	{AE24FDAE-03C6-11D1-8B76-0080C744F389}
Microsoft Scriptlet Element Behavior Handler	{5AAF51B2-B1F0-11d1-B6AB-00A0C90833E9}
Microsoft Scriptlet HiFiTimer Uses	{5AAF51B3-B1F0-11d1-B6AB-00A0C90833E9}
Microsoft Scriptlet svr om Uses	{3050f4f0-98b5-11cf-bb82-00aa00bdce0b}
Microsoft SearchBand	{30D02401-6A81-11d0-8274-00C04FD5AE38}
Microsoft SendTo Service	{7BA4C740-9E81-11CF-99D3-00AA004AE837}
Microsoft Server Configuration Notify Object	{7F368827-9516-11D0-83D9-00A0C911E5DF}
Microsoft Shell Folder AutoComplete List	{03C036F1-A186-11D0-824A-00AA005B4383}
Microsoft Shell Folder View Router	{9BA05971-F6A8-11CF-A442-00A0C90A8F39}
Microsoft Shell UI Helper	{64AB4BB7-111E-11d1-8F79-00C04FC2FBE1}
Microsoft Slider Control, version 6.0	{F08DF954-8592-11D1-B16A-00C0F0283628}
Microsoft SMTPSVC Categorizer	{B23C35B7-9219-11D2-9E17-00C04FA322BA}
Microsoft SQLServer Database Reconciler	{13D9E578-1CA8-11D0-A11B-00AA003E4672}
Microsoft StatusBar Control, version 6.0	{8E3867A3-8586-11D1-B16A-00C0F0283628}

TABLE C.1 Continued

Object	Class ID
Microsoft TabStrip Control, version 6.0	{1EFB6596-857C-11D1-B16A-00C0F0283628}
Microsoft TCP/IP Configuration Notify Object	{A907657F-6FDF-11D0-8EFB-00C04FD912B2}
Microsoft Toolbar Control, version 6.0	{66833FE6-8583-11D1-B16A-00C0F0283628}
Microsoft TreeView Control, version 6.0	{C74190B6-8589-11D1-B16A-00C0F0283628}
Microsoft TTS Engine	{E0725551-286F-11d0-8E73-00A0C9083363}
Microsoft Url History Service	{3C374A40-BAE4-11CF-BF7D-00AA006946EE}
Microsoft Url Search Hook	{CFBFAE00-17A6-11D0-99CB-00C04FD64497}
Microsoft USB PID Class Driver	{EEC6993A-B3FD-11D2-A916-00C04FB98638}
Microsoft User Extension	{4de7016c-5ef9-11d1-8c13-00c04fd8d503}
Microsoft VBA for Outlook Addin	{799ED9EA-FB5E-11D1-B7D6-00C04FC2AAE2}
Microsoft VM	{08B0E5C0-4FCB-11CF-AAA5-00401C608500}
Microsoft Wave File	{00020003-0000-0000-C000-000000000046}
Microsoft WBEM (non)Standard Marshaling for IEnumWbemClassObject	{1B1CAD8C-2DAB-11D2-B604-00104B703EFD}
Microsoft WBEM (non)Standard Marshaling for IWbemMultiTarget	{7016F8FA-CCDA-11D2-B35C-00105A1F8177}
Microsoft WBEM (non)Standard Marshaling for IWbemObjectSink	{71285C44-1DC0-11D2-B5FB-00104B703EFD}
Microsoft WBEM (non)Standard Marshaling for IWbemUnboundObjectSink	{29B5828C-CAB9-11D2-B35C-00105A1F8177}
Microsoft WBEM Anonymous pipe transport	{A4845882-333F-11D0-B724-00AA0062CBB7}
Microsoft WBEM Call Context	{674B6698-EE92-11D0-AD71-00C04FD8FDFF}
Microsoft WBEM Event filter marshaling proxy	{6C19BE35-7500-11D1-AD94-00C04FD8FDFF}
Microsoft WBEM Event Subsystem	{5D08B586-343A-11D0-AD46-00C04FD8FDFF}
Microsoft WBEM Mailslot transport	{E07D3492-32B5-11D0-B724-00AA0062CBB7}
Microsoft WBEM NT Eventlog Event Provider	{F55C5B4C-517D-11D1-AB57-00C04FD9159E}
Microsoft WBEM NT Eventlog Instance Provider	{FD4F53E0-65DC-11D1-AB64-00C04FD9159E}
Microsoft WBEM Server	{74864DA1-0630-11D0-A5B6-00AA00680C3F}
Microsoft WBEM SMTP Event Consumer Provider	{C7A3A54B-0250-11D3-9CD1-00105A1F4801}
Microsoft WBEM Uninitialized WbemClassObject for transports	{7A0227F6-7108-11D1-AD90-00C04FD8FDFF}
Microsoft WBEM Universal Refresher	{C71566F2-561E-11D1-AD87-00C04FD8FDFF}
Microsoft WBEM Unsecured Apartment	{49BD2028-1523-11D1-AD79-00C04FD8FDFF}
Microsoft WBEM View Provider	{AA70DDF4-E11C-11D1-ABB0-00C04FD9159E}
Microsoft WBEM WbemClassObject Marshalling proxy	{4590F812-1D3A-11D0-891F-00AA004B2E24}
Microsoft Web Browser	{8856F961-340A-11D0-A96B-00C04FD705A2}

• • • • • • • • • • • • • • • • •

TABLE C.1   Continued

Object	Class ID
Microsoft Web Browser Version 1	{EAB22AC3-30C1-11CF-A7EB-0000C05BAE0B}
Microsoft Windows Installer	{000C1090-0000-0000-C000-000000000046}
Microsoft Windows Installer Message RPC	{000C101D-0000-0000-C000-000000000046}
Microsoft Windows Media File Transfer Service	{503E9920-FE1F-11CF-99B0-00AA00B82E81}
Microsoft Windows Report Control	{167701E3-FDCF-11D0-A48E-006097C549FF}
Microsoft Word 2.0 Document	{00030003-0000-0000-C000-000000000046}
Microsoft Word 6.0 - 7.0 Document	{00020900-0000-0000-C000-000000000046}
Microsoft Word 6.0 - 7.0 Picture	{00020901-0000-0000-C000-000000000046}
Microsoft Word Application	{000209FF-0000-0000-C000-000000000046}
Microsoft Word Basic	{000209FE-0000-0000-C000-000000000046}
Microsoft Word Document	{00020906-0000-0000-C000-000000000046}
Microsoft Word Picture	{00020907-0000-0000-C000-000000000046}
Microsoft.Jet.OLEDB.4.0	{dee35070-506b-11cf-b1aa-00aa00b8de95}
MicrosoftRDO.RdoConnection	{9A8831F1-A263-11D1-8DCF-00A0C90FFFC2}
MicrosoftRDO.RdoConnection	{E791964C-208A-11CF-8146-00AA00A40C25}
MicrosoftRDO.rdoEngine	{5E71F04C-551F-11CF-8152-00AA00A40C25}
MicrosoftRDO.rdoEngine	{9A8831F0-A263-11D1-8DCF-00A0C90FFFC2}
MicrosoftRDO.RdoQuery	{5EBB68F5-3BF1-11CF-814C-00AA00A40C25}
MicrosoftRDO.RdoQuery	{9A8831F2-A263-11D1-8DCF-00A0C90FFFC2}
MIDI Parser	{D51BD5A2-7548-11CF-A520-0080C77EF58A}
MIDI Renderer	{07B65360-C445-11CE-AFDE-00AA006C14F4}
MIDI Sequence	{00022603-0000-0000-C000-000000000046}
MidiOut Class Manager	{4EFE2452-168A-11d1-BC76-00C04FB9453B}
MIME File Types Hook	{FBF23B41-E3F0-101B-8488-00AA003E56F8}
MimeDirItem Class	{0006F081-0000-0000-C000-000000000046}
MimeDirParser Class	{0006F082-0000-0000-C000-000000000046}
MimeDirProfile Class	{0006F084-0000-0000-C000-000000000046}
MimeDirWriter Class	{0006F083-0000-0000-C000-000000000046}
mk: Asychronous Pluggable Protocol Handler	{79eac9e6-baf9-11ce-8c82-00aa004ba90b}
MMCCtrl Class	{545AE700-50BF-11D1-9FE9-00600832DB4A}
MMCListPadInfo Class	{09474572-B2FB-11D1-A1A1-0000F875B132}
MMCTask Class	{3D112E22-62B2-11D1-9FEF-00600832DB4A}
MMStream Class	{49c47ce5-9ba4-11d0-8212-00c04fc32c45}
Mobsync	{6295DF2D-35EE-11d1-8707-00C04FD93327}
Mobsync Dll	{6295DF27-35EE-11d1-8707-00C04FD93327}
Mobsync Proxy	{6295DF2E-35EE-11d1-8707-00C04FD93327}
Module Manager for Java	{AC680B41-CDA0-11D1-A936-0080C7C575C0}
MOF Compiler	{6DAF9757-2E37-11D2-AEC9-00C04FB68820}

| TABLE C.1 | Continued |

Object	Class ID
Moniker to a Windows Script Component	{06290BD3-48AA-11D2-8432-006008C3FBFC}
Motion Blur Effect	{A380D684-4A3B-11D0-A787-00A0C91BBEE1}
Mounted Volume	{12518493-00B2-11d2-9FA5-9E3420524153}
MoveBvr Class	{C5B86F32-69EE-11d2-875F-00A0C93C09B3}
MPEG Audio Codec	{4A2286E0-7BEF-11CE-9BD9-0000E202599C}
MPEG Audio Decoder Property Page	{CC785860-B2CA-11CE-8D2B-0000E202599C}
MPEG Layer-3 Decoder	{38BE3000-DBF4-11D0-860E-00A024CFEF6D}
MPEG Layer-3 Decoder About Page	{38BE3002-DBF4-11D0-860E-00A024CFEF6D}
MPEG Layer-3 Decoder Property Page	{38BE3001-DBF4-11D0-860E-00A024CFEF6D}
MPEG Layer-3 Decoder Statistics Page	{8DD6C641-98CB-11D1-9846-00A024CFEF6D}
MPEG Video Codec	{FEB50740-7BEF-11CE-9BD9-0000E202599C}
MPEG Video Decoder Property Page	{E5B4EAA0-B2CA-11CE-8D2B-0000E202599C}
MPEG-2 Splitter	{3AE86B20-7BE8-11D1-ABE6-00A0C905F375}
MPEG-I Stream Splitter	{336475D0-942A-11CE-A870-00AA002FEAB5}
MRU AutoComplete List	{6756A641-DE71-11d0-831B-00AA005B4383}
MS Organization Chart 2.0	{E4C18D40-1CD5-101C-B325-00AA001F3168}
MS Remote	{27016870-8E02-11D1-924E-00C04FBBBFB3}
MS Stock Color Property Page Object	{7EBDAAE1-8120-11CF-899F-00AA00688B10}
MS Stock Font Property Page Object	{7EBDAAE0-8120-11CF-899F-00AA00688B10}
MS Stock Picture Property Page Object	{7EBDAAE2-8120-11CF-899F-00AA00688B10}
MSASCIILog Control	{FF160657-DE82-11CF-BC0A-00AA006111E0}
MSASCIILog Property Page	{FF160658-DE82-11CF-BC0A-00AA006111E0}
MSCustomLog Control	{FF160663-DE82-11CF-BC0A-00AA006111E0}
MSCustomLog Property Page	{FF160664-DE82-11CF-BC0A-00AA006111E0}
MSDAINITIALIZE Class	{2206CDB0-19C1-11D1-89E0-00C04FD7A829}
MSDAIPP.BINDER	{E1D2BF40-A96B-11d1-9C6B-0000F875AC61}
MSDAIPP.DSO	{AF320921-9381-11d1-9C3C-0000F875AC61}
MSDAORA	{e8cc4cbe-fdff-11d0-b865-00a0c9081c1d}
MSDAORA ErrorLookup	{e8cc4cbe-fdff-11d0-b865-00a0c9081c1d}
MSDAORA ErrorLookup	{e8cc4cbf-fdff-11d0-b865-00a0c9081c1d}
MSDAOSP	{dfc8bdc0-e378-11d0-9b30-0080c7e9fe95}
MSDASC Error Lookup	{2206CDB0-19C1-11D1-89E0-00C04FD7A829}
MSDASC Error Lookup	{2206CDB3-19C1-11D1-89E0-00C04FD7A829}
MSDASQL	{c8b522cb-5cf3-11ce-ade5-00aa0044773d}
MSDASQL Enumerator	{c8b522cd-5cf3-11ce-ade5-00aa0044773d}
MSDASQL Error Lookup	{c8b522cb-5cf3-11ce-ade5-00aa0044773d}
MSDASQL ErrorLookup	{c8b522cc-5cf3-11ce-ade5-00aa0044773d}
MSDataShape	{3449A1C8-C56C-11D0-AD72-00C04FC29863}
MSDATT	{c8b522ce-5cf3-11ce-ade5-00aa0044773d}

• • • • • • • • • • • • • • • •

TABLE C.1	Continued

Object	Class ID
MSDBGCallStack Class	{1F3C67C2-D153-11D0-BF8B-0000F81E8509}
MSDTC Component Administrator	{f27623a0-b2a1-11ce-ae4c-00aa00445589}
MSDTC Contact Pool	{f27623a1-b2a1-11ce-ae4c-00aa00445589}
MSDTDDGridCtrl2 Object	{E9B0E6D9-811C-11D0-AD51-00A0C90F5739}
MSDTHostCtrl Class	{97240642-F896-11D0-B255-006097C68E81}
MSFlexGrid General Property Page Object	{6319EEA0-531B-11CF-91F6-C2863C385E30}
MSFlexGrid Style Property Page Object	{275DBBA0-805A-11CF-91F7-C2863C385E30}
Msi custom action server	{000C1025-0000-0000-C000-000000000046}
Msi install server	{000C101C-0000-0000-C000-000000000046}
MSIDXS	{F9AE8980-7E52-11d0-8964-00C04FD611D7}
MSIDXS Error Lookup	{F9AE8980-7E52-11d0-8964-00C04FD611D7}
MSIDXS ErrorLookup	{F9AE8981-7E52-11d0-8964-00C04FD611D7}
Msie Control	{25959BEF-E700-11D2-A7AF-00C04F806200}
Msie Property Page	{25959BF0-E700-11D2-A7AF-00C04F806200}
MSIMDB	{47C4815A-F70F-11d0-8C23-00C04FC31D21}
MSIOff Control	{74304483-AC4B-11D1-A50A-00C04FD7A1BD}
MSIOff Property Page	{74304484-AC4B-11D1-A50A-00C04FD7A1BD}
MSLwvTTS 2.0 Engine Class	{D45FD31C-5C6E-11D1-9EC1-00C04FD7081F}
MSLwvTTS Engine Class	{95A893C3-543A-11D0-AC45-00C04FD97575}
MSNCSALog Control	{FF16065F-DE82-11CF-BC0A-00AA006111E0}
MSNCSALog Property Page	{FF160660-DE82-11CF-BC0A-00AA006111E0}
MSODBCLog Control	{FF16065B-DE82-11CF-BC0A-00AA006111E0}
MSODBCLog Property Page	{FF16065C-DE82-11CF-BC0A-00AA006111E0}
msodraa9.ShapeSelect	{FB6BA828-E616-11D1-8D27-00AA00B5BADA}
MsoHelp AW Search Dialog	{B58C2441-A1A3-11d1-B024-006097C9A284}
MsoHelp Key Search Dialog	{B58C2440-A1A3-11d1-B024-006097C9A284}
MSOLAP	{a07ccd00-8148-11d0-87bb-00c04fc33942}
MSOLAP Error Lookup	{a07ccd00-8148-11d0-87bb-00c04fc33942}
MSOLAP ErrorLookup	{a07ccd02-8148-11d0-87bb-00c04fc33942}
MSOLAP.ConnectDialog	{F2A39AA7-8D20-11D1-8E59-00600893AF2D}
MSOLAPAggregation Class	{B82F915F-9F4B-11D1-ABE4-00C04FC30999}
MSOLAPAggregations Class	{B82F915C-9F4B-11D1-ABE4-00C04FC30999}
MSOLAPAuxiliarie Class	{349C6AC1-A30C-11D1-ABE5-00C04FC30999}
MSOLAPAuxiliaries Class	{349C6ABE-A30C-11D1-ABE5-00C04FC30999}
MSOLAPClient Class	{AC985D53-983C-11D1-ABE1-00C04FC30999}
MSOLAPDatabase Class	{6A1B6350-99C8-11D1-ABE1-00C04FC30999}

....

TABLE C.1   Continued

Object	Class ID
MSOLAPDatabases Class	{6A1B634D-99C8-11D1-ABE1-00C04FC30999}
MSOLAPDetail Class	{6A1B6368-99C8-11D1-ABE1-00C04FC30999}
MSOLAPDetails Class	{6A1B6365-99C8-11D1-ABE1-00C04FC30999}
MSOLAPDimension Class	{6A1B6362-99C8-11D1-ABE1-00C04FC30999}
MSOLAPDimensions Class	{6A1B635F-99C8-11D1-ABE1-00C04FC30999}
MSOLAPExtLevel Class	{B82F9167-9F4B-11D1-ABE4-00C04FC30999}
MSOLAPExtLevels Class	{B82F9164-9F4B-11D1-ABE4-00C04FC30999}
MSOLAPExtMeasure Class	{B82F916D-9F4B-11D1-ABE4-00C04FC30999}
MSOLAPExtMeasures Class	{B82F916A-9F4B-11D1-ABE4-00C04FC30999}
MSOLAPLevel Class	{B82F914D-9F4B-11D1-ABE4-00C04FC30999}
MSOLAPLevels Class	{B82F914A-9F4B-11D1-ABE4-00C04FC30999}
MSOLAPMeasure Class	{B82F9153-9F4B-11D1-ABE4-00C04FC30999}
MSOLAPMeasures Class	{B82F9150-9F4B-11D1-ABE4-00C04FC30999}
MSOLAPModel Class	{6A1B635C-99C8-11D1-ABE1-00C04FC30999}
MSOLAPModels Class	{6A1B6359-99C8-11D1-ABE1-00C04FC30999}
MSOLAPPartition Class	{B82F9159-9F4B-11D1-ABE4-00C04FC30999}
MSOLAPPartitions Class	{B82F9156-9F4B-11D1-ABE4-00C04FC30999}
MSOLAPSource Class	{6A1B6356-99C8-11D1-ABE1-00C04FC30999}
MSOLAPSources Class	{6A1B6353-99C8-11D1-ABE1-00C04FC30999}
MSP Class	{11D59011-CF23-11D1-A02D-00C04FB6809F}
MSP Class	{4DDB6D36-3BC1-11d2-86F2-006008B0E5D2}
MSPersist	{7C07E0D0-4418-11D2-9212-00C04FBBBFB3}
MSPropertyTreeCtl Class	{40710C26-4BC7-11D1-8B6F-080036B11A03}
msrating.dll	{20EDB660-7CDD-11CF-8DAB-00AA006C1A01}
MSREdit Class	{2F7FC18E-292B-11D2-A795-DFAA798E9148}
MSSDBGCmdWin Class	{4FE4FFE4-D006-11D0-BF8B-0000F81E8509}
MSSDBGDocument Class	{6980ACA5-CFB6-11D0-BF8B-0000F81E8509}
MSStdFmt Format Property Page Object	{699DDBCC-DC7E-11D0-BCF7-00C04FC2FB86}
MSWC.AdRotator	{1621F7C0-60AC-11CF-9427-444553540000}
MSWC.BrowserType	{0ACE4881-8305-11CF-9427-444553540000}
MSWC.IISLog	{26B9ED02-A3D8-11D1-8B9C-080009DCC2FA}
MSWC.NextLink	{4D9E4505-6DE1-11CF-87A7-444553540000}
Msxml	{CFC399AF-D876-11d0-9C10-00C04FC99C8E}
MsxmlIsland	{379E501F-B231-11d1-ADC1-00805FC752D8}
MTSEvents Class	{ecabb0ab-7f19-11d2-978e-0000f8757e2a}
MTSLocator Class	{ecabb0ac-7f19-11d2-978e-0000f8757e2a}

TABLE C.1	Continued

Object	**Class ID**
MTSPackage	{51372af3-cae7-11cf-be81-00aa00a2fa25}
MtStream Class	{CF0F2F7C-F7BF-11d0-900D-00C04FD9189D}
MTxAS Object	{71E38F91-7E88-11CF-9EDE-0080C78B7F89}
Multi Language ConvertCharset	{D66D6F99-CDAA-11D0-B822-00C04FC9B31F}
Multi Language String	{C04D65CF-B70D-11D0-B188-00AA0038C969}
Multi Language Support	{275C23E2-3747-11D0-9FEA-00AA003F8646}
Multi-file Parser	{D51BD5A3-7548-11CF-A520-0080C77EF58A}
Multimedia File Property Sheet	{00022613-0000-0000-C000-000000000046}
Multiwiz Property Page	{6EBFA830-718B-11D1-8A98-006097B01206}
My Computer	{20D04FE0-3AEA-1069-A2D8-08002B30309D}
My Documents	{450D8FBA-AD25-11D0-98A8-0800361B1103}
My Network Places	{208D2C60-3AEA-1069-A2D7-08002B30309D}
MyDocs Drop Target	{ECF03A32-103D-11d2-854D-006008059367}
MyDocs menu and properties	{4a7ded0a-ad25-11d0-98a8-0800361b1103}
mydocs.dll	{ECF03A33-103D-11d2-854D-006008059367}
MyInfo ASP Component	{4682C82A-B2FF-11D0-95A8-00A0C92B77A9}
Name Control	{53961A09-459B-11d1-BE77-006008317CE8}
NAPSnapin Class	{5880CD5C-8EC0-11d1-9570-0060B0576642}
NdisWan Configuration Notify Object	{6E65CBC3-926D-11D0-8E27-00C04FC99DCF}
NDS Namespace Object	{51d11c90-7b9d-11cf-b03d-00aa006e0975}
NDS Provider Object	{323991f0-7bad-11cf-b03d-00aa006e0975}
Net Connections UI Utilities Class	{7007ACD3-3202-11D1-AAD2-00805FC1270E}
NetBEUI Configuration Notify Object	{A28D553A-A703-11D0-9CEC-00C04FC9BCC4}
NetMeeting Application	{3E9BAF2D-7A79-11d2-9334-0000F875AE17}
NetMeeting NmSysInfo object	{507708CC-A74A-11d2-9351-0000F875AE17}
NetShow Codec Manager	{45f9f4c0-6e5c-11d0-9292-00c04fd919b7}
NetShow ODBC Wrapper Class	{A31357D0-7242-11d0-BAA0-00C04FD91A5E}
NetShow Playback Session Manager	{81aa123e-b564-11d1-87f8-00a0c92b500f}
NetShow Real-Time Encoder Callback Class	{91985A21-C80D-11D0-A5DE-00AA00BF93E3}
Network and Dial-up Connections	{7007ACC7-3202-11D1-AAD2-00805FC1270E}
Network and Dial-up Connections	{992CFFA0-F557-101A-88EC-00DD010CCC48}
Network Common Connections Ui	{7007ACD1-3202-11D1-AAD2-00805FC1270E}
Network Configuration Component Object	{5B035261-40F9-11D1-AAEC-00805FC1270E}
Network Connection Manager Class	{BA126AD1-2166-11D1-B1D0-00805FC1270E}
Network Connection Manager Connection Enumerator Class	{BA126AD2-2166-11D1-B1D0-00805FC1270E}
Network Connections Enum	{7007ACC8-3202-11D1-AAD2-00805FC1270E}

....

TABLE C.1 Continued	
Object	**Class ID**
Network Connections Tray	{7007ACCF-3202-11D1-AAD2-00805FC1270E}
Network Context Menu Extension	{86422020-42A0-1069-A2E5-08002B30309D}
Network Install Queue	{BA126ADF-2166-11D1-B1D0-00805FC1270E}
Neutral Word Breaker	{369647e0-17b0-11ce-9950-00aa004bbb1f}
New Moniker	{ecabafc6-7f19-11d2-978e-0000f8757e2a}
NewMail Class	{AF0EB60E-0775-11D1-A77D-00C04FC2F5B3}
NMSA ASF Source Media Description Object (Ver 1.0)	{93c4a549-6b3b-11d0-ba9c-00c04fd91a5e}
NMSA Audio Transform Media Description Object (Ver 1.0)	{d4fe6225-1288-11d0-9097-00aa004254a0}
NMSA Composite Video Media Description Object (Ver 1.0)	{5c24f661-415b-11d0-ba94-00c04fd91a5e}
NMSA File System Media Description Object (Ver 1.0)	{D4FE6221-1288-11D0-9097-00AA004254A0}
NMSA File Transform Media Description Object (Ver 1.0)	{d4fe6222-1288-11d0-9097-00aa004254a0}
NMSA IP Media Description Object (Ver 1.0)	{d4fe6223-1288-11d0-9097-00aa004254a0}
NMSA Line-In Mic-In Media Description Object (Ver 1.0)	{d4fe6224-1288-11d0-9097-00aa004254a0}
NMSA Media Description Object (Ver 1.0)	{d4fe6226-1288-11d0-9097-00aa004254a0}
NMSA Session Description Object (Ver 1.0)	{d4fe6227-1288-11d0-9097-00aa004254a0}
NMSA Session Description Object (Ver 1.0)	{d4fe6228-1288-11d0-9097-00aa004254a0}
NNTP DirectoryDrop Class	{BDF68FCE-0209-11D1-85C2-00C04FB960EA}
NNTP File System Driver Prepare Class	{DEB58EBB-9CE2-11D1-9128-00C04FC30A64}
NNTP filter	{5645C8C0-E277-11CF-8FDA-00AA00A14F93}
NNTP filter	{5645C8C3-E277-11CF-8FDA-00AA00A14F93}
NNTP OnPost Script Host Sink Class	{CD000006-8B95-11D1-82DB-00C04FB1625D}
NNTP OnPostEarly Script Host Sink Class	{CD000012-8B95-11D1-82DB-00C04FB1625D}
NNTP OnPostFinal Script Host Sink Class	{CD000007-8B95-11D1-82DB-00C04FB1625D}
NntpAdmin Class	{3241F066-6D68-11D0-8950-00AA00A74BF2}
NntpAdminExpiration Class	{772BBAD1-7A22-11D0-895D-00AA00A74BF2}
NntpAdminFeeds Class	{3241F070-6D68-11D0-8950-00AA00A74BF2}
NntpAdminGroups Class	{3241F075-6D68-11D0-8950-00AA00A74BF2}
NntpAdminRebuild Class	{DEE3B231-A3C2-11D0-896E-00AA00A74BF2}
NntpAdminService Class	{3241F06B-6D68-11D0-8950-00AA00A74BF2}
NntpAdminSessions Class	{3241F07A-6D68-11D0-8950-00AA00A74BF2}
NNTPEarlyConnector Class	{CD000011-8B95-11D1-82DB-00C04FB1625D}
NntpFeed Class	{5BDDC640-AE09-11D0-8974-00AA00A74BF2}

TABLE C.1   Continued

Object	Class ID
NNTPFinalConnector Class	{CD000010-8B95-11D1-82DB-00C04FB1625D}
NntpOneWayFeed Class	{5BDDC641-AE09-11D0-8974-00AA00A74BF2}
NNTPPostConnector Class	{CD000009-8B95-11D1-82DB-00C04FB1625D}
NntpVirtualRoot Class	{28E6A820-A6C4-11D0-896F-00AA00A74BF2}
NodeInit 1.0 Object	{43136EB5-D36C-11CF-ADBC-00AA00A80033}
NodeInit 1.0 Object	{F1E752C3-FD72-11D0-AEF6-00C04FB6DD2C}
NonRootTransactionEnvoy	{ecabafad-7f19-11d2-978e-0000f8757e2a}
Notes Management Module	{00067804-0000-0000-C000-000000000046}
NPPAgent	{D413C502-3FAA-11D0-B254-444553540000}
NSC File Parser	{640999A2-A946-11D0-A520-000000000000}
NSDrive Class	{6E8E0081-19CD-11D1-AD91-00AA00B8E05A}
NSDrive Description	{692A8956-1089-11D2-8837-00104B2AFB46}
NSEPM COM Server	{05dc3bb0-4337-11d0-a5c8-00a0c922e752}
NSIEMisc Class	{2646205B-878C-11d1-B07C-0000C040BCDB}
NSLiteServer Class	{DC81C0D0-7800-11D1-BBAD-0060083178D8}
NSLiteSession Class	{B0D12372-6532-11D1-BB8F-0060083178D8}
NtaHelper Class	{ecabafbe-7f19-11d2-978e-0000f8757e2a}
NTFS Message Enumerator Class	{bbddbdec-c947-11d1-aa5e-00c04fa35b82}
NTFS Property Stream Class	{6d7572ac-c939-11d1-aa5e-00c04fa35b82}
NTFS Store Driver Class	{609b7e3a-c918-11d1-aa5e-00c04fa35b82}
NTLM Authenticator Class	{78af5016-3b7c-11d1-9326-00c04fd919b7}
NtmsMgr Class	{243E20B0-48ED-11D2-97DA-00A024D77700}
NtmsMgr Class	{3CB6973D-3E6F-11D0-95DB-00A024D77700}
NtmsMgr Class	{BF83CC10-7020-11D1-9730-00A024D77700}
NtmsSvr Class	{D61A27C6-8F53-11D0-BFA0-00A024151983}
Null filter	{c3278e90-bea7-11cd-b579-08002b30bfeb}
Null persistent handler	{098f2470-bae0-11cd-b579-08002b30bfeb}
NumberBvr Class	{ECDB03D2-6E99-11d2-875F-00A0C93C09B3}
NWCOMPAT Namespace Object	{0fb32cc0-4b62-11cf-ae2c-00aa006ebfb9}
NWCOMPAT Provider Object	{0df68130-4b62-11cf-ae2c-00aa006ebfb9}
NWLink Client Configuration Notify Object	{5BEDF7DE-98CF-11D0-B255-00C04FC9E292}
NWLink Configuration Notify Object	{050DA15F-9F13-11D0-9CE5-00C04FC9BCC4}
NWLink Configuration Notify Object	{C59938DA-9B20-11D0-9CE3-00C04FC9BCC4}
obja Class	{ecabafb0-7f19-11d2-978e-0000f8757e2a}
Object for constructing type libraries for scriptlets	{06290BD5-48AA-11D2-8432-006008C3FBFC}
Object for encoding scriptlets	{06290BD4-48AA-11D2-8432-006008C3FBFC}

TABLE C.1 Continued	
Object	**Class ID**
Object Pool Activator Class	{ecabafb6-7f19-11d2-978e-0000f8757e2a}
Object under which scriptlets may be created	{06290BD0-48AA-11D2-8432-006008C3FBFC}
objref	{00000327-0000-0000-C000-000000000046}
Obsolete Font	{46763EE0-CAB2-11CE-8C20-00AA0051E5D4}
OCATP Class	{D7546ABD-A77A-11D1-B901-00AA00585640}
OCFunc Class	{D7546AAE-A77A-11D1-B901-00AA00585640}
Office Balloons ProxyStub Factory	{E31F0409-E9D8-11d0-8A96-00A0C90C2BC5}
Office Compatible 1.0	{812034D2-760F-11CF-9370-00AA00B8BF00}
Office Graphics Filters Thumbnail Extractor	{1AEB1360-5AFC-11D0-B806-00C04FD706EC}
OfficeObj Class	{D2BD7935-05FC-11D2-9059-00C04FD7A1BD}
OfficeWebServer SyncMgr Handler	{BDEADE7B-C265-11D0-BCED-00A0C90AB50F}
Offline Files Cleaner	{effc2928-37b1-11d2-a3c1-00c04fb1782a}
Offline Files Folder	{AFDB1F70-2A4C-11d2-9039-00C04F8EEB3E}
Offline Files Folder Options	{10CFC467-4392-11d2-8DB4-00C04FA31A66}
Offline Files Menu	{750fdf0e-2a26-11d1-a3ea-080036587f03}
Offline Files Synchronization Handler	{750fdf10-2a26-11d1-a3ea-080036587f03}
Offline Pages Cleaner	{8E6E6079-0CB7-11d2-8F10-0000F87ABD16}
Old Files In Root Prop Bag	{60F6E464-4DEF-11d2-B2D9-00C04F8EEC8C}
OLE 2.0 Link	{F7A9C6E0-EFF2-101A-8185-00DD01108C6B}
OLE DB Row Proxy	{ef636392-f343-11d0-9477-00c04fd36226}
OLE DB Row Server	{ef636393-f343-11d0-9477-00c04fd36226}
OLE DB Rowset Proxy	{ef636390-f343-11d0-9477-00c04fd36226}
OLE DB Rowset Server	{ef636391-f343-11d0-9477-00c04fd36226}
OLE Docfile Property Page	{3EA48300-8CF6-101B-84FB-666CCB9BCD32}
OleCvt Class	{65303443-AD66-11D1-9D65-00C04FC30DF6}
OleInstall Class	{C3701884-B39B-11D1-9D68-00C04FC30DF6}
oleprn Class	{3E4D4F1C-2AEE-11D1-9D3D-00C04FC30DF6}
OleSNMP Class	{4F664F91-FF01-11D0-8AED-00C04FD7B597}
Online Registration Extension	{E8D83F00-CD78-11D0-B4D3-00A024BF23EF}
Open / Save As	{7629CFA2-3FE5-101B-A3C9-08002B2F49FB}
Open With Context Menu Handler	{09799AFB-AD67-11d1-ABCD-00C04FC30936}
OPWNoLink	{654C2A40-71B6-11CE-A850-444553540000}
OrderListExport	{F3368374-CF19-11d0-B93D-00A0C90312e1}
ORG10SVR 1.0 Application	{787A1520-75B9-11CF-980D-444553540000}
ORG21SVR 1.0 Application	{88738460-8CA8-11CF-980D-444553540000}
OSE.Discussion	{15F0B132-CB2E-11D1-9596-00A0C90DCA5B}

| **TABLE C.1** | Continued |

Object	Class ID
OSE.Discussions	{15F0B130-CB2E-11D1-9596-00A0C90DCA5B}
OSE.DiscussionServer	{DA1E5A8E-1A89-11D2-95C9-00A0C90DCA5B}
OSE.DiscussionServers	{DA1E5A90-1A89-11D2-95C9-00A0C90DCA5B}
OSE.Global	{15F0B134-CB2E-11D1-9596-00A0C90DCA5B}
Outlook Adult Content List Object	{0006F07C-0000-0000-C000-000000000046}
Outlook CalendarView	{00062003-0000-0000-C000-000000000046}
Outlook CardView	{00062002-0000-0000-C000-000000000046}
Outlook Central	{0006F006-0000-0000-C000-000000000046}
Outlook DocSite OLE Control	{0006F024-0000-0000-C000-000000000046}
Outlook Exception List Object	{0006F07A-0000-0000-C000-000000000046}
Outlook Express Address Book	{233A9694-667E-11d1-9DFB-006097D50408}
Outlook Express Envelope	{A08AF898-C2A3-11d1-BE23-00C04FA31009}
Outlook Express Mail Object	{06BE7323-EF34-11d1-ACD8-00C04FA31009}
Outlook Express Message List	{233A9692-667E-11d1-9DFB-006097D50408}
Outlook Express Mime Editor	{1C82EAD9-508E-11D1-8DCF-00C04FB951F9}
Outlook Express MsgTable Object	{abc00000-0000-0000-0000-000000000000}
Outlook FAT Management Module	{00067820-0000-0000-C000-000000000046}
Outlook FAT Namespace	{0006F018-0000-0000-C000-000000000046}
Outlook File Attachment	{0006F031-0000-0000-C000-000000000046}
Outlook File Icon Extension	{0006F045-0000-0000-C000-000000000046}
Outlook Finder Stub	{0006F019-0000-0000-C000-000000000046}
Outlook Form Factory	{0006F020-0000-0000-C000-000000000046}
Outlook Header OLE Control	{0006F02A-0000-0000-C000-000000000046}
Outlook IconView	{00062004-0000-0000-C000-000000000046}
Outlook Junk EMail List Object	{0006F07B-0000-0000-C000-000000000046}
Outlook Message Attachment	{00020D09-0000-0000-C000-000000000046}
Outlook Message Attachment	{0006F032-0000-0000-C000-000000000046}
Outlook Message Recall Item	{00061068-0000-0000-C000-000000000046}
Outlook Message Site Object	{0006F030-0000-0000-C000-000000000046}
Outlook My Computer Management Module	{00067821-0000-0000-C000-000000000046}
Outlook Namespace	{0006F017-0000-0000-C000-000000000046}
Outlook Network Neighborhood Management Module	{00067822-0000-0000-C000-000000000046}
Outlook Network Share Management Module	{00067823-0000-0000-C000-000000000046}
Outlook Object Model Access	{0006F069-0000-0000-C000-000000000046}
Outlook Office Explorer	{0006F01E-0000-0000-C000-000000000046}
Outlook Office Finder	{0006F01F-0000-0000-C000-000000000046}
Outlook Progress Ctl	{0006F071-0000-0000-C000-000000000046}

TABLE C.1	Continued

Object	Class ID
Outlook PSOutlookMessageSite	{00067009-0000-0000-C000-000000000046}
Outlook Recipient	{0006F011-0000-0000-C000-000000000046}
Outlook Recipient Collection Edit OLE Control	{0006F023-0000-0000-C000-000000000046}
Outlook Registered Central	{0006F005-0000-0000-C000-000000000046}
Outlook TableView	{00062000-0000-0000-C000-000000000046}
Outlook TimelineView	{00062001-0000-0000-C000-000000000046}
Outlook View Control	{0006F065-0000-0000-C000-000000000046}
Outlook View Selector Control	{0006F068-0000-0000-C000-000000000046}
OutlookAttachMoniker	{0002034C-0000-0000-C000-000000000046}
OutlookMessageMoniker	{0002034E-0000-0000-C000-000000000046}
Overlay Mixer	{CD8743A1-3736-11D0-9E69-00C04FD7C15B}
Overlay Mixer2	{A0025E90-E45B-11D1-ABE9-00A0C905F375}
OWSBrowserUI Class	{BDEADE43-C265-11D0-BCED-00A0C90AB50F}
OWSClientCollaboration Class	{BDEADEA1-C265-11D0-BCED-00A0C90AB50F}
OWSComment Class	{BDEADE41-C265-11D0-BCED-00A0C90AB50F}
OWSCommentThread Class	{BDEADE47-C265-11D0-BCED-00A0C90AB50F}
OWSDiscussionServers Class	{BDEADE4E-C265-11D0-BCED-00A0C90AB50F}
OWSEventSubscription Class	{BDEADE49-C265-11D0-BCED-00A0C90AB50F}
OWSEventSubscriptions Class	{BDEADE4A-C265-11D0-BCED-00A0C90AB50F}
OWSMiscApis Class	{BDEADE44-C265-11D0-BCED-00A0C90AB50F}
OWSNotificationSink Class	{BDEADE7A-C265-11D0-BCED-00A0C90AB50F}
OWSOfflineList Class	{BDEADEA5-C265-11D0-BCED-00A0C90AB50F}
Package	{0003000C-0000-0000-C000-000000000046}
PackagerMoniker	{00000308-0000-0000-C000-000000000046}
PageAddress Class	{47F410B9-5FA5-11D1-B647-00C04FA3C554}
PageColorPPG Class	{D62B3FF2-0463-11D1-A6F2-006097C9947C}
PageTerminals Class	{5B175DF9-6A86-11D1-B651-00C04FA3C554}
Paintbrush Picture	{0003000a-0000-0000-C000-000000000046}
Panel Property Page Object	{C27CCE3A-8596-11D1-B16A-00C0F0283628}

....

TABLE C.1 Continued

Object	Class ID
PANOSE Core Mapper	{BD84B381-8CA2-1069-AB1D-08000948F534}
PathBvr Class	{80F49562-6A9A-11d2-875F-00A0C93C09B3}
PCM Silence Suppressor	{26721E10-390C-11D0-8A22-00A0C90C9156}
PCM Silence Suppressor Properties	{40C1D161-52F2-11D0-A874-00AA00B5CA1B}
PDCubeCreate Class	{EF3694B8-3C1C-11D1-ABD2-00C04FC30999}
PDOlapAux Class	{BA2BC757-271E-11D2-8E77-00600893AF2D}
PDOlapCollection Class	{EF3694A9-3C1C-11D1-ABD2-00C04FC30999}
PDOlapCube Class	{EF3694B5-3C1C-11D1-ABD2-00C04FC30999}
PDOlapDatasource Class	{EF3694A6-3C1C-11D1-ABD2-00C04FC30999}
PDOlapDimension Class	{EF3694AC-3C1C-11D1-ABD2-00C04FC30999}
PDOlapLevel Class	{EF3694AF-3C1C-11D1-ABD2-00C04FC30999}
PDOlapMeasure Class	{EF3694B2-3C1C-11D1-ABD2-00C04FC30999}
PDOlapObject Class	{EF3694A3-3C1C-11D1-ABD2-00C04FC30999}
PDOlapReport Class	{7C504FFC-44E0-11D1-ABD4-00C04FC30999}
PDPO Class	{CCB4EC60-B9DC-11D1-AC80-00A0C9034873}
PeerDraw Class	{10072CEC-8CC1-11D1-986E-00A0C955B42E}
PeerFactory Class	{3050F4CF-98B5-11CF-BB82-00AA00BDCE0B}
Performance Property Page	{59CE6880-ACF8-11CF-B56E-0080C7C4B68A}
PerformanceAbout Class	{7478EF69-8C46-11d1-8D99-00A0C913CAD4}
PermissionChecker Class	{1BE73E22-B843-11D0-8B40-00C0F00AE35A}
PgCntObj Class	{EF88CA72-B840-11D0-8B40-00C0F00AE35A}
Phone Number Control	{53961A03-459B-11d1-BE77-006008317CE8}
Phoneme Converter	{B9F11A96-90E3-11d0-8D77-00A0C9034A7E}
Picture (Device Independent Bitmap)	{00000316-0000-0000-C000-000000000046}
Picture (Enhanced Metafile)	{00000319-0000-0000-C000-000000000046}
Picture (Metafile)	{00000315-0000-0000-C000-000000000046}
Picture Property Page	{0BE35202-8F91-11CE-9DE3-00AA004BB851}
Picture Property Page	{FC7AF71D-FC74-101A-84ED-08002B2EC713}
PipePSFactory	{0000032E-0000-0000-C000-000000000046}
Pixelate	{4CCEA634-FBE0-11d1-906A-00C04FD9189D}
Plain Text filter	{c1243ca0-bf96-11cd-b579-08002b30bfeb}
Plain Text persistent handler	{5e941d80-bf96-11cd-b579-08002b30bfeb}
Plug In Distributor: IKsClock	{877E4351-6FEA-11d0-B863-00AA00A216A1}
Plug In Distributor: IKsQualityForwarder	{E05592E4-C0B5-11D0-A439-00A0C9223196}
PlusPack CPL Extension	{41E300E0-78B6-11ce-849B-444553540000}
PointerMoniker	{00000306-0000-0000-C000-000000000046}
Policy Package	{ecabaebd-7f19-11d2-978E-0000f8757e2a}
Policy Settings Extension Snapin	{1F823A6A-863F-11D1-A484-00C04FB93753}

TABLE C.1	Continued
Object	**Class ID**
Policy Settings Extension Snapin	{3F276EB4-70EE-11D1-8A0F-00C04FB93753}
Policy Settings Extension Snapin	{ACE10358-974C-11D1-A48D-00C04FB93753}
Policy Settings Extension Snapin	{BF84C0C5-0C80-11D2-A497-00C04FB93209}
PolicyManager Class	{ecabaebc-7f19-11d2-978E-0000f8757e2a}
PoolMgr Class	{ecabafb5-7f19-11d2-978e-0000f8757e2a}
PopupMenu Object	{7823A620-9DD9-11CF-A662-00AA00C066D2}
PostAgent	{D8BD2030-6FC9-11D0-864F-00AA006809D9}
ppDSApp Class	{2AFA62E2-5548-11D1-A6E1-006097C4E476}
ppDSClip Class	{31C48C31-70B0-11d1-A708-006097C4E476}
ppDSDetl Class	{31C48C32-70B0-11d1-A708-006097C4E476}
ppDSFile Class	{1D1237A0-6CD6-11d2-96BA-00104B242E64}
ppDShowNet Class	{5C85DCB0-F967-11D0-81ED-00C04FC99D4C}
ppDShowPlay Class	{C0CD59AE-020D-11d1-81F2-00C04FC99D4C}
ppDSMeta Class	{2FEB9591-50CF-11D1-A6DF-006097C4E476}
ppDSMeta Class	{BB314F91-A010-11d1-A75A-006097C4E476}
ppDSOAdv Class	{AE1A5813-5230-11D1-A6E0-006097C4E476}
ppDSPropAdv Class	{8C4EB103-516F-11D1-A6DF-006097C4E476}
ppDSView Class	{AE1A5812-5230-11D1-A6E0-006097C4E476}
PPTP Configuration Configuration Notify Object	{6E65CBC4-926D-11D0-8E27-00C04FC99DCF}
Preview Class	{50F16B26-467E-11D1-8271-00C04FC3183B}
Primer Class	{F8860CCA-95A3-11D0-9F66-00A0C9055CAC}
PrimerMgr Class	{F8860CCC-95A3-11D0-9F66-00A0C9055CAC}
Print	{3C4F3BE5-47EB-101B-A3C9-08002B2F49FB}
Printer Data Transport	{CCDD9080-8100-11D0-B6CF-00A024BF23EF}
Printers	{2227A280-3AEA-1069-A2DE-08002B30309D}
Private Debug Manager for Java	{275D9D51-5FF5-11CF-A5E1-00AA006BBF16}
ProcedureAdditive	{4834C721-DCC9-11D0-B211-00A0C9191768}
ProcedureDistortion	{4834C722-DCC9-11D0-B211-00A0C9191768}
ProcedureEffects	{2C37C621-9C6F-11D0-9BF1-00A0C9191768}
ProcessDebugManager Class	{78A51822-51F4-11D0-8F20-00805F2CD064}
ProfferService Class	{B695EC28-8333-11D0-B21D-080000185165}
Progress Bar General Property Page Object	{C27CCE3B-8596-11D1-B16A-00C0F0283628}
Progress Dialog	{F8383852-FCD3-11d1-A6B9-006097DF5BD4}
ProjView Class	{6980ACA9-CFB6-11D0-BF8B-0000F81E8509}
PropGroupManagerObject Class	{2A005C11-A5DE-11CF-9E66-00AA00A3F464}
ProtocolsTable Class	{7669CAD6-BDEC-11D1-A6A0-00C04FB9988E}
Provider Binder for DS OLE DB Provider	{E0FA581D-2188-11D2-A739-00C04FA377A1}

· · · · · · · · · · · · · · · ·

TABLE C.1 Continued	
Object	**Class ID**
PrtSum Class	{C3701884-B39B-11D2-9D68-00C04FC30DF6}
prturl Class	{92337A8C-E11D-11D0-BE48-00C04FC30DF6}
PSDispatch	{00020420-0000-0000-C000-000000000046}
PSEnumVariant	{00020421-0000-0000-C000-000000000046}
PSFactoryBuffer	{00000320-0000-0000-C000-000000000046}
PSFactoryBuffer	{0006729A-0000-0000-C000-000000000046}
PSFactoryBuffer	{000C103E-0000-0000-C000-000000000046}
PSFactoryBuffer	{05238C14-A6E1-11D0-9A84-00C04FD8DBF7}
PSFactoryBuffer	{06210E88-01F5-11D1-B512-0080C781C384}
PSFactoryBuffer	{07970B30-A4DA-11D2-B724-00104BC51339}
PSFactoryBuffer	{08D32746-7AF6-11D0-B42A-00A0244A1DD2}
PSFactoryBuffer	{0FB15084-AF41-11CE-BD2B-204C4F4F5020}
PSFactoryBuffer	{1080B910-A636-11D0-A9EA-00AA00685C74}
PSFactoryBuffer	{28FD8302-57CF-11D0-8A3E-00A0C90349CB}
PSFactoryBuffer	{29822AB7-F302-11D0-9953-00C04FD919C1}
PSFactoryBuffer	{29822AB8-F302-11D0-9953-00C04FD919C1}
PSFactoryBuffer	{455ACF57-5345-11D2-99CF-00C04F797BC9}
PSFactoryBuffer	{48EEA71A-3775-11D1-8C96-00A0C903A1A2}
PSFactoryBuffer	{4E934F30-341A-11D1-8FB1-00A024CB6019}
PSFactoryBuffer	{53B6AA63-3F56-11D0-916B-00AA00C18068}
PSFactoryBuffer	{545A2D1A-8ECB-11D1-94E8-00C04FA302A1}
PSFactoryBuffer	{560E5A02-DEDE-11D1-A9F5-00A0248903EA}
PSFactoryBuffer	{5A435BAF-BA94-11D0-972A-0080C71CAE8C}
PSFactoryBuffer	{600FD9A3-F1D3-11D1-828E-00C04F990690}
PSFactoryBuffer	{64B8F404-A4AE-11D1-B7B6-00C04FB926AF}
PSFactoryBuffer	{66A2DB1A-D706-11D0-A37B-00C04FC9DA04}
PSFactoryBuffer	{68883F00-85D8-11D0-8A50-00A0C90349CB}
PSFactoryBuffer	{70B51430-B6CA-11D0-B9B9-00A0C922E750}
PSFactoryBuffer	{78b64540-f26d-11d0-a6a3-00a0c922e752}
PSFactoryBuffer	{7C857801-7381-11CF-884D-00AA004B2E24}
PSFactoryBuffer	{7E9EC061-F1A4-11D1-828E-00C04F990690}
PSFactoryBuffer	{888ADDCF-9993-11D0-A539-00A0C922E798}
PSFactoryBuffer	{888ADDDD-9993-11D0-A539-00A0C922E798}
PSFactoryBuffer	{8BAE8C50-4436-11D1-A540-00C04FC29CFB}
PSFactoryBuffer	{944AD531-B09D-11CE-B59C-00AA006CB37D}
PSFactoryBuffer	{98315903-7BE5-11D2-ADC1-00A02463D6E7}

TABLE C.1	Continued

Object	Class ID
PSFactoryBuffer	{A5B69200-214B-11D0-81B7-00A0C91180F2}
PSFactoryBuffer	{A9E69612-B80D-11D0-B9B9-00A0C922E750}
PSFactoryBuffer	{B196B286-BAB4-101A-B69C-00AA00341D07}
PSFactoryBuffer	{B8DA6310-E19B-11D0-933C-00A0C90DCAA9}
PSFactoryBuffer	{BD010A01-000B-11D0-D0DD-00A0C9190459}
PSFactoryBuffer	{C04EFA90-E221-11D2-985E-00C04F575153}
PSFactoryBuffer	{C5598E60-B307-11D1-B27D-006008C3FBFB}
PSFactoryBuffer	{c804d980-ebec-11d0-a6a0-00a0c922e752}
PSFactoryBuffer	{CB46E850-FC2F-11D2-B126-00805FC73204}
PSFactoryBuffer	{CD00007F-8B95-11D1-82DB-00C04FB1625D}
PSFactoryBuffer	{D2029F40-8AB3-11CF-85FB-00401C608501}
PSFactoryBuffer	{D2BD7934-05FC-11D2-9059-00C04FD7A1BD}
PSFactoryBuffer	{D97A6DA2-9C1C-11D0-9C3C-00A0C922E764}
PSFactoryBuffer	{D99E6E70-FC88-11D0-B498-00A0C90312F3}
PSFactoryBuffer	{D9E04213-14D7-11D1-9938-0060976A546D}
PSFactoryBuffer	{DC81C0CF-7800-11D1-BBAD-0060083178D8}
PSFactoryBuffer	{E8FB8620-588F-11D2-9D61-00C04F79C5FE}
PSFactoryBuffer	{E9ABBBB0-9757-11D1-83F7-00C04FA302A1}
PSFactoryBuffer	{EAA46600-E736-11D0-B988-00A0C9190447}
PSFactoryBuffer	{F808DF6F-6049-11D1-BA20-006097D2898E}
PSFactoryBuffer	{FAEDCF53-31FE-11D1-AAD2-00805FC1270E}
PSFactoryBuffer	{FE37FB02-3729-11D0-8CF4-00A0C9190459}
PSFactoryBuffer	{FE9E48A2-A014-11D1-855C-00A0C944138C}
PSFactoryBuffer	{FF736B00-82CC-11D0-9E35-00A0C916F120}
PSOAInterface	{00020424-0000-0000-C000-000000000046}
PSSupportErrorInfo	{DF0B3D60-548F-101B-8E65-08002B2BD119}
PSTypeComp	{00020425-0000-0000-C000-000000000046}
PSTypeInfo	{00020422-0000-0000-C000-000000000046}
PSTypeLib	{00020423-0000-0000-C000-000000000046}
Pubwiz Property Page	{23DA323E-7006-11D1-8A98-006097B01206}
QA Hook	{74746E21-6141-11D1-85EA-0000F81E0CE1}
QC Listener Class	{ecabafc3-7f19-11d2-978e-0000f8757e2a}
QC Marshal Interceptor Class	{ecabafcb-7f19-11d2-978e-0000f8757e2a}
QC Queue Administration Class	{ecabafc9-7f19-11d2-978e-0000f8757e2a}

· · · · · · · · · · · · · · · ·

TABLE C.1 Continued	
Object	**Class ID**
QKsAudIntfHandler	{CBE3FAA0-CC75-11D0-B465-00001A1818E6}
QKsAudioIntfHandler	{45FFAAA0-6E1B-11D0-BCF2-444553540000}
QoS Admission Control	{FD57D297-4FD9-11D1-854E-00C04FC31FD3}
QoS Admission Control	{FD57D29A-4FD9-11D1-854E-00C04FC31FD3}
QoS Admission Control	{FD57D29C-4FD9-11D1-854E-00C04FC31FD3}
QT Decompressor	{FDFE9681-74A3-11D0-AFA7-00AA00B67A42}
Quality Management Property Page	{418AFB70-F8B8-11CE-AAC6-0020AF0B99A3}
Queue Moniker	{ecabafc7-7f19-11d2-978e-0000f8757e2a}
Queued Components Player	{ecabafc4-7f19-11d2-978e-0000f8757e2a}
Queued Components Recorder	{ECABAFC2-7F19-11D2-978E-0000F8757E2A}
QuickTime Movie Parser	{D51BD5A0-7548-11CF-A520-0080C77EF58A}
RadioPlayer Class	{9C2263B0-3E3C-11D2-9BD3-204C4F4F5020}
RadioServer Class	{8E71888A-423F-11D2-876E-00A0C9082467}
RadioView Class	{847B4DF5-4B61-11D2-9BDB-204C4F4F5020}
RADIUS configuration object	{1AA7F83F-C7F5-11D0-A376-00C04FC9DA04}
RADIUS configuration object	{1AA7F840-C7F5-11D0-A376-00C04FC9DA04}
Rat Control	{BA634607-B771-11D0-9296-00C04FB6678B}
Rat Property Page	{BA634608-B771-11D0-9296-00C04FB6678B}
RDS.DataControl	{BD96C556-65A3-11D0-983A-00C04FC29E33}
RDS.DataSpace	{BD96C556-65A3-11D0-983A-00C04FC29E36}
RDSServer.DataFactory	{9381D8F5-0288-11d0-9501-00AA00B911A5}
Reconciliation interface ProxyStub Factory	{99180163-DA16-101A-935C-444553540000}
Record Control	{53961A07-459B-11d1-BE77-006008317CE8}
Recycle Bin	{645FF040-5081-101B-9F08-00AA002F954E}
Recycle Bin Cleaner	{5ef4af3a-f726-11d0-b8a2-00c04fc309a4}
Redirect Effect	{29AB59D3-7E50-11D2-B520-00A0C98C01C9}
RefDial Class	{1E794A0A-86F4-11D1-ADD8-0000F87734F0}
RefEdit.Ctrl	{00024512-0000-0000-C000-000000000046}
RegDBCompensator Class	{CB39A782-E5E4-11D1-8CC0-00C04FC3261D}
Registrar Class	{44EC053A-400F-11D0-9DCD-00A0C90391D3}
Registry Class	{C7DAE17F-D8C1-11D2-B532-00104B9A3597}
Registry Tree Options Utility	{AF4F6510-F982-11d0-8595-00AA004CD6D8}
RegWizCtrl	{50E5E3D1-C07E-11D0-B9FD-00A0249F6B00}
Remote Debug Manager for Java	{275D9D50-5FF5-11CF-A5E1-00AA006BBF16}
Remote Helper	{E423AF7C-FC2D-11d2-B126-00805FC73204}
Remote Install Computer Property Pages	{0F65B1BF-740F-11D1-BBE6-0060081692B3}
Remote Install DS Query Form	{C1293E17-534E-11D2-8424-00C04FA372D4}
Remote Install New Computer Extension	{D6D8C25A-4E83-11D2-8424-00C04FA372D4}
Remote Install Service Property Pages	{AC409538-741C-11D1-BBE6-0060081692B3}

TABLE C.1 Continued	
Object	**Class ID**
Remote Installation Services	{3060E8CE-7020-11D2-842D-00C04FA372D4}
Remote Storage Engine	{2D1E3156-25DE-11D0-8073-00A0C905F098}
Remote Storage File	{112981B2-1BA5-11D0-81B2-00A0C91180F2}
Remote Storage Media	{FE37FA01-3729-11D0-8CF4-00A0C9190459}
Remote Storage Properties	{692E33B0-AF9D-11D0-B976-00A0C9190447}
Remote Storage Recall Notification Client	{D68BD5B0-D6AA-11d0-9EDA-00A02488FCDE}
RemoteAcsSetup Class	{78FF2710-F69B-11D2-B8F2-0050040AB917}
remrras Class	{1AA7F844-C7F5-11d0-A376-00C04FC9DA04}
Rendezvous Class	{F1029E5B-CB5B-11D0-8D59-00C04FD91AC0}
Replica Class	{D2D139E3-B6CA-11d1-9F31-00C04FC29D52}
ReplicateCatalog Class	{8C836AF9-FFAC-11D0-8ED4-00C04FC2C17B}
RequestMakeCall Class	{AC48FFE0-F8C4-11d1-A030-00C04FB6809F}
Reveal Transition	{EB8F50E2-85D1-11D0-9D9D-00A0C908DB96}
Ripple	{945F5842-3A8D-11D1-9037-00C04FD9189D}
RM Enlistment Helper	{958A1709-3B44-11D1-AD74-00C04FC2ADC0}
RmsCartridge Class	{FE37FA04-3729-11D0-8CF4-00A0C9190459}
RmsClient Class	{FE37FA12-3729-11D0-8CF4-00A0C9190459}
RmsDrive Class	{FE37FA05-3729-11D0-8CF4-00A0C9190459}
RmsDriveClass Class	{FE37FA03-3729-11D0-8CF4-00A0C9190459}
RmsIEPort Class	{FE37FA08-3729-11D0-8CF4-00A0C9190459}
RmsLibrary Class	{FE37FA02-3729-11D0-8CF4-00A0C9190459}
RmsMediaSet Class	{FE37FA09-3729-11D0-8CF4-00A0C9190459}
RmsMediumChanger Class	{FE37FA07-3729-11D0-8CF4-00A0C9190459}
RmsNTMS Class	{FE37FA13-3729-11D0-8CF4-00A0C9190459}
RmsPartition Class	{FE37FA11-3729-11D0-8CF4-00A0C9190459}
RmsRequest Class	{FE37FA10-3729-11D0-8CF4-00A0C9190459}
RmsStorageSlot Class	{FE37FA06-3729-11D0-8CF4-00A0C9190459}
Role-based Security Policy	{F3CFF120-9C41-11D1-863D-0060089F6007}
Roll	{78F30B82-48AA-11D2-9900-0000F803FF7A}
RotateBvr Class	{027713F2-5FA8-11d2-875B-00A0C93C09B3}
Route Class	{DAB1A262-4FD7-11D1-842C-00C04FB6C218}
Router Configuration object for IP	{C2FE450A-D6C2-11D0-A37B-00C04FC9DA04}
Routers or Remote Access Servers	{6B91AFEF-9472-11D1-8574-00C04FC31FD3}
Routing and Remote Access	{1AA7F839-C7F5-11D0-A376-00C04FC9DA04}
Routing and Remote Access	{1AA7F83A-C7F5-11D0-A376-00C04FC9DA04}
Routing and Remote Access	{1AA7F83B-C7F5-11D0-A376-00C04FC9DA04}

....

TABLE C.1 Continued	
Object	**Class ID**
Rowset Helper Error Lookup Service	{92396AD0-68F5-11d0-A57E-00A0C9138C66}
RowsetHelper	{92396AD0-68F5-11d0-A57E-00A0C9138C66}
RTP Class	{06CE0C3A-8917-11D1-AA78-00C04FC9B202}
RTP Render Filter	{00D20921-7E20-11D0-B291-00C04FC31D18}
RTP Render Filter	{00D20923-7E20-11D0-B291-00C04FC31D18}
RTP Source Filter	{00D20920-7E20-11D0-B291-00C04FC31D18}
RTP Stream Sink Filter	{3c94d400-4188-11d0-9123-00aa00c147fa}
SAMI (CC) Reader	{33FACFE0-A9BE-11D0-A520-00A0D10129C0}
sca Class	{ecabafae-7f19-11d2-978e-0000f8757e2a}
Scale	{555278E2-05DB-11D1-883A-3C8B00C10000}
ScaleBvr Class	{E80353D3-677D-11d2-875E-00A0C93C09B3}
SCard Class	{1461AAC7-6810-11D0-918F-00AA00C18068}
SCardAuth Class	{19B7E2E2-FEBD-11d0-8827-00A0C955FC7E}
SCardCmd Class	{D5778AE7-43DE-11D0-9171-00AA00C18068}
SCardDatabase Class	{1461AACC-6810-11D0-918F-00AA00C18068}
SCardFileAccess Class	{19B7E2E3-FEBD-11d0-8827-00A0C955FC7E}
SCardISO7816 Class	{53B6AA6C-3F56-11D0-916B-00AA00C18068}
SCardLocate Class	{1461AAD1-6810-11D0-918F-00AA00C18068}
SCardManage Class	{19B7E2E4-FEBD-11d0-8827-00A0C955FC7E}
SCardSSP Class	{5A435BB0-BA94-11D0-972A-0080C71CAE8C}
SCardTypeConv Class	{53B6AA67-3F56-11D0-916B-00AA00C18068}
SCardVerify Class	{19B7E2E5-FEBD-11d0-8827-00A0C955FC7E}
SCC Quick Viewer	{F0F08735-0C36-101B-B086-0020AF07D0F4}
Scheduled Tasks	{D6277990-4C6A-11CF-8D87-00AA0060F5BF}
Scheduling Agent Service Class	{148BD52A-A2AB-11CE-B11F-00AA00530503}
Scheduling Agent Task Object Class	{148BD520-A2AB-11CE-B11F-00AA00530503}
Scheduling UI icon handler	{DD2110F0-9EEF-11cf-8D8E-00AA0060F5BF}
Scheduling UI property sheet handler	{797F1E90-9EDD-11cf-8D8E-00AA0060F5BF}
ScopeTree 1.0 Object	{7F1899DA-62A6-11D0-A2C6-00C04FD909DD}
Script Encoder Object	{32DA2B15-CFED-11D1-B747-00C04FC2B085}
Script LE	{432DC4FC-6D93-11D0-B422-00A0244A1DD2}
ScriptControl Object	{0E59F1D5-1FBE-11D0-8FF2-00A0D10038BC}
ScriptDebugSvc Class	{834128A2-51F4-11D0-8F20-00805F2CD064}
ScriptEngineSite Class	{842DFBE6-AD40-11D0-910F-0000F81E7FF2}
Scripting.Dictionary	{EE09B103-97E0-11CF-978F-00A02463E06F}
ScriptoSys Class	{FCDECE00-A39D-11D0-ABE7-00AA0064D470}

TABLE C.1 Continued	
Object	**Class ID**
Scripts (Logon/Logoff)	{40B66650-4972-11D1-A7CA-0000F87571E3}
Scripts (Startup/Shutdown)	{40B6664F-4972-11D1-A7CA-0000F87571E3}
SdoMachine Class	{E9218AE7-9E91-11D1-BF60-0080C7846BC0}
SdoService Class	{BC94D813-4D7F-11d2-A8C9-00AA00A71DCA}
SdpConferenceBlob Class	{9B2719DD-B696-11D0-A489-00C04FD91AC0}
SDSnapin Class	{BD95BA60-2E26-AAD1-AD99-00AA00B8E05A}
SDSnapin Description	{A1B9E04A-3226-11D2-883E-00104B2AFB46}
Search Results	{e17d4fc0-5564-11d1-83f2-00a0c90dc849}
Search Results - Computers	{1f4de370-d627-11d1-ba4f-00a0c91eedba}
SearchAssistantOC	{B45FF030-4447-11D2-85DE-00C04FA35C89}
Security Manager	{7b8a2d94-0ac9-11d1-896c-00c04Fb6bfc4}
Security Shell Extension	{1F2E5C40-9550-11CE-99D2-00AA006E086C}
Security Shell Extension	{4E40F770-369C-11d0-8922-00A024AB2DBB}
Security Shell Extension	{F37C5810-4D3F-11d0-B4BF-00AA00BBB723}
SecurityEnvoy	{ecabafab-7f19-11d2-978e-0000f8757e2a}
Seeking	{060AF76C-68DD-11D0-8FC1-00C04FD9189D}
SelectPPG Class	{45E7E811-02C2-11D1-A6F0-006097C9947C}
SendConsoleMessageApp Class	{B1AFF7D0-0C49-11D1-BB12-00C04FC9A3A3}
SENS Logon Events	{D5978630-5B9F-11D1-8DD2-00AA004ABD5E}
SENS Network Events	{D5978620-5B9F-11D1-8DD2-00AA004ABD5E}
SENS OnNow Events	{D5978640-5B9F-11D1-8DD2-00AA004ABD5E}
SENS Subscriber for EventSystem EventObjectChange events	{D3938AB0-5B9D-11D1-8DD2-00AA004ABD5E}
SEODictionaryItem Class	{2E3A0EC0-89D7-11D0-A9E6-00AA00685C74}
SEOGenericMoniker Class	{7E3BF330-B28E-11D0-8BD8-00C04FD42E37}
SEOMemDictionary Class	{C4DF0042-2D33-11D0-A9CF-00AA00685C74}
SEOMetaDictionary Class	{C4DF0043-2D33-11D0-A9CF-00AA00685C74}
SEORegDictionary Class	{C4DF0040-2D33-11D0-A9CF-00AA00685C74}
SEORouter Class	{83D63730-94FD-11D0-A9E8-00AA00685C74}
SEOStream Class	{ED1343B0-A8A6-11D0-A9EA-00AA00685C74}
Session Debug Manager	{68385DF9-CD7D-11D0-B443-00A0244A1DD2}

. . . .

TABLE C.1	Continued

Object	Class ID
SetBvr Class	{BA60F742-6F72-11d2-875F-00A0C93C09B3}
Setup Files Prop Bag	{60F6E466-4DEF-11d2-B2D9-00C04F8EEC8C}
SFilter Class	{49c47ce0-9ba4-11d0-8212-00c04fc32c45}
Shadow Effect	{6165A063-5F6A-11D0-B8F1-000000000000}
Shapes	{8241F015-84D3-11d2-97E6-0000F803FF7A}
Shared Task Scheduler	{603D3801-BD81-11d0-A3A5-00C04FD706EC}
ShAVColumnProvider class	{884EA37B-37C0-11d2-BE3F-00A0C9A83DA1}
ShDocProp class	{883373C3-BF89-11D1-BE35-080036B11A03}
Shell Automation Folder View	{62112AA1-EBE4-11cf-A5FB-0020AFE7292D}
Shell Automation Inproc Service	{0A89A860-D7B1-11CE-8350-444553540000}
Shell Automation Service	{13709620-C279-11CE-A49E-444553540000}
Shell Band Site Menu	{ECD4FC4E-521C-11D0-B792-00A0C90312E1}
Shell BindStatusCallback Proxy	{2B4F54B1-3D6D-11d0-8258-00C04FD5AE38}
Shell Copy Hook	{217FC9C0-3AEA-1069-A2DB-08002B30309D}
Shell DefView	{1820FED0-473E-11D0-A96C-00C04FD705A2}
Shell DeskBar	{ECD4FC4C-521C-11D0-B792-00A0C90312E1}
Shell DeskBarApp	{3CCF8A41-5C85-11d0-9796-00AA00B90ADF}
Shell DocObject Viewer	{E7E4BC40-E76A-11CE-A9BB-00AA004AE837}
Shell Drag and Drop helper	{4657278A-411B-11d2-839A-00C04FD918D0}
Shell Extension For Windows Script Host	{60254CA5-953B-11CF-8C96-00AA00B8708C}
Shell extensions for Microsoft Windows	{59be4990-f85c-11ce-aff7-00aa003ca9f6} Network objects
Shell extensions for sharing	{40dd6e20-7c17-11ce-a804-00aa003ca9f6}
Shell extensions for sharing	{f81e9010-6ea4-11ce-a7ff-00aa003ca9f6}
Shell Favorite Folder	{1A9BA3A0-143A-11CF-8350-444553540000}
Shell File System Folder	{F3364BA0-65B9-11CE-A9BA-00AA004AE837}
Shell Icon Overlay Manager	{63B51F81-C868-11D0-999C-00C04FD655E1}
Shell Name Space ListView	{43A8F463-4222-11d2-B641-006097DF5BD4}
Shell Rebar BandSite	{ECD4FC4D-521C-11D0-B792-00A0C90312E1}
Shell Scrap DataHandler	{56117100-C0CD-101B-81E2-00AA004AE837}
Shell Tree Walker	{95CE8412-7027-11D1-B879-006008059382}
shell32.dll	{3DA165B6-CC41-11d2-BDC6-00C04F79EC6B}
ShellFavoritesNameSpace	{55136805-B2DE-11D1-B9F2-00A0C98BC547}
ShellFind	{61E218E0-65D3-101B-9F08-061CEAC3D50D}
Shortcut	{00021401-0000-0000-C000-000000000046}
Simple Cut List	{A5EA8D30-253D-11D1-B3F1-00AA003761C5}
Simple File-based Log	{E16C0593-128F-11D1-97E4-00C04FB9618A}
Simple Text Reader	{D51BD5A4-7548-11CF-A520-0080C77EF58A}

TABLE C.1 Continued	
Object	**Class ID**
Slider Appearance Property Page Object	{C27CCE3D-8596-11D1-B16A-00C0F0283628}
Slider General Property Page Object	{C27CCE3C-8596-11D1-B16A-00C0F0283628}
Smart Tee Filter	{CC58E280-8AA1-11D1-B3F1-00AA003761C5}
SmartStart Class	{5D8D8F1A-8B89-11D1-ADDB-0000F87734F0}
SMTP OnArrival Script Host Sink Class	{CD000005-8B95-11D1-82DB-00C04FB1625D}
SmtpAdmin Class	{1A04EA89-9414-11D0-906F-00AA00A1EAB7}
SmtpAdminAlias Class	{1A04EA8E-9414-11D0-906F-00AA00A1EAB7}
SmtpAdminDL Class	{1A04EA90-9414-11D0-906F-00AA00A1EAB7}
SmtpAdminDomain Class	{1A04EA91-9414-11D0-906F-00AA00A1EAB7}
SmtpAdminService Class	{1A04EA8A-9414-11D0-906F-00AA00A1EAB7}
SmtpAdminService Class	{7F333A96-2BB5-11D1-BFFA-00C04FC307BD}
SmtpAdminSessions Class	{1A04EA8C-9414-11D0-906F-00AA00A1EAB7}
SmtpAdminUser Class	{1A04EA8F-9414-11D0-906F-00AA00A1EAB7}
SmtpAdminVirtualDirectory Class	{1A04EA8D-9414-11D0-906F-00AA00A1EAB7}
SmtpAdminVirtualServer Class	{1A04EA8B-9414-11D0-906F-00AA00A1EAB7}
SMTPConnector Class	{CD000008-8B95-11D1-82DB-00C04FB1625D}
SnapinAboutImpl Class	{D7FCB63B-5C55-11D1-8F00-00C04FC2C17B}
Snapshot File	{FACB5ED2-7F99-11D0-ADE2-00A0C90DC8D9}
Snapshot Viewer Control 9.0	{F0E42D60-368C-11D0-AD81-00A0C90DC8D9}
Snapshot Viewer General Property Page Object	{F2175210-368C-11D0-AD81-00A0C90DC8D9}
Snmp Snapin Extension	{7AF60DD2-4979-11D1-8A6C-00C04FC33566}
Snmp Snapin Extension	{7AF60DD3-4979-11D1-8A6C-00C04FC33566}
Snmp Snapin Extension	{7AF60DD4-4979-11D1-8A6C-00C04FC33566}
SoftDist	{B15B8DC0-C7E1-11d0-8680-00AA00BDCB71}
Software installation	{942A8E4F-A261-11D1-A760-00C04FB9603F}
Software installation	{BACF5C8A-A3C7-11D1-A760-00C04FB9603F}
Sound	{0003000D-0000-0000-C000-000000000046}
Sound (OLE2)	{00020C01-0000-0000-C000-000000000046}
Spanish_Modern Stemmer	{b0516ff0-7f1c-11ce-be57-00aa0051fe20}
Spanish_Modern Word Breaker	{0285b5c0-12c7-11ce-bd31-00aa004bbb1f}
Speech Recognition Enumerator	{E02D16C0-C743-11cd-80E5-00AA003E4B50}
Speech Recognition Enumerator/Share Object	{89F70C30-8636-11ce-B763-00AA004CD65C}
Speech Tools Grammar Compiler	{70618F72-D1ED-11d0-8FAC-08002BE4E62A}
Speech Tools Log	{B3613D9F-E26E-11d0-8FAC-08002BE4E62A}

....

TABLE C.1 Continued	
Object	**Class ID**
Speech Tools TTS Queue	{EFD0E6BA-DB5F-11d0-8FAC-08002BE4E62A}
SpeedDial	{30E7F2A0-EC4C-11ce-8865-00805F742EF6}
Spelling Control	{53961A08-459B-11d1-BE77-006008317CE8}
Spin	{3D2807C2-43DE-11D2-9900-0000F803FF7A}
SQLOLEDB	{0C7FF16C-38E3-11d0-97AB-00C04FC2AD98}
SQLOLEDB Enumerator	{DFA22B8E-E68D-11d0-97E4-00C04FC2AD98}
SQLOLEDB Error Lookup	{0C7FF16C-38E3-11d0-97AB-00C04FC2AD98}
SQLOLEDB Error Lookup	{C0932C62-38E5-11d0-97AB-00C04FC2AD98}
SrcEditor Class	{7C8780B2-793F-11D0-94AB-0080C74C7E95}
StandAloneDfs Class	{A741D3F6-31BE-11D1-9A4A-0080ADAA5C4B}
Standard COM Window	{1B0D38CF-941A-11D0-A675-00A0C903977C}
Standard Font	{FB8F0823-0164-101B-84ED-08002B2EC713}
Standard Picture	{FB8F0824-0164-101B-84ED-08002B2EC713}
stapa Class	{ecabafb1-7f19-11d2-978e-0000f8757e2a}
Start Menu	{4622AD11-FF23-11d0-8D34-00A0C90F2719}
Start Menu Task	{DDB008FE-048D-11d1-B9CD-00C04FC2C1D2}
Status ASP Component	{4682C81B-B2FF-11D0-95A8-00A0C92B77A9}
StatusBar General Property Page Object	{C27CCE39-8596-11D1-B16A-00C0F0283628}
STClient Class	{92ad68ab-17e0-11d1-b230-00c04fb9473f}
StdDataFormat Object	{6D835690-900B-11D0-9484-00A0C91110ED}
StdDataFormats Object	{99FF4677-FFC3-11D0-BD02-00C04FC2FB86}
StdDataValue Object	{2B11E9B0-9F09-11D0-9484-00A0C91110ED}
StdHlink	{79eac9d0-baf9-11ce-8c82-00aa004ba90b}
StdHlinkBrowseContext	{79eac9d1-baf9-11ce-8c82-00aa004ba90b}
StdOleLink	{00000300-0000-0000-C000-000000000046}
Steelhead Router Configuration Notify Object	{6E65CBC5-926D-11D0-8E27-00C04FC99DCF}
StillImage	{B323F8E0-2E68-11D0-90EA-00AA0060F86C }
Stream Class	{49C47CE4-9BA4-11D0-8212-00C04FC32C45}
Streaming Media Player	{cf3eb700-132b-11d0-8dbd-00aa00b90c3b}
Streaming Media Player NG	{b477ca30-3821-11d0-8de6-00aa00b90c3b}
StreamWrapper Class	{43AF3211-0887-11d1-8DCB-0080C7B89C95}
Stub Source Filter	{6B6D0803-9ADA-11D0-A520-00A0D10129C0}
Subscriber Replication Component	{4BF976C1-14CD-11D1-9A97-00AA00BB9C12}
Subscription Folder	{F5175861-2688-11d0-9C5E-00AA00A45957}
Subscription Mgr	{ABBE31D0-6DAE-11D0-BECA-00C04FD940BE}

TABLE C.1 Continued	
Object	**Class ID**
Summary Info Thumbnail handler (DOCFILES)	{9DBD2C50-62AD-11D0-B806-00C04FD706EC}
Suspeding Audio Source Object	{D4123720-E4B9-11cf-8D56-00A0C9034A7E}
SvcVwr 1.0 Object	{58221C66-EA27-11CF-ADCF-00AA00A80033}
SvcVwr 1.0 Object	{58221C6A-EA27-11CF-ADCF-00AA00A80033}
SvcVwr 1.0 Object	{DB5D1FF5-09D7-11D1-BB10-00C04FC9A3A3}
Swedish_Default Stemmer	{9478f640-7f1c-11ce-be57-00aa0051fe20}
Swedish_Default Word Breaker	{01c6b350-12c7-11ce-bd31-00aa004bbb1f}
Symantec Serialization Component	{C1172D01-751C-11D0-B6CF-00A024BF23EF}
Symantec Standard About Box	{AB481080-796C-11D0-A113-00A024B50363}
Symantec User Information Object	{5F3E04C6-4612-11D0-A113-00A024B50363}
Symantec User Registration	{5F3E04C3-4612-11D0-A113-00A024B50363}
SysColorCtrl Class	{C47195EC-CD7A-11D1-8EA3-00C04F9900D7}
System Clock	{E436EBB1-524F-11CE-9F53-0020AF0BA770}
System Device Enumerator	{62BE5D10-60EB-11d0-BD3B-00A0C911CE86}
System Information	{45AC8C62-23E2-11D1-A696-00C04FD58BC3}
System Information	{45AC8C63-23E2-11D1-A696-00C04FD58BC3}
System Information	{45AC8C64-23E2-11D1-A696-00C04FD58BC3}
System Information	{45AC8C65-23E2-11D1-A696-00C04FD58BC3}
System Information Extension	{DA6A85E0-05C7-11D1-B243-006097CAD7E2}
System Monitor Control	{C4D2D8E0-D1DD-11CE-940F-008029004347}
System Monitor Data Properties	{CF948561-EDE8-11CE-941E-008029004347}
System Monitor General Properties	{C3E5D3D2-1A03-11CF-942D-008029004347}
System Monitor Graph Properties	{C3E5D3D3-1A03-11CF-942D-008029004347}
System Monitor Source Properties	{0CF32AA1-7571-11D0-93C4-00AA00A3DDEA}
SysTray	{35CEC8A3-2BE6-11D2-8773-92E220524153}
SysTrayInvoker	{730F6CDC-2C86-11D2-8773-92E220524153}
Tab Property Page Object	{C27CCE34-8596-11D1-B16A-00C0F0283628}
TableCellPPG Class	{E01C01D0-F326-11D0-A6EC-006097C9947C}
TablePPG Class	{8F28A170-F329-11D0-A6EC-006097C9947C}
TabStrip General Property Page Object	{C27CCE33-8596-11D1-B16A-00C0F0283628}
Tabular Data Control	{333C7BC4-460F-11D0-BC04-0080C7055A83}
Tapi 3.0 Dialer Class	{FB2FF4EB-337E-11D1-9B37-00C04FB9514E}
TAPI Class	{21D6D48E-A88B-11D0-83DD-00AA003CCABD}
TAPI3 Terminal Manager Class	{7170F2E0-9BE3-11D0-A009-00AA00B605A4}

· · · · · · · · · · · · · · · ·

TABLE C.1 Continued	
Object	**Class ID**
TapiLocationInfo Class	{CB632C76-8DD4-11D1-ADDF-0000F87734F0}
Task Bar Communication	{56FDF344-FD6D-11d0-958A-006097C9A090}
Task Management Module	{00067803-0000-0000-C000-000000000046}
Telephony	{E26D02A0-4C1F-11D1-9AA1-00C04FC3357A}
Telephony	{E26D02A1-4C1F-11D1-9AA1-00C04FC3357A}
Telephony	{E26D02A2-4C1F-11D1-9AA1-00C04FC3357A}
Telephony Audio Destination	{2EC5A8A6-E65B-11d0-8FAC-08002BE4E62A}
Telephony Audio Source	{2EC5A8A5-E65B-11d0-8FAC-08002BE4E62A}
Telephony Class	{FC9E740F-6058-11D1-8C66-0060081841DE}
Telephony Controls Information Store	{F9D18BF8-E0ED-11d0-AB8B-08002BE4E3B7}
Temp Files Prop Bag	{60F6E465-4DEF-11d2-B2D9-00C04F8EEC8C}
Temporary Internet Files	{7BD29E00-76C1-11CF-9DD0-00A0C9034933}
Temporary Internet Files Cleaner	{9B0EFD60-F7B0-11D0-BAEF-00C04FC308C9}
Temporary Offline Files Cleaner	{750fdf0f-2a26-11d1-a3ea-080036587f03}
Terminal Server User Properties	{0910dd01-df8c-11d1-ae27-00c04fa35813}
Text Label Class	{54702535-2606-11D1-999C-0000F8756A10}
Text to Speech Enumerator	{D67C0280-C743-11cd-80E5-00AA003E4B50}
Text3D	{D56F34F2-7E89-11d2-9B4E-00A0C9697CD0}
TextBuffer class	{B1BF0DE1-7D27-11D0-A8AA-00A0C921A4D2}
TextManager class	{55426A33-808E-11D0-A8AA-00A0C921A4D2}
TextPackage Class	{9ADF33D0-8AAD-11d0-B606-00A0C922E851}
TextToSpeech Class	{2398E32F-5C6E-11D1-8C65-0060081841DE}
TextView class	{7BC1C9C0-7FC2-11D0-A8AA-00A0C921A4D2}
The Internet	{3DC7A020-0ACD-11CF-A9BB-00AA004AE837}
The Main wizard class for the conflict resolver	{058C1509-2201-11D2-BFC1-00805F858323}
This is the snapin created on 10/30	{B5C45061-2729-11D1-A1D7-0080C88593A5}
This snap-in administers the Microsoft Internet Information Services (IIS)	{A841B6C2-7577-11D0-BB1F-00A0C922E79C}
This snap-in administers the Microsoft Internet Information Services (IIS)	{A841B6D2-7577-11D0-BB1F-00A0C922E79C}
Thread NotificationMgr	{c733e4af-576e-11d0-b28c-00c04fd7cd22}
Thread Pool Class DLL	{d9494fc0-31d7-11d0-911f-00aa00c147fa}
ThreadManager Class	{04CCE2FF-A7D3-11D0-B436-00A0244A1DD2}
THREED CHECKBOX CONTROL	{0BA686AA-F7D3-101A-993E-0000C0EF6F5E}

....

TABLE C.1 Continued

Object	Class ID
TrayAgent	{E8BB6DC0-6B4E-11d0-92DB-00A0C90C2BD7}
Tree node callback	{E9ABBBB3-9757-11D1-83F7-00C04FA302A1}
TreeView General Property Page Object	{C27CCE32-8596-11D1-B16A-00C0F0283628}
TrialEnd Class	{438B8ECD-AD2A-11D1-ADEB-0000F87734F0}
Trident HTMLEditor	{3050f4f5-98B5-11CF-BB82-00AA00BDCE0B}
TridentImageExtractor	{7376D660-C583-11d0-A3A5-00C04FD706EC}
TriEditDocument Class	{438DA5E0-F171-11D0-984E-0000F80270F8}
TriEditParse Class	{010E6CBE-FE2B-11D0-B079-006008058A0E}
Trun Gateway Instance Class	{3BBE95FB-C53F-11d1-B3A2-00A0C9083365}
Trun Gateway Instance Scan Class	{3BBE95FE-C53F-11d1-B3A2-00A0C9083365}
Trun Gateway Tx Class	{3BBE95DA-C53F-11d1-B3A2-00A0C9083365}
Trun Gateway Tx Crash Recovery Class	{3BBE95F5-C53F-11d1-B3A2-00A0C9083365}
TRUN Tx Begin Class	{3BBE95A4-C53F-11d1-B3A2-00A0C9083365}
TrustGlobals Class	{ecabaec0-7f19-11d2-978E-0000f8757e2a}
TrustManager Class	{ecabaebb-7f19-11d2-978E-0000f8757e2a}
TypeFactory	{b5866878-bd99-11d0-b04b-00c04fd91550}
U2BASIC Authenticator Class	{d9df823c-4425-11d1-932c-00c04fd919b7}
Uninstall Prop Bag	{60F6E467-4DEF-11d2-B2D9-00C04F8EEC8C}
Uniwiz Property Page	{6EBFA81A-718B-11D1-8A98-006097B01206}
URL Exec Hook	{AEB6717E-7E19-11d0-97EE-00C04FD91972}
URL Moniker	{79eac9e0-baf9-11ce-8c82-00aa004ba90b}
URL Zone Manager	{7b8a2d95-0ac9-11d1-896c-00c04Fb6bfc4}
URLMoniker ProxyStub Factory	{79eac9f1-baf9-11ce-8c82-00aa004ba90b}
URLPicker Class	{0B89F2B1-3048-11D1-A727-006097C9947C}
User Assist	{DD313E04-FEFF-11d1-8ECD-0000F87A470C}
User Context Object	{ecabafb3-7f19-11d2-978e-0000f8757e2a}
User Context Properties Association Object	{ecabafb4-7f19-11d2-978e-0000f8757e2a}
User Data class	{7194CA22-B4D8-11D0-A8CF-00A0C921A4D2}
User Property Pages	{D707877E-4D9C-11d2-8784-F6E920524153}
UserInfo Class	{9E12E76D-94D6-11D1-ADE2-0000F87734F0}
VB Script Language	{B54F3741-5B07-11cf-A4B0-00AA004A55E8}
VB Script Language Authoring	{B54F3742-5B07-11cf-A4B0-00AA004A55E8}
VBA Collection Object	{A4C4671C-499F-101B-BB78-00AA00383CBB}
VBPropertyBag	{D5DE8D20-5BB8-11D1-A1E3-00A0C90F2731}
VBS File Host Encode Object	{85131631-480C-11D2-B1F9-00C04F86C324}

....

TABLE C.1 Continued	

Object	Class ID
VBScript Language Encoding	{B54F3743-5B07-11cf-A4B0-00AA004A55E8}
VBScript Regular Expression	{3F4DACA4-160D-11D2-A8E9-00104B365C9F}
vca Class	{ecabafb2-7f19-11d2-978e-0000f8757e2a}
VCommand Class	{66523042-35FE-11D1-8C4D-0060081841DE}
VDict Class	{582C2191-4016-11D1-8C55-0060081841DE}
Version Column Provider	{66742402-F9B9-11D1-A202-0000F81FEDEE}
VFW Capture Class Manager	{860BB310-5D01-11d0-BD3B-00A0C911CE86}
VFW Capture Filter	{1B544C22-FD0B-11CE-8C63-00AA0044B51E}
VFW Capture Filter Property Page	{1B544C22-FD0B-11CE-8C63-00AA0044B51F}
VGA 16 color ditherer	{1DA08500-9EDC-11CF-BC10-00AA00AC74F6}
Video Clip	{00022602-0000-0000-C000-000000000046}
Video File Clip	{A5EA8D31-253D-11D1-B3F1-00AA003761C5}
Video Render Dynamic Terminal	{AED6483E-3304-11d2-86F1-006008B0E5D2}
Video Renderer	{70E102B0-5556-11CE-97C0-00AA0055595A}
VideoPort Object	{CE292861-FC88-11D0-9E69-00C04FD7C15B}
VideoRenderCtl Class	{888D5481-CABB-11D1-8505-00A0C91F9CA0}
VideoSoft FlexArray Property Page/General	{AFC78D04-B917-11CE-AAE4-CE6AC0F06E88}
VideoSoft FlexArray Property Page/Styles	{2089ADC0-BE09-11CE-AAE4-CE6AC0F06E88}
VideoSoft FlexString Property Page/General	{AFC78D09-B917-11CE-AAE4-CE6AC0F06E88}
VIDProtcol Class	{C76D83FD-A489-11D0-8195-00A0C91BBEE3}
Voice Command Manager	{6D40D820-0BA7-11ce-A166-00AA004CD65C}
Voice Command Object	{A26D7620-6FA0-11ce-A166-00AA004CD65C}
Voice Dictation Manager	{35522CA0-67CE-11cf-9B8B-08005AFC3A41}
Voice Text Manager	{F1DC95A0-0BA7-11ce-A166-00AA004CD65C}
Voice Text Object	{FF2C7A52-78F9-11ce-B762-00AA004CD65C}
VolatilePolicyManager Class	{ecabaebf-7f19-11d2-978E-0000f8757e2a}
Voxware MetaSound Audio Decoder	{73F7A062-8829-11D1-B550-006097242D8D}
Voxware MetaVoice Audio Decoder	{46E32B01-A465-11D1-B550-006097242D8D}
VPN Connection UI Class	{7007ACC6-3202-11D1-AAD2-00805FC1270E}
VsHelpOptionPages Class	{854D7ACA-BC3D-11D0-B421-00A0C90F9DC4}
VsHelpServices Class	{854D7AC5-BC3D-11D0-B421-00A0C90F9DC4}
VsHtmEditorPackage Class	{75CA6903-A48C-11D0-8195-00A0C91BBEE3}
WAM REG COM LAYER	{763A6C86-F30F-11D0-9953-00C04FD919C1}
WAN Connection Manager Class	{BA126AD5-2166-11D1-B1D0-00805FC1270E}
WAN Connection Manager Connection Enumerator Class	{BA126AD6-2166-11D1-B1D0-00805FC1270E}

....

| **TABLE C.1** | Continued |

Object	Class ID
Wave Effect	{13B3D462-43AD-11D0-BDC2-00A0C908DB96}
Wave Parser	{D51BD5A1-7548-11CF-A520-0080C77EF58A}
WaveIn Class Manager	{33D9A762-90C8-11d0-BD43-00A0C911CE86}
WaveOut and DSound Class Manager	{E0F158E1-CB04-11d0-BD4E-00A0C911CE86}
WBEM DCOM Transport V1	{F7CE2E13-8C90-11D1-9E7B-00C04FC324A8}
WBEM Framework Instance Provider	{D63A5850-8F16-11CF-9F47-00AA00BF345C}
WBEM Local Address Resolution Module	{A1044801-8F7E-11D1-9E7C-00C04FC324A8}
WBEM Locator	{4590F811-1D3A-11D0-891F-00AA004B2E24}
WBEM NT5 Base Perf Provider	{FF37A93C-C28E-11D1-AEB6-00C04FB68820}
WBEM PerfMon Instance Provider	{F00B4404-F8F1-11CE-A5B6-00AA00680C3F}
WBEM PerfMon Property Provider	{72967903-68EC-11D0-B729-00AA0062CBB7}
WBEM Power Event Provider	{3DD82D10-E6F1-11D2-B139-00105A1F77A1}
WBEM Registry Event Provider	{FA77A74E-E109-11D0-AD6E-00C04FD8FDFF}
WBEM Registry Instance Provider	{FE9AF5C0-D3B6-11CE-A5B6-00AA00680C3F}
WBEM Registry Property Provider	{72967901-68EC-11D0-B729-00AA0062CBB7}
Wbem Scripting Last Error	{C2FEEEAC-CFCD-11D1-8B05-00600806D9B6}
WBEM Scripting Locator	{76A64158-CB41-11D1-8B02-00600806D9B6}
WBEM Scripting Named Value Collection	{9AED384E-CE8B-11D1-8B05-00600806D9B6}
Wbem Scripting Object Path	{172BDDF8-CEEA-11D1-8B05-00600806D9B6}
WBEM Scripting Object Path	{5791BC26-CE9C-11D1-97BF-0000F81E849C}
WBEM Scripting Sink	{75718C9A-F029-11D1-A1AC-00C04FB6C223}
WbemClassObject	{9A653086-174F-11D2-B5F9-00104B703EFD}
WbemClassObject	{EB87E1BD-3233-11D2-AEC9-00C04FB68820}
WDM Streaming Standard Data Type Handler	{73647561-0000-0010-8000-00aa00389b71}
WDM Streaming Standard Interface Handler	{1A8766A0-62CE-11CF-A5D6-28DB04C10000}
WDM Streaming VPE Property Set Interface Handler	{BC29A660-30E3-11d0-9E69-00C04FD7C15B}
WDM Streaming VPE VBI Property Set Interface Handler	{EC529B00-1A1F-11D1-BAD9-00609744111A}
Web Application Manager Object	{99169CB0-A707-11d0-989D-00C04FD919C1}
Web Application Manager Object	{99169CB1-A707-11d0-989D-00C04FD919C1}
Web Browser Applet Control	{08B0E5C0-4FCB-11CF-AAA5-00401C608501}
Web Discussions	{BDEADEB0-C265-11D0-BCED-00A0C90AB50F}
Web Discussions	{BDEADEB1-C265-11D0-BCED-00A0C90AB50F}

TABLE C.1 Continued

Object	Class ID
Web Discussions	{BDEADEB2-C265-11D0-BCED-00A0C90AB50F}
Web Folders	{BDEADF00-C265-11d0-BCED-00A0C90AB50F}
Web Page Registration Data Transport	{E5B42981-67DC-11D0-8547-00A0240B50F0}
Web Page Wizard	{E5670E37-0D2F-11D2-9E65-00A0C904DD32}
Web Printer Shell Extension	{77597368-7b15-11d0-a0c2-080036af3f03}
Web Search	{07798131-AF23-11d1-9111-00A0C98BA67D}
WebBrowserWrapper Class	{26902120-114D-11D2-8FBF-0000F80272EA}
WebCheck	{E6FB5E20-DE35-11CF-9C87-00AA005127ED}
WebCheck SyncMgr Handler	{7FC0B86E-5FA7-11d1-BC7C-00C04FD929DB}
WebCheckChannelAgent	{E3A8BDE6-ABCE-11d0-BC4B-00C04FD929DB}
WebCheckWebCrawler	{08165EA0-E946-11CF-9C87-00AA005127ED}
WebExtenderClient Class	{F6FD0A13-43F0-11D1-BE58-00A0C90A4335}
WebGate Class	{3724B9A1-9503-11D1-B86A-00A0C90DC849}
WebPub.cWebPub	{0006F08A-0000-0000-C000-000000000046}
WebView MIME Filter	{733AC4CB-F1A4-11d0-B951-00A0C90312E1}
WebViewCoord Class	{7A707490-260A-11D1-83DF-00A0C90DC849}
WebViewCoord Class	{BCFD624E-705A-11d2-A2AF-00C04FC30871}
WebViewFolderIcon Class	{844F4806-E8A8-11d2-9652-00C04FC30871}
WebViewFolderIcon Class	{e5df9d10-3b52-11d1-83e8-00a0c90dc849}
Window List in Shell Process	{ffdc1a80-d527-11d0-a32c-34af06c10000}
Windows Management Instrumentation	{8BC3F05E-D86B-11D0-A075-00C04FB68820}
Windows Management Instrumentation Backup and Recovery	{C49E32C6-BC8B-11D2-85D4-00105A1F8304}
Windows Media Administration DLL	{BF984AD0-F0B6-11cf-84BD-00AA00BF93E3}
Windows Media Administration DLL	{BF984AD1-F0B6-11cf-84BD-00AA00BF93E3}
Windows Media Audio Decoder	{22E24591-49D0-11D2-BB50-006008320064}
Windows Media Channel Manager Object	{B00464B3-67D4-11D0-A464-00C04FC29CFB}
Windows Media Multicast Wizard Control	{6EBFA82F-718B-11D1-8A98-006097B01206}
Windows Media Multiplexer	{63F8AA94-E2B9-11D0-ADF6-00C04FB66DAD}
Windows Media Network Property Page	{91643D00-4AFA-11D1-A520-000000000000}
Windows Media On-Demand Wizard Control	{23DA323D-7006-11D1-8A98-006097B01206}
Windows Media Player	{22D6F312-B0F6-11D0-94AB-0080C74C7E95}
Windows Media Program Manager Object	{7EC08DA1-69AE-11D0-BA9B-00C04FD91A5E}

⦁⦁⦁⦁⦁⦁⦁⦁⦁⦁⦁⦁⦁⦁⦁

TABLE C.1   Continued

Object	Class ID
Windows Media Program Manager Property Page	{7EC08DA2-69AE-11D0-BA9B-00C04FD91A5E}
Windows Media Services DRM Storage object	{760C4B83-E211-11D2-BF3E-00805FBE84A6}
Windows Media splitter	{6B6D0800-9ADA-11D0-A520-00A0D10129C0}
Windows Media Thinning Level Property Page	{B6D1062C-4FBE-11D1-8D85-006097C9A2B2}
Windows Media Unicast Manager Admin Control	{A5CBEE43-6C2C-11cf-BCFD-00AA00C14806}
Windows Media Unicast TraceView Control	{24DCD5F2-6DBB-11D1-BEF5-00805FBE84A6}
Windows Media Unicast Wizard Control	{6EBFA819-718B-11D1-8A98-006097B01206}
Windows Media Update	{B6353564-96C4-11D2-8DDB-006097C9A2B2}
Windows Media URL File Source	{4B428940-263C-11D1-A520-000000000000}
Windows NT Server Solution	{D857B813-5F40-11D2-B002-00C04FC30936}
Windows Script Host Network Object	{F935DC26-1CF0-11D0-ADB9-00C04FD58A0B}
Windows Script Host Shell Object	{F935DC22-1CF0-11D0-ADB9-00C04FD58A0B}
WinFaxRasterize Class	{649D583D-3401-11D1-8C47-0080C7C43E7F}
Winmgmt MOF Compiler	{C10B4771-4DA0-11D2-A2F5-00C04F86FB7D}
WinNT Namespace Object	{250e91a0-0367-11cf-abc4-02608c9e7553}
WinNT Provider Object	{8b20cd60-0f29-11cf-abc4-02608c9e7553}
WinNT System Info Object	{66182EC4-AFD1-11d2-9CB9-0000F87A369E}
WINS	{60AF234A-D7D3-11D0-ABB0-00C04FC3357A}
WINS	{60AF234B-D7D3-11D0-ABB0-00C04FC3357A}
WINS	{60AF234C-D7D3-11D0-ABB0-00C04FC3357A}
Wipe	{AF279B30-86EB-11D1-81BF-0000F87557DB}
WLBS Configuration Notify Object	{bf0eaea8-c122-11d2-94f4-00c04f72d8c4}
WMI ADSI Extension	{F0975AFE-5C7F-11D2-8B74-00104B2AFB41}
WMI Event Provider	{0725C3CB-FEFB-11D0-99F9-00C04FC2F8EC}
WMI Instance Provider	{D2D588B5-D081-11D0-99E0-00C04FC2F8EC}
WMI MSI ProviderMSIPROVApart	{BE0A9830-2B8B-11D1-A949-0060181EBBAD}
WMISnapin Class	{5C659257-E236-11D2-8899-00104B2AFB46}
WordPad Document	{73FDDC80-AEA9-101A-98A7-00AA00374959}
WSecEdit Extension Class	{803E14A0-B4FB-11D0-A0D0-00A0C90F574B}
WSecEdit Security Configuration Class	{2AABFCD0-1797-11D2-ABA2-00C04FB6C6FA}

TABLE C.1   Continued

Object	Class ID
WSecEdit Security Configuration Class	{5ADF5BF6-E452-11D1-945A-00C04FB984F9}
WSecEdit Security Configuration Class	{5C0786ED-1847-11D2-ABA2-00C04FB6C6FA}
WSecEdit Security Configuration Class	{5C0786EE-1847-11D2-ABA2-00C04FB6C6FA}
WSecEdit Security Manager Class	{011BE22D-E453-11D1-945A-00C04FB984F9}
WzConflict.sortie	{058C1536-2201-11D2-BFC1-00805F858323}
XML Data Source Object	{550dda30-0541-11d2-9ca9-0060b0ec3d39}
XML Document	{48123bc4-99d9-11d1-a6b3-00c04fd91555}
XML DOM Document	{2933BF90-7B36-11d2-B20E-00C04F983E60}
XML HTTP Request	{ED8C108E-4349-11D2-91A4-00C04F7969E8}
XML Parser	{d2423620-51a0-11d2-9caf-0060b0ec3d39}
XML Script Engine	{989D1DC0-B162-11d1-B6EC-D27DDCF9A923}
XML Viewer Behavior	{4419DD31-28A5-11d2-AE08-0080C7337EA1}
XML Viewer Moniker	{7E3FCEA1-31B4-11d2-AE1F-0080C7337EA1}
XML-based ASX Parser	{D51BD5AE-7548-11CF-A520-0080C77EF58A}
XRAY Effect	{45588FF3-51FA-11D0-8236-00A0C908DB96}
Yes/No Control	{53961A01-459B-11d1-BE77-006008317CE8}